Biodiversity and Traditional Knowledge

PEOPLE AND PLANTS CONSERVATION SERIES

Series Editor
Martin Walters

Series Originator
Alan Hamilton

People and Plants is a joint initiative of WWF,
the United Nations Educational, Scientific and Cultural Organization (UNESCO)
and the Royal Botanic Gardens, Kew
www.rbgkew.org.uk/peopleplants

Titles in the series

Applied Ethnobotany: People, Wild Plant Use and Conservation
Anthony B Cunningham

Biodiversity and Traditional Knowledge: Equitable Partnerships in Practice
Sarah A Laird (ed)

People, Plants and Protected Areas: A Guide to In Situ Management (reissue)
John Tuxill and Gary Paul Nabhan

Plant Invaders: The Threat to Natural Ecosystems (reissue)
Quentin C B Cronk and Janice L Fuller

Uncovering the Hidden Harvest: Valuation Methods for Woodland and Forest
Resources
Bruce M Campbell and Martin K Luckert (eds)

Forthcoming titles in the series

Ethnobotany: A Methods Manual 2nd edition
Gary J Martin

Tapping the Green Market:
Management and Certification of Non-Timber Forest Products
Patricia Shanley, Alan R Pierce, Sarah A Laird and Abraham Guillén (eds)

Biodiversity and Traditional Knowledge

Equitable Partnerships in Practice

Edited by Sarah A Laird

Earthscan Publications Ltd,
London • Sterling, VA

First published in the UK and USA in 2002 by
Earthscan Publications Ltd

ISBN: 1 85383 698 2 paperback
       1 85383 914 0 hardback

Typesetting by PCS Mapping & DTP, Newcastle upon Tyne
Printed and bound in the UK by Thanet Press, Margate, Kent
Cover design by Yvonne Booth
Cover photo by Sarah A Laird
Panda symbol © 1986 WWF
® WWF registered trademark owner

For a full list of publications please contact:
Earthscan Publications Ltd
120 Pentonville Road
London, N1 9JN, UK
Tel: +44 (0)20 7278 0433
Fax: +44 (0)20 7278 1142
Email: earthinfo@earthscan.co.uk
Web: **www.earthscan.co.uk**

22883 Quicksilver Drive, Sterling, VA 20166–2012, USA

Earthscan is an editorially independent subsidiary of Kogan Page Ltd and publishes in association
with WWF-UK and the International Institute for Environment and Development

A catalogue record for this book is available from the British Library

Library of Congress Cataloging-in-Publication Data

Biodiversity and traditional knowledge : equitable partnerships in practice / edited by
Sarah A. Laird ; with Miguel N. Alexiades ... [et al.].
      p. cm. — ('People and plants' conservation manuals)
   Includes bibliographical references (p.   ).
   ISBN 1-85383-698-2 (pbk.)
   1. Germplasm resources. 2. Biological diversity. I. Laird, Sarah A. II. Series.

QH430 .B54 2002
333.95—dc21
                                                                             2001006694

*This book is dedicated to the memory of Darrell Addison Posey,
a committed champion of indigenous peoples' rights, who
helped direct international attention to the issues addressed in
the following pages. His wonderful awe and reverence for life
has also made his death a great loss to the many of us who
valued his tremendous friendship*

*This book is also dedicated with love to my grandparents
Ralph and Stella Meaker who – over many years – have done
so much for all of us*

Contents

Section I: Biodiversity research relationships

Section II: Biodiversity research and prospecting in protected areas

Section III: Community relationships with researchers

Section IV: The commercial use of biodiversity and traditional knowledge

Section V: National policy context

Section VI: Conclusions and recommendations

List of figures, tables and boxes

Figures

Tables

Boxes

List of case studies

List of contributors

Chapter authors

Miguel N Alexiades
Kelly P Bannister
Charles V Barber
Lyle Glowka
Michael A Gollin
Marianne Guerin-McManus

Kerry ten Kate
Sarah A Laird
Estherine E Lisinge
Kent C Nnadozie
Flavia Noejovich
Darrell A Posey

Patricia Shanley
Brendan Tobin
Antonio G M La Viña
Rachel Wynberg

Case study and other contributors

William G Aalbersberg
Agnes Lee Agama
Paulo Amaral
P Balakrishna
Ian A Bowles
Hans Chr Bugge
Todd Capson
Amanda Collis
Tatiana Correa
Michael J De Pauw
Shivcharn Dhillion
David R Downes
Graham Dutfield
Lisa M Famolare
Anil Gupta
Camilla Harshbarger
Maurice M Iwu
Sam Johnston
Thembela Kepe

Ruth Kiew
Dillon Kim
Isoa Korovulavula
Roger R B Leakey
Patricia Madrigal Cordero
Stanley AJ Malone
Bile Mathieu
Tom Mays
William Milliken
Russell A Mittermeier
Katy Moran
Yakobo Moyini
Sally Mullard
Jackson Mutebi
Lukman Mulumba
Nouhou Ndam
Cosmas Obialor
Cecilia Oh
Gonzalo Oviedo

Daniela M Peluso
Vivienne Solis Riviera
Amy B Rosenfeld
Manuel Ruiz
Diane Russell
Elijan N Sokomba
Terry Sunderland
Hanne Svarstad
Tabe Tanjong
Martin Tchamba
Peguy Tchouto
Laura Touche
Nathalie Ward
Niall Watson
Adrian Wells
China Williams
Glenn Wiser
Wendy Yap
Jeanne Zoundjihekpon

About the authors

Miguel Alexiades is a Nuffield Research Fellow in Ethnobotany at the University of Kent at Canterbury. He is also an Honorary Research Associate of the Institute of Economic Botany, the New York Botanical Garden. He has conducted ethnobotanical research in Madre de Dios, Peru, and Beni, Bolivia, since 1985, working with a total of six different ethnic groups. His doctoral dissertation (1999, City University of New York) focused on the medical ethnobotany of the Ese Eja. He has also worked extensively with community development and indigenous primary health care projects in Peru and has published on various methodological, ethical and socio-political aspects of ethnobotany.

Kelly Bannister received her PhD in the Department of Botany at the University of British Columbia. Her doctoral research was conducted in partnership with the Secwepemc (Shuswap) First Nation (BC, Canada) as part of the Secwepemc Ethnobotany Project. She is currently a postdoctoral fellow in the Environmental Law and Policy programme at the University of Victoria, undertaking policy research on human and environmental health, focusing on research protocols and the development of an institutional model to facilitate collaborative research between universities and local communities as part of the POLIS Project on Ecological Governance. She is also a consultant in ethnobotany to several First Nations communities in British Columbia.

Charles Barber is a Senior Associate with the US-based World Resources Institute and has been based in the Philippines since 1994. He was one of the three principal authors of the WRI/IUCN/UNEP *Global Biodiversity Strategy* (1992), and has worked on biodiversity policy issues for nearly a decade. He has conducted extensive policy research and published widely on access to genetic resources, Indonesian forest policy, and Asia-Pacific marine conservation issues. He received his doctorate in Jurisprudence and Social Policy, a law degree and a Masters degree in Asian Studies from the University of California at Berkeley.

Lyle Glowka manages his own legal and policy consultancy (Biodiversity Strategies International) from Bonn, Germany. He has degrees in botany, law and environmental law from Connecticut College and Vermont Law School in the United States. He studied molecular genetics at the University of Connecticut. Lyle Glowka is a former legal officer at the IUCN Environmental Law Centre, where he focused on the legal and institutional aspects of implementing biodiversity-related treaties. His three books for IUCN include *A Guide to the Convention on Biological Diversity* (1994), *A Guide to Designing Legal and Institutional Frameworks to Determine Access to Genetic Resources* (1998) and *A Guide to Undertaking Biodiversity Legal and Institutional Profiles* (1998).

Michael Gollin has been a patent attorney for 15 years and has assisted clients with intellectual property and technology matters, including prosecution, licensing, counselling and litigation relating to patents, trademarks, copyrights and trade secrets. He has also practised environmental law, and has negotiated biodiversity access agreements in South America, Africa and the South Pacific. Michael Gollin is a partner in Venable, Baetijer, Howard & Civiletti, LLP, in Washington, DC.

Marianne Guerin-McManus, Director of Conservation International's (CI) Conservation Finance Programme, has been with the organization since 1994. As the director of Conservation Finance, she creates flexible mechanisms to fund and structure conservation projects, including debt-for-nature swap accords, trust-fund creation, bioprospecting contracts and legislative reforms. A French and US national, she is an attorney in both civil and common law and has particular expertise in international financial transactions and intellectual property law. She is a graduate of the Georgetown University Law Centre (US), the Grenoble University School of Law (France) and the Canterbury School of Law (UK).

Kerry ten Kate is head of the Convention on Biological Diversity (CBD) Unit at the Royal Botanic Gardens, Kew. Formerly a practising barrister and member of the Secretariat of the United Nations Conference on Environment and Development (UNCED) during preparations for the 1992 Rio Earth Summit, she is now responsible for coordinating the design and implementation of Kew's policies in response to the CBD. She has advised governments, companies, the Secretariat of the Convention on Biological Diversity and multilateral institutions on their strategies on access to genetic resources and the sharing of benefits, and has published on this subject and other sustainable development areas. She holds an MA in law from Oxford University.

Sarah Laird is an independent consultant with a focus on the commercial and cultural context of biodiversity and forest conservation. She has conducted research and provided advice on access and benefit-sharing issues for a range of non-governmental organizations (NGOs), governments, research institutes and community groups, most recently in Cameroon. Recent publications in this field include coauthorship of *The Commercial Use of Biodiversity: Access to Genetic Resources and Benefit-Sharing* (1999), *Benefit-Sharing Case Studies from Cameroon* (1998), *Biodiversity Prospecting in South Africa: Towards the Development of Equitable Partnerships* (1996) and *Biodiversity Prospecting* (1993). She received an MSc in Forestry from Oxford University.

Estherine Lisinge is head of the Policy Unit of WWF Cameroon Programme Office. She joined WWF in 1994 as International Treaties Officer, and has worked extensively on issues related to the implementation of the Convention on Biological Diversity. Prior to joining WWF, she was Tutorial Mistress in Law at the University of Yaounde II, in Cameroon. She is trained as a legal analyst, with a specialization in environmental law.

Kent C Nnadozie is engaged principally in environmental and intellectual property law and practice, focusing on all aspects of biodiversity and biotechnology, especially issues concerning access to, and the conservation and sustainable utilization of, biological resources and the protection of community rights. He has a BA in law and a Masters in

Business Administration. He is currently policy affairs and legal advisor to Bioresources Development and Conservation Programme (BDCP) in Nigeria, and the Executive Secretary of the Environmental Law Foundation of Nigeria. He is also a member of the International Union for Conservation of Nature and Natural Resources (IUCN) Commission on Environmental Law and an associate of the Environmental Law Institute, Washington.

Flavia Noejovich is a lawyer specializing in environmental law and indigenous peoples' rights. She is a member of the Peruvian Society for Environmental Law, and has recently worked with the World Resources Institute (WRI) on an access and benefit-sharing policy project. She has extensive experience in drafting legislation related to natural resources and indigenous peoples' rights, participating in several working groups including the Proposal of a Regime for the Protection of the Collective Knowledge of Indigenous Peoples in Peru. She has worked in training and outreach programmes for indigenous peoples relating to land and resource rights, and has participated in decision-making processes relating to the environment. She is a coauthor of the book *Participation and Consultation for Indigenous Peoples for Oil Sector Activities*.

Darrell Addison Posey was a Fellow of Linacre College and Director of the Programme for Traditional Resource Rights at Mansfield College, both at the University of Oxford, England. He was also CNPq (Brazilian National Council for Science and Technology) Visiting Research Professor at the Federal University of Maranhao, Sao Paulo, Brazil. Dr Posey was President of the International Society for Ethnobiology and a Fellow of the Linnean Society of London. He was also a recipient of the International Sierra Club's Chico Mendes Award and the United Nations Environmental Programme's Global 500 Award. He wrote or edited ten books, including the recently published 900-page volume *Cultural and Spiritual Values of Biodiversity*, and published over 200 scientific articles. Dr Posey died from cancer at the age of 53 in March 2001, in Oxford, England.

Patricia Shanley has 18 years of experience in temperate and tropical research and education, specifically on non-timber forest products. During the past eight years she has worked with forest-based communities in the eastern Amazon, concentrating on the impacts of logging on locally valued non-timber fruit and medicinals and the comparative economic value of timber and non-timber species for rural communities. In an effort to return research results to forest-based communities, Patricia Shanley has coauthored two non-timber forest product (NTFP) manuals that focus on the use and marketing of significant non-timber forest products in eastern Amazonia: *Forest Fruit Trees in the Life of Amazonians* and *Recipes without Words: Medicinal Plants of Amazonia*, both published in Portuguese. Shanley is currently a research scientist at the Center for International Forestry (CIFOR) in Bogor, Indonesia.

Brendan Tobin, a barrister from Ireland, is an independent legal consultant, specializing in international environmental law and indigenous rights. Since 1997 he has been coordinator of the Asociacion para la Defensa de los Derechos Naturales (ADN), Peru, which provides legal and technical support to indigenous peoples in natural resource management. He holds dual Irish and Peruvian nationality, and has represented Peru at the Expert Panel on Access and Benefit-Sharing, the working group on Article 8 (j) and the

Conference of the Parties of the Convention on Biological Diversity. He has published many papers and a number of books on natural resource management, access to genetic resources and protection of indigenous rights, and is a member of the Ashoka Fellowship of Social Entrepreneurs.

Tony La Viña is Director of the Biological Resources Programme of the World Resources Institute (WRI). Before accepting this position in August 1998, he was the Undersecretary for Legal and Legislative Affairs of the Department of Environment and Natural Resources of the Philippines and was instrumental in developing new policies on forestry, marine resources, climate change and biodiversity, with an emphasis on the rights of communities, particularly indigenous peoples. He also pioneered the use of consensus-building approaches in resolving environmental disputes and conflicts. He was Chief Negotiator for the Philippines in the implementation of the Conventions on Biological Diversity and Climate Change during 1996–1998 and was recognized as a lead negotiator for developing countries on these issues. Tony La Viña, who obtained his LLM and JSD from Yale Law School, is the author or coauthor of several books and articles on environmental law and policy.

Rachel Wynberg is an environmental policy analyst, academic and activist, based in Cape Town, South Africa, and at the University of Strathclyde, where she does research on the commercialization of southern African biodiversity. She works with a wide range of international and South African governmental and non-governmental organizations and is a founding member of Biowatch South Africa, an NGO dedicated to monitoring and researching the implementation of South Africa's obligations under the Convention on Biological Diversity. Rachel Wynberg has published over 50 scientific papers and technical reports and is the recipient of several environmental awards.

The People and Plants Initiative

This volume is a welcome addition to the People and Plants conservation series. It addresses the key question of how access to botanical and other biotic resources for the purposes of research or commerce can benefit biological conservation, and promote equitable and sustainable use. This matter forms a major component of the Convention on Biological Diversity. The book explores the experiences and potential roles of a variety of potential parties, including communities, researchers, professional bodies, states and commercial enterprises.

People and Plants is an initiative aimed at increasing the involvement of communities in conservation and sustainable use of plant resources. It is a partnership between WWF and UNESCO, with the Royal Botanic Gardens, Kew, taking an associate role and focusing, in particular, on provision of information and hosting a website. Since 1992, People and Plants has mounted integrated programmes of individual and group training, production of materials and institution-building in selected countries in Africa, Asia, Latin America and the South Pacific. Field activities have focused on places and themes of prime conservation importance. They have included several national parks, where agreements are needed, or are being reached, regarding the involvement of communities in their systems of management and use, and cases of unsustainable harvesting of resources of wild plants, as for wood-carving.

Several types of publications are produced (in addition to this series), including working papers, discussions papers and issues of a handbook. Training videos are also being made. Several of the books are now being published in Chinese, Spanish and sometimes other languages. Some of the other publications have been sent to over 3000 people, concentrating on active workers in developing countries.

The need for the greater involvement of communities in conservation will persist after People and Plants ends. The manuals and other publications will remain as lasting resources from the initiative, the continuing benefits of which will also persist through the activities of those individuals who have received training and the institutions and curricula that have been assisted in their development. Additionally, People and Plants is working towards the establishment of a new programme, to continue beyond the life of the programme, with the remit of identifying key issues at the interface between people and plants, determining recommended approaches and practices to tackling them, and then promulgating the results.

For further information, and to download materials, visit the People and Plants website.

Alan Hamilton
WWF Programme Coordinator, People and Plants

PEOPLE AND PLANTS WEBSITE:

www.rbgkew.org.uk/peopleplants

Foreword

Biodiversity has emerged at the centre of one of the most contentious global debates of this century. Critical to the debate are questions about how biologically endowed countries can achieve economic progress while balancing environmental and social concerns, and how equity can be built into the distribution of benefits derived from the commercialization of natural resources obtained from biologically diverse countries. In effect, biodiversity has become a platform upon which a long history of social and economic injustices that have hitherto characterized North–South relations is addressed.

The debate is complicated on many fronts, however. In part, this is due to fundamental differences across societies with regard to concepts of the environment, equity and ownership. For example, it is often assumed that traditional information is always communal, shared equally by all members of a community. My knowledge of several African tribes – including the Igbo of Nigeria (my tribe), Hausa, Yoruba, Nupe, Fulani, Bini (all of Nigeria), the Wolof, Fula, Madingo, Ga, Fanti, Ashanti, and others – indicates that while every member of a tribe has the rights to draw from the common heritage, the perfection and protection of valuable folk information is often the treasured heritage of certain families, and in some cases is restricted to specially gifted or ordained members of the community, such as traditional healers and priests.

Practical complications also arise from a widespread misconception that biodiversity research and biodiversity prospecting necessarily imply the collection and exploitation of crude resources, or knowledge, to the detriment of high biodiversity countries and communities. Significant innovations and developments have taken place in recent years, in which effective benefit-sharing in the form of technology transfer and advanced partnerships has become more the norm – both for academic and commercial research.

However, there remains a tendency on the part of some to dismiss evolutions in benefit-sharing, and to assume that all biodiversity research and prospecting partnerships are exploitative. Others, eager to make the best use possible of their indigenous resources, remain uncertain how to do so in the face of limited information and guidance. And across the board, a few professionals who have access to the information, and the communication outlets necessary, have dominated the biodiversity debate. All three of these points argue the case for making information more accessible and building understanding outside small groups of experts.

Biodiversity and Traditional Knowledge: Equitable Partnerships in Practice provides valuable information and analysis, and will advance understanding of these complex subjects and the myriad of options available to address them. It will serve as a welcome reference and guide, and can help those seeking to undertake academic and commercial research, and establish meaningful collaborations, in line with national regulations and the Convention on Biological Diversity. This manual is not based on an overly romanticized notion of traditional societies, and instead offers real tools for communities, researchers and high biodiversity countries to sustainably and equitably use their biological heritage. The authors of this volume have taken a bold step, drawing the biodiversity research and prospecting debate back to the original objectives of the Convention on Biological Diversity which acknowledge the interrelated nature of conservation, sustainable use and equity.

Maurice Mmaduakolam Iwu
Executive Director, Bioresources Development and Conservation Programme
Nsukka, Nigeria

Introduction: equitable partnerships in practice

Sarah A Laird

This book provides practical guidance on the nature of equitable research and commercial partnerships associated with biodiversity and traditional knowledge. Biodiversity is the variability within and between living organisms and the ecological systems of which they are a part, including genetic, species and ecosystem diversity (Secretariat of the Convention on Biological Diversity, 2001; Wilson, 1988). The concept of biodiversity emerged in scientific circles, gaining wider use in the 1980s, and assuming in subsequent years an ever-broader range of meanings, often as a political term (Redford and Richter, 1999; see Chapter 1).

Biodiversity research and biodiversity prospecting are the activities upon which the partnerships addressed in this book are based. **Biodiversity research** is at heart academic, and is conducted in the pursuit of primarily theoretical, rather than practical, objectives, although it may have practical spin-off applications. It incorporates a wide range of fields – including botany, microbiology, chemistry, agricultural breeding and cultural anthropology – and approaches – including field, herbarium and laboratory research (see Chapter 1). **Biodiversity prospecting**, sometimes shortened to 'bioprospecting', was first defined by Reid et al (1993) as: 'the exploration of biodiversity for commercially

valuable genetic resources and biochemicals'. It is at heart commercial, involving the search for, and collection of, resources, with an intention to commercialize (see Chapter 8).

Both biodiversity research and prospecting involve the study of biodiversity, and in some cases traditional knowledge. Biodiversity research may evolve into biodiversity prospecting, or may indirectly lead to commercialization through publications, databases and other vehicles that place information and research results in the public domain (see Chapter 4). Distinguishing between these two forms of research has proved challenging for institutions (eg University of South Pacific *Guidelines for Biodiversity Research and Bioprospecting*; see Chapter 3), governments (eg the Philippines national access and benefit-sharing (ABS) measures; see Chapter 13) and other groups. Working distinctions between the two are necessary, however, given the strikingly different financial profiles and motivations of researchers and their backers, and the important role biodiversity research plays in the management and conservation of biodiversity.

The parties involved in biodiversity research and biodiversity prospecting cover a wide spectrum of groups and individuals. They include *researchers*, who might be students, professional academics, government employees, company staff, indigenous peoples or local community members, nationals or foreigners; *institutions*, which might be universities, public research institutions, non-governmental organizations (NGOs) or corporations from a wide range of sectors; *research participants*, who might include tribal hunter-gatherers, city dwellers, the university educated, or those with little exposure to scientists; *governments*, which will set standards for both academic and commercial research, and will seek to regulate and monitor these activities at a national level; and *international agencies*, which undertake research, provide funding and set or implement international legal standards (see Chapters 1 and 12).

The scope and nature of research activities, and the parties involved in biodiversity research and prospecting, are extremely diverse. What is 'equitable' will vary significantly by case, country and the wider cultural, political, economic and social context in which research takes place. Broadly speaking, **equitable partnerships** are those which exhibit equity or 'fairness in dealing'. In common and statute law systems, 'equity' developed as separate principles of justice applied in cases not covered by the law or where the law would apply unfairly, or was too narrow or rigid in scope.

Frameworks for equitable partnerships for biodiversity research and prospecting are emerging that promote principles and practices, such as the fair and equitable sharing of benefits, prior informed consent and ongoing consultation, and adherence to standards for best practice (See Box I.1). These concepts have taken form in international policy and law, including the Convention on Biological Diversity (CBD), national access and benefit-sharing measures, institutional policies, codes of ethics and research guidelines, contracts, indigenous peoples' statements and declarations, protected areas policies, and other documents and fora.

The terms 'fair' and 'equitable' are not defined in the CBD; however, some efforts have been made to explore what they mean in relation to benefit-sharing. Bystrom et al (1999), for example, argue that fair and equitable arrangements will be reached only when the concept is understood to include a 'fair' *process* ('achieving a proper balance of conflicting needs, rights or demands') and an 'equitable' *outcome* (based on agreed *means* that are likely to render an outcome equitable, and *criteria and indicators* for equity).

This book explores a range of '*processes*' and '*outcomes*' that seek to practically realize new concepts of fairness and equity in research and commercial product development based on biodiversity and traditional knowledge. The political, commercial, scientific, social and legal context in which biodiversity research and prospecting take place is undergoing rapid change, however. This book is a response to these transformations, and a brief overview of the wider context in which it emerges follows, in an effort to help set the stage for more detailed discussion of practical efforts to implement 'equity' in subsequent chapters.

Box I.1 Equitable Partnerships in Practice: Key Terms

The following terms are commonly used in discussions of equity in biodiversity research and prospecting, and will be referred to throughout this book. Many of the following concepts are not new, and there is a great deal to be learned from their historical development, the potential for their misuse and abuse, and the ways they have been manifested in other sectors such as timber, mining, dams and oil.

Access to genetic resources

This involves obtaining samples of biological or other material that contain genetic material for the purposes of research, conservation and commercial or industrial application of the genetic material (Glowka, 1998).

Benefit-sharing

This is the sharing of benefits that result from biodiversity research or prospecting; it may involve financial or non-monetary benefits that are often distributed spatially and temporally.

Best practice

Standards of practice that are widely regarded by those in the field as representing the highest levels of conduct, and the practical implementation of core underlying principles such as conservation of biodiversity, sustainable use and equitable benefit-sharing.

Prior informed consent (PIC)

PIC is the consent of a party to an activity that is given after receiving full disclosure regarding the reasons for the activity, the specific procedures the activity would entail, the potential risks involved, and the full implications that can realistically be foreseen. The Convention on Biological Diversity requires that 'access to genetic resources shall be subject to prior informed consent of the Contracting Party providing such resources, unless otherwise determined by that Party' (Article 15 (5)). In some countries, such as the Philippines and those of the Andean Pact, PIC has been extended to local communities (see Chapters 8 and 13).

Traditional resource rights (TRR)

Traditional resources are tangible and intangible assets and attributes deemed to be of value to indigenous and local communities, including spiritual, aesthetic, cultural and economic assets. 'Traditional' implies established and respected social processes of learning and sharing knowledge that are unique to each indigenous culture (Four Directions Council, 1996). Traditional resource rights is a process and framework to develop multiple, locally appropriate sui generis – 'unique' or 'of its own kind' – systems to protect and compensate indigenous and traditional peoples for their knowledge, technologies and biological resources (Posey, 1996).

Biodiversity research and prospecting: at the juncture of change

Biodiversity research and prospecting operate at the juncture of areas undergoing significant and rapid transformation. These include: expanded commodification and privatization of biological resources; increased scientific and technological capacity to study and use genetic resources; increased globalization, use of strategic partnerships, and consolidation through mergers and acquisitions within the private sector; new obligations for prior informed consent and benefit-sharing attached to research on, and commercial use of, genetic resources; and emerging linkages formed between biodiversity conservation, sustainable use and equity. These combine to create unsteady and shifting foundations for the design of 'equitable' biodiversity research and prospecting partnerships. Some of the significant changes converging to create an area in flux are discussed later in this chapter.

New rules and norms for research

New rules governing biodiversity research and prospecting are articulated in three primary sources: international treaties (eg the Convention on Biological Diversity); national laws (eg national ABS measures; see Chapter 12); and self-regulation by professionals (eg institutional policies and codes of ethics; see Chapters 2 and 3) (Gollin, 1999). Development of standard terms in contractual agreements has also contributed a baseline for structuring research partnerships (see Chapters 9 and 10). Changes that result from these new rules include the following (Gollin, 1999; see Chapter 1):

- Biological resources are no longer the common heritage of mankind, but are subject to sovereign rights of nations.
- Biological materials are national patrimony, or heritage, subject to special treatment – they are no longer treated as commodities.
- Research on, and use of, biological materials must be linked to conservation and must respect local groups.
- Prior informed consent must be acquired before undertaking any research – from governments, institutional collaborators and local communities.
- If countries conserve their biodiversity, they should benefit from its use; research and commercial product development should 'fairly and equitably' share benefits with countries and communities.

Science and technology

Scientific and technological advances in fields such as biology, chemistry, genomics and information technology that make use of biodiversity, and in some cases traditional knowledge, are rapid. The discovery and development process is undergoing significant change, and new technologies such as combinatorial chemistry, ultra-high throughput screening and laboratories on a chip have dramatically accelerated the pace of research and development (see Chapter 8; ten Kate and Laird, 1999). In some ways, advanced scientific and technological complexity makes tracking a given biological sample seem increasingly difficult; however, the same advances can be applied – with the force of good national laws and contractual arrangements behind them – to track materials. It is, in fact, less likely today, than in the time of smuggled rubber and quinine germplasm, that the cat will definitively be 'out of the bag'. In general, however, high-biodiversity developing countries do not see the applications of new scientific and technological advances addressing their problems, although the potential for them to do so is great.

Commercial

Within and across commercial sectors – including the pharmaceutical, biotechnological, seed, crop protection, horticulture, cosmetic and phytomedical – companies enter into partnerships that allow them to participate in an increasingly specialized research process. As a result of increased fragmentation and specialization associated with biodiversity prospecting, no one individual or group tends to hold all the necessary technological infrastructure or expertise. Globally, complex networks of collaboration and partnership have become the norm (ten Kate and Laird, 1999). Partners to commercial companies are often academic research institutions, and so one result of the trend towards collaboration and out-sourcing is increased blurring between the academic–commercial research divide – a divide that was, however, never absolute (eg Brockaway, 1979).

At the same time that companies are entering into strategic research and development (R&D), marketing and production partnerships, they are also consolidating through mergers and acquisitions; and lines between sectors are blurring as companies seek cross-sector synergies to develop new knowledge and novel products. Global-life science companies – combining pharmaceutical, food, seed and chemical divisions – operating in an increasingly globalized world economy are an extreme manifestation of the trend towards consolidation,

strategic partnerships, the evolution of dynamic knowledge-based industries, and the cross-pollination of R&D, production and marketing (Mytelka, 1999; Nayak, 1999; see Chapter 9). One result of increased consolidation is that already large companies become even larger and more inscrutable, and corporate revenues dwarf the gross domestic product (GDP) of countries from which they seek to access genetic resources (see Table I.1). This has led to wariness on the part of high biodiversity countries, who cannot muster the same resources and power to negotiate and monitor partnerships.

Large life-science companies have argued that new synergies and biotechnological capacity will allow for the development of cures for a wide range of medical problems, and solutions to world hunger. However, the same consolidation, globalization and technological advances have created public suspicion of these corporations, and the willingness and abilities of governments to regulate them. The case of genetic engineering in crops, and government reluctance in the North to regulate and oversee these activities, or inform consumers, confirmed many groups' worst suspicions that advances in biotechnology are neither well-regulated nor oriented towards the public's needs (Simpson, 1999).

Intellectual property rights

The patent system – paralleling scientific and technological advances – has undergone a process of regulatory globalization and harmonization, and the scope of what is regarded as patentable has 'quietly expanded' (Drahos, 1999). In recent years, patent offices have begun to issue patents for discoveries of information already existing in the natural world, such as the genetic sequences of living organisms, and to plants, animals and microorganisms containing genes that have been modified in the laboratory. The Agreement on Trade Related Intellectual Property Rights (TRIPS) of the World Trade Organization (WTO) incorporated these trends. While intellectual property rights (IPRs) can be a powerful vehicle for allocating wealth created from the exploitation of genetic resources, and can secure financial benefits, the trend towards expanded privatization and commodification of biological and genetic resources has concerned many (Downes and Wiser, Chapter 12; Dutfield, 1999; Dutfield, 2000; Shiva, 1998). The drive towards expansion of IPRs to serve developed country biotechnology-based industries has meant that the implications for these new rules are unclear, and appear detrimental to the interest of many high biodiversity countries (Ekpere, 1999). Ultimately, 'the creation, operation, and interpretation of the patent system is linked to moral standards'; the crucial problem today is that current expansion and adaptations of the patent system are not governed by a broader public ethic, which traditionally guides the patent system, but instead largely serve private purposes (Drahos, 1999).

Traditional resource rights and the rise of the stakeholder

Within conservation and development programmes, including protected areas, there is a trend towards greater inclusiveness of a range of stakeholders. Increasingly, protected areas managers and others recognize that it is crucial to build the trust, support and ownership of local groups over conservation projects to ensure their effective implementation (eg Oviedo and Brown, 1999; see Chapter 6). There is also growing recognition of the fact that cultural diversity is closely linked to biological diversity (Posey, 1999), and that biodiversity is often at its highest in areas where the local populations are economically and politically marginalized (Dove, 1996). Increased attention has focused on the rights of indigenous peoples and local communities to 'traditional resource rights' (see Box I.1; Posey, 1996; Posey and Dutfield, 1996; see also Chapter 7). International policy instruments – such as the International Labor Organization Convention 169 Concerning Indigenous Peoples (1989), the Convention on Desertification and Drought (1994), the UN Draft Declaration on the Rights of Indigenous Peoples (1994), Agenda 21 (1992), and the Rio Declaration (1992) – address in increasingly clearer terms the rights of indigenous peoples and local communities to control and benefit from the use of their resources and knowledge. Article 8 (j) of the Convention on Biological Diversity (1992) articulates the need to 'respect, preserve and maintain knowledge, innovations and practices of indigenous and local communities embodying traditional lifestyles' as part of wider efforts to promote sustainable use and biodiversity conservation.

Indigenous peoples' groups have also outlined demands for equitable biodiversity conservation and research in declarations, statements and active participation in international policy fora – for example, the Kari-Oca Declaration and the Indigenous Peoples' Earth Charter (1992), the Mataatua Declaration on Cultural and Intellectual Property Rights of Indigenous Peoples (1993), the Statement from the Coordinating Body of Indigenous Organizations of the Amazon Basin (COICA)/UNDP Regional Meeting on Intellectual Property Rights and Biodiversity (the 'Santa Cruz Declaration', 1994), and the International Alliance of Indigenous Tribal Peoples of the Tropical Forests: the Biodiversity Convention – Concerns of Indigenous Peoples (1995) (see Chapter 7).

Conservation – sustainable use – equity

The linking of conservation, sustainable use and equity grew, in part, from the fact that most of the world's biodiversity is found in inverse proportion to technological and industrial wealth (Macilwain, 1998). Some have called its manifestation in the Convention on Biological Diversity (CBD) the 'Grand Bargain' because, in the CBD, a balance is struck between the demands of high-biodiversity developing countries to control and benefit from the use and conservation of their biodiversity, and developed-country demands that biodiversity be conserved, and industries allowed access to genetic resources (Gollin, 1993; Gollin and Laird, 1996; Downes, 1994). To a high degree, the CBD negotiation and implementation process has highlighted and allowed room for expression of North–South conflicts over

financial and natural resources, and differing conceptions of environmental problems and the meaning and value of nature (McAfee, 1999). This combination of differing agendas and perspectives is manifested in the objectives of the CBD: biodiversity conservation, sustainable use and 'fair and equitable sharing of benefits' (Article 1). In line with wider trends in the field of conservation, the CBD and other documents resulting from the United Nations Conference on Environment and Development (UNCED) bridge 'purely' environmental concerns and emerging human rights and trade issues. The CBD is a trade agreement in the sense that it establishes general and qualified terms for the trade in genetic resources; but it also acknowledges the value of non-marketed goods and services, and makes explicit ethical commitments to fairness and equity (Downes, 1994; McNeely, 1999; Bystrom et al, 1999).

Table I.1 *Gross domestic product (gdp) and annual pharmaceutical company sales, 1997 (US$ millions)*

Country (GDP ranking)/company	US$ millions GDP/ healthcare revenue (pharmaceutical sales)	
US (1)	8,083,400.0	
Japan (2)	4,706,876.7	
Germany (3)	2,128,902.8	
China (7)	962,389.2	
Brazil (8)	808,146.6	
Australia (14)	390,492.5	
South Africa (34)	129,803.3	
Malaysia (40)	97,240.4	
Bangladesh (62)	31,359.0	
Merck & Co (US)	$23,636.9	(pharmaceutical sales: 13,282.4)
Johnson & Johnson (US)	22,629.0	(7,696.0)
Ecuador (64)	19,427.9	
Novartis Group (Switzerland)	16, 376.6	(9,732.4)
Sri Lanka (75)	15,138.9	
Bristol-Myers Squibb (US)	14, 996.0	(9,932.0)
American Home Products (US)	14,484.6	(11,076.1)
Glaxo Wellcome Plc (UK)	13,087.2	(13,087.2)
SmithKline Beecham Plc (UK)	12, 783.8	(7,498.1)
Pfizer Inc (US)	12, 504.0	(9,239.0)
Costa Rica (77)	12,066.5	
Côte d'Ivoire (81)	10,453.1	
Cameroon (86)	9246.7	
Fiji (132)	2183.1	
Guyana (160)	695.0	

Source: MedAd News, September, 1998; Euromonitor, 1998

Equitable partnerships in practice

This book seeks to provide information on, and explore, a range of tools and approaches that have been employed to achieve 'equitable' partnerships. In a world permeated by social, economic and political inequality, and undergoing rapid globalization and transformation of economic, legal and scientific relations, 'equity' – a dynamic, culturally framed concept – is clearly difficult to approximate in practice. Disparities in legal and economic power, and complex political, economic, cultural and social relations, make all interventions aimed at 'equity' problematic. However, it is hoped that by developing an informed and open dialogue, based on the experiences of groups around the world, we can move closer to what constitute equitable partnerships for biodiversity research and prospecting. Empirical approaches, based on trial and error, have yielded the most valuable evolutions in standards of equity and 'best practice'. Moving from an open-access to an 'access and benefit-sharing' basis for exchange will take time and practice, and will be most effective growing from particular local conditions. As Solis and Cordero (1999) stated, in reference to the development of the 1998 Biodiversity Law in Costa Rica, it requires a 'path which is both empirical and innovative'.

It is difficult to imagine a perfect formula for equity in biodiversity research and prospecting pulled from thin air at some point down the road. Firstly, current exchanges must be placed within an historical context. The very presence of a species in a particular place is rarely devoid of a cultural, political and sometimes economic history. The trade in genetic and biological resources – including South to South – is as old as human civilization, and as complex and varied (Juma, 1989). Secondly, the genetic resource exchange is one of many forms of natural resource exploitation, most more widespread and economically significant than biodiversity research or prospecting. Numerous lessons can be drawn from efforts in the logging, mining and oil sectors to acquire 'prior informed consent' and share benefits. In many countries, the same shorthand terms for equity have been employed, and benefits such as schools, medical care, equipment, training and infrastructure have been negotiated. The ways these have, or have not, been manifested in practice, and the extent of benefit-sharing that reaches remote communities in high biodiversity regions, can be indicative of the potential for biodiversity prospecting (existing within the same economic and political structures) to realistically achieve its objectives. For example, the oil industry has undertaken broad consultations in a number of regions with indigenous peoples and local communities, and there is much to be learned from these experiences (Tobin et al, 1998). In Indonesia, the extent of consultation and percentage of timber profits that go to local communities from logging – a far more damaging activity to local livelihoods and the environment than biodiversity research or prospecting – is insignificant (Dove, 1996). As Dove (1996) put it, to extend the InBio model from Costa Rica to Indonesia effectively would require a 'different political-economic past, present and future'.

This brings us to the third point: although the CBD extends to national governments the rights to regulate access and benefit-sharing, existing relations between national governments and a range of domestic groups must be considered. Inequity that attends relations between central governments and biologically diverse 'peripheries' are often equal to, or greater than, those attending relations between more and less developed countries. The CBD as an international treaty does not address internal obstacles to achieving 'fair and equitable benefit-sharing'. However, equity in biodiversity research and prospecting partnerships is unlikely to be realized without balancing benefits accrued at a national governmental level with those at local, institutional and community levels, and without accounting for inequities built into national political and economic relations.

Throughout, a major difficulty in putting the various pieces together in ways that create equity is the fact that biodiversity research and prospecting crosses cultural, disciplinary, institutional, commercial and legal boundaries. It brings together the urban and rural, economically and politically powerful and disenfranchised, and the global and the local. It partners companies representing the latest trends in globalization, privatization and scientific and technological advances with diverse institutions, communities and countries. In order to overcome resulting misunderstandings and conflicts, and more effectively achieve equitable partnerships, a serious commitment to understanding the nuts and bolts of biodiversity research and prospecting is required.

Ultimately, this book is about tinkering and *process*. It is not a 'how to' manual, nor does it seek to promote biodiversity research and prospecting per se. It seeks, rather, to examine ways that current and future activities might better approximate 'equity' and 'fairness', and promotes an empirical basis for learning and developing new ethical and legal frameworks.

It grew from awareness of the lack of practical information available on equitable biodiversity research and prospecting partnerships. It is based on a firm belief that individuals and groups in high biodiversity countries are well equipped to address the myriad of issues raised by biodiversity research and prospecting, but are often limited by a lack of basic information. Informed local-level innovation and experiences in this area can also provide national and international policy processes with the oxygen of new ideas and the range of input needed to make them relevant and effective.

There is a great deal more information available today than even five years ago, but it remains disparate and difficult to access – much of it in 'grey' literature, policy background documents and other forms that are not readily available to any but the most invested in the issue. At the same time, even those actively involved tend to focus on the area that is most immediately relevant to them – to read papers, attend meetings and exchange ideas with those that share, more or less, their own concerns. However, a striking aspect of biodiversity research and prospecting today is its multidisciplinary and multisectoral nature.

To draft an effective national ABS measure, for example, governments must understand the main issues of concern to local communities, including effective consultation and acquisition of prior informed consent; they must be familiar with the scientific, technological and marketing elements of each industry they hope to regulate, and understand how best to maximize benefits through partnerships; they must be familiar with biodiversity contracts and the ways they reflect best practice to date, and innovative ways to share financial benefits through mechanisms such as trust funds; and they must understand how professional biodiversity researchers address ethical and legal issues raised by their research, and as manifested in institutional policies, codes of ethics, research guidelines and innovative forms of 'giving back' research results.

This book is broad in focus, and while it seeks to demonstrate the interrelatedness of the range of areas covered, it is not entirely comprehensive for any one field. Caveats can be attached to all of the approaches and recommendations included in this book and the dynamic nature of this area must be emphasized. As a result, it seeks to strike a balance between idealized and generalized positions that help drive international, and often national-level policy development, and the kind of practical detail required to implement these positions in practice. It is hoped that the book can serve different audiences, and flag issues that readers can follow up in the literature. By presenting background, case studies and analysis, the book seeks to build understanding of the principles underlying equitable partnerships, and to provide practical advice and examples from which researchers, governments, companies, indigenous peoples and local communities, and other groups can selectively draw.

Structure of the book

The book is organized into six sections:

I   Biodiversity research relationships.
II   Biodiversity research and prospecting in protected areas.
III Community relationships with researchers.
IV   The commercial use of biodiversity and traditional knowledge.
V   National policy context.
VI   Conclusions and recommendations.

These are followed by a Directory of useful contacts and resources, Contributors' contact information and a Glossary of useful terms.

Although some effort has been made to distinguish between academic and commercial research relationships (in order to avoid lumping all biodiversity research in with biodiversity prospecting, which raises a wider range of more restrictive obligations), as previously noted these distinctions are increasingly blurred. Chapters addressing specific commercial concerns are included in Section IV, but many of the issues raised in others chapters relate to commercial activities, as well.

Section I: Biodiversity research relationships – laying the foundation

Equitable academic research relationships, and widespread professional understanding of the ethical obligations raised at each step in the research process, are the foundation upon which all other biodiversity research and prospecting relationships are built. Because academic data often flow into the private sector, there are important reasons to ensure that the manner and terms under which they are collected are equitable. More significant, perhaps, is the need to instil in the academic community – which sets the standards for most research – an appreciation of the new ethical and legal envelope within which their work takes place, and the new demands that research contributes to wider social and conservation objectives (Orr, 1999; Richter and Redford, 1999). Through the process of developing codes of ethics, research guidelines and institutional policies, researchers can build awareness within their community and develop frameworks for equitable relationships.

Chapter 1 of this section introduces the rapidly changing ethical, legal and political landscape in which biodiversity research takes place today, including the new obligations and responsibilities that must be assumed by biodiversity researchers. It provides the basis from which the other chapters grow – addressing specific tools that might be employed to achieve these obligations and responsibilities.

Chapter 2 describes the efforts of a number of professional research societies to develop codes of ethics and research guidelines for members. Codes of ethics include general principles that underlie research activities (eg resource rights and self-determination of local groups), as well as those that guide the research relationship itself (eg prior informed consent, respect and equitable benefit-sharing). Research guidelines complement the framework laid down in codes by providing specific details on field practices common to a particular discipline or area of research. Discussed in this chapter is the drafting process and 'final' documents produced by the International Society of Ethnobiology, Society of Economic Botany, American Society of Pharmacognosy, American Anthropological Association and the Asian Symposium on Medicinal Plants.

In Chapter 3, we will see that a range of institutions, including the Royal Botanic Gardens, Kew, the University of the South Pacific and the Limbe Botanic Garden in Cameroon, have drafted policies to guide both academic and commercial research activities. A consortium of botanic gardens

has developed a comprehensive policy that harmonizes practices across institutions, entitled *Common Policy Guidelines for Participating Botanic Gardens on Access to Genetic Resources and Benefit-Sharing* (2001). Increasingly, institutions involved in biodiversity research and prospecting are responding to what the Association of Systematics Collections' (ASC) *Guidelines for Institutional Policies and Planning in Natural History Collections* describes as the 'increasingly complex demands on natural history collections and expertise at a time when there is rapid change in the legal and ethical standards that govern collections and research' (Hoagland, 1994).

In Chapter 4 we examine the 'flow' of biodiversity research results and information through publication. Academic publications have long served as the primary vehicle through which information on traditional use and management practices, and biodiversity research results, make their way to the public domain, and from there to the private sector. As local groups and governments seek greater control over access to information and resources today, there is increasing pressure to limit or restrict publication of certain types of data. At the same time, publications are an important manner in which researchers communicate with each other, and share their findings with wider audiences, providing a valuable basis for the development of ideas and building understanding of biological and cultural diversity. Academic and funding pressures create additional incentives for researchers to publish their results. This chapter examines some of the key issues raised by the publication of biodiversity research results – with an emphasis on the publication of cultural knowledge – and provides examples where researchers have sought to balance the need to publish with the need to respect the demands or interests of local groups.

This section concludes with Chapter 5 on 'giving back', or translating and transferring research results in ways that make them relevant and useful to local groups and applied biodiversity conservation. Although biodiversity research yields information of value to local groups – including communities, non-governmental organizations (NGOs), industry, and government – the scientific process is usually considered complete when an article has been sent for publication. As a result, most information and scientific understanding remain in the hands of researchers and sometimes policy-makers who are geographically and conceptually distant from the region of study. At the same time, natural resources held by local groups are under increasing economic and political pressure, and these groups more than ever need information and tools to effectively make decisions and defend their interests. Biodiversity research programmes should incorporate the resource management needs of local groups, and translate results into a form that will be of immediate use to these groups. While a critical element of equitable research partnerships, and a significant form of benefit-sharing, 'giving back' scientific research results is also often the most effective way that research can contribute to biodiversity management and conservation, and local development activities.

Section II: Biodiversity research and prospecting in protected areas

Protected areas are home to much of the world's biodiversity and are likely to become increasingly important as losses of biodiversity continue. Protected areas also offer infrastructure and access to biodiversity of value to research, and a stable and protected site with limited or no exploitation of resources – a critical condition for studies that monitor change over time, or require insurance that species collected will be available in the future. As a result of these and other factors, protected areas are favoured sites for both biodiversity research and prospecting, and a large number of biodiversity prospecting projects have collected material from these sites.

At the same time, protected areas are expensive to maintain, both in terms of real management and infrastructure costs, and lost opportunity costs for a country. Chronic funding shortages plague protected areas systems in even the wealthiest countries, and they are often under pressure from logging, mining, grazing and other interests that are considered more profitable. There is a need for biodiversity research and prospecting to contribute more effectively to protected area needs and funding shortages. Although implementation will vary by country, biodiversity research and prospecting can be structured to contribute more significantly to protected area and local communities' needs, both financial and informational.

Chapter 6 explores the relationship between protected areas and biodiversity research and prospecting. It is by no means a definitive study of the subject; instead, it flags issues for consideration. Case studies help to illustrate the ways in which research programmes can integrate local informational needs into biodiversity research projects – for example, through the scientific committees established at the Tai National Park in Côte d'Ivoire and Waza National Park in Cameroon. A draft policy to guide research relationships developed in Cameroon, and currently undergoing review, is provided to help promote dialogue on the value and role of such documents.

Other case studies provide examples of commercial product development from samples collected in parks prior to the

CBD – taq polymerase from Yellowstone National Park in the United States, and Sandimmune developed by Novartis from a fungus collected in Hardangervidda National Park in Norway. Steps taken by protected areas today to strike better deals and ensure benefit-sharing from research activities and any future commercial product development are addressed, including those at Bwindi Impenetrable National Park in Uganda and Yellowstone National Park.

Section III: Community relationships with researchers

Although covered throughout the book, a few core elements of equitable research relationships that involve local communities are addressed in this chapter. In particular, Chapter 7 focuses on consultation and acquisition of prior informed consent (PIC), and the use and content of research agreements. Although incorporated into many national access and benefit-sharing laws, and increasingly accepted as integral to equitable biodiversity research and prospecting relationships, effective means for researchers to acquire prior informed consent from local communities remain unclear.

Consultation is a dynamic, interactive process that goes well beyond simply informing a community of a researcher's plans. The Inuit Circumpolar Conference describes consultation as a process extending through all stages of a study, from the earliest seeking of PIC, through data collection and the use and application of findings (Brooke, 1993). Both PIC and consultations are highly dependent upon local cultural norms, and should be based upon community formal and informal organizational structures, time frames and local decision-making processes. They should also reflect the diversity that exists within communities (Four Directions Council, 1996).

As part of widespread calls for formalization of researcher–community relationships, including PIC requirements in some national ABS laws, written research agreements are proposed as useful tools for defining and clarifying the nature of research relationships. The form and extent of agreements will vary depending upon community requirements, the scale and nature of a research project, the researchers involved and the extent of community involvement. Written agreements will not be appropriate in many cases, but in others they can usefully clarify mutual expectations and obligations. Chapter 7 includes a review of some of the key elements of research agreements and provides examples from existing documents. Case studies include steps taken by researchers to acquire the prior informed consent of Ese Eja communities in Peru; the development of oral and written research agreements in Mkambati, South Africa; development of a written agreement for biodiversity prospecting research between the University of the South Pacific and the Verata community in Fiji; the use of 'know-how' licences for traditional knowledge in Peru; and the development of a model PIC protocol and form. A review of indigenous peoples' declarations and statements and the demands made regarding equitable research relationships is also included in Annex 7.2.

Section IV: The commercial use of biodiversity and traditional knowledge

Biodiversity prospecting relationships are not entirely distinct from earlier chapters, but are addressed in greater detail in this section. Commercial demand for access to genetic resources and best practice in benefit-sharing are addressed in Chapter 8. This chapter illustrates the variety and complexity of commercial use through the lens of selected sectors, including the pharmaceutical, biotech, crop protection, seed, horticulture, botanical medicine, and personal care and cosmetic. An understanding of private sector demand for access to biodiversity and traditional knowledge, the nature of discovery and development programmes, and current standards for best practice in benefit-sharing are a critical foundation for the subsequent development of national regulatory frameworks, as well as effective contract negotiation by provider countries, institutions and communities.

Chapters 9 and 10 examine biodiversity prospecting contractual agreements. Governments often set minimum terms and standards for contracts, and reserve the right to review and approve them; however, parties to contracts make important decisions relating to prior informed consent and equitable benefit-sharing. Chapter 9 provides the context within which biodiversity prospecting contracts are negotiated, addressing the relationship between national ABS measures and contracts, the negotiation of contracts and difficulties in achieving equity in contractual arrangements. Chapter 10 provides an introduction to the relationship between biodiversity prospecting contracts and existing contractual arrangements, as well as the core elements of biodiversity prospecting contracts. Examples of language from a range of negotiated contracts are provided to indicate current options agreed upon.

Chapter 11 examines one possible mechanism for sharing financial benefits generated from biodiversity prospecting: the trust fund. Drawing upon lessons learned from conservation funds, and a few case studies of biodiversity prospecting trust funds, this chapter looks at the origin of the trust fund concept, its development in the context of conservation and its application in biodiversity prospecting. Case studies include the Forest People Fund of Surinam, the Fund for Integrated Rural Development and Traditional Medicine in Nigeria, the Panama IGCB Trust Fund, and the Healing Forest Conservancy's Trust Fund Constitution.

Section V: National policy context

Chapter 12 explores the development and implementation of national access and benefit-sharing measures. It reviews the new international legal framework provided by the CBD, and discusses its implications for countries as they develop national legislation. While focusing on the scope and content of ABS legislation, the chapter also examines the broader policy decisions that must underlie and direct specific legislative choices, the importance of participatory, multistakeholder legislative development processes, and issues of administration and institutional capacity to implement new laws. Examples and case studies are drawn from experiences in Andean Pact countries, Costa Rica, the Philippines, Malaysia and South Africa.

The book concludes with Chapter 13, which offers conclusions and recommendations for a range of parties, including governments, companies, researchers, funders and granting agencies, protected areas managers, and indigenous peoples and local communities.

Given the long time frame required to publish a book, and the rapid pace of change in this field, there have been numerous developments since the case studies and other contributions were written. Readers are encouraged to consult the 'Directory of useful contacts and resources' and the 'Contributors' contact information' if they wish to obtain updates on any material in this book.

It was not possible to include codes of ethics, research guidelines, institutional policies, indigenous peoples' statements, national and regional laws, or resource material for Chapters 6 and 10 in this book. These and other useful documents referred to are available at:

www.rbgkew.org.uk/peopleplants.

People and Plants partners

WWF

WWF (formerly the World Wide Fund For Nature), founded in 1961, is the world's largest private nature conservation organization. It consists of 29 national organizations and associates, and works in more than 100 countries. The coordinating headquarters are in Gland, Switzerland. The WWF mission is to conserve biodiversity, to ensure that the use of renewable natural resources is sustainable and to promote actions to reduce pollution and wasteful consumption.

UNESCO

The United Nations Educational, Scientific and Cultural Organization (UNESCO) is the only UN agency with a mandate spanning the fields of science (including social sciences), education, culture and communication. UNESCO has over 40 years of experience in testing interdisciplinary approaches to solving environmental and development problems in programmes such as that on Man and the Biosphere (MAB). An international network of biosphere reserves provides sites for conservation of biological diversity, long-term ecological research and testing and demonstrating approaches to the sustainable use of natural resources.

ROYAL BOTANIC GARDENS, KEW

The Royal Botanic Gardens (RBG), Kew, has 150 professional staff and associated researchers and works with partners in over 42 countries. Research focuses on taxonomy, preparation of floras, economic botany, plant biochemistry and many other specialized fields. The Royal Botanic Gardens has one of the largest herbaria in the world and an excellent botanic library.

The African component of the People and Plants Initiative is supported financially by the Darwin Initiative, the National Lottery Charities Board and the Department for International Development (DFID) in the UK, and by the Norwegian Funds in Trust.

Disclaimer

Acknowledgements

Sincere thanks are due to all chapter, case study and other contributors, whose diverse perspectives and invaluable insight have made this such an interesting and collaborative project. Special thanks are due to Alan Hamilton, Gonzalo Oviedo and Tony Cunningham of WWF; Walt Reid and Chip Barber of WRI; and Rachel Wynberg of Biowatch South Africa for their patient support and help in bringing this manual to light.

Numerous individuals commented on drafts by the many chapter authors, contributed information or otherwise helped out during the course of building this manual. They include, and we would like to sincerely thank: Zayd Alathari; Bruce Aylward; Grazia Borrini-Feyerabend, Ancienne Ecole, Bugnaux; Todd Capson, STRI; Charles Chester, Fletcher School of Law and Diplomacy, Tufts University; Phyllis Coley; Gordon Cragg, National Cancer Institute, US; Tony Cunningham, People and Plants Programme; Randall Curtis; Michael Davis; Michael Davies Coleman, Rhodes University South Africa; David Downes, CIEL; Graham Dutfield, Working Group on Traditional Resource Rights; Steve Gartlan, WWF-Cameroon; Kodzo Gbewonyo, BRI; Michael Gollin, Venable, Baetjer, Howard and Civiletti, LLP; Anil Gupta, Honey Bee Network; Charlotte Gyllenhaal, University of Illinois, Chicago; Alan Hamilton, People and Plants Programme; Marthinus Horak, Foodtek, CSIR South Africa; Maurice Iwu, Biodiversity Development and Conservation Programme; Ripin Kalra, Max Lock Centre; Ruth Kiew, Botany 2000; Tom Kursar; Roger Leakey, ITE; Patricia Madrigal-Cordero; Gary Martin, People and Plants Programme; Amiya Nayak; Ruth Norris; Susanne Obigt, PhytoPharm Consulting; Gonzalo Oviedo, WWF People and Conservation Unit; Clement Patient, WWF International; Elpidio V Peria, SEARICE; Hew Prendergast, RBG Kew; Joshua Rosenthal, NIH; Steve Rubinstein; Manuel Ruiz, SPDA; Diane Russell, ICRAF; Trish Shanley, CIFOR; Jean Claude Soh, MINEF Cameroon; Vivienne Solis-Riviera, IUCN; Maui Solomon; Barry Spergel, WWF-US; Erie Tamale, WWF International; Niall Watson, WWF-UK; Nathalie Ward, Boston University Marine Programme; Helene Weitzner; Robert Winthrop, the Society for Applied Anthropology; Maureen Wolfson, National Botanical Institute, South Africa; and Abe Zachariah.

Primary funding for this manual was provided by the World Resources Institute (WRI), WWF People and Conservation Unit, and the WWF People and Plants Programme. Funding for elements was provided by UNCTAD Biotrade (geographic indications and trademarks); the Global Forest Science (grant GF-18-2000-74), for Kelly Bannister's contributions; Brazilian National Council for Science and Technology (CNPq) for Darrell Posey's contributions; the Sands Foundation, which made the trust fund chapter possible; CARPE (for Cameroon case studies); and DANIDA, which funded – through WWF International's Implementing the Convention on Biological Diversity project – the Bwindi and Tai National Park case studies. In addition, a number of institutions generously supported the work of authors on their staff, including: Biowatch-South Africa; WWF Cameroon; Bioresources Development and Conservation

Programme; the Centre for International Environmental Law; Conservation International; the Institute of Economic Botany of the New York Botanical Garden; the Royal Botanic Gardens, Kew; and the Department of Biological Sciences of the Federal University of Maranhao, Brazil. Thanks are due to all the above.

Sarah A Laird

Section I

BIODIVERSITY RESEARCH RELATIONSHIPS

Photograph by Sarah A Laird

Researcher Gabriel Leke Awang and traditional healer Michael '1911' Ngonde examining bark in the forest around Upper Buando, Cameroon

Chapter 1

Laying the foundation: equitable biodiversity research relationships

Miguel N Alexiades and Sarah A Laird

Introduction

Biodiversity research is frequently positioned at the interface of multiple junctures, such as science and the private sector; biodiversity rich but technologically poor and biodiversity poor but technologically rich nations and regions; the urban and rural; and between the economically and politically powerful and the disenfranchised (Cunningham, 1996; Dove, 1996; Macilwain, 1998; ten Kate and Laird, 1999). The result is that complex ethical questions and challenges are made more complex by rapid technological change and globalization (Alexiades, in press). Because the 'ethical envelope' (O'Riordan, 1996) – the broad moral, philosophical and political context within which biodiversity research takes place – is multidimensional and dynamic, the obligations it raises for researchers are likewise complex and constantly changing (Janzen et al, 1993). Now, more than ever, researchers need to revise their assumptions and ethical standards, taking into account economic, social, cultural and political considerations which, until recently, did not enter the mainstream academic research equation.

The entry into force of the United Nations Convention on Biological Diversity (CBD) in December 1993, and expanded recognition of the cultural and environmental rights of indigenous peoples and local communities, have created new standards for 'equity', changed the way that biodiversity research is perceived and imposed new – if not yet realized – responsibilities upon researchers. Practical or scientific objectives are no longer viewed as distinct from ethical, economic and legal obligations, obligations which biodiversity researchers are increasingly expected to incorporate into the research process.

In this chapter we discuss the broad context – the 'ethical envelope' – in which research relationships are constructed, introducing some of the important issues and questions that researchers may wish to address as they develop their fieldwork projects. We begin by providing a brief overview of the characteristics of biodiversity research itself, and then proceed to lay out some of the issues, processes and concerns that guide current discussions and tensions regarding biodiversity research. We conclude by introducing some broad guidelines of principles and questions that are treated in more detail in subsequent chapters.

The characteristics of biodiversity research

By and large, the primary objective of biodiversity research is the improved understanding of what are often threatened ecological and knowledge systems, in order to provide the valuable insights and management tools that are critical for conservation and sustainable development. In some high biodiversity regions, biodiversity research, often tied in with conservation, has become a significant economic activity (Janzen et al, 1993), although in general biodiversity research budgets are small relative to other areas of science. However, the practice of biodiversity research frequently brings to light the economic inequalities between nations and between scientists in different nations (Table 1.1).

Biodiversity research is extremely varied, both in its scope and approach. It is undertaken by researchers in fields as broad as geography, botany, zoology, microbiology, ecology, natural products chemistry, pharmacognosy, ethnobiology, genetic engineering, forestry, agriculture, rural sociology and cultural anthropology. Biodiversity research may encompass the natural, physical and social sciences. Geological mapping, studies of evolution and animal behaviour, ecological studies of gap dynamics and forest regeneration, and studies of resource use and perception may all form part of different biodiversity research initiatives, and these may or may not involve, directly or indirectly, local communities. Some forms of biodiversity research involve only a small field component, entailing the collection of such biological samples as blood, soil or plants, for example, with the bulk of the research being conducted in the lab. Conversely, biodiversity research may be largely a field-based activity, involving a forest inventory or resource management study.

To help characterize the diversity and range of activities taking place within biodiversity research, we provide an overview of who the actors are, what characterizes biodiversity research, where it is undertaken and why.

Who

Researchers

Researchers might be students (undergraduate or graduate), professional academics, government employees, nationals or foreigners, members of a local community or outsiders. The project may entail one researcher or a whole team of researchers working together at the same time, or in different phases.

Table 1.1 Relationship between number of plant ecologists and number of plant species by region

Region	Per cent of world's plant ecologists	Per cent of world's plant species
North America	43	7
Europe and North Asia	35	15
Central and South America	1	38
Sub-saharan Africa	3	16

Source: AMNH, Biodiversity Exhibit, Centre for Biodiversity and Conservation, 1998

Institutions

Researchers will frequently be affiliated with any one or more of a vast range of private and public institutions, including universities, research institutions and herbaria, government agencies, non-governmental organizations (NGOs) and grass roots organizations (GROs), or private corporations. Moreover, there may exist complex institutional partnerships that may determine how the research is carried out or in what ways the results are utilized.

Research participants

Research participants may range from tribal hunter-gatherers to city dwellers and include people who have little prior exposure to scientific research and outside agents, to those with university degrees and extensive direct involvement with researchers.

What

Research might be basic or applied, with or without a commercial component, or with varying elements of each. Community involvement in biodiversity research ranges from none, to that of providing different forms and degrees of consent and participation with regard to research design and implementation. The research may involve extremely simple, non-invasive techniques or may be highly disruptive, environmentally or culturally. Moreover, some biodiversity research may require collection of specimens, and then in varying amounts. Finally, it may last only a few days or weeks, or it may extend for years.

Where

Research might be undertaken in tropical or temperate areas, in rich or poor nations, rural or urban, inhabited or uninhabited, as well as in protected areas. Because biodiversity research tends to prioritize biodiversity rich areas, however, much research tends to be in protected areas or areas with low population densities, inhabited by subsistence farmers or indigenous peoples, and in communities which are frequently economically and politically marginalized.

Why

Research might be purely academic, undertaken in pursuit of knowledge for its own sake, with resulting products a thesis or scientific publications; it might be used strictly by a local community in contexts ranging from health, education and land rights; it might assist environmental and social impact assessments; it might address objectives of conservation and development projects; it might undertake national biodiversity inventories; it might compile community biodiversity registries of knowledge or databases for use by communities; or it might identify new (or improve existing) commercial products, be they new natural products or agricultural varieties.

5

Box 1.1 Characterizing biodiversity research

The Pew Conservation Fellows Biodiversity Research Protocols (1996) distinguish between five categories of biodiversity research to illustrate diversity in approaches with regard to local community involvement, potential commercial applications and level of extraction or collection of materials.

Non-extractive, non-commercial research

Biologists document the evolution of species and ecological patterns and processes through observation, simulation, etc, without collection of samples.

Extractive but primarily non-commercial research

This might involve the collection of samples of organisms for description, or for study of taxonomic or ecological relationships among species.

Non-extractive research with possible commercial potential

Ethnobiologists may study plants and animals without the collection of samples. These studies may involve documentation of local innovations, traditional knowledge and practices, and lead to the development of databases, or production of books, films, CDs, etc. This local knowledge may be documented to preserve or share within the community or beyond it.

Extractive research intended for commercial development

Extraction could be in small quantities, such as for biotechnological laboratories, or in large quantities for natural product development. Such research conducted by students, academic researchers, corporate researchers or local communities may be intended to develop new products based on biodiversity traditionally used by local communities or elaborated by individual innovators. It may also involve screening and analysing biodiversity, without making any reference to local uses.

Conservation research intended for protection of biodiversity

Academic researchers, NGOs, government organizations, corporate researchers or local communities may utilize all of the methods mentioned above to create effective resource management plans and biodiversity education programmes.

Biodiversity research and the changing 'ethical envelope'

The geopolitics of biodiversity

The bulk of the world's biological diversity is found in developing tropical countries, and within these countries in areas and among people who are frequently politically and economically marginalized (Dove, 1996). Moreover, the strong link between cultural and biological diversity means that biodiversity research is often conducted in close proximity to, or with the involvement of, these local communities (Maffi, 2001; Posey, 1999). These factors immediately raise a wide range of ethical issues, ranging from the researchers' relationships with local communities, to the roles of researchers as mediators between actors, agents and interests in a world permeated by social and economic inequalities.

Biodiversity and genetic resources are not only biological resources but political resources, as well (Redford and Richter, 1999). This is evident in the way issues surrounding access to, and use of, genetic resources have entered the local, national and international political arena, particularly in relation to conservation and economic development. Biodiversity-rich countries experience the pressures, opportunities and conflicts of interests associated with a mounting international environmental and corporate agenda which increasingly values, often in explicit economic terms, biodiversity and biodiversity-related cultural knowledge. There is a growing feeling that if countries are to set aside large areas for conservation purposes, at the very least they should capture a portion of the economic revenue generated by the genetic, species and ecosystem diversity they conserve (Sanchez and Juma, 1994). This argument is bolstered by increased applications for genetic resources in private-sector research and development (R&D) programmes, including those in industries such as the biotechnology, pharmaceutical, crop protection, seed, horticulture, and cosmetic (ten Kate and Laird, 1999).

Rising conflicts over access to, and use of, cultural and genetic resources are clearly expressed by the salience of biopiracy as a topic of discussion among academics, policy-makers and the general public, both in national and international fora. As a political concept, biopiracy is built on the premise that genetic resources and associated cultural knowledge are not public goods and, concomitantly, that certain stakeholders have proprietary rights over them. The legal foundation for this precept was laid down by the Convention on Biological Diversity, which recognizes sovereign states and certain groups as having rights over genetic resources. This approach has subsequently been followed up by regional and national legislative initiatives, all of which seek to define rights over genetic resources and conditions under which others' access might be granted. While many different stakeholders might agree on a general definition of biopiracy – the illegitimate appropriation or commercialization of genetic resources and associated knowledge – consensus as to what kinds of biodiversity prospecting or biodiversity research actually constitute biopiracy is probably unattainable. For example, different stakeholders often hold differing, even competing, claims to genetic resources. Individuals, family groups, communities, ethnic groups, regions and nation states may all have legitimate though often conflicting or parallel proprietary claims over the same resources. Moreover, there is likely to be little consensus as to who is and is not an appropriate representative of the various stakeholders involved, what is and what is not appropriate compensation, and even what does and what does not constitute commercialization. In any case, biopiracy has emerged as a powerful metaphor through which fear of neocolonialism in the global economy is expressed, creating a politically sensitive, emotionally charged and ethically complex backdrop for biodiversity research (Clement and Alexiades, 2000).

In an attempt to regulate commercial access to biodiversity, biodiversity rich countries have set up legislative mechanisms to control collection of materials (see Chapter 12). Distinguishing between demands for access to material and knowledge for academic or commercial research has proved difficult, and in many countries – such as the Philippines – all research is regulated in an effort to control subsequent use and set formal terms for benefit-sharing. The high media profile that biodiversity prospecting has acquired in the past years has helped polarize public opinion towards one of two stereotypes. The first of these, pervasive in industrialized nations, is that the combined efforts of new technologies and adventurous researchers can tap the enormous potential wealth of tropical forests and indigenous knowledge in order to give rise to important new cures for such diseases as cancer and AIDS. A second view, more dominant in biodiversity rich nations, shares the view that biodiversity prospecting will be extremely successful at identifying new commodities, but expresses acute concern that biodiversity rich nations and local communities will not be adequately compensated – falling victim to international 'biopirates'. Both views overestimate the involvement of the private sector in biodiversity research, and underestimate the risk and cost intrinsic to

developing new natural products (see Chapter 8; ten Kate and Laird, 1999).

A growing consensus also calls for greater stakeholder control over, and benefits from, biodiversity research and use. Stakeholders include indigenous peoples and local communities, research institutions, governments, protected areas and others. International policy instruments, such as the International Labor Organization Convention 169 Concerning Indigenous Peoples (1989), the Convention on Desertification and Drought (1994), the UN Draft Declaration on the Rights of Indigenous Peoples (1994), Agenda 21 (1992) and the Rio Declaration (1992), address in increasingly explicit terms the rights of indigenous peoples and local communities to knowledge, resources and territories. These rights include the requirement of prior informed consent and benefit-sharing associated with academic and commercial research (Posey and Dutfield, 1996; Posey, 1996). At the same time, indigenous peoples' groups have articulated their demands for an equitable research process in declarations, statements, and active participation in international policy forums (see Chapter 7).

All of these processes have created a complex, charged and rapidly shifting political environment through which researchers, with their frequent lack of adequate training or experience in these issues, may have particular difficulty navigating. As Hoagland (1994, p53) writes in the introduction to the American Association of Systematics Collections' (ASC) *Field and Research Guidelines*: 'Life is increasingly complicated for field biologists. Interest in national cultural patrimony, local economic needs, concern for private property rights, and heightened awareness of the value of biological resources have led to restrictions in field collecting in many countries.' Increasingly, researchers find it difficult to acquire permits for research and collections in countries in which they have worked for many years, and many bemoan the development of governmental approaches that assume the worst intentions on the part of researchers. Governments of biodiversity rich countries, on the other hand, frequently feel the pressure of public opinion and the need to restrict biopiracy, while lacking information or understanding of biodiversity research and the way in which researchers set standards for their own practices. As a result, governments are often given little choice but to say 'no' to research badly needed for their own national biodiversity conservation programmes.

Biodiversity research and the Convention on Biological Diversity

Biodiversity researchers have significantly contributed to raising public awareness regarding the alarming loss of biological and cultural diversity. In conjunction with the conservation community, they also helped to spawn a utilitarian argument for conservation: the loss of biodiversity means the loss of species with medical and other applications, while a parallel process of acculturation is leading to the diminishing of traditional ecological knowledge, including that on medicinal uses of plants. Researchers are now confronted with the implications of the successful transmission of this message around the world, including implementation of the Convention on Biological Diversity (CBD). The CBD explicitly links conservation with use – both in the sense that sustainable use is necessary to conserve a wide range of biological diversity, but also in that 'use' (including research) must contribute to conservation and wider development needs through equitable benefit-sharing.

The CBD provided the first comprehensive policy approach to biodiversity conservation, and in doing so incorpo-

rated 'explicitly ethical provisions' (McNeely, 1999). Activities directed at the conservation of biodiversity, including research, now 'must be based upon an explicit understanding of the values that are promoted through different types of production systems and institutional arrangements' (McNeely, 1999, p29). In the CBD policy process, including implementation at the national level, practical and scientific approaches to conservation – including biodiversity research – are now often evaluated and viewed through the lens of the geopolitical and ethical considerations discussed above.

One consequence of this trend is that biodiversity research now takes place in a very different ethical, scientific, commercial and policy context than it did ten years ago. Specifically, shifts include:

- Biodiversity is now the 'national patrimony' of host countries and not the 'common heritage of mankind'.
- Genetic and species diversity are seen as having commercial potential, often as an 'informational' (rather than purely 'material') basis for product development, which in turn is harder to track.
- Biodiversity research is called upon (and expected) to contribute to conservation and sustainable development, and a large portion of biodiversity research today is funded under a broad conservation umbrella.
- The rights of indigenous peoples and local communities to control and benefit from biodiversity research are recognized and increasingly formalized in policy instruments and documents developed by indigenous peoples' groups.
- Biodiversity research relationships are required to be 'equitable' and include the 'fair and equitable sharing of benefits' (CBD, Article 1).

Development of a concept of ethics in biodiversity research circles

Ethics and the social sciences

Discussions of ethics in relation to research participants, the profession and governments became a central concern in anthropology during the 1960s, when the Vietnam war and the role of anthropologists in military intelligence operations, and the US government-sponsored Project Camelot in Latin America precipitated a thorough reexamination of the role of science in society (Wax, 1987; Akeroyd, 1984). As a result, many professional societies, including the Society for Applied Anthropology, the American Anthropological Association and the British Sociological Association, developed specific codes of conduct during the 1960s and 1970s. Discussions pertaining to ethical behaviour and revisions of codes of conduct continue to this day. Akeroyd (1984) sees this change as a reflection of a continuous shift in power relations between social scientists, sponsors, citizens and governments following:

- broad changes in the social, economic, administrative, legal and political contexts and constraints of social research;
- the institutionalization and professionalization of social scientific research; and
- a growing recognition that knowledge is 'not only a source of enlightenment but also of power and property and, therefore, it entails the power to both harm and to benefit those studied' (Akeroyd, 1984, p134).

Today, ethical debates often centre on the interaction of the fieldworker and the research hosts, and deal with issues of informed consent and whether or not benefit or harm might result for the communities under study. For example, the American Anthropological Association's Committee on Ethics deals increasingly with issues involved in the relationships between anthropologists and their informants or host groups, including: protection of human subjects; informed consent; anonymity of informants and communities; payment of informants; exploitation of informants; and the failure to foresee the repercussions of one's research on the peoples being studied (see Box 2.4; Hill, 1987).

Ethics and the life sciences

As with the social sciences, concern with ethics within the medical establishment can be traced to the mid 1960s, leading to the creation of the field of bioethics (Fox, 1990). Over the past decades, bioethics has dealt with a broad range of issues, including patient confidentiality, truth-telling, informed consent in medical treatment and experimentation, the rights of prolonging or terminating life, and ownership and transplant of body parts or genetic materials (Marshall, 1992).

Unlike their colleagues in the social and medical sciences, ethical concern for the social impact of research is recent among natural scientists. To date, many natural scientists have not been 'accountable to a wider range of social and political opinion when researching and presenting results' (O'Riordan, 1996). Rather, ethical concerns within the natural sciences focus mostly on research misconduct, including data fabrication, falsification and plagiarism (eg Office of Science and Technology

Policy, 1999), as well as on broader environmental ethics and animal welfare (Farnsworth and Rosovsky, 1993; Cooper and Carling, 1996).

Given burgeoning public attention to ethical issues in science, Farnsworth and Rosovsky (1993) argue that it is time for ecologists to begin to question the ethical assumptions implicit in their field research. Their paper focuses on the ecological impacts of collections and research (eg destructive sampling, manipulation of ecosystems, observation of animals in the field), but their arguments apply to broader ethical issues raised by biodiversity research. They have found that although scientists are increasingly called upon to justify research on economic and ethical grounds, and are asked to advise policy-makers on environmental issues, they remain reluctant to address ethical issues raised by their research. The reasons for this include a desire to keep a low profile, the belief that potential benefits of the knowledge acquired far outweigh any short-term harm, and the difficulties of perceiving the negative effects of research while in the field (Farnsworth and Rosovsky, 1993). To this we might add a distinct philosophical legacy, which claims that science is morally and ethically neutral and which dissociates science from politics or, more generally, from problems that emerge as a result of unequal power relations.

Ethics and biodiversity research

Beginning in the early 1990s, a number of initiatives emerged to bring ethics to the forefront of biodiversity research (eg Posey, 1990, 1994; Greaves, 1994; Reid et al, 1993; Janzen et al, 1993; Cunningham, 1993). These were developed in response to the changing geopolitical context described above and include the establishment of committees on ethics and codes of ethics and research guidelines drafted by professional groups specializing in forms of biodiversity research. These groups include the International Society of Ethnobiology, the Society for Applied Anthropology, the Society of Economic Botany, and the American Society of Pharmacognosy (see Chapter 2). The ASC published *Guidelines for Institutional Policies and Planning in Natural History Collections* in response to a 'new world reality' and rapid changes in the 'legal and ethical standards that govern collections and research'(Hoagland, 1994, p1). Some of the key institutions involved in biodiversity research and prospecting drafted institutional policies to provide guidance to staff and some transparency to the research process, including distinctions made between commercial and academic research (see Chapter 3).

While commendable and essential, such initiatives cannot address the full range of issues raised by biodiversity research in the new geopolitical context. For example, whereas 'intellectual property rights' – used as a catchall term to describe local community and indigenous peoples' rights to control and benefit from the research process – are now broadly recognized, the implementation of these rights, from choosing a representative voice to setting up access and benefit-sharing arrangements, continue to raise many unresolved issues. Some guidelines and policies, such as those of the International Society of Ethnobiology (ISE), explore and address these issues in greater detail. In the end, however, the development of ethical norms in biodiversity research is a process, and current efforts reflect the ongoing struggle biodiversity researchers face as they seek to balance the demands of 'science' within their disciplines, and new obligations emerging at a time of multiple transitions.

Biodiversity research relationships as intercultural communication

Beliefs about what constitutes ethical and unethical research behaviour are inextricably related to broader moral values and philosophical assumptions, which are in turn culture-specific. As Marshall (1992) points out, 'ethics and values cannot be separated from social, cultural and historical determinants that regulate both the definition and resolution of moral quandaries'. As a corollary, anthropology can play a vital role in helping understand the 'cultural underpinnings that sustain and reinforce ethical constructs' (Marshall, 1992, p62), and help develop a cross-cultural model for the exploration of ethical questions raised by biodiversity research.

As pointed out at the outset, biodiversity researchers frequently serve as brokers between different worlds – rural and urban, the economically and politically disenfranchised and powerful, the academic and commercial, Southern and Northern, and so on. Many of the issues and questions raised by biodiversity research are issues that anthropologists have examined and explored for quite some time. These include issues relating to the articulation between local and global agents and processes; questions surrounding the appropriation of culture and cultural knowledge; issues of representation (how academics, media and local communities think about and represent each other); and the assumptions or implications of such categories of social organization as 'community' or 'ethnic group'. The concerns, approaches and conceptual tools of socio-cultural anthropology are central to many of the issues in biodiversity research, and are raised by such concepts as prior informed consent, equitable benefit-sharing and notions of 'property' and ownership of knowledge and resources.

New responsibilities for biodiversity researchers

Changed perceptions of biodiversity research, pressure to conserve biodiversity, scientific and technological developments, the increased presence of market forces in science and conservation, the commodification of culture and of biodiversity, and the political mobilization of indigenous peoples and local communities around the environment and resource rights have shifted the ethical envelope for biodiversity research. Researchers face new, and previously unimagined, responsibilities. Ethical issues now extend to include those raised by new notions of biodiversity – as national patrimony, as information with commercial value, as a subject of conservation efforts and as an expression of cultural diversity. Researchers are asked to not only inform communities, local institutions and governments of the purpose of their research, but to account for their needs in the research process – to inform, respect, serve and benefit these stakeholders. Areas that once amounted to 'common courtesy' (Hoagland, 1994) are now incorporated into regulations that formally stipulate the terms for 'equitable' research relationships.

At the same time, researchers are often asked to link even the most basic biodiversity research to conservation and sustainable development in increasingly concrete ways (Richter and Redford, 1999). In some cases, this means establishing partnerships with policy, extension and education groups, and repackaging research results into forms that inform resource management practices and influence decision-making at community, corporate and governmental levels (see Chapter 5). In other cases, researchers are required to view their work as an economic activity like any other, and are asked to pay 'conservation overhead' along with other users, in order to help off-set the host countries' costs of maintaining biodiversity and making it available for study (Janzen et al, 1993). Finally, researchers are asked to examine the implications of their research, including issues raised by the dissemination and publication of research results and disposition of collected materials (see Chapter 4). In summary, a sample of the new responsibilities which biodiversity researchers must face include:

- clarification to both host country governments and collaborating communities of the broader principles upon which research is based; ensuring that these are in line with the objectives of the CBD and other international instruments;
- linking research with biodiversity conservation; incorporating 'application' of research results to address conservation and development problems into a research project;
- undertaking consultations with local communities in order to receive prior informed consent and to 'touch base' throughout the research process on issues such as: mutual expectations, publication and dissemination of collected materials and research results and benefit-sharing;
- clarification of proprietary rights to data and research results, particularly with regard to recorded traditional knowledge and materials sent to ex situ collections;
- articulation of the ways in which research will benefit: collaborating communities, local and national conservation and development priorities, and host country institution and capacity-building;
- clarification of any potential commercial use of the research (even if not immediately evident to the researcher) and any visible or invisible commercial partners;
- clarification of the expectations and agendas of funders and sponsors of research, as well as home institutions.

In sum, existing academic norms are largely insufficient for biodiversity research in many countries today. While many researchers consider the practical manifestation of new obligations bureaucratic and cumbersome, few participate in the CBD and related processes outside of expressly scientific concerns. Professional biodiversity research bodies are all but absent. Groups that advocate an interpretation of any biodiversity research involving collection of material as 'biopiracy' are a stronger voice and have captured greater public and governmental attention.

Access and benefit-sharing regulations usually apply to both academic and commercial research, and are widely considered damaging to the research process within the biodiversity research community. Regressive permitting and regulatory procedures for biodiversity research have usually been drafted with limited or no involvement on the part of actual researchers, however. Researchers can help policy-makers draft reasonable and effective laws and develop permit procedures that do not act as disincentives to biodiversity research. The benefits of biodiversity research are often abstract, and it is all too easy for governments pressured by fears of 'biopiracy' to say 'no' to any research – even those addressing issues of inequity. Biodiversity researchers, therefore, bear an additional responsibility today: active participation in national- and international-level policy processes.

These new responsibilities are projected onto researchers at a time of considerable pressure. Although there is more money allocated to funding biodiversity research than at any time before, an overall sense of shortage persists in the research community, and the increasing number of biodiversity researchers feel they seek funds in a highly competitive environment. Moreover, the general weakening of the public sector has motivated a broad shift and growing dependence of academic and research institutions on the private sector, creating new pressures and conflicts of interests among scientists.

Meanwhile, academic advancement criteria have not changed, and the type of applied, multidisciplinary research most valuable for conservation and development in host countries and communities is poorly rewarded, and often even discouraged (Orr, 1999). There is enormous pressure to narrow one's focus and to specialize, and to publish research results in a manner that often runs counter to providing host communities and research institutions greater control over the information flow (see Chapter 4). Funders and sponsors of research often require wide dissemination of results and fast turnaround times, allowing little room – and, to date, little funding – to incorporate appropriate consultations on a national, institutional and community level, as well as innovative benefit-sharing.

While scientific disciplines are increasingly specialized, the literature continues to expand, and researchers often find they can barely keep abreast of developments in their own field. To adequately address the legal, ethical, social and multidisciplinary issues raised by their research, and to master the complex international and national policy dialogue underway today, researchers need time and support they do not have. As a result, many biodiversity researchers have backed away from engagement in issues raised by their research, while at the same time resenting new obligations as obstacles established by the uninformed. Ultimately, this is an untenable position. As Farnsworth and Rosovsky (1992, p469) point out, while researchers may resist society's 'sometimes burdensome, stereotypic, and simplistic delineation of our roles, we are nonetheless answerable to an ethic generated by that society'. The current state of affairs argues strongly for a support system within the research community; specifically, institutions, funders and professional researcher groups must begin to shoulder the responsibility of addressing these issues and setting standards for best practice in biodiversity research.

Formalization of research relationships through institutional policies, codes of ethics, research guidelines and other written standards for best practice, and the process through which they are drafted, provides guidance to individual researchers and draws out ethical issues and values embedded in research. Such issues include:

- Do researchers still adhere to the 'common heritage of mankind' paradigm of exchange?
- Do researchers understand research results to be so important that they outweigh considerations of consultation with local communities?

- Do researchers understand the potential commercial applications of their research results?
- Do researchers understand their new legal obligations?

Written policies and codes can, in turn, influence the legal, policy and ethical environment to which they respond, and have often been used as reference documents for language employed in access and benefit-sharing legislation, policy and agreements. By articulating researcher positions, they help communicate to others the responsibilities that researchers are willing to shoulder, and allow incorporation of researchers' perspectives into the ongoing policy dialogue.

Conclusion

It is not only in the field of biodiversity research that scientists are asked – just as their fields narrow and specialize – to shoulder broad legal, moral and ethical responsibilities. Agriculture, genetics, medicine, nuclear physics and other forms of scientific research are called upon today to answer to wider concerns on the part of society. Science has always taken place within an 'ethical envelope', and links between biodiversity research and corporate development are not new (Brockway, 1979). However, in today's world of improved communications, of globalized markets and intensified articulation between the local and global, of blurring divisions between commercial and academic research, and when the implications of scientific and technological developments are beyond the grasp of any but the most expert, researchers have increased obligations to make clear the ethical framework within which they operate.

Biodiversity researchers have helped put a set of issues on the international stage with which they must continue to actively engage, even though these have taken unanticipated forms. As we will see in the following chapters, some institutions and professional research groups have begun to draft institutional policies and to develop codes of ethics and guidelines for research through their professional societies. Others – although still too few – participate in a serious and informed fashion in the national and international discussions surrounding such policy processes as the CBD. Finally, researchers help build more equitable research relationships by following the rhetoric through to realization in the field, through means such as appropriate consultation, benefit-sharing and development of innovative forms of 'giving back' research results to local stakeholders.

Chapter 2

Professional society standards for biodiversity research: codes of ethics and research guidelines

Sarah A Laird and Darrell A Posey

A number of professional research societies have developed and issued documents to articulate ethical values embedded in research and set standards for *best practice*. These documents are variously referred to as codes of ethics, voluntary codes, codes of practice, statements on ethics, guidelines and research protocols. In many cases there is little distinction between them; for the purposes of this chapter we will use the terms **code of ethics** (*codes*) and **research guidelines** (*guidelines*) to describe two broad categories of document. Codes of ethics articulate underlying principles and the philosophical basis for research. Research guidelines outline standards of practice, and although some stand alone, they are also appended to codes of ethics to provide practical guidance. These might include: guidelines for publications and databases; guidelines for disposition, or distribution and use, of collected materials; guidelines for students; or guidelines for commercial research.

This chapter will address *codes* and *guidelines* of particular relevance to biodiversity research, although there is a great deal to be learned from fields such as medicine, psychology, sociology, archaeology and social work, and others that have grappled with ethical issues for many years. Some of these are also reevaluating their professional standards in light of new developments in biodiversity and biotechnology research. Professional societies in these fields have developed codes and other documents to guide (and sometimes dictate) research practices.[1] Although the terms *code* and *guidelines* are used by many organizations, the way professional groups enforce them varies from recommended standards followed at the researcher's discretion, to expelling members who do not follow the societies' guidelines, to actual punishment, such as removal of rights to practise a profession.

From the outset, the importance of the *process* of developing these documents must be emphasized – it is impossible to overemphasize the importance of dialogue and awareness-raising that occurs in the evolution of codes and standards. Through internal dialogue on ethical and practical issues associated with research, awareness is raised and standards evolve within the research community in ways that allow researchers to more effectively address the changing ethical and legal 'envelope' in which their work takes place. This has included, in recent years, responding to the demands and concerns of indigenous peoples and local communities as expressed in a range of declarations and statements (see Chapter 7). Codes and guidelines focus dialogue and create 'talking points' to guide this process, and help researchers – often from very different backgrounds and perspectives – to share understanding and develop frameworks for equity as a community. The objective should be to develop an 'ethical culture' in which ethical considerations are expressed at all stages of research and broad understandings are built. There is a great deal of potential to only superficially implement written documents; as a result, the primary responsibility of societies is to build broader consensus on principles and standards of best practice through the process of code development and the creation of ethical committees. At the same time that this process and these documents respond to external events, they also help shape those events. For example, in rapidly emerging ethical areas with no existing legal framework – such as biodiversity research, and what is known as 'access and benefit-sharing' – codes and standards of practice are often used to guide or inform legislative processes. Numerous draft access and benefit-sharing laws, such as those in Brazil, were informed by, or directly drew language from, statements, declarations and codes of ethics drafted by researchers and indigenous peoples' groups.

What is a code of ethics?

A **code of ethics** is a public moral system that encourages, requires or prohibits certain forms of behaviour considered rational and ethical for those who ascribe to it or whose professions adopt the agreed forms of behaviour and norms. A public moral system includes ideals that encourage certain types of behaviour, and rules which must be followed (American Anthropological Association, 1998). As O'Riordan (1996) put it: 'Any code of practice has to be believed in, with emotional conviction; it should not just be regarded as a rule of good field research.'

Codes of ethics, therefore, include general principles that underlie and enhance prior rights upon which equitable research activities are based (eg rights of communities and ecosystems studied), as well as principles that guide research practices (eg honesty, transparency and confidentiality). The International Society of Ethnobiology's (ISE's) code of ethics, for example, is introduced with a broad range of principles (eg principles of prior rights; self-determination; inalienability; and traditional guardianship), as well as those that guide the research relationship itself (eg principle of active participation; full disclosure; prior informed consent (PIC) and veto; confidentiality; respect; active protection; precaution; compensation and equitable sharing; supporting indigenous research; the dynamic interactive cycle; and restitution).

What are research guidelines?

Research guidelines provide details on current standards of best practice in research and are most effectively drafted to deal with what the American Anthropological Association (AAA, 1998) refers to as 'special context' research. Thus the Society of Economic Botany (SEB) and the American Society of Pharmacognosy (ASP) have issued 'guidelines' in an effort to address some of the issues raised by their particular research niches. Guidelines, at their most effective, will provide specific information and guidance on researcher behaviour and practice, such as language employed; social and environmental impacts; sampling methods; prior informed consent; disposition of research results and collections; and publication and entry into databases of information. The more narrow the research area, the more specific the guidelines can be drafted. The ISE, for example, has developed *Guidelines for Research, Collections, Databases and Publications* and has appended these to its code of ethics. While still quite general, the guidelines offer detail on practical issues associated with acquiring and distributing data not covered in the code.

In 1991, in response to a noted absence of national government regulation on the collection and exchange of plant genetic resources, the Food and Agriculture Organization (FAO) issued a *Draft International Code of Conduct for Plant Germplasm Collecting and Transfer*. The code of conduct was intended to provide guidance to national governments until such time as they implement national access and benefit-sharing measures. The code includes: objectives and definitions; nature and scope; relationship with other legal instruments; collectors' permits

(authority for issuing, contents of an application for collection, granting of permits); responsibilities of collectors and appropriate behaviour pre-, during and post-collection; responsibilities of sponsors, curators and users; and reporting on, monitoring and evaluating observance of the code. There also exist ongoing efforts on the part of ex-situ genetic resource collections to issue codes of conduct or guidelines for the transfer and exchange of material, such as the MOSAIC Code for Culture Collections (see Chapter 8).

Guidelines for Equitable Partnerships in New Natural Products Development: Recommendations for a Code of Practice (Cunningham, 1993) provides guidelines on the type of consent required from government on responsibilities and procedures that should be followed by researchers before, during, and after collection, on responsibilities of sponsoring organizations and on monitoring and evaluation. In another example, the *Indigenous Plant Use Newsletter* in South Africa published *Useful Guidelines and Tips for Fieldworkers* that provides general guidance on ways to establish equitable relationships with communities, as well as detail on recording appropriate information on ecological, botanical and medicinal use of species (Gericke, 1996).

In other cases, codes – 'outlining public moral systems' – are combined with guidelines. The Pew Conservation Fellows Biodiversity Research Protocols (1996), for example, begin with 'Principles Underlying these Guidelines'. The guidelines themselves then provide relatively concrete information on how researchers might go about acquiring prior informed consent (PIC) from communities; negotiations and compensation associated with commercial research; and steps that might be taken by professional societies, academic institutions and funding agencies to further ethical research practices. The guidelines remain quite general, however, given the range of research practices and issues they address, and the highly varied political, cultural, social, environmental and economic contexts in which researchers work. Recommendations for researchers are classified into those that 'must', 'usually should' and 'might' be carried out.

The Manila Declaration (1992), on the other hand, grew out of a meeting of Asian scientists working on medicinal plants, spices and other natural products, and the result is much more directed guidance (see Box 2.5). The declaration begins by addressing the broad ethical issues associated with the use of Asian biological resources, but then includes in appendices both a 'code of ethics' for foreign collec-

tors of biological samples (resembling something more like guidelines), and 'contract guidelines', which provide specific detail on the amount of material collected, payments and broader benefit-sharing.

There is a great deal of variety in approaches to combining both principles and practical research guidance. The Archaeological Institute of America (AIA), for example, begins with a brief introduction to basic principles, which is called the 'code of ethics', followed by the AIA code of professional standards, which details researchers' responsibilities to the archaeological record, the public and colleagues. The Register of Professional Archaeologists (RPA) begins with a code of conduct outlining researchers' responsibilities to the public, colleagues, employees and students, and employers and clients; it then provides standards of research performance to guide practices in the field.

Are codes of ethics and guidelines necessary?

There is often resistance within professional societies to the development of codes of ethics. This grows from a fear of the potential misuse of the term 'ethics' and efforts to control behaviour in the name of public morality. Many researchers also feel that the moral principles inherent in codes of ethics – such as 'autonomy, non-maleficence, beneficence and justice' – have little relevance for their practical fieldwork (Cassell and Jacobs, 1987). For example, in the case of both the ASP's and the SEB's guidelines, there was significant resistance to what were perceived as 'dictatorial' (Cragg, ASP, pers comm, 1999) and 'authoritarian' (Theodoropoulos, SEB, pers comm, 1999) codes. Within the SEB,

several members stated their opposition to an 'authoritarian code which might run roughshod over some members' deeply held convictions, or be too inflexible to deal with unusual situations' (Theodoropoulos, SEB, pers comm, 1999). As one member wrote, it would be preferable that 'any recommendations made are not disguised under the broad terminology of a code of ethics, but rather are couched more precisely in terms of recommended guidelines for plant collection, and the like' (Tyler, 'Letter to the SEB', 1994).

But practical decisions frequently have ethical ramifications, and it is often difficult to recognize an ethical dilemma when encountered. In fields such as anthropol-

BOX 2.1 THE PEW CONSERVATION FELLOWS BIODIVERSITY RESEARCH PROTOCOLS (1996)

Anil Gupta (Centre for Management in Agriculture, Indian Institute of Management, Ahmedabad, and SRISTI and Honey Bee Network)

The Pew Conservation Fellows developed ethical guidelines based on the guiding principles that:

- Research is an educational process for all concerned (even if opportunities of learning may not always be reciprocal or balanced).
- Proprietary rights for scientific knowledge cannot be fundamentally different from the rights of producers and providers of traditional knowledge and contemporary innovations.
- A need exists for respecting local cultural values and norms, as well as for fair and equitable sharing of benefits among various stakeholders.

In 1994, a meeting was held by several scholars, including some non-Pew scholars, to address ethical issues raised by biodiversity research. Access to biodiversity and associated knowledge systems invariably involves making judgements about various kinds of accountabilities of the parties involved. Gupta (1994) identified seven types or loci of accountability, which formed the basis of discussion at the meeting. Additional background materials compiled for, and presented at, the meeting included existing codes of ethics and statements of different organizations and professional societies (Churcher, 1997).

The guidelines resulting from this meeting deal with four kinds of relationships between researchers and local communities:

1 non-extractive, non-commercial research;
2 extractive but primarily non-commercial;
3 non-extractive but with possible commercial potential; and
4 extractive for commercial developments.

It is obvious that ethical obligations cannot be set in each case in the same manner and, consequently, certain aspects of the guidelines are phrased using the words 'must', 'should' and 'may'. The scholars realized that different professionals and political communities may have a genuine difference of opinion on these guidelines, but hoped that they would provide ground for further progress.

How much information is sufficient and when should negotiations among people and outsiders be considered satisfactorily concluded will become evident only through experimentation. Clearly, one cannot take advantage of the generosity of local communities and individuals. In this context, the Pew Fellows Ethical Guidelines clearly distinguish four stages in the negotiation of the terms of access to local biological resources:

1 when access occurs;
2 when a new use is discovered;
3 when a product is developed; and
4 when commercialization occurs.

ogy, ethnobiology, pharmacognosy, ecology, conservation biology and others that raise complex issues and obligations, misunderstandings and conflicts will inevitably arise. In the 'Preamble' to the Pew Conservation Fellows Biodiversity Research Protocols (1996), it is pointed out that some researchers inadequately acknowledge their collaborators' contributions, or betray their best interests without any intention of doing so: 'ironically, they actually have conformed to the prevailing professional norms. These norms must change, for they have been inadequate in ensuring equity and respectful exchanges'.

Aspects of codes of ethics and guidelines will not amount to much more than putting down in one place what is already 'common sense and courtesy' (Hoagland, 1994). However, other elements will require significant rejigging of existing ethical outlooks and practices, including (in the case of biodiversity research) the removal of the 'common heritage of mankind' basis for exchange, and shifts in responsibilities that have accompanied the entry into force of the Convention on Biological Diversity (CBD) and the rise in indigenous peoples' resource rights (see Chapter 1).

The Society of Conservation Biology does not have a code of ethics, although one of the society's stated goals is to 'promote research and the maintenance of the highest standards of quality and ethics in this activity'. However, the society does address ethical issues through the publica-tion of articles in its journal, *Conservation Biology*. In one such article, Colvin (1992) argues for a code of ethics for research in the developing world as a way to bridge the gap between scientists and the public, and to foster mutual respect, sharing of knowledge and resources, and to create balance in a relationship that has been described as 'academic imperialism' (the flow of data and specimens primarily in one direction – from the developing to the developed world).

Formalizing and articulating under-standings and obligations already embedded in fields of research is particu-larly important in today's ethical, political and legal research environment. Principles articulated in codes of ethics can help researchers develop and maintain an ethical framework for fieldwork (AAA, *Code of Ethics*, 1998; see Box 2.2). Guidelines can complement this frame-work by providing specific details on field practices common to a particular disci-pline or area of research. Codes of ethics and guidelines can help researchers reflect on, and attempt to improve, current practices, as well as increasing sensitivity to and regulating behaviour within the research community (Cassell and Jacobs, 1987). As Maui Solomon (pers comm, 1999) put it: 'the greatest strength of any code of ethics or conduct is its appeal to the moral conscience of the researcher. Until there are legally binding frameworks in place, codes of conduct and research guidelines will be the most effective behav-iour modification tools.'

Combining codes of ethics and research guidelines

The most effective approach to addressing the range of issues raised by biodiversity research is a combination of codes of ethics and research guidelines. For example, in the case of the ISE and the Manila Declaration, professional research

BOX 2.2 DEVELOPING A VOLUNTARY CODE OF CONDUCT FOR CONSERVATION RESEARCH AND COMMUNITY BIODIVERSITY REGISTERS IN INDIA

P Balakrishna (IUCN)

The fourth meeting of the Conference of the Parties to the Convention on Biological Diversity (CBD) requested countries to look at the development of guidelines and codes of best practice for access and benefit-sharing arrangements (Decision IV/8.3). Consideration is now being given to non-legal frameworks under the umbrella of voluntary codes of conduct (VCCs). VCCs are now under development by individual institutions and groups. One of the earlier efforts is underway in India, where the MS Swaminathan Research Foundation, Madras, is developing a VCC for activities relating to agrobiodiversity conservation and the development of community biodiversity registers (see Chapter 4). In 1995, the development of community biodiversity registers began in India as a way to document biodiversity and associated knowledge at the village level. As this programme evolved, the registers came to be seen as store houses of information on biodiversity and traditional knowledge, and the potential for their use in claiming rights over resources and knowledge emerged. However, until recently, issues associated with prior informed consent and the reaching of mutually agreed terms with communities whose knowledge was collected were not considered. With this in mind, the MS Swaminathan Research Foundation developed a voluntary code of conduct to guide such activities in the spirit of the CBD. The code was developed through a wide consultation process, involving non-governmental organizations (NGOs), fieldworkers, lawyers, scientists and policy-makers. The application of the code at the field level is still under experimentation, but it shows promise as a possible prelude to implementing Article 8 (j) of the CBD. A VCC for community biodiversity registers must consider the following questions:

- Who owns the genetic resources?
- How can prior informed consent (PIC) be obtained?
- What are material transfer agreements (MTAs)?
- Who is authorized in the community to provide PIC and sign MTAs?
- Who will manage the community biodiversity register?
- Who will have access to the register?
- Will the register be used as an official document in order to settle disputes?

The ethical principles underlying the VCC include: clear communication on the purpose of initiatives such as the development of the register, its uses and possible future implications; capacity-building within the community; and community ownership of the register. Information exchange with the community must be transparent and participatory. By honouring these principles, a sense of partnership can be established between researchers and communities.

Development of suitable institutional structures based on non-legal methods, such as the VCCs, may act as models for effective implementation of the CBD. With the marked transition to ethical and equitable partnerships as envisaged under the CBD, VCCs can play an important role in developing, on a case basis, a flexible and practical approach to help change legal regimes and research relationships.

Box 2.3 Elements of a code of ethics and research guidelines

Preamble

The preamble describes the context in which research takes place, the professional society's objectives and why the society decided to develop a code.

Principles

These are the underlying principles that determine ethical research relationships; they can be divided into those that underlie any equitable relationship (eg self-determination, resource rights) and principles that guide practical fieldwork and ownership/dissemination of results (eg PIC, confidentiality, transparency, benefit-sharing).

Researcher responsibilities

Some codes are structured around researcher responsibilities, rather than principles. Following on a statement of principles, a code might include a section on 'researcher responsibilities', including responsibilities to people whom they study; scholarship and science; the public; sponsors; and students and trainees.

Scope and application

This describes to whom and what activities the code will apply and the ways in which this will occur.

Process

This section explicitly acknowledges the ongoing, dynamic nature of code and guideline development, including articulating the process through which the documents were developed and adopted, and the process for ongoing revision and discussion.

Appendices

I Research guidelines

Guidelines can provide standards for academic research practices and might be grouped together into a single document. Different guidelines might also be drafted to address the range of 'special context' issues raised by varying types of research, including:

1   Before research
    *   Prior informed consent: what this involves, including PIC from the full range of stakeholders (eg government, collaborating universities and research institutions, indigenous peoples and local communities).
2   During research
    *   Ongoing, dynamic consultations;
    *   Equitable benefit-sharing (specific forms benefit-sharing might take; methods for distribution);
    *   Researcher behaviour (respect, transparency, etc).

3 Post-research
- Disposition of collections;
- Publication and entry into databases of field data (conditions attached, necessary consent, implications of doing so, etc).

II Guidelines for developing research agreements
In some cases it will be appropriate to develop written agreements outlining the relationship between researchers and local institutions, and researchers and local communities; guidelines might guide researchers through the elements of such agreements.

III Guidelines for commercial research
Guidelines can provide details on issues and practices that must be followed for commercial research, building on those provided for academic research relationships.

IV Other documents of relevance to research
These might include codes, international and national laws, indigenous peoples' declarations, institutional policies and other documents to which researchers should adhere. A single code or guideline cannot possibly cover all issues, and other documents can act as a complement and provide a context to a given code or guidelines.

groups drafted a generalized code of ethics to articulate principles embedded in equitable research relationships, as well as those that guide researcher behaviour. A number of guidelines – addressing a range of 'special context' research issues – were then appended to the code of ethics to provide practical guidance to fieldworkers.

In some cases, it will be appropriate for researchers to follow a variety of ethical codes and guidelines, and to balance obligations incurred from various roles and statuses. No single code or set of guidelines can anticipate the unique circumstances of every situation (AAA *Code of Ethics*, 1998). For example, the National Association for the Practice of Anthropology (1998) has drafted its own version of the AAA Code of Ethics – *Ethical Guidelines for Practitioners* – that incorporates issues unique to applied anthropology. A number of codes and guidelines include reference in appendices to additional codes, guidelines, laws and other documents that might also govern research practices.

By developing both a code and research guidelines, what should be a strong statement of principles (the code) and very specific guidance for field researchers (the guidelines), will be less likely to be watered down and generalized. By folding into a single document a hodgepodge of concerns, professional research groups often make standards for best practice vague and confusing. Documents have no real impact on the ethical and practical behaviour of member researchers, and spur limited discussion or interest on the part of researchers.

Box 2.4 The American Anthropological Association Committee on Ethics: evolution of a code of ethics

In 1965, the AAA's executive board received expressions of concern over the US government's support of social science research in foreign countries. This research was alleged to assist the government in their insurgency and counterinsurgency activities. The most notorious example was Project Camelot in Chile, in which the army was believed to clandestinely fund social science research to prevent public revolts against the government of Chile. Public outcry associated with this project, the war in Vietnam and later conflicts raised ethical questions: concerns that anthropology's resultant bad reputation might close off future field opportunities abroad, and the information gathered would be used by the US government to control, enslave or damage communities under study.

In this context, in 1965 the AAA formed a Committee on Research Problems and Ethics, which drafted the first code of ethics, a 'Statement on Problems in Anthropological Research and Ethics', adopted in 1967. In 1968 the executive board appointed an official Interim Committee on Ethics to make recommendations on the nature of a standing committee on ethics and issues involving ethical relationships. The committee was also asked to address issues of means by which standards of ethics could be enforced (an issue that has never been resolved). The committee proposed an elected Standing Committee on Ethics and presented a draft code of ethics. Some members of AAA objected to the committee as being itself an 'unethical' structure. Nevertheless, a standing COE was elected in 1970, with its first case the complex and controversial issues associated with research in South-East Asia considered 'clandestine' and supportive of US government counterinsurgency efforts. Since that time the COE has dealt with grievances associated with collegial relationships (plagiarism, faculty–student relationships, tenure, etc), ownership over data, discrimination of various kinds and issues involved in relationships between anthropologists and their informants or host groups. The latter include:

- protection of human subjects;
- informed consent;
- anonymity of informants and communities;
- payment of informants;
- exploitation of informants; and
- the failure to foresee the repercussions of one's research on the peoples being studied.

Although still present, the issues that once received the bulk of the COE's attention have changed since the Vietnam war because of: termination of the war; the increasing number of anthropologists and the variety of contexts in which they work, especially in applied areas; the increase in economic and political involvement by anthropologists; and increased competition for jobs and contract funds. There is also increased debate on whether anthropologists working for companies should engage in confidential research, not made available for public view. Overall, a clear shift in emphasis has taken place within the COE since 1972 from cases dealing primarily with general ethical issues to an emphasis on interpersonal and intergroup disputes (ie grievance cases).

The COE has proven largely ineffectual in resolving grievance cases, since the AAA has no 'teeth' to resolve such disputes, nor the institutional capacity to do so. The AAA's Principles of Professional Responsibility grew out of a very unpopular war and were directed more to the ethical problems of that era than to those of today. The many diverse ethical problems that confront anthropologists working in a wide variety of non-academic contexts are not adequately covered in the current code, nor is the code likely to be able to deal with all of them. Developing and revising the code has taken up the bulk of the COE's time, and 'it appears to be a never-ending process, as it should be'.

Today, the COE is working to answer fundamental questions about its mission. Who should it serve? What should its role and function be? Should it handle grievance cases or confine itself to activities and publications dedicated to educating anthropologists on matters of ethics? It is felt that the AAA should develop a new, very general, code of ethics relevant to all professional anthropologists and not get bogged down in the ever-increasing number of 'special context problems', which might be addressed in more specialized codes of ethics, drafted by specialized anthropological organizations to suit their specific needs.

Source: excerpted from Hill, 1987

The process of developing a code of ethics and research guidelines

A code of ethics and research guidelines are dynamic documents. They grow from a long process of dialogue and discussion among researchers, and once formulated and adopted, continue to evolve in the light of changing ethical, scientific, political and other factors. The process of developing a code and guidelines is as important as the product, which will be 'less a set of categorical prohibitions engraved in stone, than a series of aspirations, admonitions and injunctions to be considered, discussed and periodically altered' (Cassell and Jacobs, 1987, p2). The documents reflect an assumption that the majority of persons affected by the code agree that there are shared ethical principles, although there is unlikely to ever be definitive agreement on the nature of problems and solutions (AAA, 1998; Akeroyd, 1984).

This section will review the process through which some of the codes and guidelines for biodiversity research have been developed. The age and size of professional groups varies dramatically, and this diversity is reflected in the ways in which codes of ethics are developed. The AAA, for example, has spent more than 30 years working intensively on ethical issues, and today's code of ethics is the result of a process involving formation of various committees, drafting of documents, review at annual meetings and the evolution of understanding through case studies and discussion in the AAA's *Anthropology Newsletter*. The SEB and the ISE are much smaller and younger societies, and they represent a smaller niche, or sub-set, of research activities. As a result, the process through which these groups developed codes and guidelines was shorter and more focused. The following sections briefly discuss the ISE's, the ASP's and the SEB's code and guideline development process.

International Society of Ethnobiology (ISE)

Since its founding in Belém, Brazil, in 1988, the ISE has worked to develop principles for collaborative and equitable research relationships with indigenous peoples and local communities. The process by which this group has addressed issues raised by ethnobiological research is a valuable example of how younger societies can – in a directed and targeted fashion – develop codes of ethics and standards for research best practice in the field. The original draft documents were developed primarily as the basis for dialogue and as a tool for awareness-raising, not only of members but also of the larger public. The intention was not to exert control over people's behaviour, but to present points for discussion and facilitate a process through which the community of researchers could agree on the underlying principles upon which their work should be based. After many years of dialogue, a code of ethics was ratified only in 1998 were and research guidelines drafted.

The first ISE statement – the **Declaration of Belém** – incorporated broad calls for prior informed consent, benefit-sharing and awareness-raising. Over the course of the next ten years, these issues received greater international coverage, and the ISE responded with an internal process that culminated in the ratification in 1998 of a code of ethics and guidelines for research.

At its Fourth International Congress of Ethnobiology (ICE), held in Lucknow, India, in 1994, the ISE committed itself to build upon the principles outlined in the Declaration of Belém, in order to develop a new constitution, code of ethics and standards of conduct. The Global Coalition for Bio-Cultural Diversity (GCBCD) – the educational and policy wing of the ISE – coordinated the development of these documents, including holding a series of workshops at the Fifth International Congress, held in Nairobi, Kenya, in 1996. Workshops at Nairobi were divided into two parts: a pre-congress drafting session and an open symposium during the five days of the conference itself. The pre-congress workshops sought to:

- review the draft code of ethics and standards of practice prepared by the GCBCD; and
- evaluate 43 indigenous and traditional peoples' statements, declarations and guidelines to develop a comprehensive list of demands and expectations that these groups have of the scientific community.

Twelve individuals – including indigenous representatives – participated in pre-workshop sessions. The demands of indigenous groups were organized by topic and written on individual pieces of paper. The pre-workshop participants reviewed the draft code and guidelines, and compared them with the language and demands of indigenous groups as separated out on the pieces of paper. The draft documents were revised and brought to the full congress as part of the symposium Ethics and Ethnobiology, which involved four hours of open discussion and hearings held across the five-day duration of the congress. Between 80–90 per cent of the 250 congress participants took part in the symposium during the course of the congress. A refined code of ethics and a set of guidelines for action were developed. The code of ethics outlines the principles according to which ethnobiological research should be conducted, and the guidelines for action specify issues associated with 'best practice', including data management, cultural and genetic resource collections and publications. These documents were then circulated broadly for comment to all ISE members, as well as to indigenous and traditional peoples' groups, other professional societies and non-government organizations.

Prior to the Sixth International Congress, held in Aotearoa, New Zealand, in 1998 and hosted by the Maori communities and tribes of Maatatua, 44 people from 12 countries met for a four-day pre-congress workshop in order to prepare a revised document for the entire congress that would incorporate all consultations and suggestions received through the lengthy consultation process. Following this review process, a final code of ethics was ratified by those attending the Sixth International Congress. Congress participants deemed that it was premature to discuss the draft *Guidelines for Research, Collections, Databases and Publications*, and these were deferred to the ethics committee for further consultation and revision in preparation for a final debate and vote for adoption at the Seventh International Congress, held in 2000 at the University of Georgia, Athens, US.

The American Society of Pharmacognosy (ASP)

The ASP also undertook a multiyear process of drafting documents and holding workshops at annual meetings. In 1992, issues associated with natural products research were raised at the annual meeting in Williamsburg, US. In 1993, at the ASP annual meeting in San Diego, the use of terms to describe a written document providing guidance to researchers was discussed. As mentioned, there was significant opposition to the term 'code of ethics', and so 'guidelines' became the accepted term. In 1994, an ad hoc Committee on Indigenous Materials was established to draft a set of guiding principles for members of the society to follow in undertaking research using indigenous knowledge and resources (Cragg et al, 1997). The committee reviewed policies in effect at various institutions and companies available at the time, and drafted a paper entitled 'Natural Products Drug Discovery and Development: New Perspectives on International Collaboration' (Baker et al, 1995). The committee then prepared a resolution and draft guidelines that were published in the ASP newsletter (vol 32, no 1) in 1996. ASP members were invited to comment, and in July 1996 the resolution and guidelines were presented to ASP members attending the 37th annual meeting of the society at the University of California, Santa Cruz. They were approved with no dissenting votes and a few abstentions. There has not been a great deal of discussion of these issues since approval of the guidelines, but it is thought that most ASP members take them seriously and abide by the terms (Cragg et al, 1997; Cragg, pers comm, 1999).

The Society for Economic Botany (SEB)

The Society for Economic Botany initiated the process of developing what are now known as *Guidelines of Professional Ethics of the Society for Economic Botany* in 1990. A two-hour ethics roundtable was held at the annual meeting of the society at the University of Wisconsin, Madison, US. Based on this meeting, draft guidelines were prepared and circulated in the SEB newsletter, with a call for comments. One individual responded; this response was published in the April 1991 newsletter. The autumn 1993 newsletter included a report from the ethics committee and a list of eight other newsletters dealing with ethical issues, in order to help raise awareness with the membership. In

BOX 2.5 THE MANILA DECLARATION AND MELAKA ACCORD

Ruth Kiew (Botany 2000 Asia)

Growing concern about the behaviour of foreign scientists who collect biological materials for pharmaceutical companies overseas was voiced at several Asian conferences, including the Symposium on the Development of Drugs from Plants in Manila in 1989, the Botany 2000 Asia Workshop in Perth in 1990 and the Asian Coordinating Group for Chemistry in China in 1990. Widespread concerns and frustrations on the part of a diverse group of scientists led to the crystallization of the Manila Declaration at the Asian Symposium on Medicinal Plants, Spices and Other Natural Products (ASOMPS) in Manila in 1992.

As the subtitle of the Manila Declaration, *The Ethical Utilization of Asian Biological Resources*, makes clear, this declaration was a call for an ethical code of behaviour by foreign scientists with fair and equitable collaboration. This ethos covered four broad aspects:

1   The natural biological heritage of each country should be respected and explored for the benefit of that country, including the sharing of royalties.
2   Collaboration with foreign scientists should be conducted on a mutually acceptable basis and, where possible, should include training of local scientists and technology transfer.
3   Legislation should be developed to cover the collection and export of materials, and equitable royalty and licence arrangements.
4   Traditional knowledge must be recognized as significant intellectual property.

While every country obviously wants to benefit economically from its natural resources, two additional concerns were voiced that are particularly relevant for this region. The first is that the potential economic value of organisms, particularly in rainforests and coral reefs, is an argument easily understood by politicians who can then see the benefits of conserving natural ecosystems. If benefits accrue only to industrialized countries, however, the incentive to conserve areas in pristine condition is removed.

The second is that most Asian countries now have adequate scientific facilities to carry out research. It is intensely frustrating to local scientists to be denied the excitement of finding potentially useful biochemicals, or to describe new species, when raw materials are taken out of the country for analysis without any opportunity for collaboration or training. In addition, there are many cases where promised results of analysis carried out overseas are not made known, even when required as a condition for the acquisition of material. This also has the more serious implication that industrialized countries can exclude the country of origin from any claims to royalties or other benefits.

The fact that diverse groups of scientists, natural products chemists, plant taxonomists and pharmacologists shared common frustrations, coupled with the recalcitrance of several overseas organizations to enter into any form of collaboration, resulted in overwhelming acceptance of the Manila Declaration. The Manila Declaration sets out a series of recommendations based on the principle of collaboration and includes two appendices: a 'Code of Ethics for Foreign Collections of Biological Samples' and 'Contract Guidelines' for the provision of biological materials.

Although wholeheartedly endorsed by the Asian scientific community working in these fields, it had no impact on the behaviour of some foreign organizations. Indeed, from throughout the region reports surfaced that some foreign organizations, on contacting local institutions to purchase biological material and being told that they should abide by the Manila Declaration, disappeared only to resurface at a more remote or less well-off institution unfamiliar with the Manila Declaration, and willing to be paid on a per sample basis.

These concerns and frustrations were voiced at the next ASOMPS meeting held in Melaka in 1994. It was felt that the spirit of collaboration proposed in the Manila Declaration had failed and that a firmer commitment through legislation (preferably on a regional basis, eg under the umbrella of the Association of South-East Asian Nations – ASEAN) was necessary. This resulted in endorsement of the *Melaka Accord: Towards the Development of Legislation to Protect Biodiversity*.

The Melaka Accord also emphasized that editors of scientific journals should require publications based on material from outside their country to cite in the acknowledgements the permits of permission for acquiring the material. Papers should not be published if the material was not acquired through proper channels. However, until now the great majority of editors have ignored this responsibility.

In its emphasis on developing legislation, the Melaka Accord resulted in an informal meeting in Kuala Lumpur of a small group of scientists from ASEAN countries to try to develop a common form of legislation. As always with legislative matters, especially in a field unfamiliar to law-makers, this has proceeded slowly. In the meantime, the Philippines and the state of Sarawak, Malaysia, have enacted legislation which, while well meaning, has in some cases made collaboration for bona fide scientists more difficult, if not impossible. This was foreseen at the Manila ASOMPS conference, where it was hoped that equitable collaboration would result without the necessity of bureaucratic legislation.

the spring of 1994, revised guidelines were published in the newsletter and at the 1995 meeting of the council the guidelines were formally accepted, subject to ongoing revision, by a 5:4 vote. Ethical issues continue to be addressed at annual meetings and in the newsletter, which in 2000 began a new question and answer column on ethics (SEB, 1999). One member of the ethics committee suggests that this 'living, changing exchange of ideas will be more valuable than a static code. After all, we cannot foresee what new issues will develop in coming decades' (Theodoropoulos, pers comm, 1999).

BOX 2.6 FEDERAL FUNDING CODES: THE CANADIAN TRI-COUNCIL POLICY STATEMENT ON ETHICAL CONDUCT FOR RESEARCH INVOLVING HUMANS

Kelly Bannister (University of British Columbia – UBC)

While this chapter discusses standards for biodiversity research at the level of professional societies, it is important to note also the role of ethical codes at the level of federal-funding bodies, which not only govern federally funded research but often form the bases for ethical codes set by academic institutions. In Canada, for example, the *Tri-Council Policy Statement on Ethical Conduct for Research Involving Humans* governs all research supported by the Medical Research Council of Canada (MRC), the Natural Sciences and Engineering Research Council of Canada (NSERC) and the Social Sciences and Humanities Research Council of Canada (SSHRC). The Tri-Council policy statement recently underwent an extensive review and revision by the Tri-Council Working Group on Ethics during 1994–1997, taking into account numerous existing ethical codes and guidelines as well as the related work of scholars in a diversity of fields (*Draft Code of Ethical Conduct for Research Involving Humans*, 1997). Final revisions were approved by the three councils in 1998. The current Tri-Council policy statement includes (among others) sections on free and informed consent, privacy and confidentiality and research involving aboriginal peoples. The section on research involving aboriginal peoples is currently in abeyance awaiting negotiations with First Nations groups. In the meantime, guidance on research involving aboriginal and other groups can be found in the 1997 recommendations of the Tri-Council Working Group on Ethics Involving Collectivities. These are posted on the UBC Centre for Applied Ethics web page (www.ethics.ubc.ca) under the title of the 'Code of Ethical Conduct on Research Involving Human Subjects' (Michael McDonald, pers comm, 2000).

Two points are worthy of highlighting, in light of the above. Firstly, investigators who receive federal research funding in Canada are compelled to be aware of the Tri-Council policy statement and to ensure that their research is in compliance with this 'top-down' requirement. Secondly, the opportunity exists for influencing ethical policies at the federal and institutional levels through a 'bottom-up' approach, and indeed a responsibility to do so is implicit, as researchers confront the issues, strive to address them within the framework of the governing ethical policy, and in the process gain valuable insights on further revisions that may be required to achieve the stated goal of the Tri-Council policy statement: 'to help researchers, Research Ethics Boards and administrators of institutions develop and maintain the highest standards of ethical conduct in research involving humans'.

Source: Draft Code of Ethical Conduct for Research Involving Humans, 1997; Tri-Council Policy Statement on Ethical Conduct for Research Involving Humans (http://www.ncehr-cnerh.org)

Conclusion

Codes of ethics and research guidelines are an important element in the process of formalizing biodiversity (including traditional knowledge) research relationships. In conjunction with institutional policies and research agreements, they offer researchers an opportunity to make explicit the ethical issues embedded in their research, and to articulate standards for research best practices. Biodiversity research is often conducted in developing countries, where the bulk of biodiversity is held and where people live in closer proximity to, and depend upon, biodiversity to a greater extent for their survival. As a result, biodiversity research raises a number of issues that have not customarily been dealt with in large umbrella professional research organizations. Fields such as anthropology, ecology and botany have addressed ethical issues. However, for the most part they have not yet incorporated obligations to protect the 'knowledge, innovations and practices' of indigenous and local communities as prescribed under the CBD and issues raised by the growing recognition of indigenous peoples and local-community environmental, human and cultural rights associated with biodiversity.

Codes of ethics and research guidelines will become increasingly important tools for the communication of researchers' approaches to the many complex ethical and practical issues raised by biodiversity research today, and can help inform the process through which governments draft legislation to regulate biodiversity research. Additionally, as an increasing number of countries develop legislation regulating the collection, use and transfer of genetic resources and traditional knowl-edge, researchers must ensure that their practices adhere to these laws. Nevertheless, many researchers remain ignorant of the legal ramifications of their work. Professional societies can provide an important service to members by informing them of their legal responsibilities, providing frameworks for addressing these issues in the form of codes of ethics and guidelines, and building understanding within the research community of the dramatically changing legal landscape.

More specialized professional bodies in fields such as economic botany, ethnobiology and pharmacognosy have taken steps to address these new challenges, and many researchers in these fields are at the front line of the evolving ethical debate. However, the bulk of researchers remain unaware of the new ethical envelope within which biodiversity research takes place, and the majority of codes and guidelines today remain vague and undirected – reflecting the difficulties in mastering the new paradigm within which biodiversity research takes place. A 'do' and 'don't' list is not usually the most appropriate approach; but specificity in ethical considerations raised at each stage of research is critical. By institutionalizing a process of development and revision of codes and guidelines, professional societies can help raise awareness and ensure that members remain abreast of rapid ethical developments surrounding biodiversity research. Only through the development of an ethical culture within the research community, in part resulting from this ongoing process, will the complex and case-specific application of the principles underlying codes of ethics be possible.

Table 2.1 *Elements of codes of ethics and research guidelines*

Code or guidelines	Elements	Prior informed consent	Researcher behaviour/ benefit-sharing	Publication and distribution of data
American Anthropological Association (AAA) *Code of Ethics* (June 1998 version)	I Preamble II Introduction III Research • responsibility to people and animals with whom anthropological researchers work and whose lives and cultures they study • responsibility to scholarship and science • responsibility to the public IV Teaching • responsibility to students and trainees V Application VI Epilogue VII Acknowledgements (process of developing the code) VIII Other relevant codes of ethics	Researchers should obtain in advance the informed consent of persons being studied, providing information, owning or controlling access to material being studied, or otherwise identified as having interests which might be impacted by the research. Degree and breadth of informed consent varies by project and policy context. Informed consent is a dynamic and continuous process that should begin in the project design phase and continue through implementation. Informed consent does not necessarily require a written or signed form. "It is the quality of the consent, not the format, that is relevant.'	Ethical obligations include: to avoid harm or wrong, understanding that the development of knowledge can lead to change which may be positive or negative, respect the well-being of humans and non-human primates; work for long-term conservation of archaeological, fossil and historical records; consult actively with the affected individuals or groups, with the goal of establishing a working relationship that can be beneficial to all parties involved.	Researchers must determine in advance whether their hosts/providers of information wish to remain anonymous or receive recognition and make every effort to comply with those wishes. Researchers must present to their research participants the possible impacts of the choices and make clear that, despite their best efforts, anonymity may be compromised or recognition fail to materialize. Researchers should utilize the results of their work in an appropriate fashion and whenever possible disseminate their findings to the scientific and scholarly community; but they must also consider carefully the social and political implications of the information they disseminate.
International Society of Ethnobiology (ISE) *Code of Ethics* (1998) and *Guidelines for Research, Collections, Databases and Publications* (Draft 3, 1998)	I Preamble II Purpose III Principles • prior rights • self-determination • Inalienability • traditional guardianship • active participation • full disclosure	Principle of prior informed consent and veto: PIC must be obtained before any research is undertaken. Indigenous peoples, traditional societies and local communities have the right to veto any programme, project or study that affects them. PIC	Researchers must follow: • principle of respect; • principle of active protection; • principle of precaution; • principle of compensation and equitable sharing; • principle of supporting indigenous research;	*The Guidelines for Research, Collections, Databases and Publications* give special attention to issues raised by ownership of, and control over, research data and collections. They include the requirement for PIC, agreement on disposition of collected

Code or guidelines	Elements	Prior informed consent	Researcher behaviour/benefit-sharing	Publication and distribution of data
	• PIC and veto • confidentiality • respect • active protection • precaution • compensation and equitable sharing • supporting indigenous research • dynamic interactive cycle • restitution IV Adoption of principles by ISE V Appendix I: international declarations and instruments; ISE *Guidelines for Research, Collections, Databases and Publications*	assumes that all potentially affected communities will be provided complete information regarding the purpose and nature of the research activities, as well as probable results, including all reasonably foreseeable benefits and risks of harm (be they tangible or intangible) to the affected communities.	• principle of the dynamic interactive cycle; • principle of restitution. The *Guidelines for Research, Collections, Databases and Publications* calls for PIC, agreements, good faith, sharing of information and data.	materials, shared authorship, and ongoing monitoring and review of the research relationship that includes approval at each step of the ways in which data can be published or used.
The American Society of Pharmacognosy (ASP) *Guidelines for Members* (1992)	I Resolution II Guidelines for implementation • compliance with national and international legal and professional researcher declaration, standards • PIC • equitable partnerships • training and technology transfer to build source country capacity • compensation for development of a	'In sampling... members and their source country collaborators will make good faith efforts to obtain the prior informed consent of the relevant parties and to safeguard the legitimate rights of such communities.'	Collaborations will reflect 'equitable partnerships in the sustainable use and development of biological materials in the source country and the exchange of results of the biological and chemical evaluation of materials in a confidential and timely manner.' Training and technology transfer will be provided to build source country capacity. Activities damaging to the conservation and sustainable	All parties participating in research will be recognized for their contribution of material and/or knowledge to the development of a commercial product.

- commercial product research will have a minimal impact on the conservation and sustainable use of biodiversity

use of biodiversity will be avoided or minimized.

Society for Economic Botany (SEB) *Guidelines of Professional Ethics of the Society for Economic Botany* (1995)	1 Members of the SEB have responsibilities to the public.	Members will communicate clearly and honestly to all individuals with whom they work; this includes individuals who may be affected by the objectives and possible consequences of the research. If the research has a commercial objective, researchers will make that explicit to those studied and will disclose the expected commercial results.
	2 Members of the SEB have responsibilities to those studied.	Researchers will comply with all rules and limitations that local people, their communities or their institutions place on the research. They will not 'trick' people into revealing 'secret' information. They will offer to supply any reports or materials resulting from the research. If the research has commercial applications, they will 'do all in their power to ensure that compensation is paid'.
	3 Members of the SEB have responsibilities to host governments and other host institutions.	Researchers will comply with all regulations and supply reports and specimens to perform specified services (eg seminars and training). They will help enhance the physical and human resources of their collaborators' institutions.
	4 Members of the SEB have responsibilities to the profession.	Researchers will respect any request for confidence by those providing data or materials, provided that the maintenance of such confidence does not compromise other ethical considerations. They will respect individuals' right to anonymity and privacy of those they work with when it is requested.
	5 Members of the SEB have responsibilities to those who support their research that are consistent with the ethical guidelines of the SEB.	

35

Code or guidelines	Elements	Prior informed consent	Researcher behaviour/ benefit-sharing	Publication and distribution of data
Pew Conservation Fellows *Biodiversity Research Protocols: Guidelines for Researchers and Local Communities Interested in Accessing, Exploring and Studying Biodiversity* (1996)	I Preamble II Principles underlying these guidelines III Scope of the guidelines • non-extractive, non-commercial research • extractive but primarily non-commercial research • non-extractive research with possible commercial potential • extractive research intended for commercial development • conservation research intended for protection of biodiversity IV Guidelines consist of: • approval • initial disclosure of information • involvement and negotiation • compensation and other terms of access • professional societies, academic institutions and funding agencies	Informed consent should be obtained within limits of practicality. In most cases the researchers should obtain clearance from the appropriate state government authority and, where applicable, from institutions of indigenous peoples. Outlines under 'Initial Disclosure of Information' the types of information researchers should provide to communities when first seeking access.	Researchers should communicate in locally understood languages. They will share findings at different stages with the providers; they must not engage in bribery or make false promises. They must provide documents and hold meetings to acquire PIC and update communities. Researchers must help broker benefit-sharing for commercial research at different stages in product research and development. They should work with institutions and professional societies to improve standards for good conduct and practice by researchers.	Researchers and communities must agree on a protocol of acknowledgements, citations, authorship and inventorship as applicable, either citing local innovators or conservators, or respecting requests for anonymity. Professional societies, academic institutions and funding agencies should encourage citation of intellectual contributions of local innovators, communities and groups.
Seventh Asian Symposium on Medicinal Plants, Spices and Other Natural Products (ASOMPS VII)	I Introduction II The Manila Declaration III Appendix 1: Code of Ethics for Foreign Collectors of Biological Samples	Researchers must obtain permission for all collections. For all collecting, the authorizing agreement(s) should include provision for any subsequent commercial	Researchers should respect the regulations of the country visited; obtain permission for collections; leave a complete set of adequately labelled	Researchers should send copies of research reports and publications; acknowledge collaborators and host institutes in research reports and publications.

The Manila Declaration concerning the Ethical Utilization of Asian Biological Resources (1992) Code of Ethics for Foreign Collectors of Biological Samples (Appendix 1) Contract Guidelines (Appendix 2)	IV Appendix 2: Contract Guidelines	development that may eventually arise.	duplicates with local institutes; not collect rare or endangered species without permission; collect no more material than is needed; leave copies of photographs, slides and other materials; send research reports. For commercial collections, limits are set on the amount of material to be collected; payments and benefit-sharing are specified; reporting requirements are included; it is necessary to avoid destructive harvesting; add value (eg preparation of extracts) in country to samples.	
American Folklore Society *A Statement of Ethics: Principles of Professional Responsibility (1988)*	I • Preamble • relations with those studied • responsibility to the public • responsibility to the discipline • responsibility to students • responsibility to sponsors, including one's own and host governments • epilogue	The aims of the investigation should be communicated, as is possible, to the informant. The anticipated consequences of the research should be communicated as fully as possible to the individuals and groups likely to be affected.	Folklorists' primary responsibility is to those they study. Where there is a conflict of interest, these individuals must come first. Folklorists must do everything in their power to protect the physical, social and psychological welfare of their informants and to honour the dignity and privacy of those studied. There should be no exploitation of individual informants for personal gain. Fair return should be given to them for all services.	Informants have the right to remain anonymous. The right should be respected both where it has been promised explicitly and, as much as possible, where no clear understanding to the contrary has been reached. These strictures apply to the collection of data by means of cameras, tape recorders and other data-collecting devices, as well as to data collected in interviews. There is an obligation to reflect on the foreseeable repercussions of research and publication on the general population being studied.

Note

1 For a listing of codes, see the 'Directory of useful contacts and resources' at the end of this book; see also the codes online included in the 'Professional Ethics Resources on WWW' put out by the Centre for Applied Ethics: www.ethics.ubc.ca/resources/professional/codes.html, and 'Biodiversity Research Protocols' compiled by Tegan Churcher for the Pew Fellows: http://geography.berkeley.edu/ProjectsResources/BRP/BRP.html.

Chapter 3

Institutional policies for biodiversity research

Sarah A Laird and Rachel Wynberg

This chapter describes ways in which research institutions have developed policies to address issues raised by biodiversity research and prospecting. We look at steps taken to distinguish between commercial and academic research, the process through which policies are developed, and differences in approaches required for institutions in the North and those in the generally biologically richer but technologically poorer South. These issues are illustrated by case studies throughout, including more detailed examination of the experiences of the Limbe Botanic Garden, Cameroon, and three research institutions in South Africa.

What are research institutions and how are they involved?

Research institutions involved in biodiversity research and biodiversity prospecting include universities, botanic gardens, natural history museums, government research institutes and other non-profit institutions that receive some level of support from public funds. The primary objectives of these institutions include expanded human understanding of the natural world; research to address specific public needs, such as the development of new medicines; education and training; and – more recently incorporated – biodiversity conservation.

Most research institutions undertaking biodiversity research and prospecting do not have formal policies that guide the activities of researchers in the field, or set terms for prior informed consent or benefit-sharing. Instead, such institutions traditionally adhere to long-standing practices understood by staff as 'best practice', and this generally does not include written institutional policies. However, in many institutions there have been rapid developments on this front over the past ten years, partly in response to the Convention on Biological Diversity (CBD), and particularly in those institutions that collect biological material. Institutions that have drafted policies to guide the work of their staff and collaborators include botanic gardens, natural history museums and universities. In some cases, however, there is significant resistance to the development of policies, both from members of staff and external researchers, who perceive such initiatives to be unnecessarily bureaucratic and restrictive to their research. Researchers with a strong interest in ethics have often found that the most effective way to influence practices in their field is through their professional societies and the development of codes of ethics and research guidelines (see Chapter 2).

Why develop an institutional policy?

Research institutions often house large ex-situ collections of materials, many of which they exchange with other institutions as part of a long academic tradition, and sometimes as an obligation connected to public funding. They also conduct a large portion of ongoing field research and collections in biodiversity rich countries, and increasingly collect materials for commercial partners. As the international policy context in which biodiversity research and prospecting and the exchange of materials in ex-situ collections evolves, the need for institutional policies grows. As the Association of Systematics Collections' (ASC's) *Guidelines for Institutional Policies and Planning in Natural History Collections* explain (Hoagland, 1994, p1):

> *'Natural history museums face a new world reality. There are increasingly complex demands on natural history collections and expertise at a time when there is rapid change in the legal and ethical standards that govern collections and research. Institutions without clear missions, goals and policies are increasingly handicapped.'*

Increasing calls for clarity and transparency in the activities of non-profit research institutions, in line with evolving international standards, will require institutions to formalize their policies on such issues as prior informed consent from stakeholders in source countries; the conditions under which material may be supplied to third parties; strategies for benefit-sharing; and adherence to the CBD, the Convention on International Trade in Endangered Species of Wild Fauna and Flora (CITES) and other international treaties. The ASC guidelines recommend that institutions establish policies addressing broader ethical issues that underline research practices (Hoagland, 1994, p47):

> *'While individuals associated with a collecting organization invariably owe allegiance to a code promulgated by their profession, it is important for a collecting organization itself to establish its own ethics policy. Such an ethics policy assures adherence to the organization's mission, maintenance of a positive work environment and attention to obligations owed its current public and posterity.'*

Working towards a comprehensive policy for academic and commercial research

As part of a wider trend in the scientific community, many research institutions conduct both commercial and academic research, forming partnerships with a diverse array of public- and private-sector agencies. One of the more intractable issues this raises is the difficulty of distinguishing between commercial and academic research, and the increasingly grey divide and overlap between the two research areas. Policies are invaluable in clarifying this distinction and the different ways in which consent for activities should be sought and benefits shared.

In general, two approaches have been adopted in an attempt to clarify research objectives. The first approach, embraced by some of the institutions most actively involved in commercial biodiversity prospecting activities – such as the New York Botanical Garden, the Missouri Botanical Garden, Strathclyde Institute of Drug Research (SIDR) and the US National Cancer Institute – is to develop institutional policies to specifically address the commercial acquisition of natural products. Such policies tend to be short and focused on issues raised by a specific exchange of material and the partnership upon which it is based. Common elements of these policies include (see Table 3.1):

- a review of the institutional mission;
- clarification of the ways in which commercial collaborations can contribute to achievement of the mission;
- affirmation of the institutional commitment to international treaties such as the CBD and CITES;
- a requirement for the prior informed consent of source countries, sometimes including local communities; and

- a description of the benefit-sharing package, primarily with respect to publications and royalties.

A second approach, adopted by other research institutions, including the Royal Botanic Gardens, Kew, and the University of the South Pacific, is to develop a more comprehensive policy that addresses issues such as prior informed consent, supply and exchange of collected materials and benefit-sharing in the case of both academic and commercial research. While specific provisions cover the unique considerations associated with commercial use, the inclusion of academic research in the policy creates a foundation from which all collections are 'cleared' by source countries and local communities, and for a distinction to be made between commercial and academic collections.

The University of the South Pacific (USP) *Guidelines for Biodiversity Research and Bioprospecting* directly address 'the very considerable difference between basic scientific research in biodiversity ... and bioprospecting for commercial ends'. It also acknowledges that 'the dividing line between them is not always clearly demarcated'. Section A of the policy covers 'biodiversity research', and Section B 'bioprospecting'. When biodiversity research – which is defined to include a range of collecting, surveying, cataloguing, dissemination and assessment activities – 'leads to bioprospecting', the terms included in Section B then apply. Bioprospecting is defined as 'any research on biodiversity where the intent is to collect, sample or survey living organisms with a view to screen or prospect for potentially useful substances or genetic resources ... by its nature bioprospecting

Table 3.1 *Institutional biodiversity prospecting policies*

Institution	Biodiversity prospecting policy	Institutional mission and relevance of bioprospecting	Distinction between academic and commercial research	Adherence to international and national law and prior informed consent	Benefit-sharing	Environmental impact of collections
The Royal Botanic Gardens (RBG), Kew	*Policy on Access to Genetic Resources and Benefit-Sharing:* this includes the annex 'Policy of RBG Kew on Benefit-sharing in Connection with Commercial Contracts for Pre-CBD Genetic Resources', January 1998 (Replaced in June 1999 with the *Common Policy Guidelines for Participating Botanic Gardens on Access to Genetic Resources and Benefit-Sharing* and RBG Kew's supplementary annex on commercialization) Replaces the 1992 'Conditions of acceptance of plant material from external collaborators (the supplier) for	The RBG Kew mission is to 'ensure better management of the Earth's environment by increasing knowledge and understanding of the plant and fungal kingdoms – the basis of life on earth'. To achieve this mission, RBG Kew uses its collections and the skills of its staff in systematics, horticulture and conservation.	'RBG Kew will supply genetic resources subject to the terms of any permits or MTAs under which they were received from Suppliers. RBG Kew will supply genetic resources to Recipients who meet its criteria. Emphasis will be placed on supplying genetic resources to support the conservation of biological diversity and the sustainable use of its components, and to build capacity in taxonomy and other systematics to help meet these objectives.' The 'special case of commercial use by Recipients of genetic resources obtained from RBG Kew' is covered in a separate section of the policy.	RBG Kew intends to honour 'the letter and spirit' of the CBD, CITES and other international, regional and national laws and policies concerning biodiversity. It will obtain the prior informed consent of the country providing the genetic resources and the stakeholders as required by law in the country in question and according to best practice. Stakeholders may include relevant departments of central government, local authorities, private individuals such as landowners, indigenous peoples, local communities and NGOs.	'RBG Kew will make share the benefits arising from access to genetic resources and derivatives fairly and equitably with the Source Country and appropriate stakeholders within it' (3.1). Monetary benefits include an upfront payment, medium-term milestone payments, and royalties; 50% of net revenue from royalties received by RBG Kew arising from commercial use of genetic resources will be shared with source country and other stakeholders, as appropriate; monetary benefits will be paid into the Kew Benefit-Sharing Fund to support activities such as training and information	reasonable efforts to

Institution	Policy	Scope of activity	Application of policy	Benefits
	collaborative studies in the Biochemistry Section of the RBG Kew Memorandum of Understanding'			exchange. Monetary and non-monetary benefits will vary by case. An indicative list includes: scientific information and research results; technology transfer; training; joint research and development; employment of locals; in kind benefits.
The New York Botanical Garden (NYBG)	'Statement of Policy Regarding Biodiversity Prospecting with Collaborating Organizations', January 1996	The NYBG 'engages in biodiversity prospecting, an activity which includes the discovery, documentation, research and development of new commercially viable medicines, foods, fibres, fuels, or other products from plants and fungi. The results of biodiversity prospecting have broad applications for the benefit of the public in agriculture, industry and the health sciences.'	'This policy applies to the NYBG's activities in biodiversity prospecting with other organizations. It does not apply to the NYBG's relationship with individuals engaged in biodiversity prospecting or to the NYBG's activities in basic research in systematic and economic botany.'	• Sharing of data. • Joint authorship of all resultant publications. • 'NYBG will pay 50% of net royalties [received by NYBG] to any organization or collectively to organizations that collaborated substantively in the product's discovery or development.' • 'The NYBG believes that all organizations participating in collaborative biodiversity prospecting will gain, if not financially, then by the advancement of shared scientific goals.'

Institution	Biodiversity prospecting policy	Institutional mission and relevance of bioprospecting	Distinction between academic and commercial research	Adherence to international and national law and prior informed consent	Benefit-sharing	Environmental impact of collections
The Missouri Botanical Garden (MBG)	*Natural Products Research Policy,* October 1994	The mission of the MBG is 'to discover and share knowledge about plants and their environment, in order to preserve and enrich life'.	'Botanists of the research Division of the MB collect, process and curate herbarium specimens to promote the goals of basic botanical research. As part of separate research endeavours, MBG botanists may also collect samples for evaluation and development of plant derived products... Researchers of the MBG's Research Division will only engage in the collection of samples for evaluation and potential commercial development when such goals have been clearly stated.'	Full prior informed consent of all appropriate government agencies must be obtained. All research activities will be conducted in accordance with the provisions of the CBD and CITES. All 'appropriate parties are aware of project activities'. All permits for collection and export of plant samples have been obtained and regulations of participating countries are followed, as well as the regulations of the USDA. MBG will work only with reputable source country institutions that can represent the national interests.	Where necessary and appropriate, MBG personnel will offer to serve as liaisons to facilitate negotiation of agreements between source-country institutions and other organizations for whom samples are collected. MBG will make its best effort to ensure: 'an appropriate percentage of the profits generated by any products developed will return to the source country...MBG will only enter into commercial research agreements with a provision ensuring that royalties will be paid to the source country in the event a discovery is marketed and generates profits.... MBG will not receive any	'MBG botanists will collect plant specimens and samples in a manner that will minimize impact to any population, species or ecosystem. Collections of large samples will be designed and monitored to ensure that neither population size nor genetic diversity is significantly impacted'.

percentage of such royalties'. Source countries will have first right of refusal to develop an appropriate and sustainable supply of raw material. Opportunities for research originating as a direct result of any programme are shared in an equitable manner between MBG and collaborating source country institutions. The intellectual contribution of researchers, traditional healers and others is respected, and MBG 'respects the intellectual property rights that protect their input' to the research process.

The Natural History Museum (NHM), London	*Bioprospecting Policy*, October 1996 Included in *Life and Earth Sciences Collections: Curatorial Policies and Collections Management Procedures*, 1998	The NHM mission is 'to maintain and develop our collections and use them to promote the discovery, understanding, responsible use and enjoyment of the natural world'. The NHM, 'with our	Will act in accordance with the provisions of the CBD relevant to bioprospecting. 'When participating in bioprospecting outside the UK, we will operate in a contractual framework which	The NHM 'will only supply samples for bioprospecting purposes when the agreement between the host country and the body purchasing the samples provides the fair and equitable sharing of benefits arising from	'Appendix 6: Code for collecting biological and geological specimens'; includes details on acceptable collecting practices: 'Every effort will be made to avoid unnecessarily destructive or environmentally

Institution	Biodiversity prospecting policy	Institutional mission and relevance of bioprospecting	Distinction between academic and commercial research	Adherence to international and national law and prior informed consent	Benefit-sharing	Environmental impact of collections
		substantial reference collections of biological specimens from all regions of the world, and our expertise in collecting, authoritatively identifying and classifying biological organisms', can play an important role in bioprospecting. 'Recognizing the potential benefits to the custodians of biological resources and to humanity, we are willing to participate in bioprospecting which uses material newly collected for these purposes.'		includes agreement from an appropriate government agency in the country concerned. We will not collect and supply samples for screening without the prior informed consent of the host country.'	their commercial or other utilization. In drawing up bioprospecting agreements, we will take account of the rights, interests and practices of indigenous peoples. We expect that, by working cooperatively with local organizations, we will help to strengthen the taxonomic capacity of countries providing the biological resources.'	damaging sampling'.
The International Cooperative Biodiversity Groups (ICBG: US NSF, NIH, USAID)	'Principles for the treatment of intellectual property and the sharing of benefits associated with ICBG sponsored research', 1997	The ICBGs were formed to serve the basic goals of 'drug discovery, economic development, and the conservation and sustainable use of biological diversity'.	ICBG collaborations involve commercial partners to assist in the drug discovery component of the project. Agreements should anticipate 'tension between traditional scientific ethics of	Projects must respect and comply with relevant international conventions such as the UN CBD and national ABS laws, which should be 'observed rigorously' in the development of agreements and	'Equitable distribution of benefits should accrue to all those who contribute to a commercialized product, whether they are members of the consortium or not, including research institutions and local	

		public access to information...and indigenous or commercial partners for confidentiality of information with potential commercial value, pending protection through patenting or other means'.	the conduct of research'. The prior informed consent of local peoples should be based on full disclosure of information; 'indigenous concepts of intellectual property should be respected'; the best practice to acquiring PIC is written agreement.	or indigenous people who provide useful traditional knowledge... ideally compensation begins flowing early in the collaboration through initial payments, training, equipment or services, to provide near term conservation incentives.'	
University of the South Pacific (USP), Pacific Island countries	*Guidelines for Biodiversity Research and Bioprospecting, 1997*	The rich biodiversity of the tropical South Pacific region encompassed by the USP member countries represents the heritage of its people at both the national and community levels, and its sustainable use holds the key to their future well-being and security. Much of this biodiversity remains undiscovered and undescribed and its value both real and potential is largely unknown. The [USP] recognizes that	'Biodiversity research of the tropical South Pacific region is considered basic research which is a fundamental and required component of research and teaching at the University of the South Pacific. It is not the intent of these guidelines to impede the conduct of such work...where biodiversity research leads to bioprospecting, however, it must automatically fall under the guidelines for bioprospecting provided in Section B, and proposals	Written consent of recognized representatives of resource owners for access to collecting areas must be acquired.	MOAs must address patent rights; IPR of resource owners must be protected and benefits to be shared between resource owners, researchers, and companies made clear; resource owners should be involved in collections, and trained in collection and conservation techniques of species with potential commercial value; as high a level of research on useful compounds should be	Bioprospecting using rare, endangered or restrictive species is prohibited; and collection must be conducted in a manner not detrimental to the environment; this may include a stated size limit of samples, on a species basis; if large re-collections are to take place, a researcher must provide USP with funds to monitor impacts.

Institution	Biodiversity prospecting policy	Institutional mission and relevance of bioprospecting	Distinction between academic and commercial research	Adherence to international and national law and prior informed consent	Benefit-sharing	Environmental impact of collections
		priority must be given to assist its member governments in the conduct of both basic and applied research on biodiversity'.	must follow the format provided in Annex 2... The University recognizes the very considerable difference between basic scientific research in biodiversity...and bioprospecting for commercial ends.' The policy elaborates upon the distinction between academic and commercial research, acknowledging the difficulty in doing so.		conducted within the region as possible; nationals should be trained in such work; voucher specimens should be deposted.	
The Council for Scientific Research (CSIR), South Africa	*CSIR (Division of Food Science and Technology) Policy on Bioprospecting, 1999* *CSIR's Research Approach to Bioprospecting, 1999* *CSIR's Policy on Partnerships for Bioprospecting, 1999*	The CSIR is one of South Africa's main scientific and research institutions. The overall objective of bioprospecting at CSIR is to 'unlock the economic and social benefits inherent in South Africa's rich biodiversity and associated indigenous knowledge through a nation-wide	Policy documents focus on the commercial exploitation of South African plants. A memorandum of understanding establishes a bioprospecting consortium between the CSIR and major research institutions in the country, but is focused exclusively on 'adding value to	It is CSIR policy to 'act in accordance with the CBD and all related national legislation'. The policy makes no specific reference to prior informed consent.	'The CSIR will only engage in bioprospecting research when provision for the fair and equitable sharing of the benefits arising from their commercial or other utilization is agreed upon. In drawing up bioprospecting agreements, we will take account of	

research and development project'. indigenous plants and indigenous knowledge systems through bioprospecting'. Collaboration is to 'create a benefit for the South African economy'.

the rights, interests and practices of indigenous peoples. We expect that, by working cooperatively with local organizations, we will provide the scientific and technological partnership which will permit communities to benefit from their indigenous knowledge.' Some of the more tangible benefits received thus far from collaborations with foreign institutions include the transfer of anti-cancer screening technology from the NCI to the CSIR, and the development of a medicinal plant extraction facility at CSIR, through the technical and financial support of Phytopharm and Pfizer.

has commercial implications'. By making clear the distinction between these two forms of research, while acknowledging the difficulty in doing so, communities, government and other groups can feel more comfortable that the institution is tackling in a comprehensive manner the complex array of issues raised by their research.

A recent undertaking to develop a comprehensive policy and harmonize practices in the botanical garden community has resulted in *Common Policy Guidelines for Participating Botanic Gardens on Access to Genetic Resources and Benefit-Sharing* (2001). Botanic gardens and seed banks house up to a third of the world's vascular plant species, most collected before entry into force of the CBD (Dove, 1998). The *Common Policy* was developed by a group of 17 botanic gardens to harmonize approaches to accessing genetic resources and sharing benefits (see Box 3.1; ten Kate, 1999, UNEP/CCBD/ISOC/Inf.2; UNEP/CBD/ISOC/Inf.1). The policy, including model material transfer agreements, broadly tackles the mechanics of exchange that underlie the acquisition and supply of genetic resources, and standards for both academic and commercial best practice. Each institution will now add detail and emphasis, reflecting the local context, and begin the laborious process of implementation. This is likely to be especially challenging for developing country institutions that lack both the finances to create additional posts and the mechanisms to track genetic resources that are being acquired by these institutions or supplied to third parties. Early experiences suggest that this process will require considerable awareness-raising and capacity-building, especially among staff of botanical gardens who have traditionally focused upon biological and ecological work rather than upon the difficult social and political issues raised by biodiversity research and prospecting.

Which of the two approaches adopted is to be recommended? While useful as the basis for agreements, a narrow institutional policy focus on commercial exchanges of materials belies the complex overlap and relationship between academic and commercial collections. In fact, many of the early biodiversity prospecting policies have evolved into more comprehensive policies over time. Within institutions whose mission and core activities involve the collection and exchange of genetic resources, and traditional knowledge associated with those resources (for example, through databases, publications and herbarium labels), it is common for academic collections to end up with commercial applications. Uncertainties surround the use to which a collection might be put in the future, either by the original institution or by a third party institution to whom material is supplied as part of academic collaborations. A more comprehensive approach can help resolve issues likely to arise in the future about collections made in the past, and can include 'trigger points' that determine whether a project is academic or commercial in nature. Additionally, this can help to resolve confusion associated with existing collections, including an institutions' treatment of material obtained prior to the CBD's entry into force (UNEP/CBD/COP/3/Inf. 46; ten Kate, 1997).

In addition to uncertainty surrounding end-users of collected resources and knowledge, many research institutions support field collections through commercial partnerships, thereby further blurring the academic and commercial divide. For example, northern botanic gardens and universities, such as the New York Botanical Garden, the Missouri Botanical Garden and the University of Illinois

Box 3.1 Common Policy Guidelines for participating botanic gardens on access to genetic resources and benefit-sharing

China Williams (Royal Botanic Gardens, Kew)

The entry into force of the Convention on Biological Diversity (CBD) in December 1993 and its subsequent ratification by 175 parties provides a new mandate for botanic gardens and presents them with both policy and practical challenges. If the ex-situ collections held in botanic gardens are to be of value to science and conservation, they must be maintained and improved. To achieve this, continued access to plant, fungal, microbial and animal genetic resources is essential. The exchange of genetic resources between botanic gardens is also necessary in order to facilitate taxonomic and other scientific research and to ensure that the levels of diversity held in ex-situ collections are adequate for conservation. Additionally, botanic gardens act as an important 'clearing house' as the genetic resources they collect may be supplied to a wide range of organizations, including other botanic gardens, universities' research institutions and industry.

The CBD and national laws on access to genetic resources have introduced certain legal obligations with which botanic gardens must comply. However, in some important respects (eg access to collections made prior to the entry into force of the CBD), there is little legal or policy guidance for botanic gardens. By taking a voluntary, proactive approach to find a clear and practical way to operate in the current situation, botanic gardens can help devise solutions which meet the requirements of the CBD and relevant national law, and which are appropriate to their activities. As there are some 1775 botanic gardens in the world, if each garden were to adopt its own approach on access to genetic resources and differing material transfer agreements, the exchange of materials could become extremely complicated and time consuming. In order to facilitate access to genetic resources directly from countries of origin and through exchange with other botanic gardens, it is highly desirable that botanic gardens harmonize their policies, practices and agreements.

With this in mind, 17 botanic gardens from Australia, Brazil, Cameroon, Canada, China, Colombia, Malaysia, Germany, Ghana, Mexico, Morocco, the Russian Federation, South Africa, the UK and the US have been working together in a project coordinated by the CBD Unit of the Royal Botanic Gardens, Kew, and funded by the UK Department for International Development. Botanic Gardens Conservation International and the International Association of Botanic Gardens have also taken part. The objectives of the project, which started in November 1997, have been to develop a harmonized approach for the participating gardens on access to genetic resources and the sharing of benefits that implements the letter and spirit of the CBD; to produce model material-transfer agreements for the acquisition and supply of genetic resources by botanic gardens; and to prepare a publication explaining the choices made and their implications.

The project has involved four workshops for participants. The first was held at the Royal Botanic Gardens, Kew, in December 1997 and the second at Kirstenbosch Botanical Garden in Cape Town, South Africa, in September 1998. At the third workshop, hosted by the Institute of Botany in Beijing during 17–19 May 1999, the representatives from 14 botanic gardens from 11 countries who attended agreed by consensus on the language of the Common Policy Guidelines (CPG) summarized below.

The fourth and final workshop was held in November 2000 in Cartagena, Colombia. Here, the group agreed a set of non-legally binding principles, which will form the basis for more detailed institutional policies (for more information on the CPG and the process, see www.rbgkew.org.uk/conservation).

The Common Policy Guidelines are divided into the following sections.

Section 1

Section 1 sets out the five objectives of the CPG:

1   to ensure that activities of participating gardens (PGs) involving access are consistent with all applicable law;
2   to promote cooperation between all users of genetic resources;
3   to establish conditions that facilitate access;
4   to promote the fair and equitable sharing of benefits arising from the use of genetic resources; and
5   to encourage other botanic gardens to adopt the CPG and a harmonized system of access to genetic resources and benefit-sharing.

Section 2

Section 2 provides common definitions for all terms used in the document, consistent with definitions used in the CBD.

Section 3

Section 3 states the principles of the CPG, that PGs will, when acquiring genetic resources from in situ conditions (as far as possible and when appropriate), obtain prior informed consent from government; when acquiring genetic resources from ex situ collection, obtain prior informed consent from the body governing the collection; acquire and supply genetic resources under material transfer agreements that satisfy these principles; maintain records to track the acquisition, supply and benefit-sharing of genetic resources; and share benefits arising equitably with the country of origin and other stakeholders.

Section 4

Section 4 sets out conditions for acquisition under the CPG. When acquiring in situ material, PGs will obtain PIC from government where required, and will make reasonable and sincere efforts, in a material acquisition agreement (MAA), if possible, to clarify the roles and responsibilities of all parties to the agreement; to obtain and record the consent of stakeholders; to ensure that all handling of material has been in accordance with all applicable law; and to clarify the terms and conditions of use in writing.

When acquiring material from a documented ex-situ source, PGs will obtain PIC from the governing body of the ex situ collection and will make reasonable and sincere efforts, in an MAA if possible, to clarify the roles and responsibilities of all parties; to ensure in writing that the material was acquired and is being supplied in accordance with all applicable law; to ensure all handling of material has been in accordance with all applicable law; and to clarify terms and conditions in writing.

When acquiring material from other ex situ sources, PGs will ensure that acquisition conforms with all applicable law and will make reasonable and sincere efforts to ascertain that the materials were obtained by the provider in accordance with the CBD.

Section 5

Section 5 sets out the importance of establishing appropriate systems of records, tracking and management so that PGs can follow the acquisition, use and supply of material in order to implement the CPG, including sharing benefits from the use of genetic materials.

Section 6

Section 6 sets out conditions for supply under the CPG. PGs will clarify, where possible in a material supply agreement (MSA), whether the supply is for commercial or non-commercial purposes. They will supply material on terms that honour the conditions on which the material was originally acquired. In addition, PGs will supply material under agreements that oblige the recipient to share benefits arising from the use of the material; not to commercialize without the consent of the providing PG; and not to pass genetic resources, their progeny or derivatives on to third parties without ensuring that they enter into written agreements containing terms that are no less restrictive. As far as possible, PGs will treat material acquired prior to the entry into force of the CBD and those acquired after its entry into force in the same manner.

Section 7

Section 7 sets out the CPG's commitment to benefit-sharing and the obligation on PGs to share benefits arising from the use of this genetic material, their progeny and derivatives fairly and equitably with the country of origin and other stakeholders. Where possible, PGs should also share benefits arising from the use of pre-CBD material.

Section 8

Section 8 states that implementation should be progressive and should be regularly reviewed. The PGs recognize that the CPG should continue to develop and respond to feedback and suggestions, and encourage the wider participation in the process of other botanic gardens and all other individuals, groups and organizations dealing with genetic resources.

Annex 1

Annex 1 contains two model agreements, a model MAA and a model MSA. These have been prepared for illustrative purposes to demonstrate the kind of terms and conditions that should be contained within a transfer agreement that is consistent with the CPG.

Annex 2

Annex 2 is the ratification list containing the names of PGs that have formally adopted these Common Policy Guidelines by sending a letter of adoption to China Williams or Kerry ten Kate at RBG, Kew.

Programme for Collaborative Research in the Pharmaceutical Sciences (PCRPS), undertake field research funded by commercial companies, but with collections made by staff who also work in source countries on an academic basis (see Table 3.2). This is also the case with many Southern research institutions, such as the National Botanic Institute and the Council for Scientific Research (CSIR) in South Africa, the University of Yaounde in Cameroon and the University of the South Pacific in Fiji. Many institutional researchers are now tarred as 'biopirates' because of an inability for those both inside and outside of the institution to distinguish between academic and commercial activities. Staff undertaking basic research with no commercial support often resent these commercial partnerships, which they see as jeopardizing ongoing, and more important, institutional academic research. A policy can help to clarify distinctions between institutional academic and commercial research, and by setting out institutional principles can reassure collaborators that the institution adheres to current standards of best practice.

Table 3.2 *Examples of research institution commercial partnerships in the 1990s*

Non-profit research institution	Examples of commercial partners and countries of collection
North	
The New York Botanical Garden (NYBG)	Pfizer – US National Cancer Institute (NCI) – Latin America Merck – US and Latin America
Missouri Botanical Garden	Monsanto – Africa NCI – Africa
University of Illinois PCRPS	Monsanto – South-East Asia (Vietnam, Laos) Glaxo – South-East Asia (Vietnam, Laos) Bristol-Myers Squibb – South-East Asia NCI – South-East Asia
Royal Botanic Gardens (RBG), Kew	Glaxo – RBG Kew's ex-situ Living Collections and Herbaria – global
South	
National Botanical Institute (NBI), South Africa Council for Scientific Research (CSIR), South Africa	Ball Horticulture – South Africa Phytopharm – South Africa Pfizer – South Africa
The University of the South Pacific, Fiji	Strathclyde Institute of Drug Research (SIDR) – Fiji
National Institute of Biodiversity (InBio), Costa Rica	Merck NCI Bristol-Myers Squibb Givaudane Roure Indena Analyticon

The process of developing a policy

Institutional policy development is a process (see Box 3.2) and no single institution can be expected to master quickly the complex and extremely involved policy dialogue currently underway relating to access and benefit-sharing. However, nor can they afford half measures. Staff should be designated or hired to address these issues, and the implementation of policies – and not merely drafting of documents – must be given priority. An important part of a comprehensive institutional approach is the development of follow-up strategies to ensure implementation and acceptance of the policy, as well as its refinement and adaptation over the years in light of lessons learned, and changing legal, ethical and scientific trends. The process by which a policy will be further refined, developed and implemented should be made clear within the policy document itself. The RBG Kew policy, for example, highlights the need to build internal capacity to implement the policy, and to constantly revise the policy in accordance with rapidly evolving standards of accepted best practice. Steps outlined in the policy to do this include: developing guidelines for staff on how to implement the policy; an improved collections strategy; more detailed policies on the acquisition of genetic resources by RBG, Kew; more detailed policies on access and benefit-sharing for information acquired with genetic resources (eg ethnobotanical data); and procedures for monitoring, evaluating and enforcing the policy.

The importance of perpetually refining and updating policies is evidenced by the activities of staff at the Missouri Botanical Garden. In 1994, the Missouri Botanical Garden was one of the first botanical gardens to draft a biodiversity prospecting policy, which at the time was considered a fairly progressive document for a large institution. However, staff in charge of the policy now consider it 'drastically in need of revision...as a first effort it suffers as many first efforts do'. A more holistic approach, involving not only biodiversity prospecting agreements, but also specimen exchange and loan, plant material exchange and other issues, is now underway in collaboration with the Botanic Gardens Policy Project described above (Jim Miller, pers comm, 1999).

The US National Cancer Institute (NCI) has developed a succession of documents that outline NCI policies on access and benefit-sharing and act as the basis for agreement with source countries in which they collect samples. The first such document was developed in the late 1980s and issued in 1990 as a 'Letter of Intent'. Today, the NCI employs a 'Letter of Collection' (introduced in 1992) and – in countries in which a greater portion of drug discovery and research take place – a 'Memorandum of Understanding' (1995). At each step advances have been made with respect to the range of benefits to be shared with source countries, the extent of their involvement in the research process, and the role of source countries as active partners in negotiations should a commercial product be developed (ten Kate and Laird, 1999).

Likewise, the US government-funded (National Institutes of Health (NIH), National Science Foundation (NSF) and US Department of Agriculture (USDA)) International Cooperative Biodiversity Group's *Principles for the Treatment of Intellectual Property and the Sharing of Benefits Associated with ICBG Sponsored Research* have evolved alongside

BOX 3.2 THE INSTITUTIONAL POLICY DEVELOPMENT PROCESS: STEPS IN POLICY DRAFTING AND IMPLEMENTATION

Review and strategize

Hire or designate an individual inhouse to draft a review of the 'state of the art' and develop a strategy for institutional policy development.

Designate a driver

Appoint or hire individuals to spearhead policy development and implementation.

Develop a support committee

Develop a small committee to provide support to the process. The committee should include individuals from inside the institution and a few key experts, or external advisors, to reflect a range of perspectives and stakeholder interests. Include individuals from countries in which the institution conducts research – even if their involvement is largely by e-mail or post.

Develop a list of stakeholders to be involved in the policy process and consult broadly

Identify a broader group of stakeholders who receive information about the process and can contribute to the process through commenting on documents, attending workshops, etc.

Disseminate information

Ensure that the coordinating individuals and the support committee have copies of institutional policies, codes of conduct, national ABS laws and relevant policy and background papers; work to build capacity in this area from the earliest stage; bring in visiting speakers and lecturers to educate the committee and staff; have staff and the committee meet with researchers, NGOs, government officials and others with experience in the CBD, ethical research practices, etc to flesh out ideas developed through internal consultations.

Consult internally

Hold consultations within specific departments and levels of the institution, as well as joint meetings with individuals representing different departments, in order to bring altering viewpoints together.

Draft first version of policy

The coordinating individual/team, in conjunction with outside and internal advisors, drafts a first version of the policy; included are recommendations for the institutional structures required to effectively implement and revise the policy. The committee then reviews and comments on the policy and plan for implementation. A broad policy will more effectively cover a diverse range of situations, but region- or project-specific guidelines may be needed to supplement the broader policy and provide more detailed guidance in the field.

Internal consultation on policy

The revised draft policy and recommendations for implementation are sent around internally to all staff for review, and individual departments hold meetings with the policy coordinator to provide feedback.

Revision of policy

The policy is revised, based on feedback from staff.

Broad consultation on policy

The revised policy is sent to the broad stakeholder group for feedback and advice, particularly institutions and individuals in countries where research takes place. Workshops take place where necessary.

Revision of policy

The policy is revised, based on feedback from the broad consultation.

Development of implementation strategy and priority actions

An implementation strategy is developed, including provisions detailing how it will be implemented, necessary 'next steps' to this end, and the process for revision over time to allow changes in light of lessons learned and shifting legal, ethical and scientific contexts.

Establish institutional structures

Steps are taken to establish the institutional structures necessary to implement the policy – ie fundraising proposals sent out, staff hired, office space and facilities made available.

Adoption of policy

The policy is formally and publicly adopted.

Ongoing monitoring

The committee is adapted as necessary but remains in existence as an advisory and monitoring arm to the policy implementation staff, and meets several times a year to review progress and address concerns.

Dedicated attention

One full-time and dedicated staff person (or more, depending upon the institution's size) works exclusively on implementing the policy, including participating in international meetings and other fora impacting policy development, implementation and ongoing revision and refinement.

standards for best practice. The original principles grew out of a 1991 conference held by the involved US government agencies (Schweitzer et al, 1991). These principles were further articulated and refined by International Cooperative Biodiversity Groups (ICBG) staff members (Grifo, 1996; Rosenthal, 1998). They were finally moved into the 'Request for Applications', which legally outlines the principles to which grantees should comply (NIH/NSF/USDA, 1998). Specific changes incorporated over the years include:

- highlighting the need for formal, independent legal advice for source countries and organizations;
- more specific discussion of contract elements and types;
- default ownership of samples by host country governments and organizations; and
- recognition of the role of community ownership and the attendant rights and responsibilities for an informed consent process (J Rosenthal, pers comm, 2000).

The incremental manner in which the University of Illinois PCRPS (see Box 3.3) has worked towards developing a policy is typical of most large research institutions in which the differing agendas and approaches of departments of research, finance, intellectual property and boards of trustees must be juggled and balanced. Few institutions have a dedicated policy unit, as is the case at RBG, Kew, which makes quick and directed policy development more difficult.

Largely in response to the Common Policy for Botanic Gardens on Access to Genetic Resources and Benefit Sharing (2001), the National Botanical Institute (NBI) of South Africa is adopting a more holistic approach towards the use of genetic material, including model material-transfer agreements for both acquisition and supply, as well as policies on benefit-sharing and traditional knowledge. Although such policies are not yet in place, the NBI has entered into an important biodiversity prospecting agreement with Ball Horticulture (Case Study 3.1). It is significant that the development of this agreement was considerably stalled by the lack of national legislation to guide negotiations, and the absence of an institutional policy on such issues as benefit-sharing, prior informed consent and intellectual property rights to which the agreement could defer. In the absence of these standards, the issues were clouded, suspicions ran high and stakeholders – brought together to debate the agreement – were concerned that provisions of the CBD could be neglected or counteracted. Interestingly, and perhaps unfairly, the willingness of the NBI to make transparent the terms of its agreement with Ball Horticulture (not common practice in most institutions) allowed for unprecedented public scrutiny and criticism of the case.

Box 3.3 The University of Illinois, Chicago's PCRPS:
evolution of an institutional policy

The University of Illinois, Chicago's (UIC) PCRPS has spent over ten years working towards a policy for their biodiversity research and prospecting activities. Beginning with staff involvement in developing the National Cancer Institute's (NCI's) 'Letter of Intent' in 1988, the following ten years saw various points of refinement of internal positions on PIC, benefit-sharing and other issues. Key events are described below:

- 1986: NCI-supported collections begin.
- 1988: Contracted collecting institutions – including PCRPS – collaborate on the drafting of a 'Letter of Intent', issued in 1988, and outlining NCI responsibilities associated with access and benefit-sharing.
- 1991: UIC PCRPS involvement in collecting additional raw material of a promising *Calophyllum* species in South-East Asia draws the attention of the Sarawak government to these issues; subsequently a state access and benefit-sharing (ABS) law is passed.
- 1992: The United Nations Conference on Environment and Development (UNCED) is held in Rio de Janeiro in 1992; issues associated with 'access and benefit-sharing' attain international prominence.
- 1993: Beginning of PCRPS collaboration with Glaxo which catalysed the need for a policy for benefit-sharing (staff had previously relied on the NCI documents to guide collecting overseas). Staff made a public statement that 50 per cent of any royalties received by UIC would be shared with source countries; this was in line with standard practice at the time, including at botanic gardens such as NYBG and RBG, Kew.
- 1994: PCRPS staff helped to coordinate an American Society of Pharmacognosy meeting on intellectual property rights (IPRs) in Costa Rica; staff present the framework for a policy, subsequently published in the *Journal of Ethnopharmacology* in 1996.
- 1995: PCRPS begins a research collaboration in Ecuador, including discussion of ABS issues, and contents of potential agreement.
- 1996: Collaborators from Ecuador visit UIC to discuss IPRs, coauthorship and other benefit-sharing issues with PCRPS staff and the Intellectual Property Office of UIC. Andean Pact Decision 391 shifts parameters of discussion, and after much negotiation the collaboration was dropped in 1998 due to issues on which agreement could not be reached.
- 1997: Internal discussions are held within UIC Intellectual Property office and PCRPS on the CBD, benefit sharing, best practice, etc in order to prepare a policy for inclusion in an ICBG proposal.
- 1998: PCRPS receives the ICBG grant and begins negotiations with parties in Vietnam and Laos; a 'benefit-sharing package' is developed involving specific sharing of royalties with source country institutions, UIC and inventors. A trust fund is established to support benefit-sharing in Vietnam and Laos.
- 1999: The development of a benefit-sharing plan for the ICBG provided the institution with the opportunity to examine the potential elements of an internal policy. A comprehensive institutional policy still does not exist, but staff are now interested in pursuing something of the kind based on their experiences over the past years.

Source: DD Soejarto, pers comm, 1999

CASE STUDY 3.1

INSTITUTIONAL RESPONSES TO BENEFIT-SHARING IN SOUTH AFRICA

Rachel Wynberg (Biowatch South Africa/Graduate School of Environmental Studies, University of Strathclyde)

Introduction

Benefit-sharing is a much bandied-around buzzword, conjuring up visions of community empowerment and enrichment, and partnerships that are altruistic and equitable. The concept is particularly associated with the CBD, which requires fair relationships to be developed between those commercializing biodiversity (largely companies in technologically advanced countries of the North) and those providing the genetic resources (generally the biologically rich South). Similar language is peppered throughout literature on the issue, from official UN documents through to popular publications. But how far are we in implementing these noble principles?

Because research institutions are often at the forefront of developing bioprospecting agreements – mediating between different interests and determining benefit-sharing packages – their experiences provide some interesting answers. Depending on a range of variables – such as business and legal acumen, technological and scientific capacity, commitment to conservation and social justice principles, financial status and autonomy, policy environment and experience in product development – good deals or bad deals may be brokered. Three case studies are examined below, drawing on agreements developed by three research institutions active in the bioprospecting field in South Africa:

1   an agreement between the Council for Scientific Research (CSIR), a parastatal research institution, and the UK-based company Phytopharm to develop an anti-obesity drug;
2   an agreement between the National Botanical Institute (NBI) and the US-based company, Ball Horticulture; and
3   a project underway between Rhodes University and the National Cancer Institute (NCI).

Adding value and equity to South Africa's biodiversity

In South Africa, benefit-sharing has been catapulted into the spotlight as an issue requiring urgent attention to justify conservation as a legitimate land use. Issues of equity are especially pertinent to the country, having had a long history of injustice, dispossession and discrimination through years of apartheid policies. Included in this history were forced removals of black communities from land to be later designated for conservation purposes, and the removal of people's rights to use natural resources for their livelihoods. These iniquities, combined with a past neglect of social problems in South African conservation practice, have resulted in the widely held perception that biodiversity conservation serves the recreational interests of the privileged elite and is irrelevant to the majority of South Africa's people.

Slowly attitudes are changing, largely through a realization of the potential economic benefits to be gleaned from the country's biodiversity through such activities as tourism and the development of new medicinal, cosmetic and food products.

Certainly, opportunities abound. As the third most biologically diverse country in the world, South Africa contains between 250,000 and one million plant species, a large number of which occur nowhere else in the world. Few countries can boast having an entire plant kingdom within national borders – the Cape Floral Kingdom – and the highest recorded species diversity of any similar-sized region in the world. Joined with well-developed institutions and research capacities in the country, these attributes provide an extremely favourable environment for bioprospecting – the exploration of biodiversity for commercially valuable genetic and biochemical resources (Laird and Wynberg, 1996; 1997).

Adding value to the country's natural resources is well recognized as an important avenue for economic development in South Africa. This recognition exists despite previous approaches that disregarded indigenous genetic resources and prohibited practices such as traditional healing. With biodiversity now globally recognized as an important resource for new commercial products, various government initiatives are responding to potentially lucrative opportunities. The Innovation Fund, for example, an initiative of the South African Department of Arts, Culture, Science and Technology, identifies biotechnology and 'value addition with respect to exploitation of our natural flora and fauna' as two of three focal areas warranting the allocation of scarce government funds. The Indigenous Knowledge Programme, coordinated by the same department, similarly includes a focus on opportunities associated with biodiversity in its aims to 'unearth, promote and protect the African heritage'.

The government's policy on biodiversity, formulated in response to its obligations under the CBD, stipulates as a key goal the need to ensure that benefits derived from the use and development of South Africa's genetic resources serve national interests (DEAT, 1997). Furthermore, it identifies as a priority the development of legislative and institutional measures to control access to genetic resources and ensure equitable benefit-sharing. Specifically, the policy sets standards for best practice through a number of requirements for the development of bioprospecting agreements, ranging from scientific capacity-building through to the protection of traditional knowledge (see Box 3.4). Underpinning all of these intents is the commitment from government to reduce social inequality and improve the quality of life in poverty-stricken areas.

Does policy mean practice?

How are these policies and initiatives reflected in bioprospecting practice in South Africa and are existing approaches the best way to secure benefits for the country? How are the most marginalized communities to benefit from ongoing deals? How is the conservation of South Africa's rich biological and cultural heritage being enhanced by bioprospecting? And are we witnessing business as usual, or a fundamental turnabout in approaches to benefit-sharing and a real commitment to equity?

In an attempt to answer these questions, three ongoing bioprospecting projects in South Africa have been examined. For each case, the national policy on bioprospecting – as described in Box 3.4 – is used as a benchmark and checklist against which 'best practice' can be assessed. This assessment is included in Table 3.3, which also summarizes the main components of each agreement. While each project has yet to generate profits and is at a different stage of development – from initial collection and screening/analysis, through to clinical trials – they nonetheless reveal interesting trends with respect to bioprospecting and benefit-sharing in South Africa. An overview of each case is presented below, followed by a detailed assessment in Table 3.3.

BOX 3.4 BIOPROSPECTING POLICY IN SOUTH AFRICA: SETTING STANDARDS FOR BEST PRACTICE

- What is the environmental impact of collecting material and how has biodiversity conservation been strengthened by the project?
- Was the prior informed consent of communities or landowners obtained/Will the prior informed consent of communities be obtained?
- How was consent from government obtained?
- How has the reconstruction and development of South Africa been promoted?
- How has economic development been promoted in marginalised parts of the country?

- Who are the intended beneficiaries of the project?
- What benefits have/will holders of traditional knowledge obtain/ed from the project?
- What mechanisms exist to disburse funds to beneficiaries?
- What initiatives exist to ensure collaboration with other local research institutions?
- To whom have intellectual property rights for intended products been conferred?
- How has South Africa's science and technology capacity been enhanced by the project?

The Development of an anti-obesity drug : CSIR and Phytopharm/Pfizer

The first project concerns the development of an appetite suppressant (dubbed 'P57') derived from a species of *Hoodia*, a succulent plant indigenous to southern Africa and long used by the San to assuage hunger and thirst. The appetite suppressant is considered to have the potential to become the first blockbuster drug to be derived from an African plant and is to be commercialized into a prescription medicine with an estimated market potential of more than US$3 billion (Foodtek, 1998). The US, which represents the largest opportunity for obesity drugs, has some 35 to 65 million obese individuals.

A licensing agreement for the further development and commercialization of the product has been signed between the CSIR, a research institute in South Africa, and Phytopharm plc, which specializes in the development of phytomedicines. The CSIR is one of the largest scientific and technological research organizations in Africa, employing approximately 3300 staff and currently performing about 12 per cent of all the industrial research and development on the continent. Some 40 per cent of its income is derived from the government, and the remaining 60 per cent from contract research work for its clients.

Further development and marketing of the drug is to be undertaken by US-based pharmaceutical giant Pfizer, which has been granted an exclusive global licence by Phytopharm for worldwide commercialization. Phytopharm, in turn, will receive up to US$32 million in licence fees and milestone payments. Milestone payments to the CSIR are linked to the performance of P57 in clinical trials, and although cited as 'substantial', have not been publicly disclosed. However, projected royalties to the CSIR through licensing the patented technology are 'expected to amount to hundreds of millions of

Table 3.3 *Does policy mean practice? Key bioprospecting agreements in South Africa*

Policy element	CSIR–Phytopharm/Pfizer	NBI–Ball	Rhodes–NCI
Environmental impact of collecting	Plants are being grown in the Northern Cape to avoid overharvesting in the wild. Policy states that material will be acquired with 'minimum disturbance to local ecosystems'.	Not stipulated in the agreement but conservation is a primary objective of the NBI.	A feasibility study would be required for large collections and opportunities for mariculture would be investigated if the need arose.
Prior informed consent of landowners and/or holders of traditional knowledge	Collectors request permission from property owners (generally farmers) who are required to sign a form if they are willing to donate the plant material. It is, however, uncertain how landowners benefit from the arrangements.	NBI will abide by the International Food and Agriculture Organization (FAO) Code of Conduct for Germplasm Collecting and Transfer. The NBI is also currently developing its own policy on prior informed consent, based on the *Common Policy Guidelines on Access to Genetic Resources and Benefit Sharing* being developed by 15 botanic gardens.	Not stipulated. (Although marine resources are nationally owned, collections are likely to be most appealing in protected areas. This would require a detailed process of planning with protected area managers).
Prior informed consent of government	Project has met with government approval.	Several consultations have been held with the South African Department of Environmental Affairs and Tourism. Royalties from successful products will be invested in a trust fund to be used for the development of local horticulture and botany, and other conservation and rural development projects in the areas from which plants are collected.[1]	Permission to prospect was obtained from the South African Department of Environmental Affairs and Tourism. Project has resulted in:
Strengthening of biodiversity conservation	Conservation benefits are unknown.		• a complete collection of voucher specimens lodged at local museum; • underwater slides of 250 invertebrate and algal species; • a comprehensive computer database of biological and global positioning systems (GPS) information; • valuable taxonomic information and identifications funded by the NCI and the Coral Reef Research Foundation; and

Policy element	CSIR–Phytopharm/Pfizer	NBI–Ball	Rhodes–NCI
			• biological samples to provide baseline markers for toxic metal concentration studies.
Promoting community and economic development in marginalized parts of the country	Bulking-up projects occur in the impoverished Northern Cape, from where the plant originates. However, disadvantaged and marginalized communities are not involved in these projects.	The agreement does not commit Ball to investing in product development in South Africa. Instead, in rather weak language, Ball will give 'special consideration' to investing in the local development and growing of products 'wherever appropriate and feasible'.	In obtaining licencees, the NCI requires the applicant to seek as its first source of supply the natural products available from South Africa. If this is not possible, an amount of money is to be granted to the government for conservation projects.[2]
Fund disbursement	Policy states that provision will be made for the fair and equitable sharing of benefits, but it is unclear how the CSIR will disburse funds generated from the successful commercialization of the drug. Funds generated return to a common pool at the CSIR, which is not specifically earmarked for the conservation of biodiversity or for remuneration to holders of traditional knowledge.	Profits generated from the agreement will be placed in a trust fund managed by the NBI board.	Project is still in the early stages. Would support the idea of a national trust fund to manage any profits generated.
Benefits derived by holders of traditional knowledge	The plant being developed has a long history of use among the San (and more recently among the military) as a thirst quencher and appetite suppressant. Although it is CSIR policy to 'take account of the rights, interests and practices of indigenous peoples' and to develop 'equitable collaboration agreements' with traditional healers, it is not clear how these principles are incorporated into the project.	The agreement excludes use of materials for medicinal or natural product purposes. There is no known traditional development of horticultural varieties. Knowledge about the plant species is largely confined to scientific knowledge generated by NBI staff and scientists in other South African research institutions.	No known traditional usage of the marine material collected.

Benefits derived by landowners	Not stipulated. Much of South Africa's biodiversity falls within private ownership, and there is a lack of clarity regarding the way in which the state asserts ownership over such resources.	Not stipulated. A mix of private and public landowners is likely to be affected by the agreement.	Not stipulated. Most of the area under investigation is publicly owned.
Coordination with other research institutions	A bioprospecting consortium has been formed between the CSIR and several parastatal research institutions and universities, although the Phtyopharm-Pfizer agreement does not appear to involve any of these partners.	Not stipulated.	Collaborations with the Coral Reef Research Foundation, the Universities of Port Elizabeth and Western Cape, East London Museum and other foreign and national research institutions. Ongoing discussions for an umbrella project for all marine bioprospecting in South Africa.
Institutional policies and codes of conduct	A broad policy on bioprospecting has been adopted by the CSIR.[3]	Ball Horticulture has no policy on bioprospecting. NBI adheres to *Common Policy Guidelines for Botanic Gardens* and the Model Material Acquisition Agreement developed by this group. NBI is additionally developing a code of conduct for staff and a policy on benefit-sharing.	See the People and Plants website (www.rbgkew.or.uk/peopleplants) for more information on the NCI policy. Rhodes University has no specific policy on bioprospecting.
Intellectual property rights	A patent has been taken out on extracts from *Trichocaulon* or *Hoodia* species by individuals at the CSIR. By default, the government and the CSIR have ownership over the patent.	Ball is granted an exclusive licence to commercialize plant material provided by NBI and is entitled to obtain a patent or plant breeder's right certificate on superior products developed. Ball will pay royalties on successful products, the proportion of which will vary according to the extent of breeding and technology used to develop the plant.	This depends on whether the discovery is made by NCI or Rhodes University. Either way, the inventing organization is required to collaborate with the source country, and any licensee of a drug is required to negotiate the terms of collaboration with the source country organization or government. Royalties would be determined once a promising drug is discovered and a separate agreement would then be negotiated.

Policy element	CSIR–Phytopharm/Pfizer	NBI–Ball	Rhodes–NCI
Technology transfer and strengthening South Africa's science and technology capacity	An FDA-approved medicinal plant extraction facility has been constructed at the CSIR and funded by Phytopharm and Pfizer. Research capacity is to be built in the drug development arena.	No clear commitments for Ball to invest in technology transfer. Royalties will be used for capacity-building in botany and horticulture. NBI staff and others will do internships at Ball facilities and give seminars in South Africa. A greenhouse is to be built in South Africa as part of a soft loan by Ball to the NBI.	There will be interaction and collaboration between research institutions in South Africa and the US; training of chemistry and taxonomy PhD students and learning techniques for chemical analysis and preliminary screening; capacity-building of South African scientists through exchange programmes with Northern institutions; and research publications.
Regional linkages	Not known, but the plant being investigated transcends national boundaries.	Not stipulated.	While the importance of developing regional collaborations is recognized, this is not addressed by the project.

Rand per annum for the lifetime of the patent'. It is anticipated that any money made by the CSIR will get invested back into the organization or into providing scientific services; no proportion of projected royalties has been earmarked for conservation, nor for benefit-sharing with holders of traditional knowledge about the plant. Pfizer and Phytopharm have paid for the construction of a Food and Drug Administration (FDA)-approved medicinal plant extraction facility at the CSIR for the pilot scale manufacture of P57, to be used in phase II and III clinical trials (Foodtek, 1999). With first commercial sales of the product forecast for 2003, horticultural trials have already been established at two locations in the country to provide supplies of the drug for trials.

Importantly, this project forms part of a much larger bioprospecting programme for the CSIR. Through the Chemical and Microbial Products Programme of the CSIR's Division of Food Science and Technology, a major bioprospecting project has been launched, aimed at investigating most of the country's 23,000 plants for commercially valuable properties over the next ten years (www.csir.co.za). To obtain ethnomedical information for the project, the CSIR has developed an agreement with a 'committee of 10' traditional healers, said to be representative of a large number of healers in South Africa – a fact disputed by many. Additionally, the CSIR has spearheaded a bioprospecting consortium comprising various research institutions and universities, including the Agricultural Research Council, the Medical Research Council, the National Botanical Institute and the Universities of Cape Town, the North and the Western Cape'.[4] Although still embryonic, the coming together of these key institutions in a collaborative venture for bioprospecting is extremely significant, indicating a likely hub of bioprospecting activities in the country. 'Getting it right' with Phytopharm and Pfizer is thus enormously important and precedent setting.

Exploiting South Africa's horticultural potential: the National Botanical Institute and Ball Horticulture

The second project involves an agreement between the National Botanical Institute (NBI) and the giant Chicago-based Ball Horticulture. The NBI is a public institution that aims to 'promote the utilization and conservation of, and knowledge and services in connection with, Southern African flora', and also to promote the economic use and potential of indigenous plants.[5] This it does through, inter alia, managing the various botanical gardens and herbaria in South Africa, conducting environmental education and outreach programmes, undertaking scientific research on plants and maintaining and developing databases about southern African flora. The organization employs over 600 people and manages an operating budget of some $5.5 million (1996), 85 per cent of which it receives from parliament. Ball Horticulture is the world's largest multinational horticultural company, holding 40 per cent of the US market in bedding plants and pot plants, and 25 per cent of the European market.

The five-year agreement, which is the first North–South bioprospecting agreement in the horticulture sector, will see the NBI using its expertise to select South African plants of horticultural interest to Ball, both from its living collections and from the wild. Any selected or hybridized varieties of these plants will be patented by Ball, and the NBI will receive a cut of profits for 20 years following the plant's introduction to the market. Additionally, Ball will pay the expenses of two staff members at NBI and a soft loan of US$125,000 towards the building of greenhouse facilities, where plants will be propagated before being sent to America.

Much controversy has surrounded the agreement, largely because of the public nature of the NBI, and the use of public funds to develop collections and expertise that are now commercially attractive. Considerable criticism has additionally accompanied the benefit-sharing provisions of the agreement, which are perceived to badly under-value South Africa's national heritage, to raise ethical issues around the patenting of life, and to neglect national imperatives towards job creation and the reconstruction and development of South Africa. A key reason for these deficiencies is because of the underdevelopment of the South African horticultural industry – and thus weak bargaining power of the NBI. The NBI, however, has justified the agreement as a long-overdue opportunity for South Africa to obtain benefits from indigenous genetic resources, and a 'world first' for horticulture that could set precedents for access and benefit-sharing arrangements in other developing countries (Gosling, 1999).

Investigating anti-cancer compounds from marine biodiversity: Rhodes University and the National Cancer Institute

A collaboration between Rhodes University in the Eastern Cape of South Africa and the National Cancer Institute (NCI) in the US comprises the third project under consideration. In this instance, an agreement between the two institutions forms the basis for a joint programme to investigate coastal and marine macro-organisms and algae from South Africa for their potential as anti-cancer agents. This agreement is a blend of two standard NCI agreements (its 'Letter of Collection and Memorandum of Understanding') developed for collaborations with source country organizations to stipulate access and benefit-sharing arrangements. First collections have already taken place in Algoa Bay with scientists from the US Coral Reef Research Foundation and the University of Port Elizabeth (South Africa); later collections and identifications will additionally include the East London Museum (South Africa) and possibly other research institutions working with marine natural products. Material will be extracted and tested in the NCI screens, and some isolation projects will also be done at Rhodes University and possibly other US institutions. In all cases, extracts are only provided to organizations signing a material transfer agreement that guarantees the rights of South Africa in terms of collaboration and compensation in the event of commercialization (Cragg, NCI, pers comm, February 1999).

The project differs from the cases described above in that it represents an early stage of research; the NCI is also a non-profit research institution funded exclusively by the US government and not directly engaged in commercializing products. Similarly, the main interest of Rhodes University in the collaboration is to train students and to advance knowledge about natural products and biodiversity under the umbrella of drug discovery, not to generate profits from a successful product (M Davies Coleman, Rhodes University, pers comm, February 1999). This is in contrast to the approaches of the NBI and the CSIR, where the agreement is focused on commercialization and the emphasis is placed upon financial rewards. Nonetheless, the collaboration brings with it the obvious potential for commercialization, as well as a range of non-monetary benefits. The possibility of the initiative to form an umbrella for marine bioprospecting in South Africa, and to link up with the bioprospecting programme at the CSIR, further underscores the significance of the project. An agreement between the CSIR and the NCI to investigate South African plants has already resulted in the transfer of anti-cancer screening technology from the NCI to the CSIR, suggesting an opportunity for the local testing of marine species.

Taking stock

The examples above include some of the better-known bioprospecting projects in South Africa, and together they illustrate certain common features, lessons and pitfalls associated with research institutions in developing countries that are engaged in the business of bioprospecting. Firstly, and perhaps most importantly, they suggest that bioprospecting brings with it only a limited set of benefits. Countries wanting to commercialize their biodiversity need to do so as part of an overarching and multifaceted strategy that considers bioprospecting as one of many different options to reap benefits from biological resources. Bioprospecting per se is unlikely to solve national conservation and development problems, and needs to be complemented by a set of comprehensive and innovative approaches towards the consumptive and non-consumptive use of biodiversity. This may, for example, include the development of local phytomedicine industries that add value to resources already in use; or it may be through focused efforts to support community-driven projects on natural product development or tourism. It may also be through lobbying to bring about necessary policy changes. Effective tenure reform, for example, is likely to yield far more significant social and biodiversity benefits than bioprospecting in the long-term; likewise, there are benefits in the proper valuing in national accounting systems of services provided by natural resources.

Having said this, the examples described do illustrate that bioprospecting can play an important role in strengthening scientific institutions and building the capacity of researchers. A general observation, however, is that such benefits tend to be more meaningful in cases where provider countries already have high levels of technological and scientific capacity – a situation pertinent to South Africa but that is not typical of most developing nations. Collaboration between industry and local research institutions can, additionally, facilitate much-needed taxonomic work, through activities such as the collection and identification of samples. While it could be argued that these activities would occur as a matter of course to enable screening and analysis to take place, they nonetheless provide new taxonomic knowledge about biodiversity – a field that is desperately underfunded in South Africa.

Unsurprisingly, issues that receive inadequate attention in the projects described are those that have historically not been tackled by scientific institutions in South Africa – poverty alleviation, job creation and the reconstruction and development of the country. Although opportunities to address development needs present themselves in the cases examined (for example, the bulking-up or local development of products), these are not stipulated as requirements in the agreements. Neither has attention been given to developing innovative conservation projects in areas where collections take place or for exploited resources. Instead, the argument is presented that it would be 'nice if possible to do these things', but only if they prove to be economically competitive. With the high risks and costs involved in research and development for new pharmaceutical, horticultural and other products, social responsibility plays second fiddle. The reality is that developing country institutions simply lack the technological and marketing know-how to insist on fairer deals, a fact brought home by the NBI case study, where the absence of a strong domestic horticultural industry considerably weakened the institution's negotiating position with Ball.

A question that must be asked is the extent to which research institutions should be held responsible for determining more meaningful benefit-sharing packages, and for mediating between the wide range of different interests that bioprospecting brings. Many of the issues raised by bioprospecting are inherently difficult to resolve, and require guidance in the form of a national vision and approach. Such leadership is sorely lacking in South Africa and is thwarted by inadequate coordination between government departments, a lack of capacity and a poor understanding of the nature of the problem. Although a broad national policy on bioprospecting has been adopted, legal and administrative mechanisms to implement the policy are still not in place. All of the examples described cite frustration in obtaining policy guidance from government and the difficulties of operating in an institutional vacuum. Fundamental issues concerning the ways in which traditional knowledge should be rewarded, approaches to the patenting of biological resources and national systems of equitably disbursing funds derived from royalties have simply not been addressed by government. The lack of legal certainty on such issues as ownership of biological resources further muddies the waters.

An important lesson to emerge is the inadequacy of policy as a sole mechanism to control access to genetic resources and determine parameters for benefit-sharing. All of the cases analysed indicate that while the general ethos expressed by institutions involved in bioprospecting may concur with national policy, these sentiments are not fully articulated in the details of negotiated agreements (see Table 3.3). This negligence of policy requirements suggests that without effective bioprospecting legislation and the necessary institutional arrangements for implementation and monitoring, South Africa is likely to be short changed. Legislation is required not only to guide possible foreign collaborators, but also to strengthen the bargaining arm of local institutions. Unfortunately, South Africa's isolation through the apartheid years is still reflected in the naivety with which local institutions receive foreign commercial collaborations, and the lack of capacity of local institutions to engage with and comprehend the very powerful interests that tend to drive such partnerships. For South Africa to glean significant benefits from her biological resources, urgent efforts must be made to build such capacity, to establish legal parameters for access to genetic resources and benefit-sharing, and to place bioprospecting within the context of a coherent and long-term strategy for commercialization of the country's natural heritage.

Institutional policies in the North and South

Despite the fact that most of the world's biodiversity is located in the developing countries of the South, a great deal of the research on biodiversity and traditional knowledge emanates from research institutions in the biologically poorer North. Worldwide, the bulk of research institutions are found in industrialized countries of the Northern hemisphere, and most scientific research on biodiversity and traditional ecological knowledge is funded by Northern agencies and channelled through Northern institutions. As a result, the manner in which these institutions regulate the activities of their staff, and set terms for 'equitable' research relationships, can have tangible impacts thousands of kilometres away.

Institutional policies developed in biologically rich countries with developing economies tend to raise issues not captured by their Northern counterparts. For example, the perennial funding and technical capacity constraints of developing country institutions suggest the need for policy to prescribe forms of benefit-sharing from foreign partners that help to build the capacity and infrastructure of the institution. Partnerships with foreign institutions are seen as a way to build long-term benefits for the institution through training, supply of equipment, access to publications and, in some cases, funds. In some countries, institutional policies are also a way to make transparent the terms under which genetic resources are passed to Northern academic or commercial concerns. Increasingly, institutions in the South are asked to account for samples shipped elsewhere and to explain the terms under which they do so. The development of policies in the South also provides a base from which consultations can be held regarding the institution's role in the country and responsibilities to the 'national patrimony'.

In South Africa, these issues have featured prominently in discussions to develop biodiversity prospecting agreements within two parastatal organizations, the National Botanical Institute (NBI) and the Council for Scientific Research (CSIR) (see Case Study 3.1). Both institutions receive a substantial proportion of their funding from the government and thus are accountable to the South African taxpayer. For both the NBI and the CSIR, criticism has focused, amongst other things, on the inadequate recognition given in bioprospecting agreements – with Ball Horticulture and Phytopharm/Pfizer respectively – to the developing country needs of South Africa. While 'soft' benefits such as research publications and scientific cooperation are built into the agreements, more concrete development benefits such as job creation tend to be given scant regard. Although a careful balance needs to be struck between commercial interests and the wider social and national interests, important questions remain as to the ultimate beneficiaries of these agreements.

In Cameroon, the Limbe Botanic Garden initiated a policy-development process as part of a strategy to become self-sufficient in the world of botanic gardens and conservation projects (see Case Study 3.2). Staff realized that in order for the institution to survive in the long term, collaborating institutions in the North would have to rethink the nature of their relationship with a developing country institution (ie to consider them more equal partners, while more effectively sharing benefits). A policy was a useful way to formalize these new relationships, while helping the institution to fulfil its objectives to the country under the CBD and CITES.

Institutions in tropical countries are notoriously and chronically underresourced and underfunded, and historically – in exchange for limited hand-to-mouth resources – have played junior partner to developed country research institutions. A relationship of imbalance has evolved which is often supported by funding, scientific and institutional traditions, despite increasing rhetoric and calls at the international policy level for capacity- and institution-building. Tropical country research institutions, in fact, often subsidize researchers from the North – providing housing, vehicles, staff time and information. In return, many do not receive useful data, training, acknowledgement of contributions in publications or even reports on joint research.

Biodiversity research has expanded dramatically over the past decade. Calls for institution- and capacity-building have grown alongside calls for more inventories, taxonomic reviews and better understanding of disappearing species. While funding is still disproportionate to the amount of work required, there has been a growth in funds allocated for biodiversity research and conservation projects. But can it be said that the budgets of developing country botanic gardens, universities and research institutes have grown over the past ten

CASE STUDY 3.2

LIMBE BOTANIC GARDEN POLICY ON ACCESS TO GENETIC RESOURCES AND BENEFIT-SHARING, COLLABORATIVE RESEARCH AND DATA AND INFORMATION EXCHANGE

Sarah Laird, Tchouto Peguy, Limbe Botanic Garden/Mount Cameroon Project, Terry Sunderland, African Rattan Research Programme, and Nouhou Ndam, Limbe Botanic Garden/Mount Cameroon Project

Located within South-West Province, Cameroon, the Limbe Botanic Garden (LBG) is an attractive institutional base for researchers from overseas. It is the only botanic garden in the country, is home to the regional herbarium with highly trained and experienced staff and is easily accessible from international airports. The town of Limbe itself is situated on the coast, at the foot of biologically diverse and spectacular Mount Cameroon, and is a lively town 'known for its enjoyment', an informational brochure reads.

The Limbe Botanic Garden is a technical unit of the Ministry of Environment and Forestry (MINEF) with the mission 'to provide facilities and services for collaborative research, education and training in support of biodiversity conservation in the Mt Cameroon region and beyond'. Although bilateral funding is currently provided by the UK Department for International Development (DFID) – formerly the Overseas Development Agency (ODA) – in 1994 special dispensation was given to the garden by the Cameroon government that enabled funds raised through both direct grants and collaborative research to contribute to the long-term maintenance and development of the institution itself. In addition, with strong technical links to the Royal Botanic Gardens, Kew, and other international research institutions, as well the burgeoning interest in the 'conservation and development' of Cameroon's biodiversity on the part of international funders, LBG was increasingly perceived as having a crucial role in the initiation of collaborative research programmes.

By 1994 the Limbe Botanic Garden was receiving increasing numbers of requests from researchers around the world to act as an institutional base for their work in the region. In some cases, these 'requests' came in the form of research proposals in which the institution was, often unknowingly, featured as a local counterpart – commonly with little or no provision for formal institutional support. Many overseas researchers saw national research institutions within Cameroon as little more than a jumping-off point for their work, and relationships were almost always formed on a personal – rather than an institutional – basis. In order to build the scientific and technical capacity of the institution, therefore, staff came to realize that they must also work to redefine the role of the tropical country institution in science. Formalizing research relationships through a written policy and agreements with researchers was seen as one way to work towards this end.

During this time, an involved and complex debate was also underway within the government of Cameroon, research institution, university, NGO and protected area circles resulting from the potential commercial development of compounds extracted from *Ancistrocladus korupensis*. *A. korupensis* was collected within the Korup National Park in South-West Province in 1987, and the compound michellamine-B subsequently showed great promise in the US National Cancer Institute's natural products screening programme. The CBD had recently been signed by the government of Cameroon, and issues relating to 'access and benefit-sharing' and 'equitable research relationships' were high on the national agenda (Laird, Cunningham and Lisinge, 1999). Staff at the Limbe Botanic Garden felt that, as a national research institution, it was their obligation to:

- ensure that the operating principles underlying any research collaborations in which the botanic garden was involved were clear; and
- clarify the responsibilities of visiting researchers.

An institutional policy was drafted and circulated for comment in 1994. A long process began in which staff capacity to address these issues was developed, and the various elements of implementing an institutional policy were explored. For example a Unified System of Charges for Scientists Visiting the Mount Cameroon Project Area was developed and put in place to address one aspect of research relationships. The broader range of issues that must be considered in an institutional policy, however, were not fully expressed until the culmination of this process in the 1999 draft *Policy on Access to Genetic Resources and Benefit-Sharing, Collaborative Research, Data and Information Exchange*.

Importantly, parallel to the policy-development process, institutional structures were examined, and a research coordinator post, with responsibility to achieve transparency, mutually agreed terms, shared objectives and benefit-sharing, was established. It is a truism to say that institutional policies are only as good as the staff and institutional structures that exist to implement them. However, all too often resources are not made available to implement policies effectively. A major concern on the part of researchers worldwide is that institutions and managers of protected areas will draft policies but lack the staff to implement their terms, so all research will grind to a halt or reaching an agreement will take many months.

The 1999 draft *Policy on Access to Genetic Resources and Benefit-Sharing, Collaborative Research, Data and Information Exchange* was 'developed to implement the provisions of the CBD and national laws on access and benefit-sharing, to provide sufficient information for partners to understand what they can expect when they deal with LBG and to promote dialogue and good practice within the international community'. The policy covers:

- the acquisition of genetic resources;
- the supply of genetic resources;
- collaborative research;
- conditions relating to access to the LBG/Mount Cameroon Project data;
- the fair and equitable sharing of the benefits arising from the use of genetic resources.

The current LBG policy grows in large part from the Botanic Garden Policy on Access and Benefit-Sharing Pilot Project, funded by the UK Department for International Development and coordinated by the CBD Policy Unit of the Royal Botanic Gardens, Kew (see Box 4.1). However, it grafts onto the framework policy document developed by the 17 botanic gardens involved in this project, and the better elaborated Royal Botanic Gardens, Kew, policy on *Access to Genetic Resources and Benefit-Sharing*, a range of issues and relationships of direct concern to the LBG. These include issues relating to collaborative research (including a research agreement drawn largely from the 1994 LBG draft document), relationships with local communities, and conditions attached to the use of the extremely valuable data collected and housed by the LBG/Mount Cameroon Project (MCP).

Indicative benefits elaborated in the policy (and drawn from the Kew policy) that might result from the use of data and research collaborations include:

- taxonomic, ecological and other information, through research results, publications and educational materials;
- the transfer of technology such as software and know-how;
- training in science, in-situ and ex-situ conservation, information technology and management and administration of access and benefit-sharing;
- joint research and development, through collaboration in training and research programmes, participation in product development, joint ventures and coauthorship of publications;
- training of the local communities in parataxonomy, village mapping, participatory rural appraisal (PRA) and ethnobotanical techniques;
- paid use of local guides, scientists and facilities;
- in the case of commercialization, monetary benefits such as royalties.

Attached to the policy are copies of the standard 'Agreement for the Supply of Biological Material', standard 'Conditions for Loan of Herbarium Specimens', standard 'Agreement on Conditions on Access to the Mount Cameroon Project Data in the BRAHMS and TREMA databases', and a standard 'Research Agreement'. The 'LBG/Mount Cameroon Project Research Agreement', based closely on the 1994 document drafted by the LBG, requires that:

- Researchers obtain appropriate permits from the Cameroon Ministry of Scientific and Technical Research (with assistance from LBG if necessary).
- Researchers work with MCP/LBG staff (and provide appropriate training).
- For any research involving collection of plant materials, a duplicate set of all specimens collected, as well as their label information, should be left with the LBG and the national herbaria.
- Correct documents (eg phytosanitary certificate, certificate of origin, CITES exportation permit, where necessary) are acquired for plant material before it is dispatched.
- Plants or materials may not be passed to a third party without written consent from LBG/MCP.
- Benefits must be shared with communities, LBG/MCP and government, including research results, copies of publications and acknowledgement of MCP/LBG in publications.
- Commercialization of plant 'material or any progeny or derivatives thereof' may not be commercialized without the written permission of MCP/LBG, subject to a separate agreement.
- 'Ethnobotanical information and indigenous knowledge must be appropriately acknowledged in publications, and agreements reached with local experts supplying the information as to equitable sharing of benefits arising from the research, including financial payments.
- Copies of reports and publications should be provided to MCP/LBG; joint publications are preferable.

- Upon completion of their fieldwork, researchers may be invited to give a lecture or presentation of their work, and/or to conduct training prior to departure.
- Researchers will pay research-related charges as agreed and as set by the MCP/LBG.

Financial benefits and responsibilities of researchers included in the 1994 draft policy comprise set fees for vehicle use; employment of village guides and porters, project contract workers and project civil servants; a contribution to village development funds; bench fees for use of the herbarium; and a management fee that amounts to 10 per cent of local costs incurred as part of the overall budget. Current fees, as elaborated in the 1999 draft policy, are set according to use of vehicles, equipment, staff time, etc.

A more involved policy development process was undertaken in 2001, culminating in a package of institutional policy documents. Implementation and testing of these policy documents will take place during 2002. A copy of *The Limbe Botanic Garden Policy on Access to Genetic Resources and Benefit Sharing* (2001) is available on the People and Plants website at www.rbgkew.org.uk/peopleplants.

years? Compare the multimillion dollar budget of any donor-funded conservation project in a high biodiversity country with the operating budget of the local university's botany department or national herbaria or wildlife school. It is critical that attention is given to strengthening national institutions in developing countries in order to coordinate, effect and support the scale of biodiversity research proposed for the future.

The political, economic and social problems that plague many countries are often used to justify a lack of investment in institutions. However, the directed and transparent sharing of benefits with institutions specified by policy and research agreements can help to circumvent some of these problems. Expenditure of funds and effort on the conservation of biodiversity in high biodiversity countries should include bringing onboard local institutions dedicated to education and research. Building institutions is one of the more effective ways to magnify the effects of benefits generated by both biodiversity research and biodiversity prospecting.

'Users' of biodiversity – including researchers – should include in their budgets overheads for the institutions at which they are based overseas, and not only their home institutions. Northern institutions can better guide their own researchers, and can ensure that collections of data and material are done in accordance with 'best practice' by developing, implementing and revising institutional policies. Developing country institutions have long collaborated with scientists from other countries and have relied heavily on their expertise to develop their research and knowledge base, and management plans for protected areas. Such countries will continue to depend upon outside expertise; but increasingly this can be done according to terms set by institutions based in those countries. In order to do this, institutional policies and research agreements are required to create a framework within which all research contributes to institutional survival and conservation and development activities in the areas in which research takes place.

Institutional policy as a commitment to best practice

Clear standards for best practice are emerging from existing institutional policies, national and international law and the guidelines developed by professional researcher societies and indigenous peoples' groups. These include the prior informed consent of all stakeholders; sharing of benefits; clear agreement on the supply and exchange of materials and knowledge collected; and a commitment to innovative partnerships that seek to build capacity and infrastructure in partner institutions in high-biodiversity developing countries.

The process through which institutions develop policies is in itself an invaluable exercise that allows groups to come to terms with rapidly evolving understandings of 'equitable' research relationships. It also allows for hidden assumptions and internally inconsistent approaches within institutional departments to come to light. In some ways, addressing these issues requires dramatic shifts in the way research has been undertaken to date. But in a world of increased commodification of both knowledge and biological resources, and where the lines between public and private research are increasingly blurred, these are critical shifts to make.

Notes

1   Press release on the NBI–Ball access and benefit-sharing agreement (NBI, August 1999)
2   'Memorandum of Understanding between Rhodes University, South Africa and the Developmental Therapeutics Programme, Division of Cancer Treatment, Diagnosis, and Centres, National Cancer Institute', 17 March 1998
3   The policy can be found at: http://www.csir.co.za
4   'Memorandum of Understanding between the Council for Scientific and Industrial Research, the Medical Research Council, the National Botanical Institute, the Agricultural Research Council, the University of the North, the University of Cape Town, and the University of the Western Cape'
5   Forest Act 122 of 1984 and Forest Amendment Act 53 of 1991

Chapter 4

Publication of biodiversity research results and the flow of knowledge

Sarah A Laird, Miguel N Alexiades, Kelly P Bannister and Darrell A Posey

The publication of biodiversity research results is an important factor that shapes the flow of knowledge and information between and within different groups, including local communities, academia, industry, the media and the general public. Embedded in a complex web of local and global social relations, such flows raise issues relating to proprietary rights and to power relations between different groups. In this chapter we identify some of these issues and discuss conflicts of interest that emerge as researchers simultaneously seek to fulfil professional obligations while developing socially responsible research partnerships. While we place more emphasis on questions relating to cultural knowledge, many of the processes and questions that we examine also pertain to other types of environmental knowledge.

We begin our discussion by examining the role of publication within the academic establishment. We then discuss some of the issues raised by the publication of cultural knowledge, including the implications of documentation, dissemination and appropriation. Finally, we provide some examples of how professional societies, funding bodies, sponsoring institutions and individual scientists have addressed these issues, both in the past and today. By introducing some of the key questions that direct contemporary debates, and by summarizing contemporary approaches to address these issues, we hope to help researchers engage in productive discussions regarding the future of biodiversity research, while developing more socially responsible research partnerships and publication practices.

Publication and academic traditions

Publications are the principal means through which researchers share their findings within and beyond their academic fields and institutions. By providing a crucial basis for the validation and development of new ideas within and between disciplines, publications form a core element of the scientific process and estab-lishment. Not surprisingly, then, peer-reviewed publications serve as the currency through which scientific credibility, prestige and advancement are determined. In this way, institutional reward and advancement policies and increasingly competitive funding structures perpetuate the 'publish or perish' dilemma. As a result, researchers may be tempted to prioritize publication over other important considerations. One set of problems emerges when publications include cultural knowledge over which other groups have proprietary claims, or where publication of such knowledge has direct or indirect repercussions on other stakeholders. This has become increasingly the case in recent years, following increased media, public and corporate interest in cultural knowledge and its concomitant commodification (Alexiades, in press).

In recent years, a growing number of charges of 'biopiracy' have been levelled against individual researchers and scientific institutions, particularly in the tropics. While these accusations frequently overestimate the degree to which scientists directly engage in biodiversity prospecting, publication of academic research may involve two elements intrinsic to the concept of biopiracy: unauthorized appropriation and commodification of cultural knowledge or genetic resources. Because different stakeholders, communities, ethnic groups or nation states have different and even conflicting needs and proprietary claims over genetic resources and associated knowledge, and because many of these stakeholder groups do not necessarily recognize the rights of other stakeholders to represent them or their interests, it is unlikely that there will be much consensus as to what constitutes legitimate or illegitimate appropriation. In the meantime, however, scientists have the ethical and professional responsibility to obtain permission for publication of cultural knowledge and negotiate appropriate relationships.

Even if academic researchers do not directly accrue material benefits from the publication of scientific reports, the fact remains that such publications provide the basis for researcher salaries, grants and prestige, which in turn contribute directly to economic security and institutional advancement. Moreover, the increased privatization of science through corporate funding and through structural readjustments in large public institutions is creating new contexts in which academic publications contribute to the appropriation of cultural knowledge and genetic resources by industry (ten Kate and Laird, 1999; Parry, 1999).

While publication is equally important in all fields of research, within the applied and industrial sciences, the publication process is often regulated by such mechanisms as patents, delayed publication and employer–employee agreements, all of which are designed to protect costly investments in research. In contrast, the ethic of free and unimpeded flow of information, through such means as symposia, publications and verbal and written discussions, is still prevalent among university and museum-based researchers in whole-organism biology (Janzen et al, 1993). Having said that, it is important to note that even among academic researchers most information does not really begin to 'flow' until the researchers have established certain proprietary rights, notably through publication (Janzen et al, 1993).

There are signs that the increased privatization of science is already undermining the ethic of free-flow of information. As the chairman for the American Association for the Advancement of Science (AAAS) Committee on Scientific Freedom and Responsibility noted at a recent conference entitled Secrecy in Science, increased privatization of science has 'resulted in a new regime of secrecy which is very concerning to the scientific community' (*The New York Times*, 6 April 1999). Increasingly, such regimes of secrecy may respond not only to the interests of industry, but to those of other stakeholders claiming proprietary rights over the research process (see Case Study 4.1).

CASE STUDY 4.1

PEOPLE, PLANTS AND PUBLISHING

William Milliken (Royal Botanic Garden, Edinburgh)

Publishing academic research results: reaching a compromise

Countless books have been published on the medicinal plants of indigenous groups and regions of the world, and virtually every issue of any scientific journal dealing with economic botany or ethnobotany includes at least one contribution on the subject. In general, these books and papers make no reference to the issue of intellectual property rights, nor do they include any mention or discussion of how the recording or publication of the information might be beneficial or detrimental to the people who supplied it. There are, of course, exceptions to this; but the fact remains that most ethnobotanists or ethnopharmacologists, though willing to pay lip service to the issues of intellectual property rights in theoretical discussion, will tend to ignore them entirely when it comes to the publication of their work. There are various reasons for this. Firstly, scientists tend to dissociate themselves from the implications of their research. Secondly, scientists have the ability to convince themselves that publication in the academic forum is separate from the world of commerce. Thirdly, most scientists are under very considerable pressure to publish as much as possible as soon as possible.

Between 1993 and 1995, while working for the Royal Botanic Gardens (RBG), Kew, I collected ethnobotanical information in the northern Brazilian Amazon (state of Roraima), focusing particularly on medicinal plants. The principal objectives of this work were: to research the anti-malarial plants of the region, with the aim of promoting the most effective species as alternatives for the growing dependence on pharmaceuticals; and to catalogue the medicinal plants of the Yanomami Indians with the aim of producing a practical guide for use by health workers. The work with the Yanomami was carried out jointly with the anthropologist Bruce Albert.

Although the main purposes of the work were practical ones, nevertheless as researchers working for academic institutions we were expected to publish our results in the scientific forum. Unwilling to place in jeopardy the intellectual property rights of the people with whom we had been working, we originally prepared a manuscript that omitted to mention the specific names of any of the plants that they use. The purpose of the paper was not so much to publish the knowledge of the Yanomami as to publish the fact that they possess the knowledge. This was intrinsically interesting since it had been held, up to that time, that these people possess no significant pharmacopoeia (this is far from the case). The paper included analyses and discussions (in the context of Amazonian ethnobotanical knowledge) of the methods of preparation and administration of the medicines, of the uses to which the plants were put and of the family-level composition of the pharmacopoeia. The reason for the omission of specific plant names from the text was clearly explained in the first paragraph of the paper (ie that no functional legal system was in place for the protection of intellectual property in this context).

Initially, we submitted the article to the *Journal of Ethnopharmacology* – a leading publisher of articles on medicinal plant use. The manuscript was returned with the explanation that whereas the referees recognized this as a significant and valuable contribution, it was not their policy to withhold data from the reader. We then submitted it to *Economic Botany*, who replied in a similar vein. Although the reasons for our approach were understood by the referees, it was felt that this would set an unacceptable precedent.

After much wrangling, which delayed the eventual publication by more than a year, a mutually acceptable 'compromise' was reached. Having conducted a fairly thorough literature search of the published medicinal uses of the species with which we were dealing, we agreed to name only those species that had widely been reported elsewhere as having been used in the same way. If their use was widespread and already in the public domain, we felt that we would not be jeopardizing any potential financial or other benefit which the Yanomami might stand to gain from this knowledge.

Some time later, I submitted two more manuscripts to *Economic Botany*, one being a further report on the Yanomami pharmacopoeia (after further fieldwork) and the other being an account of the anti-malarial plants known and used in the state of Roraima. I took the same approach of restricting the data (ie referring to species in the latter anti-malarial paper only when they were widely known or published as having that property). When the other members of the genus were well known in this context (but not the particular species), then the plant was referred to by its genus only, and likewise families.

Once again we reached an impasse. While it was accepted by the journal that it was reasonable to restrict the raw data, it was felt that the subsequent discussion of the 'whole' data set, of which only a part was visible, was inappropriate. Reluctant to limit the discussion in this way, we then searched for another alternative and eventually suggested the inclusion of voucher specimen numbers. In modern ethnobotanical works these serve as hard references to the sources of the information included in the paper, and are normally listed together with the species names. In this case we suggested inclusion of the voucher specimen numbers alone for plants that were included in our discussion/analysis of the data but that had not been named. Of course, if the specimens were widely distributed around the herbaria of the world, this would have effectively overridden the data restriction, since anybody sufficiently interested (not very likely) would be able to track down the names via the voucher numbers. However, in this case the numbers referred to a collection that had been kept separate from the main collection in Kew. While not available for public consultation, these specimens nonetheless provide a permanent point of reference for the data.

This, then, was the final formula. It was arrived at after a great deal of 'toing and froing' and caused very substantial delays to the publication of our work. Whether or not it was worth the effort, and whether or not the arrangement that we arrived at was a widely applicable and acceptable one, is open to question.

Issues associated with publication as a way of returning benefits to local communities

At the same time that we were publishing our papers on the medicinal plants of the Yanomami, we were also preparing an illustrated field guide. The guide was to be produced in an easily usable form providing basic information on the character of the plants, their medicinal uses, the ways in which they are prepared and administered, and background information on the known medicinal properties or uses of the species. It was written in Portuguese and illustrated.

The guide to the medicinal plants of the Yanomami was intended neither as an academic publication nor as a commercial one. On the contrary, its specific purpose was to help the Yanomami to retain an important part of their traditional knowledge, thus helping to control their increasing dependence upon external medical support, a very real problem in some communities. It was designed as a resource for health workers, educators and for the Yanomami themselves.

For a number of reasons, most of which are connected to the fact that their lands are rich in precious minerals and lie across an international border, the Yanomami are facing a period of change and threat. The horrors of their experiences during the Roraima gold rush of the late 1980s and early 1990s are well known and will not be repeated here. In many such situations, where a previously isolated culture with an oral tradition suddenly finds itself confronted with the juggernaut of Western civilization, one of the first casualties is their traditional knowledge of medicinal plants. The mechanism by which this occurs varies, but often starts with the introduction of new epidemic diseases such as influenza and measles. Since no traditional cure for these introduced diseases exists, people start to die. If they are lucky, Western medics will arrive and perform apparently miraculous cures. The fact that the foreign doctors are able to cure something that their own healers cannot engenders the belief that foreign medicine is more powerful than their own, and confidence in traditional knowledge is lost. When the young people lose interest in the seemingly irrelevant knowledge of their elders, it only takes a generation or two for that part of their heritage to be lost entirely.

Again, publication of this information, albeit in a form intended to be of benefit to the Yanomami, raised a difficult moral dilemma. One cannot ignore the possibility that the information will, through its publication, fall into the hands of unscrupulous individuals or companies who may develop it for their own profit with no thought for the people who discovered it. In this way a potential source of future revenue for the indigenous people may have been lost. On the other hand, there is the likelihood that unless something is done soon, then an important part of this information will disappear from the oral tradition – a significant loss to those people at the practical level.

The question, therefore, was not only how to go about publishing the guide but whether to do so at all. Our original intention was to produce an informal publication (ie to print and distribute it ourselves). Then it was suggested that since copies of this document would inevitably become available outside theYanomami communities, it would be better if it were published in a more formal manner – clearly stating that the information therein is the intellectual property of the Yanomami and should be respected and treated as such. Finally, just as the manuscript was nearing completion, the intellectual property rights issue became such a hot potato in Brazil that it seemed unwise to proceed until the situation had been resolved.

That is where we stand now. Although a small part of the information has since been modified as a Yanomami-language-only document for use as a teaching resource for an education project run by a non-governmental organization (NGO) in the Yanomami area, the full manuscript is unpublished. There is a risk that it will become, at least for some Yanomami communities, an historical document.

Biodiversity research and publications

As noted above, biodiversity research publications, which include journal articles, books, manuals, databases and other written and electronic forms of expression, raise important social, political and ethical questions. Consequently, newly recognized obligations, as expressed in the Convention on Biological Diversity (CBD) and elsewhere (see Chapter 1), emphasize the need to clarify through a process of a consultation some fundamental issues such as prior informed consent, full disclosure of research objectives and appropriate negotiation of the terms of research relationships. These terms include the ways in which results might be published or disseminated, and how benefits resulting from dissemination ought to be shared. While by far the greatest concerns have arisen in relation to the publication of cultural knowledge, publication of biological data has also raised a number of concerns, particularly related to the distribution of threatened or commercially valuable endemic species, or those of special sacred or cultural significance to local communities.

Primary issues associated with the publication of biodiversity research results relate to joint authorship and sharing of data. All too often, communities and local research institutions share their time and knowledge with visiting researchers, who in turn do not return their results in ways that are relevant to the needs of local groups or conservation efforts – or in a language that can be understood. Many participating groups now build into the consent process a requirement that all publications (and sometimes raw data) resulting from research undertaken in their community (in conjunction with their institution) or in their country are shared locally. Increasingly, institutional policies and professional codes of ethics call for both the sharing of research results and, when appropriate, joint authorship of publications as well. As a result, a new trend may be emerging in which scientists help develop written materials and other tools specifically in order to reciprocate the flow of knowledge (eg Lacaze and Alexiades, 1995; Shanley et al, 1998), and in publications authored or coauthored by local research participants (eg Chau Ming et al, 1997; Chiqueno et al, 1994; Ventoncilla et al, 1995).

The flow of cultural knowledge

Much knowledge within communities is not distributed equally; rather, it is distributed and exchanged according to particular norms and criteria, all of which may be disrupted by the publication process. For example, many societies restrict certain forms of specialized knowledge to particular members of their society, according to age, lineage or gender. Specialized knowledge may flow only through those who are initiated or accepted in defined (often secret) segments or born into certain families or households, and divulging information outside the group may carry severe penalties. Thus, the flow of information in indigenous societies is complex and frequently related to the maintenance of group or sub-group identities that, in turn, work to maintain the ethnic distinctiveness of the tribe, community or indigenous nation. This is partly why removal or transfer of information from the group through publication can threaten internal and/or external stability. In effect, publication raises concerns that knowledge may be misrepresented and thus weakened, or inappropriately used (Bannister and Barrett, in press; Mann, 1997).

Sharing of information can also sometimes be dangerous for the person who provides the data – for example, if the knowledge itself is sensitive, or if it reveals controversial views about other factions or individuals in the community. This is why some authors or sources may seek anonymity. Furthermore, it may be necessary to keep the name of the community anonymous if information about it is sensitive and restrictive, or if publication can draw undue and unwanted attention (Akeroyd, 1984). Studies of mixed-race communities, for example, frequently 'protect' individual racial identities by changing the names of individuals and entire communities or regions (eg Posey, 1979). Publications about exotic and particularly beautiful spots or about rare natural resources can attract unwanted land speculation or tourism, or encourage collection of protected or endangered plants. Clearly, an ethical decision needs to be made in each case based on an informed discussion with research participants regarding the risks and benefits involved with any given approach.

These complexities make it difficult to clearly lay out universal 'rules' for how information on cultural or environmental knowledge might be published and used. While researchers often employ discretion in the release of their own research results, few communities or local participants attach conditions to the recording and dissemination of cultural knowledge. However, indigenous peoples' groups and professional research societies increasingly raise these as important issues. A trend is emerging towards greater consultation with groups regarding publication of their cultural knowledge. For example, the UN Commission on Human Rights (1995) states that 'researchers must not publish information obtained from indigenous peoples or the results of research conducted on flora, fauna, microbes or materials discovered through the assistance of indigenous peoples without identifying the traditional owners and obtaining their consent to publication'.

Likewise, the *Pew Scholars Initiative Guidelines for Researchers and Local Communities* (1996) require that researchers 'agree on a protocol of acknowledgements, citation, authorship and inventorship as applicable, either citing local innovators or conservators, or respecting requests for anonymity'. The *International Society of Ethnobiology Code of Ethics* repeatedly calls for a high level of community control over the information dissemination and publication process – including prior informed consent, joint authorship and anonymity if requested – and identifies these as key issues to be revisited throughout the life of a research project, as part of the 'dynamic interactive cycle' of consultation.

The precautionary principle

Bannister and Barrett (in press) propose application of the precautionary principle to issues of publication and dissemination of cultural knowledge. They argue that publications present opportunities for uncontrolled appropriation and exploitation of traditional knowledge and resources by third parties. Because third party users do not interact directly with providers of the knowledge, they rarely assume obligations to communities from where the knowledge originated, and are often unaware of negative impacts that may result from knowledge appropriation. Thus, a mechanism is needed that would require *all* users to seek consent through *direct* interaction with indigenous communities. The precautionary principle – which calls for proactive efforts to predict and prevent potentially harmful outcomes of actions, even without 'scientific proof' that harm will result – could provide guidelines for such a mechanism in the ethnosciences (Bannister and Barrett, in press).

Publication and the politics of recording cultural knowledge

Publication of cultural knowledge reflects power relations between researchers and research participants, and raises a number of ethical, social and political questions with regard to representation and property rights. Some of these include the following:

- Who has rights to access, publication and authorship of knowledge?
- Who determines those rights, and based on what criteria?
- What are the implications of publishing, in terms of validating or commodifying cultural knowledge, and what effect do these have on community internal and external dynamics and well-being?

These questions raise complex issues that require consideration and discussion with research participants in order to attain an acceptable level of informed and consensual agreement.

In some cases, publication of ethnobotanical knowledge may help to validate or legitimize cultural knowledge, thus consolidating the status of some community members in relation to others: for example, elders in relation to younger generations, research participants in relation to non-participants, or local communities in relation to society at large. In effect, then, publications have the potential of endowing certain participants with prestige, a powerful resource in the mediation of interpersonal and social relations. One might argue, for instance,

that anthropology and ethnobiological publications have helped to 'legitimize' indigenous knowledge systems and indigenous cultures, have attracted public attention, and therefore have helped to create a political environment that has favoured certain forms of indigenous political agency. Likewise, publications have served as powerful vehicles for cultural and political self-determination among disenfranchised groups, and have been employed to 'conserve' and record threatened systems of knowledge (see Case Studies 4.1 and 4.2). The effects of publications on power relations between different actors are complicated and frequently ambivalent, however. This is not only because some actors are empowered in relation to others, but also because certain views, versions and representations of knowledge and culture are advanced over others.

Information pertaining to the abundance or distribution of particular natural resources and the histories of their utilization may also have important political implications in terms of how, when and by whom these are used. Such information can advance or negate specific territorial or management claims of different interest groups, particularly in cases where conflicts over land or resource use exist. In Cameroon, for example, the Forestry Law of 1994 provides for a new category of forest, the 'community forest', which is dependent upon the development of management plans that, in turn, depend upon sound baseline data.

BOX 4.1 REGISTRIES OF BIODIVERSITY-RELATED KNOWLEDGE

Publications and databases have been suggested as tools to protect indigenous people and local community interests. One method proposed is 'defensive publishing', which places information in the public domain to block a patent application based on this knowledge (The Crucible Group, 1994). Another is the compilation – usually in electronic database form – of community registries of biodiversity-related knowledge. Registries of knowledge are ordered collections or repositories of information. Originally developed as tools to allow communities to better manage their resources and associated knowledge, they are increasingly seen as a way to promote, protect and either claim rights over, or prevent appropriation of, traditional knowledge. Where those outside the community have access to the information contained in the database, there are conditions attached that ensure community control over subsequent use and benefit-sharing.

A number of indigenous and local communities have found registries and databases to be useful tools for organizing their knowledge in a way that allows protection and improved management of their resources and intellectual and cultural heritage, in the face of external economic, cultural, political and social pressures. Examples include the People's Biodiversity Registers, sponsored by WWF India, and the Honey Bee database of farmers' innovations and creative practices in India. The Inuit of Nunavik and the Dene in Canada have also developed databases of traditional knowledge, in order to better define research priorities and strategies for their lands (IUCN, 1997). The Inuit of Nunavik database contains information on land use and resources, and grows from 15 years of systematic interviewing of Inuit concerning their knowledge and understanding of the land and resources. The database has informed decisions relating to commercial fisheries, tourism and environmental impact assessment methodologies (Simon and Brooke, 1997).

Source: Downes and Laird, 1999

Publications can undermine as well as strengthen processes of self-determination in other ways. Publishing of ethnobotanical data, for example, automatically converts cultural knowledge into a public resource, making it difficult for the group in question to negotiate specific terms of compensation for the subsequent commercial use of that knowledge. As a result, in some cases the same process of validation that may accord certain political and management advantages may simultaneously create other disadvantages. Registries of biodiversity-related knowledge have been established in order to promote the advantages of publication, without incurring the disadvantages (see Box 4.1).

Schoenhoff (1993) argues that the transfer of knowledge from oral to written, printed and electronic forms implies movement across cultures and symbolic translations of ideas. Each expert along the way, and their associated 'community of belief', will leave a mark on the knowledge documented. The medium in which an item, complex or system of knowledge is embedded, expressed or recorded arguably shapes and changes the nature of the knowledge itself, as well as the way in which human beings interact with it.

This process of translation of cultural knowledge from one domain to another does not take place amidst egalitarian social relations. The case has been made that 'scientification' of knowledge (mainly through publications) can further disempower certain social actors by reducing them to 'information-bearing systems'. Thus, some have questioned the merit of validating the scientific value of indigenous knowledge at the expense of indigenous forms of representation. As a result, the extent to which printed or electronic data relate to cultural knowledge can be questioned, which in turn raises questions about the value of databases and registries as a tool for the 'conservation' of culture and knowledge. Although only touched upon here, these points are included to highlight the complexity of the issues raised by the publication of research results, the role of publication and the objectives served.

Professional research organizations and publications

Publication of data is often linked to broader discussions of 'ownership' of knowledge and cultural resources, sometimes referred to as 'intellectual property rights' (IPRs) – used as a catchall term for the rights of communities to own and control their knowledge and resources (Greaves, 1993; Fowler, 1993). While most codes of ethics acknowledge the power associated with data publication and dissemination, and resulting researcher responsibilities, few clarify the role or authority of local groups in this process.

An exception is found in the International Society of Ethnobiology (ISE) *Code of Ethics* (ratified in 1998) and draft *Guidelines for Research, Collections, Databases and Publications*, which provide special attention to issues associated with ownership over, and control of, data and field collections. Through a process described as a 'dynamic interactive cycle', the research relationship promoted in the ISE documents is constantly revisited, and terms agreed to at the beginning (including the ways in which data might be entered into databases, published or otherwise disseminated outside the community) are re-evaluated by researchers and communi-

ties in light of newly emerging issues. The fact that the ISE felt it necessary to develop guidelines to specifically address the issue of collections, databases and publications highlights their importance both as an integral element of ethnobiological research, as well as a focal point for increasing concerns expressed by indigenous peoples and traditional communities.

A basic aspect of the 'dynamic interactive cycle' is also that unless the researcher can expect to fulfil all phases of research – such as guarantees of equitable and secure terms that regulate the flow of information and materials, including the meaningful return of useful results to the community – then the project should not be started in the first place. Specific suggestions for ways to resolve these issues are not provided by the ISE guidelines, however. Rather, prior informed consent (PIC) is highlighted as a process and framework through which an agreement ought to be reached at the outset, and specific terms and conditions are amended and modified as necessary as the research relationship unfolds (see Chapter 7 and Annex 7.1).

In another example, the Melaka Accord (adopted in 1994) calls for editors of scientific journals to require details of legal collection permits for all materials acquired. If researchers cannot provide details of the permits, then the manuscript should not be published (see Chapter 2). Likewise, requirements have been proposed to address permission issues and to ensure that sources of cultural knowledge are adequately acknowledged in publications and conference presentations. For example, Bannister and Barrett (in press) suggest that editorial boards should require that the original knowledge holders be cited as the primary source of cultural knowledge in journal articles, in a manner consistent with that expected for academic citation of any other source of information or ideas. Anil Gupta (pers comm, 2000) recommends that professional research organizations require that papers not be published or accepted for presentation at professional conferences unless they have already been shared with the knowledge providers in their language. He also seeks proper attribution to information and knowledge providers, and evidence of full disclosure and prior informed consent that ensure the rights of communities to control their knowledge.

As early as 1948, the American Association of Anthropology (AAA) passed a *Resolution on Freedom of Publication* addressing efforts to suppress, alter or dispose of research results in ways that amount to suppression or curtailment of academic freedom. The resolution also covers the need to avoid publishing data that may harm individuals or groups from which information is obtained. Researchers must be free to interpret and publish their findings without censorship and interferences, provided that 'the interests of the persons and communities or other social groups studied are protected'. However, questions emerge as to who typically decides what constitutes these 'interests' and how such interests should be 'protected'. The voices of 'persons and communities or other social groups studied' ought to be considered integral to decision-making processes.

It is still not uncommon, however, to hear incorporated into ethical debates discussion of whether a community's wishes override those of 'science'. In a case study published in the AAA's newsletter, for example, a researcher related a situation in which he was told during ethnographic research in the south-west US that non-material culture – beliefs and practices – were not the property of non-Indians and should not be published. The researcher respected their wishes but asked (Cassell and Jacobs, 1987):

> 'Do the wishes of my consultants override the need of science for an ethnographic description of a little-known culture that is becoming Westernized? Would it be ethical to produce a work that would appear only after all of my consultants are dead, which could be 20 or 30 years? Or does the right to privacy, which my consultants insisted on, have to be observed as long as the people maintain their independent existence?'

In another example, the conclusions emerging from a 1991 workshop organized by the US National Institutes of Health (NIH), US Agency for International Development (USAID) and the National Cancer Institute (NCI) to address the relationship between 'Drug Development, Biological Diversity and Economic Growth' identified as an 'immediate' priority 'the completion of species and traditional-knowledge inventories, which should include provisions for information dissemination. These inventories need to be developed using electronic databases with wide access' (Schweitzer et al, 1991). Since this time, considerations associated with community control over the dissemination and use of their knowledge have been brought to the attention of researchers within these institutions. Institutional policies and agreements used by the NIH and NCI now demonstrate a greater awareness of the need to receive the consent of communities before publishing and disseminating field results. For example, the NCI now requires all potential grantees in the natural products area to provide documented evidence of plans to procure proper permits (collection and export), and statements signed by themselves and authorized officials of their institutions, assuring that equitable benefits will be returned to appropriate source country organizations and/or indigenous peoples in the event of discovery of novel drugs (Cragg, NCI, pers comm, 2000).

The 1997 International Cooperative Biodiversity Groups (ICBG: NIH/NSF/AID) *Principles for the Treatment of Intellectual Property and the Sharing of Benefits Associated with ICBG Sponsored Research* state:

> '*Agreements and research plans should anticipate the tension between the traditional scientific ethic of public access to information, including publication of results, and the understandable desire of indigenous or commercial partners for confidentiality of information with potential commercial value, pending protection through patenting or other means.*'

In a similar vein, the *Pew Conservation Fellows Biodiversity Research Protocol* (1996) states that 'Just as the proprietary rights of scientific knowledge are well established and respected, such rights are due to the producers and providers of traditional knowledge and contemporary innovations from local communities.'

Funders' and sponsors' expectations for publishing

Funding agencies (particularly governmental) and sponsors of contract research (often companies, or companies in conjunction with public institutions) commonly attach conditions to the ways that field data can be used, published and disseminated. Governments usually require widespread distribution of material in the public domain, while companies restrict access to, and use of, information in ways that serve their objectives. A third group, private foundations, also expects researchers to publish their findings but generally attaches fewer specific guidelines or conditions, although many foundations assume rights over research results produced by their staff.

It is often the case that funders and sponsors of research do not recognize discretionary powers to control dissemination of research results at the levels of researcher, community and individual members of a community. It is also often the case that researchers do not understand their legal obligations to publicly disclose their research results, or cede control over dissemination to a company. These are critical issues that need to be clarified early in the research process.

For example, the University of Oxford, UK, assumes full rights over any discovery produced by any student enrolled in the university. Professors and technical employees can claim up to 50 per cent of royalties produced from a discovery, following negotiation, with the university retaining at least a 50 per cent share. International aid agencies often assume complete intellectual property rights over products that result directly or indirectly from research they fund.

Government funding usually comes with a requirement that data and findings are shared with the public and, in some countries, with the private sector. It is a tacit assumption that US National Science Foundation (NSF)-funded research (funded by US taxpayers) will be put into the 'public domain' through publication in scientific journals or entry into electronic networks (Janzen et al, 1993). This raises significant concerns for groups such as those surrounding Glacier National Park in the US who negotiated with the US National Park Service to retain control over the use of 'new data' collected in their communities, but ran into problems since government laws and regulations prohibited this form of control (Ruppert, 1994; Ruppert, pers comm, 1998).

Contract research also raises significant questions about control over data. A standard clause in agreements vests rights to all data collected to the agencies paying for the work, which are often companies. Some agreements allow use of the data by the researcher only if a proposed publication is approved by the agency, and others require that all field data be turned over to the financing agency, which then decides if it will ever be used and in what manner (Fowler, 1993). Data are often owned by an agency, which has control over accessibility and dissemination of the information and which may keep it secret or use it in unethical ways, whether or not to the approval of the anthropologist, the researcher's informants or the people studied (Hill, AAA, 1987). Grievances brought to the attention of the American Anthropological Association (AAA) Committee on Ethics are often tied to disputes over the ownership, confidentiality, public accessibility and rights of publication to data derived in connection with contract research, particularly for government and private corporations (Hill, AAA, 1987).

Precautionary and innovative approaches to the publication and dissemination of research results

Individual researchers and communities have developed innovative ways to address issues associated with the publication of biodiversity research results; but this is still an evolving area, and most efforts of this kind run counter to the status quo and face significant opposition. The following section will discuss and provide examples of how individual researchers and groups determine how and what to publish, and how they control the distribution of published material.

Determining how and what to publish

How can a researcher protect groups' rights to control the recording, dissemination and use of cultural knowledge, while continuing to participate in the scientific exchange of ideas and information?

Milliken attempts to answer this question, balancing community and scientific needs in the field of ethnobiology (see Case Study 4.1). Some difficulties that he

---

BOX 4.2 RESEARCHERS' CHECKLIST FOR PUBLISHING RESULTS

Know your legal and ethical obligations

- Are you aware of the international and national laws (eg the Convention on Biological Diversity (CBD), national access and benefit-sharing measures), professional codes of ethics and institutional policies that create obligations with regard to the recording, publication and dissemination of research results?

Know the implications of your work

- Have you thought about the general internal and external political and legal implications of publishing data?
- Have you thought about where the results will end up and the potential interest of third parties in the information?

Inform, consult and agree

- Have groups been adequately consulted and granted prior informed consent for the ways in which knowledge and information is recorded, and the ways it might be disseminated?
- Do communities and local institutions seek joint authorship?
- Do individuals or groups wish to remain anonymous, and how will this be ensured?
- Has agreement been made on the return of data, publications and the language and form they will take?
- Have the conditions attached to data by funders or sponsors been made clear to research collaborators and participants?

Explore new paradigms for publishing

- Have you explored innovative ways of protecting knowledge or information?
- Have you explored ways to return data in forms of value to local groups?

---

confronted resulted from scientific pressures to publish 'as much as possible as soon as possible'; researcher tendencies to dissociate themselves from the implications of their research; and a reluctance to acknowledge that publication in the academic forum is not distinct from the world of commerce. After long negotiations with scientific publishers, Milliken devised the compromise of publishing the names and uses of only those species widely published as having been used in the same way elsewhere, and included only the genus of those species with restricted or specialized use to the Yanomami with

whom he worked (Milliken and Albert, 1996; Milliken, 1997). The introductory paragraph to one of the published papers (Milliken and Albert, 1996) is as follows:

'Although this paper is primarily a discussion of the medicinal plants used by a group of Yanomami Indians, and those plants have been collected and identified using rigorous ethnobotanical procedures, only those medicinal species whose properties are widely used and which are already well documented have been mentioned

by name. *This is a deliberate attempt to combine protection of the intellectual property rights of those people with scientific reporting. It is hoped that it will help to emphasize the urgent need for a satisfactory and equitable solution to an issue which ethnobiologists ought not to be able to ignore.'*

Other researchers have followed similar protocols, restricting the disclosure of ethnobotanical information to species that have already been published (eg Alexiades, 1999), or not including species names (eg Sheppard, 2000), as a way of preventing the data being incorporated into such literature databases as NAPRALERT. Cunningham (1996) relates a case in which the Martu aboriginal people in Australia considered publication of common and widespread uses acceptable, but requested that vernacular names of localized plants not be published. In this way, any outsider interested in these plants is required to work through local communities, allowing them greater control over the use of these species in the future.

As mentioned above, in the US case of the review draft 'Memorandum of Understanding (MOU) Regarding Proposed Ethnographic Research in Glacier National Park', efforts were made to define and attach conditions to the publication and dissemination of 'new data' collected as part of an ethnographic research project. New data was defined in the MOU as: 'any ethnographic information collected through research procedures conducted during the course of the Research Contract (including, but not limited to structured or unstructured interviews, survey instruments, participant observation, video, and audio taping, photography), and not previously recorded or otherwise documented'. The MOU states that 'intellectual property

rights to this information' are retained by those providing it, and that:

'...the individual Tribes shall determine the disposition (storage and manner of use) of any New Data. The National Park Service agrees to use any and all New Data only after consulting with and gaining permission from official representatives of the Tribes. Original field notes, photos, videos and sound recordings of New Data will reside with the designated offices of appropriate Tribes, and only general summaries of New Data will be made publicly available, but only with the explicit permission of the affected Tribes'.

Community control over the publication and dissemination of newly recorded data is clear and strongly stated, however; this form of control was considered in conflict with US federal laws and regulations, and the MOU was never adopted (Ruppert, 1994; see Chapter 7).

Concerns similar to those outlined by Milliken have influenced the approach of ethnobotanical researchers working with the Secwepemc (Shuswap) First Nation in Canada. The Secwepemc Ethnobotany Project – a collaborative, interdisciplinary research programme focusing on Secwepemc plants, language and culture – was initiated in 1991 in consultation with, and with the support of, the Shuswap Nation Tribal Council, the Secwepemc Cultural Education Society and many Secwepemc elders and researchers. One of the several aspects of the Secwepemc Ethnobotany Project was an investigation of the chemical properties of Secwepemc food and medicinal plant resources (Bannister, 2000). While the chemical research took a *process*- rather than a *product*-oriented approach to investigating plant–human interrelationships, there has been widespread outside interest expressed in the findings.

In this case, adhering to a precautionary ethic has meant forgoing funding offers by interested third parties and deferring publications of the phytochemical data until a community review and approval process (specified in a research agreement with the Secwepemc Cultural Education Society) has had time to take place. Addressing concerns about dissemination of cultural knowledge and supporting indigenous rights to protect cultural knowledge and traditional resources, then, may require recognizing and challenging academic policies that inadvertently encourage the exploitation of indigenous knowledge. Such policies include rewards based on publication, industrial partnerships that focus on applied or patentable research and university ownership policies.

Furthermore, the research agreement that governs Secwepemc medicinal plant research included the following explicit statement of ownership and provisions for future use: 'the Secwepemc Nation has control over access to the traditional plant knowledge, as well as to potential development of any marketable products (such as drugs or pharmaceuticals) that may be discovered as a result of the traditional knowledge shared during the course of this research' (Bannister and the SCES, 1997).

At the time this agreement was made, it was perceived by the contracting parties to offer satisfactory protection of Secwepemc rights. However, it is now clear that the protection offered by such research agreements is limited beyond the contracting parties themselves, and (if not linked to formal means of protection, such as intellectual property rights) is greatly diminished after publication. In light of current trends to privatize and commercialize, concerns have been expressed that publication and dissemination of cultural

knowledge may be inappropriately or prematurely forcing indigenous peoples 'into considering IPR protection mechanisms simply as a defensive strategy to prevent others from employing them first' (Bannister, 1999, p11). The fact that publication prior to an intellectual property rights application can also invalidate the potential for utilization of intellectual property rights protection mechanisms (eg patents and trade secrets) highlights both the powerful role that publication can play in control of knowledge, and the importance of adequate time to enable decision-making processes – something that the academic process neither encourages nor rewards (Bannister, 1999).

Controlling the distribution of published material

How can groups publish cultural knowledge for their own purposes, while at the same time controlling the way it is disseminated and used?

In many cases, indigenous peoples and local communities seek the publication of their knowledge as a way of recording, conserving and making certain types of information available for education purposes. Around Kinabalu National Park in Sabah, for example, Dusun communities living outside the park sought to record and publish their knowledge of commonly used medicinal species as a way to make it available to other community members and subsequent generations, while restricting outsiders' access to the resulting publication. The result was a protocol for distribution, which attaches conditions to the ways in which the information might be distributed and used (see Case Study 4.2).

Concerns associated with control over this type of publication led Milliken and others to forgo production of a medicinal plant guide for the Yanomami, although in this case publication would directly serve

Box 4.3 The growing role of databases:
conflicting trends in access

Until the early 1970s, printed publications were the primary means for scientific information dissemination; but developments in information technology mean that an increasing proportion of information is now held in electronic form in databases. Databases are primarily comprised of information published in printed form, but documents are increasingly published exclusively in electronic form and disseminated through the Internet. This trend is likely to continue (Bhat, 1997). Databases such as NAPRALERT and MEDLINE, as well as 'academic' databases such as those on economic botany developed by botanic gardens, serve as key focal points for information exchange associated with genetic resources and traditional knowledge. NAPRALERT (NAtural PRoducts ALERT), for example, is compiled from ethnomedical source literature scanned since 1975 from some 125,000 journal articles, books, abstracts and patents. It supplies information on the chemistry, pharmacology, biological activity, taxonomic and geographical distribution, and ethno-medical uses of around 110,000 natural products and 120,000 organisms. Information from approximately 600 new articles is scanned in each month (Bhat, 1997).

Databases also represent the point at which conflicting trends of thought associated with the exchange of information converge. On the one hand, they reflect a global move towards the free flow and accessibility of information through electronic means. Indeed, it is rare that recommendations for improved biodiversity research management and communication between institutions overlook improved and more accessible databases. On the other hand, biodiversity, economic botany, medicinal plant and other databases inadequately address the need to restrict access to information on genetic resources and traditional knowledge in order to allow providers greater control over their use. For example, NAPRALERT does not have any procedures in place to regulate the use of traditional knowledge, although some staff members are exploring possible options (Gyllenhaal, pers comm, 1999). NAPRALERT is made available for free to non-profit users in developing countries, which is a significant benefit, amounting to roughly US$400,000 in value per year (Gyllenhaal, pers comm, 2000). However, this is not widely considered adequate in today's post-Convention on Biological Diversity (CBD) paradigm of exchange, in which source countries and communities seek control over access, as well as benefit-sharing (Gupta, 1995).

In time, it is possible that access to scientific collections, records and databases and associated benefit-sharing will be regulated through legislative means (Glowka, 1998). Another possibility is to grade information in databases, placing differing levels of restrictions according to the type of knowledge. While common and widely reported knowledge may continue to be considered as public information, access to specialist or previously unpublished knowledge may be subject to consent or to benefit-sharing conditions.

Steps to grade and restrict access to information on species use (and possibly distribution) might be incorporated into institutional policies. For example, in its Workshop on Data Sharing and Database Ethics, the Association of Systematics Collections (ASC) reported that the 'ASC supports maximum access to scientific information, while ensuring that the institutions and scientists who provide the information to users outside the scientific community are recognized for their contribution, and have the support needed to continue their service to society' (ASC, 1992; see also Hoagland, 1994, on institutional policies on documentation and databases). Institutions claim proprietary rights to their databases in ways that can incorporate community and other providers' interests, alongside those of institutions and researchers who act as brokers of knowledge and information.

Clearly, the ability to control information already entered into databases is limited. However, institutional policies can seek to correct imbalances in past collection and dissemination practices, much as they are attempting to do with large ex-situ herbarium or germplasm collections. The Royal Botanic Gardens, Kew, for example, seeks to bring the exchange of all collections (including those made prior to the entry into force of the CBD) up to the standards promoted by the CBD. Information collections should also be held to higher standards for best practice, and database managers should participate in institutional-, national- and international-level discussions that seek to establish equitable research through all stages of data-gathering, dissemination and use. The push for faster and freer exchanges of knowledge and materials should be balanced against the rights of communities and source countries to control the way their knowledge and resources are exchanged and used.

the needs of the community (see Case Study 4.1). In other cases, health manuals have been produced including only well-known and previously published plants (eg Lacaze and Alexiades, 1995).

In Australia, the library at the Australian Institute for Aboriginal and Torres Strait Islander Studies restricts access to culturally sensitive information. Terms are attached to access published materials, including the following (Cunningham, 1996):

'Any purchaser or subsequent reader shall abide by a specific condition placed on secret/sacred material in this book by Aboriginal men and/or women. All knowledge relating to those rituals (sites) is normally confined to the men and/or women who have been inducted into them. Many Aboriginal people are eager to have this material recorded and published as a matter of permanent record. Because much of this material is secret/sacred it may cause great distress if it is discussed with any Aborigine before it has been established that he/she has the correct standing in his/her society and is willing to participate in discussion.'

A readers advisory was employed by Elisabetsky and Posey (1994) in the introduction to a paper presenting information on uses of plants for gastrointestinal disorders by Kayapo medical experts (see Box 4.4). Although not legally binding, the advisory was included as a way to attach moral and ethical conditions to the use of the information presented in the paper. Since the most common route by which published data makes its way to commercial laboratories is through databases – which collate published research results – it is unlikely that this advisory will pass through the system of exchange. Nevertheless, it might serve as the basis for challenges to any patents based on the knowledge presented.

The mode chosen for dissemination of the cumulative years of research conducted by numerous investigators as part of the Secwepemc Ethnobotany Project (see the previous section) takes into account many of the concerns that have been raised in this chapter. To assist in keeping Secwepemc plant knowledge and resources both accessible for community needs and under the control of the Secwepemc First Nation, an alternative publication avenue has recently been established – two manuscripts are soon to be copublished by the Secwepemc Cultural Education Society itself.

BOX 4.4 A READER'S MORAL AND ETHICAL ADVISORY: ONE APPROACH TO PROTECTING TRADITIONAL KNOWLEDGE

In a 1994 publication of data resulting from years of research in Brazil with the Kayapo Indians, Elisabetsky and Posey (1994) advise readers in an opening section on 'intellectual, cultural, and scientific property', that:

'The data were obtained with full consent of the Kayapo people. The paper is published in the spirit of joint partnership with the Kayapo to advance knowledge for the benefit of all humanity. Any information used from it for commercial or other ends should be properly cited and acknowledged: any commercial benefits that should accrue directly or indirectly should be shared with the Kayapo people.'

While this opening paragraph will not carry legal weight in most countries, and it is difficult to attach it to the data once it enters into databases, subsequent publications and other forms derived from the original publication, it 'nonetheless carries a universal force of moral and ethical standards and obligations' (Posey et al, 1996). Since no national legislation was in place within Brazil at the time, the authors considered the use of this paragraph as one way to help prevent commercial use of the information without further negotiations with communities. The advisory might also provide some legal basis to require benefit-sharing with communities should a commercial product be developed, and encourage more thought and attention on the part of researchers to the issue of publishing data in forms that make it readily available to industry, with no conditions attached.

Source: Elisabetsky and Posey, 1994; Elisabetsky, pers comm, 1999; Posey et al, 1996

Conclusion

Publications are a central feature of the research process today. As a result, there is significant reluctance to interfere with publishing in ways that might slow down, alter or impede publication of research results and findings. It is widely believed, particularly among natural scientists, that the free dissemination of information serves the greater good, and that – with the exception of the most flagrant cases (and these have been addressed in depth by many professional research groups) – publications do not damage or harm; at most, they restrict opportunities for gain. Such a view expresses a political and social

naiveté that economic, social and technological changes in the latter part of the 20th century have made untenable. The increased commodification of biodiversity and of biodiversity information, the improvements in data storage, management and communication systems, and the continued expansion of the global economy into the most remote communities mean that researchers must face new expectations and be prepared to meet new obligations. These include creating, supporting and, indeed, *advocating* alternatives to the publishing status quo, and drawing on fair and respectful guidelines,

Dusun communities' efforts to control distribution of a medicinal plant manual around Kinabalu National Park

Agnes Lee Agama (People and Plants Initiative, South-East Asia)

The park

Kinabalu National Park encompasses a protected area of approximately 754 square kilometres (km^2) and has been ranked as the sixth highest global biodiversity centre in the world. This area consists of extensive lowland and montane forests and high-altitude vegetation that provide a rich habitat for up to 6000 species, 1000 genera and over 200 families occurring in the flora (Beaman and Beaman, 1998). Mount Kinabalu (4098m) sits as the centrepiece of Kinabalu Park some 83km from the state capital of Kota Kinabalu and is visited by over 200,000 tourists per year. The park is administered by Sabah Parks, a government body that is directly responsible for the management of nature parks in the state of Sabah. The Projek Etnobotani Kinabalu (Kinabalu Ethnobotanical Project), an ethnobotanical division of Sabah Parks established in 1992, has been compiling a floristic inventory of Mount Kinabalu. The project has trained up to nine Dusun villagers to collect plant specimens from areas in and around Kinabalu National Park. Collections have been made from over 100 locally named sites from a range of natural and anthropogenic habitats, with specific instructions to collect plants that have known uses for Dusun communities.

The people

The Dusun people live in several villages (100 to 2000 people per village), located outside the park boundary in settlements ranging in elevation from sea level to 2000m. Most communities are subsistence swidden rice farmers, who have been involved in small-scale cash cropping and trade, although an increasing number are now becoming involved in the cash economy, with villages closer to the park headquarters engaging in formal employment under the park. As increasing urbanization and national development policies seep into the rural interior, the Dusun have become increasingly involved in the market economy by intensifying cash cropping, harvesting and sale of non-timber forest products, and participating in tourism initiatives. Introduction of state legislation, the expanding cash economy, wage labour, compulsory education and Christianity continue to convert Dusun villagers to modern living. As this increasing level of acculturation decreases Dusun interaction with the surrounding forest, so does the degeneration of traditional institutions, such as traditional healing, decrease Dusun dependency upon medicinal plants. Traditional knowledge of plants is rapidly fading because mechanisms for transmitting traditional knowledge are disappearing, and the effects of the modernizing social context continue to discourage Dusun people from reinforcing their knowledge.

The plant manual project

In 1998 a joint project was initiated under the Projek Etnobotani Kinabalu and the People and Plants Initiative in South-East Asia to compile an educational resource manual, specifically to be used by local communities, that will integrate data from the last six years of community ethnobotanical collections. The main objectives of this collaboration were to:

- return the results of the Projek Etnobotani Kinabalu to local Dusun communities;
- revitalize and reinforce traditional knowledge of plants among Dusun communities;
- promote environmental awareness of forest resources through the use of community educational materials.

A series of joint consultations was carried out with the 20 Dusun villages involved in the ethnobotanical collections to discuss proposals for the content, format and target audience for the educational resource. As a result of these discussions, local communities decided to produce a plant manual to be used by local Dusun communities that would list the names and uses of 40 commonly used medicinal plants. Issues raised by local communities during these sessions also included uncertainty about protecting intellectual property rights over the knowledge of plant uses, long-term monitoring of the distribution and use of the manual and the option of restricting distribution to participating communities. It was also decided that further consultation should be continued to explore ways in which the community could establish mechanisms that would enable a higher sense of community-control over the production, circulation and application of the traditional knowledge. An action committee comprising 20 representatives from each village was established to continue consultations with the project team. This manual would be seen as an initial step towards future efforts at compiling more indepth accounts of ethnobotanical knowledge among Dusun communities.

The protocol

Although the project attempted to integrate existing Projek Etnobotani Kinabalu data into the compilation process, several unforeseeable logistical problems (eg fatal virus infection of the database and inconsistent scientific determinations on herbarium specimens) prevented this from happening as planned. Instead, the project team initiated new attempts to collect and verify data on the 40 plants with the help of local communities from each of the 20 participating villages. Voucher specimens were sent for independent identification at the Royal Botanic Gardens, Kew, the Forest Research Centre in Sandakan, and inhouse by Sabah Parks staff and colleagues.

In light of the ethnobotanical information being collected from 'new' sources, the action committee voiced renewed concerns regarding establishing mechanisms to monitor and protect the circulation and application of this knowledge once the manual is complete. Thus, upon completion of the manual, a workshop was conducted in collaboration with the Projek Etnobotani Kinabalu, People and Plants Initiative in South East Asia and the action committee representing the 20 villages. The objectives of the workshop were to:

- address the concerns of local communities regarding access to the plant manual;
- discuss options of how local communities can specify and monitor the circulation and application of the manual by potential users;
- draft a protocol document that would propose measures defining the access to, distribution and use of the manual.

Draft distribution protocol for the plant manual *Wakau, Kayu Om Sakot:Tubat Tinungkusan Sinakagon Kadazandusun*, 16 September 1998 (updated 8 October 1998)

Kiau Bersatu, Kiau Nuluh, Kiau Toburi, Mantanau, Melangkap Baru, Melangkap Kapa, Melangkap Nariou, Melangkap Tiong, Melangkap Tomis, Monggis, Nalumad, Pinawantai, Takutan, Toruntungon, Ulu Kukut
in collaboration with People and Plants South-East Asia and Sabah Parks

Draft Protocol Document for the Distribution of the Medicinal Plant Manual *Wakau, Kayu, Om Sakot: Tubat Tinungkusan Sinakagon Kadazandusun*

Rationale
Traditional knowledge is being lost due to a variety of factors including:

- A lack of contact between elders and youth.
- Influence of schools: less time is spent on teaching about medicinal plants in the national curriculum.
- The young are not interested and tend to migrate away from villages.
- Hospitals and pharmaceutical medicines are easily accessible, thus replacing medicinal plants.
- Village elders are forgetting traditional knowledge because they are not using traditional medicines anymore.
- Apprenticeship systems of transmitting knowledge have disappeared.
- New religions discourage its use, particularly in relation to taboos and magic associated with the practice of traditional medicines.
- People are losing confidence in traditional medicine.
- Children spend less time with their parents, especially in the fields, and are thus less exposed to plants.
- Forested areas are disappearing.
- People are more interested in 'modernization'.

Protecting and conserving traditional knowledge
The best ways to protect and conserve traditional knowledge are:

- establish medicinal plant gardens in villages for educational purposes;
- parents and elders must take responsibility for teaching the younger generation;
- conserve medicinal plant reserves near villages for educational purposes;
- practical teaching through use, processing and application of medicinal plants;
- documentation of knowledge in publications, such as this manual, posters and audio-visual materials;
- form part of the school curriculum, but in collaboration with local communities to ensure that teaching is concurrent with maintaining local traditions;
- conduct seminars, workshops and exhibitions.

The *primary objective* in producing this manual is to document and help conserve traditional knowledge on the part of the 16 villages that participated. There are some concerns regarding distribution of the manual and the use of information contained therein:

- Outside people might make commercial use of the plants, without the knowledge or permission of the communities or the sharing of benefits with the communities who have been involved.
- Outside people might publish other books based on the information in this manual.
- Traditional knowledge might be used in inappropriate ways.
- People might come into village areas to collect plants without the permission of the community.
- People might overharvest the medicinal plants.
- Outsiders who use the book might not take the medicine properly.

As a result, the following distribution policy has been developed for the manual.

Distribution Protocol for the Plant Manual *Wakau, Kayu, Om Sakot: Tubat Tinungkusan Sinakagon Kadazandusun*

1 One copy of the manual will be distributed to each household within each of the participating villages.
2 A meeting will be held in each village to ensure that all community members are aware of this distribution policy.
3 Distribution of the manual to neighbouring villages will be granted upon submission of a written application and granting of approval by the committee. Any applicants that have been approved are bound by this distribution protocol. Applications will be considered based on the application guidelines that have been determined by the committee.
4 Distribution of the manual to visitors, scientists and schools will be decided upon written application to the committee.
5 Researchers and visitors who are interested in the manual will be encouraged to visit communities to interact with the people regarding their culture with the permission of the committee, the village headman and the Village Safety and Development Committee.
6 WWF and Sabah Parks will each receive a specified allocation of copies of the manual, but will adhere to this distribution policy and any other policies developed by the committee to address the concerns of the communities as expressed above.
7 There will be a sticker label placed inside each copy of the book which states the terms under which each copy is released.

Buuk nopo ti nga' tua' di pininggisaman mantad kampung-kampung.
Buku ini adalah hasil dari kampung-kampung:
This book is the result of joint efforts by the following villages:
Kiau Bersatu, Kiau Nuluh, Kiau Toburi, Mantanau, Melangkap Baru, Melangkap Kapa, Melangkap Nariou, Melangkap Tiong, Melangkap Tomis, Monggis, Nalumad, Pinawantai, Takutan, Toruntungon, and Ulu Kukut.

1. *Pogoduhan do popodual buuk diti.*
   Dilarang menjual buku ini.
   Sale of this book is prohibited.
2. *Pogoduhan do popintahak buuk diti kumaa tulun do suai.*
   Dilarang mengedar buku ini kepada pihak lain.
   Distribution of this book to any other party than those cited above is prohibited.

3. **Pogoduhan do poposurat kawagu nunu nopo id suang buuk diti, toi ko' poposurat id suang database komputer.**
   Dilarang menerbitkan sebarang maklumat, atau memasukkan ke dalam database komputer.
   Publication of information contained within this book or inclusion in a database is prohibited.

4. **Pogoduahan do momoguno toilaan id suang buuk diti di maan do ponginda-puan.**
   Dilarang menggunakan maklumat dari buku ini untuk tujuan perniagaan.
   Under no circumstances is the information contained in this book to be used for commercial purposes.

5. **Pogoduhan do momoguno om popinwangkar toilaan nokosurat id suang buuk diti poinkuro pia kowaya-wayaon nung aiso kasaga'an mantad id AJK.**
   Dilarang menggunakan dan mengedar maklumat dari buku ini dalam bentuk lain yang tidak diluluskan oleh AJK.
   Any use or distribution of the information contained in this book in ways not approved by the committee is prohibited.

6. **Ontokon om adaton isai nopo i adapatan amu' mamayaan dilo' kapantangan-kapantangan di nokosurat.**
   Tindakan dan denda akan dikenakan pada sesiapa yang didapati melanggar peraturan-peraturan yang dinyatakan.
   Anyone found disregarding the stated regulations will be penalized.

_____

tandatangan penerima
Signature of recipient

tarikh:
Date:

_____

tandatangan dan cop AJK
Signature and stamp of committee

tarikh:
Date:

_____

8 The effectiveness of the distribution policy will be re-evaluated by the committee in six months' time.
9 The composition of the committee is as follows:
- representatives of each of the participating villages (all TMGK members are automatically members of the committee);
- representatives of Sabah Parks;
- representatives of WWF.

The majority of committee members will be from the communities. Participating villages are encouraged to establish TMGK branches in their own village.

Source: This protocol was drafted with the mutual agreement of all participating communities in the Community Research Agreement Workshop, 15–17 September 1998, at the Mesilau Nature Resort Kundasang, organized by the People and Plants Initiative in South-East Asia (WWF Malaysia) and Sabah Parks. Community members representing their villages were: Sopinggi Ladsou and Gampat Saborong (Kiau Nuluh); Ginting Gumu and Golakin Somidin (Kiau Bersatu); Kasimin Gindai and Louis Kabun (Kiau Toburi); Lumabai Balensiu (Melangkap Baru); Bakait Garob and Lorin Lugas (Melangkap Tomis); Sualin Sidan (Melangkap Kapa); Yangan Nangan (Melangkap Tiong); Indoh Galing (Melangkap Nariou); Dius Tadong and Miul Kasum (Takutan); Jahinin Ratimin (Nalumad); Salimah Bakarung and Asong Rumbai (Pinawantai); Joemeh Tan Sang Hock (Monggis); Raimon Rudin (Ulu Kukut); and Morini Gapaya (Mantanau). Other participants and resource people were Agnes Lee Agama, Sarah Laird, Jannie Lasimbang, Claudia Lasimbang, Joesph Guraat, Wendy Yap, Rusaslina Idrus, Alan Hamilton, Gary Martin, Ludi Apin, Sugarah Juanih and Ansow Gunsalam.

such as provided by the precautionary principle.

Researchers must also be aware of the rapidly changing legal and ethical paradigm of exchange within which biodiversity research currently takes place. The resources and knowledge upon which biodiversity research is based are no longer considered freely available goods, and the rights of groups managing biodiversity to control access to these materials and their knowledge are increasingly upheld. A balance between scientific requirements for the free exchange of information and ideas, and the rights of countries and communities to exert control over the flow of information, can and must be reached. In order to effectively create this balance, however, researchers – including institutions and funding agencies that motivate the existing incentive system – must take it upon themselves to further explore options for meeting both the needs of scholarship and those of host communities and countries.

Chapter 5

'Giving back': making research results relevant to local groups and conservation

Patricia Shanley and Sarah A Laird

A great deal of research is underway to assess and characterize biodiversity and associated resource management systems. This research yields information critical to the design of conservation programmes and national strategies for biodiversity conservation and furthers scientific understanding of threatened ecosystems. However, researchers and research institutions generally regard the scientific process as complete once an article is sent to press. The result is that most information and scientific understanding generated by researchers remains in the hands of scientists, academics and policy-makers geographically and conceptually distant from the region of study. Rarely are research programmes designed in a way that incorporates the resource management needs of local groups, nor are results put in a form that communities can employ when making resource management decisions. And yet, local groups are widely considered key stewards and stakeholders in biodiversity and forest conservation today.

In part, this situation results from the fact that the outlook and skills necessary to extend and disseminate results are not often found within the organizations that collect and analyse scientific data (Orr, 1999). Education and extension groups in the industrialized North acquire scientific data and make valuable use of it in their outreach programmes, but these groups are traditionally small and underfunded in poorer and more biologically diverse regions of the world. For example, school children in the temperate North are taught that while tropical forests cover only 7 per cent of the Earth's surface, they contain 50 per cent of the world's species and are the lungs and medicine chest of the earth. This information is taught not only in schools, but is also displayed for Northern consumers on candy bar wrappers, shampoo bottles and in coffee table books. Villagers living within tropical forests, however, are not privy to such information. Most live unaware that leading world scientists predict the demise of the forests they call home – in only a few decades.

The result is that governments, conservation organizations, researchers and companies often promote or make land-use decisions without fully informing or involving the local populations most affected. At the same time, groups living in close proximity to forests or high biodiversity zones are often badly in need of scientific data that can assist them in negotiations with logging companies, the development of management plans for community forests, assessing the relative value of a given forest area for non-timber forest products versus agriculture, and so on. Increasingly drawn into national and global economies and politics, remote groups more than ever need information and tools to effectively participate, and negotiate their position, in this broadened context.

Traditionally considered distinct from science, education and extension can effectively be twinned with research through institutional or departmental collaborations. Many researchers will not have the skills or interest to translate and transmit their data to local groups; but if they are aware of the importance of this activity, they can forge alliances to ensure this results.[1] Some researchers – as we will see in the case studies – integrate science and extension in their research design. The fields of education, development and rural agriculture extension have for decades worked to effectively transfer information to local groups – including through workshops, manuals, theatre and farmer-to-farmer exchanges – and there is much to be learned from these experiences (eg Chambers, 1983; Kowal and Padilla, 1998; www.oneworld.org/odi). Unfortunately, communication between most biodiversity researchers and these professionals has been limited.

We have seen in other chapters in this section the critical importance of laying a solid foundation for equity – the need for ongoing consultations with communities, prior informed consent, continual reassessment of relationships and innovative sharing of benefits. This chapter addresses an often overlooked element of equitable research relationships and an invaluable form of benefit-sharing: returning data in forms relevant to local groups and applied conservation.

A growing awareness of the need for 'giving back'

A new, more equitable approach to sharing – or 'giving back' – scientific results can be built into the scientific process, and there are increasing calls for this approach. For example, the *International Society of Ethnobiology Code of Ethics* (1998) incorporates the concept of a 'dynamic interactive cycle' for research in which projects should not be initiated unless all stages can be completed. This includes 'training and education as an integral part of the project, including practical application of results' (see Chapter 2). In an editorial for *Conservation Biology*, Colvin (1992) recommends a 'code of ethics for research in the third world' that suggests, among other points, that researchers 'help develop educational outreach programmes and interpretative centres that include... research results, reflect the knowledge and values of indigenous cultures, and can be used by both visitors and the local community'.

In India, the Honey Bee Network has worked to transform the paradigm of benefit-sharing to include professional accountability towards those whose knowledge and resources are studied. Researchers realized that their work was published mainly in English, and in ways that remained unavailable and not immediately useful to local groups. As part of their work, the Honey Bee Network shares scientific knowledge in local languages and pools both formal scientific and so-called 'informal' solutions to resource management problems developed by people around the world in order to share experiences across communities (Gupta, 1995; 1999; see Case Study 5.1).

CASE STUDY 5.1

THE HONEY BEE NETWORK: TRANSFORMING THE PARADIGM OF BENEFIT-SHARING

Anil Gupta (Centre for Management in Agriculture, Indian Institute of Management, Ahmedabad, and SRISTI and Honey Bee Network)

The Honey Bee Network evolved ten years ago in response to an extraordinary discomfort with my own conduct and professional accountability towards those whose knowledge I had written about and benefited from. I realized that my conduct was no different from that of other exploiters of rural disadvantaged people, such as moneylenders, landlords, traders, etc. They exploited the poor in the respective resource markets, and I exploited people in the ideas market. Most of my work had remained in English and thus was accessible only to those who knew this language. While I did share findings of my research with the providers of knowledge through informal meetings and workshops, the fact remained that I sought legitimacy for my work primarily through publications, mainly in English and in international journals or books. The 'income' that had accrued to me had not been shared explicitly with the providers of the knowledge. I argued with myself that I have spent such considerable time and energy in policy advocacy on behalf of knowledge-rich, economically poor people. But all of this was of no avail when it came to being at peace with myself. That is when the idea of Honey Bee came to mind.

Honey Bee is a metaphor indicating ethical as well as professional values which most of us seldom profess or practise. The honey bee does two things which we researchers often do not: it collects pollen from flowers, and the flowers don't complain; and it connects flower with flower through pollination – apart from making honey, of course. When researchers collect knowledge from farmers or indigenous people, unlike the flower they sometimes complain. Similarly, by communicating only in English, French or other global languages, researchers do not facilitate communication between people who supply their knowledge. The Honey Bee Network has tried to correct both of these problems. We acknowledge the innovations of local groups, linking them with innovators' names and addresses, and ensure a fair and reasonable share of benefits arising out of any use of the knowledge. At the same time, we insist that this knowledge be shared in local languages so that people-to-people communication and learning can take place.

Honey Bee acts as a knowledge network that pools solutions developed by people across the world in different sectors and links not just the people, but also formal and informal science. The network has collected more than 8000 innovative practices to date (predominantly from dry regions). It is obvious that people cannot find solutions for all problems, and that those solutions they do find may not always be optimal. There remains scope for value addition and improvement in efficiency and effectiveness in all communities. A strategy for development that does not build upon what people know, and excel in, is neither ethically sound nor professionally efficient.

SRISTI, a global non-governmental organization (NGO) set up few years ago, provides organizational support to the Honey Bee Network around the world. It is a network of oddballs who experiment and do things differently. Many of them end up solving problems in a very creative and innovative manner. But the unusual thing about these innovations is that they remain localized and are sometimes unknown to other farmers in the same village. Lack of diffusion cannot be considered a reflection on the validity of these innovations. The innovations could be technological, socio-cultural, institutional and educational in nature, contributing to the conservation of local resources and generation of additional income, or reduction or prevention of possible losses. Farmers have developed unique solutions for controlling pests or diseases in crops and livestock, conserving soil and water, improving farm implements, devising various kinds of bullock or camel carts for performing farm operations, storing grain, conserving landraces and local breeds of livestock, conserving aquatic and terrestrial biodiversity, etc.

The scope for linking scientific research with farmers is enormous. We are beginning to realize that people's knowledge systems need not always be considered informal just because the rules of the formal system fail to explain innovations in another system. For example, the soil classification system developed by many local people is far more complex and comprehensive than the US Department of Agriculture (USDA) classification systems. But it is important to note that not all the knowledge held by people in biodiversity rich, economically poor regions and communities is traditional, carried forward in fossilized form from one generation to another, collective in nature, and known to all members of a community.

There is much to be learned from the knowledge and innovations of rural people around the world. However, scientific and commercial research should be undertaken with the prior informed consent of people, and benefits should be shared concerning any use of traditional knowledge. Scientific papers should acknowledge those who supplied the information and knowledge upon which they are based, and research results should be shared with those who contributed their knowledge, in local languages and locally useful forms.

In another example, The Max Lock Centre at the University of Westminster, London, is undertaking research to 'improve the exchange and transfer of research knowledge'. The ongoing study proposes to suggest ways and means of making research more relevant to the needs of the target communities and research knowledge easily available in a practical format to those communities (Max Lock Centre, 1999; see Box 5.1). In Costa Rica, a consortium of institutions, including the National University of Heredia, The Open State University, the Ministry of Environment and Energy, and IUCN-Mesoamerica, have joined to develop a programme that combines wildlife research, production of extension materials and training. In the early stages, the project is working through consultations with local communities to acquire prior informed consent (PIC) for the research, and to more effectively design and implement the research phase in ways that respond to concerns or needs raised during consultations (see Case Study 5.2).

This chapter includes five ongoing case studies that illustrate some of the ways in which researchers incorporate innovative information transfer into project design. These cases are drawn from a range of subject areas (eg medicinal plants, marine biology, low-impact logging, wildlife management and conservation, and non-timber forest products) and describe how data are being disseminated in a meaningful way to a wide range of audiences, including sawmill owners, school children, ranchers, rural villagers and women's associations.

CASE STUDY 5.2

COMMUNITY PARTICIPATION IN TRAINING AND PRODUCTION OF EDUCATIONAL MATERIALS FOR WILDLIFE CONSERVATION IN COSTA RICA

Vivienne Solís Rivera and Patricia Madrigal Cordero (Wildlife Thematic Area, IUCN-Mesoamerica)

The Osa Peninsula is one of Costa Rica's most biologically diverse regions, as well as being of great importance because of its natural, social and cultural riches. This region, located in the south-eastern part of the country's southern Pacific zone, covers an area of approximately 150,000 hectares, with vegetation characteristic of tropical and sub-tropical rainforest. The area contains 12 different types of ecosystem, including mangroves, herbaceous lagoons, herbaceous swamps, Yolillo palm swamps, mountain forests and cloud forests.

The Osa Peninsula is populated mainly by colonists who have settled in the area over the past 50 years. Large migrations to this region were triggered by the shortage of land in Costa Rica and Panama, the opening of the Inter-American highway, the establishment of the Banana Company and the discovery of gold in the area. The region is also home to the Guaymi indigenous group, which has long inhabited the border-lands between Costa Rica and Panama and retains its rich cultural heritage.

The creation of various protected areas in the region has been marked by conflict. In order to establish the Corcovado National Park, hundreds of people were expelled from their lands. The government banned gold mining activities in the area in order to prevent their negative impact on the environment and it imposed a total hunting ban. As a result of these measures, local inhabitants have come to regard the 'protected areas' policy as one that is at odds with opportunities for their social development.

Many groups, institutions and organizations have given priority to biodiversity conservation in this zone and to improving the quality of life of the local inhabitants; but there has been a lack of coordination and articulation between the different initiatives and projects. Often lacking is a real involvement of the communities in the decision-making process for local development and the conservation of natural resources.

In Costa Rica, most conservation training materials have been designed by technicians or biologists. However, experience has shown that it is also essential to consider the economic, social, legal and cultural implications of conservation. With this in mind, in 1998 the Dutch embassy approved funding of the project Community Participation in Training Processes and the Production of Educational Materials on Conservation of Wildlife Species. This project is currently being implemented in an inter-institutional manner by the World Conservation Union (IUCN-Mesoamerica), the Open State University (UNED), the Regional Master Programme of Wildlife Management, the National University (PRMVS-UNA) and the Protected Areas National System of the Ministry of the Environment and Energy (SINAC-MINAE).

The project is based on the fundamental belief that in order to have a real impact and to change the attitudes of communities towards their environment, it is first necessary to gather information that shows how different individuals, ethnic groups or genders use or perceive the importance of wildlife resources in their daily lives. It is also based on the idea that the design of training materials incorporating this information should respond to the needs, interests and visions of different people, in order to have a greater impact on their attitudes and guarantee the sustainable use of natural resources.

The first challenge of this project was to initiate a process of field research to gather information from four peasant communities and one indigenous group concerning their relationship with wildlife. All of these communities live in areas surrounding three important protected zones: Corcovado National Park, Piedras Blancas National Park and the Alto Laguna Indigenous Reserve.

Traditionally, this type of information has been gathered in the conservation areas and in the local communities without considering the obligations of the research centres, students and various institutions to respect the 'intellectual property rights' of those who provide the information. For this reason, and in observance of the country's biodiversity law that includes regulations to protect and conserve traditional knowledge, a project code of ethics was drafted. This code requires us to obtain prior informed consent from the communities for gathering information from them and to use their information and associated knowledge in accordance with their expectations. We found communities unaccustomed to being asked for 'permission' to work in their living areas and with their members. The code also addresses the need to share benefits and receive community consent to disseminate information collected. It was produced in English and Guaymi.

Our first task was to organize a workshop with the communities to discuss and make known the contents of the code of ethics and the objectives of the project, and introduce the researchers who would visit the communities to gather information. As part of the project, we designed a survey with a series of interdisciplinary questions formulated in conjunction with local communities. Information on biological and cultural aspects of local community relationships to biodiversity was gathered during the first research phase of the project. The results of the survey show that local communities experienced unpleasant events, such as evictions, when the protected areas were established. Subsequent restrictions on the use of wildlife resources, lack of information, neglect and lack of financial opportunities engendered feelings of discontent with the conservation laws and the related institutions. Despite this, some local people are aware of the benefits of the wildlife areas and the need for their conservation, provided that the local populations are given opportunities to earn income and obtain basic services. However, most of the people in the communities surveyed cannot read or write well, do not perceive the complex interrelationships within ecosystems and the problem of extinction, do not understand the main functions of the Osa Conservation Area or of MINAE, and the concept of the state is alien to their lives.

This type of information will be used in the next phase of the project, in which we will seek to give back information gathered in each community and subsequently compiled and analysed. Development of conservation and resource-management outreach materials will result from a joint process with communities, in a manner consistent with the rhythm and pace of life in these communities. Materials will then be disseminated to a broader range of communities and groups in the region.

BOX 5.1 THE MAX LOCK CENTRE OUTPUT GUIDE: PROVIDING ADVICE ON COMMUNICATION TO 'KNOWLEDGE MINERS'

An output guide for researchers is under development by The Max Lock Centre of the University of Westminster, London, with support from the UK Department for International Development. The guide is intended to provide UK and other Northern researchers – or 'knowledge miners' – with information on ways to make research more inclusive of beneficiaries and to better communicate results. Current experience shows that access to research knowledge is poor, particularly for potential users, limiting its value. The intention is to improve access to knowledge, and establish a route or network to enable target groups to condition and influence the research undertaken in their name. The intended outcome is a two-way flow of information, relevant research and practical solutions (Max Lock Centre, 1999). The output guide will provide prompts to encourage effective communication at each stage of the research process, including checklists on a stage-by-stage basis. The objectives of the guide are to:

- improve the information base for sound decision-making;
- increase the penetration and accessibility of existing and new research;
- lengthen its active life;
- improve the diversity and practicability in use;
- promote innovation in the communication process; and
- foster needs-led research where the user's wishes feed into the process from the outset.

Source: The Max Lock Centre, 1999; www.wmin.ac.uk/builtenv/maxlock/default.htm

Why 'give back'?

Most biodiversity researchers feel an affinity for the ecosystems and communities that they study or with whom they work. Indeed, most proposals for biodiversity research include in the project's objectives their service to these ecosystems and communities. But how do researchers generally propose to make this connection? This is accomplished, primarily, by building understanding and organization of the subjects and, secondly, by providing information that will influence policy-makers and the general public, and might also be adopted by applied conservation projects.

While these are important objectives, another significant way that research results can be magnified to serve communities and conservation is by taking the results and, effectively, returning them to the groups and communities in or around which they were generated. As described in the case studies, research designed and directed to serve local resource-management needs, and shared in ways that allow groups to make informed decisions about long-term resource use, often has surprisingly significant – albeit localized – effects. As we move through conservation fad after conservation trend, often with mixed results, concrete small steps in a positive direction seem an increasingly sufficient objective.

Not only is 'giving back' research results to local stakeholders (rural and

Box 5.2 Culture-based approaches to research design: Teaching survey principles in a Fijian community

Diane Russell and Camilla Harshbarger

The WWF South Pacific Programme and the Biodiversity Conservation Network (BCN) developed a workshop to teach survey principles to community members involved in conservation and development initiatives. The workshop consisted of six steps:

1 what is action research;
2 different types of research;
3 survey concepts;
4 outline/design questionnaire;
5 implementation;
6 analysis.

The purpose was to expose people to survey concepts, such as sample frame, unit of analysis and bias. Many participants had taken part in informal data-gathering exercises, but few had any experience in carrying out surveys. Surveys were usually implemented by outsiders. More important, however, was to introduce notions of objectivity and scientific method. In Fiji, most information is gathered in large group meetings where there is little if any lag time between getting the information and the leadership making a decision on what to do. Only the higher status people typically speak up in meetings, and there was no tradition of testing assumptions about the root causes of problems – people assumed that they knew the cause.

Surveys make people get out and talk to others as individuals, and to think about testing assumptions. Participants saw clearly, however, that surveys are not always appropriate methods of obtaining certain kinds of information. One question developed on the sample survey instrument concerned ranking of important fish species. Many respondents could not make sense of the question. After much discussion, it turned out that most local fishers do not go out looking for specific fish but go out to fish and pick up what they find. The ranking did not make sense to them. Participants decided that a focus group of fishers was a better method to learn about the way in which fishers make decisions about what and where to fish. This method would lead the researcher to understand which species end up being most used. The administrators of a tikina, or county of eight villages, implemented a household survey and kept the data for themselves. They felt that their survey was much more professional and accurate than any other surveys that had been compiled by outsiders.

Source: BCN and WWF-South Pacific Programme, 1998

urban communities, governments, industries, conservation projects, etc) an important ethical responsibility that should be taken up by researchers, there are also practical reasons to do this that serve immediate scientific and conservation objectives, as well. Some reasons why a researcher should work to give back results in locally relevant forms include:

• Local stakeholders represent a critical set of actors who will determine if and how natural resources are used and protected. Generally far from enforcement agencies, these groups determine how and if policies are manifested on the ground, and the ways in which resources are managed.

- The knowledge of local populations is an invaluable perspective in examining data. Their specific commentary and critiques of research can serve as a local test of methods and results (see Box 5.2; Richter and Redford, 1999). As Anil Gupta (pers comm, 1999) said, it is common that when research results are handed back to local groups, they say something like: 'Oh, is that why you were asking that question... I didn't tell you the full story because I didn't know the full context for your inquiry – now that I know it, I will tell you something I did not tell you earlier.'

- By returning the results of research locally, the information can be immediately applied. Data fed into the scientific publication circuit can take years to emerge, and must compete for policy-makers' attention in an avalanche of published documents.

- Local groups often have key research questions that they want addressed and their livelihoods, and conservation of local resources and habitats, may depend upon concrete answers.

Forms of 'giving back'

There are many ways in which researchers can 'translate' their data into forms that are immediately relevant to local groups and conservation. These include written sources (such as manuals, illustrated booklets, curricula, colouring books and technical books) as well as oral and in-person sources (such as interactive workshops, seminars, theatre, travelling shows, music and lectures). In part, the choice of medium will depend upon the objectives to be served, as well as the intended audience. Local audiences will vary, and will include rural and urban communities and organizations, companies (eg loggers, ranchers, commercial agriculture), governments and applied conservation and development projects. Materials should be dynamic and constantly revised in light of feedback and experiences (Pyke et al, 1999).

For example, we see in the Eastern Amazon case study that communities are struggling with ways in which to determine the value of their forests in order to strike better deals with loggers and to assess whether a given area is more valuable to the community for its non-timber products (game, medicine, fruits) or for its timber rights. In this case, given the geographic distance across which communities are grappling with these issues, illustrated manuals (that make them accessible to the illiterate as well as literate), exchanges between groups and travelling theatres and workshops were found to most effectively capture the key scientific results, and allowed for broad dissemination (see Case Study 5.3).

The Institute of People and the Environment of the Amazon (IMAZON) also sought to share results from many years of research, but their primary objective was to educate loggers and the forest products industry (see Case Study 5.4). They chose workshops and seminars, field days, videos and a forest handbook that translates scientific data into concrete technical assistance for an audience unlikely to wade through scientific papers

BOX 5.3 FORMS OF 'GIVING BACK' DATA

There are many ways of translating data into valuable forms for local groups, and the method selected will depend upon both the groups and the objectives you seek to serve. Below are some ideas that might be considered.

Oral

Interactive workshops and seminars: for many industry groups, technicians, and government officials, this form of exchange will prove most useful; structured loosely, and involving field trips or site-based interaction, they can help to create dialogue and awareness.

Theatre and travelling shows: rural and urban groups alike often respond better to stories, enacted by fellow community members or visitors, which relay lessons learned in a more engaging format than a lecture or seminar. In the realm of theatre, people find it possible to relay information that they might normally find embarrassing to share. In some cases, travelling theatres and shows have proven invaluable for neighbouring communities and groups to share lessons they have learned with each other.

Exchanges: exchanges between groups with like needs and backgrounds but from differing geographical regions can be an extremely effective means of transferring information. When neighbouring stakeholders present information to each other in culturally appropriate forms, there are many benefits. Firstly, language, expressions and manner of communication are clearly understood. Secondly, trust is more readily built; information is better accepted from 'insiders' because they have no motivation to 'sell' ideas. Thirdly, individuals in one region may have personally experienced the positive or negative effects of particular land-use decisions, and are able to relate the consequences in a far more moving and convincing way than an outside extension agent.

Music: songs are a powerful method of cultural expression. New or familiar songs that integrate research findings into lyrics can convey not only relevant scientific facts but also embody the feelings of cultural loss surrounding ecosystem impoverishment. Music has the additional benefit of migrating from community to community on its own, thereby carrying messages across geographical distances.

Lectures: in some cases, presentation of scientific results in a fairly standard academic format will be appropriate and useful, particularly for local research institutions, universities and sometimes government departments. Even in these forums, however, it is important to occasionally integrate aspects of the presentation styles listed above. Standard format lectures are far less memorable than those eliciting audience participation.

Written

Manuals and illustrated booklets: the content of manuals will vary greatly. Some may be illustrated guides to local uses and management of species, intended for largely illiterate audiences who are concerned about the loss of their cultural knowledge and seek in some way to record and validate this knowledge; others may take the form of field guides that local groups can sell to tourists or can use in managing resources; others may be hands-on technical manuals that help local groups better manage resources or negotiate with commercial and government representatives interested in local resources and lands. When seeking to reach semi-literate and illiterate populations, it is critical to test illustrated materials with local people; rural persons, in particular, exhibit acute perceptivity regarding the size and shape of fruits, leaves and wildlife, and have well-developed opinions on natural resource processing and management techniques.

Curricula: teachers in high-biodiversity developing countries often have limited access to materials that assist in teaching about the local environment, traditional use of resources and wider environmental concerns; researchers can provide an invaluable service by translating their results into forms that are easily adopted by teachers in the classroom.

Colouring books: children respond well to colouring books in their local language or vernacular; colouring books allow them to become engaged in the subject and are important education and learning tools.

Books: publication of books can help to disseminate information more widely that otherwise might not reach a broad cross-section of society; however, many groups cannot afford books, and researchers should be clear on who this form of dissemination can reach – generally academic and governmental, rather than the rural and urban poor.

in search of sustainable management techniques. Scientific publications are the priority product for IMAZON. However, as a group also committed to changing practices on the ground in the Amazon Basin, they realized the need to publish popular articles that could help change public perceptions of the forest, and to provide technical information of immediate value to forest managers and loggers.

In Belize, traditional healers asked researchers to help them produce a book for teaching children, and which might serve as a reference for, and validation of, threatened medicinal plant knowledge. The published book includes both local knowledge and clinical information gathered by researchers in the US through databases and literature. Other products include colouring books for children and a video used in local schools to teach the importance of traditional knowledge (Balick and Arvigo, 1998).

The Jump with Whales programme in the eastern Caribbean tailors its materials in ways that create a sense of ownership and feeling of being 'at home' in young and old alike. Colouring books for children, curricula material for schools, and a *BLOWS! Newsletter* distributed free to schools have all helped to translate scientific data into forms that build wider awareness of marine mammal conservation, and a constituency 'to bring about changes in attitudes and values while instilling a sense of heritage for stewardship of the marine environment' (see Case Study 5.5).

CASE STUDY 5.3

EMPOWERING COMMUNITIES TO SLOW DEFORESTATION: TRANSFER OF ECOLOGICAL AND ECONOMIC RESEARCH RESULTS IN THE EASTERN AMAZON

Patricia Shanley

In the late 1980s and early 1990s, as the logging industry in Eastern Amazonia faced diminishing stocks of timber in the immediate vicinity of sawmills, loggers began seeking timber from ever-increasing distances. The penetration of logging roads into remote areas caused contact between two formerly distinct worlds: the timber industry and isolated rural communities. Tempted by quick cash, many villagers quickly sold large tracts of timber for meagre sums. Consecutive episodes of timber extraction, however, left communities with ever-diminishing stocks of game, fruit and fibre resources. In the wake of rapid impoverishment of their resource base, families along the Capim River basin in Para, Brazil, and representatives of the Rural Workers' Union of Paragominas began to question the costs and benefits of logging and to consider whether there might be forest management alternatives to logging in which forest products other than timber could be marketed. Lacking sufficient technical knowledge of forestry, they began searching for scientific collaborators to inventory their forests and determine if non-timber forest products might offer greater promise than timber.

The resultant research project coordinated by Woods Hole Research Centre/EMBRAPA scientists continued over a four-year period, documenting the present contribution of non-timber forest resources to rural livelihoods, assessing the comparative value of timber and non-timber resources and determining whether key non-timber forest resources from selectively logged *terra firme* forests could be sustainably managed and profitably marketed. However, although the research offered new contributions to scientific understanding of non-timber forest products, it fell markedly short of adequately meeting the communities' needs. Graphs and tables generated by conventional research are meaningless to households dependent upon the forest for their daily livelihoods. Unprepared, illiterate and in an extremely poor negotiating position, many villagers continued to trade large expanses of forest or trees for meagre sums.

To combat this destabilizing trend, forest residents need clear, relevant information to evaluate the costs and benefits associated with intact forests. They need to understand which species of fruit and medicinal plants are critical to day-to-day livelihoods and which offer more to the domestic economy when left standing than when cut. Many smallholders require assistance in inventorying their forest resources, measuring fruit and/or medicinal oil production, comparing the financial value of timber and non-timber products and mapping. Clearly, an initiative was needed in which relevant scientific information was given back in locally appropriate ways. To accomplish this, a few women from rural communities, together with the lead researcher, formed a group called *Mulheres da Mata*, whose specific objective is to return relevant scientific data to local communities. In spite of many cultural, socio-economic and geographical obstacles to returning research results, the group has reached hundreds of communities with positive outcomes in terms of improved forest management. Key features that assisted communities to capture, understand and use the information are presented below.

300 fruits
R$60

R$2

10 fruits

=

Source: Shanley et al (1998)

Figure 5.1 *'Giving back' research results in the Eastern Amazon: illustrating results from scientific study in ways that can be used by local communities. Here values for forest fruits derived from many years of ecological and marketing research are compared with the price that logging companies offer communities for the timber of the same species*

Conduct locally relevant research

Research questions and decisions regarding which species to study were jointly agreed upon during a consultative process with community members. Notably, the fruit and medicinal species of greatest value to villagers had received little to no scientific study. The ecological and economic information needed to answer the communities' queries regarding the comparative value of timber and non-timber forest products was also not available or accessible. To determine whether a tree was more valuable for its wood, fruit or resin, smallholders required basic information regarding densities and fruit production. In addition, market prices were needed to compare the economic value of fruits, fibres, game and medicinals to timber.

Recognize limits and strengths of traditional and scientific knowledge

While local knowledge was key in pointing researchers toward the locally most important species, their fruiting and flowering cycles and the types of wildlife that dispersed their seeds, the knowledge base of communities was insufficient to provide data necessary for modern land transactions and timber negotiations. For example, local estimates of fruit production varied by tenfold; estimates of fruit tree densities were widely variable; and knowledge of forest boundaries was vague and inconsistent. Likewise, the knowledge of the research team was woefully insufficient to even begin recommending alternative forest management options. The team did not know which species of trees were most valuable to hunters, which copaiba trees might produce oil, the impact of logging and fire on locally valued trees, or the regeneration potential of valued forest fruit trees.

Integrate local and scientific knowledge

The inclusion of decades-long, local understanding of fruit and medicinal species strengthened the research immeasurably, and made the results relevant to, and respectful of, local knowledge. The research/education process also taught our team where local expertise was limited and where scientific expertise could help complement local knowledge and empower communities. For example, villagers did not know how to inventory their forest holdings; how to measure the number of cubic metres per tree; or how to calculate the market value of game, fruit and fibre. In addition, traditional plant knowledge, eroded through years of purchasing pharmaceuticals, needed strengthening. Consultations with phytochemists, pharmacologists and botanists assisted the team to discern which local remedies had been scientifically proven to be most effective against particular illnesses, and clarified proper preparation techniques and dosages.

Offer ongoing, preliminary results

The long-term time frame necessary to generate rigorous data was in sharp contrast to that of the villagers' time frame. Villagers were in desperate need of land-use alternatives immediately, not five years from now. To provide results more swiftly to communities, the research team offered preliminary data and results, some of which were immediately useful in comparing the value of their timber and non-timber resources, in assessing the subsistence value of their forest, and in preparing effective medicinal plant remedies.

Display results in local units and language

Participatory presentations by local residents ensure that language is appropriate to the audience. Since language determines who enters a discussion, who is heard and who is not heard, it is important to eradicate needless technical terms and introduce only select scientific vocabulary. For many individuals, metric measurements, net present value and US dollars are not meaningful units of assessment. In presenting results, it is critical to understand how local residents think and speak regarding the size of their land holdings, weight measurements, economic value and tree size. For example, while scientists measure diameter at breast height of a tree (dbh), villagers often speak in terms of a tree's circumference. Number of trees per hectare may be meaningless to residents in regions where hectare is an unfamiliar term and where trees occur in densities of less than one per hectare. Similarly, to communities who have scant access to cash, describing a tree's worth in monetary terms may be little understood. Comparisons using commonly sold agricultural commodities may be more easily comprehended (eg the timber of one tree may be worth one sack of manioc flour, whereas the fruit of the same tree is worth ten sacks of manioc flour).

Recognize local value of biodiversity

Research results demonstrated that although forest resources offered substantial economic input to families, this was infrequently accounted for at the household level. For some families, the value of the forest for game, fruit and fibres is implicit; for others, free commodities from the forest are little valued. One household calculated that from one hectare, on average, they annually consumed the equivalent of approximately US$200 in fruit, fibre and game. In 1998, if they sold the logging rights of that hectare to a logger, they would receive a mere US$36. Recognition of the substantial input of natural resources to this family's livelihood greatly assisted neighbours to better understand the value of their standing forests.

Such recognition can be encouraged through increasing access to market prices, costs of substitute goods and costs of valued-added products. For example, guessing games in which families estimated how many kilogrammes (kg) of game a neighbouring hunter had caught (63kg) and its corresponding economic value in the market place (US$126) assisted the community understand the value of certain game-attracting tree species. US$2 offered by the logger for one piquiá (*C. villosum*) tree is clearly not worth the loss of the 30 kg of protein-rich game, valuing US$60, that one hunter captured beneath that tree.

Include women

Suffering disproportionately from forest impoverishment, women, although reticent to take part in workshops, generally offered powerful voices. As caretakers of the health and nutritional needs of the family, women know and use many forest products and therefore can offer significant input towards recognizing both the subsistence and market benefits of forest management. For example, women knew how to prepare remedies for malaria when distance or cost prohibited access to pharmaceutical preparations. In hard times that prohibited purchase of store-bought products, women ingeniously employed forest fruits combined with tree oils to make soaps. Women brought a voice of caution and thrift to timber negotiations, prohibiting disadvantageous deals and conserving fruit trees. When women of one community became involved in land-use decisions, they banned any further timber sales.

Improve market/regulatory knowledge base

Negotiations between industry representatives and smallholders are largely uniform, resulting in deals that neglect to consider the basic nutrition and health care needs of forest-based communities. Not accustomed to bargaining, villagers often accept whatever is offered, many unaware of downstream values for their resources. For example, one farmer traded his 75 hectares (ha) of forest for a broken rifle; another sold three pau d'arco (*Tabebuia* spp) trees for the equivalent of US$36 when the downstream value for the cubic metres present in the three trees equalled US$600. However, when villagers became aware of the value of timber and the increasing market value of fruits, some opted to process and sell fruit in lieu of timber. For example, one bag of fruit offered 25 times the value that a logger was offering for the entire fruit tree. Two litres of medicinal oil from a copaiba tree commanded 30 times the price offered for the tree's timber. Although there are significant socio-economic and ecological obstacles to marketing forest products, the knowledge that fruits, fibres and medicines can command high prices gives villagers reason to pause before selling valuable trees.

Catalyse the learning process with new, useful, challenging concepts

Although research results demonstrated that intact forests held a net present value far in excess of their current timber value, both policy-makers and rural residents routinely ignore the substantial 'invisible' income in fruit, game and medicinal plants that intact forests hold. For instance, one villager traded scores of primary forest trees for a rustic stove. Another community sold the timber rights to hundreds of hectares of forest for a few thousand dollars with which they purchased bicycles, radios and liquor. New language, information and concepts, however, can challenge prevailing notions and habits. We discovered that clearly presented economic arguments, demonstrating the stark value of intact as opposed to logged forests, assisted villagers to question and to think more openly about forest management options. Although foreign, the concepts embedded in 'forest reserve' and 'forest corridor' were of potentially great importance to villagers. These terms were introduced through maps, posters and discussions.

Participation and innovation

But how to disseminate ecological, market and medicinal plant information to a wide range of audiences? Clearly, ordinary means of information transfer through scientific publications to local residents would be inappropriate. Instead of presenting scientific data in threatening forms such as graphs, tables or written words, we wove information into locally familiar forms of communication such as role playing, posters, songs and interactive dialogue. For example, the comparative economic value of fruit and timber was demonstrated through realistic role-plays featuring downtrodden harvesters, cunning loggers and shrewd fruit buyers. Hunters proudly depicted the economic importance of game-attracting fruit trees on posters while healers displayed examples of local bark, root and herbal remedies, comparing their price (free from the forest) to prices of pharmaceutical drugs (costly). During workshop intervals, villagers sang locally popular tunes that were infused with historic, economic and ecological lyrics on forest value.

We discovered that skits and lyrics infused with these realistic stories of forest loss, and incorporating solid economic and ecological data, provided a new knowledge base on which communities can make more informed decisions. Entertaining yet sobering, participatory presentation of research results through skits and songs awakened villagers to new ways of thinking. Once aware that the fruit or oil production of a tree may be worth 25 times that of the value the logger offers for the entire tree, or that the downstream value of sawn wood is worth 10 to 20 times that offered locally for crude wood, smallholders tend to pause before entering into disadvantageous land and timber deals.

Extend dissemination beyond the research area

Many communities who have participated in workshops demonstrated significant changes in forest management practices. Some negotiated more effectively with loggers, sold fruit in lieu of timber, restored degraded lands, and created fire barriers and forest reserves. In spite of the surprising success of workshops within scores of communities, our team of village extensionists realized that the wave of logging, ranching and fire was far too strong to be significantly altered by a small band of foot-travellers. In order to offer basic data to smallholders with which they could more effectively make their forest-management decisions, not scores but thousands of remote communities needed ecological and economic information.

When requests for workshops exceeded our ability to meet them, we decided that we needed a new way of reaching isolated communities. The ecological and economic data, stories, songs and lore presented in workshops were placed on paper in an illustrated form with a descriptive text. The books are disseminated to rural workers' unions, women's associations, forest managers and rural community groups. Six months to one year after workshops with the books are conducted, the team returns to the community to determine if and what type of changes have resulted. Return visits demonstrate that workshops conducted in regions outside of the research area proved successful in catalysing positive land-use decisions. By returning results in a culturally captivating form to communities, the extension team of rural women also made the unexpected discovery that the information presented this way was also more accessible to policy analysts, conservation organizations and urban citizens. Requests for workshops from urban groups, policy-makers and non-governmental organizations attest to this.

Conclusion: equity in information transfer

Predatory timber extraction is not only unsustainable from a local perspective, but from a state and national perspective in terms of maintaining a viable timber industry for the future. To combat this destabilizing trend, rural residents, industry representatives and policy-makers need clear, relevant information to evaluate the costs and benefits associated with timber and non-timber forest products. What is needed is a full assessment of the relative value and contribution of forest resources to the region's economic, nutritional and health status. It is fundamental to understand which species are critical to day-to-day livelihoods and which offer more to the economy standing than cut.

Although conservation and development projects throughout the world have compiled massive data sets in ecological, resource management and non-timber forest resources, few have managed to extend the results in a useful way to local communities. Scientists who collect data are not required or encouraged to give it back to the communities where it was generated or to make it accessible in the policy realm. Communities dependent upon natural resources are frequently comprised of disadvantaged members of society, such as women and the rural poor, who have scant access to information. The results of this research indicate that innovative transfer of relevant information can be an effective means of achieving meaningful conservation and development goals, and of improving equity for forest-based communities.

CASE STUDY 5.4

FOREST EDUCATION IN THE EASTERN AMAZON: THE CASE OF THE FOREST MANAGEMENT PILOT PROJECT

Paulo Amaral and Tatiana Corrêa (Institute of People and the Environment of the Amazon – IMAZON)

Through a forest management pilot project, IMAZON has developed a strategy to disseminate both scientific and wider educational information. It is felt necessary to disseminate the results to a large and varied audience. The forest sector's actors are anxious for information to help better use and manage forest resources. The scientist should therefore create high-quality technical information for this audience, and should seek to draw the media, government and society into debate on resources in the Amazon.

The problem

The Brazilian Amazon is home to the largest tropical timber reserves in the world. Logging in the Amazon began in the 18th century but until 1970 it was low volume. Today the Amazon produces about 28 million cubic metres (m^3) of roundwood, or 80 per cent of national production. This represents only approximately 4 per cent of tropical wood exports on the international market; but in the next decade this situation could change due to the depletion of forest resources in Asia (Veríssimo and Amaral, 1996).

Logging in Amazonia can be characterized as 'forest mining'. First the loggers exploit the high-value species. Later, during short breaks, they come back to the exploited forest looking for smaller high-value trees species. This type of exploitation creates new roads and trails, resulting in forest deterioration. If, after the first exploitation, the forest was left to recuperate, its canopy would close and the forest would return to its 'primary' condition. By 1990 only approximately 3 per cent of wood production in the region was from managed forests. Forest management was confined to research stations, and the timber industry remained a spectator in the process. In addition, forest management studies were located in remote areas, and results disseminated only to the academic public. Results did not present a rigorous cost-benefit analysis of forest management: the kind of information commercial loggers are interested in (Uhl et al, 1997).

In response to this situation, during the 1990s, IMAZON's forest-management pilot project sought to better integrate research activities and education. In order to reach the production sector, the project began to work with a mill that owned 200 hectares, located in Paragominas, Eastern Amazon. The study compares two neighbouring plots: one exploited without planning and the other with forest management. The results reveal that forest management has economic advantages over unplanned exploitation. In general, positive results include waste reduction, more efficient use of equipment, accident reduction and greater productivity. However, the most important discovery about forest management is related to harvest cycles: good management can reduce the harvest cycles from 70–100 years (without management) to 30–40 years (with management) (Uhl et al, 1997). This means that forest management can double wood production. In some cases, the loggers would need half of the forest area used at present to supply their demand.

Dissemination

Upon completing the forest-management pilot project, our goal was to reach the wood sector's actors in order to educate them about the benefits of sustainable management of forest resources. Our strategy was to develop several means to disseminate the results of the pilot project, including field days, videos, handbooks, field courses, seminars and publications.

Field days

Seven field days were held in order to present and discuss the main project results with loggers, government experts, forest researchers, forest engineers and undergraduate and high school students. Approximately 120 people participated in this activity, the majority being loggers. The main lesson we learned from this experience is the need to emphasize the wider purpose of the experiment and the message we hoped to transmit. In addition, it is important to prepare a guide to research results that answer the questions in a succinct way.

Video

The images of an exploitation scene demonstrate visually and powerfully the advantages of forest management. We prepared an 18-minute video, which won an award for the best script at the National Festival of Ecological Video in 1994. The video presents the high damage and waste incurred by predatory exploitation, as well as the economic and ecological advantages of forest management.

The video's primary target was the wood sector's actors (loggers, workers in the timber industry, experts and researchers). However, it reached a larger audience, including high school students, workers, educators and decision-makers. The video has been shown in several national and regional TV programmes and workshops that focused on forest issues in the Amazon. More than 300,000 people have watched the video in the last three years. Groups that have been using the video are drawn from the government, schools, rural peoples' organizations, international agencies (eg US Agency for International Development (USAID), Gesellschaft für Technische Zusammenarbeit (GTZ)) and support institutions. We produced 400 copies of the video, of which 50 are in English. We learned that to reach several levels of audience (from illiterate people to experts), a video should not be too long (18 minutes in this case).

Forest handbook

We also present the results of the pilot project in a forest handbook that targets forest experts, loggers, exploitation managers and community leaders. The handbook is 150 pages in length, includes more than 150 illustrations and maps and is divided into 11 chapters. In general, the forest handbook teaches, step by step, how to implement forest management from forest inventory, through exploitation planning, harvest and skidding, to silvicultural treatments following exploitation.

To produce the forest handbook, we gathered previously analysed scientific data and translated the results into a less technical and more accessible language, determined in light of the target audience. Figures were considered critical in transmitting the information.

Field courses

Short field courses are a direct and intensive means of disseminating information and training people in forest management techniques. We tested this model of extension through seven courses (about five days long), for a total of 110 people. Four courses were offered to students and forest engineers; two for small rural producers in Rondônia State, and another was directed at high school students (agriculture specialization). One of these courses involved the main institutions working on forest management, including IMAZON, Tropical Forest Foundation (FFT), University of Amazonas, University of Pará, Brazilian National Institute for Agriculture and Livestock (EMBRAPA) and the Institute of Environmental Research for Amazônia (IPAM). The courses bring together a diversity of experiences from mill, communities, extractive reserves and Indian lands.

Seminars

In the last four years we participated in multiple seminars and gave dozens of presentations in academic fora and workshops directed at the private sector, government, development banks, and rural community and small producer organizations. The five main IMAZON researchers presented approximately 100 papers to a total audience estimated at 8–10,000 people. IMAZON elaborated criteria for participation in conferences and seminars:

- The seminar objectives should relate to our study areas.
- The seminar importance should be weighed in terms of expected audience and media coverage.
- Exchange of information and professional relationships should be encouraged.

We learned through experience that a good presentation is not enough to maintain a debate on our results, and that written summaries of our presentations are important aids in this regard.

Scientific and non-scientific papers

In general, scientific publications are the priority product resulting from our research. Popular dissemination of the research results follows a completed scientific version of our work. During six years of the pilot project, we published 16 papers in international journals such as *Scientific American, Bioscience, Forest Ecology and Management, Forest Science, Conservation Biology, Unasylva, Environmental Conservation and Ecological Applications*. We have also published articles for newspapers and non-scientific magazines, mainly in Brazil. Based on the circulation of all these publications, we estimate that more than 100,000 people have read at least our article summaries.

Conclusion

We believe that high-quality scientific information and up-to-date research themes involving economic, social and ecological discussions are essential to promote the changes in forest management in the Amazon region that are our primary objective. However, in order to achieve sound forest management, the wider public, forest sector and government must be involved. It is essential, therefore, that information and technical advice are disseminated in ways that allow changes in timber exploitation in order to slow or halt forest destruction in the Amazon.

CASE STUDY 5.5

Jump with Whales

Nathalie Ward (Boston University Marine Programme)

Jam to the music, move your feet,
Sing with the whales, wiggle to the beat.
Jump up and dance with dolphins in the street,
It's a whale party, see who you can meet.

Unless conservation education is rooted within a local system of knowledge and meaning that supports and justifies it, conservation practices will not be maintained because there will be no cultural ballast keeping conservation efforts steady in the face of changing circumstances. Jump with Whales is a conservation education programme in the eastern Caribbean designed to teach children about the basic biology of whales and dolphins, and the conservation considerations necessary for healthy populations to exist. Funded in 1994 by the International Fund for Animal Welfare (IFAW) and the Whale and Dolphin Conservation Society, Jump with Whales is tailored to the social, cultural and economic context of the eastern Caribbean. The educational materials incorporate my research and knowledge of whales and dolphins in the region (and that of other researchers in the field) with local knowledge about whales. The first objective was to develop interpretive materials that engage learners by using a vernacular context to create an 'at home' sense of ownership about whales and dolphins and the places they inhabit. To date, three children's books have been published.

Jump with Whales is an ABC colouring book of whales and dolphins for preschool and young elementary school children. *Whales and Dolphins – Inside and Out* is a workbook for children aged 7 to 11 which outlines anatomy and behaviour basics. *Jam with Whales* is a children's and teachers' workbook for ages 7 to 14 which explores the whales' multidimensional underwater world of sound, communication and acoustics.

Jam with whales, it's a calypso thing,
Wind up and get ready to sing.
Dolphins squeal, whistle and chirp,
Whales click, moan and even burp!

Jam with whales under the sea,
They make sounds like you and me.
Some whales sing to attract a mate.
Others use sounds to catch their bait.

Jump with Whales is designed to link local knowledge and scientific knowledge systems. In addition, the programme aims to integrate the study of marine mammals into the elementary science curriculum; to offer teachers an innovative hands-on curriculum; to advance partnerships between schools, ministries of education, and citizen involvement in marine mammal perception; to increase protection and conservation of marine mammal habitats which have been historically minimized in the Caribbean; to advocate pro-conservation policy in international marine policy assemblies; and to enlighten media communications regarding endangered marine species.

The Jump with Whales programme emphasizes the importance of place-based education initiatives that include the life experience and sphere of reference of the learner. If students do not understand or relate to the materials being taught, they are not engaged and easily can become alienated from the subject. For place-based education to be relevant, it has to include a wide variety of perspectives in all phases of planning, developing, teaching and learning. Local-based education has an opportunity to create new interpretive methods that kindle commitment or define problems of emerging relevance to locals. Effective programmes create a constituency to bring about changes in attitudes and values while instilling a sense of heritage for stewardship of the marine environment.

These innovative books and accompanying whale newsletters – *BLOWS!* – have been distributed to children for free through the support of a range of international organizations, some of which have also supported an out-reach education programme for fishermen in the eastern Caribbean, through the production and free distribution of the field guide *Whales and Dolphins of the Caribbean*. Jump with Whales marine mammal education programme was embraced by island nations of the Windward Islands (Dominica, St Lucia and Grenada) as part of a wider conservation effort to protect marine endangered species of the region. Jump with Whales methodology is designed to be a template for any marine endangered species, with specific aims of enhancing public appreciation, enjoyment and understanding of marine fauna. This approach emphasizes the importance of local values and socio-economic needs of local populations as a concurrent objective of species and habitat protection.

Lessons learned and issues raised

The case studies and other efforts to link dissemination of results with research have yielded some significant lessons and have flagged key issues that researchers might consider in the design of their research programmes. These include lessons associated with the ways in which data are translated and transmitted, as well as lessons connected to the broader research context in which 'giving back' takes place.

Lessons learned in 'giving back' scientific data

Lessons learned include the following:

- Conduct locally relevant research, in response to locally articulated needs.
- Provide research results in a range of forms as you go through the data collection and analysis process.
- Present economic value and units of measurement appropriate for different audiences; to be most effective this may entail using non-monetary value systems and non-metric local measuring systems.
- Integrate traditional and scientific knowledge, usually highly complementary, when returning results.
- Understand how and why local groups use and manage resources in the ways that they do – this will help make your contribution accurate, relevant and useful.
- Provide information on the range of options available to groups, and not only those a researcher considers optimal – this will help to ensure that recommendations and information are

adequately placed in the decision-making reality that local groups face.

- Catalyse the learning process with new, useful and challenging concepts – do not assume that local groups are aware of all possible outcomes and options.

- Be innovative and creative in coming up with ways to transmit your information and lessons to communities – for example, explore the use of posters and songs and interactive dialogue to relay what is customarily illustrated in scientific graphs and charts or technical language.

- Extend dissemination beyond the study area – neighbouring groups and communities often face many of the same challenges and information shortages; train local collaborators to extend results to neighbours.

- Encourage local stakeholders involved in generating information to give back the information, blending in their knowledge, experience and perspectives.

- Reflect local social, economic and cultural norms when 'giving back', and seek to make the audience feel at home with the information and the message.

Broader issues associated with 'giving back' scientific data

Broader issues include the following:

- Researchers are often limited by the availability of funds. Education and extension are an additional cost that many feel they have neither the time nor money to afford. It is important, therefore, that funders not only respect this additional cost within a proposed budget, but – when possible – seek to promote 'giving back' as a standard part of the research they fund, including in some cases assisting in linking research and extension institutions.

- Researchers tend to look upon information transfer as a 'lower' endeavour, and one not of immediate relevance to their work. Academic promotion systems do not generally reward the multidisciplinary, applied work that 'giving back' entails, nor the manuals and other products that do not enter the peer review system. Professional societies might help to promote the concept of the 'dynamic interactive research cycle', as well as 'giving back' results within research institutions and universities unaccustomed to considering this part of the research process.

- Researchers' and local groups' time frames are often markedly different. Local groups' livelihoods or resource-management decisions may require immediate access to information, while journal articles presenting scientific data may take months or years to emerge. Researchers should seek to share preliminary results within a reasonable time frame with local groups.

Note

---

1   For a valuable review of collaboration and coordination between extension/development and research/service organizations, including lessons learned from experience in farm forestry by the CONSEFORH (Honduran Dry Forest Species Conservation and Silviculture Project), see Kowal and Padilla, 1998.

Section II

BIODIVERSITY RESEARCH AND PROSPECTING IN PROTECTED AREAS

Photograph by Sarah A Laird

Limbe Botanic Garden field botanist Wilfred Mukete collecting Ancistrocladus korupensis *in forest near Korup National Park, Cameroon*

Chapter 6

Protected area research policies: developing a basis for equity and accountability*

Sarah A Laird and Estherine E Lisinge

Research in protected areas

The roughly 27,000 protected areas in the world today are home to much of the world's biodiversity and are likely to become increasingly important as repositories of this dwindling resource. Protected areas also often offer infrastructure and access to biodiversity that are of value to research and to collectors of materials for academic or commercial purposes. Research in high biodiversity countries has received increased attention and funding in the last decade, and there has been a rise in calls in international fora for national biodiversity inventories, taxonomic initiatives and other research activities geared to better understanding and organizing information on biodiversity. The role of research as an economic, as well as scientific, activity within protected areas is likely to increase in the coming years.

Protected areas offer researchers both biologically diverse and protected sites, and important services. Protected areas provide logistical (eg vehicles, housing, trained staff, field equipment) and administrative support (eg assistance with permits, computers). The staff are knowledgeable about the ecosystems, local communities, and political, social and economic context of the area in which research takes place; they know the history of an area and scientific research undertaken there to date. Protected areas also offer researchers a stable site with limited or no exploitation of resources – a critical condition for studies that monitor change over time, sometimes for decades.

But protected areas are not cheap to maintain. Countries pay both direct management and opportunity costs to maintain their biodiversity and make it available to researchers. Chronic funding shortages and limitations in institutional capacity are some of the most consistently cited obstacles to effective protected area management; 6 of the 14 Caracas Declaration principles call for measures to increase institutional effectiveness. A recent survey found that only 1 per cent of protected areas worldwide are considered

---

*   Two valuable annexes to this chapter, 'A shifting paradigm: indigenous peoples and protected areas' by Gonzalo Oviedo and 'The Convention on Biological Diversity and protected areas' by Sam Johnston, are available on the People and Plants website at: www.rbgkew.org.uk/peopleplants/manuals/biological/annexes1.htm

---

BOX 6.1 WHAT ARE PROTECTED AREAS?

Niall Watson (WWF-UK)

Protected areas serve multiple purposes: as stores of valued biodiversity (whether ecosystem species or genetic diversity), suppliers of natural products, protectors of water supplies, centres for tourism, education and recreation, and as cultural assets. In the world today, there are some 27,000 protected areas, covering almost 8 per cent of the Earth's land surface. The establishment of marine protected areas currently lags far behind those on land, although this too is beginning to change.

Protected areas have been defined as:

- 'an area of land and/or sea especially dedicated to the protection and maintenance of biological diversity, and of natural and associated cultural resources, and managed through legal or other effective means' (IUCN et al, 1994); and
- 'a geographically defined area which is designated or regulated and managed to achieve specific conservation objectives' (Convention on Biological Diversity, Article 2).

Public perception of protected areas is, in many instances, limited to national parks or nature reserves (large natural areas set aside for the benefit of a nation's citizens); but a much broader diversity of protected area types exists, often under a bewildering array of different names. Australia alone uses some 45 different protected area names, while globally over 140 names have been applied to protected areas of various types. To distinguish between the nature and type of protected areas and to give greater clarity to the role of protected areas within conservation planning and sustainable land use, the World Conservation Union (IUCN) and its World Commission on Protected Areas (WCPA) have expanded these basic definitions into six categories of protected area (see Box 6.2). The categories reflect a gradient of management intervention from little or no intervention in categories I and II to greater management in category IV, through to the sustainable use reserve of category VI, where the protected area is set up to allow use of natural resources.

As these new protected area categories demonstrate, the principle underlying modern approaches to establishing and maintaining protected areas is flexibility and diversity. There is a distinct trend away from *exclusive* management models towards *inclusive* models that include a higher degree of local participation and access. Ownership and management is similarly not limited to the state but can include, for example, local government, local and indigenous communities, private landowners, and even industrial holdings and collaborative undertakings between different permutations of these.

'secure' and that a large portion of protected areas amount to little more than 'paper parks' (Stolton and Dudley, 1999). Various methodologies suggest that 10 per cent of the world's different ecosystems need to be within a protected area network to ensure a degree of representation that would provide the basis for long-term in-situ conservation of biodiversity (Johnston, 2000). However, some argue that if 10 per cent of the land of a country with a small tax base is set aside for

---

BOX 6.2 IUCN PROTECTED AREA CATEGORIES ADOPTED AT THE 1994 GENERAL ASSEMBLY

- *Category Ia: strict nature reserve/wilderness protection area managed mainly for science or wilderness protection* – an area of land and/or sea possessing some outstanding or representative ecosystems, geological or physiological features and/or species, available primarily for scientific research and/or environmental monitoring;
- *Category Ib: wilderness area* – protected area managed mainly for wilderness protection; large area of unmodified or slightly modified land and/or sea, retaining its natural characteristics and influence, without permanent or significant habitation, which is protected and managed to preserve its natural condition;
- *Category II: national park* – protected area managed mainly for ecosystem protection and recreation; natural area of land and/or sea designated to: (a) protect the ecological integrity of one or more ecosystems for present and future generations; (b) exclude exploitation or occupation inimical to the purposes of designation of the area; and (c) provide a foundation for spiritual, scientific, educational, recreational and visitor opportunities, all of which must be environmentally and culturally compatible;
- *Category III: natural monument* – protected area managed mainly for conservation of specific natural features; area containing specific natural or natural/cultural feature(s) of outstanding or unique value because of their inherent rarity, representativeness or aesthetic qualities or cultural significance;
- *Category IV: habitat/species management area* – protected area managed mainly for conservation through management intervention; area of land and/or sea subject to active intervention for management purposes in order to ensure the maintenance of habitats to meet the requirements of specific species;
- *Category V: protected landscape/seascape* – protected area managed mainly for landscape/seascape conservation or recreation; area of land, with coast or sea as appropriate, where the interaction of people and nature over time has produced an area of distinct character with significant aesthetic, ecological and/or cultural value, and often with high biological diversity; safeguarding the integrity of this traditional interaction is vital to the protection, maintenance and evolution of such an area;
- *Category VI: managed resource protected area* – protected area managed mainly for the sustainable use of natural resources; area containing predominantly unmodified natural systems, managed to ensure long-term protection and maintenance of biological diversity, while also providing a sustainable flow of natural products and services to meet community needs.

Source: IUCN, 1994

---

conservation, it must contribute to the intellectual and financial capital of that country at least as much as if it were used in other ways. Conserved areas, it is argued, should be seen as another kind of land use, one with costs and benefits like any sector (Janzen et al, 1993).

In Costa Rica, researchers at the National Institute of Biodiversity (InBio) have developed the concept of 'conservation overhead' in which both academic and commercial research contribute directly to the information base and costs of maintaining protected areas. However, because researchers have long viewed access to biodiversity as unrestricted, costs for 'conservation overhead' have not been widely incorporated into research proposals to date. As Janzen et al (1993) put it: 'This introduces into research an accountability factor beyond the experience of most academics, who at best feel indebted to the granting agency and to their peers. Yet, the conserved wildland is, in a sense, a kind of granting agency insofar as it sustains the cost of keeping the organisms alive and maintains the infrastructure that all researchers use.'

While protected areas clearly offer benefits to researchers, scientific data generated by research institutions are, in turn, vital to the understanding and managing biodiversity within protected areas. Investigations into ecology, taxonomy and sustainable management are critical tools for the development of management plans. Even basic research contributes in multiple, if indirect, ways to a comprehensive understanding of species and ecosystems. As a result, many protected areas managers have entered into partnerships with scientists in order to generate useful data, and many are loath to discourage research activities of any kind. Few protected areas have sufficient budgets to cover their most basic research needs, and most will 'take what they can get'.

Spurred by changing attitudes on the relationship between science and conservation, protected areas managers are redefining the role of research. In this new approach, research is part of a collaborative strategy that both addresses pressing conservation and management information needs, and serves the longer-term interests of science and understanding of biodiversity. Many feel that given the pace with which biodiversity is being lost, scientific research must incorporate applied elements, or otherwise help protected areas conserve biodiversity in the short term. Otherwise, five or ten years down the road, the object of researchers' attentions will no longer be available for study.

In some cases – such as in the Tai National Park in Côte d'Ivoire (see Case Study 6.1) and Waza National Park in Cameroon (see Case Study 6.2) – this has meant the development of scientific committees that set research agendas based on priority needs for local conservation and sustainable development. To date, research priorities have often been determined by people based outside the protected area, and reflect the fashions and agendas of foreign scientific and funding institutions – the bulk of which are found in the North. In contrast, protected area scientific committees, such as those in Côte d'Ivoire and Cameroon, both seek to attract researchers willing to work within the park's agenda and review and approve applications based on the relevance of research to the park. This includes developing innovative ways for even basic research projects to generate benefits – whether equipment, training, funds for more applied research, or integrating a project component that collects and analyses data of relevance to park management. In this way it is hoped that basic science – necessary for the long-term understanding of complex ecosystems and their management – is not discouraged, but that the research activities themselves contribute towards shorter-term conservation and sustainable use objectives.

In the Tai National Park, for example, the Scientific Council develops research priorities for the park and reviews applications sent to the Ministry of Higher Education and Scientific Research (MESRS) in light of its research agenda. In Cameroon, the Waza National Park's recently launched Scientific Council approves research applications, in

CASE STUDY 6.1

THE TAI NATIONAL PARK IN CÔTE D'IVOIRE:
DEVELOPING RESEARCH RELATIONSHIPS THAT BENEFIT THE PARK AND LOCAL COMMUNITIES[1]

Jeanne Zoundjihékpon, Bilé Mathieu and Michael J De Pauw
(WWF Côte d'Ivoire)

The Tai National Park

Situated in the south-west of Côte d'Ivoire, the Tai Forest represents one of the last remnants of West African dense humid forest, having survived the great periods of the quaternary era (Riezebos, 1994). It is highly diverse, with a number of endemic species (Guillaumet, 1967; 1994; Aké Assi, 1984; Oates, 1983; Allport et al, 1994). As a result of its biological diversity, the Tai National Park (TNP) has attracted the attention of the international research and conservation community.

The history of the national park goes back to 26 April 1926 when a park refuge was created with a surface of 960,000 hectares (ha). Since this time, the park refuge has undergone several subsequent transformations. Decree 72.544 of 28 August 1972 established the TNP for the propagation, protection and conservation of wild animal and plant life for scientific and educational purposes, and for public recreation. On 28 April 1978, the TNP was included as a biosphere reserve as part of the United Nations Educational, Social and Cultural Organization's (UNESCO's) Man and the Biosphere (MAB) Programme. On 17 December 1981, the TNP was included as a world heritage site by UNESCO.

In 1993, the TNP was placed under the management of the autonomous PACPNT (Autonomous Conservation of the TNP project) for a seven-year trial period. If this approach is effective, the project could become a model for the management of other national parks in Côte d'Ivoire. Core funding is supplied by KfW (the German Kredietanstalt für Wiederaufbau) and by the Ivorian Ministry of Environment and Forests through its DPN (Department for the Protection of Nature). Additional financing is supplied by MESRS/DR (the Department of Research of the Ivorian Ministry of Higher Education and Scientific Research), GTZ (the German Gesellschaft für Technische Zusammenarbeit), WWF and Tropenbos-CI, the Tropenbos Foundation in Côte d'Ivoire. Each of these partners has its own responsibility in pursuing the long-term protection of TNP. GTZ deals with training and sustainable development activities in the area surrounding TNP. WWF is responsible for surveillance and training of park wardens, and Tropenbos-CI coordinates the scientific research component of the project.

Research permitting process

Research is the only legally authorized activity within the park. Researchers wishing to work in the TNP must apply for permission to the Ministry of Higher Education and Scientific Research (MESRS). Applications are coordinated by the TNP Scientific Council, which was established to prioritize and guide research activities in the TNP. The Scientific Council comprises some 20 members and includes all project partners, representatives of local communities and non-governmental organizations (NGOs) working in the area. The permanent core of the council includes MESRS, Ministry of Agriculture and Livestock (MINAGRA), PACPNT and the Tropenbos-CI.

The Scientific Council reviews requests to conduct research in the TNP in light of park objectives and research priorities set by the council, and interest to avoid damage to the park, and advises MESRS, which authorizes research based on this advice. Authorization papers are then sent to the DPN, which grants permits to enter the park. Thus, research activities within the TNP are subject to the granting of a dual authorization:

1   a research permit granted by the research department of the MESRS following recommendations made by the Scientific Council;
2   an entry permit into the TNP delivered by the Department for the Protection of Nature of the MINEF.

These permits include both general and case-specific obligations that bind researchers. General obligations include sharing of research reports (three copies for MESRS and two for MINEF); good researcher behaviour and conduct in the field; respect for rules of the park; and avoidance of damage to the park through research.

The Scientific Council undertakes consultations with a range of affected stakeholders – including local communities and NGOs active in the area – in order to identify priority needs for research and any concerns associated with the research process. The council draws up a multiyear research plan or 'PPA'. The most recent plan was elaborated by Tropenbos in 1994 and revised and adopted in April 1997. Research priorities for TNP identified in the PPA include, in particular:

•   inventory of the current knowledge on biological diversity of the park, and synthesis of existing information and knowledge of the TNP;
•   study of means to restore biological diversity in the exploited areas;
•   identification of the indicators for maintaining biological diversity in the park;
•   analysis of the costs and benefits derived from the conservation of the park;
•   study of species of special concern;
•   optimal use of land;
•   ecological interactions important for the conservation of biological diversity;
•   influence of human activities on the biological diversity of Tai National Park and its surrounding area;
•   social and cultural perception of the forest by local communities;
•   participation of local communities in the management of Tai National Park and the study of mechanisms employed in participatory land-use planning;
•   identification of new sources of food and monetary income for the local communities.

The Tropenbos Foundation coordinates the implementation of research and integrates results in ways that are relevant for park management. Many research activities proposed for the TNP will not fall within the PPA, but the council often approves them in order to further scientific understanding of important problems. For example, the World Health Organization (WHO) has undertaken studies related to the Ebola virus in the park.

The TNP is the only protected area in Côte d'Ivoire with a functional Scientific Council. The Scientific Council acts as a mechanism for granting prior informed consent for research in the park, but has no legal means to enforce the conditions it attaches to research. To date, issues raised by the Convention on Biological Diversity (CBD) are not explicitly incorporated into the permitting process. A national access and benefit-sharing framework is needed to guide research within the TNP and elsewhere in Côte d'Ivoire, in keeping with recommendations made by the summit of Organization of African Unity (OAU) heads of state in June 1998 in Burkina Faso.

Ways in which biodiversity research might benefit the park and local communities

Some 2500 publications have been written on the biological diversity of the TNP. Although a review of several decades of research in and around Tai National Park has been compiled into a book, *Le Parc National de Tai, Côte d'Ivoire* (Riezebos et al, 1994), many of these publications are not made available in French and few are disseminated to park staff or within the country. It is often the case that even MESRS does not have access to critical information generated by studies of biological resources. Decree 96,613 of 9 August 1998 established a Centre for Research in Ecology (CRE) to help coordinate ecological research by setting up a network for information and data exchange concerning ecology and the environment; and to promote regional and international cooperation in the field of ecological research. The centre is working to gather and make available documentation concerning each of the parks and reserves in Côte d'Ivoire.

Research can generate a range of benefits for the country, and it is important to ensure that these benefits are realized. For example, research generates data and collections that are important for national conservation efforts, including providing information important for park management and policy development. Research can include training of national researchers and research assistants in the park; and researchers can produce results in materials that are useful for local communities and also for ecotourists. For local communities, research projects can provide training, build infrastructure in the village and help with micro-enterprise projects. In Paule Oula, for example, some researchers paid for a school, educational materials and teachers' salaries. The population can also benefit from increased income from ecotourism.

For the park, research provides invaluable data on plant and animal species and helps with more effective in-situ or ex-situ conservation. For example, in the TNP, research results helped to develop a domestication programme, *Coula edulis*, which furnishes wood resistant to termites and *Tieghemella heckelii* (Makoré), a species in great demand. This project aims to domesticate forest trees prized by farmers and to reduce pressure exerted on the park. In another project, researchers are extending their results to farmers regarding green fertilizers, such as *Pueraria spp*, *Mucuna spp* or *Chromolaena odorata*, which can replace chemical fertilizers. Finally, research has also drawn attention to the enormous biological diversity of the TNP, and has led to national and international attention on the park.

In order for these benefits to be realized, however, a core of problems must be resolved, including: lack of translation of publications into the working language (French); poor dissemination of research results; lack of monitoring results and poor communication between researchers and park managers; and limited translation of research results into a useful form for local communities and non-specialists. By addressing these problems, government ministries, the Centre for Research in Ecology, and the Scientific Council, in collaboration with the Tropenbos Foundation, can help to establish the basis for equitable research relationships in line with the objectives of the Convention on Biological Diversity.

conjunction with the Ministry of Environment and Forestry (MINEF) and the Ministry of Scientific Research (MINRES). The Waza Scientific Council, like that in Tai National Park, is also investigating ways to better define the nature and scope of relationships with researchers through the development of policies and codes of behaviour (see Case Study 6.2).

In Bwindi Impenetrable National Park (BINP) in Uganda, one of the last strongholds of the mountain gorilla, staff are also working to establish a system in which researchers are accountable to the BINP management, as well as to government ministries, in order to ensure that the terms of the research proposals and park regulations are strictly observed. Because there is no formal mechanism to monitor the activities of researchers within the park, 'several incidences when park field staff have noted discrepancies with some data collection methods and the types and amount of specimens collected by some researchers' have been reported (see Case Study 6.3).

In addition to promoting applied research projects in protected areas, therefore, managers are also working to clarify researchers' responsibilities relating to prior informed consent, behaviour in the field and the sharing of benefits. The intention here is to bring research relationships up to international standards of 'best practice' as outlined in codes of ethics developed by professional scientific societies (see Chapter 2); research institution policies (see Chapter 3); national and international law (see Chapter 12), such as the Convention on Biological Diversity (CBD) (see Box 6.3); and indigenous peoples' and local community declarations and statements (see Chapter 7). The core elements of equitable research relationships emphasize the need to seek prior informed consent from government, communities and institutions; share benefits; and behave in the field in a manner consistent with ethical norms (see the draft policy in Case Study 6.2).

Academic and commercial research: the dwindling divide

Protected areas must also grapple with an issue relevant to all research relationships: the growing convergence of academic and commercial research projects, agendas and the flow of data and biodiversity 'information' between sectors. The commercial applications of samples, material and traditional ecological knowledge have expanded in recent years. At the same time, non-profit research institutions in both the North and South are supplementing declining institutional budgets with funds raised through commercial partnerships (see Chapter 3). For example, collections of the forest liana

Ancistrocladus korupensis in the Korup National Park, Cameroon, in 1987 were undertaken as part of research collaborations between the non-profit Missouri Botanical Garden (MBG) and the Centre for the Study of Medicinal Plants, Yaounde, on behalf of the US National Cancer Institute (NCI). The commercial implications of the collections were unknown to either park managers or government at the time, and this created a great deal of confusion when a promising anti-HIV compound – michellamine B – was identified in plant samples (Laird et al, 1999).

CASE STUDY 6.2 DEVELOPMENT OF PROTECTED AREA RESEARCH POLICIES IN CAMEROON

CASE STUDY 6.2

Sarah A Laird, Estherine E Lisinge (WWF, Cameroon), Tabe Tanjong (WWF, Cameroon) and Martin Tchamba (WWF, Northern Sudanian Savannah Project)

Protected areas within Cameroon are divided into the following categories: national parks, wildlife reserves, hunting blocks, game ranches, wildlife sanctuaries and buffer zones. The protected area system currently consists of seven national parks, seven wildlife reserves and one wildlife sanctuary, which together account for 4.4 per cent of the national area. Most of the protected areas in the country are the site of conservation and development projects of some kind, funded by international donors and managed by a consortium of international non-governmental organizations (NGOs) and aid agencies. Between 1986 and 1997 donors invested more than US$40 million in protect area management in Cameroon, the largest and most consistent to Korup National Park (Culverwell, 1997). More than twice that has been spent on rainforest conservation projects until 1995 (Burnham, 2000). Protected areas are home to a large portion of biodiversity research undertaken in the country, conducted by staff of international aid agencies, overseas research institutions and professional researchers and students based in Cameroonian institutions.

In 1999, the WWF Cameroon Policy Unit initiated a project to investigate the potential for protected area research policies to better define terms for researcher–protected area relationships in line with the objectives of the Convention on Biological Diversity (CBD). The elements of research relationships investigated included the need for prior informed consent, behaviour during the research process and benefit-sharing. Numerous individuals from government, protected areas management, botanic gardens, universities, NGOs and international research institutions were interviewed, in order to determine the nature of research underway within the country and key issues that might be addressed in a policy. A draft policy has been formulated and is under review by government and protected area managers.

During interviews conducted in 1999, concerns were consistently raised that researchers do not make the objectives and implications of their research transparent, and that benefits are rarely shared in any structured manner. In no case did individuals seek to restrict research activities within Cameroon, and many highlighted the importance of international research institutions in helping to build an understanding of Cameroon's flora, fauna and ecosystems, given the limited funding available at a national level for such activities today. However, staff at protected areas and national research institutions felt that researchers should more effectively collaborate with protected area managers in order to maximize the potential contribution of their work to immediate conservation and sustainable use issues within Cameroon. Some of those interviewed reported a resistance by international researchers – accustomed to working according to their own agendas and time frame – to adopt a more collaborative approach with institutions and protected area managers. Such measures were perceived as a time-consuming and 'bureaucratic' way for non-scientists to interfere with the research process and for individuals of sometimes dubious integrity to profit personally, rather than building capacity either within the country or the protected area.

Most interviewees representing research institutions, government and protected areas felt that by developing a written policy, protected areas could ensure that research is transparent, that all involved agree to the terms of collaboration, and that research could better serve national and local conservation and development objectives. Most felt that this could be done in a way that did not needlessly hamper research or force researchers to spend excessive amounts of time acquiring approval, although for some this was a very real concern. The draft *Research Policy for Protected Areas* is an effort to strike a balance between the immediate needs of protected areas managers and those of researchers. It seeks to make research relationships transparent and relevant for conservation while providing the clarity and efficiency required by researchers.

National policy framework

Protected areas and national research institutions play a key role in implementing Cameroon's obligations under CBD and national legislation, including the 20 January 1994 Law regulating Forestry, Wildlife and Fisheries and the 1996 Framework Law on the Environment. Article 65(1) of the latter, for example, requires that:

> *'...scientific exploration and biological and genetic resource exploitation in Cameroon shall be done under conditions of transparency and in close collaboration with national research institutions and local communities, and should be profitable to Cameroon. The exploration and exploitation should be done under the conditions stipulated by the international conventions relating thereto, duly ratified by Cameroon, especially the Rio Convention of 1992 on biodiversity.'*

The enabling decree intended to provide a framework for collaboration between foreign researchers and Cameroon research institutions, however, has not yet been enacted, making it difficult to apply this article (Bokwe et al, 1999). Protected areas and national research institutions can take significant steps towards realizing these provisions of the law and can contribute – through on the ground efforts at institution policy development – a pool of practical experience to inform drafting of the decrees of application.

The 1994 Forestry Law, Section 12, stipulates that 'the genetic resources of the national heritage shall belong to the State of Cameroon. No person may use them for scientific, commercial or cultural purposes without prior authorization.' The 1994 Forestry Law, and its Decree of Implementation, created a new category of 'non-permanent' forests – the community forest – in which residents living in the periphery of the national forest estate might manage up to 5000 hectares of state forest (Article 27(4) of the decree). This is conditional upon the elaboration of management plans and an agreement between communities and the forestry administration (Articles 11 and 15 of the decree). Management plans will require a foundation of scientific data, including density, distribution, regeneration, population structure and other areas required for the sustainable use of a range of forest products. Demand for scientific data of this kind – generated at sites throughout the country – will be of increasing importance for the management of the forest estate, both in proximity to protected areas and elsewhere.

Benefits resulting from research collaborations

Benefits resulting from the research process will vary by project and site. The Ministry of Scientific and Technical Research (MINREST) requires as part of its research-permitting process that copies of reports be left with collaborating organizations, that the input of Cameroonian institutions is acknowledged in reports and that specimens of all plant material collected are lodged in the National Herbarium. Most protected area managers would like to go much further, promoting through a collaborative approach the tailoring of research design, data collection and analysis to assist in addressing immediate conservation and management problems. In addition to the generation of more immediately relevant research data, benefits that might result from a more collaborative approach to research, and cited in interviews, include:

- the return of publications, technical reports and data to protected areas managers;
- joint publications;
- training of local researchers, community members and protected area staff in data collection and field techniques, scientific methodologies, etc;
- assistance provided by collaborating research institutions in species identification and analytical tools;
- donation of equipment, including 'know-how' (eg computers);
- species checklists and field manuals or guides;
- information relevant to basic ecological monitoring and species management;
- employment of local population;
- development of young students' and researchers' careers;
- development of rural areas (through assistance with road or bridge-building, health centres, education);
- fund-raising assistance; and
- financial income (eg a percentage of the research operating budget).

It was felt by many that the nature and extent of benefits should be weighed against the assistance provided by the protected area, the scale of the research project and the relevance of the research to protected area management.

Core areas that were considered central to a protected area policy included terms for the research relationship, need for prior informed consent and transparency and the sharing of benefits. In addition, many felt that protected areas policies should dictate appropriate behaviour on the part of researchers in the field. Most commonly cited was the need for researchers to respect traditional customs and build solid relations with local communities with whom they work. A number of poor experiences were cited, involving researcher disregard of local customs, theft of project equipment, abuse of protected area staff and promises made relating to assistance, including provision of literature, that were never followed through. It was felt that policies should incorporate traditional laws and customs where relevant, and that the process of seeking prior informed consent, sharing benefits and monitoring research relationships should fall in line with the customary practices of local communities.

Two cases within Cameroon in which policies are under development to guide research relationships, and which yield lessons of relevance for the development of protected area policies, are found at the Mount Kupe Forest Project and the Waza Logone Project. In each case, a process to develop a framework for equitable research relationships is underway.

The Mount Kupe Forest Project: draft Guidelines for Visiting Researchers at Mount Kupe

The Mount Kupe Forest Project (MKFP) was reopened in November 1997 by WWF, under contract with the government of Cameroon (GoC), as a designated Global Environment Facility (GEF) site. All GEF sites in Cameroon are coordinated by the Ministry of Environment and Forestry (MINEF), Yaounde. The MKFP is not a protected area, and as a project does not carry the same authority; but in exchange for research cooperation and assistance it is exploring ways to better define equitable research relationships.

The GEF component of the project – 'Conservation and Management of Biodiversity' – is responsible for implementing biological research and monitoring on Mount Kupe and the adjacent forests of Bakossiland, with preliminary investigation of Mount Nlonako and the adjacent Bakaka Forest Reserve. The MKFP encourages both pure and applied research in the natural sciences within the project area in order to enhance data collection, building of technical expertise and collaboration as a means to generate data critical to management of the forests and useful in building 'interest and income' in local communities (Introduction to the draft *Guidelines for Visiting Researchers at Mount Kupe*, 1997).

The draft *Guidelines for Visiting Researchers at Mount Kupe* were developed in order to achieve the objectives outlined above. The MKFP's objective of conserving biodiversity in the area is dependent upon a good relationship with local communities and local and national government. However, due to the small size of the forest under project management, its endangered flora and fauna and the topography of the area, MKFP staff felt that research and tourism might conflict with the maintenance of MKFP relationships with communities and government. Experiences with visiting researchers that prompted the drafting of guidelines included cutting of transects and other destructive practices without the consent of project staff or local communities. It was also found to be rare that data collected in the project area were returned to the project or local communities; project staff found it enormously difficult to track down and gain access to reports and raw data. At times, visiting researchers developed inappropriate relationships with local community members, which were contrary to project standards and, in some cases, created bad feeling between the project and local communities. The guidelines were drafted to respond to these and other concerns associated with research undertaken in the project area.

The draft guidelines categorize relationships between visiting researchers and MKFP staff, in order to rank priorities for the provision of financial, logistical and technical assistance given by the MKFP. Priority is given to WWF/MKFP research consultants hired to undertake specific research projects for MKFP, followed by collaborating institutions and individuals addressing project objectives in their research, Cameroonian students and overseas volunteers, and finally overseas visiting researchers and independent research projects wishing to undertake fieldwork in the MKFP study area.

Guidelines include the following provisions:

- Timeline for applications: this comprised, at a minimum, three months in advance of intended fieldwork.
- Possible forms of assistance provided by the MKFP: this might include obtaining research permits; transport to and from airports; use of laboratory facilities; accommodation; provision of trained field guides; technical assistance; etc. If a research proposal is considered to have particular applied interests to the MKFP, the project

may provide logistical, administrative, technical and, in some cases, financial support. 'The degree to which researchers are given assistance is discretionary and judged on merit, standards and the anticipated value of the work to the Project.'

- Benefits to be received by MKFP: benefits include the right to discuss research undertaken; copies of raw field data at the end of fieldwork; provision of preliminary reports on results according to an agreed-upon schedule; final drafts of papers prepared for publication, as available; three copies of published papers; acknowledgement of WWF/MKFP and MINEF for relevant aid in reports and publications.
- Obligations and responsibilities of researchers: researchers must obtain research permits, collecting permits and certificates of origin for specimens. Collection of living animals and plants for commercial export trade is expressly prohibited. Collections for scientific purposes may be undertaken with relevant government and MKFP approval, but require formal applications to justify the collections well in advance of the task.
- Research behaviour in the field: under a section entitled 'Traditional Customs', researchers are 'politely requested to inform and obtain permission from local leaders for access to the forest and to respect local standards of dress, behaviour and religious belief'. Field protocol includes the following:
  1 Respect the needs of local forest stakeholders, fellow researchers and short-term visitors to the mountain.
  2 Entering caves and crater lakes is prohibited unless approved by the MKFP.
  3 Transect-cutting may only be performed with prior approval. This should be non-destructive and limited to saplings < 2cm diametre at breast height (dbh) and must never include climbers, tree ferns or *Ucca* species.
  4 Avoid damage to vegetation (beyond reasonable collecting activities and clearance of undergrowth for campsites).
  5 For personal safety, use only designated campsites and ensure that a colleague and the MKFP are aware of your plans when you are at remote sites.
  6 Use only existing fallen wood for making fires.
  7 Return all litter from camping to a suitable waste dump in the village.
  8 Avoid disturbance to stream sediments, including large sunken logs.
  9 Avoid washing with soap in streams or other natural bodies of water.
  10 Refrain from eating bushmeat.

The guidelines remain in draft form and are not legally binding. Given the increasing number of researchers visiting the project area, however, staff are leaning now towards a written form of research agreement that would make transparent and binding an agreed relationship between researchers, their home institutions, MKFP and communities.

Developing a Scientific Council to guide research in the Waza National Park

The Waza National Park was created in December 1968 to promote tourism, conservation and protection for the wildlife and ecosystems of the region. In 1982, Waza became a United Nations Educational, Social and Cultural Organization (UNESCO) biosphere reserve. Covering 170,000 hectares, Waza supports five primary vegetation types, forming a mosaic of savanna forms in the west and open grass floodplains in the east of the park. Wildlife is abundant and includes elephants, waterfowl, lions, giraffe, red-fronted gazelle and ostrich. Waza attracts the largest number of tourists of any park within Cameroon and has been the site of a large number of research projects over the past few decades (Culverwell, 1997; Bobo Kadiri et al, 1998).

More research has taken place in Waza than in any other protected area in Cameroon, resulting in more than 200 published and unpublished papers. However, in only a few cases has research proven of immediate use for park management and conservation objectives. In most cases, results were not made available to park managers, and there have been only sporadic and inconsistent collaboration and training of Cameroonian researchers and staff. In many cases, park staff were not aware of research projects until the researchers arrived at the park to begin work. Staff in MINEF who were responsible for protected area management were likewise in the dark. Local communities, too, were in large part unaware of the nature of research, and – as in many places in Cameroon – were paid as porters or guides, but were not informed of the objectives of the work.

Waza National Park is the only protected area within Cameroon with a management plan, and based on this plan the Waza Scientific Council was created. Following the elaboration of management plans for other protected areas – beginning with the Dja Reserve and Korup National Park – MINEF will establish scientific councils in those protected areas as well. One function of these councils will be to help develop and implement a policy to guide research activities.

To address issues of comanagement, coordination and wider park management issues, in 1997 the Waza Scientific Council (Conseil Scientifique Waza) was established. The council has responsibility for drafting research priorities for the park, promoting this agenda to researchers and providing guidance to researchers on their behaviour in the park. It also advises the Park Committee on management issues based on scientific information.

In 1999 MINEF signed Decision 'Portant organisation et fonctionnement du Conseil Scientifique du Parc National de Waza', and Decree No 0732/A/MINEF/DFAP/DAJ, 'Rendant executoire le Plan Directeur d'Amenagement du Parc National de Waza', which provide for implementation of the management plan and details of the council's mission, composition and activities. The council meets twice a year and includes members from government, NGOs and research institutions. The Waza Scientific Council's objectives include the following:

- analyse research conducted in the Waza National Park and surrounding area;
- identify research priorities;
- identify the potential for research to contribute to applied research;
- contribute to the formulation of regulations and policy for the park and surrounding area;
- propose a management system for the conservation of resources;
- develop applied research data to establish management plans;
- comment on and review management plans for the park and surrounding areas;
- comment on and review annual work plans;
- evaluate internally the activities in the annual workplan.

The Waza Scientific Council began its activities with a review and evaluation of research undertaken to date. Building upon this foundation, the council is now working to develop a research programme, including a strategy for prioritizing and monitoring research. This includes identifying research needs raised by specific resource management issues, such as those associated with gum arabic, fuelwood, thatching grass and the harvest of fish from water holes. Also promoted are studies on the population dynamics of wildlife species upon which little or no research has been undertaken (eg elephant, cob, topi, gazelle, roan antelope) and the environmental impact of park management activities, such as enlarging waterholes and management of fire.

In addition to MINREST and MINEF, the Waza Scientific Council must now also grant consent for research activities prior to their initiation. If a proposed research project has little immediate relevance to applied conservation and management needs, the council will encourage researchers to incorporate an applied element, or will levy a small fee – now contemplated at 15 per cent of field budgets – to be directed towards applied research in the area. The council also intends to produce an outline of its research priorities, distributed to government ministries and research institutions, to guide the emphasis and approach of research projects in the future. Clarification of benefits expected by the park (which will be incorporated within the outline's collaborative approach with researchers in the future) will include training of local staff; collaboration with Cameroon institutions and researchers; copies of research results; payment of local staff, park workers, members of local communities; and an overhead fee (eg 15 per cent of total research budget or field expenses).

An example of the ways in which research can be conducted to benefit both the park and local communities is the wildlife survey underway by the WWF, Northern Sudanian Savannah Project. Biologists cannot undertake this type of massive survey on their own, and these types of research projects are not of interest to many scientists. Through the Benoue National Park survey, 22 game guards and park managers have been trained to collect data under the supervision of scientists, including training on research techniques and methodologies, as well as the use of global positioning systems (GPS), compasses and other equipment. The wildlife survey involves 75 20km transects, which is more than this trained team can handle; as a result, the project has also recruited from local villages. 30 men from the villages are paid for six weeks of work, but longer-term employment in monitoring is also envisioned. At present, three trained villagers are permanently employed for vegetation surveys, data collection in experimental fire management blocks and the evaluation of habitat use by wildlife. Research collaboration with villages has had the added benefit of changing attitudes to the park. In the beginning, some village members did not want to participate because they thought poaching in the park was more lucrative; most came to realize, however, that helping with the research was more consistently paid. One of the most notorious poachers in the area – killing on average ten elephants a year, and obviously very knowledgeable – has recently joined the survey teams as a permanent tracker.

The Waza Scientific Council will develop a park-researcher policy to help make the research process transparent, be of value to park management and yield important benefits for the park and local communities. MINEF is interested in applying a researcher policy to other protected areas with management plans. There is increasing interest in the ability of government and protected area management to provide a flexible framework in order to promote collaborative research activities that contribute to effective management of the protected area system, and also benefit local communities. The draft policy under development by WWF, Cameroon Policy Unit, in conjunction with MINEF, the Mount Kupe Forest Project, the Waza Logone Project and other projects and protected areas will serve as a first step in this process of policy development.

For an update on this process and the documents, contact the Policy Unit at WWF Cameroon Programme Office (www.wwfcameroon.org).

Draft research policy for protected areas in Cameroon

Preamble

The mission of _____ [protected area] is to: conserve biodiversity and promote the sustainable use and management of resources within the protected area and surrounding communities [include language from mission statement].

Research is a valuable contribution to protected area management, and scientific data is critical to the development of an understanding of the genetic, species, ecosystem and cultural diversity found within and around _____ [protected area]. The management of _____ recognizes the value and importance of collaborations with national and international research institutions in developing an understanding of the _____

Research must, however, be conducted in a way that does not damage genetic, species, or ecosystem diversity, and equitably benefits local groups. Research activities in _____ [protected area] must honour the letter and spirit of the Convention on Biological Diversity (CBD), the Convention on the International Trade in Endangered Species of Wild Fauna and Flora (CITES), and other international, regional and national laws and policies concerning biodiversity and human rights.

In _____ 19__, the _____ [protected area] and the Ministry of Environment and Forestry (MINEF) established a _____ [Scientific Council]. The _____ [council's] objectives are to develop research priorities for _____ [protected area] management, promote its research agenda and seek funding to support critical research needs, to set standards for and monitor researcher behaviour within the protected area and local communities, and to develop and implement a coherent policy for research within _____ [protected area].

Research should, where possible, be designed in line with the research priorities set by the Scientific Council. Where this is not possible, data collection and analysis should be modified to incorporate an applied element, as agreed by protected areas managers and the researcher.

Researchers will contribute a set percentage of field operating costs [or total research budget] to _____ [Scientific Council/protected area] to support applied research addressing conservation and management needs, to train staff and local communities in research methodologies, and to support the scientific understanding, and immediate conservation and management needs of _____ [protected area].

_____ [protected area] recognizes the close links between cultural and biological diversity. Living within or in proximity to _____ [protected area] management zone, are the following ethnic groups and communities: _____, _____, _____. Their consent to any research undertaken on their knowledge, resources or lands must be acquired prior to the initiation of any research, and their culture, traditions and customary law respected.

Researchers are required to acquire the prior informed consent of relevant stakeholders within Cameroon, including government, protected area management and local communities (where appropriate) prior to beginning field research. Researchers are expected to share benefits with stakeholders as detailed below.

Professional researcher codes of ethics, guidelines, institutional policies, international agreements and indigenous peoples' statements and declarations articulate the principles and practices that – together – form a standard for current best practice in research. Appended to this policy, and a resulting agreement between the protected area and researcher, they act as a guide to current standards within the research community. _____ [protected area] management has on hand a range of documents of this nature, but researchers are asked to provide codes of ethics for their discipline, as well as their institutional policy. This will help build the capacity of protected area management in this field, and will make clear to both researchers and protected area managers the current norms for best practice in the researcher's field.

Commercial collections will not be allowed in _____ [protected area] without the full consent of the protected area managers and relevant government ministries [MINEF and MINRES]. Any known commercial end use of research, data or collections must be made explicit in the agreement between the protected area and researcher. Materials collected may only be passed to commercial parties with the written consent of the government of Cameroon and the protected area, and in line with existing national and international law and policy.

The _____ [protected area] recognizes that students cannot fulfil the same standards for benefit-sharing as professional researchers, and will come to an agreement reflecting the limited access of students to institutional resources. However, students will be encouraged to use their experience reaching agreement with _____ [protected area] to expand their understanding of the importance of collaboration and the structuring of transparent, equitable research relationships.

National and international researchers will be required to follow the standards laid out in the policy; requirements for benefit-sharing are likely to be reduced in the case of national researchers, although supply of research results and publications, training and other benefits that amount to common courtesy will be required.

Objectives of the policy

The objective of this policy is to ensure that research is conducted in a collaborative manner, and where possible incorporates the research priorities and objectives of _____ [protected area]. Research should promote and assist in the conservation of biodiversity and sustainable use of its components, and should not cause damage to biodiversity. The policy seeks to ensure that research is conducted in a manner respectful of local traditions and cultures, and that the informed consent of involved stakeholders, including _____ [protected area], local communities and the government of Cameroon (GoC), is received prior to initiation of a research programme and that benefits are shared (as below).

Scope of the policy

The Research Policy is intended to primarily address academic research relationships, but may also act as the basis for commercial research agreements. The scope of the policy includes:

- *non-extractive non-commercial research* (eg ecological research in which samples are not collected);
- *extractive non-commercial research* (eg botanical research involving collection of specimens); the potential commercial use of collections housed in other institutions is noted, and these institutions are obligated to receive written consent from the _____ [protected area] and the GoC prior to passing material to third parties;

- *non-extractive research with commercial potential* (eg ethnobotanical research on local people's knowledge of species use);
- *extractive research intended for commercial development* (eg biodiversity prospecting involving collection of samples);
- *conservation research* contributing directly to _____ [protected area] management objectives, and undertaken at its behest or with its approval.

Definition of terms

Best practice: minimum standards set for behaviour or practices that reflect both the spirit and the letter of the Convention on Biological Diversity and other international and national instruments, professional researcher codes of ethics, indigenous peoples' statements and institutional policies.

Benefit-sharing: sharing of benefits that arise out of the research process and the information and resources that are collected.

Biodiversity: the variability among living organisms and the ecological complexes of which they are a part, biological diversity or 'biodiversity'; includes genetic, species and ecosystem diversity.

Biodiversity prospecting: the exploration of biodiversity for commercially valuable genetic and biochemical resources.

Conservation: the management of human use of the biosphere so that it may yield the greatest sustainable benefit to current generations while maintaining its potential to meet the needs and aspirations of future generations.

Customary law: traditional and locally specific system of jurisprudence, embedded in indigenous peoples' and local communities' culture and language.

Endemic: restricted to a specific region or locality.

Prior informed consent: the consent of a party to, or affected by, an activity that is given after receiving full disclosure regarding the reason for the activity, the specific procedures the activity would entail, the potential risks involved and the full implications that can realistically be foreseen.

Protected area: an area of land and/or sea especially dedicated to the protection and maintenance of biological diversity and of natural and associated cultural resources, and managed through legal or other effective means.

Researcher: refers to both the individual conducting research and the sponsoring or contracting institutions on whose behalf the researcher conducts research.

Scientific council: body established in _____ [protected area] to develop a research agenda, mediate and monitor research relationships and set standards for 'best practice' within the protected area.

Stakeholder: a person or organization affected by, or with an interest in, the activities at stake. Stakeholders involved in protected area relationships with researchers include government ministries, local government, local communities, NGOs and protected areas managers.

Sustainable use: management of resources in a way that meets the needs of current generations but can be maintained indefinitely without compromising the ability to meet those of future generations.

Traditional ecological/environmental knowledge: a body of cumulative and dynamic knowledge built up by a group of people after generations of living in close contact with nature. It includes systems of classification, a set of empirical observations about the local environment and a system of self-management that governs resource use.

Institutional relationships and responsibilities

Management of _____ [protected area] is entrusted to _____ [protected area management], to be undertaken in conjunction with the Ministry of Environment and Forestry (MINEF). Under decree _____/_____, a Scientific Council was established to develop a research agenda for _____ [protected area] and to set standards for researcher relationships.

In developing a research policy, the protected area managers [and Scientific Council] act as representatives of both national and local interests. As such, they will consult directly with representatives of government, national research institutions, NGOs and local communities in an effort to determine the most effective research strategy for the protected area, and to ensure that the perspective of a range of stakeholders within Cameroon is represented.

Collaborative bodies in which the _____ [protected area] management are involved, and through which these consultations will take [took] place include: _____ [community joint management associations; government committees; NGO or donor working groups, etc].

Review of research applications

_____ [protected area] will establish the following structures [within the Scientific Council] to efficiently and quickly review research proposals to work in _____ [protected area]: _____ [sub-committees, focal points, key individuals, etc]. The time required to process an application will, in most cases, not be more than _____ [weeks/months].

Ongoing review and implementation of the policy

Periodic review of the research policy will take place, including – in the first year of implementation – at the three annual meetings of the Scientific Council and through _____ [detail other channels for review]. The review will take into account the relationship of the research policy to new legislation and policy drafted to implement the Convention on Biological Diversity and other national and international measures.

Adherence to national and international law

All research conducted within protected areas must adhere to relevant national legislation, as well as regional and international law and policy, such as the Convention on Biological Diversity (CBD) and the Convention on the International Trade in Endangered Species (CITES).

National laws of particular importance to research relationships include the 20 January 1994 Law Regulating Forestry, Wildlife and Fisheries, and its implementing decrees, and the 1996 Framework Law on the Environment.

Under Article 65(1) of the Framework Law on the Environment, 'scientific exploration and biological and genetic resource exploitation in Cameroon shall be done under conditions of transparency and in close collaboration with national research institutions and local communities, and should be profitable to Cameroon. The exploration and exploitation should be done under the conditions stipulated by the international conventions relating thereto, duly ratified by Cameroon, especially the Rio Convention of 1992 on biodiversity.'

The 1994 Forestry Law (Section 11) stipulates that 'the genetic resources of the national heritage shall belong to the State of Cameroon. No person may use them for scientific, commercial or cultural purposes without prior authorization'.

Elements of agreement between _____ [the protected area] and the researcher

Prior informed consent
Prior to initiating research, researchers must acquire the informed consent of relevant government ministries [MINRES and MINEF], local communities (where applicable) and _____ [protected area] [as represented by the Scientific Council].

Government
Researchers must enter the country on a research visa. Researchers must obtain a research permit from the Ministry of Scientific and Technical Research (MINREST) before beginning research. _____ [protected area] might assist in this process, and in so doing would require a written application, copy of the research proposal, CV, six passport photographs and the _____ CFA fee, including _____ CFA for the permit and _____ CFA processing fee for _____ [protected area]. All collecting permits and certificates of origin are the responsibility of the researcher.

Protected area
Researchers must receive the full consent of _____ [Scientific Council/protected area management], following the submission of a research proposal [application]. Included in a proposal to _____ [Scientific Council/protected area management] should be:

- details on the research: where it will take place, when and how, including the proposed field methodology;
- type of information/data to be collected and in what form;
- the ways in which the data and information collected will be used in the short and long term;
- the manner in which local communities will be involved in the research process;
- copies of funding proposals for the research project, including budgets or a description of funding support if there is no formal proposal;
- information on the funding agency and conditions they attach to research results;
- CVs of researchers;
- copies of permits;
- an analysis by the researcher of the foreseen impact on the biological subjects of the research and on the habitats in which they occur;
- forms of benefit-sharing anticipated in the short, intermediate and long term (see below);
- professional codes of ethics and guidelines from the researcher's field;
- affiliated institutional policies, if they exist.

Local communities

The _____ [protected area] works through joint management agreements with local communities, and requires their participation in decision-making on issues that affect their land, resource management strategies and knowledge. Researchers must receive the prior informed consent of all communities with whom they will work. Researcher–community relationships should be designed to promote benefit-sharing and achievement of sustainable use objectives relevant to the community. Communities have the right to decline involvement in the research – to veto or say 'no' to a collaboration or research project. The acquisition of prior informed consent from local communities should be undertaken in conjunction with protected area staff and will include disclosing to the community:

- the purpose of the research and interest of the individual researchers in conducting this activity;
- the nature and purpose of the research, including the duration, geographic area and collecting methods;
- the identity of those carrying out the activity and its sponsors, and the terms set by affiliated institutions and sponsors;
- possible consequences or risks entailed by this activity;
- destination of knowledge or material that is to be acquired, its ownership status and the community's ability and rights to control its use once it has left the community;
- any commercial interest that the researcher or funders have in the research, or material and knowledge collected;
- the nature of benefits to result for the community (eg copies of reports or documents, training, employment, etc).

During the consultation process researchers must:

- ensure that the community at large and the range of stakeholders are incorporated into the process (eg by holding a public meeting);
- explain the codes, guidelines, policies and other standards to which the researcher adheres and experiences with implementation in other areas;
- emphasize the researcher's intention to respect cultural and legal traditions, and to avoid conducting research on sacred, secret or confidential areas without express prior informed consent from the community;
- emphasize the right of communities to not be involved or participate in the research.

The consultation process will be facilitated by _____ [protected area/Scientific Council], which will make its best effort to coordinate effectively and quickly the process of acquiring prior informed consent, but respects the communities' right to determine the appropriate timeline according to which consultations are undertaken.

The research process

While undertaking research, researchers are required to adhere to high standards of behaviour, collecting practice and benefit-sharing.

Researcher behaviour

Researchers are required to behave in a way that is respectful of local culture and traditions, customary laws and the integrity of the environment. This will include the following:

- adhere to local cultural norms and the terms of the prior informed consent (PIC) agreement with communities in conducting interviews and research in villages or surrounding areas; rights to privacy, confidentiality and anonymity should be respected;
- collect all waste and deposit it in a suitable site agreed by _____ [protected area management] and local communities;
- use only those campsites designated by _____ [protected area management];
- use only existing fallen wood for making fires;
- avoid disturbance to stream sediments;
- avoid washing with soap in streams and other natural water bodies;
- refrain from eating bushmeat;
- avoid sacred and environmentally sensitive sites unless authorized by _____ [protected area management] and local communities;
- treat protected area staff, local communities and others with respect;
- pay agreed-upon rates for employment and do not negotiate rates down.

Collections

Collections should not deplete populations of the biological material collected and should exhibit particular sensitivity in collecting any material used by local people.

Collections should not include rare and endangered species unless with the permission of _____ [protected area management/GoC].

Destructive harvesting, such as removal of roots, bark, bulbs or whole plants, must be made clear and done only with the permission of _____ [protected area management]. Only agreed-upon quantities may be removed.

No more material than is strictly necessary should be collected [set amount or type by species and site].

The _____ [protected area] should be informed of the whereabouts of any rare or endangered species that are found.

Transect-cutting may take place only with the approval of _____ [protected area]; if undertaken, transects should be minimally destructive and limited to _____ [specified area] and should never include _____ [specified area].

A duplicate of all specimens collected, and their label information, must be lodged in the National Herbaria [and others, as detailed].

Benefit-sharing

The object of benefit-sharing is to achieve fairness and equity and to create incentives for the conservation of biological diversity and the sustainable use of its components. During the research process, benefits should be shared with _____ [protected area] and local communities (where appropriate). Specific benefits to be shared will be identified prior to initiation of the research, during the prior-informed consent consultation, as described above. Benefits will vary by case and circumstance. An indicative list of benefits that flow from the research process follows:

- training of protected areas staff in scientific techniques, use of equipment, methodologies, etc;
- training of local community members in the same;
- supply of equipment;

- employment of staff and local community members;
- transfer of technology such as hardware, software and know-how associated with their use;
- training in information technology and management;
- supply of publications and written or photographic materials;
- provision of a 'conservation overhead' fee of ___ per cent of [field operating/ total research] budget; the provision of an overhead fee and calculation of the rate will be dependent upon the scale and nature of the research project, the provision of in-kind and non-monetary benefits that might offset the fee, the status of the researcher (eg student or professional, national or international) and other factors.

Protected area contribution to research

The protected area will provide to researchers, according to the following fee schedule and terms (and agreed on a case basis):

- vehicles : _____ CFA per day/km;
- staff: _____ [elaborate fees for different levels of staff];
- housing: _____ CFA per day;
- use of administrative infrastructure (computers, photocopiers, phone, etc);
- access to libraries, copies of publications, etc held by protected area staff;
- briefings on previous research conducted in the area, ecology, history and other areas relevant to the research process.

Post-field research follow-up

The researcher–protected area relationship does not end with the collection of data and materials in the field. Researchers will continue to hold obligations regarding the disposition of collected material, benefit-sharing and reporting to _____ [protected area/Scientific Council].

Disposition of collected material

All required documents (phytosanitary certificate, certificate of origin, CITES export permit) must be acquired prior to the dispatch of collected material.

Duplicate specimens may only be deposited in those institutions agreed to, as part of the prior informed consent process, unless written approval is received by _____ [protected area/ Scientific Council].

Researchers may not transfer material or any progeny or derivatives thereof to any third party without the prior informed consent, in writing, of _____ [protected area management/Scientific Council], and then under legally binding written agreement containing terms no less restrictive than those contained in this agreement, unless otherwise agreed in writing by _____ [protected area management/Scientific Council].

As agreed, the _____ [protected area/Scientific Council] and local communities (where appropriate) must be updated on the status of data analysis and publication.

Research data – and not only publications – should be shared with the protected area and, where requested, local communities.

Researchers must adhere to restrictions placed on the publication of traditional knowledge.

Benefit-sharing

Benefits to be shared with _____ [protected area] and local communities following field research, and as agreed by researchers and _____ [protected area/Scientific Council], include:

- copies of publications in French or in English;
- copies of photographs or slides taken during field research;
- analysis of data in a manner that is of value to protected area management;
- continued supply of publications relevant to protected area management and assistance with information and networking (including notification of impending conferences and publications of importance to the protected area);
- transformation of scientific findings into a form useful for education, outreach and other programmes (eg manuals on the management of useful species and field guides for visitors and tourists to the protected area);
- summary of the policy implications of research findings, where appropriate.

Reporting, monitoring and evaluation

Researchers should update the _____ [protected area/ Scientific Council] and local communities (as agreed) on the status of the research process, data analysis, publication and key findings. Reports of _____ pages, detailing _____ [findings, developments, etc], should be submitted [twice a year/quarterly].

Term and amendment of the research agreement

The research agreement between _____ and the _____ [protected area/Scientific Council] will be in effect as of _____, and will remain in effect until _____.

   Agreement between the researcher and _____ [protected area/ Scientific Council] will include clear protocols that either party can use to break the agreement. Acceptable reasons for breaking this agreement include: _____, _____, _____.

   The mechanism for resolving grievances is as follows: _____.

   During the course of the research, the agreement between the researcher and _____ [protected area/Scientific Council] may be amended through the following process: _____ [submission of a written request prior to quarterly Scientific Council meeting; agreement to resolve and amend the agreement at the meeting; etc]

SIGNED BY

_____   _____
Protected Areas Manager/ Scientific Council   Date

_____   _____
Researcher   Date

_____   _____
Government representatives (MINEF/MINRES)   Date

_____   _____
Local community representative (where applicable)   Date

Attach side agreement with community (where applicable)

Attached documents
Examples of documents that might be appended to a protected area policy and research agreement, and to which research relationships should adhere in letter and spirit, include the following.

Professional codes of ethics and research guidelines
- *American Anthropological Association (AAA) Code of Ethics;*
- *International Society of Ethnobiology (ISE) Code of Ethics and Draft Research Guidelines;*
- *Society of Economic Botany (SEB) Guidelines;*
- *Association of Systematics Collections (ASC) Guidelines;*
- *The Food and Agriculture Organization (FAO) Code of Conduct for Plant Germplasm Collection and Transfer;*
- *American Society of Pharmacognosy (ASP) Guidelines;*
- *Biodiversity Research Protocols* (Biodiversity and Ethics Working Group of Pew Conservation Fellows, 1997);
- *Manila Declaration and Code of Ethics for Collectors* (1992);
- *Declaration of Belem* (1988).

Institutional policies
- *Common Policy Guidelines for Participating Botanic Gardens on Access to Genetic Resources and Benefit-Sharing* (2001).

Biodiversity prospecting policies
- Missouri Botanical Garden (MBG);
- New York Botanical Garden (NYBG);
- Natural History Museum, London (NHM).

Indigenous peoples and local community guidelines, declarations and statements
- *Mataatua Declaration on Cultural and Intellectual Property Rights of Indigenous Peoples* (1993);
- *Kari-Oca Declaration and the Indigenous Peoples' Earth Charter* (1992);
- 'Statement from the COICA/UNDP Regional Meeting on Intellectual Property Rights and Biodiversity' (the Santa Cruz Declaration, 1994);
- *Indigenous Peoples Biodiversity Network: Indigenous Peoples, Indigenous Knowledge and Innovations and the Convention on Biological Diversity* (1996)
- *WWF/IUCN/WCPA Draft Principles on Indigenous Peoples and Conservation* (1999);
- *The Global Coalition for Biocultural Diversity Covenant on Intellectual, Cultural and Scientific Resources* (1994);
- *The Inuit Tapirisat (Canada) – Negotiating Research Relationships in the North* (1993);
- Prototype Guidelines for Environmental Assessments and Traditional Knowledge (World Council of Indigenous Peoples).

International treaties/statements
- Convention on Biological Diversity (CBD, 1993);
- Convention on the International Trade in Endangered Species of Wild Fauna and Flora (CITES);
- *UN Draft Declaration on the Rights of Indigenous Peoples* (1993);
- *Principles and Guidelines for the Protection of the Heritage of Intellectual Property* (1995).

CASE STUDY 6.3

BUILDING A BASIS FOR EQUITABLE RESEARCH RELATIONSHIPS IN BWINDI IMPENETRABLE NATIONAL PARK, UGANDA[2]

Jackson Mutebi (CARE Development through Conservation – CARE-DTC, Uganda), Lukman Mulumba (Manager Afritech (U) Ltd, Uganda) and Yakobo Moyini (EMA Ltd, Uganda)

Bwindi Impenetrable National Park

Bwindi Impenetrable National Park (BINP) is located in south-western Uganda (latitude 0° 15′ to 1° 81′ south, and longitude 29° 35′ to 29° 50′ east). BINP covers a total area of 330.8 square kilometres (km^2) and represents 5.4 per cent of Uganda's gazetted natural forest estate. BINP is a major water catchment area and a source of many rivers that drain into Lakes Edward and Mutanda. These lakes, in turn, form part of the catchment of the River Nile and the hydrological balance of the region and the country.

BINP is part of the Albertine Rift Valley refugium, one of the most biologically diverse forests in Uganda and Africa. It is characterized by a great diversity of plant and animal species with a large number endemic to the Albertine region. The park supports at least 120 species of mammals, making it one of the most prominent forests in Africa in terms of mammalian species richness. The primate species in BINP account for 58 per cent of those in Uganda. The park is particularly known for being home to half of the population of the world's remaining mountain gorillas (*Gorilla gorilla berengei*). Avian, insect and reptile diversity are also notable.

BINP became a national park in 1991. Before that, the area was a central forest reserve (CFR). In Uganda, as elsewhere, national parks have the highest conservation status of all protected areas. Under a national park status, community access to biological resources for extractive utilization is severely limited. Forest reserves, on the other hand, allow for the sustainable harvest of biological resources under various permitting systems. Consequently, while prior to 1991 communities could harvest timber and non-wood products with permission from the Uganda Forest Department, under its present status of a national park, extractive utilization is largely prohibited except in multiple use zones.

The human population densities in the areas surrounding BINP are much higher than the national average, ranging from 151 to 301 individuals per square kilometre. The average annual population growth rate is also high at 3.5 per cent per annum. The rapid population growth in the areas surrounding BINP has placed acute demands upon the area's natural resource base. Furthermore, the local people around BINP are, generally, poor and in the past have relied exclusively on the forest for their livelihoods. Activities previously carried out when the area was a CFR included logging, mining, hunting, cultivation, bee-keeping and collection of herbs, firewood, poles and materials for basket-making – particularly during the breakdown of government authority in the 1970s and 1980s. The pressure on BINP has been exacerbated by poor agricultural practices, which have led to land degradation and thus low crop yields and poverty, thereby reinforcing the desire to encroach on park resources.

Organizations working with BINP include CARE Development through Conservation (CARE-DTC), the International Gorilla Conservation Programme (IGCP) and the Institute of Tropical Forest Conservation (ITFC). These groups have initiated activities aimed at reducing tension created with local communities when Bwindi was converted from a central forest reserve into a national park.

Research activities within BINP

Most of the research undertaken thus far in BINP has been carried out by graduate students. Many of these students have come from universities outside of Uganda, although numerous nationals conduct research sponsored and supported through ITFC and other institutes. These research projects have greatly contributed to the inventory of species in Bwindi and the establishment and management of the park's Multiple Use Programme (MUP); for the most part, student theses reports have been made available to park managers and other researchers. The bulk of research undertaken in BINP is ecological research and includes studies on the distribution of duikers and canines; the role of multiple use in reducing illegal activities in the protected area; ecology and distribution of useful species, such as *Faurea saligna*, *Loeseneriella apocynoides* (omugyega) and *Smilax anceps* (ensuri); and routine ecological monitoring overseen by the ITFC.

However, it is generally believed that biodiversity prospecting within Uganda is largely conducted under the guise of academic scientific research, and that at times academic research itself is improperly monitored and is undertaken without appropriate permits. For example, in 1997 a group of British researchers were intercepted on the island district of Kalangala with over 70 animal and plant specimens; they did not have research permits to allow collections. Since 1996, a PhD student from the US has been collecting plant samples containing bioactive compounds in and around BINP; but BINP staff remain unclear about the final use and destination of the samples and information collected. Concerns have also focused on the collection and export of *Prunus africana* bark. As a result of these and other experiences, BINP staff members have grown increasingly wary of research partnerships and are developing ways to better define and monitor research activities.

National institutional context: development of access and benefit-sharing measures

Biodiversity prospecting activities in Uganda are not well documented, principally because there is a lack of appropriate and effective mechanisms for regulating and monitoring access to genetic resources and benefit-sharing. As a result, genetic material is leaving the country with little or no benefits accruing to the government and local communities.

Activities underway to address access and benefit-sharing issues within Uganda include national consultations recently organized by the National Environment Management Authority (NEMA) in conjunction with the Natural Chemotheraupetics Research Laboratory (NCRL) and the Uganda National Council for Science and Technology (UNCST). Financial and technical support were provided by WWF and the African Centre for Technology Studies (ACTS). NEMA and UNCST have used results of the consultations to prepare draft regulations for access to genetic resources that were discussed at a national workshop at the end of 1999. The Uganda Wildlife Society (UWS), ACTS and the World Resources Institute (WRI) have also produced legal and policy options for developing appropriate legislation to govern access to genetic resources. At the same time, the National Drug Authority (NDA) has established an ad hoc advisory committee on herbal medicines with terms of reference that include licensing, control of production, supply and import and export of herbal medicines. The National Agricultural Research Organization (NARO), through the Plant Genetic Resources Committee, has prepared draft *National Regulations for Plant Germplasm Collection and Transfer*. Despite the foregoing, there is still a lot that needs to be done, including implementing a coordinated approach to develop comprehensive measures and guidelines on access, and designating a single government agency responsible for granting prior informed consent (PIC) for any requests, whether they are academic or commercial.

Regulation of academic and commercial research within BINP

Activities within BINP today are largely guided by the 1996 Wildlife Statute within the overall framework of the National Environment Statute 1995. The regulation of research activities prior to 1991, when BINP became a national park, was the responsibility of the Uganda Game Department and the Uganda Forest Department, with coordination by the Uganda Institute of Ecology (UIE). However, since UIE's expertise lay mostly in savanna woodland ecosystems, the newly established Institute of Tropical Forest Conservation (ITFC) of Mbarara University of Science and Technology (MUST) was appointed to manage all research in BINP in 1991 on behalf of Uganda National Parks. This arrangement was upheld when Uganda National Parks and the Uganda Game Department were amalgamated to form the Uganda Wildlife Authority (UWA).

Application procedure

Research within BINP, as in any wildlife protected area, is authorized by the executive director of UWA. A researcher submits a research proposal to the coordinator of monitoring and research of UWA. The coordinator may, in turn, liaise with ITFC to establish the relevance of the research to Bwindi. ITFC will then endorse the research proposal when satisfied with its quality and substance. On the strength of the ITFC endorsement, the monitoring and research coordinator submits a recommendation for approval, through the deputy director of planning, monitoring, research and concessions, to the executive director. The executive director then writes a letter of approval, including guidelines and/or other relevant background, to the chief park warden, BINP. The letter also serves as the researcher's introduction to the park authorities. ITFC is normally informed of the letter by either the park authorities or the researcher. It is important to note that it is not yet a requirement that a copy of the research proposal is sent to the chief park warden, BINP.

Approval by UWA does not automatically allow the researcher to commence investigations. The legal institution for all research in the country is the Uganda National Council for Science and Technology (UNCST). The researcher submits the proposal simultaneously to both UWA and UNCST. However, the latter will not issue the ultimate authority to conduct research until the researcher obtains approval from UWA.

Once both UWA and UNCST have given their approval, the researcher takes the letter of introduction to the chief park warden for recognition of his/her presence in the park. If the researcher is attached to ITFC, then he or she reports to ITFC's offices in the park. However, independent researchers may also require some support from ITFC by way of identifying and/or providing field assistants and porters. On its part, the park may, on request, provide patrol rangers.

Monitoring research activities in BINP

Currently, no effective and formal mechanisms or guidelines exist for monitoring the activities of researchers inside the park on the part of BINP or ITFC. BINP management expects researchers to adhere to guidelines discussed with headquarter staff. ITFC monitors by allocating field staff to accompany the researchers into the forest. However, usually it is only when something goes wrong, and it is reported either by field assistants or patrol rangers, that park management has the opportunity to react – a characteristic 'management by crisis'. A key issue here is that for both BINP and ITFC, institutional capacity to carry out effective monitoring of research activities is severely limited. At monthly salaries of about US$80, it is not difficult to imagine how field assistants or park patrol rangers may be easily compromised by unscrupulous researchers.

Experiences in coordinating and monitoring research in BINP

Research in BINP, particularly by foreign researchers, has not been well coordinated and monitored in the past. Although most researchers obtain permission from both UWA and UNCST, neither the chief park warden nor the management of ITFC has adequate control over what authorized researchers actually do. There have been several incidences when park staff members have noted discrepancies with some of the data collection methods, and the types and amounts of specimens collected by some researchers. Some wardens and patrol rangers of BINP feel strongly that many researchers collect more specimens than is required. The park management is now asking the UWA head office to design a system that makes all researchers in BINP accountable to the chief park warden in order to ensure that the terms of the research proposals, as well as the park by-laws and regulations, are strictly adhered to.

Another area of great concern is the use of the local people's indigenous scientific knowledge without due recognition and acknowledgement by researchers. Most of these researchers, both foreigners and nationals, use local people in data collection either as field assistants or as key informants, especially the resource-expert elders. While these people provide useful information to researchers, it is unfortunate and shameful that they are hardly acknowledged – at a minimum. It would be helpful to mandate that the local people or 'traditional scientists' who provide information are acknowledged by documentation in the final scientific reports, and even in copyrights and patents. Furthermore, the acknowledgement should be passed on to the concerned individuals in writing and, where possible, fair and equitable compensation should be made to them.

Ensuring that research benefits BINP and local communities

There are plans underway at UWA headquarters to address many of these issues. The Monitoring and Research Coordination Unit has produced the *Wildlife Monitoring and Research Policy*, duly approved by the UWA board of trustees. Research priorities for protected area management have been drafted by UWA, and researchers will be encouraged to address these priorities in their research plans. For example, the ecological dynamics of BINP are not yet well understood, and information to utilize several management tools (such as fire management) are missing; economic values of species and the park also remain relatively unknown. Academic and commercial research is expected to generate data and information on these important parameters. Through their work, both academic and commercial researchers can help to train park staff in the areas of taxonomy, interpretative work and sample collection. A better understanding of the ecological dynamics of the park will enhance conservation and development efforts. In addition, researchers will be required to conform to the rules and regulations stipulated in the research plan.

The communities surrounding BINP might also gain from benefit-sharing programmes, including direct features such as employment, sale of produce and provision of low-cost and simple tourism services. Adequate academic and commercial agreements might also ensure that downstream royalties are made available to the park, local communities and overall conservation and development efforts (see Table 6.1). UWA experiences chronic funding shortages, and it is hoped that research can help contribute to its ongoing costs. At the moment, UWA cannot pay its way and a substantial share of its development and recurrent expenditure comes from external assistance.

Table 6.1 *Possible benefits from research*

Benefits	Direct beneficiaries		
	BINP	Local communities	Conservation and development
A Benefit-sharing			
1 Revenue-sharing		✓	
2 Resource-harvesting – multiple use		✓	
3 Support for community development project		✓	
4 Revenue substitution		✓	
5 Agricultural extension services		✓	
B Direct benefits (employment, sales of produce, provision of tourism services)	✓	✓	
C Downstream royalties	✓	✓	✓
D Data, information, publications	✓	✓	✓
E Training	✓	✓	
F Skills and better management practices	✓	✓	✓
G Regulating access to genetic resources and enhanced sustainability	✓	✓	✓
H Monitoring plan	✓		✓

Lessons learned in sharing benefits with local communities from the Revenue-Sharing Programme

The Revenue-Sharing Programme (RSP) was adopted as a policy in 1994 but is now a statutory requirement, having been provided for in the Wildlife Statute 1996. The overall purpose is for a wildlife-protected area to share part of its revenues with the surrounding communities. Unfortunately, there was limited public consultation and community involvement during both the establishment and elaboration of the RSP. The communities did not have much input in determining the percentage of revenues collected that should accrue to them.

In Bwindi, originally, 12 per cent of the revenue from gorilla permits was set aside for revenue sharing, of which 2 per cent went to the National RSP Consolidated Fund for other protected wildlife areas that do not generate significant revenues to meet some of their operating costs. Another 2 per cent went to the three districts in which Bwindi is located. The remaining 8 per cent went directly to the local communities. However in 1996, parliament enacted the Wildlife Statute 1996 and provided for 20 per cent of gate fees only; in effect, it abolished the previous arrangement of sharing 12 per cent of all revenues. At current rates of about US$40 for gate fees and US$250 for a gorilla-trekking permit, under the old provision (12 per cent of all revenue) the local communities would be entitled to US$34.80 per visitor compared to the new regime's (20 per cent of gate fees) benefit of US$8.

The RSP was initially administered by the Park Management Advisory Committee (PMAC) and the Park Parish Committees (PPCs), which were formed to act as direct links to the local communities in order to implement the RSP. Due to the lack of negotiating power and weak institutional capacity, there are recent moves to transfer local community responsibilities to the Production and Environment Committees (PECs) of the various levels of local government. The PECs at district, sub-county, parish and village levels are made up of elected members of the respective local councils.

Funds from the RSP are disbursed to support community development projects in the adjacent parishes but not as cash payments to individuals. To date, over 21 community projects have been approved and funded from the RSP. The funding level was up to a maximum of US$4000 for each project. A total of slightly more than US$100,000 has so far been shared with the neighbouring communities under the RSP, far exceeding any contribution that government has ever made for developments in the area covered by the programme.

Although the idea of revenue-sharing is good in principle, its implementation modalities need to be refined with the participation of all the stakeholders. Although the beneficiary communities are represented and appear to have significant voting power (through either the PMAC or the PECs), in reality they do not have much say over how much they should get. There are many important lessons in benefit-sharing that can be learned from RSP operations for communities surrounding BINP, including the following:

- The concept of revenue-sharing was agreed upon by the park authorities and the supporting projects and agencies. The park also decided on the amount of money to release to the communities. Community participation should have been sought on the purpose and rationale of revenue-sharing and the amount of money to be remitted to the community.
- The disbursement of money to communities has brought hope to the community that, after all, some tangible benefits are beginning to trickle in. It is seen as a gesture of goodwill on the part of the national park authorities to which communities are eager to respond. However, the programme created too high expectations among some of the local people and their confidence has gradually waned because of some apparent delays in realizing the support from the RSP funds for their projects.
- Local communities decided to use the initial money from revenue-sharing on community – rather than individual – projects for two main reasons. Firstly, originally, everybody had equal access to forest products, so the revenue-sharing money should fund projects where all have equal access, such as schools, clinics and roads. Secondly, the park authorities and supporting agencies indicated a preference for community projects over individual projects.
- The decision regarding what project a community should implement was taken in view of the volume of money received from the park. A sum of 50 million Uganda shillings (Ush) was available to the 21 parishes adjacent to BINP for the first disbursement of the revenue-sharing money. Each parish was to receive up to four million Ush; as a result, all the 21 projects funded in the first phase of the programme are very similar: schools of two to four classrooms, sub-dispensaries and roads. No funds went to an income-generating project.

- Community members, especially the community leaders, appreciate the role played by park authorities and supporting agencies and projects in guiding them on how to design, implement and monitor the various projects. Many of the people feel that without this guidance much of the money could have been misused by a minority elite, and no visible projects would have resulted on the ground.

- The revenue-sharing programme is beginning to pay off: people's attitudes are beginning to change positively. An example is a case narrated to us in Nyambale Parish, Kabale District. Mr Kiiza of Nyambale had lost the entire crop in his Irish potato garden to monkeys that came from the park. When he discovered this in the morning, he decided to take the matter to court at the sub-county office. However, a group of fellow village mates, who were assembled at one of the village bars, pleaded with him not to take the park management to court. They reasoned with him that the monkeys had recently 'built' a school for the whole parish (Ihumga Primary School), whereas Mr Kiiza had never contributed even a eucalyptus pole towards the old classrooms. Kiiza gave up the case. In another incident during September 1997, fire broke out in Mushanje and spread into the park. The local community, on its own initiative, put out the fire. The exercise took three days.

- Communities feel that the next financial disbursement should support individual families to enable them start income-generating activities. Many say that this could be achieved by putting the money in the local credit and savings schemes, known locally as 'Biika oguze'. People do not like the idea of putting the money in commercial banks, which make borrowing only possible for a few elite. 'The money is safer when banked within the community,' stressed one Ziimbeihire of Nyamabale Parish.

- The changes in percentage of park revenue to be set aside for revenue-sharing are a source of worry to both the communities and park management who disburse the money. Unless policy-makers review the new guidelines, the future of revenue-sharing is seriously threatened.

Recent developments

A number of recent developments will contribute to creating a more effective framework for equitable research relationships within BINP. These include the following:

- The Ministry of Tourism, Trade and Industry, under which UWA falls, initiated a review of the Wildlife Policy 1995. A draft, titled *Wildlife Policy 2000*, has been produced and awaits cabinet approval. Thereafter, amendments will be made to the existing Wildlife Statute 1996.

- Drawing upon the *Wildlife Policy 2000*, UWA developed a *Monitoring and Research Policy* that gives strong endorsement to the regulation of access to genetic resources. The policy was approved by the UWA board of trustees and is now operational. The policy clarifies research application procedures, reporting requirements and allowable quantities of specimens for collection.

- The Monitoring and Research Unit of UWA has developed a comprehensive research database that will be used to store data on various research activities in the wildlife-protected areas, including Bwindi. The Monitoring and Research Unit has also developed a geographic information system-based (GIS) ecological and socio-economic monitoring system called MIST for both savanna and forest ecosystems.

- A forestry sector policy is being formulated and some of its provisions will have relevance to Bwindi. After approval by cabinet, the policy will be translated into an enabling legislation to replace the Forests Act 1964, Cap 246.
- The World Bank-supported Protected Area Management for Sustainable Use (PAMSU) Project is aimed at building capacity at park level, among others. Bwindi will be a significant beneficiary of this support. The project will contribute to building capacity for more effective monitoring of various research activities in the park.
- The Environmental Law Institute and Uganda Wildlife Society have produced *Legal and Institutional Options for Governing Access to Genetic Resources in Uganda* (April 1999).
- The National Environment Management Authority (NEMA) has produced *Draft Regulations on Access to Biological Resources and Benefit-Sharing in Uganda*. The most current version of the draft was dated 23 April 1999. The regulation is a subsidiary legislation meant to enable the enforcement of Section 45, sub-section 1 of the National Environment Statute 1995, which mandates NEMA to develop guidelines and measures that specify:

'...(a) appropriate arrangements for access to the genetic resources of Uganda, by non-citizens of Uganda including the fees to be paid for that access; (b) measures for regulating the export of germplasm; (c) the sharing of benefits derived from genetic resources originating from Uganda; and (d) any other matter which the Authority considers necessary for the better management of the genetic resources of Uganda.'

The regulation will also assist with the enforcement of Part X (Sections 66, 67, 68 and 69) of the Wildlife Statute 1996, which deals with international trade in species and specimens.

In Norway, a fungus – *Tolypocladium inflatum* – was collected in 1969 by a Sandoz Co scientist while on vacation in Hardangervidda National Park. In 1983, years after the original collection, the company launched the product Sandimmun, based on cyclosporin A produced by *T. inflatum* in fermentation. An improved version of the product was launched in 1994 by the company now known as Novartis, generating US$1.7 billion in sales in 1997 alone (see Case Study 6.4). In another example, a microorganism collected in 1966 from the extreme environment of thermal pools in Yellowstone National Park in the US yielded an enzyme with a variety of biotechnological applications that gener-ates annual sales of around US$200 million (in contrast, the annual operating budget of the US National Park Service is US$20 million). This experience led the National Park Service to examine options for controlling access to resources and requiring benefit-sharing, and resulted in the 1997 Cooperative Research and Development Agreement (CRADA) between Diversa Corporation and Yellowstone. Under this agreement, Diversa will provide the park with up-front financial payments, equipment, training and royalties should a commercial product be developed (see Case Study 6.5; ten Kate et al, 1998; Chester, 1996).

However, even in cases where park managers try to structure equitable

BOX 6.3 THE CONVENTION ON BIOLOGICAL DIVERSITY
AND PROTECTED AREAS

The term 'protected area' is defined in Article 2 of the Convention on Biological Diversity (CBD) as 'a geographically defined area which is designated or regulated and managed to achieve specific conservation objectives'. Paragraphs (a), (b), (c) and (e) of Article 8 contain specific references to protected areas and provide that parties should:

- establish a system of protected areas or areas where special measures need to be taken to conserve biological diversity;
- develop, where necessary, guidelines for the selection, establishment and management of protected areas or areas where special measures need to be taken to conserve biological diversity;
- regulate or manage biological resources important for the conservation of biological diversity whether within or outside protected areas, with a view to ensuring their conservation and sustainable use; and
- promote environmentally sound and sustainable development in areas adjacent to protected areas with a view to furthering protection of these areas.

The central role of protected areas has been repeatedly emphasized in the decisions of the Conference of the Parties (COP), which regularly reviews the implementation of the CBD, considers and adopts amendments to the Convention and establishes subsidiary bodies as required. The COP meets on a regular basis, with the fifth regular meeting held in Nairobi in May 2000. Parties to the CBD have consistently identified their efforts to develop and maintain their national protected area system as the central element of their strategy to implement the CBD. The provisions of the CBD and decisions of the COP promote an approach to protected areas that does not 'lock up' resources found within the protected area network, but rather promotes their integration into the national economy in a sustainable and equitable manner. Protected areas will be one of three main topics for the seventh meeting of the COP, likely to be in either 2003 or 2004, and as a result will be the focus of work of various subsidiary bodies of the CBD preceding this meeting.

At the same time that the CBD calls for the conservation and sustainable use of biodiversity, it also seeks to promote the 'fair and equitable sharing of benefits' arising from the use of genetic resources. To do this, the Convention recognizes the sovereign rights of States over their natural resources and requires that access to genetic resources be on 'mutually agreed terms', and subject to the 'prior informed consent' of Contracting Parties. Scientific research based on genetic resources should be undertaken with the full participation of Contracting Parties, and any benefits derived from 'the commercial and other utilization of genetic resources' must be fairly and equitably shared (Article 15).

'Access and benefit-sharing' is considered one of the CBD's 'cross-cutting' issues, and is closely linked to a number of other issues, in particular Articles 8 (j), 11, 16, 17, 18 and 19. Other cross-cutting issues addressed by the Conference of the Parties include biosafety, the rights of indigenous and local communities under the Convention (also known as Article 8 (j) issues), intellectual property rights, indicators, the Global Taxonomic Initiative and alien species. Cross-cutting issues have an important role to play in bringing cohesion to the work of the CBD as they provide the substantive bridges or links between ecosystem themes.

Provisions within the CBD relating to in-situ conservation and protected areas, access and benefit-sharing, the rights of indigenous and local communities, the Global Taxonomic Initiative and other programmes aimed at furthering scientific understanding of biodiversity converge at the point where researchers enter into relationships with protected areas management. Protected area policies for researchers operate at this point of convergence, drawing from both thematic and cross-cutting issues under the CBD.

Sources: Johnston, 2000; www.biodiv.org; Johnston's annex to this chapter at www.rbgkew.org.uk/peopleplants

commercial arrangements, they must wrestle with the enormous public and political attention focused on the highly controversial area of biodiversity prospecting, and the speed with which issues are advancing. For example, the Yellowstone–Diversa agreement was recently the subject of a lawsuit in the US, and is suspended pending an environmental impact study with public input (Chester, 1999). Although park managers, through this agreement, attempted to share in revenue streams produced by commercial collections undertaken for years under non-obligation scientific research permits, watchdog groups were concerned that the public was not consulted, the details of the agreement remained confidential and the potential environmental impacts of collections were not known (Smith, 1999).

This case amply demonstrates the difficulties that park managers face under changing paradigms of both commercial use of biodiversity and protected area management. 'Use' of park resources lies far outside the traditional paradigm of park management; however, most first-round biodiversity prospecting collections involve minimal or no damage to species (Chester, 1999). Yellowstone park managers were seeking to gain from new forms of commercial research, and to employ new models of protected area management that link sustainable use and conservation. However, wider public

consultation and greater transparency will be necessary in order to ensure a level of comfort with the rapidly evolving role of protected areas.

In many countries, commercial collecting partnerships are seen as a way to support chronically underfunded protected areas. For example, one of the International Cooperative Biodiversity Groups (ICBG) supported by the US government is randomly collecting material in the Cuc Phong National Park (CPNP) in Vietnam. ICBG funds are applied immediately to pay staff, upgrade infrastructure and support conservation and income-generation projects. Both milestone and royalty payments will be paid – via a trust fund – to the park. If a plant species collected in Vietnam is developed into a commercial product, the ICBG benefit-sharing plan provides that financial benefits returning to Vietnam are shared between the park and the National Centre of Science and Technology (NCST). By partnering with the CPNP, ICBG staff members not only gain access to biologically diverse samples, but also increase the immediate conservation benefits resulting from their project. CPNP managers, in turn, acquire badly needed support for park infrastructure, training, and research (DD Soejarto, pers comm, 1999).

The National Institute of Biodiversity (InBio) in Costa Rica also conducts commercial collections in protected areas as a way to fund biodiversity research,

CASE STUDY 6.4

NOVARTIS'S GOLDEN EGGS FROM A NORWEGIAN GOOSE

Hanne Svarstad (University of Oslo), Shivcharn Dhillion (Agricultural University of Oslo) and Hans Chr Bugge (University of Oslo)

The following is a case study of biodiversity prospecting in Hardangervidda National Park in Norway. Sample collection was undertaken 30 years ago, in the context of open access predating entry into force of the Convention on Biological Diversity (CBD). The Swiss corporation Novartis generates annual revenues in excess of US$1 billion a year from the 'Norwegian goose'; but Norway, as the source country, does not share in the 'golden eggs'. This case can provide lessons that are relevant today, when Norwegian coral reefs are subject to biodiversity prospecting under a system that remains unregulated.

Tourists with a camera and plastic bags

The Swiss pharmaceutical company Sandoz began its screening programme for anti-fungal antibiotics in 1958. Since then, employees on business trips and on holiday have routinely carried plastic bags for the collection of soil samples for the screening of micro-organisms (Tribe, 1998). In 1969, Dr Hans Peter Frey, working as a biologist at Sandoz, spent a few weeks' holiday in Norway with his wife. During the trip, Dr Frey collected more than 50 soil samples (Frey, pers comm, 1998).

Like other scientists and colleagues, Dr Frey believed that such collections were useful for the development of new medicines and other products (ibid). When Dr Frey and his wife arrived in Oslo, they rented a car and drove to Bergen. On the way, they crossed through the mountain plateau of Hardangervidda National Park, occasionally stopping to take pictures of the scenic views. Dr Frey used the opportunity of these stops to collect soil samples (Frey, pers comm, 1998.). The selection of collection sites was, in fact, based entirely on aesthetic considerations.

Back in Switzerland, Frey's soil samples became subject to Sandoz's test procedures. In 1972 a strong immunosuppressive property was found in the biochemical cyclosporin A, produced by *Tolypocladium inflatum* Gams (hyphomycetes), a fungus from Hardangervidda. An additional 11 years were spent on research and development before a medicine was ready for the market.

Novartis and the golden eggs

Sandoz and Ciba Geigy, both with headquarters in Basle, Switzerland, merged in 1996 to form Novartis. At the time, this was the largest corporate merger in history. The new company presents itself as the world's leading life science company (see www.novartis.com). It produces commodities for human health care, agrobusiness and nutrition. At the end of 1997, Novartis employed 87,239 people, a decline from 116,178 during the previous year (Novartis, 1998). Novartis's total sales in 1997 were US$21.5 billion (CHF 31.2 billion) (*European Chemical News*, February 1998). Based on sales, the company is ranked as the world's second largest pharmaceutical company (*European Chemical News*, March 1997).

In 1983 Sandoz introduced Sandimmun to the market. Based on cyclosporin A, the medicine helped transplant patients to avoid rejection of new organs. An improved formulation called Sandimmun Neoral was launched in 1994 (Novartis Pharma AG,

1998). Sandimmun and Sandimmun Neoral are Novartis's leading pharmaceutical products today, generating revenues in 1997 of US$1.2 billion (CHF 1.8 billion) (Gjersvik, Novartis Norge AS, 17 March1998). Worldwide, some 200,000 transplant patients were reported to have used the cyclosporin A medicines in 1996 (Tribe, 1998).

Novartis produces cyclosporin A by isolation from large-scale fermentation broth cultures of *Tolypocladium inflatum*. As the fungus grows, it produces cyclosporin A, and at saturation the biochemical is extracted. Although *T. inflatum* has been found in several countries, the Norwegian isolate has proven the most suitable for production of the drugs. After collecting the original sample from Hardangervidda, it has not been necessary to go back to recollect samples for either research or production. The original culture has been easy to perpetuate. The company's production of cyclosporin A has therefore always been based on the strain from Hardangervidda (M Dreyfuss, pers comm, 1998; Å. Gjersvik., pers comm, 1998). Thus, when Dr Frey returned from his holiday, he not only brought with him the key to a new important medicine, but he also brought his company a 'goose that lays golden eggs'.

Fungal biodiversity and Hardangervidda

There are an estimated 1.5 million species of fungi, with most still undescribed (Webster, 1997). Fungi have an essential role in maintaining ecosystems. They participate in nutrient cycling, decomposition and various obligatory symbioses (Webster, 1997; Hooper et al, 1995). In addition, fungi provide various benefits to humans from fermentation used in baking and brewing, controlling agricultural pathogens and producing antibacterial compounds that yield novel biochemical products. *T. inflatum* demonstrates the potentially immense medical and economic value of fungal diversity.

Hardangervidda, where *T. Inflatum* was found, is the largest mountain plateau and the southernmost arctic plateau in Europe, covering some 4000 square kilometres (km^2). It is the habitat for a number of arctic animals, plants and fungi in Europe, and is the grazing area for Europe's most important stock of wild reindeer. In 1981, Hardangervidda National Park was established close to the road along which Dr Frey made his crucial collection. It constitutes the largest national park in Norway. A 'protected landscape' has also been established in the area – having somewhat less stringent protection criteria than a national park.

Open versus regulated access

Before collecting soil samples, Dr Frey did not acquire any permits from the Norwegian government, and no papers were filed with customs when the Freys flew home from Bergen (Frey, pers comm, 1998). During that time, there was no regulation of access to biodiversity aimed at securing benefit-sharing, and it would be difficult to conclude that Norwegian law was violated when the soil samples were removed from Hardangervidda and taken out of Norway. However, this case demonstrates the potential value of Norwegian biodiversity, and argues in favour of establishing access and benefit-sharing regulations to guide collections undertaken today.

In a situation of regulated access, Norway would have a reasonable claim of 2 per cent annual royalties on sales of products derived from *T. inflatum* and collected in Norway (Svarstad et al, 2000). In 1997, 2 per cent of gross sales of Novartis's two medicines produced from the Hardangervidda fungus amounted to US$24.3 million. Royalties are generally calculated on net sales, but even a smaller figure would significantly contribute to local health care, scientific capacity building and conservation programmes.

Norway is a rich country, but funding for protected areas such as the Hardangervidda National Park are always more limited than those managing protected areas would wish. The state budget for this purpose has been very limited for a number of years, and remains well below the norms established by the International Union for Conservation of Nature and Natural Resources (IUCN) (Deputy Director Harald Smith Ruberg, Ministry of Environment, pers comm, 1999). Increased funds would make it possible to more effectively protect a wider and more representative range of ecosystems, an expensive undertaking within Norway since national law generally requires that landowners are compensated. Furthermore, within existing protected areas, including Hardangervidda National Park, support for basic maintenance and restoration is needed. For example, improved control and supervision of park lands, marking of the park's borders and restoration of traditional paths that have been partly destroyed by motorized traffic are cited as outstanding needs. Increased funding would also make it possible to improve research, as well as education and extension activities that increase public appreciation of the rich natural and cultural heritage of Hardangervidda. Such activities are quite limited today.

In 1999 German researchers began screening microbes collected on Norwegian reefs by submarine. A new regulation that dates from March 1999 lays down a general principle of precaution for fishing activities to avoid degradation of coral reefs. In one area, bottom-trawling is prohibited; but protected areas have not been established for coral reef ecosystems. At the same time, Norwegian access and benefit-sharing regulations remain non-existent, inside or outside national parks. Therefore, new 'golden eggs' may be 'hatched' without the source country sharing the benefits. In order to change this situation, new legal instruments must be established in Norway to implement the access and benefit-sharing (ABS) provisions of the CBD. The regulation must be strong enough to secure a reasonable share of any golden eggs, while not being so time-consuming and unpredictable as to strangle the goose. Benefit-sharing should be channelled to address three key, and often underfunded, areas: conservation programmes, including those in protected areas; scientific research on biodiversity; and health care.

conservation and support the national system of conservation areas. InBio was established by the Ministry of Environment and Energy (MINAE) as a private non-profit organization to help conserve, study and 'use' the country's biological diversity. As laid out in a cooperative agreement between MINAE and InBio, InBio will provide roughly 10 per cent of the total annual budget of any project to the country's conservation areas, and 50 per cent of any financial benefits resulting from commercial product development received by InBio. Of the US$1,135,000 advance payment made to InBio by Merck & Co in 1991,

for example, US$100,000 was provided to MINAE (Sittenfeld and Gamez, 1993). To date, InBio's biodiversity prospecting agreements have yielded more than US$390,000 to MINAE; US$710,000 to conservation areas; US$710,000 to public universities; and US$740,000 to cover activities within InBio, primarily the national biodiversity inventory (ten Kate, 1999). InBio's commercial partnerships include those with Diversa (US), Bristol-Myers Squibb (US), Givaudane Roure (Switzerland–US), Indena (Italy), Analyticon (Germany), La Pacifica (Costa Rica) and the British Technology Group (ten Kate, 1999).

CASE STUDY 6.5

ACCESS TO GENETIC RESOURCES AND BENEFIT-SHARING IN A PROTECTED AREA: AN AGREEMENT BETWEEN YELLOWSTONE NATIONAL PARK AND THE DIVERSA CORPORATION[3]

Kerry ten Kate, Laura Touche, Amanda Collis and Adrian Wells
(Royal Botanic Gardens, Kew)

The benefit-sharing agreement

This case study examines a benefit-sharing partnership between the Yellowstone National Park (YNP) and the Diversa Corporation under a Cooperative Research and Development Agreement (CRADA) signed on 17 August 1997. Diversa had already been sourcing thermophilic micro-organisms from the park's geothermal features for three years, under a series of research specimen collection permits. The CRADA creates a legal, benefit-sharing framework for Diversa's continued work, including the development and commercialization of enzymes and other compounds discovered during investigations of samples obtained in YNP. The agreement is regarded by YNP as a 'model' for future partnerships of this type.

The YNP–Diversa CRADA is initially valid for five years; following its termination, any benefit-sharing obligations would survive. Under the agreement, Diversa paid YNP an upfront fee. This is offset against future royalty payments that the YNP will receive from Diversa should a product developed from a YNP genetic resource prove profitable. The company has also transferred equipment to YNP, such as DNA extraction kits and DNA 'primers', and has trained park staff in recent molecular biology techniques. In return, Diversa gains continued access to YNP's thermophilic microbes and can use these for product development.

Key players in drafting the agreement

Yellowstone National Park

Yellowstone National Park (YNP) is located in the northern Rocky Mountains, United States, and spans an area of 8992 square kilometres. Established in 1872, YNP is the world's first modern national park and is both a US Biosphere and a World Heritage Site.

YNP is estimated to contain 60 per cent of the world's geothermal features (Yellowstone Media Kit, 1999). Thermophilic micro-organisms thrive in these features, in temperatures of between 40° and 93° Celsius (Lindstrom, 1997). As 'extremophiles', such microbes contain unique enzymes and bioactive compounds, and are thus of great interest to bioprospectors for product development and industrial application. It is estimated that less than 1 per cent of the micro-organisms living in Yellowstone's 10,000 thermal sites have been identified (Yellowstone, 1999).

YNP is owned and managed by the National Park Service, one of the US federal land management agencies under the control of US Department of the Interior. YNP's management regulates scientific research within the park, including access to biological resources, by means of research specimen collection permits (as stipulated in the *Code of Federal Regulations* – 36 CFR, Sections 1.6 and 2.5) and, more recently, by CRADAs.

The Diversa Corporation

The Diversa Corporation is headquartered in San Diego, California. Diversa specializes in the discovery, development and manufacture of novel enzymes and bioactive compounds sourced from extremophile organisms. In addition to YNP, the company has bioprospected in Iceland, Costa Rica and Indonesia. It has isolated more than 600 enzymes.

World Foundation for Environment and Development (WFED)

WFED is a non-governmental organization based in Washington, DC. It facilitates negotiations over access to, and sustainable use of, genetic resources. Since 1995, WFED has worked with YNP to develop a scientific, research-focused, bioprospecting programme at the park. It also coordinates the Yellowstone Thermophiles Conservation Project.

The context: research on Yellowstone's thermophilic microbes

The partnership was shaped by the discovery in 1966 of a thermophile named *Thermus aquaticus*, obtained from YNP during a collection by researchers from Indiana University (Brock and Freeze, 1969). An enzyme, thermostable DNA polymerase (Taq polymerase), was isolated from *T. aquaticus* by a private company in 1984 (R Lindstrom, Yellowstone Center for Resources, pers comm, 1998). Taq polymerase catalyses DNA synthesis and can be used repeatedly to 'bulk up' DNA samples – a process termed the polymerase chain reaction (PCR) (Madigan et al, 1997). PCR is used in a wide range of biotechnological applications and annual sales of PCR equipment exceed US$200 million (Lindstrom, 1997).

YNP has received no direct share of these profits given that the 1966 collection did not take place subject to a benefit-sharing agreement (Wolf, 1994). During 1994–1995, YNP therefore decided that its future research agreements must provide for benefit-sharing, should products derived from YNP's genetic resources be commercialized by research partners (P Scott, WFED, pers comm, 1998).

Policy framework

Ownership of Yellowstone's genetic resources

Title 36 of the US *Code of Federal Regulations* (CFR) provides that all specimens collected in a national park under research permits belong to that park. As specimens are gathered on national land, the ultimate owner is the federal government, with whom title remains under any agreement permitting research on those specimens.[4] The YNP–Diversa CRADA does not, therefore, grant Diversa title to the samples it collects in YNP; but it does allow Diversa to patent any innovations based on specimens and to commercialize resultant products, subject to benefit-sharing with YNP.

Yellowstone research specimen collection permits

YNP issues permits for access to, and use of, its biological resources pursuant to Title 36 of the CFR. Diversa's activities in YNP are governed by such permits.[5]

Section 1.6 of Title 36 of the CFR empowers a national park superintendent to issue permits 'consistent with applicable legislation, Federal regulations and administrative policies', having determined that collection work will not adversely affect 'public health and safety, environmental and scenic values, natural or cultural resources, scientific research, implementation of management responsibilities, proper allocation and use of facilities, or the avoidance of conflict amongst visitor use activities'.

Section 2.5 of Title 36 of the CFR establishes that park superintendents may only issue permits for collecting specimens to 'an official representative of a reputable scientific or educational institution or a State or a Federal agency', and for scientific research or resource management. Permits may not be issued if the removal of specimens will damage the park's ecosystem.

Consistent with Title 36 of the CFR, the 'Yellowstone Permit Application' requires all specimens collected and not consumed by authorized research to be accessioned and catalogued into YNP records, and housed either at the park museum or with an agreed outside repository under an Outgoing Loan Agreement. The National Park Service reserves the right to designate such a repository in the interests of science, and to approve and restrict transfers between repositories.

Although 'Yellowstone Research Specimen Collection Permits' state that specimens 'shall be used for scientific and educational purposes only', the park superintendent may explicitly authorize commercialization. CRADAs provide the legal framework for such commercialization.

Cooperative research and development agreements

The 1986 US Federal Technology Transfer Act (15 USC 3710a *et seq*) encourages cooperative research and technology transfer between the federal government and the private sector. The act authorizes a private company to enter into a CRADA with a 'federal laboratory facility', contributing funds and expertise for collaborative work in exchange for access to federal property (eg specimens or patents, and rights in resultant discoveries). Designated 'federal laboratories' are authorized to enter into CRADAs. The Department of the Interior approved YNP's self-designation as a federal laboratory facility for the purposes of the act.

Section 2.1(c) of Title 36 of the CFR prohibits YNP from any 'sale or commercial use of natural products'. For the purposes of CRADAs, however, Yellowstone distinguishes between 'natural products', on the one hand, and 'research results' on the other. That is, 'natural products' taken from YNP are not equivalent to useful applications of any 'research results' derived from investigations of YNP specimens. The park does not, therefore, regard section 2.1 (c) applicable to the genetic information that Diversa obtains from microbes for product development (P Scott, WFED, pers comm, 1998).

Process for establishing the arrangements

Stakeholder participation

At the Old Faithful Symposium in September 1995, YNP managers announced their intention to seek commercial profits generated by products developed from YNP's extremophiles. They sought the response of the public and other stakeholders, such as universities and biotechnology companies. Although there was agreement that YNP should enter into such commercial partnerships, no consensus was reached over benefit-sharing arrangements appropriate to YNP's circumstances (R Lindstrom, YCR, pers comm, 1998). Park staff and the WFED, which YNP had hired in order to assist its negotiations with Diversa, therefore consulted the National Biodiversity Institute (InBio) in Costa Rica, which had seven years of experience with access and benefit-sharing agreements with companies.

Negotiations between Yellowstone and Diversa

YNP and WFED used the Department of Interior's CRADA policy, as outlined in its handbook *Technology Transfer: Marketing Our Products and Technologies (A Training*

Handbook for the US Department of the Interior), as a guideline for negotiations with Diversa. The US National Institutes of Health were consulted over whether the royalty rates offered by Diversa were comparatively fair.

The CRADA was amended in 1998, following its examination by US government officials for consistency with existing regulations and government policy. Changes to the terms of the CRADA raised the value of non-monetary benefits to YNP from a total of US$75,000 over the five-year period of the contract to the same value each year. The royalty range was also increased to above 10 per cent in the event that a product attains sales of between US$50 million to US$200 million (E Mathur and C Ericson, Diversa Corporation, pers comm, 1998).

Non-governmental organizations (NGOs) have challenged the CRADA, alleging that it violates the Federal Technology Transfer Act because YNP is not a 'federal laboratory' within the meaning of the act and that the agreement involves the extraction and exchange of natural resources, not merely the transfer of laboratory-related equipment. Other allegations concern insufficient provision for public scrutiny of the agreement and violations of YNP's governing acts[6] that prohibit the sale or commercial use of the park's natural resources (Edmonds Institute, 1997). The agreement became the subject of two law suits. In March 1999, a federal judge ruled in favour of NGOs, suspending the contract and ordering YNP to conduct an environmental impact study of bioprospecting activities subject to greater public consultation. However, NGOs failed in their appeal against a ruling by the Department of Interior, which preserved the confidentiality of royalty rates agreed between YNP and Diversa. The press subsequently published these rates (Smith, 1999).

Content of the arrangements: inputs

Yellowstone National Park
In addition to granting Diversa access to the park's microbial resources, YNP scientists contribute expertise to the partnership, including detailed knowledge of the characteristics of individual geothermal sites.

Diversa
Diversa staff undertake collection work in YNP in collaboration with park officials. The company's subsequent research is based on molecular biology and functional genomics, and aims at developing recombinant natural products. DNA is isolated from raw microbial samples. It is then introduced into easily grown microbial hosts in order to generate a 'gene library'. The DNA is then screened for the expression of novel enzymes and bioactive compounds using high-throughput robotic screens. Diversa is already developing enzymes sourced from YNP's thermophilic microbes to bleach pulp for paper manufacture and to 'stone wash' blue jeans.

Content of the arrangements: benefits

Monetary benefits
Under the CRADA, Diversa must pay YNP an upfront fee of US$100,000 in five annual instalments of US$20,000. This fee is offset against YNP's potential receipt of royalty payments, derived from net sales of any products developed by Diversa from YNP's genetic resources. The agreed royalty rates range up to 10 per cent for different categories of product, depending upon Diversa's commercial interests in them. On sales of industrial or pharmaceutical products developed from the park's microbes, YNP will

receive a royalty of 0.5 per cent. On sales of 'research reagent or diagnostic' products derived from YNP's genetic resources, the park will receive a 3 per cent royalty (Smith, 1999). For 'native enzymes' purified from cultured microorganisms sourced from YNP, the rate increases to 8 per cent. Should any products achieve net sales of between US$50 million and US$200 million, YNP will receive a royalty of more than 10 per cent. The park will also receive 10 per cent of net revenues derived from the licensing, assignment or sale of copyrighted work, such as books, journals, articles or genetic codes (Smith, 1999). However, while the CRADA law allows Yellowstone to retain upfront annual payments from Diversa, it must share any royalty payments with the National Park Service, meaning that some of Yellowstone's financial benefits will be shared with other parks.

Diversa will itself obtain net profits on sales of products. In addition, the WFED has been paid US$28,000 for supporting negotiations between YNP and Diversa (J Varley, Yellowstone Center for Resources, pers comm, 1998).

Non-monetary benefits
The CRADA provides that Diversa must provide YNP with non-monetary benefits to the value of US$75,000 per year over its five-year term. Diversa's contributions to park staff include DNA extraction kits and DNA 'primers' for polymerase chain reaction (PCR), used to detect target DNA. Diversa scientists and park staff regularly work together, and the latter are trained in the latest molecular biology techniques for park projects, including DNA fingerprinting techniques for the detection of *Brucellosis* in Yellowstone bison. This training is worth an estimated US$15,000 per year (Smith, 1999).

Diversa, in turn, benefits from access to biological resources under the CRADA and from rights to commercialize products based on material obtained from YNP both during and prior to the CRADA. Diversa also benefits from the expertise and logistical support of YNP staff.

Support for conservation activities[7]

The Yellowstone Thermophiles Conservation Project
The CRADA provides that monies due to YNP must be paid into a government account earmarked for the Yellowstone Thermophiles Conservation Project. The project is a collaboration between YNP, WFED, the Yellowstone Park Foundation and the National Park Foundation. The project has three areas of activity.

Microbial biodiversity conservation activities
The project's conservation activities aim to:

- improve understanding of YNP's microbial biodiversity in order to enhance habitat protection and resource management activities;
- develop and maintain a coordinated network of ex-situ culture collections to complement YNP's in-situ conservation efforts, enabling species identification, authentication and preservation; and
- improve in-situ and ex-situ culture collection and preservation strategies.

Scientific research and data management
The project will encourage study of YNP thermal habitats to promote the discovery and description of new microbial forms, biochemical compounds and habitats. It will also explore the development of an integrated database for information on habitats and

other scientific data in order to benefit YNP's microbial conservation and management practices. Key objectives are to improve understanding of the spatial and temporal distribution of YNP's microbial diversity, and to enhance methodologies for the characterization, isolation and identification of its microbial communities.

Public outreach and education
The project seeks to raise public awareness of the value of national parks and biodiversity through, amongst others, publications, presentations, field workshops and field excursions. It will also explore innovative biodiversity management practices that can be adapted for application elsewhere.

Collections in the Norwegian and Cameroon cases cited above pre-dated the Convention on Biological Diversity and the shift in the paradigm of exchange for genetic resources. Today, collections are more effectively monitored by governments and watchdog groups, and the need for an agreement laying out the terms for collections and benefit-sharing is more widely recognized. However, this creates added obligations on protected areas managers to clarify their relationships with researchers. A primary means to provide such clarification and shared understanding is to formalize the terms of all research and specimen collection through standardized yet flexible policies and agreements (see Case Study 6.2).

Protected areas managers must also be prepared to describe and defend these agreements to the wider public, and stay abreast of the rapidly evolving debate surrounding access and benefit-sharing associated with genetic resource collections. This will require building significant capacity within protected area staff to address the range of legal, ethical and political issues raised by many forms of research today. There is clear commercial interest in biological diversity contained within protected areas, but the main lesson to be drawn from the previous examples is not the potential for enormous financial gain, which is highly uncertain. Rather, the principal need is for clarity and agreement in research relationships.

National access and benefit-sharing measures and protected areas

Increasingly, national measures drafted to implement the access and benefit-sharing (ABS) provisions of the CBD incorporate provisions that affect research in protected areas (see Chapter 12 for a discussion of national ABS measures). In Costa Rica, for example, the consultation process leading up to the 23 April 1998 Biodiversity Law included discussion of the distinction between commercial and academic research, and the relationship between

protected areas, conservation and research. Under the law, prior informed consent of 'the regional councils of the Conservation Areas' is required for access (Solis, pers comm, 1999; Solis Rivera and Madrigal Cordero, 1999). Likewise, in the Philippines under the 1994 Executive Order 247, collectors must obtain the prior informed consent of local protected areas management boards (see Chapter 12). In contrast, during the consultation process leading up to Decision 391, 'Common Regime on Access to Genetic Resources of the Andean Pact', protected areas received limited attention. However, regulations imposed by the decision could have immediate, and potentially negative, impacts on biodiversity research in those sites (see Box 6.4).

In South Africa, a country renowned for its outstanding system of protected areas, a similar situation prevails. No specific policies exist to govern access and benefit-sharing in protected areas, and thinking and awareness about the issues remains embryonic. Slowly this is changing, and conservation bodies are now starting to develop policies and permitting procedures to differentiate between academic and commercial research in protected areas. This has been in response both to South Africa's biodiversity policy, and to escalating requests from collectors and potential collaborators. With no less than ten agencies responsible for protected area management in the nine provinces of the country, and an absence of national access legislation and leadership on the issue, difficulties surround the ways in which

benefit-sharing might be implemented. The chequered history of protected areas in South Africa – deeply linked to resource alienation and forced removal of communities – makes this issue especially sensitive and critical to resolve if conservation is to be accepted as a legitimate land use in South Africa (R Wynberg, pers comm, 1999).

Protected area managers can play an important role in national consultative processes that address access and benefit-sharing issues and that develop national measures to implement the CBD. Such managers can contribute valuable perspectives on effective in-situ conservation, and can provide insight into some of the practical ramifications of approaches to ABS regulation. However, effective participation in this process requires capacity and understanding of the elements of equitable research relationships, international standards of 'best practice' for researchers and commercial use of biodiversity. Ongoing capacity-building is also a necessary precursor to, and by-product of, a protected-area policy consultation and drafting process.

Local communities and protected area research

Although the term 'protected areas' has long suggested places without people, in the past decade protected area management and philosophy have dramatically shifted, making them more flexible in aim, definition, size and approach. Protected areas objectives might include watershed protection, demarcation of indigenous territory, extractive reserves and the maintenance of culturally significant sites. The 1994 IUCN categories for protected area management reflect and incorporate this diversity in approach, and recognize that local communities are important

stakeholders in protected area management (Dudley and Stolton, 1997). There is a trend away from exclusive management models towards inclusive models that include a high degree of local participation, recognize the link between nature and culture, and employ collaborative approaches that incorporate the traditional resource rights of local communities (see Box 6.5; Oviedo's annex to this chapter (www.rbgkew.org.uk/peopleplants); Oviedo and Brown, 1999; Oviedo, 1998; WWF/IUCN/WCPA, 1999).

BOX 6.4 RESEARCH IN PROTECTED AREAS IN THE CONTEXT OF DECISION 391 OF THE ANDEAN PACT

Manuel Ruiz (Peruvian Society for Environmental Law)

During the development and negotiation of Decision 391 of the Andean Pact, 'Common Regime on Access to Genetic Resources', limited reference was made to the issue of access and benefit-sharing in protected areas of member states. Although, at the time, discussions made it clear that biological and genetic resources located within protected areas were undoubtedly the property of the state, little attention was given to specific national regulations for protected areas, including the potential to link existing regulations with the new access regulatory system.

Decision 391's definition of access refers to 'obtaining and utilizing genetic resources conserved in *ex situ* and *in situ* conditions, its derived products or, if it be the case, its intangible components, with the purpose of research, biological prospecting, conservation, industrial application or commercial use, among others' (Article 1). Its scope establishes that it is 'applicable to genetic resources of which Member States are countries of origin' (Article 3). It is clear from this that Decision 391 applies to all areas within national jurisdiction, with no distinction made as to whether genetic resources are marine, coastal, Andean or Amazonian, or whether resources are located in an ex-situ conservation centre or a protected area.

Decision 391 has but one very clear reference to access to genetic resources in protected areas. The Sixth Complementary Disposition establishes that 'when access is requested for genetic resources or its derived products from protected areas, the applicant will comply with provisions of Decision 391 and with specific national regulations on the matter'. Therefore, not only is an applicant required to undergo regular access procedures established in Decision 391, and therefore obliged to present a formal application and enter into an access contract with the state, they must also comply with national legislation related to research activities in protected areas. Furthermore, if samples were to be collected of CITES protected species, another layer of approval must be sought, and complying with the administrative process becomes even more complex.

The case of Peru offers an example of the increasingly complex structures created for research in protected areas. Through Supreme Decree 010-99-AG of 7 April 1999 the government of Peru approved the Director Plan for Natural Protected Areas, which lays out the policy and regulatory framework for management and administration of the different categories of protected areas in the country. Point 2.3 of Chapter II establishes the specific requirements for general scientific research in protected areas and also specifically refers to biodiversity prospecting. Under this decree, access to genetic resources is subject to the objectives of the protected area, the land-use plan and the management plan for the particular area. These requirements are in addition to those established in Decision 391; but the authority responsible for granting research permits in protected areas (INRENA) is different from the likely access competent authority.

If the process of receiving permits – even for basic academic research – to work in protected areas becomes too complex, researchers might avoid working in these areas. Although the objective – to achieve equitable research relationships and ensure benefit-sharing – is admirable, burdensome regulations and administrative procedures that consume time and imply costs might become a primary obstacle not only for biodiversity prospecting, but also for valuable academic scientific research in protected areas.

A number of protected areas have developed joint management agreements with local communities, and in many areas research activities are undertaken with a significant degree of local participation. In Bwindi Impenetrable National Park (BINP) in Uganda, for example, revenue-sharing and multiple use programmes have helped improve community–park relations and community participation in conservation activities, while enhancing local people's sense of ownership and collective responsibility for the park (see Case Study 6.3; Mutebi et al, 1997). BINP staff are also trying to protect local communities' rights to control access to, and benefit from, their traditional ecological knowledge, as part of wider efforts to set standards for research relationships (see Case Study 6.3).

Throughout the world, protected areas have in many cases been overlaid on lands traditionally used and managed by local communities. Areas viewed as 'pristine wilderness' were often, in fact, territory where local communities gathered products, farmed or fished or were used for a range of cultural purposes (Tuxill and Nabhan, 1998). In the US, for example, the establishment of many national parks – including Yosemite and Yellowstone – involved the expulsion of indigenous people and restriction of traditional hunting and gathering practices (Tuxill and Nabhan, 1998). These lands continue to have cultural importance to contemporary tribal societies. Today, in an effort to better understand the cultural significance of these areas, and to design resource management plans in line with this understanding, the US National Park Service (NPS) funds ethnographic research in collaboration with tribal communities. As part of this research, what is called 'ethnographic resources' are collected through research on specific geographic locations, animal or plant materials, or

mineral deposits important to cultural life (Ruppert, 1994).

But research seeking to better understand the relationship between local communities and resources held in a protected area often raises complex issues of its own. In the Glacier National Park, which has strong historical and contemporary ties to the Blackfeet, Kootenai and Salish tribes, tribal representatives expressed concern about the type of data to be collected by the NPS, the sensitivity of researchers to its meaning for the tribes, and the release of this information into the public domain. For example, information about sacred sites, vision-questing and the use of plants and minerals for ceremonial purposes was considered highly sensitive. Tribal representatives were also wary because many researchers had come through in the past, collecting cultural information, and had provided nothing in return – not even research results. As a result, park researchers and tribal groups developed a memoranda of understanding for the proposed research process (Ruppert, 1994; see Chapter 7). For example, the US National Park Service recently signed a 'Memorandum of Understanding Regarding the Gathering of Plant Resources for American Indian Traditional Cultural–Religious Purposes from National Park Lands with the Kabib Band of Paiute Indians, the San Juan Southern Paiute Tribe, the Moapa Paiute Tribe, the Las Vega Paiute Tribe and the Paiute Indian Tribes of Utah'. This agreement places limits on the amount and type of material collected, and sets terms for the behaviour of researchers during collections.

Indigenous people and local communities often have long historical as well as contemporary relationships with land and resources held in protected areas. Protected area management increasingly

Box 6.5 WWF and IUCN/WCPA Principles on Indigenous/Traditional Peoples and Protected Areas

Principle 1

Indigenous and other traditional peoples have long associations with nature and a deep understanding of it. Often they have made significant contributions to the maintenance of many of the Earth's most fragile ecosystems, through their traditional sustainable resource-use practices and culture-based respect for nature. Therefore, there should be no inherent conflict between the objectives of protected areas and the existence, within and around their borders, of indigenous and other traditional peoples. Moreover, they should be recognized as rightful, equal partners in the development and implementation of conservation strategies that affect their lands, territories, waters, coastal seas and other resources, and in particular in the establishment and management of protected areas.

Principle 2

Agreements drawn up between conservation institutions, including protected-area management agencies, and indigenous and other traditional peoples for the establishment and management of protected areas affecting their lands, territories, waters, coastal seas and other resources should be based on full respect for the rights of indigenous and other traditional peoples to traditional, sustainable use of their lands, territories, waters, coastal seas and other resources. At the same time, such agreements should be based on the recognition by indigenous and other traditional peoples of their responsibility to conserve biodiversity, ecological integrity and natural resources harboured in those protected areas.

Principle 3

The principles of decentralization, participation, transparency and accountability should be taken into account in all matters pertaining to the mutual interests of protected areas and indigenous and other traditional peoples.

Principle 4

Indigenous and other traditional peoples should be able to share fully and equitably in the benefits associated with protected areas, with due recognition to the rights of other legitimate stakeholders.

Principle 5

The rights of indigenous and other traditional peoples in connection with protected areas are often an international responsibility, since many of the lands, territories, waters, coastal seas and other resources which they own or otherwise occupy or use cross national boundaries, as indeed do many of the ecosystems in need of protection.

recognizes this relationship and the importance of bringing local communities on board as stakeholders. Protected areas policies for researchers should also incorporate specific provisions that reflect the rights of communities to be informed, grant consent and share in the benefits from research (see the draft policy in Case Study 6.2). In Cameroon, a tendency for researchers to involve local community members only as porters and guides, and not fully inform them of the nature and extent of research, has raised a great deal of suspicion on the part of local communities and government officials, who conclude that researchers are, in fact, in search of gold or diamonds. This type of confusion obviously creates significant problems for protected area management.

Protected area research policies can make clear to researchers – many of whom will not be familiar with the area or people – the ways in which prior informed consent should be sought, appropriate researcher behaviour and the types of benefits that should be shared. Indigenous peoples' statements and declarations, or other documents appropriate to the local situation, might be appended to a research policy to further guide researchers (see the draft policy in Case Study 6.2). Issues raised by research on indigenous peoples' and local communities' lands, resources and knowledge have been well articulated, and although documents will need modification on a case-by-case basis, they can provide invaluable guidance to researchers and protected areas managers (see Chapter 7).

Research policies and their effective implementation

Protected areas are home to much of the world's biodiversity and the site of a great deal of biodiversity research and some biodiversity prospecting. Protected areas are, in many ways, at the front line of changes in the way genetic resources are viewed and conservation programmes conceived – including the grouping of conservation, sustainable use and equitable benefit-sharing objectives under the Convention on Biological Diversity. At the same time, protected area management and philosophy are undergoing their own – institutionally parallel but closely linked – shift towards greater inclusiveness.

As a result of these factors, there is a growing need for protected areas to rationalize and formalize their relationships with researchers. To this end, written policies – supported by and reflecting international and national law, professional researcher standards for best practice and the concerns of indigenous people and local communities – can prove a valuable tool. Research policies bring transparency and accountability to research relationships, both for protected area managers and for researchers who complain of unreasonable or unclear expectations on the part of local institutions.

In order to make the most effective use of policies, however, protected area managers must institute the capacity to implement a policy, including processing research applications quickly and efficiently. Under the new protected area and genetic resource exchange paradigms, it is not only researchers who must bear new responsibilities, but protected areas as well – for building internal capacity, achieving efficiency and transparency in process and the effective sharing of benefits to serve conservation and sustainable use objectives. Researchers asked to share benefits should be able to feel that their contributions are effectively and transparently managed, and are applied to shared conservation objectives. Protected areas policies should account for national-level systems of permitting, and the approval and agreement process should integrate affected government ministries, where possible, to allow for a streamlined approach. This requires a concerted effort to develop administrative and institutional capacity, including the following:

- build know-how within protected area and government staff relating to equitable research relationships and access and benefit-sharing issues under the CBD;
- establish a multistakeholder scientific council, or comparable body, to set priorities for research, draft and implement research policies, monitor research relationships and oversee sharing of benefits; composition of this body might include protected areas managers, as well as representatives from government ministries, active institutional collaborators and researchers, local communities and NGOs;

- help to establish a streamlined permitting process that efficiently, and with transparency, integrates the range of relevant governmental, protected area and local community requirements and regulations;
- establish trust funds or other bodies to manage financial benefits;
- institute an ongoing process of capacity-building, and policy and institutional review and development.

Notes

1 This case study was undertaken by WWF, with support from the Danish Agency for Development Assistance (DANIDA), as part of the Implementing the Convention on Biological Diversity Project.

2 This case study was carried out on behalf of WWF EARPO.

3 This case study summarizes a submission to the Executive Secretary of the Convention on Biological Diversity by RBG, Kew, 22 April 1998. The original study was based on an involved research process, including interviews with: Terrance Bruggeman, Eric Mathur and Carolyn Ericson, Diversa Corporation; Preston Scott, World Foundation for Environment and Development (WFED); John Varley and Robert Lindstrom, Yellowstone Center for Resources; Peter Thomas, US Department of State; Daniel Piller, Hoffman-LaRoche; Andrew Kimbrell, International Centre for Technology Assessment (ICTA); and Leslie Platt, American Type Culture Collection (ATCC).

4 Text of standard letter from the Yellowstone Park superintendent to cooperating researchers, Ref N2621 (YELL) and Environmental Law Institute, 1996.

5 'Research Authorization', 'Request to Perform Research in Yellowstone National Park', 'Permit Application', National Park Service, Yellowstone Centre for Resources, PO Box 168, Yellowstone National Park, WY 82190

6 Title 36 of the CFR, the Enabling Act of the National Park Service and the National Parks Organic Act (1916) define YNP's operational parameters.

7 Information provided by Preston Scott, WFED, March 1998.

Section III

COMMUNITY RELATIONSHIPS WITH RESEARCHERS

Photograph by Patricia Shanley

Women with copaiba oil, tapped from a forest tree in Capim, Brazil. Processing and marketing non-timber forest products is one element of a project that seeks to build on research to help local communities with their development and conservation objectives

Chapter 7

Building equitable research relationships with indigenous peoples and local communities: prior informed consent and research agreements

Sarah A Laird and Flavia Noejovich

Introduction

This chapter examines two elements of equitable relationships between researchers and indigenous peoples and local communities currently under discussion and development: prior informed consent (PIC) and research agreements. There is a rich and growing body of literature on wider issues raised by biodiversity research and prospecting, and indigenous peoples and local communities. Within this chapter we will not adequately reflect this body of work, and refer readers to the References section at the end of this book which includes many useful citations on these subjects. Aspects of and issues raised by these relationships are also addressed in other chapters in this manual, including those on biodiversity research relationships (see Chapters 1–5), contracts (see Chapter 9) and national measures (see Chapter 12).

We begin by briefly covering the legal and policy context in which these relationships occur, including human, cultural and environmental rights that provide the foundation for equitable relationships. We then explore PIC and effective consultations throughout the research process. The elements of research agreements are discussed, supported by case studies from South Africa and Fiji, followed by annexes that examine the realization of PIC in the field, and review issues relating to research relationships raised in indigenous peoples' declarations and statements.

Box 7.1 provides examples of definitions of the terms 'local communities' and one type of local community – 'indigenous peoples'. These terms have different meanings and implications in different countries and regions around the world. There is great diversity not only between, but also within communities. Communities might be rural, small and marginalized, or live in proximity to large urban areas with many members living in cities, some as government officials. Members of communities – old and young, male and female, wealthy and poor, the healer and the councillor, and so on – might have dramatically different perspectives and agendas. As a result, it is

---

BOX 7.1 INDIGENOUS PEOPLES AND LOCAL COMMUNITIES: DEFINITIONS

Tribal peoples: tribal peoples in independent countries whose social, cultural and economic conditions distinguish them from other sections of the national community, and whose status is regulated wholly or partially by their own customs or traditions or by special laws or regulations (ILO Convention 169).

Indigenous peoples: peoples in independent countries who are regarded as indigenous on account of their descent from the populations who inhabited the country, or a geographical region to which the country belongs, at the time of conquest, or colonization, or the establishment of present state boundaries, and who, irrespective of their legal status, retain some or all of their own social, economic, cultural and political institutions (ILO Convention 169).

Indigenous cultural communities or indigenous peoples: a homogeneous society identified by self-ascription and ascription by others which has continuously lived as a community on communally bounded and defined territory, sharing common bonds of language, customs, traditions and other distinctive cultural traits, and which through resistance to the political, social and cultural inroads of colonization, became historically differentiated from the majority of Filipinos (Department Administrative Order, No 96-20, Section 2.1 'Implementing Rules and Regulations for Executive Order 247, the Philippines').

Indigenous and local communities: indigenous, Afro-American and local communities are human groups whose social, cultural and economic conditions distinguish them from other sectors of the national community, who are governed totally or partially by their own customs or traditions or special legislation, and who, regardless of their legal status, conserve their own social, economic, cultural and political institutions or parts thereof (Decision 391, Andean Pact).

Local community and indigenous population: a human group differentiated by its social, cultural and economic conditions, organized, in total or in part, according to its own customs and traditions or by special legislation, and preserving, regardless of legal status, separate social, economic and cultural institutions, or parts thereof (Draft Brazil Bill of Law No 306/95).

Local community: a group of people having a long-standing social organization that binds them together whether in a defined area or otherwise; it shall include indigenous peoples and local populations, and shall where appropriate refer to any organization duly registered under the provisions of this act to represent its interest (Community Intellectual Rights Act, 1994, Third World Network).

---

extremely difficult to generalize about what constitutes a 'community' and an equitable research relationship with local groups. Annex 7.1 provides ample evidence and argument for a cautious approach to this type of generalization.

At the same time, it is very difficult to generalize about the scale and nature of research addressed in this chapter. Research involving indigenous peoples and local communities might do so in a number of ways, including:

- basic natural science (eg geological mapping, studies of evolution, animal behaviour or ecological relationships, such as gap dynamics) that involves seeking access to local peoples' territory and resources, and often the collection of samples to be stored in ex-situ collections;
- academic research in ethnoecology, anthropology or other fields that involve the direct study of local cultures as well as land and resources;
- research undertaken by conservation groups or others seeking to build upon and apply traditional knowledge to local or national conservation and development problems; and
- commercial research undertaken on behalf of companies that involves seeking access to people's land, and the collection of samples and often knowledge.

The same underlying principles for equity apply in all cases (for an indicative list, see those in the International Society of Ethnobiology's *Code of Ethics*, and Inuit Tapirisat, 1993); but the research process involves communities and accesses knowledge and resources in different ways.

Research projects vary not only in approach, but also in size, longevity and the number and type of researchers or staff involved. For example, researchers might be students or professional academics, or might work for companies; a project may run for ten years or one month, and may involve 20 field collectors or a single graduate student. Research may or may not involve collections of samples (see Chapter 1; Pew Scholars, 1996). Commercial research, in particular, gives rise to a range of unique considerations; issues involved in negotiations and contracts between companies and local communities are addressed in Chapter 9.

This chapter provides a general overview relevant to a cross-section of researcher–community relationships. There are many dangers that emerge when employing a generalized approach of this kind, and it is hoped that communities and researchers will not take the following as a prescription or model. Rather, we suggest that readers pick and choose, pulling from the material as is found useful, following up with suggested readings and contacting the groups mentioned for further elucidation and advice.

The legal and policy context

During the last decade the development and implementation of environmental law has increasingly reflected the close relationship between the environment and human rights. The documents adopted at the United Nations Conference on Environment and Development (UNCED) in Rio de Janeiro in 1992, for example, straddle environment, trade and human rights law. Indigenous peoples and local communities have also been more widely

incorporated into the environmental policy-development process and programmes that work to encourage sustainable use of resources. Within international fora such as the Convention on Biological Diversity (CBD) Conference of the Parties (COP), the Intergovernmental Panel on Forests and the Food and Agriculture Organization (FAO) Commission on Plant Genetic Resources, and more recently the dialogue initiated

BOX 7.2 THE AYAHUASCA PATENT CASE: INDIGENOUS PEOPLE'S STAND AGAINST MISAPPROPRIATION

Glenn Wiser (Center for International Environmental Law)

For centuries, shamans of indigenous tribes throughout the Amazon Basin have processed the bark of *Banisteriopsis caapi*, along with other rainforest plants, to produce a ceremonial drink known as 'ayahuasca' or 'yagé'. The shamans use *ayahuasca* in religious and healing ceremonies to diagnose and treat illnesses, meet with spirits and divine the future. According to tradition, *ayahuasca* – which means 'vine of the soul' in the Quechua language – is prepared and administered only under the guidance of a shaman. Indigenous peoples have characterized the *ayahuasca* vine as a religious and cultural symbol analogous to the Christian cross or Eucharist.

The Coordinating Body of Indigenous Organizations of the Amazon Basin (COICA), an umbrella group that represents over 400 indigenous tribes of the region, was thus stunned to learn in 1994 that an American citizen, Loren Miller, had obtained a US plant patent on a purported variety of *B. caapi*, which he dubbed 'Da Vine'. Miller propagated his plant from a cutting acquired from an indigenous person's garden in Ecuador. He claimed in his patent application that the plant had a different physical appearance from other forms of *caapi* and was 'being investigated for its medicinal value in cancer treatment and psycho-therapy'. However, neither he nor his company, International Plant Medicine Corp, ever developed any commercial applications from the patent.

After prolonged and often heatedly acrimonious exchanges, COICA failed to convince Miller to voluntarily relinquish his patent. Consequently, COICA, joined by the Coalition for Amazonian Peoples and Their Environment and the Centre for International Environmental Law, filed a request before the US Patent and Trademark Office (PTO) asking the PTO to reexamine the patent and cancel it. Agreeing with the requesters that they had raised 'substantial new questions of patentability', the PTO granted their request for a reexamination and subsequently rejected Miller's patent claim on 3 November 1999.

COICA noted in its reexamination request that the Plant Patent Act was designed to reward the efforts of growers who develop new varieties of crops, such as fruit trees or grapevines. The act thus requires applicants to show that a plant is a new variety, distinct from other forms, and not found in an uncultivated state. In his patent application, Miller claimed that 'Da Vine' had new and distinctive physical features from other forms of *B. caapi*, particularly in its flower colour. But according to Professor William A Anderson of the University of Michigan, a leading expert on the plant family to which *B. caapi* belongs, the features described in the patent are typical of the species as a whole, and were documented as 'prior art' in the specimen collections of major US herbaria. Concurring that it could see no patentable distinctions between those specimens and 'Da Vine', the PTO admitted that Miller's claim failed to satisfy the Plant Patent Act. This is apparently the first time that the PTO has broadened the concept of prior art to include mounted herbarium specimen sheets.

Although the PTO rejected the *ayahuasca* patent claim, its decision highlights several shortcomings of the reexamination process as it currently stands. The PTO agreed with COICA that medical or therapeutic use could not have formed the basis for granting the patent, because Miller's claim merely alleged that 'Da Vine' had useful medical characteristics without stating in any way how they might be new and distinct from those characteristics found in other forms of *caapi*. But in doing so, the PTO managed to side step the question of whether the knowledge and use of a plant by generations of indigenous peoples should constitute prior art under the patent rules.

The PTO also determined that two specimen sheets accessioned by major herbaria more than a year before the 'Da Vine' patent was filed – but after the filing of an earlier application that was subsequently abandoned – were not 'bona fide prior art references'. But the only publication that Miller relied upon to establish the putative difference of his plant was also published after the earlier application date. This inconsistent treatment allows patent applicants to 'grandfather' the effective cut-off date for prior art by abandoning an application in favour of a new one, and then supporting their new claims by picking favourable prior art while ignoring unfavourable prior art.

This treatment of prior art indicates other, serious problems. By law, plant patents cannot be awarded for plants 'found in an uncultivated state'. But in order to challenge a patent such as Miller's on the grounds that a plant is found in an uncultivated state, a requester must produce prior-art 'printed publications' demonstrating that the plant occurs naturally (as *B. caapi* does). Such publications might not have existed at the time a patent application was filed. Accordingly, an applicant such as Miller could obtain a wild, previously undescribed plant, distinguish it by comparing it to varieties that *had* been described, assert it had been obtained from an indigenous person's garden, and then claim it as a new variety eligible for plant patent protection. Even if someone could later prove that the patented plant occurred naturally in the wild, the PTO would not grant a reexamination request on that basis unless the requester could submit prior-art printed publications dating from before the original application submission. The PTO apparently believes this scenario is perfectly acceptable under the law. It took at face value Miller's assertion in his application that 'Da Vine' had been 'discovered growing in a domestic garden in the Amazon rainforest of South America'. In the PTO's opinion, the origins of a plant and the question of whether it is identical to plants growing wild nearby are irrelevant to patentability.

The *ayahuasca* patent case is a rare example of the reexamination process actually working to protect the interests of indigenous and local communities. The applicant's abuse of the Plant Patent Act was apparent, the affected indigenous peoples were unusually well organized, and their legal arguments were clearly documented by prior-art references in a form acceptable to the PTO. Most cases in which corporations appropriate indigenous knowledge through the patent laws are less clear cut. The law assumes that anyone whose interests are harmed by a patent will object to it through the existing legal processes. But that ignores the reality that indigenous peoples throughout the developing world usually have no means of discovering that their biological and/or genetic resources have been claimed by US commercial interests. (It took COICA eight years to find out about Miller's patent.) Even if they do, they will rarely have the financial resources to successfully prosecute an objection. Moreover, the standards for prior art place them at an even greater disadvantage, because the PTO does not recognize their unwritten knowledge, practices and innovations as prior art upon which a reexamination request can be granted. Until the PTO reevaluates its policy in light of the needs of such peoples, and until a reliable system exists that both respects the concerns of indigenous peoples and allows patent examiners to verify whether a patent claim is relying upon their traditional knowledge, abuses of the system will likely continue.

Note: For more information and updates on this case, contact: Glenn Wiser at the Centre for International Environmental Law, Washington, DC, and visit the CIEL website at www.ciel.org/biodiversity/BiodiversityIntellectualProperty.html.

Box 7.3 What is Traditional Ecological Knowledge?

Traditional ecological knowledge (TEK) is also known as cultural knowledge, folk ecology, ethnoecology, traditional environmental knowledge, indigenous knowledge and knowledge of the land. Martha Johnson of the Dene Cultural Institute in Yellowknife, Canada (1992) defines TEK as:

> '...a body of knowledge built up by a group of people through generations of living in close contact with nature. It includes a system of classification, a set of empirical observations about the local environment, and a system of self-management that governs resource use. The quantity and quality of TEK varies among community members, depending upon gender, age, social status, intellectual capability and profession (hunter, spiritual leader, healer, etc). With its roots firmly in the past, traditional environmental knowledge is both cumulative and dynamic, building upon the experience of earlier generations and adapting to the new technological and socioeconomic changes of the present.'

Traditional resources?

Traditional resources are tangible and intangible assets and attributes deemed to be of value to indigenous and local communities, including spiritual, aesthetic, cultural and economic. Resources describe all that sustain communal identity, express history, are manifest in nature and life, sustain the pride of unique heritage, maintain a healthy environment, and from which emerge sacred and spiritual values. 'Traditional', according to the Four Directions Council, is the 'established and respected social process of learning and sharing knowledge that is unique to each indigenous culture'. Traditional resources include plants, animals and other material objects that have sacred, ceremonial, heritage or aesthetic and religious qualities, as well as economic and social values (Posey, 1996).

within the World Intellectual Property Organization (WIPO), indigenous peoples and community groups have argued for and secured greater awareness of their rights. At the same time, these groups have developed internal capacity and external collaborations necessary to defend these rights, including, in some cases, bringing legal action to defend their traditional knowledge. For example, patents on indigenous knowledge and resources have recently been challenged, including that filed for *ayahuasca*, a sacred plant used for generations by indigenous peoples in South America (see Box 7.2).

The rights of indigenous peoples and local communities to protect their collec-tive property has been recognized in international conventions such as the 1993 Convention on Biological Diversity (Articles 8 (j) and 10 (c)), the 1994 Convention on Desertification and Drought and the 1989 International Labour Organization Convention 169 Concerning Indigenous Peoples. As yet, however, no international legal mechanism unequivocally recognizes the inviolable property rights of indigenous peoples over their collective traditional knowledge (Posey, 1996), although at a national level the Peruvian Biodiversity Law clearly recognizes indigenous knowledge as the 'cultural patrimony' of the people who hold it (see Chapter 13). It is widely felt that in order to effectively and comprehensively recognize and protect the traditional resource rights of indigenous peoples, a sui generis system must be developed that incorporates the unique considerations associated with traditional ecological knowledge (TEK) (see Box 7.3) and biological resources (Posey, 1996; Posey and Dutfield, 1996; Nijar, 1996; Tobin, 1997).

'Indigenous peoples are entitled to the recognition of the full ownership, control and protection of their cultural and intellectual property. They have the right to special measures to control, develop and protect their sciences, technologies and cultural manifestations, including human and other genetic resources, seeds, medicines, knowledge of the properties of fauna and flora, oral traditions, literature, designs, and visual and performing arts' UN Draft Declaration on the Rights of Indigenous Peoples (1993).

International policy processes have introduced equity and resource rights-based vocabulary into the everyday language of scientists, non-governmental organizations (NGOs), and governments. National consultations for access and benefit-sharing measures commonly incorporate terms such as *participation*, *consultation*, *benefit-sharing*, *prior informed consent* and *equitable*. These terms reflect an evolving view of biodiversity and natural resource conservation that is increasingly linked to community empowerment, resources rights and a vision of sustainable development that incorporates respect for, and benefit-sharing with, traditional stewards, managers and owners of resources and knowledge.

Table 7.1 includes some of the more significant bodies of international and national law that converge to create the legal and

'Subject to its national legislation, respect, preserve and maintain knowledge, innovations and practices of indigenous and local communities embodying traditional lifestyles relevant for the conservation and sustainable use of biological diversity and promote their wider application with the approval and involvement of the holders of such knowledge innovations and practices and encourage the equitable sharing of benefits arising from the utilization of such knowledge, innovations and practices' Article 8 (j) of the Convention on Biological Diversity.

policy environment in which academic and commercial research with indigenous peoples and local communities takes place. National access and benefit-sharing measures are addressed in Chapter 12, and a range of 'soft law' documents, such as codes of conduct and institutional policies, are covered in Chapters 1–5.[1]

Rights underlying equitable partnerships and collaborations

Equitable research relationships are most likely to result when based on a bundle of basic rights, including rights to self-determination, autonomy and territory, as well as basic human and cultural rights (Posey, 1996; ISE, 1998). As stated by the International Alliance of Indigenous Tribal Peoples of the Tropical Forests and the International Working Group for Indigenous Affairs (1997):

Table 7.1 *International and national laws that impact research relationships*

International conventions*	'Soft law'**	Bodies of national and state law
Convention on Biological Diversity (CBD), 1992	Rio Declaration, 1992	Access and benefit-sharing measures (Chapter 13).
UN Convention to Combat Desertification in Countries Experiencing Serious Drought and/or Desertification, Particularly in Africa, 1994	Agenda 21, 1992	Intellectual property rights, including industrial property law, patent law, trademarks, denomination of origin, plant breeders' rights, etc
International Labor Organization (ILO) Convention 169 Concerning Indigenous Peoples in Independent Countries, 1989	Forest Principles, 1992	Natural resource and environmental regulations (eg forestry, wildlife, water and fishing, biodiversity, conservation and protected areas, agriculture, wildlife)
UN International Covenant on Civil and Political Rights	Universal Declaration of Human Rights, 1948	Measures for the protection of traditional knowledge (eg Peru's draft Indigenous Knowledge Law; Biodiversity Law 7788, Costa Rica; Andean Pact Decision 391; the Philippines Executive Order 247; Peru's Biodiversity Law 26839)
UN International Covenant on Economic, Social and Cultural Rights (ECOSOC)	UN Draft Declaration on the Rights of Indigenous Peoples, 1994	Land tenure
	United Nations Educational, Social and Cultural Organization's (UNESCO's) cultural documents (eg 1985 UNESCO and World Intellectual Property Organization – WIPO – Model Provisions for National Laws on Protection of Expressions of Folklore Against Illicit Exploitation and Other Prejudicial Actions)	Laws for the protection of the rights of indigenous peoples (eg over land, natural resources, customary law, provisions for participation and consultation)
	Declaration on Indigenous Peoples (Organization of African Unity – OAU)	Constitutions
	Food and Agriculture Organization (FAO) International Code of Conduct for Plant Germplasm Collecting and Transfer	Aboriginal treaties (in some countries)

Note: * International conventions are legally binding.
** Soft laws do not legally bind signatory governments, but they do place a moral obligation to conform with their provisions upon parties, and in many cases convert into compulsory norms over time.

'Any discussion on indigenous peoples and forests has to address the totality of our rights: our identity as peoples, our territoriality, our cultural heritage, our customary law and our political institutions which are framed by our fundamental right to self-determination... Partnership and participation can only take place between equals and in conditions where our fundamental rights remain intact. We are rightsholders, not stakeholders. No activity should take place on our territories without our free and informed consent; we insist that we have the right to control our own resources.'

Additional rights that underlie equitable research relationships include community rights to control traditional knowledge and natural resources; access to information; consultation over activities relating to natural resource exploration and exploitation in indigenous and community territory; alternative systems for conflict resolution; as well as recognition of indigenous customary law that incorporates the collective nature of certain rights. Time and practice have demonstrated that equitable relationships are most effectively established with prior and careful recognition of these basic rights. A study of 15 recent international declarations and statements concerning the rights of indigenous peoples was undertaken to elucidate the views and primary concerns associated with research relationships, and these are summarized in Annex 7.2 (Dutfield, Annex 2).

Prior informed consent and consultation

It is now widely accepted that the participation of local communities and indigenous peoples in projects relating to natural resource use on their lands, including research, is not only a requirement for the exercise of other important human rights but also provides substantial benefits for the project. These include enhancing possibilities for effective implementation of projects, eliminating potential conflicts, securing the confidence of local populations and local buy-in to the proposal and promoting greater understanding between the parties (World Bank, 1996; Borrini-Feyerabend, 1997; Tobin et al, 1998). International agreements such as the ILO Convention 169 make direct reference to the rights of indigenous peoples to participation and consultation. As a result, there exist an increasing number of valuable experiences regarding consultation between public and private sector actors and indigenous peoples that can inform the process through which researchers consult with communities (eg Barsh and Bastien, 1997; Emery, 1997).

Community 'participation' can take many forms and, in practice, has different meanings. In the context of receiving PIC for research, we simplify a very complex area into the following categories:

- information distribution: a one-way flow of information from one party to another;
- consultation: a two-way flow of information between parties in a manner that assists in subsequent decision-making;

- negotiation: a meeting of 'equals' in which the intended products are legally binding agreements that respect and define rights and obligations between parties for the future (see Chapter 10 on commercial contracts);
- collaboration: a joint venture, or joint decision-making process in which all parties have an equal say in the development of a project;
- community controlled research or 'empowerment': when decision-making and design are in the hands of communities.

Information distribution is not a sufficient means by which communities can grant informed consent for research activities. *Consultation* and *collaboration* are the most common ways in which researchers will seek PIC and research agreements will be developed. *Community controlled research* is today an exceptional, if increasingly important, form of research. Community controlled research occurs when communities set research agendas and the terms for research collaborations. Community controlled research can include self-demarcation, inventories of traditional resources, environmental/social impact assessments and resource management plans (Posey, 1995). The Kuna Yala in Panama, for example, launched a programme in 1983 to establish and manage a forest reserve, including conducting interdisciplinary research to assist in forest management (see Box 7.4). The Inuit of Nunavik in northern Quebec, Canada, initiated a large-scale research programme in order to develop a database on their use and knowledge of the land base and resources, in order to help with the management and sustainable development of Nunavik (Simon and Brooke, IUCN, 1997). In India, a People's Biodiversity Registers Programme is underway to document and provide a record of local

knowledge, revitalize local knowledge, alert conservationists of the need to protect knowledge as well as resources, and to protect local biodiversity and knowledge from misappropriation by companies. Protocols guiding the collection and dissemination of data are currently under development (Gadgil, 1998).

Limitations to achieving true community participation are many, however, and terms such as 'consultation' and 'participation' are easily coopted by powerful state and private-sector actors who seek to force unwanted projects on communities (Pimbert and Pretty, 1995). Limitations include the following (Borrini-Feyerabend, 1997):

- Full local participation and empowerment are best developed in democratic societies.
- The concept of participation may be alien to some cultures and groups.
- National governments may not support local participation and empowerment, particularly if they regard them as threats to their own authority.
- A participatory approach may not be viable because of local political opposition and lack of institutional support.
- Participatory processes require investment of time and resources that may not be available.
- The process of participation often requires expert facilitation and clear objectives, in order to avoid chaotic meetings and general loss of direction for the initiative.

Prior informed consent

Research tends to be most valuable for local groups when they are actively involved in the design or management of a research programme. In most cases,

BOX 7.4 THE KUNA YALA

In Panama, the Kuna Yala launched an initiative in 1983 to set aside 60,000 hectares of forest as a nature reserve, and to document their resources and knowledge using integrated Kuna and Western scientific techniques. To do this, they realized that they would need to set standards for the practices of outside researchers, with whom they collaborate. The Kuna Yala design of a researcher–community relationship has served as the basis for a number of other communities developing written agreements with researchers.

The manual *Programa de Investigacion Monitoreo y Cooperacion Cientifica* provides an outline of Kuna objectives with regard to forest management, the conservation of biological and cultural diversity, scientific collaboration and research priorities, and establishes guidance for researchers, including the types of benefits that must accrue to the Kuna. It recognizes the need for collaborations between Kuna and Western scientists in order to better document and manage their cultural and natural resources. However, all research is geared toward providing the Kuna with the information necessary to better manage their forests and marine resources, and in some cases to revive local cultural traditions. Guidelines for visiting scientists include the following requirements:

- Develop a proposal outlining the timing, extent and potential environmental and cultural impact of a research programme. This must then be approved by the Scientific Committee of PEMANSKY (the Study for the Management of the Forested Area of the Kuna Territory).
- Provide PEMANSKY with written reports of the research and two copies of any publications in Spanish.
- Provide PEMANSKY with copies of photographs or slides taken during the research programme.
- Include in their research programme Kuna collaborators, assistants, guides and informants, and undertake training in relevant scientific disciplines.
- Provide descriptions of all species new to science.
- Receive approval for the collection of species from the Scientific Committee of PEMANSKY. All collections must be done in a non-destructive manner, may not include any endangered species and may not be used for commercial purposes. Samples of all collected specimens must be left with PEMANSKY to be added to collections at the University of Panama.
- Undergo an orientation into the culture of the Kuna Yala, and respect the norms of the communities in which they work.

The procedures also forbid the introduction of exotic plant or animal species, or the manipulation of genes. Research is restricted to certain areas of the reserve, is prohibited in some sites, such as ceremonial or sacred sites, and is controlled in other specific sites, such as some forest areas under community management.

Source: PEMANSKY, 1988; Chapin, 1991

however, research agendas will be set by researchers, who must then consult with communities to receive their PIC for the proposed activities. The term **prior informed consent** broadly means the consent of a party to an activity that is given after receiving full disclosure regarding the reasons for the activity, the specific procedures the activity would entail, the potential risks involved and the full implications that can realistically be foreseen.

In the Convention on Biological Diversity, Article 15 requires that 'Access to genetic resources shall be subject to prior informed consent of the Contracting Party providing such resources, unless otherwise determined by that Party' (Article 15.5). In some national access and benefit-sharing measures written to implement the Convention – such as those of the Philippines and the Andean Pact countries – the requirement PIC has been extended to local communities. In this way, 'tiers' of required PIC have been established. An academic or commercial researcher must receive PIC from both the government and the local communities whose resources or knowledge are to be collected. However, the process by which academic and commercial researchers obtain the PIC of local communities remains unclear in most countries.

PIC will most effectively take place within a dynamic consultative process. The term PIC can suggest something that is completed and not revisited. However, in practice research relationships require ongoing revision over time in light of changing and evolving circumstances, and informed consent will be necessary at a number of stages in the research process. It is unlikely that all issues that might arise in the course of a research project will be anticipated prior to initiation of that project. Having said this, the first level of PIC – that provided prior to the initiation of work – will require disclosure of information and communication of objectives. Posey and Dutfield (1996) recommend full disclosure of the following, in writing, in the local language:

- the purpose of the activity;
- the identity of those carrying out the activity and its sponsors, if different;
- the benefits for the people or person whose consent is being requested;
- possible alternative activities and procedures;
- any risks entailed by the activity;
- discoveries made in the course of the activity that might affect the willingness of the people to continue to cooperate;
- the destination of knowledge or material that is to be acquired, its ownership status and the rights of local people to it once it has left the community;
- any commercial interest that the performers and sponsors have in the activity and in the knowledge or material acquired; and
- the legal options available to the community if it refuses to allow the activity.

In a similar vein, the Pew Scholars Initiative (1996), in its *Proposed Guidelines for Researchers and Local Communities Interested in Accessing, Exploring and Studying Biodiversity*, suggest the following initial disclosure of information. The researcher:

- should carry out all communications in the local language;
- must explain the nature and purpose of the proposed research, including its duration, the geographic area in which research would take place, and research and collecting methods;
- must explain the foreseeable consequences of the research for resources, people and accessors, including the potential commercial value;
- should explain the potential non-commercial values, such as academic recognition and advancement for the researcher;

- should explain any social and/or cultural risks;
- must notify the community at large by some means (eg public meeting);
- should consider explaining the guidelines that the researcher is following, as well as his/her practice in previous similar research projects;
- should be willing to provide copies of relevant project documents, or summaries thereof, preferably including the project budget, in the local language; in the case of commercial prospecting, researchers must share such documents;
- must agree on a protocol of acknowledgements, citation, authorship, inventorship as applicable, either citing local innovators or conservators or respecting requests for anonymity;
- must share findings at different stages with the providers;
- must not engage in bribery or making false promises.

In many cases, the initial step of granting PIC – undertaken as part of early consultations – should be followed by a series of consultations during the course of the research project. For example, in *Negotiating Research Relationships in the North*, the Inuit Tapirisat of Canada (1993) begin with the requirement of PIC, but move on to calls for more involved consultation, including the collaborative design of research to serve community needs, benefit-sharing and monitoring and evaluation:

- Informed consent should be obtained from the community and from any individuals involved in research.
- In seeking informed consent, the researcher should at least explain the purpose of the research; sponsors of the research; the person in charge; potential benefits and possible

problems associated with the research for people and the environment; research methodology; and the participation of, or contact with, residents of the community.
- Anonymity and confidentiality must be offered and, if accepted, guaranteed except where this is legally precluded.
- Ongoing communication of research objectives, methods, findings and interpretation from inception to completion of projects should occur.
- If, during the research, the community decides the research is unacceptable, the research should be suspended.
- Serious efforts must be made to include local and traditional knowledge in all stages of research, including problem identification.
- Research design should endeavour to anticipate and provide meaningful training of aboriginal researchers.
- Research must avoid social disruption.
- Research must respect the privacy, dignity, cultures, traditions and rights of aboriginal people.
- Written information should be available in the appropriate language(s).
- The peer review process must be communicated to the communities, and their advice and/or participation sought in the process.
- Aboriginal people should have access to research data, not just receive summaries and research reports. The extent of data accessibility that participants/communities can expect should be clearly stated and agreed upon as part of any approval process.

PIC of research participants has long been an important issue in academic research circles, but the importance of the concept has grown lately in discussions surrounding ethics (Wax, 1987; Hill, 1987; see Chapters 1 and 2). The American Anthropological Association (AAA) Code of Ethics, for example, states that anthropological researchers 'should obtain in advance the informed consent of persons being studied, providing information, owning or controlling access to material being studied, or otherwise identified as having interests which might be impacted by the research'. The code goes on to emphasize that the process of receiving PIC is dynamic and continuous, and should begin in the stages of project design and continue through implementation 'by way of dialogue and negotiation with those studied'. Informed consent in the AAA's code of ethics is not considered to necessarily imply or require a particular written or signed form, and the emphasis is on the 'quality' of the consent, rather than the 'format'.

Broader consultation

Informed consent, therefore, should be sought both prior to and throughout implementation of a research project, as part of dynamic consultations (see Box 7.5). It is a process, rather than an event, that 'should evolve and develop throughout the lifetime of a project' (see Case Study 7.1; see also Annex 7.1). Through consultations, communities participate in a project – via workshops, meetings, public audiences, informal discussion and other means – well beyond 'simply informing the community' of plans or 'taking community members into account as experts on local conditions and priorities' (Schwartz and Deruyterre, 1996). The Inuit Circumpolar Conference describes consultation as a process extending through all stages of a study, from the earliest seeking of PIC, through data collection and the use and application of findings (see Box 7.6; Brooke, 1993). In the *International Society of Ethnobiology* (ISE) *Code of Ethics* (1998), this process is referred to as 'the Dynamic Interactive Cycle', in which 'all projects must be seen as cycles of continuous and ongoing dialogue' (see Chapter 2).

Consultations between researchers and communities involve cross-cultural communication, in which 'one person's knowledge base is packaged and transferred (communicated) in a form that others may understand and from which they can derive meaning to enrich their (different) knowledge base' (Borrini-

---

BOX 7.5 WHAT IS 'CONSULTATION'?

Consultation provides to the party consulted notice of a matter to be decided in sufficient form and detail, and with enough time, in order to allow that party to prepare its views on the matter. It offers an opportunity to present such views to the party obliged to consult, and full and fair consideration by the party obliged to consult of any views presented (the Yukon Umbrella Agreement in Canada, Emery, 1997).

Public consultation is 'the process of engaging affected people and other interested parties in open dialogue through which a range of views and concerns can be expressed in order to inform decision-making and help build consensus. To be meaningful, consultation should be carried out in a culturally appropriate manner, with information in local languages distributed in advance' (IFC, 1998).

'Community consultation means that the community, planners and lending agency staff enter into a dialogue in which the community's ideas and priorities help shape projects. The final design of the project reflects community responses received during consultative dialogues' (Schwartz and Deruyterre, IDB, 1996).

Box 7.6 The Inuit Circumpolar Conference: Guidelines for effective consultation

The Inuit Circumpolar Conference produced a report for the Arctic Environmental Protection Strategy (AEPS) that included guidelines for the stages and elements of working with indigenous peoples and indigenous knowledge. The following steps were included under the design and consultative process stages.

Design stage

A research committee is formed and ethical and methodological guidelines are defined through a participatory process involving all stakeholders.

Research committee

The research committee designs and oversees all phases of the collection and documentation of indigenous knowledge. It establishes the methods, devises a consultation process and develops a detailed study design that extends to data analysis and presentation of findings. Most importantly, it ensures that the views and priorities of the affected indigenous population are included in the earliest discussions of methodology and project design. The committee reviews objectives, methodologies and procedures which other similar projects have used elsewhere. The research committee comprises representatives of all stakeholders from the communities, region and economy covered by the study.

Consultation

The consultation process extends through all stages of the study, including: discussion about concerns or points of view that give shape and definition to the research project; setting research priorities and study objectives; identifying the study components and procedures for data collection and analysis; interpreting findings and drawing conclusions; applying the findings and conclusions; and monitoring their application in any work or project resulting from the study.

Establishing ethical guidelines

Through a consultative process, the research committee establishes and enforces ethical guidelines and codes of conduct governing the research. Ethical guidelines for researcher behaviour recognize the need for full negotiation by affected indigenous peoples through all stages of the research process. They also reflect indigenous concerns about political implications of research projects carried out on their territories, and about the way research findings are used. Guidelines are needed in order to safeguard access to data and information while at the same time controlling their use.

Preparing a field guide

Preparation of a field guide forms part of the consultation process. Its purpose is to explain the research project to all participants in the research process, including: the need for the research; its objectives; methods and procedures for collecting and processing information; units or categories of information to be collected; and the rights, responsibilities and ethical principles to be respected and adhered to throughout the project.

Source: Brooke, 1993

Feyerabend, 1997). Effective dialogue will require recognition and respect for vastly different fundamental understandings of the universe, customary laws that reflect relationships between man, land and nature, and respect for the decision-making processes and representative structures of local groups (Narby, 1997; Diaz-Polanco, 1995; Emery, 1997; see Annex 7.1). Consultations should make use of existing community-based formal and informal organizational structures, oral communication and time frames appropriate for consensus decision-making and local cultural norms (almost certainly longer than those to which researchers are accustomed). The Resource Management Law reform process in New Zealand, for example, provided a range of alternative mechanisms for Maori participation that responded to Maori cultural preferences, including the following (Crengle, 1997):

- an intensive set of *hui* (meetings) on *marae* (customary community meeting places);
- an open-door policy on accepting and incorporating submissions at any time in the review to more easily accommodate tribal time frames;
- provision of a free phone service for recording oral submissions;
- comprehensive funding and human resource assistance to tribal organizations for preparing written submissions;
- meeting personal and travel costs of participants in *hui*.

There also exists diversity within communities that must be considered during consultations (Four Directions Council, 1996; see Case Study 7.1). For example, an elder might emphasize the long-term effects of a collaboration based on an ability to see many generations into the future, while a project manager will have a more short-term approach; the differing needs of all parties must be satisfied for a project to succeed (Emery, 1997). An example from the Blackfoot Confederacy in North America amply illustrates the complexity in adequately representing the range of individuals and groups within a community (see Box 7.7).

The process of acquiring informed consent and conducting adequate consultations prior to and during

BOX 7.7 THE BLACKFOOT CONFEDERACY

The Blackfoot Confederacy in North America is comprised of several allied nations, each of which is divided into several territorially localized clans. Each nation also has its own unique system of 'societies' that are voluntary associations of women or men who have special skills, knowledge and responsibilities. Although one language is spoken through the confederacy, ecological knowledge is divided among the clans and 'societies'. The natural history of particular places is generally clan-level knowledge. Relationships with the animal and spirit worlds provide knowledge for this purpose. The possession of different kinds of hunting or foraging knowledge, by comparison, varies by species: clans for berries and small animals, 'societies' for some large animals such as bison, and individual specialists for the most powerful animals such as bears. Women tend to hold knowledge of medicinal and food plants, and men possess most knowledge of animals. A complete model of the Blackfoot ecosystem can therefore only be reconstructed through the cooperation of all segments of the population; no one individual or group possesses, or has the right to share, all of the relevant data.

Source: Four Directions Council, 1996

CASE STUDY 7.1 NO QUICK FIX: DESIGNING AGREEMENTS TO SUIT COMPLEX AND DIVERSE SOCIAL CIRCUMSTANCES; THE CASE OF MKAMBATI, SOUTH AFRICA

Thembela Kepe (University of the Western Cape) and Rachel Wynberg (Biowatch South Africa)

Understanding the context

South Africa's post-apartheid government has embarked on several policy-driven programmes that aim to reduce social inequality and to improve the quality of life in poverty-stricken areas. The land reform programme is arguably one of the most challenging tasks. Following more than three centuries of conflict over land, which were characterized by inequality, dispossession and exploitation, the government is currently trying to set right the wrongs of the past. Included in this history is the forced removal of people from their land, which was to become designated for various purposes, including biodiversity conservation (Wynberg and Kepe, 1999). One example of this is the Mkambati Nature Reserve, located on the Wild Coast of the Eastern Cape Province, South Africa. This short case study illustrates some of the lessons that have been gleaned from working with communities in the Mkambati area.

The area known as Mkambati is situated in north-eastern Pondoland and falls within the former Transkei, one of the areas reserved for blacks and given independence by the apartheid government. Mkambati comprises three areas which are under different tenure regimes: the Kanyayo communal settlements, comprising seven villages and about 800 households; 11,000 hectares (ha) of state land used as a parastatal agricultural project; and a 7000ha state-owned nature reserve. The inhabitants of the area are Xhosa-speaking people, who generate their livelihoods through a mixture of arable and livestock farming, the collection of natural resources and a range of off-farm sources, including remittances and pensions (Kepe, 1997). Conflict over land in Mkambati dates back to 1899, when Paramount Chief Sigcawu agreed to the allocation of an area of land for use as a leper colony (Kepe, 1997). The area was demarcated and fenced off in 1920 and subsequently taken over as a nature reserve in 1977, after the health institution had closed down. Currently, there is substantial conflict in the area stemming from competing claims for land rights, and the designation of Mkambati as an anchor project area for the government's Wild Coast Spatial Development Initiative.[2] Kepe (1997) highlights the difficulties of identifying and differentiating between 'communities' contesting for the land and other natural resources, and of the complexity and uncertainties in understanding the term 'community'. These difficulties are further complicated in a society such as South Africa, where transition and rapid social change result in a situation where new communities are emerging and former communities disintegrating (Kepe, 1999). Work with communities in these circumstances is highly challenging and requires an extremely sensitive approach to be taken. These factors are underscored by recent research experiences in the Mkambati area, described below.

Designing a research project

In 1996, a social research project was initiated by the Programme for Land and Agrarian Studies (PLAAS) at the University of the Western Cape, South Africa. The research made use of the environmental entitlements approach to study interactions between livelihoods, social institutions and environmental change on the Wild Coast area. While the study was mainly academic, its main findings were aimed at policy formulation and local resource management strategies. A fundamental component of the research project comprised the development of agreements between researchers and the different social actors within the study area.

Structuring agreements to address concerns

Consent to conduct the research in the area was sought and received from a wide range of social actors who entered into various agreements with the researcher depending upon the different sets of concerns and issues articulated (see Table 7.2). As the following examples show, the nature of the research agreement varied according to the needs and interests of different stakeholders. At Mkambati there was no one community to negotiate with, and each social actor determined a new set of parameters. Although people were, on the one hand, interested in knowing the kind of agreements developed with others (eg household members wanting to know what the chief or political leader said), at the same time they were not prepared to be bound by other people's agreements.

At Mkambati, three main groups of social actors were identified, each group also comprising its own levels of diversity:

1   those involved in managing the two state-run institutions in the area (Mkambati Nature Reserve and Transkei Agricultural Corporation (TRACOR));
2   leaders from the village; and
3   resource users.

Government institutions

Personnel from the two state-run institutions in the area constituted one of the main groups of social actors. For both institutions, verbal agreements were entered into between the researcher and the state institution following lengthy explanations about the research, conveyed through letters, e-mails, telephone conversations and face-to-face meetings. The managers agreed to give the researcher access to geographical areas under their control, on condition that the research activities would not result in substantial social and ecological disturbances within these areas. The researcher, in turn, undertook to share the research findings with the two institutions in the form of publications, a workshop and informal contacts.

Village leadership

A second group of social actors was the village leadership, comprising the chief, headmen and other political leaders. This was the first group of social actors to be consulted within the village. Here proposed research was described to the leadership through an *imbizo*, or villagers' discussion session. With the previous government's history of unwelcome intervention in the area, the leaders were initially concerned that the research may be another ploy by the government to take over control of their natural resources, particularly land, forests and the coastline. Following assurances from the researcher, including the presentation of a letter of introduction from the head of department at the university, some verbal agreements were entered into.

Table 7.2 *Designing agreements in Mkambati*

Social actor	Main issues and concerns	Type of agreement	Elements of the agreement
Government	Research activities should not result in social and ecological disturbances.	Verbal, with each institution	• Government to grant researcher access to study areas. • Researcher undertakes to minimize social and ecological disturbances. • Researcher to share research findings through publications, a workshop and informal contacts.
Village leadership	There was suspicion that the research was another government ploy to take control over the community's natural resources.	Verbal	• There was community support for research provided it did not directly result in loss of control over land resources. • Researcher to conduct research ethically and to seek consent of all those interviewed. • Researcher to conduct workshop on research findings and provide reports. • Researcher to remunerate villagers for goods and services enjoyed.
Resource users:			
Domestic users of medicinal plants	Family-specific knowledge might be divulged.	Verbal	• Users to share experiences and knowledge. • Researcher to treat information with sensitivity and share with people who could positively intervene in the area. • Researcher not to disclose names of users or specific information communicated. • Findings of the study to be shared through a workshop or with individuals.
Gatherers and sellers of medicinal plants	Collectors from other areas would enter the area and compete for limited resources.	Collective, verbal	• Researcher will not intentionally encourage new collectors to the area. • Research findings will emphasize problems experienced by collectors. • Collectors were assured anonymity. • Findings of the study to be shared through a community workshop or with individuals.
Traditional healers	Specialized knowledge would be divulged.	Individual, verbal	• Researcher to focus only on common knowledge in the public domain. • Researcher to pay a consultation fee if requested. • Research findings to be shared with individual healers.
Illegal resource users	Names of individuals and actions would be divulged and lead to prosecution.	Verbal	• Researcher to acknowledge the legitimacy of reasons for illegal use. • Researcher not to divulge names of people or actions. • Resource users to share information and allow observations to be made. • Findings of study to be shared through community workshop.

Firstly, the Kanyayo recorded their support for the research on the condition that it did not directly result in the loss of control over land resources by the villagers. Secondly, the researcher undertook to conduct the research in an ethical manner, to explain the purpose of the work to villagers and to seek the individual consent of all those interviewed during the process. Thirdly, a commitment was made by the researcher to provide reports and to conduct a workshop on the findings of the research with the villagers. Fourthly, the researcher undertook to remunerate villagers properly for all goods and services that the researcher enjoyed, unless it was clearly stated from the onset that the villagers were offering these purely as an act of generosity. Lastly, the Kanyayo leadership agreed to allow the researcher to attend most village meetings, provided that this was not accompanied by any unsolicited interventions by the researcher.

Resource users

A third group of social actors with whom the researcher entered into agreements comprised those utilizing resources in the area. These were the key social actors in the research process, as the study sought to learn from their experiences and analysis with regard to the use of natural resources. Diverse groups of resource users exist in the area, but those collecting and using medicinal plants provide an illustration of the different types of agreements developed with this particular group of social actors.

Three types of users of medicinal plants were identified by the study, each requiring the development of a different research agreement: ordinary villagers who gathered and used medicinal plants for members of the household; people who collected medicinal plants for sale; and traditional healers.

Domestic users of medicinal plants

Medicinal plants were widely gathered and employed for household use in the area by ordinary villlagers. This particular group included adults and children within the household. The most common plants that were collected were those that treated minor ailments such as colds (eg *Artemisia afra* or *umhlonyane*). Most of these plants were very common in the village and could often be found around the homestead. Because people did not really separate the use of medicinal plants from other resources such as fuelwood, research agreements were entered into with this group as part of those developed for the broader household study. Additionally, because most plants were used for common remedies, there was little secrecy accompanying information conveyed. Those families who perceived their knowledge of a certain plant to be special would simply not identify it.

In terms of the general household research agreements, social actors resolved to share their experiences and knowledge with the researcher, especially if it could result in improvements in their livelihoods. The researcher, in turn, undertook to treat the information received with sensitivity and to share it with relevant people who could positively intervene in the area. Household members were also assured that their names or specific information they communicated would not be shared with others (including other villagers and outsiders in general) if they so wished. Under these circumstances, only the general analysis (without names of plants and people) would be shared. The researcher agreed to share the findings of the study with individuals if this was requested, as well as with all villagers through a workshop.

Gatherers and sellers of medicinal plants

A second category of users of medicinal plants in the area included those people who gather large amounts of medicinal plants to sell in the markets of Durban and Johannesburg. These plants are purchased primarily by traditional healers or chemists. In the study area, those collecting and selling the material are mostly poor single women who, more often than not, did nor know the different uses of the plants they collected and did not require special training other than learning to recognize the plants.

Research agreements entered into with these social actors were achieved collectively, since women were often constituted as collection groups. The collectors agreed to share information on the plants with the researcher on the condition that this would not result in collectors from other areas coming into their area and competing for limited resources. While the researcher could not provide an absolute guarantee in this regard, he undertook not to intentionally encourage new medicinal plant collectors to the area. An additional agreement formulated was that the research findings should emphasize the problems experienced by these women, such as diminishing plant resources, long distances travelled to the markets and lack of safety while in the bigger cities. Like many of the other agreements developed within the village, collectors were assured anonymity where requested, as well as feedback through a workshop or as individuals.

Traditional healers

Traditional healers represented a third category of medicinal plant users in the village. Healers were either male or female and worked mostly on an individual basis within the region. Some travelled further afield to places such as Durban, Johannesburg, uMtata and so forth, selling their products and services. Some, and particularly women, collected these plants in bulk to sell to other healers.

Research agreements were entered into with individuals of this group, rather than as a collective. Within this group there was a great deal of secrecy. The researcher undertook to respect that secrecy and to not seek detailed knowledge of medicinal plants used to make specialized mixtures. Through prompting from some of the healers, the researcher additionally agreed to pay a consultation fee as other people would have done. This was especially necessary if the interview or field-visit period was lengthy, thus taking away from collection time or possible consultations by clients. Not all traditional healers requested this small fee for interviews. Because this group did not really work as a collective, the researcher undertook to share the findings of the study with them as individuals.

Illegal resource users

Numerous villagers collected resources illegally, and it is useful to reflect on the types of agreements developed with this group. Illegal activities included the harvesting of fuelwood from forest reserves, grass from the nature reserve and the growing and selling of *Cannabis sativa* (marijuana). These agreements were obviously very sensitive and required a long process of trust-building between the resource users and the researcher. Once trust was established in the researcher, a process of establishing agreements was initiated. In most of these cases the researcher had to acknowledge (but not necessarily condone) the legitimacy of reasons for the resource user's actions. The researcher also undertook not to use names or examples that could lead to prosecution of the resource users. The resource users, in turn, committed themselves to share information and allow observations to be made. This commitment was made in the hope that the researcher would report their condition and justify the actions being taken. Since illegal resource-harvesting activities were undertaken by many throughout the village (except for *Cannabis sativa*), it was agreed that a community workshop would be the best place to share the findings of the study at various stages of the research.

Conclusion

The successful development of agreements at Mkambati highlights important lessons that have broad application to other social research projects. Firstly, recognition must be given to the fact that communities are not homogeneous entities that represent a collective and uniform group. They are, instead, comprised of individual social actors whose socio-economic goals and conditions vary considerably. Secondly, agreements must be regarded as continuous, dynamic processes that should evolve and develop throughout the lifetime of a project as social and environmental conditions change. Thirdly, researchers must be continuously aware of social differences and power relations within the community and wary of those who claim to represent the interests of others. Finally, the difficulties of developing agreements must not be underestimated. Building trust and developing relationships with communities takes time and patience, and may require the allocation of additional human or financial resources. These elements must be factored into research programmes and funding proposals, which should be sufficiently flexible to accommodate unforeseen matters that arise. At Mkambati, the principal researcher shared both the language and culture of the community. This was undoubtedly a major factor accounting for the development of successful agreements. Researchers working in the field need to be acutely sensitive to the significance of personalities in research projects, and to the importance of building bridges and gaining mutual respect where cultures and languages differ. It is through implementation of these basic principles that a mutually beneficial relationship can be developed between communities and those engaged in research in communities.

community-based research is not a quick and easy one, and will add both time and costs to a researcher's project. In order for researchers to comply, it will be necessary for somewhat larger budgets and longer time frames to be factored into proposals for funding than has been standard practice to date. These changes in the planning and budgeting of research programmes should become common practice, and might be institutionalized by major granting agencies.

The extent and scope of a consultation process will vary by scale and nature of a research project. Because consultations take place during the life of a research project, it is important to view them as a process, involving different stages and objectives, including: preparation (securing PIC); project planning (developing research to serve community needs in order to minimize negative impacts and maximize positive returns/benefits); and monitoring and evaluation (assessing and revising project activities according to agreed upon principles and objectives).

Consultation as a **preparatory mechanism** will:

- involve information exchange;
- include capacity-building;[3]
- identify interests and concerns of parties;
- assist in building confidence and a

relationship of trust between parties and establish the basis for long-term transparent and respectful communication between them.

Consultation during **project planning** will help to:

- identify expectations and opinions regarding the project;
- define the process for achieving and monitoring parties' objectives (including the negotiation of agreements, benefit sharing provisions, etc);
- define the consultation mechanisms (workshops, public meetings, etc);
- ensure the PIC of relevant communities for research activities.

Consultation as a form of **monitoring and evaluation** will help to:

- identify whether information exchange and opportunities for participation are adequate to ensure ongoing informed decision-making by communities;
- identify changes necessary in project implementation;
- evaluate and supervise compliance with the obligations assumed;
- identify possible conflicts, where possible, before they arise.

In order for consultations to succeed, they must adhere to a set of basic standards for 'best practice'. Based on experience with oil industry consultations with indigenous peoples in Peru, Tobin et al (1998) developed the following criteria for a successful consultation. Consultations must be:

- carried out in good faith: all affected peoples have the opportunity to fully and actively participate;

- timely: carried out prior to significant decision-making;
- inclusive of all sectors of society affected, with a bias to securing participation of marginalized sectors, in particular women, youths and elders;
- locally inclusive: in order to ensure the greatest level of participation by affected communities;
- significant: must be substantive and result in real decision-making;
- continuous: held throughout the planning, design, implementation and evaluation of the project;
- informed: in order to enable communities to make judgements regarding potential impacts;
- facilitated: with sufficient funding to enable indigenous peoples to attend relevant decision-making fora, prepare commentaries on technical documents and diffuse information pertaining to the relevant activity amongst its people, as well as to contract necessary technical and legal support services;
- reported: with precision to ensure that information regarding indigenous concerns is well documented and taken into consideration in decision-making processes;
- respectful of the culture, laws and representative organizations of indigenous peoples;
- equitable: ensuring benefit-sharing reflects the desire of the indigenous peoples as a whole;
- non-coercive: without threat of economic force or retaliation or any other form of force as a means to induce acceptance of any project or agreement.

Box 7.8 Checklist for developing an effective consultation process

Begin consultation at the earliest possible stage of project design

- Request permission of local groups before entering onto their territories or visiting communities with offers in return for provision of resources or knowledge.
- Hold visits and meetings with the local population and distribute information regarding the proposed research.
- Identify representatives and contact points for future development of an agreement on research objectives and activities.
- Disclose information early; use information disclosure to support the consultation throughout, provide meaningful information and ensure that the information is accessible (IFC, 1998).
- Upon permission of communities, collect information regarding the project area, its population, their problems and interests, in order to have a better understanding of the context in which the potential project will be developed, and to incorporate and address local needs and concerns.
- Inform communities of what may be expected of them, activities to be carried out on their lands and the potential impacts (eg limits on the use of areas or species by the local communities, constant presence of outsiders in the area, need to maintain contact with the community, whether there is a wish to obtain information from the communities regarding resources or characteristics of the area).
- Respect the traditions, customs and languages of participants and seek bridges that help to overcome cultural differences and mistrust of outsiders.

Build the confidence of communities

- Secure the earliest possible involvement of communities.
- Identify and involve traditional decision-making authorities and representative organizations.
- Do not exclude anyone.
- Show due respect for customary law and traditions.
- Avoid making offers of gifts to individuals or of tying so-called assistance.
- Provide all the information necessary for informed decisions.
- Offer sufficient opportunity for local groups to make known their opinions.

Identify stakeholders and their rights over land, natural resources and associated knowledge

- Identify local communities and/or indigenous peoples directly or indirectly affected by the research.
- Identify holders of land and resource rights where research/collection is to occur.
- Identify relevant national, state and local authorities with jurisdiction over the area and activities.
- Identify individuals or authorities whose support or opposition to the project may affect its outcome.
- Identify organizations or individuals with knowledge and social, cultural or environmental information of value to the research.
- Include all stakeholders, including elders, youth and women's participation.

'Since women will put different items on the agenda for discussion and review, make sure that they are included as the community organizes to participate. It is also important to increase and support women's capacity to participate, as many of them will not have "formal" positions in the community which will automatically lend themselves to this, and their extensive responsibilities to caring for their families can make participation difficult' (Emery, 1997).

Agree upon acceptable logistical and administrative frameworks for consultation

- Identify measures for information exchange and access.
- Identify capacity-building and other needs/potential benefits for communities.
- Ensure that there is wide understanding of the intended process, the community's legal rights and the ways in which they can influence the process for the duration of the project.
- Identify need for independent advisers, monitors and access to legal support.
- Identify further need for interpreters, where appropriate.
- Establish a structure and time frame for the process in line with the wishes of communities.
- Identify consultation mechanisms most appropriate for the circumstances and parties involved (eg workshops, public audiences, visual presentations, informal discussions, etc); informal discussions are an important element of community consultations, since they have the advantage of enabling divergent interests to be considered (Borrini-Feyerabend, 1997).
- Establish jointly the themes, frequency and agenda for meetings for the duration of the project.
- Clarify decisions to be made jointly and the weight given to different considerations.
- Establish means to review the effectiveness of ongoing consultations for the duration of the project, and accessible mechanisms for resolution of conflicts.

Research agreements

To date, there exist few examples of written agreements between researchers and communities.[4] However, there are increasing and widespread calls for the formalization of researcher–community relationships. At international, national, professional researcher, NGO, and indigenous peoples' organizational levels, calls have been made for the requirement of PIC and local control over use of knowledge and resources, including research. These have included calls for written documen-tation of the consent process (eg indigenous peoples declarations; the Andean Pact Decision 391; the Philippines Executive Order 247; WWF, 1996; Posey and Dutfield, 1996; IUCN, 1997; PACOS, 1998; ISE, 1998).

The US government-funded International Cooperative Biodiversity Groups' (ICBG) *Principles for the Treatment of Intellectual Property and the Sharing of Benefits*, for example, calls for 'the development of written agreements with a community following complete and formal presentation of the Groups' goals and methods' as the 'best practice' for acquiring PIC. The International Society of Ethnobiology's (ISE's) *Guidelines for Research, Collections, Database, and Publications* (Draft 3, 1998; see Chapter 2) state that no research, collection, database or publication project shall be undertaken until 'an agreement is reached, in writing and/or tape recording, using local language whenever possible, with each potentially affected community, after full disclosure, and prior informed consent ... regarding the relevant equitable benefit-sharing from, compensation for, restitution for, and ownership of the collection, database or publication'.

Whether growing from a community-designed research programme or the interests of an outside researcher, written agreements can be useful tools for defining and clarifying the nature of a research relationship. Through the process of consultation leading up to an agreement, communities and researchers can come to a better understanding of where and how their goals converge. The final document is therefore less important than the process by which it is reached, since it will express relationships previously articulated and agreed upon during this process.

In most cases, written agreements should not make the research process unnecessarily bureaucratic and restrictive for ethical and conscientious researchers. If relationships are well defined, resulting from an effective consultation process (see Box 7.8), drafting a written agreement should be straightforward and quite simple. If, on the other hand, relationships are poorly defined, the process of developing a written agreement can clarify potential concerns, state the underlying objectives of the relationship in ways that will hold true over time, and will avoid confusion and inconsistent and unrealistic expectations.

As Barry Evans (1998) described it:

'*...developing a meaningful relationship and understanding between diverse parties is all too often a haphazard affair conducted under difficult circumstances. Poor communication, language barriers, time pressure, money, hidden agendas, lack of and unequal knowledge of the process and substance can all hinder the process of developing an understanding between parties. Consequently, the process is often truncated or bypassed, resulting in unnecessary conflict.*'

As a result, Evans and others at WWF in the South Pacific are working to develop *A Guide to Developing (a Memorandum of) Understanding Within and Between Parties Involved in Community-Based Recording and Use of Ethnobotanical Knowledge.*

An agreement will also bring to the surface what may be implicit in research collaboration but may not come to light otherwise. For example, in some countries government-funded research results must be published in entirety, and in others government-funded research institutions are required to pass results with commercial value on to companies. Public disclosure laws are often not well understood by the funding agencies or the individuals seeking to conduct research. In the United States, for example, both raw data and published results may be open to the public under various laws and regulations (Ruppert, pers comm, 1998; see Chapters 2 and 4).

A case can be made that all commercial research collaborations should involve formal written agreements, and that if such agreements are deemed culturally inappropriate, the research should not take place. Commercial research grows from a sector in which the written word is central to communication and confirmation of shared objectives and understandings. If a community is ill prepared to undertake written agreements with a company, then it is unlikely to be able to monitor the research relationship over time (see discussion of commercial agreements in Chapters 9 and 10). For example, in Fiji staff at the University of the South Pacific worked closely with the Verata community to build understanding and capacity to undertake an agreement for the supply of samples for commercial research purposes (see Case Study 7.2). Based on their experience with biodiversity prospecting projects involving local communities, staff at Conservation International (CI) developed a 'Prior Informed Consent Protocol and Form'. The PIC form acts as a covenant to allow commercial research to begin with mutual understanding of the nature and implications of a project; it precedes and sets the stage for a subsequent contract (see Annex 7.3).

Commercial written agreements may begin with a **memorandum of understanding** (MOU), or PIC form, as proposed by Conservation International, that sets down the general framework of a future agreement. This may include reference to the agenda and rules for future negotiations, as well as the scope of proposed discussions and parties involved. An MOU can act as a written record of a verbal agreement. In cases where there is general agreement on the scope of the terms for which further negotiation is required, then a **letter of intent** (LOI) to continue negotiations in good faith may be drafted (see Chapter 10). The letter of intent should be clearly written, setting down all relevant facts regarding the parties, the collection area and the resources to be collected, including relevant traditional knowledge.

The contents of the letter should be read out loud to participants and a version in the language(s) of participating communities should be prepared. A letter of intent may be very useful for indigenous peoples who have negotiated the major terms of an agreement but wish to give further thought to the matter or seek legal review of the proposal before signing a binding contract.

The distinction between commercial and academic research is blurred, however. Many academic researchers collect resources and knowledge for commercial companies. Less directly, but more commonly, most companies acquire information on traditional uses of species via academic publications and databases (see Chapter 4). This provides another reason for academic researchers to ensure their relationships with communities are well defined and are based on PIC (including the manner in which data and recorded knowledge are distributed outside of the community).

Research agreements must be flexible enough to address the dynamic and evolving nature of research relationships. This is particularly true for smaller projects involving long-term relationships between researchers and communities, minimal or no collecting of material, and in which monitoring and evaluation of collaborations is ongoing. In those cases, verbal agreements might often suffice, but should be based on a core set of principles and elements similar to those contained in written agreements (see Case Study 7.1). If it is decided that a written document is not appropriate, it is still important to resolve issues relating to mutual responsibilities, expectations for benefit-sharing and the underlying objectives a research collaboration is intended to serve. As a result, the following discussion of elements, and examples of approaches and language used by groups from around the world,

BOX 7.9 DO YOU NEED A WRITTEN DOCUMENT? A SAMPLE OF THE PROS AND CONS

Pros

A sample of the pros includes the following:

- Mutual expectations are clarified: this occurs on the part of both researchers and communities.
- Confusion is removed.
- The research relationship is formalized over time; interpretations are unlikely to change with a written document as years pass.
- The relationship is protected from overreliance on the involvement of one or a few individuals.
- In some cases, parties are legally bound by the document.
- Interpretation of the research relationship takes a form which can be shared widely and made clear to a large number of people.
- Researchers and local groups are morally bound to a set of principles and objectives.
- Researchers are made aware of the need for PIC and respect of local cultures, and are forced to adapt accordingly.
- Agreements promote and push forward a shift in the researcher–community relationship paradigm (see Chapter 2).
- Agreements incorporate the principles expressed in professional codes of conduct and institutional policies (see Chapters 3 and 4).
- Although they are most effective when the legal and institutional framework is in place, agreements can be used as a tool for setting terms and requiring benefit-sharing when appropriate legal frameworks do not exist.
- The process of reaching agreement can clarify distinctions between communally and individually owned information or knowledge within the community.

Cons

A sample of the cons includes the following:

- Written documents are often culturally inappropriate.
- Written documents are a Western approach to clarifying objectives.
- Agreements take too much time and are bureaucratic.
- Written documents go against a more friendly atmosphere of research collaboration.
- Written agreements require too much time and investment for short-term research projects.
- They can create division among community members.
- For commercial agreements, communities need legal or other expert assistance (perhaps not readily available) in order to develop, monitor and evaluate compliance.
- The transaction costs for commercial agreements can be well beyond the reach of local communities (see Chapter 10).
- The history of indigenous peoples' experiences with written agreements is not a good one – agreements and 'legally' agreed terms have been used to undermine community interests.
- Agreements can be made with the wrong party or parties within a community.

can serve as a guide in developing a range of equitable partnerships.

The form and extent of agreements might also vary depending upon the scale and nature of the research project and the researchers involved. For example, communities might set different standards for researchers from, and still residing in, the community, researchers from the community based at national institutions outside of the community, national researchers not part of the community, foreigners of various types, undergraduate students, postgraduate students, and so on. The level of involvement of communities in a research project will also influence the extent of the agreement – is research conducted on territories of communities, but with little active involvement? Are communities involved in the research process? Is traditional ecological knowledge under study? Two or three tiers of agreements or approaches might be most appropriate. Each agreement will reflect distinct cultural, academic and legal contexts.

Any agreement – verbal or written – will take shape in the context of existing traditional legal norms. For some communities, customary law will play a critical role in the negotiation, design and resolution of disputes associated with agreements. As The Four Directions Council (an organization of North American indigenous peoples) warns (1996):

> '...indigenous peoples possess their own locally specific systems of jurisprudence with respect to the classification of different types of knowledge, proper procedures for acquiring and sharing knowledge, and the rights and responsibilities which attach to possessing knowledge, all of which are embedded in each culture and

its language... Any attempt to devise uniform guidelines for the recognition and protection of indigenous peoples' knowledge runs the risk of collapsing this rich jurisprudential diversity into a single "model" that will not fit the values, conceptions or laws of any indigenous society.'

Community research agreements are one possible 'tool' that can be used to control access to knowledge and resources, set terms for equitable relationships and define benefits that will be shared. They will be most effective, however, when supported and complemented by other measures, including international and national law (see Chapter 12) and researchers' professional codes of conduct and institutional policies (see Chapters 2 and 3).

Community research agreements: summary of key elements

Community research agreements, community protocols, community codes of conduct and memoranda of understanding are terms used to refer to written forms of agreement between communities and outside researchers. They are often used interchangeably, but can represent a range of approaches and relationships. The emphasis in the following discussion is on academic research relationships, although many of the same principles apply to commercial research; commercial agreements are discussed in greater detail in Chapters 9 and 10.

Introduction/executive summary

Written research agreements are not common practice and can serve a wide range of community and researcher objectives. It is useful, therefore, to introduce

CASE STUDY 7.2 BUILDING A COMMITMENT TO CONSERVATION AND SUSTAINABLE MANAGEMENT: THE ROLE OF A FIJIAN COMMUNITY IN A BIODIVERSITY PROSPECTING PROJECT

William G Aalbersberg (University of the South Pacific), Isoa Korovulavula (SPACHEE) and Diane Russell (Biodiversity Conservation Network), with John E Parks (World Resources Institute)

Overview

During the colonial era in Fiji, the rights of native Fijians were taken into consideration to a greater extent than in many other colonies. As migrants from other countries and labourers primarily from India moved to Fiji, a large proportion of the land was reserved for the indigenous Fijians. This land could not be sold or otherwise permanently alienated. As a result of this policy and the continuity of local political structures, indigenous Fijian villages have a deep social and ecological grounding. There is a tremendous sense of place. Land-owning *mataqali* or family groups continue to manage lands in their territories, and often that control extends as far into the sea as local boats can go. Government consults with chiefs on fishing licences and other permits for the use of resources, and outsiders pay leases to the *mataqali* for such uses as hotels, dive areas, plantations and even access roads.

Verata is a *tikina* or county comprised of eight villages within the province of Tailevu, on the eastern shore of Viti Levu. It is a highly important locale in Fiji – one of the first sites where Fijians consider their ancestors to have settled. The chiefly families retain great prestige, and Verata people maintain ties with many other *mataqali* throughout the land. Activities carried out in Verata thus have resonance throughout the country. In addition, Verata is not far from Suva, so there is very active participation of Suva residents from Verata in the development of their area. (See Box 7.10.)

University of the South Pacific (USP) and Verata

The relationship between Verata and the University of the South Pacific (USP) is woven from many threads. One strand goes back to the early 1970s to the relationship between USP Professor of Natural Products Chemistry Bill Aalbersberg and his teacher of the Fijian language during his stint as a Peace Corps volunteer. Another strand was added during 1993–1995 with the 'Community-Based Biodiversity Conservation' surveys carried out by USP Professor of Pacific Islands Biogeography Randy Thaman, who had also been a teacher of the son of the paramount chief of Verata.

As staff at USP began to investigate the potential for biodiversity prospecting to provide an alternative and low-risk source of income for local communities, thus creating an incentive for sustainable development and biodiversity conservation, Verata seemed a natural choice. The project team included a consortium of groups, including USP and the South Pacific Action Committee on Human Ecology and the Environment (SPACHEE), a local environmental non-governmental organization (NGO). They contacted traditional Verata and government authorities to vet the idea of a biodiversity prospecting project. The team then met with the community to discuss the project concept and the nature of potential community participation. In normal generous spirit,

---

BOX 7.10 VERATA DEMOGRAPHICS AND ECOSYSTEMS

Population (1995 census): 1571 residents in 319 households. In addition, there are 643 urban residents with rights in Verata.

Number of villages: 8.

Number of mataqali: 49 live in Verata, directly controlling a total of 503ha of land.

Total area of Verata tikina *and* qoliqoli *(traditional marine management area):* 95km^2 (marine) + 140km^2 (terrestrial).

Main revenue generating activities: selling *yaqona* (kava) and *dalo* (taro); harvesting sea creatures such as *beche de mer*, mud lobster, sea cockle; fishing; land rents.

Key habitats: coral reefs, mangroves, riverbanks, shoreline, garden areas and secondary forest.

---

the community was eager to share its traditional cures with the rest of the world and trusted that the project team would protect its interests. People were concerned that marine stocks seemed to be decreasing but felt helpless to address the problem as sea resources provided a major source of income. The idea of having 'taboo' areas to allow for species regeneration was discussed and the question arose whether there would be compensation for 'lost' revenue. It was decided that income generated from the biodiversity prospecting project might be used to cover such costs, and would be at the discretion of the community.

USP then drafted a proposal to the Biodiversity Conservation Network (BCN), which provided initial funding for a 'planning grant', during which time arrangements were to be made with a biodiversity prospecting partner and further consultations with communities undertaken. The original project concept was to work only in Ucunivanua, the chiefly village of Verata. During discussions with the high chief of Verata, the chief expressed his wish that the project would involve all eight villages of Verata. A primary objective of the project was to link biodiversity prospecting (as an alternative income-generating activity) to conservation of local resources. A series of workshops was held in 1996 to identify priority conservation issues for the communities.

At a normally scheduled Verata Tikina Council meeting, 'mayors' from each village, many of whom had attended the workshops, brought forward concrete steps for discussion and possibly legal adoption concerning improved resource management and conservation. Around this time, members of the Verata Tikina Council were nominated by the Verata people to attend discussions with representatives from SmithKline Beecham (SKB). SKB staff came to Fiji in November 1995 to discuss a biodiversity prospecting agreement. The SKB lawyer noted that he had not previously held legal discussions with community and NGO representatives in such an open manner. In June 1996, SKB closed its natural products research division in the US, and with it the prospect of possible collaboration. USP was given six months by BCN to locate a new partner and found the Strathclyde Institute of Drug Research (SIDR) in Glasgow, Scotland. SIDR and USP signed an agreement in April 1997, in which SIDR would act as a broker for Verata's samples. It was more than a year later that an associated agreement between USP and Verata was signed, due to delays in translation, review by a village-appointed lawyer and the need to bring the high chief of Verata and vice-chancellor of USP together for a signing ceremony. During that time verbal consent was given by the high chief for the project to continue.

The USP and Tikina Makawa O Verata Agreement, 1998

The agreement between USP and Tikina Makawa O Verata outlines the nature of the USP–SIDR agreement, the three-year BCN implementation grant, details associated with the supply of samples, PIC and benefit-sharing. USP agrees to pay Verata every three months the entire sum of extract licence fees received by USP from SIDR associated with extracts from Verata. BCN will cover the cost of transport, subsistence costs of collectors and costs of extraction and shipping. If the BCN project is not in force, the fee paid to Verata will be the extract licence fee less legitimate costs of collecting and shipping, expected to not exceed 30 Fiji dollars per sample.

Benefits to be shared with the Verata include:

- extract licence fees, as above (to be targeted, at the discretion of the community, for development, resource management and health improvement projects);
- assistance in cataloguing biological diversity and management of resources;
- assistance in the commercial development of other non-timber forest products;
- legal support in contract negotiations, including translation of agreements into the Fijian language and provision of a lawyer, at no cost, of Verata's choice;
- a variety of types of training, including approximately six people in collecting and preparing samples; six in methods of biodiversity monitoring; and six in socio-economic monitoring;
- preference to suitably qualified people of Verata to fill any project positions; and
- future financial benefits should a commercial product be developed, to be distributed 'on an equitable basis to be negotiated by USP, Verata and the Government of Fiji'; it is expected that any royalty received from SIDR will be equally divided between the three parties.

The Verata agree to establish a trust fund to manage extract licence fees (see Chapter 11). USP agrees to provide ongoing updates on project developments to the communities through written documentation, attendance at Verata Tikina Council meetings, workshops and other means.

The SIDR paradigm solely involves cash benefits to its partners. As SIDR could contract only with a legal entity, sample licensing fees were paid to USP to be passed on in full to a Verata conservation trust fund. (This was established in early 1999 after considerable work by a Suva-based group of Verata people who had been delegated to do this by the Verata Tikina Council.) In-kind benefits were provided for in the BCN grants to USP in order to enhance its ability to add value to samples by screening and active principal isolation, and to Verata for enhancing their knowledge and skills. These included training in biological monitoring and community resource management.

Training for community sample collectors and collection activities

Each village was invited to appoint two members interested in, and knowledgeable about, local plants to become sample collectors. About ten people, several of whom had been part of the biological monitoring training, assembled at the training site. Marika Tuiwawa, a botanist in the biology department at USP, had worked with Professor Aalbersberg to develop a list of plants to be collected based on those desired by SIDR and those identified in Verata by Professor Thaman's rapid rural assessments. 65 plants were collected in one and a half days, and an additional 40 on another collection day a few months later. Verata has a much richer marine than terrestrial biodiversity because much of the land consists of grasslands and secondary forests and further marine collections have been made by USP scuba divers.

At the request of the community, a major focus of the project has been marine resource management. Following a series of workshops, the Verata Tikina Council established the following marine conservation measures: a ban on commercial fishing licences; a ban on killing turtles; size limitations on gill nets; a ban on coral harvesting; and establishment of 'taboo' (no-take) zones. To support implementation of these measures, the project trained communities in the biological monitoring of two indicator species that they selected. Results show significant increases in marine resources, with greater increases in populations in the taboo areas compared with the harvested ones.

The activities supported by BCN – taking place prior to the arrival of any income from biodiversity prospecting – proved critical in building local awareness of conservation priorities and sustainable resource management. Conducted in conjunction with sample collection, these activities have allowed the Verata monitoring teams to develop an expertise in environmental impact assessments and resource-surveying techniques that other agencies have made use of, and communities have set aside 'taboo' areas to provide a reprieve for threatened species. Through these activities, biodiversity prospecting became tied to conservation. Community commitment to conservation, and the building of skills and confidence to sustainably manage their resources, must be a primary goal of any benefit package resulting from a biodiversity prospecting venture.

the agreement with an explanation of why an agreement was developed (eg to serve wider community interests; clarify expectations), a review of the general principles underlying the agreement and a summary of the core elements. A summary also provides a synopsis more accessible to a large audience not in need of detail.

Parties to the MOU

This section includes the names, addresses and contact details for the parties to the agreement. In addition to communities and researchers, all third parties (eg affiliated institutions and companies) should be included. Any policies, codes of conduct or operating procedures issued by these institutions or companies should be appended to the agreement. All 'invisible' as well as 'visible' interests should be represented (eg funders, affiliated institutions).

Principles and objectives

The underlying principles and objectives of the research relationship should be clarified in order to avoid misunderstandings between parties and to help ensure that, over time, the original intent of the research relationship is upheld. Principles and objectives can range from the very general to the specific. They might reflect the wider issues that communities hope to address through the research collaboration, or might only cover the purpose of a specific study. They can also serve to clarify issues within the community, such as distinctions between communally and individually owned information, knowledge and resources.

Definition of terms and scope

The terms used in an agreement must be clear to all parties involved. Lack of clarity in terms used can result in a confusing agreement that is difficult to implement and monitor over time. Key terms might include, for example: 'community', 'researcher', 'data', 'traditional ecological knowledge', 'culturally appropriate amounts', 'collections', 'best practice', 'access' and 'benefit-sharing'.

National policy and legal context

National legal and policy frameworks – including measures relating to access and benefit-sharing, environment, intellectual property rights and human rights – will influence the formation and legal nature of written agreements (see Chapters 9, 10 and 12; Gollin and Laird, 1996). For example, in the US Glacier National Park, an MOU negotiated between the National Park Service (NPS) and local tribes was considered unenforceable by the US Interior Department Solicitor's Office (see Box 7.11). A range of federal laws, regulations and agency policies constrained the NPS from considering ownership of intellectual property (Ruppert, 1994).

Contractual agreements between parties from different legal jurisdictions, or for activities to be carried out in several jurisdictions, also usually require a 'choice of law' that will be used to interpret the meaning of an agreement's language (Downes et al, 1993). In the case of community research agreements, the relationship between customary, national, state and international law should be clarified where possible (Downes et al, 1993; Shelton, 1995). For many researchers, coming to grips with the national policy context – often internally inconsistent – will be difficult. For large-scale research projects and all commercial research, however, it is critical to do so.

Communities may also need technical and legal advice in order to enter into an agreement. The provision of this form of capacity-building can be built into the consultation process.

Process by which agreement was reached

It is valuable to review in writing the process by which agreement is reached in order to ensure transparency in the short term, and greater understanding of the considerations that contributed to development of an agreement in both the present and into the future. The type of 'checklist' offered in Box 7.8 for effective consultations could be fleshed out and modified according to local practice, and included in the agreement.

Responsibilities of Researchers

The responsibilities of collaborating parties at different phases in the research process should be clearly articulated. It might be useful to break the research process down into three phases, each with its own set of responsibilities.

Phase 1 (prior to initiating research: consultation and PIC): Researchers should consult with communities, seek PIC and might sign a written agreement.

Phase 2 (during the research process: data collection and ongoing consultation): This will include responsibilities associated with respect for the local culture and environment (eg avoidance of sacred sites, adherence to cultural norms in conducting interviews); fees to be paid; behaviour of researchers in the community (including details such as picking up waste and appropriate dress); and training of local community members (see, for example, Box 7.12). The Arctic Environment

---

BOX 7.11 THE GLACIER NATIONAL PARK PROJECT

The Glacier National Park, in the United States, has strong historical and contemporary ties to the Blackfeet, Kootenai and Salish tribes. The US National Park Service (NPS) contracted with a researcher to gather information on contemporary uses of park resources by these tribes. To initiate this work, the researcher and park officials met with tribal representatives in 1992 to receive permission for this study. Tribal representatives were concerned about the type of data collected, the sensitivity of researchers to its meaning for the tribes and the release of this information into the public domain. For example, information about sacred sites, vision-questing and the use of plants and minerals for ceremonial purposes was considered highly sensitive. Tribal representatives were also wary because many researchers had come through in the past, collecting cultural information, and provided nothing in return, including information on the research they conducted. As a result, a memorandum of understanding (MOU) was drafted for the proposed research project between the NPS, the Glacier National Park, the confederated Salish and Kootenai tribes of the Flathead Nation and the Blackfeet tribe.

The MOU addressed the following five areas:

1 It defined the concept of 'ethnographic resource' – any natural or cultural resource, landscape or natural feature linked by an ethnic community to the traditional practices, values, beliefs and/or ethnic identity of that community – and the types of information related to these resources that the park needed for its planning process.
2 It specified the kind of information or data that would qualify to be protected by tribal rights to intellectual property. This information was called 'new data' resulting from interviews detailing cultural information not found in other sources.
3 It placed stipulations on the use of 'new data' by the park for planning, decision-making and public education purposes. These stipulations also specified the tribes' right to recall or deny the use of these 'new data' by the park if the use to which they were put was considered inappropriate to the tribe.
4 It outlined the tribes' right to grant or deny permission for publication of 'new data'.
5 It defined a process of dispute resolution.

The federal agencies deemed that the MOU conflicted with federal laws and regulations, however, and this agreement was never implemented.

Source: Ruppert, 1994

Protection Strategy (1993), for example, states that: 'Interviewers should regard themselves, and behave, as participants in a collaborative effort of inquiry with local people. Sensitivity, patience and experience are crucial qualities for this collaboration.' Through an ongoing process of consultation, researchers and communities should also revise or modify previous research objectives and expectations.

Phase 3 (follow-up): Follow-up might involve sharing of publications and other benefits, updates on data analysis, inclusion of analysis relevant to community resource management and translation of results into local languages. The Inuit Tapirisat of Canada (1993), in their guidelines for research, state that: 'Aboriginal people should have access to research data, not just receive summaries and research reports. The extent of data accessibility that participants/communities can expect should be clearly stated and agreed upon as part of any approval process.'

Responsibilities of local communities

In addition to clarifying the responsibilities of researchers, a written agreement should articulate the responsibilities of local communities. Because communities do not usually recruit researchers into their area, and there will be tremendous variation by case, it is difficult to generalize on community responsibilities. However, agreements might try to ensure that all information provided by the researcher is communicated effectively within the community and that community interests are well represented. Equitable distribution of benefits throughout the community might also be included as a community responsibility. Because consultations will include, and PIC will be acquired from, individuals selected to represent community interests, these forms of communication and benefit distribution will be likely but not guaranteed in all cases. Logistical matters should also be clarified, including, for example, the provision of housing, structures to hold collections and assistants, guides and informants, for a set number of days and at an agreed fee. Communities might also agree to process researchers' requests for PIC in an agreed amount of time.

Responsibilities of other collaborators

Researchers are generally affiliated with universities, research institutions, conservation projects or other groups. Collected resources might be housed in botanic gardens, herbaria, and other ex-situ collections. Communities might be members of a federation representing a wide geographic area, or might work closely with a local council in developing their relationships with researchers. National and local authorities in charge of indigenous peoples' issues might significantly impact the realization of research objectives. Third parties might be involved as evaluators, monitors and arbitrators of the research relationship and of benefit-sharing. The nature and scope of involvement of all parties, and their responsibilities, should be clarified in a written agreement

Benefit-sharing

Benefits resulting from research collaborations can take monetary and non-monetary form, and will vary depending upon whether research is academic or commercial. Both monetary and non-monetary benefits should be clearly identified in the body of the written agreement. In the case of academic research, monetary benefits include fees paid to assistants and guides, payment for the use of facilities and infrastructure and possibly small grants to village development and other community funds.

Non-monetary benefits – often considered of greater value than monetary benefits over time – might include: training of community members; equipment and infrastructure support; copies of publications; coauthorship of publications; production of manuals and other documents in forms of use to communities (see Chapter 5); photographs; building of

BOX 7.12 THE AWA FEDERATION

The Awa Federation is a legal institution which administers 101,000 hectares held under communal title by the Awa in Ecuador and makes collective decisions regarding its use, as well as working on the development of socio-economic infrastructure. The Awa acquired legal recognition of communal title to their land in 1995. Prior to this time, they were considered 'wards of the state' and their territory a 'forest reserve' of the communal settlement of the Awa people. Since 1995 the Awa have demarcated their territory by planting a 50-metre wide border with fruit trees and by patrolling and securing their boundaries. Due to the botanical and ethnobotanical wealth of the Awa and their lands, a number of research institutions have begun collaborations with the Awa. In 1993, the *Convenio – Reglamentos para la Realizacion de Estudos Cientificos en el Territorio de la Federacion Awa* was developed to set terms for research relationships. It includes the following provisions:

- All scientists must ask for written permission to carry out studies. The written request for permission must include a description of objectives, size and composition of research party, length of research programme, species or object of study, and the manner in which this research will benefit the Awa community.
- The request for permission must be given with a minimum of two months' notice (widely dispersed communities only meet four times a year for four days).
- More than five people to a research group is prohibited.
- More than one group of scientists are prohibited from entering at the same time (this and the preceding provision are intended to minimize the cultural impact of the research process).
- Local guides and informants must accompany all scientists.
- The collection of animals, insects or plants for commercial purposes is prohibited.
- Only three specimens of each species are to be collected – one each for the research group, the Awa Federation and the Tobar Donoso Project in Quito (this was later increased to allow for larger numbers).
- The removal of any object from Awa territory not approved by the federation is prohibited (the main concerns are cultural artefacts and property, including stone mortars found in the forest and believed to be possessions of the ancestors).
- Scientists must dispose of their own waste.
- The prices established by the Awa Federation for their services are as follows: members of each scientific group must contribute to the federation 1000 sucres in order to enter Awa territory; guides and informants receive 700 sucres per day; cooks, cleaners and other workers receive 500 sucres per day; members of scientific groups from Ecuadorean universities or institutions pay only 500 sucres per day to enter Awa territory.
- It is not permitted to provide gifts or money outside of the established regulations.
- Scientists who do not respect these rules or Awa organizations and cultures will be expelled immediately.
- The Awa Federation must receive acknowledgement in publications.

Permission to collect in Awa territory requires two tiers of permission: firstly, the researcher must secure permission from the Awa and, secondly, they must obtain permission from the government.

local commercial capacity or community-based industries; provision of medical services; and so on. The *Declaration on the Protection of Traditional Knowledge and Expressions of Indigenous Cultures in the Pacific Islands* (1999), for example, calls for training in scientific, legal and information management areas in order to support a system to protect indigenous culture. Non-monetary benefits will grow directly from the consultation process and will reflect the type of research undertaken.

A Plan for the distribution of benefits

The distribution of monetary and non-monetary benefits within a community should be clarified in the agreement in order to ensure transparency and clarity of intent over time. Benefits for other collaborators (eg botanic gardens and host institutions) in the research process should also be clarified. Janzen et al (1993) suggest that any research project should provide a roster of in-country entities likely to receive the various compensations, that the nature of compensation should be spelled out, and that the legal and logistical reason for such a distribution should be explained. In Peru, benefits must legally be shared between the state (which claims as national patrimony the country's genetic resources) and communities (which claim as cultural patrimony their traditional knowledge).

At the community level, the *Covenant on Intellectual, Cultural and Scientific Resources* (1994) states that compensation should be 'equitably shared within and among groups, and...is in a form that strengthens the community and ethnic group'. This is difficult in cases where groups share knowledge of species use and cross national borders; different levels of sharing may be necessary, depending upon local customary law. Following disruption of traditional decision-making authorities in many areas, new local-, national-, regional- and even global-level organizations have grown up that might assist in negotiations between communities. As we see in the case of traditional healers' organizations in South Africa, minimal institutional and sometimes legal infrastructure is required for effective benefit-sharing (see Box 7.13).

Trust funds are increasingly used to distribute financial benefits to communities and others according to agreed-upon objectives. The Healing Forest Conservancy, for example, has recently launched a trust fund with the Bioresources Development and Conservation Programme in Nigeria; a few of the International Cooperative Biodiversity Groups' (ICBGs') programmes have similarly made use of community trust funds; and the Tikina Verata in Fiji has established a biodiversity trust fund to administer funds from biodiversity prospecting (see Chapter 11).

Disposition of collected information

Conditions attached to data and collections that might be addressed in an agreement include the following (see Chapter 4):

- community access to raw data;
- the need for communities to be regularly updated on the status of data analysis, publication and materials held in ex-situ collections;
- the publication or entry into databases of information collected;
- the housing (and numbers) of specimens collected; and
- the requirement of PIC from the community for any distribution, publication or housing of information or materials.

Box 7.13 Traditional healers and biodiversity prospecting in South Africa: overcoming constraints to meaningful benefit-sharing

Rachel Wynberg (Biowatch South Africa)

Traditional healers are playing an increasingly prominent role in bioprospecting in South Africa, and their experiences are demonstrating the difficulties of putting benefit-sharing into practice and the importance of political and social stability to achieve this goal. The country's exceptionally diverse biodiversity, rich traditional knowledge and well-developed scientific capacity provide key attractants to companies developing new drugs, crops or natural products; to date, traditional healers have been approached by several companies including Shaman and Marshall Chemicals. Traditional healers have also recently entered into an agreement to commercialize indigenous plants with the Council for Scientific Research (CSIR), a parastatal institute based in South Africa undertaking scientific and technological research.

Through such developments traditional healers are rapidly recognizing the economic potential of their knowledge. This follows many years of traditional medicine being marginalized and traditional healers persecuted by colonial and apartheid governments. It also follows a long history of exploitation, initiated by colonial botanists who used traditional knowledge of plants to identify species of commercial potential, and the subsequent commercial development of South African species by foreign companies. Few if any of the benefits of such commercialization have been returned to the people from whom knowledge was derived. With the upsurge of interest in South African flora, it is crucial to redress this situation; but an array of complex constraints makes implementation of this requirement a difficult task.

Lack of information and understanding regarding the ownership of traditional knowledge

Perhaps the most crucial constraint that prevents meaningful benefit-sharing with healers is the lack of information and understanding regarding the ownership of knowledge about South African biodiversity. Knowledge obtained is often difficult to attribute to a single community or individual, having evolved over centuries and having been passed down from one generation to the next. While some knowledge is unquestionably unique to a certain community or region and is of a specialized nature, biological resources and knowledge often cross political boundaries in the region and may be a shared resource among communities. Complicating matters are the varying levels of expertise among healers and the growth of charlatans in the business. Benefit-sharing arrangements clearly need to take account of these circumstances through local, national or regional arrangements. Moreover, they need to recognize that existing Western intellectual property systems, which reward individuals or legal entities, may well be inappropriate to traditional knowledge systems, which are often of a collective nature.

Absence of a unified voice to represent traditional healers

For appropriate benefit-sharing mechanisms to be developed, however, healers need to engage in bioprospecting with a unified voice. Unlike many other African countries where a single organization may represent the needs and interests of the traditional healer community, there is no single national champion of traditional medicine in South

Africa. Instead, some 200 to 300 organizations exist, many of which are considered spurious, competing intensely for members, membership fees and recognition. The country's turbulent past has undoubtedly played no small role in this divisive situation, now deeply rooted in local politics and associated power struggles. Without a coherent and unified organizational base, it has been extremely difficult for the needs of healers to be democratically and strongly represented within policies and laws. Because of the difficulties involved in dealing with a multitude of organizations, it has also resulted in companies or institutions developing bioprospecting agreements with individual healers, rather than ensuring that benefits reach the broader community. Recently, an attempt has been made to constitute a single umbrella organization for healers in South Africa, although it is too early to tell whether this will successfully establish itself as a neutral and widely accepted body.

Lack of organizational skills and capacity

A major factor precluding the healer community from obtaining meaningful benefits from bioprospecting deals is their lack of organizational skills and capacity. Most associations suffer from insufficient management capabilities, poor exposure to the issues and high levels of illiteracy. Negotiating an even-handed and equitable agreement under these conditions presents enormous problems.

Few benefits to the disempowered

Because of this situation, those healers who have reaped benefits from bioprospecting initiatives in South Africa tend to be those who are better organized and empowered. For example, a recent agreement between the CSIR and the Traditional Doctors' Committee to evaluate the commercial potential of indigenous plants came about through approaches to the CSIR by individual healers who were 'more forward looking and progressive in their approach'.[5] The committee is a group of ten healers, constituted specifically for the purposes of the agreement. While there is a tacit agreement that these individuals will liaise with traditional healer organizations and spread benefits more broadly than themselves, this responsibility rests on the healers involved and does not form part of the agreement with the CSIR. No products have yet been developed and it is still too early to determine the outcome of this approach; but it would appear that few safeguards are in place to guarantee the rights of the 300,000 healers estimated to practise in South Africa

No law to protect traditional knowledge and guide benefit-sharing

Finally, there needs to be government commitment and action to enable bioprospecting to reap suitable returns for traditional healers and other holders of traditional knowledge, as well as for the conservation of an increasingly threatened biota. Although it is government policy to protect traditional knowledge and to develop laws to control access to genetic resources and stipulate benefit-sharing requirements, these have not yet been developed. Ongoing efforts are thwarted by a lack of capacity within government to regulate and monitor existing laws, as well as poor understanding regarding the issues involved. Although there is widespread support for a benefit mechanism, such as a national trust, this has yet to be implemented. The use of traditional knowledge, either through consultation of databases or through direct approaches to healers by companies or middlemen, thus takes place in a policy vacuum, with virtually no guidance from government. All of these issues require urgent attention if benefit-sharing is to move beyond its current rhetoric.

The process by which PIC and mutual agreement are reached for uses not covered in the initial agreement should also be clarified.

Reporting, monitoring and evaluation

The process by which research relationships will be monitored and evaluated over time should be clarified in the written agreement. Requirements for meetings with the community, and the timing, scope and submission of reports by researchers, should be detailed. Standards against which the relationship is evaluated (eg elements of the written agreement) should be explained. In some cases, particularly commercial collaborations, outside evaluation of compliance with the agreement and monitoring by a third party may be helpful (see Chapter 9). The community should also be involved in monitoring activities in the field.

Exclusivity and confidentiality

Exclusivity of research relationships should be clarified. It is assumed that for academic relationships exclusivity is not required. However, commercial agreements will often involve a period of exclusive access to resources or knowledge. Communities will likely not wish to enter into this type of arrangement but should clearly state this in the agreement. The *Covenant on Intellectual, Cultural, and Scientific Resources* (1994), for example, emphasizes 'non-exclusivity of relationships, meaning that both parties are free to enter into agreements with other parties'.

Confidentiality issues are central to academic as well as commercial research relationships. Community members might expressly state that information not otherwise publicly available on traditional cultures, or traditional use of species, may not be disclosed without the PIC of the community. For example, an MOU between the Zion National Park and Paiute Indians in the United States – *MOU Regarding the Gathering of Plant Resources for American Indian Traditional Cultural-Religious Purposes from National Park Lands* (1998 draft) – requires that:

> 'Information shared with the PARKS by the TRIBES or by individual tribal members, related to gathering activities, shall be considered sensitive and confidential. As such, the PARKS shall protect such information from public disclosure to the maximum extent practicable under law and regulation.'

The types of information that may be shared, and those off-limits to researchers, should be spelled out in the agreement.

Dispute resolution

Clear protocols for resolution of disputes should be included in an agreement, including the role of customary law and bodies. The United Nations Educational, Social and Cultural Organization's (UNESCO's) Commission on Human Rights on the Protection of the Heritage of Indigenous Peoples (UNESCO, 1995), for example, states that: 'In the event of a dispute over custody or use of any element of an indigenous peoples' heritage, judicial and administrative bodies should be guided by the advice of indigenous elders who are recognized by the indigenous communities or peoples concerned as having specific knowledge of traditional laws.' Dispute resolution for commercial research relationships is expensive, so the agreement should make clear who will cover the cost (see Chapter 9).

Term and amendment

Agreements should include clear protocols on the ways in which agreements can be modified and parties can break the agreement, including listing acceptable reasons for breaking it (Janzen et al, 1993). This process will integrate the results of monitoring and evaluation activities. By keeping the duration of an agreement relatively short, the need for renegotiation might be kept to a minimum (Grifo and Downes, 1996). However, given the dynamic nature of community–researcher relationships, it is important to keep an agreement as flexible and open to amendment during the course of the research relationship as possible.

For example, in the MOU between the Zion National Park and Paiute Indians in the United States *(MOU Regarding the Gathering of Plant Resources for American Indian Traditional Cultural-Religious Purposes from National Park Lands)* the section on 'Term and Amendment' refers to the agreement as a 'living' document that 'may require changes or alterations to meet new or changing circumstances'.

Annex

Annexed to the agreement should be copies of relevant supporting material that provide background and context to the agreement. This information will help to make the collaboration as transparent, and information as accessible, to the largest numbers as possible.

Materials that might be attached include:

- copies of funding proposals for the research project;
- information on the funding agency and their requirements relating to research results;
- CVs of the researchers;
- copies of permits;
- indigenous peoples' statements/declarations and/or other documents supported by the community;
- copies of state/provincial, national and international laws or policies relevant to the collaboration;
- professional codes of conduct to which researchers adhere;
- affiliated institutional/company policies.

Annex 7.1 Prior informed consent: the anthropology and politics of cross-cultural exchange

Miguel N Alexiades (Institute of Economic Botany, the New York Botanical Garden) and Daniela M Peluso (Columbia University)

Introduction

Prior informed consent (PIC) has become an important tool in mechanisms that regulate the use and access to biological diversity and that implement the rights of such stakeholders as the nation state and indigenous and local communities over these resources. As critically important as PIC is to self-determination and to equitable models of exchange between researchers and research subjects or participants, we can immediately anticipate several difficulties in its implementation. These difficulties, in turn, emerge from the socio-economic, cultural and political reality in which most research initiatives are embedded.[6] For one thing, researchers can not realistically foresee all the potential risks and implications of their research, firstly, because cause–effect relations are extremely complex and, secondly, because the techno-logical, social, political and economic circumstances that determine the conse-quences of research – particularly of published research – will inevitably change in unpredictable ways (see Chapter 4). Biotechnology, information technology, the global economy and the privatization of science, for example, have all had a tremen-dous impact on how genetic resources and ethnobotanical information are valued, used or misused, and has done so in ways that were hardly foreseeable to our colleagues several decades ago (see Chapter 1). Some of the unforeseeable conse-quences of research may thus ultimately prove to be the most important ones.

PIC involves two other subtler, and perhaps more important, challenges than that of researchers recognizing and predict-ing the implications of their work. Firstly, PIC hinges on the ability of researchers to successfully communicate what are often complex, abstract and culturally alien concepts across cultural differences created by differences in nationality, ethnicity, socio-economic class, level of academic instruction or personal, historical or social experience. Typically, then, PIC implies a process of cross-cultural communication and therefore of translation between categories. This process of translation becomes increasingly complex and problematic the more divergent the experi-ences, categories, precepts and assumptions of the different parties involved.

In addition, as all other forms of social exchange, PIC negotiations are inevitably embedded in a matrix of unequal global, national and local power relations, relations over which individuals have little, if any, control. The structural inequalities that permeate most social relations tend to undermine attempts to facilitate genuine participation and equitable forms of exchange. The process of PIC is thus contin-gent and limited by our ability to address the challenges imposed by human commu-nication and human power relations. We suggest that this shortcoming can only be addressed partially at best, and then only through adequate training and, most importantly, through a genuine sense of respect and responsibility towards those with whom we work.

In this annex we examine some of the implications of PIC as a form of political and cross-cultural exchange.[7] Our intention is not to deconstruct PIC but, rather, to identify and illustrate some of the difficulties that may emerge as we attempt to implement it in the field. Using examples from our own research in Amazonia, we examine how each component of PIC – 'consent' that is 'informed' and 'prior' to research – raises different though mutually interdependent challenges. We also attempt to offer some suggestions on how some of these difficulties may be broached, suggesting that PIC is best viewed as part of an ongoing 'dynamic interactive cycle' of consultation (International Society of Ethnobiology, 1998; see Chapter 2). That is, we see PIC as a dynamic and interactive process, not an event, through which researchers and research participants explore options, identify common goals and build consent.[8]

The implications of 'consent'

To the extent that different people and groups of people have different definitions and expectations regarding the nature, purpose and boundaries of consent, consent is a cultural and hence somewhat arbitrary category. As external agents, we represent and assume culture-specific models of social exchange and interaction, and these are likely to differ from those of research participants.[9] As such, there will most likely be discrepancies in how we and our research partners understand, value or seek consent. Kaufert and O'Neil (1990), for example, explored the signing of consent agreements between health professionals and native Canadians, and found that while the former emphasized biomedical understandings of disease and therapy, native patients approached consent from an experiential basis, drawing on cultural understandings of illness and disease, inter-

pretations of hospital regulations and the clinician's behaviour, and meanings attached to intergroup relations in the broader society.

Our own field experience in Amazonia suggests that among egalitarian non-industrialized societies, consent is inextricably related to notions of exchange, in turn based upon trust and relationships that can only be developed over time. Genuine consent for many research activities is unthinkable outside of the context of personal relationships that were established through the continuous cycle of exchange of services, goods and friendship. This process and context-based approach may contrast with more contractual notions of consent, where agreements are forged outside of the context of personal relations, and where consent is viewed as an event. In communities with little experience with external agents and/or contractual agreements and exchanges, PIC may need to be structured quite differently than in communities with more experience in this regard.[10] Given the broad range of circumstances in which research is structured, it is clearly impossible to lay down absolute rules on how consent should be negotiated. We suggest more equitable research partnerships will be developed when these are based on an understanding of how social, economic and political exchange is structured in the communities with whom we work, and when our intervention seeks to minimize the destructive impact on these institutions and on the ability of their actors to make decisions in an informed and free manner.

An ethnocentric approach to informed prior consent would assume that research participants need to 'understand' the nature and implications of the research process in order to give their approval, in contrast to a relativistic approach where consent is organized, structured and carried out according to the terms, conceptual notions and systems of exchange used by the research participants. In this case, PIC not only involves a process of translation, but also of accommodation and compromise on behalf of the researcher. As a form of exchange, PIC in these cases is moulded and negotiated by actors using different cultural and economic models.

Consent is always negotiated within a socio-political context, and as such is not only a cultural category but a political tool as well. Researchers, at least from the perspective of local peoples, are frequently associated with centres of economic and political power: the state, universities, research institutions, international foundations and/or cities, for example. The articulation between researchers and local communities thus typically takes place in a broader social environment characterized by asymmetrical power relations, which in turn has profound implications for how consent can be, and is, negotiated. For one thing, communication between researchers and research participants rarely takes place on a *tabula rasa*: our research participants most likely will have had experiences with other external agents, and thus may have concerns and expectations that may or may not be realistic. The genuine dialogue proposed by the concept of PIC thus needs to be historically and politically informed, and by definition requires the researcher's will and ability to compromise his or her needs. Otherwise, the process of PIC can easily become a disguised or implicit form of coercive intervention.

The consent process is contingent upon recognizing appropriate stakeholders and representatives to these stakeholders. The individuals we work with are social actors with memberships in diverse, often competing, social institutions, including households, extended families, kin, communities, institutions, ethnic groups and nation states. Which of these stakeholder groups should be included in the consent process? While some of these stakeholders are easily identified and incorporated into the consent process, others may easily slip by unnoticed. Our own field experience suggests that this is a potentially serious problem because our choices have political repercussions in terms of the relationship between different stakeholder groups. One

example from our own doctoral fieldwork among the Ese Eja, conducted between 1994 and 1996, may illustrate this problem.[11]

As with many Amazonian groups, several parallel systems of leadership coexist in Ese Eja communities. 'Traditional' forms of authority and leadership emerge from the structure of social organization, which in this case is patrilineal and uxorilocal, meaning that people inherit their identity from the father, but that couples reside with the woman's family. Households, in turn, form spatial and political clusters or extended family groups. The older man in each extended family effectively acts as a leader or representative of sorts. Though this person has no direct authority over those in his extended family, his prestige and social standing grant him a certain amount of power in influencing group-level decisions among his extended kin. These older men, or *etii*, form something loosely akin to an elders' council and represent one form of political authority.[12]

By definition however, *etii* are older and frequently not as bicultural as some of the younger and schooled Ese Eja, who have much greater contact with the national culture. It is these younger Ese Eja who are chosen as mediators between the community and external agents. Ese Eja communities today, by law, have a leadership council consisting of a president, vice-president, secretary and treasurer. This political structure modelled after that of the nation state serves to articulate the community with external agents. Its ability to effectively mediate internal conflicts and dynamics, however, is generally quite limited. This is because the skills and attributes required of mediators with external agents are usually incompatible with those required by mediators of internal affairs. Generally, the younger bicultural men who hold political positions lack the age, prestige and social networks necessary to successfully mediate internal affairs. As a result, among the Ese Eja one can recognize two types of leaders; 'external' leaders who reflect and effect Ese Eja relations with the outside world, and 'internal' leaders, who mediate many aspects of internal relations.

When we first began to work with the Ese Eja in the late 1980s, we were immediately directed by the Ese Eja, by the regional indigenous federation and by our colleagues to the 'official' political leaders of the community, and it is these actors whom we first identified as 'official' mediators. After some time, however, it became apparent that these leaders had limited say in community internal affairs. Though not as approachable, the older men and women were clearly important actors who needed to be involved in discussions. Moreover, it also became apparent that while these elders recognized the importance and value of young leaders, they frequently resented their power and scoffed at their attempts to exert authority in domains customarily not theirs. It was only with time and after making several mistakes that we began to recognize some of the subtleties of Ese Eja social and political organization and its relevance to our relationship with our hosts. In our subsequent negotiations and interactions with Ese Eja communities, we have sought to incorporate different political and social actors in our discussions and consent process. Not surprisingly, each has required a different approach and format. While community-level meetings and formal mechanisms and institutions familiar to the nation state and its agents are important and relevant to one dimension of Ese Eja political organization, other important discussions and negotiations need to take place at individual, household and family-level discussions, bringing in different types of communication tools and using different concepts.

By consciously or involuntarily choosing one group of political actors over others, external agents and researchers can undermine certain forms of political authority within the social groups with which they interact. This process is, in turn, facilitated by the fact that different stakeholder groups have different abilities to articulate their claims in the consent process. Not surprisingly, nation states have been most successful at establishing these claims, as evidenced by the growing international and national legislation guaranteeing national sovereignty over genetic and cultural resources. To varying degrees, indigenous organizations and communities have also been able to successfully articulate their agendas and position themselves as stakeholders. Other stakeholders – notably less bicultural individuals or families, older people and women – may remain invisible to the naïve or inexperienced researcher, raising the question of how much responsibility researchers and external agents have to identify such stakeholders, or at least identify the impact their research has on them.

Communities, ethnic groups and all other social groupings are not homogeneous entities: they are internally diverse, fluid and frequently fractured configurations of actors with diverse attitudes, experiences, values and perceptions and needs. Contact between indigenous peoples and external agents, be they explorers, traders, missionaries, the state, development programmes, oil companies, ecotourism firms or researchers, has also helped to shape and create leaders and representatives. We have already noted, for example, how indigenous communities have political structures that reflect, and which were created in order to allow, articulation of the community with the nation state. As a corollary, indigenous groups that have had less contact with external agents frequently do not have the social and political structures that external agents need in order to articulate themselves directly in the community. The fact that all human communities are permeated with internal divisions and conflicts of interests does problematize consent. More importantly, it is all too easy for third parties, consciously or not, to exploit these internal cleavages to further their own agendas. Indeed, this strategy of 'divide and conquer' has historically been used by a broad range of agents of intervention, including the state, missionaries and development projects, with considerable success. One ethnographer's confession that in the course of his fieldwork he had, in a way, 'set out to exploit the tensions that divided the community' (Metcalf, 1998, p336) is a reflection more of the rarity of academic honesty than of the rarity of such interactions taking place in the field. Clearly, this raises important challenges to such concepts as equity and consent. At the very least, as researchers we must develop greater personal accountability for the impact of our research agendas and must establish a consent process that is as consensus-based as possible.

The implications of 'informed'

Besides being an exercise in power relations, PIC is also an exercise in communication. Communication between individuals is always complicated by the fact that all people, even as speakers of the same language, have a different body of experience and 'culture' that is used to interpret what they see and hear. As a result, 'misunderstandings' are as much a part of human communication as 'understandings'. The more those engaged in communicating with each other differ in their body of knowledge and experience, the more challenging communication becomes. While this problem is most dramatic and apparent with speakers of different languages who, in effect, cannot understand each other, there are many other situations where misunderstandings are more subtle and perhaps, as a result, more dangerous.

For consent to be informed, it requires that our collaborators understand the full implications of our presence and proposed research. This, in turn, requires a process of translation, which becomes harder as researchers and research participants share less in their experience and understanding. Concepts as basic to researchers and the consent process as 'university', 'academic publications', 'foundation' or 'research' may be alien, and thus require explanation and translation. In some cases, then, the process of PIC includes providing partici-

pants with the necessary background information, conceptual skills and experience to process and evaluate the specific research proposal. As part of our own fieldwork, we conducted workshops and showed audiovisual materials to introduce and discuss our field techniques and the characteristics of such research products as academic publications and herbarium specimens. We also accompanied younger, more bicultural, collaborators on their trips to town, introducing them to the local university, herbaria and libraries and allowing them to meet other Ese Eja more familiar with research and its implications.

While some might criticize these actions for subverting the 'traditional' role of the scientist as an objective observer, we believe that researchers are inevitably agents of intervention and contact. Moreover, in our case, it was clear that we were accepted, at least in part, precisely because we were expected to act as favourable agents of contact and as vehicles through which our collaborators could access external material and political resources. This put us in an extremely difficult position, which we sought to navigate by facilitating contact with institutions and concepts that we felt would strengthen the ability of the Ese Eja to successfully mediate their subsequent relations to the world of *deja*, or 'non-Ese Eja'.

The implications of 'prior' consent

Effective communication is contingent upon having a suitable level of linguistic and cultural competence; yet such competence is primarily gained through the process of enculturation that occurs when researchers spend a considerable amount of time living in the communities in which they wish to work. PIC thus presents researchers with another dilemma: the need to communicate effectively with research participants before they have had a chance to develop effective communication skills. For inexperienced researchers, therefore, the 'prior' and 'consent' aspects of PIC are not easily reconcilable.

There are at least two complementary approaches to this problem. One is for inexperienced researchers to work closely in their PIC negotiations with other researchers or intermediaries, who in turn may have greater cultural and linguistic competence and who are familiar with the history and dynamics of the social groups in question. A second approach is to view PIC as a step-wise feedback process, whereby different stages of the research are introduced in sequence over time, and according to the nature of the relationship between researchers and community members.

During our doctoral fieldwork with the Ese Eja we adopted such an approach. We divided our research into a series of overlapping stages, each of which was based on extended discussions, ongoing dialogue and increased enculturation within the native culture and language. Upon arriving within the community, we discussed our research goals in broad terms, emphasizing that although we were hoping to develop a long and productive relationship, we were only seeking permission to live in the community for a few weeks, in order to get to know each other. The Ese Eja have had state schools in their communities for two decades now, and so are familiar with the concept of a school and of 'formal' education. We explained that we were students, and that part of our training required us to conduct a study and write a book. We explained that we wanted to come live with them for some time, getting to know each other and learn the language, and that during our time there we wanted to be of as much assistance as possible in ways that mattered to the community. We enlisted some of the things with which we had experience; this included different aspects of community development, and some of this experience was interesting to our hosts. After a discussion among themselves, several people expressed that in the past 'outsiders' had come in, 'taken things out' and left nothing behind. We reiterated our willingness to break that pattern and asked what we could do. The community voted to let us live with them and we were asked to contribute to the upcoming celebrations for the community's anniversary, and to provide some books for the school. In addition, we were asked to share some of the medicinal plant knowledge we had acquired through our work with other groups with our hosts. We spent several weeks living in the community, engaging in 'participant observation', learning the language and, above all, getting to know each other as people.

After several weeks, we had begun to establish personal relationships with individuals and had participated in the daily work of different households in the community. At that point, we held another meeting in which we presented and discussed a next stage of research that would involve some semi-structured household interviews in which we collected baseline demographic, health and natural resource-use data. We thus structured our research into a series of phases, each of which gave us and our hosts a series of tools in order to evaluate the form and content of the next phase. Repeated meetings helped process the cumulative experience gained over the months, allowing the community to absorb new information, evaluate us and our work and articulate more clearly and confidently their own needs and expectations. Over time, our commitment and our collaboration with our hosts grew out of this relationship, which in the end led to a participatory and bilingual health manual (Huajo-Huajo et al, in preparation), to the use of slides, tapes and video in a process of intercommunity communication, and to other forms of reciprocal exchange.

This approach incorporates the principle of 'the dynamic interactive cycle' where projects are seen as 'cycles of continuous and ongoing dialogue' (ISE, 1998). This process 'should be initiated in the project design and continue through implementation by way of dialogue and negotiation' (American Anthropological Association, 1998).

Conclusion

Difficult choices need to be made regarding the troubling fact that researchers, as all external agents, are inevitably, implicitly or explicitly agents of change and intervention. The process of social research inevitably transforms the very reality it seeks to observe. Indeed, people often welcome or put up with researchers because they see them as vehicles of contact with external resources – political, financial or material.

Ultimately, consent is an exercise in power relations and in communication, both of which become immeasurably more complicated in the context of cross-cultural contact, and given the legacy of inequality and exploitation that underscores most exchanges between external agents and rural communities. We suggest that the wider the cultural gap, the harder it is to obtain genuine PIC. Enculturation, including linguistic competence, and genuine respect and concern for the people with whom we work are absolute prerequisites for PIC. When researchers lack the necessary skills and experience they should consider using adequate intermediaries who can assist in creating a more effective dialogue and consent process. Ultimately however, PIC hinges on a personal and profound commitment to create professional relationships which are as honest and equitable as possible.

Annex 7.2 Indigenous peoples' declarations and statements and equitable research relationships

Graham Dutfield (Working Group on Traditional Resource Rights, Mansfield College, Oxford University)

A survey was carried out of 15 recent international declarations and statements concerning the rights of indigenous peoples in order to elucidate the views and concerns of indigenous peoples concerning equitable research partnerships. These particular statements and declarations were chosen for three reasons. Firstly, they are quite well known and influential, being perhaps the most frequently cited of all such documents. Secondly, the texts of each statement were agreed upon by representatives of indigenous peoples from various countries and can therefore be said to indicate a broad international consensus concerning the issues they address. Although not all were written by indigenous peoples, all of them reflect the authentic views of a large number of indigenous peoples' organizations that had

met together to discuss matters that were of common concern.[13] Third, they are all intended for a large international audience, including indigenous peoples, national and international policy-makers and intergovernmental organizations, and as a consequence are sophisticated, carefully worded and well informed.

It can be summarized from the outset that many of these declarations and statements indicate that researchers must do more to build trust with the indigenous communities with whom they wish to collaborate *before* the research takes place. There is evidently quite a lot of suspicion towards scientists, which is why some of these statements oppose such activities as bioprospecting and registering traditional knowledge. On the other hand, indigenous peoples do not seem completely opposed to

Table 7.3 *Types of demands*

Type of demand	Statement number*
Ownership/inalienable rights over knowledge and resources	1, 2, 3, 4, 5, 6, 7, 8, 9, 10, 11, 12, 13, 14, 15
Prior informed consent	1, 2, 3, 4, 10, 11, 12, 14, 15
Participation	3, 4, 7, 12, 13, 14, 15
Right of veto over research and/or access to lands, knowledge and resources	1, 8, 10, 12, 14, 15
Moratorium on bioprospecting	5, 10, 11, 12, 13, 15
Full disclosure of research results	1
Compensation/benefit-sharing	2, 3, 4, 7, 12, 14, 15
Restitution	2, 4, 10, 11, 14, 15
Codes of ethics to guide research partnerships	5, 7, 8

Note: * Numbers refer to Box 7.14.

228

BOX 7.14 STATEMENTS AND DECLARATIONS OF INDIGENOUS PEOPLES

1 *Declaration of Principles of the World Council of Indigenous Peoples* (1984)
2 *Kari-Oca Declaration and the Indigenous Peoples' Earth Charter* (1992)
3 *Charter of the Indigenous Tribal Peoples of the Tropical Forests* (1992)
4 *UN Draft Declaration on the Rights of Indigenous Peoples* (1993)
5 *Mataatua Declaration on Cultural and Intellectual Property Rights of Indigenous Peoples* (1993)
6 *Julayinabul Declaration Regarding the Wet Tropics World Heritage Centre* (1993)
7 'Recommendations from the Congress, Voices of the Earth: Indigenous Peoples, New Partners, the Right to Self-Determination in Practice' (1993)
8 'Statement from the COICA/UNDP Regional Meeting on Intellectual Property Rights and Biodiversity' (*Santa Cruz Declaration*) (1994)
9 'UNDP Consultation on the Protection and Conservation of Indigenous Knowledge' (*Sabah Declaration*) (1995)
10 'Final Statement from the UNDP Consultation on Indigenous Peoples' Knowledge and Intellectual Property Rights' (*Suva Declaration*) (1995)
11 *Principles and Guidelines for the Protection of the Heritage of Indigenous Peoples* (1995)
12 *International Alliance of Indigenous Tribal Peoples of the Tropical Forests: the Biodiversity Convention – the Concerns of Indigenous Peoples* (1995)
13 *Indigenous Peoples' Biodiversity Network: Indigenous Peoples, Indigenous Knowledge and Innovations and the Convention on Biological Diversity* (1996)
14 *Results of the International Meeting of Indigenous and Other Forest-Dependent Peoples on the Management, Conservation and Sustainable Development of All Types of Forests: a Contribution to the Intergovernmental Panel on Forests* ('Leticia Statement') (1996)
15 *Second International Indigenous Forum on Biodiversity: Submission to the Workshop on Traditional Knowledge and Biological Diversity* (1997)

---

sharing their knowledge once a climate of trust and good faith has been established.

The main demands relating to equitable research relationships that can be gleaned from the statements and declarations are included in Table 7.3.

Ownership and/or inalienable rights over resources and knowledge

Recognition that indigenous peoples own their knowledge and have inalienable rights over their lands and resources is expressed in all of the statements. For example, the *Declaration of Principles of the World Council of Indigenous Peoples* (1984) states that:

'Indigenous peoples have inalienable rights over their traditional lands and over the use of their natural resources which have been usurped, or taken away without the free and knowledgeable consent of Indian peoples' (paragraph 10).

They tend to consider knowledge, resources and territories as inextricably linked. Thus, their ownership of one implies their ownership of all. According to the *Mataatua Declaration on Cultural and Intellectual Property Rights of Indigenous Peoples* (1993):

'Indigenous flora and fauna is inextricably bound to the territories of indigenous communities and any property right claims must recognize their traditional guardianship' (paragraph 2.6).

Researchers should certainly not assume that access to indigenous peoples' knowledge, resources and territories is freely accessible but, rather, should understand that such access is negotiable.

Prior informed consent

The requirement that PIC should commence before research is another very common demand. Paragraph 61 of the *Kari-Oca Declaration and the Indigenous Peoples' Earth Charter* (1992) states as follows:

'Indigenous peoples must consent to all projects in our territories. Prior to consent being obtained the peoples must be fully and entirely involved in any decisions. They must be given all the information about the project and its effects. Failure to do so should be considered a crime against the indigenous peoples.'

Similarly, according to the *Charter of the Indigenous Tribal Peoples of the Tropical Forests* (1992):

'All investigations in our territories should be carried out with our consent and under joint control and guidance according to mutual agreement; including the provision for training, publication and support for indigenous institutions necessary to achieve such control' (Article 45).

Participation in research and decision-making

Almost as common was the demand that indigenous peoples are granted the right to participate in all activities and decisions affecting them, including scientific research. For example, the *Principles and Guidelines for the Protection of the Heritage of Indigenous Peoples* (1995) state that:

'Researchers and scholarly institutions should make every possible effort to increase indigenous peoples' access to all forms of medical, scientific and technical education, and participation in all research activities which may affect them or be of benefit to them' (paragraph 38).

With respect to decision-making, the 'Leticia Statement' (1996) claims that:

'Genuine participatory mechanisms need to be developed which allow Indigenous Peoples and other forest dependent peoples a decisive voice in evaluations of deforestation processes and the evolution of appropriate policy responses.'

Right of veto over research and/or access to lands, knowledge and resources

Although the right of veto over research and access is implied in the right to prior informed, some of the statements demand this right explicitly:

'[We urge Pacific governments to] incorporate the concerns of indigenous peoples to protect their knowledge and resources into legislation by including "Prior Informed Consent or No Informed Consent" (PICNIC) procedures and exclude the patenting of life forms' (*Suva Declaration*, 1995, paragraph 5.1).

Furthermore: 'No activities must take place on Indigenous Peoples' territories without their full and informed consent through their representative institutions, including the power of veto' ('Leticia Statement', 1996).

Moratorium on bioprospecting

Several of the more recent statements incorporate this demand. Thus the indigenous peoples' Second International Indigenous Forum on Biodiversity calls for:

'A moratorium on all bioprospecting and/or collection of biological materials in the territories of Indigenous Peoples and protected areas and patenting based on these collections until acceptable sui generis *systems are established'* (1997)

Full disclosure of results

This demand featured in only one of the statements but a number of them expressed an interest in the outcome of scientific research on their knowledge, resources and territories. For example, the World Council of Indigenous Peoples' declaration (1984) states that:

'Indigenous peoples and their designated authorities have the right to be consulted and to authorize the implementation of technological and scientific research conducted within their territories and the right to be informed about the results of such activities' (paragraph 18).

Moreover, the 1995 principles and guidelines call on 'all researchers and scholarly institutions' to:

'take immediate steps to provide indigenous peoples and communities with comprehensive inventories of the cultural property, and documentation of indigenous peoples' heritage, which they may have in their custody' (paragraph 32).

They also call for a:

'return [of] all elements of indigenous peoples' heritage to the traditional owners upon demand, or obtain formal agreements with the traditional owners for the shared custody, use and interpretation of their heritage' (paragraph 33).

Compensation/benefit-sharing

Indigenous peoples not only demand compensation for the use of their knowledge and resources, but also want to decide on the nature of the compensation provided:

'The sharing of the benefits derived from the use of indigenous knowledge [should] include[s] other rights, obligations and responsibilities such as land rights and the maintenance of indigenous cultures to facilitate the transmission of knowledge, innovations, practices and values to future generations' (Second International Indigenous Forum on Biodiversity, 1997, paragraph 8).

Furthermore, 'Any benefits from territories of Indigenous Peoples and other forest dependent Peoples must primarily be for their own local use and in accordance with principles of benefit-sharing established by them' ('Leticia Statement', 1996).

Restitution

Indigenous peoples in some of these statements demand full restitution, repatriation and/or other forms of legal recourse when knowledge or resources are taken from them without authorization. Thus, the 1995 principles and guidelines state that:

> 'National laws should guarantee that indigenous peoples can obtain prompt, effective and affordable judicial or administrative action in their own languages to prevent, punish and obtain full restitution and just compensation for the acquisition, documentation or use of their heritage without proper authorization of the traditional owners' (paragraph 25).

Codes of ethics to guide research partnerships

In four of the statements indigenous peoples urge governments, scientists, academic and other organizations, and indigenous peoples themselves to adopt, develop or comply with ethical standards and guidelines, such as codes of ethics and conduct. The statement from the Voices of the Earth Conference recommends that (1993): 'Governmental and non-governmental organizations, as well as scientific and professional groups, should develop codes of ethics and conduct regarding respect for indigenous peoples and their intellectual, cultural and scientific property' ('Cultural, Scientific and Intellectual Property', paragraph 3).

The *Mataatua Declaration* (1993) calls on indigenous peoples *rather than just external agencies* to 'develop a code of ethics which external users must observe when recording (visual, audio, written) their traditional and customary knowledge' (paragraph 1.3).

Annex 7.3 Prior informed consent: protocol and form

Marianne Guerin-McManus (Conservation International) and Dillon Kim (Conservation International)

Introduction

'The primary moral justification of the obligation to obtain informed consent is respect for autonomous action' (Ruth R Faden and Tom L Beauchamp).

Local communities and governments claim that it is because of their cultivation, preservation and use of plants that the biodiversity found on their lands has resulted in valuable medicines for the rest of the world. Pharmaceutical companies claim that it is their research efforts that add value to the raw samples extracted from these biodiverse regions for world consumption. These biodiversity collectors want local communities and governments to preserve these areas, but communities demand compensation to make this conservation effort worth their while. Often, this has led to heated conflict between the two groups. Today, however, a previously improbable collaboration between local communities and the private sector may be the key in satisfying the agendas of both, as well as in achieving the overall conservation of these biologically significant areas.

To facilitate this collaboration, collectors of biodiversity are increasingly attempting to obtain informed consent by the local community before researching and developing the indigenous community's natural resources into marketable goods. By obtaining informed consent, collectors demonstrate their commitment and concern for the community's sovereignty over its own natural resources as per the directive from the Convention on Biological Diversity (Articles 15 (4), 15 (5)). The purpose of obtaining informed consent is to fully apprise the local community of the intentions of the collector. The anticipated result of obtaining informed consent is that both parties fully understand the cooperative nature of the proposed project, and understand the potential benefits that might result from the sharing of community knowledge regarding natural resources.

In order to obtain informed consent, an understanding is required by both the collector and the local community of the property law that will govern the transaction. Instruction in the field of patents and other intellectual property tools may be necessary in order for a truly informed consent to exist. This may involve considerable effort since the concept of a legal intellectual property framework may be completely at odds with the indigenous population's traditional beliefs about the 'ownership' of these resources. There must be considerable effort to bridge this gap of understanding between the collector and the native populations since this lack of baseline understanding will prevent any meaningful discussion from taking place. These differences must therefore be reconciled before informed consent can exist.

The process of consent is essentially the result of a continuous dialogue between the two parties. The community must have *sufficient information* to make an intelligent judgement about their situation. This requires full disclosure by the collector of the purpose of collection as well as an opportunity for the community to ask questions of the collector. The community or community representative must also be *competent* in order to comprehend the information presented and must be able to *understand* the consequences of the decision at hand. Finally, the decision must be made *voluntarily* without outside interference or coercion. It is important when determining whether the consent was voluntary to take into consideration the bargaining power and options for the parties. For instance, a community in extreme poverty will be more likely to settle for less in a deal in their desperation for other amenities. Situations such as this cannot be considered voluntary and the parties must be aware of this potential pitfall.

If the entire process of dialogue is successful and a sufficient 'meeting of the minds' occurs between the two parties, then informed consent can exist. PIC is not a contract per se but instead sets the stage for a more detailed delineation of the arrangement. Hopefully, the informed consent will be seen over time as a kind of gatekeeper that serves to sharpen the dialogue between the parties involved in the bioprospecting deal.

Framework for obtaining informed consent

The difficulty in establishing a model consent form that adequately documents the initial agreement between the collectors and indigenous communities is that each individual situation will require a unique approach. As a result, the process will largely depend upon the good faith of the negotiating parties, who will be required to work out the extent of the details that are needed to adequately describe what exactly is being agreed upon. Despite the wide range in variation amongst the consent forms, there are many common concerns that will arise throughout the course of these types of negotiation.

This annex tries to document some of the considerations and gives an example of what a consent form may look like. However, it should not be treated as a model form to blindly follow; a form would be antithetical to the improvisational nature required of such agreements. The idea of obtaining informed consent should not be looked upon so much as a contract but instead should be looked upon as an instructional tool. Consequently, the ongoing discussion with, and education of, the community should continue even after the consent document is signed.

The dialogue between the negotiating parties should be recorded whenever possible for the benefit of all of those involved in the consent process. A transcript would be extremely helpful in determining the *intent* of the negotiating parties, which is crucial in any agreement process. The agreement should also be flexible to alteration if the background conditions surrounding the initial consent have unpredictably changed to a considerable degree over time. This would prevent any party from being locked into a deal that they had not intended. The initial consent agreement, therefore, must be reviewed periodically to ensure that the arrangement is an accurate representation of this process of consent.

Box 7.15 Basic checklist and sample consent form

Basic checklist outlining aspects of consent form

1 A full transcript or notes of all the discussions and explanations given to date

- The full details of everything that needs to be understood when obtaining consent can not pragmatically be put into one document. A transcript thus becomes absolutely essential in helping to determine the exact nature of the agreement and the intent of the parties. A possible suggestion would be to create an official transcript that could be referred to in the consent form and subsequent contracts or agreements.

2 Date and location of meeting

- A convenient forum should be provided in order to encourage participation by all interested parties. The forum should most likely be in the area in which the collectors plan to utilize the most community knowledge and resources.

3 Parties to the agreement

- It is important to note who is negotiating and in what capacity they are acting. If the representative is speaking for a group, it becomes critical to assess the nature of that representation and how well informed the represented group is of the decision-making process. The objective is to reduce the likelihood of corruption and 'capture' at the top and legitimize the use of representatives in the negotiations.
- Great efforts should be made to identify and include the parties who will be affected by the decision. Documentation of this effort will enhance the legitimacy of the consent.
- The official country government should be taken into account. However, it should be noted that not all governments support their indigenous communities and vice versa.

4 Substance of the agreement

- The intentions of the parties should be expressed in a clear and concise manner with an opportunity for each party to ask questions in order to clarify what is at stake. It is not adequate simply to state that a full explanation was given. Instead, more detail of what was communicated is important in determining whether consent was obtained through a genuine understanding of the situation.
- The agreement should be sensitive to the difficulties presented when the signees are unfamiliar with concepts that are fundamental to the understanding of the agreement. The notion of property and, in particular, intellectual property should be understood by all parties before any discussion of consent can occur. A transcript of the proceedings would be particularly useful here since the requisite level of understanding of crucial concepts could be ascertained by analysing the level of dialogue.
- The projected scope of the planned research should be included. This involves initial predictions of what the collector hopes to find and what the collector will do with the information or resource. It should be understood that the more the scope of the project deviates from the initial projections, the less convincing is the informed consent.

- There should be some mention of what the benefits to the community may be if the product or information is found to be marketable. This would be evidence that the discussion occurred with the required baseline understanding by both parties of the implications of the consent.
- The project's time period should be specified. A finite time period will ensure a continuous process of obtaining the consent of the local community that is crucial to the legitimacy of the activity.

5 Signatures of the parties granting consent

- A signature should be understood by all parties as a recognition of the terms outlined in the process of obtaining consent. In particular, the binding nature of signing documents should be adequately understood by all parties.

Sample Consent Form

This agreement represents the result of an ongoing process and dialogue between ____ [party A] and ____ [party B] since contact was first initiated between the two parties on ____ [date or approximate date]. (See transcript, pp [000–000].)

A meeting was held on ____ [date] at ____ [location of the meeting] between ____ [parties including the collector, the country encompassing the region and the indigenous group]. Effort was made to establish the relationship between the official country government and the indigenous group. Effort was also made to determine that the representative indigenous group in the contract was indeed the historical occupier of the land from which collection is to occur. There is also documentation that this group has been the primary steward of the resource. Effort was shown to exist in determining that the representatives who will sign or give consent are truly representative of the people who will be affected by the decision. These efforts are to ensure the integrity of this agreement and of the collection process. (See transcript, pp [000–000].)

During the dialogue process, the collector has fully explained to the source country government and to the local indigenous people about his/her objectives of collection. The collector fully explained the potential benefits and profits that could result from collection. The collector specified, if applicable, the specific sample to be collected. There is reasonable understanding by the collector that the source country and the local indigenous people fully comprehend and adequately interpret what he/she hopes to find and develop and the results and consequences of consent. If any knowledge of the local indigenous people is to be utilized, that is mentioned here. This section requires extensive proof through documentation. (See transcript, pp [000–000].)

The time frame for the research is specified. The scope of the area to be searched will be defined with continual analysis and research in order to ensure that the local indigenous people occupy all of that land area. (See transcript, pp [000–000].)

The specifics of the consent are outlined: what is agreed upon, by whom, when the agreement is to take place, where the research will be carried out, and the potential gains for both through this agreement. (See transcript, pp [000–000].)

_____

Signatures to the consent with an understanding by all parties of the binding nature of signatures. (See transcript, pp [000–000].)

Translated copies are to be kept for all parties involved.

Notes

1   For a more comprehensive discussion of the legal and policy context briefly addressed here, see: Working Group on Traditional Resource Rights (www.users.ox.ac.uk/~wgtrr); Posey, 1996; Posey and Dutfield, 1996; IWGIA, 1997 (http://hem1.passagen.se/iwgia); IBPN (ipbn@web.net); Glowka, 1998; Tobin, 1999; Gómez, 1997; Garcia Hierro, 1997; Ardito, 1997: Graves, 1994; IUCN, 1997.

2   The Spatial Development Initiative Programme emerges directly from the government's macro-economic strategy and aims to generate employment and 'sustainable economic growth and development' through attracting private investment to regions that are perceived to be underutilized.

3   The Shell Camisea Project in Peru, for example, involved an extensive process of consultation and participation that was subject to ongoing revision. This process included workshops on capacity-building, law, characteristics of petrol operations and environmental impact assessment. Aside from concerns associated with the operation itself, and the reasons for Shell's decision to discontinue its operations, it is certain that the communities involved are now better prepared to defend their rights and to negotiate benefit-sharing agreements with any company that may in the future seek to exploit the Camisea oil field then they were when Shell entered in 1994. For further discussion of the Shell project in Camisea, see la Torre Lopez, 1998 and Camisea's web page: www.camisea.com.

4   To facilitate the exchanges of information between individuals and groups with an interest in community research agreements, contact details and documents will be posted on the People and Plants Conservation Series website, www.rbgkew.org.uk/peopleplants/manuals/index.html.

5   Personal communication from Marthinus Horak of the CSIR, November 1999

6   Our discussion is mostly focused on research that is performed in cross-cultural contexts: that is, where researchers are from nationalities, regions, ethnic groups, social class, professions or levels of academic instruction that differ from those of all, or most, research participants. Most research fits into this definition of 'cross-cultural' even though different contexts may raise problems that vary in degree and kind to those described here.

7   Some authors suggest that in some instances, application of Western ethical standards of informed consent represents a form of ethical imperialism (Angell, 1998; Newton, 1990; cited in Marshall, 1992).

8   We use the term 'research participants' to describe the people who are directly and indirectly involved and or impacted by our field research. Thus, we include not only people who are directly involved in the research, as subjects, informants, collaborators or partners, but also their kin and neighbours whose lives will be directly or indirectly affected by our research.

9   Clearly, there are instances where researchers are community members, in which case the role of researchers as external agents is not as evident. However, even in these cases community researchers tend to collaborate or work closely with such external agents as state and private institutions.

10 As critical as developing deep and meaningful personal relationships is, such relationships create a new set of ethical problems, at times making it easier to compromise one's commitment to informed consent. As the American Anthropological Association (AAA) notes: 'researchers who have developed close and enduring relationships...with either individual persons providing information or with hosts must adhere to the obligations of openness and informed consent, while carefully and respectfully negotiating the limits of the relationship' (AAA, 1998). Metcalf (1998, p327) observes that 'all such relationships [between anthropologists and their hosts] are at least potentially exploitative. We make use of those who befriend us; we have the power to damage those to whom we are most

indebted'; this weighs heavily on anyone who has developed close personal relationships with their research hosts.

11 Ese Eja is the self-denominated term for an Amazonian Tacana group living in a number of communities in the border regions of Bolvia and Peru, close to the lowland foothills of the Andes. We conducted our doctoral fieldwork in two communities, between 1994 and 1996, though we had previously worked extensively with these and other Ese Eja groups (eg Alexiades, 1999; Peluso, in preparation).

12 This category, whose literal translation is 'old', has different meanings and connotations. An *etii* (plural, *etiikiana*) is an old person, but *etii* is also used to describe the eldest man within an extended family group. This is the meaning we employ in our discussion. Another category of *etii* refers to yet another, now extinct, leadership status. These men reportedly exerted considerable authority in military and other group decisions. This last category of *etii* began to decline at the time of intensified contacts between the Ese Eja and the nation state at the turn of the century, leading to its disappearance during the mid 20th century.

13 Numbers 4 and 11 in Box 7.14 were drafted by the UN Working Group on Indigenous Peoples (WGIP) in response to the many submissions, proposals and suggestions provided by indigenous peoples' organizations attending the annual WGIP meetings.

Section IV

THE COMMERCIAL USE OF BIODIVERSITY AND TRADITIONAL KNOWLEDGE

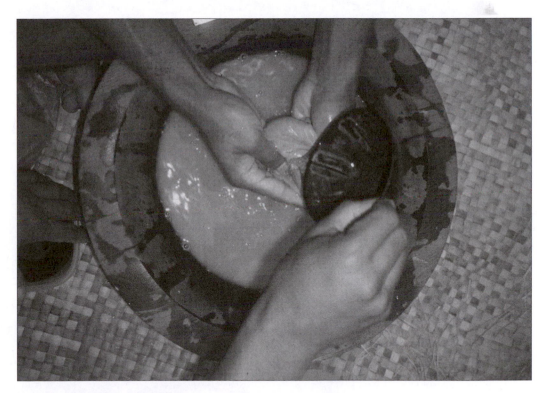

Kava (Piper methysticum) prepared in the South Pacific. Kava has been used traditionally in the region for thousands of years, and recently became a top-selling botanical product on international markets

Biodiversity prospecting: the commercial use of genetic resources and best practice in benefit-sharing

Sarah A Laird and Kerry ten Kate

Introduction

The world's biological diversity is distributed largely in inverse proportion to scientific and technological capacity (Macilwain, 1998). As a result, many biologically diverse countries with developing economies and limited scientific infrastructure do not actively participate in rapid scientific and technological advances that make new and varied use of genetic resources. At the same time, companies and research institutions based in developed countries seek diversity and novelty in the genetic resources they study and use, and many look outside their borders for new leads. The Convention on Biological Diversity (CBD) promotes more equitable use and exchange of genetic resources, redrawing ethical and legal norms established over a long history of genetic resource trade and commercialization, and seeking to balance the needs of both technologically and biologically endowed countries.

Informal, as well as commercial, trade in genetic resources is as old as human civilization. One of the earliest recorded plant-collecting expeditions was sent out from Egypt in 1495 BC to the land of Punt (Somalia/Ethiopia) to obtain frankincense-producing species of *Boswellia* (Juma, 1989). Europeans' search for spices, and subsequent colonization, furthered state-supported collection of genetic resources, resulting in a vast transfer of such resources, expanded cultivation of existing crops and the introduction of new ones. By the 18th century, botanic gardens – originally established as medicinal gardens attached to European universities in the 16th and 17th centuries – were brokering the transfer of a wide range of species around the world. These included coffee, oranges, bananas, cinchona and mahogany (Juma, 1989; Table 8.1).

Years of exchange across cultures and continents means that many genetic resources have passed outside of their original countries of origin, and today many are found in vast ex-situ collections housed in developed countries. At the same time, much biodiversity (such as micro-organisms) located within developed countries remains poorly understood, and its commercial potential

Table 8.1 *Examples of genetic resources transferred before the 20th century*

Species	Common name	Origin	Destination and date (if known) of transfer(s)	Primary areas of production today
Theobroma cacao	Cocoa	Lower slopes of Andes	Central America (circa 0AD), Gulf of Guinea islands (1600s), South-East Asia (1670s)	Ghana, Brazil, Nigeria
Coffea arabica	Coffee	Ethiopia	Arabia (unknown; 1200s?), Java (1690s), India (late 1600s), Brazil (1727), Uganda (1900)	Brazil, Colombia, Côte d'Ivoire
Musa spp	Bananas	India – New Guinea region	Near East/Mediterranean (700–1000), East Africa (before 1000?)	Central and South America, Africa, Asia
Camellia sinensis	Tea	China	Java (1690), India (1818), Sri Lanka (1870s), Malawi (1886)	India, Sri Lanka, China
Hevea brasiliensis	Rubber	Amazon	Sri Lanka, Singapore (1870s)	Malaysia, Indonesia
Catharanthus roseus	Rosy periwinkle	Madagascar	Europe (early 1700s)	US, India, also pan-tropical weed
Cinchona spp	Cinchona, quinine	Andes	Java (1854), India (1861)	Quinine, largely replaced by synthetic anti-malarials
Zea mays	Maize, corn	Mexico	Throughout New World (pre-1490s), East Africa (1498), Spain (1500)	US, Europe, China, Africa
Ipomoea batatas	Sweet potato	Tropical America	Polynesia (1250s–1390s), Spain (early 1500s)	Africa, Asia
Citrullus lanatus	Watermelon	Africa	South-West Asia (circa 2000 BC), America (1500s)	Dry tropics/sub-tropics
Sorghum bicolor sub-spp *Bicolor*	Sorghum	Sahel	India (3200–2500 BC), Mediterranean (100–300), North America (1850s)	Africa, India
Manihot esculenta	Cassava	Tropical America	Gulf of Guinea islands (late 1500s), Madagascar (mid 1700s)	Africa, America
Eucalyptus spp	Gum	Australia	India (1790), Africa (1800s)	Pan-tropical/sub-tropical

Source: Purseglove, 1979; Prendergast, et al, 1998; Vaughan and Geissler, 1997; Tewari, 1992; Juma, 1989

is, as yet, unexplored. As a result, many researchers today conduct research on genetic resources readily available in situ or ex situ at home. However, the extraordinary diversity and novelty of genetic resources found in high-biodiversity regions remains a valuable source of leads for new product development, and many companies continue to seek access to these materials.

Numerous concerns are associated with current collecting activities, and the disposition of existing ex-situ collections of resources. For some, any commercial use of genetic resources is 'biopiracy', because it is felt that the legal and policy environment does not adequately ensure prior informed consent and adequate benefit-sharing (Shiva, 1998; www.RAFI.org; www.GRAIN.org). For others, however, fair and equitable benefit-sharing arrangements within the context of a suitable policy framework can be in the interests of all the stakeholders involved, including governments, research institutions, communities and companies in both provider and user countries. However, poor understanding of markets, a dearth of experience in establishing partnerships and inadequate or unclear policy frameworks mean that there are currently relatively few success stories to support this position. A number of features of the transfer of genetic resources and the discovery and development of products make the monitoring and enforcement of access and benefit-sharing agreements extremely difficult, as a number of authors have observed (Zerner, 1999; Parry, 1999; ten Kate and Laird, 1999).

Among these features are the route by which material travels from countries of origin to the private sector, the many hands through which they pass from collection to commercialization, the fact that the product which is commercialized is frequently not physically linked to the original genetic resources collected, but may have been manufactured from scratch based on modifications of chemical structures originally found in nature, and the difficulty of tracking the exchange of genetic resources and their derivatives. The use of genetic material and biochemicals contained in genetic resource samples has become increasingly specialized, and companies and researchers in academia often treat research activities as confidential, thus rendering their use beyond the grasp of the lay person.

By revealing some of the scientific and economic uses to which genetic resources pass after field collection, we hope that this chapter can help to provide the basis from which governments, individuals and institutions can structure equitable relationships with commercial partners (see ten Kate and Laird, 1999). In this chapter, we offer some basic information on the ways in which selected industries use biodiversity, their demand for access to genetic resources and practices in benefit-sharing. The intention is not to promote commercial use per se, but to contribute to wider understanding of the mechanics of biodiversity prospecting so that when commercial use takes place, it is informed and according to current standards of best practice.

What is biodiversity prospecting?

Biodiversity prospecting encompasses a wide range of commercial activities, including the pharmaceutical, biotechnology, seed, crop protection, horticulture, botanical medicine, cosmetic and personal care and food and beverage sectors (ten Kate and Laird, 1999). Lines between commercial sectors are increasingly blurred, through mergers and acquisitions (eg Glaxo Wellcome and SmithKline Beecham; Monsanto and Pharmacia & Upjohn; and Pfizer and Warner Lambert) and strategic partnerships in research and development (R&D), production and marketing. These make use of cross-sector synergies to develop new knowledge and novel

---

BOX 8.1 DEFINITION OF TERMS

Biodiversity prospecting: the exploration of biodiversity for commercially valuable biological and genetic resources

Genetic resources: genetic material of actual or potential value; genetic material means any material of plant, animal, microbial or other origin containing functional units of heredity (see Convention on Biological Diversity, Article 2)

Best practice: standards of practice that are widely regarded by those in the field as representing the highest levels of conduct, and the practical implementation of core underlying principles such as conservation of biodiversity, sustainable use and equitable benefit-sharing

---

products. In large part driven by the emergence of biotechnology within the pharmaceutical, food, seed and chemical industries, new, knowledge-based oligopolies are increasingly formed both within and across industry segments (Mytelka, 1999). Life science companies – combining pharmaceutical, food, seed and chemical divisions under one umbrella – are the most visible manifestation of this trend towards consolidation, strategic partnerships, the evolution of dynamic knowledge-based industries, and the cross-pollination of R&D, production and marketing (Mytelka, 1999; Nayak, 1999). Major life science companies include Aventis, Novartis, Astra-Zeneca, DuPont, Monsanto and Dow AgroSciences (Nayak, 1999).

As biotechnology becomes ubiquitous in industry, virtually every commercial sector makes use of genetic resources in some manner. The biotechnology sector uses bacteria to remove unwanted by-products in the paper and packaging industry; incorporates novel enzymes in the baking industry and uses micro- and other organisms in the human diagnostics industry, valued during 1999 in the US alone at US$2.5 billion (GEN, 1999). Researchers are constantly exploring new uses of genetic resources, such as their potential as starting materials for the development of fibreglass, brake fluid and other components in the automobile industry (see Box 8.10). The pharmaceutical and agriculture industries have received the lion's share of attention directed at biodiversity prospecting; but, in fact, they represent just part of a diverse range of commercial activities involving the use of genetic resources.

The CBD does not mention 'biodiversity prospecting' per se, but contains an article on access to genetic resources, which is an inevitable part of biodiversity prospecting activities. The CBD and subsequent national-access legislation regulate access to genetic resources for non-commercial scientific research, such as taxonomy, as well as for potentially commercial purposes, and are thus broader in application than biodiversity prospecting.

Biodiversity prospecting (often contracted to 'bioprospecting') was first defined as 'the exploration of biodiversity for commercially valuable genetic resources and biochemicals' (Reid et al, 1993). 'Exploration' and 'prospecting' are critical components of the definition. The word 'prospecting' has unfortunate negative connotations of heedless exploitation, but also suggests the *search* (for resources or knowledge), *collection* and/or *acquisition*, and an *intention to commer-*

cialize which characterize biodiversity prospecting. Applying this definition to certain kinds of activity reveals those activities that are properly understood as bioprospecting, and those that involve the use of natural resources in other ways but do not amount to bioprospecting. The bulk trade in commodities, sales of timber or cut flowers, the collection of known non-timber forest products, such as high-intensity protein sweeteners for local and regional trade, and mining for minerals do not constitute biodiversity prospecting. Neither do sales of raw plant material such as *Catharanthus roseus*, *Taxus* spp or *Strophanthus* spp, destined for the manufacture of pharmaceutical drugs, nor the continued sale of products based on genetic resources. Biodiversity prospecting involves the investigation of genetic resources or biochemicals for new commercial leads. Academic research may involve the study of genetic resources, and may give rise to commercial applications, but research only becomes biodiversity prospecting once the researchers spot the commercial potential and conduct their investigations with this in mind.

Understanding the commercial use of genetic resources is a critical prerequisite for equitable agreements, effective national laws and a realistic assessment of national, institutional and community objectives associated with these activities. It can help to provide the basis from which governments, individuals and institutions can structure equitable relationships with commercial partners, and to develop national strategies that simultaneously promote domestic and international research on native genetic resources, the conservation of biodiversity and the fair and equitable sharing of the results arising from its use.

Biodiversity prospecting: a review of selected sectors[1]

Variety in bioprospecting

As this chapter will show, there is considerable variation in the manner in which genetic resources are used in the pharmaceutical, botanical medicine, crop protection, seed, horticulture, personal care and cosmetics sectors, and in other areas of biotechnology, such as bioremediation. Between these industry sectors, and within each one, there is diversity in:

- the size of industries and markets for products;
- the role of natural products in these markets and percentage of sales contributed by genetic resources;
- the relationship between commercial products and the genetic resources from which they are developed.

Size

Table 8.2 reveals a wide range in market figures. The global market for pharmaceuticals is now more than US$300 billion a year, and for agricultural produce in excess of this (although commercial sales of the agricultural seed from which much of this is produced is just some US$30 billion). Sales in the botanical medicine industry are not much more than US$20 billion, and those of ornamental horticultural products lie between US$16–$19 billion. The cosmetic and personal care industry has annual sales between US$50–$75 billion a year (depending upon classification of companies), but the 'natural' component of this industry is not more than US$3 billion. Top companies in the pharmaceutical industry have sales averag-

245

Table 8.2 *World's top companies in selected industry sectors, and annual sales by sector and company*

Pharmaceutical US$300 billion (US$75 billion)* 1998 figures	Crop protection US$30 billion (US$0.6–$3 billion) 1997 figures	Agricultural seed US$30 billion 1997 figures	Horticulture US$16–$19 billion (US$1.8 billion for sales of horticultural seed by top seven companies)	Botanical medicine US$20 billion (top ten German phyto-medical companies) Jan–Nov 1999 figures	Cosmetic and personal care US$75 billion (US$3 billion) 1998 figures
Merck & Co, US (US$13.69 billion)**	Novartis, Switzerland (US$4.2 billion)	Pioneer Hi-Bred, US (US$1.8 billion)***	Takii, Japan (US$430 million)	Schwabe (US$277.8 million)	L'Oreal Group, France (US$10.4 billion)*****
Johnson & Johnson, US (US$8.56 billion)	Monsanto, US (US$3.13 billion)	Monsanto, US (US$1.2 billion)	Sakata, Japan (US$390 million)	Madaus (US$193.13 million)	Procter & Gamble Co, US (US$7.38 billion)
Novartis, Switzerland (US$10 billion)	Zeneca, UK (US$2.67 billion)	Novartis Seeds, Switzerland (US$900 million)	Seminis, US (US$380 million)	Lichtwer (US$175.22 million)	Unilever, The Netherlands and UK (US$6.74 billion)
Bristol-Myers Squibb, US (US$12.57 billion)	DuPont, US (US$2.52 billion)	Groupe Limagrain, France (US$700 million)	Novartis, Switzerland (US$225 million)	Bionorica (US$147.97 million)	Shiseido Co, Japan (US$4.18 billion)
Roche, Switzerland (US$9.94 billion)	AgrEvo, Germany (US$2.35 billion)	Advanta, The Netherlands	Ball, US (US$180 million)	Schaper U Bruemmer (US$141.2 million)	Estee Lauder Co, US (US$3.6 billion)
Aventis, France (US$13.52 billion): merger of Rhone Poulenc and Hoechst	Bayer, Germany (US$2.25 billion)	Agribio Tech, US (US$460 million)	Nunhems/Sunseeds, The Netherlands (US$130 million)	Pohl Boskamp (US$132.51 million)	Johnson & Johnson, US (US$3.24 billion)
Pfizer, US (US$12.23 billion)	Rhône Poulenc, France (US$2.2 billion)*·*	KWS, Germany (US$390 million)	Limagrain, France (US$100 million)	Steigerwald (US$120.65 million)	Avon Products, US (US$3.17 billion)
SmithKline Beecham, UK (US$7.71 billion)	Cyanamid, US (US$2.12 billion)	Seminis, US (US$380 million)		Krewel (US$116.39 million)	Kao Corp, Japan (US$2.4 billion)
Glaxo Wellcome, UK (US$13.25 billion)	Dow AgroSciences, US (US$2.05 billion)	Takii, Japan (US$310 million)		Meuselbach (US$116.39 million)	Wella Group, Germany (US$2.35 billion)
Abbott Laboratories, US (US$2.6 billion)	BASF, Germany (US$1.85 billion)	Sakata, Japan (US$280 million);		Biocur (US$106.59 million)	Beiersdorf AG, Germany (US$2.35 billion)
		Kaneko, Japan (US$280 million)		Hoyer-Madaus (US$98.66 million)	

Notes: * Estimated sales derived from genetic resources, if different from total sales (ten Kate and Laird, 1999); ** Companies are ranked by health-care revenue; sales figures included for each company are for 1998 sales of pharmaceuticals only (*MedAd News*, September 1999); *** Sales figures are for 1997, for seed sales only and not groups sales; ***** Sales figures are for 1998 (WWD, 1999); *·*. In 1999, Hoechst and Rhône Poulenc merged to form Aventis, whose sales will exceed those of Novartis

Sources: Pharmaceuticals: *MedAd News*, September 1999; Crop protection: *Agrow World Crop Protection News*, 1998; Seed: International Seed Trade Federation (FIS), December 1998; Horticulture: Assinsel/FIS, 1998, www.worldseed.org/~assinsel/stat.htm; Botanical medicine: IMS, 1999; Cosmetics and personal care: WWD, 1999

ing around US$10 billion on pharmaceutical products, in cosmetics and personal care between US$2–$10 billion, and the global sales of botanical medicine companies are rarely in excess of US$200 million. The annual turnover of top seed companies such as Pioneer Hi-Bred, Monsanto and Novartis generally lies between US$1 and US$2 billion, and several smaller companies have turnovers of a few hundred million US dollars a year.

The role of genetic resources in market figures

The impact of products derived from genetic resources on market figures also varies significantly between sectors. In the pharmaceutical industry, natural products contribute somewhere between 25–50 per cent of total sales of products on the market. Commercial botanical medicines, ornamental horticultural products and sales of agricultural seed are 100 per cent natural products; 'natural' personal care and cosmetic products make up less than 10 per cent of global sales in this sector today. Since 'biotechnology' can be defined as the application of biological organisms, systems and processes to the provision of goods and services (OECD, 1994; 1998), all categories of biotechnol-

ogy products, from enzymes and metabolites to processes such as bioremediation systems, have involved genetic resources in their development and manufacture.

Commercial products and genetic resources

The relationship between commercial products and genetic resources also varies within sectors. For example, in the pharmaceutical and crop protection industries, commercial products might be chemically identical to the pure natural product, might start with a natural product that is then chemically modified, or might result when the parent structure comes from nature, but the final product is synthesized to a design based on a natural template. 'Natural' personal care and cosmetic products include active ingredients isolated from natural sources, as identified in high-throughput screens, standardized extracts that include set amounts of chemical markers, or extracts of whole plants containing all the constituents found in a given plant. The product base for personal care and cosmetic products might be from genetic resources or, more commonly, synthetic or based on petrochemicals.

Markets and access: the use of genetic resources and traditional knowledge by various industry sectors

Pharmaceuticals

Global sales of pharmaceuticals are currently some US$300 billion a year (*The Economist*, 1998). Pharmaceutical companies have grown an average of 12 per cent over the past five years (*Science*, 1999). North America, Europe and Japan are home to both the majority of consumers and almost all of the large research-based

pharmaceutical companies, including their R&D departments. The pharmaceutical industry is dominated by a core of large multinational companies, the top ten of which represent around a third of global sales (see Table 8.2). Many of these companies are getting larger, as they merge and acquire other companies in order to achieve economies of scale, a larger pool of funds for increasingly expensive research and development programmes, and sometimes to acquire a new drug in another company's 'pipeline' (*The Economist*, 1998).

Pharmaceutical companies are traditionally vertically integrated and conduct the full range of activities from the earliest stages in the discovery process, through to the marketing of drugs. Beginning with the rise of biotechnology (biopharmaceutical) companies in the early 1980s, smaller, innovative companies are springing up that specialize in certain stages in the research process and fill an important niche in the industry. Strategic partnerships have become the norm in the pharmaceutical industry, and in 1997 alone 374 agreements were set up between large pharmaceutical firms and small drug discovery companies. In the US, more than half of the substances currently in clinical trials originated outside the laboratories of the biggest pharmaceutical companies (*C&EN*, February 1998). Government agencies, non-profit research organizations and academic institutions also play a key role in the research process. Although the largest companies continue to market the vast majority of drugs, the research and development process usually involves numerous players.

BOX 8.2 DRUG DISCOVERY AND DEVELOPMENT

Pharmaceutical research and development (R&D) is the process of discovering, developing and bringing to market new ethical drug products. Drug discovery and development activities were once carried out sequentially, but today they often take place at the same time and in conjunction with each other.

Drug discovery

This is the process by which a lead is found, including the acquisition of materials for screening; identification of a disease and therapeutic target of interest; methodology and assay development; advanced screening; and identification of active agents and chemical structure.

The development of a drug by screening consists of two parts: developing a screen to detect biological activity of interest and finding the chemical compounds (both synthetic and of natural origin) to test in the screens. There are two main kinds of screens: mechanism-based screens and whole-organism screens. Compounds to be screened might be man-made 'synthetic' chemicals, including those produced through combinatorial chemistry or natural products.

Drug development

This includes chemical improvements to a drug molecule, animal pharmacology studies, pharmacokinetic and safety studies on animals, followed by phase I, II and III clinical studies in humans. Clinical evaluation phase I studies include safety and pharmacological profiling, usually taking less than a year. Phase II are pilot efficacy studies, involving 200–300 volunteer patients and taking on average two years. Phase III are extensive clinical trials on 1000–3000 volunteer patients, lasting around three years. Phase IV studies are conducted after a drug is approved in order to extend the range of applications for a drug, and to reformulate it in ways to be more effective.

Source: OTA, 1993; Christofferson and Marr, 1995; PhRMA, 1998

The pharmaceutical industry is the most research intensive in the world. In 1997, US- and UK-based companies spent roughly 20 per cent of all sales on R&D, and in Japan this figure was 12.5 per cent (PhRMA, 1998; ABPI, 1998; JPMA, 1998). Estimates for the cost to develop a new drug are now around US$500 million (PhRMA, 1999; ABPI, 1998). The bulk of this is spent on development, with only 37 per cent spent on the discovery phase. It is common within the US, Europe and Japan for a third of research budgets to be spent on clinical trials, which absorb a larger portion of R&D budgets and time than any other category (Shearson Lehman Brothers, 1991; PhRMA, 1999). Estimates for the time required to develop a drug are between 10 to 18 years, largely due to the lengthening clinical trial phase (JPMA, 1999; PhRMA, 1999). Of 5000–10,000 compounds screened, only one is estimated to become an approved drug (PhRMA, 1998).

Trends in R&D and the role of natural products

Scientific developments in the fields of biochemistry, molecular biology, cell biology, immunology and information technology are transforming the process of drug discovery and development. Advances in molecular biology and genomics produce a previously inaccessible range of disease targets for the development of new drugs. New scientific technologies – such as combinatorial chemistry, high-throughput screens and laboratories-on-a-chip – provide unprecedented numbers of compounds to test in high-throughput screens, as well as better ways to turn the new knowledge into conventional molecules and those produced by biotechnology, for testing. At the same time, trends in the financial and management decision-making process

influence R&D, including pressure to reduce cycle times and costs and the need for significant breakthrough therapies (Carte, 1997).

In this environment, natural products are often viewed as too slow, costly and problematic. Combinatorial chemistry, which can rapidly generate vast numbers of chemical compounds for screening, has created real pressures on natural-products research departments to deliver viable leads. However, natural products continue to hold key advantages: diversity and novelty resulting from years of evolution. Furthermore, improvements in the technology associated with purifying and analysing compounds in complex mixtures have decreased the time involved in separating and analysing natural products (RFS, *Science*, 1999). Combinatorial chemistry and natural products are increasingly seen as complementary, rather than competing, sources of new compounds for screening.

In fact, although some companies have recently scaled down or closed natural products programmes, including Abbott Laboratories, SmithKline Beecham and Shaman Pharmaceuticals, all of the world's top pharmaceutical companies either run natural-products discovery programmes in-house or through wholly owned subsidiaries. Within these companies, natural products form one small part of R&D budgets – usually occupying only between 1–5 per cent. However, natural products continue to hold a disproportionate significance for the bottom line of these same companies.

Newman and Laird (1999) demonstrated, for example, that the contribution of natural products to sales in the world's top pharmaceutical companies ranged from 10 per cent to more than 50 per cent. In the case of Merck & Co, for example, natural product or natural product-derived drugs accounted for 50.6 per cent of 1997 sales. Cholesterol-lowering Zocor (simvastatin), derived from a natural product and the world's top-selling drug, earned Merck & Co sales of US$3.58 billion in 1997 and US$3.95 billion in 1998 (*MedAd News*, May 1998; May 1999). Of the 25 best-selling drugs world-wide in 1997, 42 per cent of sales came from biologicals, natural products or entities derived from natural products, with a total value of US$17.5 billion (Newman and Laird, 1999). Key products driving Bristol-Myers Squibb's record sales in the first quarter of 1999 included the cholesterol-lowering natural product Pravachol (pravastatin), showing 9 per cent growth and first quarter sales of US$486 million (total 1997 sales of US$1.44 billion; 1998 sales of US$1.64 billion), and the anti-cancer drug Taxol (taxotere), derived from the Pacific yew tree (*Taxus brevifolia*), with 31 per cent growth and sales of US$329 million in the first quarter of 1999 (1998 sales of US $1.2 billion) (Mirasol, 1999; *MedAd News*, May 1999).

In a 1997 study, Grifo et al (1997) analysed the top 150 proprietary drugs from the US National Prescription Audit for the period of January–September 1993. The audit is a compilation of virtually all of the prescriptions filled in the US during this time, and the data are based on the number of times a prescription was filled. They found that 57 per cent of the prescriptions filled contained at least one major active compound 'now or once derived or patterned after compounds from biological diversity'. Cragg et al (1997) analysed data on new drugs approved by either the US Food and Drug Administration (FDA) or comparable entities in other countries between 1985–1995, focusing on the areas of cancer and infectious diseases. They found that of the 87 approved cancer drugs, 62 per cent are of natural origin or are modelled on natural product parents, and of the 299 anti-cancer drugs in pre-clinical or clinical development, the figure was 61 per cent.

Natural product drug discovery is likely to continue as an element of pharmaceutical R&D, if on a modest scale relative to other discovery tools. However, as scientific and technological advances

---

BOX 8.3 RELATIONSHIPS BETWEEN NATURAL PRODUCTS AND FINAL COMMERCIAL PRODUCTS

Natural products contribute in a range of ways to commercial drug discovery, including:

- *Biologicals or biopharmaceuticals:* an entity that is a protein or polypeptide either isolated directly from the natural source or more usually made by recombinant DNA techniques, followed by production-using fermentation; also viral and bacterial vaccines and blood products.
- *Natural products:* an entity that, although occasionally manufactured by semi-synthesis or even total synthesis, is chemically identical to the pure natural product.
- *Derived from a natural product:* an entity that starts with a natural product that is then chemically modified to produce the drug.
- *Structural class from a natural product:* this is material where a parent structure came from nature and then materials were synthesized de novo but following the natural template.

Source: Newman and Laird, 1999

continue to evolve, the nature of industry demand for genetic resources will also change. Current trends are towards smaller numbers of targeted samples, rather than the large bulk collections typical during the 1980s. R&D approaches fall in and out of favour within this industry with great speed, suggesting that national governments should not only have sufficient understanding of R&D while drafting national access and benefit-sharing (ABS) measures, but should continue to follow developments closely in subsequent years.

Biotechnology

'Biotechnology' means the application of biological organisms, living systems and processes to the provision of goods and services (OECD, 1994; 1998). Biotechnology companies apply enzymes and use biologically active compounds derived from genetic resources as an integral part of processes and products in almost every industry sector. The biotechnology industry is relatively young and still evolving. In the early 1980s, biotechnology was primarily an academic enterprise that used molecular biology, recombinant DNA technology, genetic engineering, biochemistry, plant and animal sciences and immunology research as the basis from which to develop new products. During the past 20 years, the biotechnology industry has matured into a sector based on the intensive use of knowledge, capital and human resources, with more than 5000 companies worldwide, market capitalization of around US$200 billion and annual sales of some US$50 billion (Nayak, 1999). Biotechnology has become so ubiquitous that it is difficult to identify an industry into which it has not been integrated; as a result, it is difficult to treat it distinctly from the other sectors covered here.

Biopharmaceutical companies represent the largest segment of the biotechnology industry and a part of the pharmaceutical industry that is swiftly growing in importance. Biopharmaceuticals currently contribute 11 per cent of the sales of the top 25 blockbuster drugs; however, their market share is likely to grow significantly, with anticipated sales in 2005 of US$20.4 billion (GEN, 1999). Biopharmaceutical companies produce human therapeutic products – such as proteins, vaccines and monoclonal antibodies – using biotechnological techniques. In 1998 there were 75 biopharmaceuticals on the market and 35 more slated for FDA approval. Over 350 biopharmaceuticals produced by 140 pharmaceutical and biotechnology companies are currently under development (Laird and ten Kate, 1999; Newman and Laird, 1999).

Agricultural biotechnology is the second largest segment of the biotechnology sector. Companies modify plant and animal genes to produce organisms with desirable properties, such as pest resistance, improved nutritional profiles or the ability to make chemicals more economically. Genetic engineering has already produced a raft of recombinant seed products, including delayed-ripening tomatoes, herbicide-resistant cotton, insect-resistant corn and fungus and virus-resistant crops. In 1998, total commercial planting of biotechnology crops developed by Monsanto alone comprised more than 22.3 million hectares worldwide, out of a total acreage for all biotechnology crops planted in the world that year of more than 30 million hectares. In 1998, the market potential for pre-farm gate uses of biotechnology was estimated to be in the range of US$50–$70 billion (ten Kate, 1999a). Post-farm gate opportunities were estimated at around US$500 billion (*AgBiotech Bulletin*, 1998).

In addition to healthcare and agriculture, several other markets for biotechnology products and processes, such as environmental biotechnology, industrial enzymes, biocatalysts, diagnostics, biomaterials and bioenergy, are growing rapidly (ten Kate, 1999b). Many 'environmental technologies' use biotechnology to save energy and materials, and to reduce, treat or dispose of waste. Some environmental technologies focus on pollution prevention. The estimated global annual market share of biotechnology for cleaner production in the chemicals, pharmaceuticals, paper and food-and-feed industries has been estimated at between US$56 billion and US$120 billion (OECD, 1998). Another estimate suggests that some 20–30 per cent of the total environmental technology market now consists of products or services with a major biotechnology component, representing an annual turnover of US$50–$75billion (OECD, 1994). Bioremediation and biotreatment involve the use of biological processes to treat waste. Micro-organisms are capable of degrading many pollutants and contaminants, and developments in bioprocesses have made this both a technological possibility and economically attractive. The bioremediation sector is growing at roughly 10 per cent a year, compared with the overall growth of the environmental technology market of 4-5 per cent per year. The annual market size for soil remediation in the European Community (EC), Japan and the United States during the years 1990 and 2000 has been estimated as US$10 billion and roughly US$25 billion, respectively (OECD, 1994).

For an estimated half of biotechnology companies, in common with most industry sectors, collection by staff is comparatively insignificant as a method of acquiring genetic resources. For these companies, culture collections are the main source of genetic resources. Such collections may be national or international, or those held in universities or other companies. However, biotechnology companies are relatively unusual among industry sectors in that, for a large proportion of biotechnology companies (perhaps some half of them), collection by their own staff is the predominant manner in which they acquire genetic resources (ten Kate, 1999b).

Most kinds of microbial genetic resources are poorly known and characterized, compared with the plant and animal kingdoms. For example, it is not unusual for some 15–30 per cent of fungi found in some investigations to be unknown to science, and about 1700 new species of fungi are described each year (Stackebrandt, 1994). Using modern molecular techniques that do not rely on the need to obtain a pure culture of micro-organisms, which can be difficult, it is apparent that there is a huge diversity of micro-organisms in all natural habitats. For this reason, some companies collect in their own backyards, feeling that there is plenty of diversity there to explore. Others focus on extremophilic micro-organisms that can withstand extreme conditions of temperature, pressure, acidity or alkalinity, or other dramatic conditions in which conventional organisms could not survive. Extremophiles are valued by industry, since they contain enzymes with possible applications in similar extreme conditions in industrial processes. One famous example is Taq DNA polymerase, an enzyme isolated from pink bacteria and mat samples collected in 1966 from the outflow channel of Mushroom Spring at Yellowstone National Park, at a temperature of about 69° Celsius. The application of the polymerase chain reaction (PCR), using the Taq polymerase enzyme for genetic fingerprinting and other applications, relies entirely on the stability of the enzyme at relatively high temperatures.

European sales of Taq polymerase alone reached US$21 million in 1991. Annual global sales of PCR enzymes are thought to be in the range US$50–$100 million (UNEP/CBD/SBSTTA/2/15).

Crop protection

The global agrochemical market (including herbicides, insecticides, fungicides, plant growth regulators, rodenticides and molluscicides, but excluding fertilizers) was US$30.2 billion in 1997. Sales of herbicides accounted for 48 per cent of the market, insecticides for 27 per cent, and fungicides for 20 per cent. In 1996, the top 20 agrochemical discovery companies controlled 91 per cent of the total market (Agrow, 1998a). In 1997, sales of crop protection products by the top ten companies alone were 84 per cent of the global market. Companies from North America and Europe generated almost two-thirds of world sales of agrochemical products in 1997 (*British Agricultural Association Annual Review*, 1998).

The three main approaches to crop protection – chemical control, biological control and genetic improvement of the crop plant itself – use genetic resources in different ways (ten Kate, 1999). Chemical-control methods use chemical compounds to kill pests. Natural products that operate by chemical control can include compounds isolated from nature and not changed chemically, semi-synthesized derivatives (modifications of compounds isolated from nature) and even synthetic compounds built from templates originally discovered from natural products. Behaviour-modifying chemicals use naturally derived and synthetic versions of signalling chemicals from living organisms, such as pheromones, to create insect traps and disrupt mating; growth regulators (which can also be natural products) are other chemical methods used to control pests.

Screening for the discovery and development of chemical pesticide R&D is broadly similar in approach to that for screening for pharmaceutical discovery and development; but the economics of crop-protection product development are very different. To develop a new commercial chemical pesticide can cost between US$40 million and US$100 million (compared with the US$250–$500 million of pharmaceuticals) and can take from 8 to 14 years. The discovery stage (which consists of two parts, the first covering initial screening and the second, development of a promising 'lead') typically costs US$10–20 million and can last up to four years. The development stage involves developing a lead emerging from the discovery process into a candidate pesticide for product approval. This phase is likely to cost between US$25 million and US$60 million and take a further three years. The greatest costs during the development phase are associated with generating the safety information on the toxicology, environmental impact and effect on non-target organisms of the potential product. After this, a further one to three years are needed for the candidate pesticide to complete the regulatory procedure required for product approval, which adds a few more million dollars to the cost of product development. In practice, some of the work involved in the first two phases can be conducted concurrently.

Biological methods of crop protection apply the living organism itself and include toxic protein-producing bacteria, baculoviruses, fungal pesticides, bacterial pesticides and the use of beneficial, predatory organisms. Biological control is highly dependent upon access to genetic resources in the form of living organisms. At US$80 million, biopesticides still represent a niche market since they are often relatively costly, have a narrow environmental window for efficacy, shorter shelf life and special handling requirements. The naturally occurring bacterium *Bacillus thuringiensis* (Bt) accounts for the major part of the biological control market. There are over 30 recognized subspecies of the bacterium, each producing different insecticidal toxins, and work continues to isolate strains with new toxins and to manipulate the Bt genes that encode toxin production using both recombinant and other methods (Georgis, 1997). Annual sales of Bt products as pesticides are now some US$60–$70 million. It would appear that many major crop-protection companies are beginning to divert significant research into biocontrol, and to integrate biological and chemical control as part of their programmes on integrated pest management (IPM); several smaller companies specialize in a growing range of biocontrol products.

The research and development process for microbial biocontrol agents can involve the study of receptors and the screening of strains of microbes for their biological activity. The major difference is that biocontrol agents apply the living organism itself, while chemical pesticides use compounds extracted or derived from micro-organisms and other genetic resources, as well as totally synthetic compounds. The research and development process for biological control agents that employ insect predators differs significantly from that for chemical pesticides. The approach is largely based on traditional biology, studying the nature of plant disease and the behaviour of natural predators. Researchers find natural enemies of pest species and, using literature searches, ascertain their potential beneficial effects. Greenhouse trials demonstrate how effective the predator is against the pest. Once a predator with proven potential has been identified, a plan to rear it on a commercial scale is formulated. The introduction of pest and disease resistance into crops themselves through genetic engineering and traditional crop breeding is another approach to crop protection, and is covered under plant breeding in the following section on 'Seed'.

Seven per cent of current crop-protection products were developed from research programmes involving access to genetic resources (although the resources may have been obtained from within the company's own collections), but these products only account for around 2 per cent of the sales of crop-protection products, since the synthetic products on the market are responsible for higher sales. Crop-protection products that, however distantly, owe their origin to nature comprise roughly 10 per cent of the annual global sales of crop-protection products. However, discovery of new products from wholly synthesized analogues once modelled on a template from nature does not require access to genetic resources (although the resources may have been obtained from within the company's own collections) (ten Kate, 1999a).

Seed

In 1996, Rabobank reported that there were over 1500 seed companies in the world, 600 of which were based in the US and 400 in Europe, and that private seed companies competed with government to procure and distribute seed in only 28 per cent of the countries of the world (Rabobank, 1996). Today, there are several thousand companies (depending upon whether the term 'seed company' is used to embrace firms involved in trade as well as production). A trend to privatize seed production and distribution, and, in some countries, plant breeding, too, means that the private sector is now producing and distributing seed in more than 50 per cent of the countries of the world (Patrick

Heffer, ASSINSEL, pers comm, December 1998).

In 1998, US$30 billion of the US$50 billion total global market for seed consisted of the commercial sale of seed. Seed bred and distributed by the public sector accounts for approximately US$10 billion, or 20 per cent of the global market for seed, and sales of farm-saved seed worldwide account for the complement. 31 per cent of the commercial sale of seed was accounted for by the 23 largest companies. The 1998 turnover of the top ten seed companies accounted for 23 per cent of the world market for commercial seed, and the three biggest companies alone – Pioneer, Monsanto and Novartis – together account for 13 per cent of global sales, with combined turnovers of US$3.9 billion (FIS/ASSINSEL, 1998).

Over the last few decades, in common with other areas of the 'life sciences', the commercial seed industry has witnessed a number of major mergers and acquisitions. In 1997, Monsanto acquired Holden's Seeds, said to be the source of 35 per cent of the parental lines used by independent corn breeders, for US$1 billion, as well as Brazil Agroceres, the largest seed company in the Southern Hemisphere, for an estimated US$70 million (RAFI, 1998; Bell, 1997). During 1998, Novartis acquired Ciba Seeds and Northrup King Seeds and Monsanto became the second-largest seed company. Monsanto's family of seed companies, now called the Monsanto Global Seeds Group, owns Agracetus Inc, Agroceres, Asgrow Agricultural Seeds, Cargill Seed International, Dekalb, Hartz, Holden's Foundation, Hybritech, NatureMark and PBI.

After the life science industry giants, the Rural Advancement Foundation International (RAFI, 1998) distinguishes two other tiers of company: large multinational firms and small- and medium-sized enterprises. 'Second-tier' companies include multinational firms with interests in agrochemicals and pharmaceuticals, such as Advanta, AgrEvo, Dow AgroSciences, KWS AG, and Groupe Limagrain and several large companies whose primary focus is the commercial seed trade, such as Takii (Japan), Barenbrug (the Netherlands) Svalof Weibull (Sweden), Cebeco-Handelsraad (the Netherlands) and Sakata (Japan). This tier of companies has seen its own share of mergers and acquisitions. The third tier comprises the small- and medium-sized independent seed companies, of which there are about several thousand, a small proportion of which will be actively engaged in plant breeding.

When seed companies obtain new material, they generally do so via a collector or an intermediary. Most collecting activities are conducted by universities, government breeding institutions and international organizations. The most common sources of germplasm for companies are the national collections and gene banks, followed by international gene banks, then universities and occasionally botanic gardens and culture collections. These intermediaries acquire genetic resources from around the world, either by mounting collecting expeditions or being sent samples by similar organizations worldwide.

Many different individuals and organizations are involved in characterizing, selecting and improving agricultural materials. Agricultural genetic resources often change hands several times, being altered, improved and bred by public and private organizations around the world before they are commercialized. A university researcher might collect seed from a local market, grow it up and observe it over a few generations, select the best seed, and pass it to a public gene bank, which might enhance the material and provide the resulting pre-bred seed to a private company. The company might breed the cultivar with its own lines and obtain regulatory approval to release the new commercial cultivar.

Development and release of a new, modern variety typically takes 8 to 15 years and costs in the range of US$1–$2.5 million, for a traditionally bred variety, to US$25–$75 million to develop a transgene that might be used in many genetically modified varieties. The research and development cycle of new seed varieties generally involves three overlapping phases: selection and pre-breeding, breeding and product approval. These phases differ slightly where the R&D involves genetically modified organisms, since the high-technology biotechnological research tools needed for genetic engineering require extra investment and the costs of regulatory approval are higher.

In countries where the public sector plays an important role in seed breeding, the work of public-sector scientists would typically take some 80 per cent of the time needed to develop a new variety. However, they would take just 30–35 per cent of the entire expense, since the breeding work conducted by the public sector would involve materials in earlier stages of development. Once the public sector announces that certain material is available and is passed to the private company, the remaining 20 per cent of the time needed to develop a finished commercial variety typically takes 65–70 per cent of the research and development budget for a new variety. According to the companies we interviewed in this sector, breeders in the public sector commonly pass their pre-bred materials to private companies for no more than a nominal fee, such as US$5 to US$20, or for a slightly greater sum that might, for example, enable the public agency to purchase a computer, but certainly not to cover the costs of the research.

Horticulture

The horticulture market can be broadly divided into the market for vegetables and the market for ornamental products. The former is considerably greater than the latter, as is shown by the relative size of the market for vegetable seed, compared with that for flower seed. In 1996, annual global sales of horticultural seed, including flower and vegetable seed for the commercial and private markets, were approximately US$1.75 billion (Rabobank, 1996). Of this, the commercial market for vegetable seed (ie the market for seed sold to companies which would raise vegetables from it) was estimated at US$1.6 billion. Tomato seeds alone accounted for about half of this, and sales of flower seed made up the remaining US$150 million. The markets for vegetable and flower seed have grown in the last two years, and in 1998, sales of horticultural seed by the top seven companies alone were some US$1.8 billion (see Table 8.2). Within the market for horticultural seeds, the US, the Netherlands, France and Japan are the most important suppliers (Rabobank, 1996; FIS, 1998). While these figures exist for the commercial market for vegetable seed, no reliable data are available on the global market for finished fruit and vegetable produce because of the complexity of the supply chain and the vast range of different products, as well as the general shortcomings of market data in the field of horticulture (ten Kate, 1999).

By comparison with the agricultural and vegetable seed industry, ornamental horticulture is a very modest market, probably lying between US$16 billion to US$19 billion (wholesale value). The annual global-export market for potted plants and cut flowers is nearly US$6 billion. The 'big three' producer countries of horticultural produce are the Netherlands (leader of world floriculture production, valued at US$4.7 billion annually); Japan, which has 47,489 hectares under horticultural production (but this will cover fruit and vegetables, as well as flowers); and the USA, which is the leader in garden flower production with a market of US$1.3 billion (Floriculture Crops Summary, 1997). The ornamental horticulture industry comprises five main areas:

1   herbaceous ornamental horticulture (including annual bedding plants, some potted plants such as impatiens, petunia and geranium);
2   woody ornamental horticulture (a relatively minor component of ornamental horticulture, including shrubs, trees, etc);
3   cut flowers;
4   foliage plants (which includes non-flowering potted plants); foliage plants are sometimes absorbed into the other categories, with flowering plants included in herbaceous ornamentals and non-flowering plants in woody ornamentals; and
5   bulbs (bulbs are sold as potted plants, cut flowers and starting materials sold commercially to be grown into potted plants and cut flowers).

While many horticultural companies – from the single nurseryman to the multinational company – are engaged in growing, distributing and selling ornamental varieties, far fewer are involved in working with genetic resources to develop new commercial ornamental products. Companies breeding ornamental plant varieties fall into three main categories: a small group of multinational companies that account for the majority of sales worldwide; a slightly larger cohort of mainly national companies; and several hundreds of small- and medium-sized enterprises, which together account for

only a modest share of the global market.

Just some ten major multinational seed companies are responsible for roughly 90 per cent of global sales of seed of ornamental varieties and for breeding the vast majority of the ornamental plants that are subsequently raised and distributed, often through a long chain of organizations. The five leading flower-seed companies alone represent 80 per cent of the global market for seed for cut flowers and bedding plants (rather than for vegetatively propagated plants; pers comm Patrick Heffer, FIS, March 1999). The horticulture divisions of these companies have annual turnovers of between US$60 million and US$100 million, employ many thousands of staff worldwide and market many millions of units of plants each year. They dominate the market for the world's top-selling ornamental varieties. The four top-selling ornamental herbaceous varieties worldwide are impatiens, petunia, geranium and pansy. The major multinational horticulture companies dedicate substantial research budgets to the development of new products. The combined annual research and development budgets of these companies generally lie between US$50 million and US$100 million.

The second group of companies, numbering some 25–50, are middle-ranking firms, with turnovers in the bracket of US$5–$50 million and from 100 to several hundred employees, of whom 10 per cent or less will be plant breeders. Generally focusing on a narrower range of products than the major multinationals, these companies make an important contribution to the remaining 10 per cent or so of global sales of ornamental varieties.

Finally, several hundred small- and medium-sized enterprises, from the one-man nursery to the company with 50 to 100 employees, select and breed ornamental varieties for sale. Their turnover may

257

be from as little as US$10,000 or US$20,000 per annum up to a few million dollars each year, and they are likely to operate on a very modest acreage.

Some ornamental plants are produced by seed, but most of the big-cut flowers are vegetatively propagated from cuttings. Until as recently as a few decades ago, most of the ornamental plants developed were open-pollinated (inbred) varieties; since then, the vast majority of varieties that have reached the market have been F1 hybrids. The production of F1 hybrids often involves hand pollination of the female plants, which requires considerable manpower. The largest companies often employ several thousand employees in production sites around the world.

Ornamental horticulture companies involved in developing new products may be interested either in improving existing varieties (for example, by introducing a line with a new colour of flower), or in introducing or developing entirely new species. The main product portfolio of the largest companies lies with new varieties of 'standard' plants, such as the top-selling species listed above; but companies in group one are increasingly involved in developing more unusual 'new' species, such as kangaroo paw and gazanthus.

The time needed to develop a new variety from scratch can range from one or two years to more than ten, and the cost from virtually nothing to some US$5 million. Several commercial breeders suggested that to develop a new F1 hybrid would take between five and ten years, generally from five to eight years.

Botanical medicine

Sales in the global botanical medicine industry are estimated to grow to US$22 billion by the year 2000. Europe dominates the market with US$7.2 billion in 1997 sales, 50 per cent of which are contributed by Germany. Asian markets were roughly US$3 billion in 1997, and Japan US$2.5 billion (Gruenwald, 1999a). The Chinese-finished traditional medicine (TCM) sector was estimated to have US$3.7 billion in sales in 1996 (Yuquan, 1998). Fastest growth in the botanical medicine industry is found in the United States, where annual growth rates averaged between 10–20 per cent during 1994–1998, with 1998 retail sales of botanical medicines an estimated US$3.87 billion (Brevoort, 1998). However, by late 1999 growth in the US market appeared to be levelling off (Blumenthal, 1999).

Top-selling products vary significantly by region and country, but botanical medicine sales increasingly reflect a cosmopolitan global economy. Ginseng, *Echinacea*, St John's wort, and garlic are a few of the species found in stores around the world (see Table 8.3). In general, top sellers tend to dominate markets. For example, the top-ten selling botanicals in Europe represent approximately one third of the total market (Gruenwald, 1999a). In the United States – a market more heavily driven by media and fads – the top ten sellers represent somewhat more than 50 per cent of annual sales.

Most of the top-selling botanical medicines are derived from species native to, or naturalized in, the regions where they are sold. Lange (1998) found that of the more than 2000 medicinal and aromatic species in trade in Europe, two-thirds are native to Europe. Asian species play an increasing role in international botanical medicine markets, due to the rise in the popularity of TCM. African and Latin American species tend to have a smaller role, with significant exceptions including devil's claw (*Harpagophytum procumbens*), pygeum (*Prunus africana*) and yohimbe (*Pausinystalia johimbe*) from Africa, and cat's claw (*Uncaria* spp) and Pao d'Arco (*Tabebuia* spp) from Latin

Table 8.3 *1998 top ten best-selling Botanical Medicines in Europe and the US*

Europe	US
Ginkgo biloba	Echinacea
St John's wort	St John's wort
Saw palmetto	*Ginkgo biloba*
Valerian	Garlic
Ginseng	Saw palmetto
Garlic	Ginseng
Echinacea	Golden seal
Horse chestnut	Aloe
Black cohosh	Siberian ginseng
Vitex agnus castus	Valerian

Source: Gruenwald, 1999; Richman and Witkowski, 1998

America. Increased academic research on species from high biodiversity areas, however, has meant growing commercial interest in those that have shown promise in the laboratory, such as kava (*Piper methysticum*) from the South Pacific.

Botanical medicine products can take a number of forms, but in all cases are produced directly from whole plant material and contain a large number of constituents and active ingredients working in conjunction with each other, rather than a single, isolated compound, as is the case for pharmaceuticals. Botanical medicines are sold as:

- **raw herb material**: dried or fresh;
- **extracts**: which represent a greater concentration of the original material produced through separation of the active material with the aid of a solvent;
- **standardized extracts**: which are standardized to one or more chemical markers; and
- **phytomedicines**: which are standardized to a few groups of active marker compounds, and sometimes eliminate other compounds found in the original plant material.

The botanical medicine industry is currently in flux, moving towards greater globalization, on the one hand, and consolidation of companies, on the other. Despite these trends, the industry remains fragmented, and plant material might pass through many hands before arriving as a finished product at retail outlets. Broadly, the industry can be divided into:

- **supply companies**: cultivators or wildcrafters of raw plant material; wholesalers of raw plant material, including exporters, traders, brokers and agents; and bulk-ingredient processing companies;
- **manufacturing and marketing companies**: some high-level processing companies (many with 'branded' or trademarked lines) and manufacturers (including labelling and packaging) of finished products; and
- **consumer sales**: brokers and distributors of finished products to retail outlets; retail outlets, including those of mass and specialty markets; and direct sales in the form of mail order, multilevel marketing, Internet or e-commerce, and sales through health-care providers.

BOX 8.4 CURRENT TRENDS IN THE BOTANICAL MEDICINE INDUSTRY WITH RELEVANCE TO THE DEMAND FOR NEW NATURAL PRODUCTS

Current trends include the following:

- There is increasing consumer demand for alternative medicine as a complement to pharmaceutical drugs and modern health care, which are perceived as limited in scope and having too severe side effects.
- There is acceptance of botanical medicines by national and commercial insurance companies.
- Expanded research has improved the legitimacy of botanical medicines; many of the top-selling botanical medicine products are popular due to research results produced primarily in European laboratories.
- The rise in green consumerism has increased demand for 'natural' medicine.
- Increased advertising budgets and media attention have attracted consumer interest.
- In the United States, changes in the regulatory environment have made the manufacture and marketing of botanical medicine more attractive.
- The entry of large pharmaceutical and over-the-counter (OTC) companies (eg Bayer AG, Warner Lambert, SmithKline Beecham, and American Home Products – Centrum) has helped spur the expansion of the botanical medicine industry within the mass market.
- Globalization and consolidation at all levels (including retail, wholesale and supply of bulk ingredients and raw materials) is on the rise.
- Increased emphasis on safety, efficacy and quality has changed the types of product in demand and requirements placed on suppliers of raw material and bulk ingredients.

To date, botanical medicine companies in the United States conduct only limited research on botanical medicines; once a product is launched on the market, a company cannot claim exclusive rights and therefore cannot recoup its investment in R&D. In contrast, many European and Asian countries have traditions of linking government, academic and industrial research in botanical medicine that create strong foundations from which commercial product development grows. This system encourages a certain conservatism with regard to developing products from species new to the market, but provides a framework within which botanical medicines are approved in a timely and affordable manner, while ensuring safety and efficacy. In the long run, therefore, this environment will provide more stable markets and demand for new, as well as established, botanical medicine products. Overall, research on botanical medicines is likely to increase in the coming years due to the entry of large pharmaceutical and over-the-counter (OTC) companies with vast R&D budgets, and increasing calls for safety, efficacy and quality control on the part of US consumers.

Of significant concern in this industry is the manner in which raw materials are sourced. Global demand for high-quality botanical medicine products has focused greater attention on raw material quality; but the same attention has not been paid to the sustainability and equity of collect-

---

BOX 8.5 CITES AND THREATENED BOTANICAL MEDICINE SPECIES

As a result of commercial pressures on wild populations, a number of medicinal species have been placed on CITES (Convention on the International Trade in Endangered Species of Wild Fauna and Flora) appendices. CITES regulates international trade in animals and plants through a system of permits and licences, protecting species from excessive trade by listing them in appendices. Appendix I includes species threatened with extinction, and for which trade in wild material is generally prohibited. Appendix II species can be traded with proper permits. Medicinal species on CITES Appendix II include: *Sarracenia* spp, *Aloe ferox, Pterocarpus santalinus, Rauwolfia serpentina, Prunus africana, Panax quinquefolius, Hydrastis canadensis* and *Podophyllum hexandrum*.

Source: Sheldon et al, 1996; Robbins, 1998; Lange, 1998b; Lange, 1999

---

ing practices. Suppliers of raw materials are customarily bargained down to low prices that cannot support sustainable practices for many species or adequate livelihoods for collectors.

There is a trend towards the sourcing of cultivated material; but wild sources will continue to play an important role for species difficult to cultivate, for those with small markets and for those whose wildcrafting can be sustainable and cultivation uneconomic. Furthermore, wildcrafted material is often cheaper, and species new to the market are unlikely to have been in extensive cultivation previously. Given the rising fortunes of this industry, and the spectrum of environmental concerns raised by its activities, it is time for companies and industry associations to address current sourcing practices in which raw materials are viewed as cheap bulk commodities.

Natural personal care and cosmetic

The natural personal care and cosmetic market is experiencing rapid growth worldwide, averaging 8–25 per cent. It is estimated that natural personal care and cosmetic products will make up 10 per cent of the annual US$55+ billion personal care and cosmetic market. Natural personal care and cosmetic sales came to US$2.8 billion in 1997, featuring most prominently in product categories such as hair products (23 per cent of sales), skin care (38 per cent) and bath items (12 per cent) (NBJ, 1998).

Personal care and cosmetic products are sold in prestige, mass and alternative markets. *Prestige markets* are characterized by higher-priced products with limited distribution; *mass market* products are lower priced and widely available, including through pharmacies and supermarkets. *Alternative markets* include direct marketing, health food stores and other non-traditional channels for product sales. Many of the products sold as 'natural' fall within the alternative market category.

Companies active in the natural personal care and cosmetics sector can be grouped into two broad categories: supply companies, and manufacturing and marketing companies. Supply companies include suppliers of raw, bulk botanical material – exporters, traders, brokers and agents – that sell to a range of industries including cosmetic, botanical medicine, pharmaceutical, nutrition and food, dyes, pet products and household products. A small portion of raw material suppliers – usually in conjunction with manufactur-

---

BOX 8.6 WHAT IS 'NATURAL'?

Although widely used in association with personal care and cosmetic products, natural ingredients are used in commercial products in a variety of ways. The majority of products marketed as natural, in both prestige and mass markets, include only negligible quantities of natural material, often solely for marketing purposes. Other products contain scientifically validated active ingredients of natural origin, most likely combined with synthetic processing agents, colorants, fragrance and other non-natural ingredients. These products tend to emerge from large R&D efforts that include high-throughput screens. Marketing may not highlight the natural origin of the active ingredients, and will instead emphasize efficacy and therapeutic potential.

Other products might contain scientifically or traditionally validated active ingredients of natural origin; but all other ingredients will also be of natural origin (this does not include petrochemicals, animal products and alcohol). Marketing and company identity are likely to be tied closely to '100 per cent natural' ingredient claims, and companies tend to be small and focused on niche markets and 'green' or health-food store consumers.

---

ing and marketing companies – source-certify 'green' or 'fair trade' raw material for product manufacture. Generally, however, companies have little idea of the fashion in which raw materials are sourced, and the sustainability and equity problems plaguing the botanical medicine industry also apply to natural cosmetic and personal care products.

Specialty chemical ingredient manufacturers also fall under the category of supply companies. These companies conduct a significant portion of R&D in the industry, and current trends lead them to seek out larger numbers of 'performance-enhancing' and therapeutic compounds (Fost, 1997). Increased demand from manufacturers for natural ingredients in stable and useful form has created a supplier market of chemical companies that provide popular natural ingredients and develop 'new' ones by processing and recombining biological products. Specialty chemical suppliers also increasingly test new ingredients, supplying finished product manufacturers with a product dossier substantiating all claims.

Manufacturing and marketing companies vary in size and in approach, some with turnovers of less than US$10 million, and others with multibillion dollar sales. In the category of 'beauty sales' – including fragrance, make-up, skin care, hair care, cellulite creams, deodorant and shaving creams – the US had the largest number of companies (28) in the top 75, followed by France (13), Japan (8), Germany (7), Italy (7), South Korea (5), UK (3), and Brazil (2) (WWD, 1999). Today, most manufacturing and marketing companies feature a natural product line, and for some this is a great deal more than a marketing ploy. Companies such as Estée Lauder and Elizabeth Arden (of Unilever's Home and Personal Care Division) conduct advanced research on natural products, including screening for active ingredients.

In response to consumer demand for natural and therapeutic products, the industry increasingly seeks leads and raw materials for product development in the natural world. Botanicals, marine organisms, vitamins and other natural products

---

BOX 8.7 TRENDS THAT CONTRIBUTE TO RISING DEMAND FOR NATURAL PERSONAL CARE AND COSMETIC PRODUCTS

Such trends include the following:

- increasing consumer sophistication, including demand for higher quality, awareness of ingredients and interest in all things 'natural';
- stagnant markets for product areas, which leads to a search for new ingredients to make products more exciting to consumers;
- the entry of mass and prestige companies (and their large advertising budgets) to an area previously served by niche market companies;
- changing demographics that create demand for a wider range of products, including for the ageing and for men; and
- increasing demand for therapeutic – or cosmeceutical – products that repair damaged tissues, smooth, protect from the sun, moisturize and provide other therapeutic actions.

---

provide active compounds that contribute to product efficacy, assist with improved delivery systems and replace petrochemicals, artificial preservatives, surfactants and other synthetic ingredients. As Jon Anderson of Estée Lauder wrote: 'The research trend is moving towards the development of highly refined raw materials of natural origin with defined constituents imparting specific biological effect to benefit healthy skin. Ingredients target mechanism-based systems to modulate enzymes or receptors present in the skin to prevent and protect skin from damage or to repair damaged skin' (Anderson, 1996).

Most companies obtain ideas for new products and ingredients from literature, databases, trade shows and other secondary sources in their home countries. To acquire materials for further research or formulation, companies contact supply companies. A long and complex chain of raw-material exchange is involved in both product development and the sourcing of raw materials for product manufacture. In some cases, the relationship between the manufacturing company and source country is closer, particularly in those companies founded by individuals with a strong interest in the environment. Examples include Ales Group (France), Aveda Corporation (US), The Body Shop (UK), Neals Yard (UK), Tom's of Maine (US), Yves Rocher (France) and Rainforest Nutrition (US). Large companies commissioning natural-product sample collection to feed high-throughput screens also have closer ties to source countries. Intermediaries hired to provide samples collect materials much as they would for pharmaceutical companies (they are often the same organizations).

Demand for access to genetic resources

The previous section outlined the diversity of approaches to R&D in different industry sectors, and between companies within a particular industry sector. The manner in which companies seek access to genetic resources and traditional knowledge, and the ways in which they use these resources, reflect this diversity. This section examines the types of material that companies acquire, who collects genetic resources, the role of ex-situ collections as sources of genetic resources for industry, and the relative importance of geographic diversity and traditional knowledge.

The scale of sample acquisition by companies varies enormously. For example, small pharmaceutical companies may have focused acquisitions programmes in which they obtain just 10 to 100 targeted samples a year. They may seek certain specific samples to complete their collections. At the other extreme, companies operating ultra high-throughput screens may seek upwards of 10,000 new samples a year.

Types of material acquired

Taken as a whole, industry has an interest in every conceivable kind of genetic resource. Given the enormous variety of approaches to R&D and the choice of starting material between industry sectors – and even within each sector – it is difficult to generalize about the kinds of material that companies seek to acquire. While the majority of companies in the pharmaceutical industry, for example, balance an interest in plants and micro-organisms, some focus primarily, or even exclusively, on particular fungi or animal toxins. Many small- and medium-sized enterprises concentrate their research efforts entirely on one kind of genetic resource, such as a particular species of plant or category of micro-organism, or on compounds isolated from samples taken from sharks, frogs, leeches or venomous insects.

The botanical medicine, horticulture and seed industries are primarily plant-based industries. However, there is a growing interest in marine organisms and fungi in the botanical medicine trade, and the advent of genetic engineering has led to a growing number of crop plants that incorporate genetic resources from other kingdoms, from the *Bacillus thuringiensis* bacterium to fish gene-coding for cold tolerance. Some cosmetic and personal care companies operate marine prospecting programmes and investigate novel therapeutic actions in micro-organisms, although the bulk of 'natural' cosmetic products contains botanical ingredients. The biotechnology industry devoted to products in fields other than pharmaceuticals and agriculture conducts a great deal of its research on micro-organisms, but also has interests in many other categories of genetic resources. The basis for the crop protection industry is plant genetic resources; but chemical crop-protection products and biological control systems also make use of a wide range of micro-organisms and insects.

The form samples take when supplied to companies also varies. Pharmaceutical, biotechnology and crop-protection companies often receive material as raw samples (such as dried plant and soil samples) or extracts (organic or aqueous). Some samples may have been selected on the basis of ethnobotanical information or will be supplied with such information. Some companies acquire 'value-added' genetic resources. Typically, these could be samples supplied with the results of screening, pre-bred crop lines, identified bioactive compounds or even data emerging from product trials (usually as part of collaborative partnerships). However, to date, the majority of samples obtained from developing countries has little value added.

Some groups – such as the US National Cancer Institute (NCI) and the partnerships formed under the International Cooperative Biodiversity Groups (ICBG) programme – are working to ensure that a larger portion of discovery and value-adding research takes place in source countries. Such projects build the capacity to accomplish this as part of joint research programmes. Assisted by the development of best practice in benefit-sharing arrangements, countries with the requisite scientific and institutional infrastructure will increasingly be able to supply value-added products to companies, often protected by intellectual property rights, thereby enabling source country institutions to capture a larger share of the benefits.

Criteria for sample collection

In companies operating high-throughput screening programmes in the pharmaceutical, crop protection, biotechnology and even cosmetics and personal care sectors, a number of different approaches are commonly used to select samples for screening:

- *Random/blind:* collections are conducted on a random or 'serendipitous' basis within a given geographical area in order to obtain a representative, but random, sample of local diversity.
- *Ecology driven/biorational:* collections are based on an understanding/observation of ecological relationships between species that might lead to the production of secondary compounds.

- *Chemotaxonomic:* collections are based on knowledge of taxa with certain classes of compounds of value to research and screening.
- *Ethnobotanical:* collections are based on indigenous peoples' or local communities' uses of species.

In plant breeding, materials are generally selected for breeding efforts based on known, desirable characteristics – such as pest, disease or drought tolerance, or (in the case of the ornamental horticulture industry) an aesthetically pleasing feature, such as the shape and colour of the flower or the colour and pattern of the foliage. Breeders learn of such potentially useful traits from their own observations of materials within their collections, from databases and relevant literature (such as the journals *Crop Science* and the *UK Plant Breeding Abstract and Plant Breeding News*) and from partnerships with research organizations. These organizations offer them the service of keeping them up to date with developments and may pre-select materials for use in company breeding programmes. In the botanical medicine and personal care and cosmetics industry, new products are similarly selected for further research or commercial product development in response to trade and academic literature, databases, trade shows and advice or data provided by intermediaries and collaborators.

Collectors of genetic resources

The acquisition of genetic resources involves a range of parties and approaches. A small minority of the genetic resources acquired by the private sector are actually collected by the staff of the companies themselves. The vast majority of samples are, however, obtained from intermediaries such as:

- commercial brokers and importers of material who acquire genetic resources from around the world;
- research institutes, gene banks, universities, botanic gardens, culture collections and other such organizations that collect in source countries abroad and maintain collections in the country where they are based; and
- similar organizations based in source countries themselves.

A large percentage of collections are still made by intermediary organizations based outside of source countries, often in the country where the company itself is located. However, increasing numbers of source country-based intermediaries collect specimens on behalf of, or together with, client companies. For example, the National Institute of Biodiversity (InBio) in Costa Rica has entered into collection and supply agreements with Merck & Co; Bristol-Myers Squibb (US pharmaceutical companies); Phytera (US biotech company); INDENA (Italian manufacturer of botanical extracts and phytochemicals for the pharmaceutical, botanical medicine, cosmetic, food and other industries); Givaudane Roure (Swiss–US company interested in new fragrances); and Analyticon (German service and contract research company) (ten Kate, 1999b). Through the US government-sponsored International Cooperative Biodiversity Groups (ICBG), Monsanto, American Home Products and Bristol-Myers Squibb are also collaborating with a number of source country partners to acquire genetic resources (Rosenthal, 1998; Baker et al, 1995).

The natural personal care company Aveda Corporation has developed a joint product-development programme with the indigenous Yawanawa community of the Gregorio River area in Acre, Brazil (Waddington and Laird, 1999). Croda Inc, a provider of high-quality raw materials and specialty chemicals to many markets, particularly the personal care and cosmetic, has formed a collaboration with the non-profit group Conservation International (CI) for the supply of sustainably produced rainforest products for the development of a natural raw material line (Morris and Laird, 1999). In the botanical medicine and natural personal care and cosmetics industries, raw-material supply companies undertake a large portion of industry research on 'new' commercial products, including – as in the case of Croda Inc, brokered by CI – forming direct links with source countries.

A few botanical-medicine marketing companies work directly with source countries and local communities, developing partnerships based on the search for new leads. These include Axxon Biopharmaceuticals (Nigeria/US), which works in Nigeria, Cameroon, Guinea, Ghana and South Africa; Shaman Botanicals (US), with partnerships in 30 countries; and Nature's Way (US), which, in Vietnam, participated in a multiyear process to develop an endemic ginseng product new to the market (Laird and Burningham, 1999).

A second group of intermediaries – particularly the small commercial brokers – collects or acquires specimens with no particular client in mind at the time of acquisition, but with the specific aim of supplying the samples to other organizations, including industry.

A third group of intermediaries, largely comprising non-profit research institutions such as universities and botanic gardens, often collects genetic resources for its own academic research programmes, but may subsequently allow companies access to the specimens in its collections.

In all industry sectors, genetic resources generally pass through several hands, from the initial collector to the company that markets the final product, with value being added to the material by each intermediary organization along the way. For example, in the field of biotechnology, a university may collect a soil sample and deposit a strain of a microorganism in a culture collection. The culture collection may allow a biotechnology company to access the strain, and the company may screen the strain for potential industrial applications. The biotechnology company may isolate a useful enzyme from the strain and formulate an enzyme preparation that can make a certain industrial process more efficient. It may then license the resulting product to a chemical company for use in its manufacturing process.

To take another example, the path for a new ornamental variety from the wild or someone's garden to a retail outlet can involve several stages. A botanic garden may collect an attractive plant sample, grow it and select the best plants over several generations and supply these to a horticultural breeding company, which may conduct research and development on the plant, produce seed (or vegetative propagating material) of the new ornamental variety and supply it to a broker. The broker may prime the seed (for example, conditioning it for germination and enhanced performance, or coating it so that it is easier to sow by machine), then distribute the seed internationally to plug producers or directly to wholesale growers. The plug producers may germinate the seed supplied by the broker and, when the seedlings are some five or six weeks' old, distribute them to wholesale growers. If the wholesale growers received seed direct from brokers, they will plant the seed and raise seedlings. If the seed was already germinated and raised into young seedlings by plug producers, the wholesale growers will simply raise the seedlings for a further few

weeks and sell the young plants to local retail outlets. The retail companies will then sell the final potted plants to the public.

Libraries and ex-situ collections

There are two basic sources of material for discovery and development: materials from in-situ conditions in natural habitats, such as forests, savannahs, farmers' fields and oceans, and materials from ex-situ collections, where they are held outside their natural habitat in a variety of facilities, such as zoos, aquaria, culture collections, gene banks and botanic gardens. Ex-situ collections are an increasingly valuable source of genetic resources for companies, particularly in light of the regulation of collecting activities in source countries. Indeed, in addition to the concentration of collecting activities into fewer countries, companies report greater recourse to ex-situ collections as one result of the Convention on Biological Diversity (ten Kate and Laird, 1999, Chapter 10).

As well as obtaining samples from ex-situ collections maintained by other organizations, companies in the pharmaceutical, crop protection, plant breeding, biotechnology and horticulture sectors generally maintain their own ex-situ collections of genetic resources. Pharmaceutical companies build and maintain libraries of compounds, extracts or dried plant material that they can use in their screening programmes. Companies' libraries are used for in-house research and may also be licensed to other companies or exchanged with commercial partners. Combinatorial chemistry has made it possible for small, highly specialized firms to develop libraries of synthetic compounds. An exclusive library of around 100,000 molecules can be hired for US$1 million today (*The Economist*, 1998). Natural product libraries take many years to build and are usually smaller. The US NCI, for example, has built a library of 150,000 natural product extracts and 400,000 compounds.

In the crop-protection sector, public-sector institutions and companies maintain libraries of genetic resources, including samples of seed, soil samples, pure microbial cultures, pathogenic fungi, enzymes, extracts from microbial cultures or plants and compounds such as pheromones. Biotechnology companies rely heavily on ex-situ culture collections for the provision of samples, and also obtain samples from 'search and discovery' companies, commercial partners, university staff and, on rare occasions, gene banks. In the pharmaceutical, biotechnology and crop-protection sectors, a category of 'search and discovery companies' has emerged. These firms specialize in building libraries of genetic resources, which they license to larger companies. Some such companies are spin-offs from university departments. They collect and isolate new compounds, sometimes obtained in the course of the university's academic research.

The seed industry maintains vast private libraries of genetic resources, built up by acquiring and breeding plants for many decades. Corporate collections contain elite strains of seeds that represent the companies' breeding efforts to date. Unadapted, 'exotic' materials form only a small proportion of company collections, which are mainly 'adapted' or 'improved' lines. National gene banks, 'in trust' ex-situ collections maintained by the international centres of the Consultative Group on International Agricultural Research (CGIAR) and smaller collections held by universities are also important sources of material for private-sector breeders. Collections held by these organizations generally contain a higher proportion of primitive and unadapted

materials than those within companies. For example, 40,000 of the 130,000 entries for wheat in CIMMYT's (the Centro Internacional de Mejoramiento de Maiz y Trigo) collections are landraces.

Demand for geographic diversity

Private-sector collections of genetic resources are increasingly confined to a small number of countries in which companies have established partnerships and find a conducive legal and policy environment for access to genetic resources. However, the diversity ensured by broad geographic and ecological sampling is considered of high value to many industry research programmes that may complement the materials acquired from in-situ conditions with samples from geographically diverse origins held in ex-situ collections.

In the pharmaceutical industry, serendipitous, randomly based screening programmes aim to test as much biological – and therefore chemical – diversity as possible. Although the hypothesis that geographic diversity produces chemical diversity is not fully proven, companies do seek out collections from a broad geographic base. Some of the larger companies screen samples from over 20 countries in a year.

In the seed sector, demand for 'foreign' or 'exotic' material for crop breeding remains significant, despite a relatively low overall representation of such material in the genome of new varieties. Exotic germplasm may bring useful traits, but breeders prefer to use germplasm from locations with similar environmental conditions, as it will already be adapted to the locations where it will ultimately grow. Genetic engineering has facilitated the rapid assimilation of genetic material into elite strains not only from very different agro-ecological conditions but from differ-

Box 8.8 Ex-situ collections:
benefit-sharing into the future

The access and benefit-sharing provisions of the Convention on Biological Diversity (CBD) do not apply to collections made before the CBD entered into force in December 1993. Strictly speaking, organizations holding such pre-CBD collections are not obliged to obtain permission from countries of origin before supplying them, or to share with countries of origin the benefits arising from their use. However, a growing number of ex-situ collections can see the rationale for abiding by the letter and spirit of the CBD, and are developing policies and codes of conduct requiring them to do so. To begin with, even before the CBD, many materials were collected under permits (which are effectively contracts between those acquiring genetic resources and the body issuing the collecting permit). These permits may not have allowed the commercialization of the materials, so any proposed commercial use by ex-situ collections or those who receive materials from them may require additional permission. Secondly, many ex-situ collections rely for their scientific work on continuing access to new specimens. They are aware that countries may not be willing to allow collecting expeditions by ex-situ collectors who they know supply historical collections to companies without seeking the countries' permission or sharing the benefits with them.

Two examples of voluntary codes of conduct developed in recent years by ex-situ collections in order to ensure fair and equitable partnerships are the *Common Policy Guidelines for Participating Botanic Gardens* and the *MOSAIC Code for Culture Collections* and other organizations handling microbial genetic resources. The *Common Policy Guidelines* are described in Chapter 3.

To implement such policies requires the management of collections, data and staff in such a way that the ex-situ collection can honour the commitments it made in the terms under which it acquired the specimens. Considerable concerns have been raised about the difficulties of tracking or controlling successive uses of, and modification to, the materials collected. Observers have noted that ex-situ collections of material – whether herbarium specimens or seeds placed in cryogenic storage – can be kept for hundreds of years, and that by the time the material is eventually used, records of where it was collected and under what terms may be unavailable (Parry, 1999).

Although tracking and controlling successive uses of materials will always pose a significant challenge to equitable benefit-sharing, the policies developed by ex-situ collections often set out in some detail the nature of records that must be maintained in order to enable collections to be 'curated' in line with the policy commitments. Typically, it is necessary to record and maintain data on their acquisition, including information on the provider; country of origin; collector; collection date and number; accession number; taxa; prior informed consent and conditions of use (eg as contained in permits and/or material acquisition agreements); and other relevant data associated with the acquisition of accessions. Subsequently, it is necessary to 'track' specimens, or to maintain records of the location of specimens of genetic resources, their progeny and derivatives in order to follow their distribution and use within the ex-situ collection itself and their supply to other organizations. In the case of supply to other organizations, the providing ex-situ collection will need to record and maintain data on the supply of genetic resources, their progeny and derivatives, including information on the recipient and the terms of access and benefit-sharing under which they were supplied. The records concerned can be kept in a variety of ways, from accessions databases to labels on specimens (such as herbarium sheets).

ent taxonomic kingdoms. Nonetheless, the bulk of 'exotic' germplasm used in breeding programmes tends to be obtained from areas with similar agro-ecological conditions.

Botanical medicine and natural personal care and cosmetic companies demonstrate an increased interest in materials from around the world. On the one hand, companies in the cosmetic industry operating high-throughput screening programmes are in search of chemical diversity along the lines of pharmaceutical companies. Some botanical medicine companies in search of new and promising medicines are also seeking out new leads overseas, particularly as scientific research on species previously unknown to the trade, from regions such as Africa and Latin America, validates traditional use and identifies active compounds. On the other hand, these companies operate in sectors dominated, in many countries, by marketing and media. Novelty remains an important way in which to differentiate a company in a competitive marketplace, and may be sought more for marketing than for scientific purposes.

Demand for traditional knowledge

The sectors addressed in this chapter have their roots in traditional knowledge – that is, they grow from long histories of traditional management and the improvement of food and medicine, and from complex cultural relationships between people and the natural world that also include spiritual and aesthetic concerns. Even today, direct links can still be made between many commercial products on sale and knowledge systems dating back millennia. For example, of the approximately 120 pharmaceutical products derived from plants in 1985, 75 per cent were discovered through the study of their traditional medical use (Farnsworth et al, 1985). Grifo

et al (1997) demonstrated that for the base compound in most of the top 150 plant-derived prescription drugs, commercial use correlates with traditional medical use.

The established link between traditional use and commercial products, however, has often led to an overestimation of the role that traditional knowledge plays in current research and development efforts; and there is confusion associated with the ways in which companies access traditional knowledge incorporated within R&D programmes today.

The botanical medicine, cosmetic and personal care, pharmaceutical and, to a lesser extent, crop-protection sectors seek traditional knowledge to help guide product research and development activities, but they do so in different ways (see Table 8.4). Although they grow directly from age-old practices and traditional systems of knowledge and species management, the horticulture, seed and biotechnology industries appear to make little direct use of traditional knowledge in their R&D programmes today. Companies do not conduct field ethnobotanical collections and only rarely, if ever, use traditional knowledge gathered from second-hand sources such as literature.

Those industries that do make use of traditional knowledge – the botanical medicine, cosmetic, pharmaceutical and crop-protection industries – largely do so through literature and databases, rather than field collections. The movement of traditional knowledge from a community to the wider public domain, and from there into the private sector, does not take place primarily in the commercial domain. Rather, publication of academic research results is the most common route by which traditional knowledge makes its way to the private sector (see Chapter 4). The issues associated with these activities, and resulting responsibilities of researchers, are addressed in Chapters 1–5.

Table 8.4 *The use of traditional knowledge by industry sectors*

	Manner of use	*Source*
Pharmaceutical	Traditional knowledge (TK) is not considered a useful tool during the early stages of high-throughput screening; but once an active compound is identified, most companies use TK (when available) to guide subsequent research. A (very) few companies direct their research programmes based on TK; some will use traditional knowledge as the basis for setting up screens to select for competing (or better) compounds with similar bioactivity (ie as a reference compound to select more active synthetic analogue compounds).	Literature, databases, intermediary brokers A minority of companies commission field ethnobotanical collection; ethnobotanical information is often attached to samples as an 'add on', even if collections are primarily chemotaxonomic or ecology driven.
Biotechnology	Many biotechnology applications (eg brewing and bread-making) are based on traditional knowledge dating back millennia, but contemporary biotechnology makes little use of TK.	
Crop protection	A small proportion of companies use TK to guide the collection and screening of samples; as with pharmaceuticals, once activity is demonstrated, TK is sometimes used to decide on the direction of subsequent research.	Literature, databases
Seed	Companies make little use of TK, but they do use germplasm that has been pre-bred by other organizations to which genes from traditional varieties may have made an important contribution.	
Horticulture	Many popular ornamental varieties and horticultural vegetable crops owe their existence to traditional domestication and selection over long periods of time. However, TK is rarely used in the selection and breeding of new horticultural varieties today.	
Botanical medicine	TK is used as the basis of identifying potential new product development; safety and efficacy studies; formulation; is widely used in marketing commercial products; and sometimes is used in developing wildcrafting or cultivation strategies for raw materials.	Literature, databases, tradeshows, Internet, etc; middlemen brokers will follow up on leads in literature with local communities and research institutions. Rare cases in which the literature leads marketing companies to conduct field-based research on species of promise; this is directed, rather than bulk-collecting, research.
Personal care and cosmetic	TK is used as the basis of identifying potential new leads, and to direct research on the commercial potential of species; it is used in safety and efficacy studies; is widely used in marketing commercial products; and sometimes is used in developing sourcing strategies for raw materials.	Literature, databases, tradeshows, Internet, etc; occasionally, middlemen brokers will follow up on leads from the literature with local communities. Companies conducting high-throughput screening will commission the collection of ethnobotanical samples with identified uses; other companies have entered into direct field-based partnerships with communities to use their TK in product development.

Best practice in benefit-sharing

Benefit-sharing varies dramatically across and within sectors, and recent trends respond in varying degrees to national and international policy developments, such as the Convention on Biological Diversity (ten Kate and Laird, 1999). As a result, a flexible and highly informed approach to access and benefit-sharing measures at a national level is the most effective (see Chapter 12).

Overall, there is a gradual but noticeable trends towards more creative benefit-sharing, and the development of standards of benefit-sharing 'best practice', involving monetary and non-monetary benefits in the short, medium and long term. This trend reflects the evolution of public opinion, NGO advocacy, private-sector responses to source-country demands and the initiative of intermediary institutions that have tried to broker the interests of provider country groups and commercial users. Widely publicized cases, such as the agreement between InBio and Merck in Costa Rica, have served to some extent as a template for the development of subsequent benefit-sharing arrangements. However, there is a growing appreciation that what is 'fair and equitable' is likely to differ substantially across industry sectors, product areas and individual research and development programmes, and that successful benefit-sharing arrangements are those tailored to the specific circumstances of an individual case. These are guided by growing agreement on basic standards of best practice. The following is a brief review of current practice in benefit-sharing in selected sectors.

Pharmaceuticals

The global market for pharmaceuticals, and the research budgets and profit margins of companies in this sector, are relatively high compared with those of other industry sectors using genetic resources. This fact, coupled with extensive collecting and the high-throughput screening programmes of the 1980s, has led to greater attention to, and experience in, establishing benefit-sharing arrangements in this sector than in any other. The partnerships of pharmaceutical companies attracted international attention before the principles of prior informed consent (PIC) and benefit-sharing were articulated in the CBD.

Today, it is usual for pharmaceutical companies to pay royalties on net sales of commercial products, which was not the case ten years ago. Milestone payments at key stages in the development process, in addition to the initial fees for samples or grants to cover research, are also common. A 'package' of non-monetary benefits to accompany monetary benefits has evolved over the past ten years, and includes provision of the involvement of source-country scientists in collaborative research, the supply of literature or in-kind benefits such as medical assistance. Perhaps most significantly, the capacity of source countries to engage in value-added research has grown over the past decade, and many companies are increasingly open to collaborations at a higher level in the discovery and development process.

Biotechnology applications other than in health care and agriculture

Biotechnology companies often obtain for free samples that were collected by university researchers. Licensing agreements for access to value-added genetic resources and biotechnologies are rarely seen by companies in this sector as 'benefit-

BOX 8.9 MONETARY FORMS OF BENEFIT-SHARING

The following comprises some indicative figures for different forms of monetary benefit-sharing, based on a range of cases. While actual amounts vary enormously across the pharmaceutical sector, these figures, yielded from available data (see Laird and ten Kate, 1999) reflect typical ranges.

Fees for samples ($US)

- $25–$200/kg dry weight plant sample;
- $100–$200/25g plant solvent extract;
- $20–$140 microbial cultures;
- $60–$100 fungal samples.

Advance payments

This involves supporting the implementation of an agreed and well-defined work plan and covering operational costs. It is defined on a case basis.

Milestone payments ($US) (an example from one case)

- First patent filing: $5000;
- Initiation of phase I clinical study: $10,000;
- Initiation of phase III clinical study: $25,000;
- Filing of National Drug Authority (NDA) or equivalent: $50,000.

Royalties (on net sales)

Raw material: 0.5–2 per cent
- Raw material (eg dried plants, soil samples) and basic extracts (organic or aqueous): 0.5–2 per cent.

Value added: 1–4 per cent

- Ethnobotanical information: 1–4 per cent;
- Material supplied with some results from screening: 2–3 per cent;
- Identified bioactive compound (with known structure and test tube activity): 1–4 per cent.

Clinical data: 2–15 per cent
- Animal model data supplied with identified bioactive compound: 2–6 per cent;
- Clinical data supplied with identified bioactive compound: 5–15 per cent.

Factors which affect the magnitude of royalties (relevant to many sectors)

- Current market rate of royalties;
- Likely market share of a given product;
- Relative contribution of the partners to the inventive step and development;
- Degree of derivation of the final product from the genetic resource supplied;
- Provision of ethnobotanical data with the sample for some companies.

Source: ten Kate and Laird, 1999

sharing'. Instead, they are seen as an inevitable part of the bargain in order to maintain access to quality samples, to enjoy the advantages of collaboration with high-calibre scientists and to remain competitive in the future. Rather than initiating benefit-sharing arrangements of their own, biotechnology companies often follow the lead of intermediary organizations such as culture collections, which are increasingly supplying materials under material transfer agreements (MTAs). Genetic resources may have passed through many hands before reaching companies, and benefit-sharing with source countries is relatively rare and is usually confined to cases in which companies collect genetic resources themselves, or establish arrangements with intermediary institutions overseas. Such benefit-sharing agreements that exist typically involve technology transfer and training, as well as commitments to pay royalties. The sharing of information and capacity-building often arise informally as part of business relationships.

Crop protection

Crop-protection products are often developed by departments or subsidiaries of companies that are involved in pharmaceutical development. Libraries of compounds and gene-based materials may be tested for use in both areas, and the technologies for sourcing and screening materials are also broadly similar, although the economics of product development in the sectors are extremely different. Where such links with a pharmaceutical company exist, crop-protection companies are more likely to be familiar with the CBD and current practice in benefit-sharing, and to include aspects of benefit-sharing in their agreements with suppliers of genetic resources. However, the crop-protection industry also has some similarities with the seed industry in that basic research is often conducted in the public sector, from which genetic resources are passed, often for free, to industry. Furthermore, most crop-protection companies have synthesis programmes that use strategies involving model compounds based on templates originally discovered from nature as natural products. Since product discovery of this kind does not entail seeking access to new genetic resources, crop-protection companies have seen little rationale for sharing the benefits that arise from the development of such commercial products. This contrasts with the pharmaceutical industry, where royalty arrangements generally guarantee benefit-sharing, however modest, for derivatives of genetic resources, even for wholly synthesized analogues.

Seed

Benefits are shared in a more indirect fashion in the seed industry than the pharmaceutical industry. It is common for many seed companies to obtain genetic resources for free or for a nominal handling fee, particularly if the germplasm acquired is 'unimproved' – although licensing agreements are common for access to elite germplasm. Many actors are involved in the chain from initial access, through pre-breeding and commercial development, to sale of the final product to the farmer or consumer. The gradual privatization of the seed industry in many parts of the world, and the growing use of licences as more seed is patented, mean that sophisticated agreements do occur toward the end of this chain. However, benefits do not pass back directly along the chain to each contributor, particularly as the vast majority of the materials used have been obtained from collections maintained by seed companies themselves or by national governments.

BOX 8.10 DEVELOPMENT OF NEW MATERIALS AND BENEFIT-SHARING IN THE MOTOR INDUSTRY

R R B Leakey (School of Tropical Biology, James Cook University)

At first sight there would seem to be little in common between building top-of-the-range deluxe cars, agroforestry and poverty alleviation. However, in the early 1990s, Daimler-Benz set up an environment department to examine the durability and quality of their products, their life cycle, the opportunities for recycling parts and the possibility of applications for natural materials in vehicle production. One of the outcomes was the decision that the company should support basic and applied research on the use of renewable natural materials in automobile manufacturing. To do this, it established the Poverty and Environment in Amazonia (POEMA) Programme, in cooperation with the Federal University of Pará (UFPA) at Belém, Brazil, and a cooperative called PRONAMAZON. Working with local communities POEMA established activities in various sectors, such as basic sanitation, health and education, multistrata agroforestry, renewable energy and the processing of non-timber forest products (Mitschein and Miranda, 1998).

The basic research at UFPA examined the suitability of a range of products, such as fibres, dyes, oils and rubber from Amazonian plants for industrial use by the company. The result was the creation of 'flexiform' from natural fibres (eg sisal, Curauá) in a polypropylene matrix made from natural oils and resins, as an alternative to fibreglass for use in interior panelling of vehicles. These are now fitted to C-class Mercedes-Benz cars, as are several other natural product components, such as coconut fibre headrests, manufactured by PRONAMAZON in local communities around Belém, in Para State. Daimler-Benz sees positive commercial, as well as environmental and development, benefits from the transition from dependence on fossil resources to renewable resources. Among the commercial benefits from 'flexiform', for example, are its 20 per cent lower weight than conventional materials and its shock resistance and freedom from splintering. In addition, the manufacturing process has lower energy requirements and the material causes less wear and tear on manufacturing tools. Similar opportunities are seen for a range of other products, such as reinforced fibre composites (Kübler, 1998). Daimler-Benz envisage that these products and approaches will also become components of their lorry, train and aircraft manufacturing industries

The raw materials being grown for Daimler-Benz by subsistence farmers include coconut fibres, jute, sisal. Curauá (*Ananas erectifolius*), Ramie (*Boehmeria nivea*), castor oil, rubber, cashew oil, Andiroba (*Carapa guianensis*) and indigo (Indigofera arrecta). These are grown together with a wide range of food crops and other trees producing indigenous non-timber forest products of household importance for the farmers, within agroforestry mixtures composed of seven storeys, with advice from POEMA (Mitschein and Miranda, 1998). These have been found to provide a monthly income of US$353 by the 12th year, an increase of fourfold to fivefold over a typical minimum salary.

At its recent environment forum in Magdeburg, Germany (12–14 July 1999), DaimlerChrysler, the company formed through the merger of Daimler-Benz and Chrysler Corporation, announced their new partnership with the World Bank to expand private–public-sector activity in sustainable development activities. The company also announced plans to repeat the Brazilian experience close to another of its factories, this time in South Africa. Meanwhile, in Brazil, the POEMA programme has been expanded to become BOLSA AMAZONICA and to extend its activities to other parts of Amazonia.

The majority of researchers in agriculture view the unrestricted, reciprocal access to genetic resources as the major benefit 'shared' through the current informal system of exchange. Nevertheless, the sharing of research results, access to technology and capacity-building also take place predominantly in the public sector, though sometimes in private relationships. These benefits are often not linked to access to specific germplasm, but flow between institutions engaged in collaborative crop research that involves access to germplasm.

Horticulture

Benefit-sharing is almost unheard of in the field of commercial ornamental horticultural development, particularly among the many small companies and amateurs involved in collecting and breeding ornamental horticultural plants. Some commercial arrangements do exist that involve royalties and payment of fees, and a number of in-kind benefits might be shared, including reciprocal access to plant material between non-commercial organizations and acknowledgement of the name of the provider of the genetic resource in the name of the cultivar subsequently developed by a breeder. Supply of equipment, training and other non-monetary forms of benefit-sharing have resulted from some commercial partnerships. Horticulture companies that breed new ornamental varieties tend to conduct the majority of research in-house and rarely enter into the joint research programmes common in the pharmaceutical and seed industries. Collaborative research does take place but tends to revolve around the development of production protocols for the commercial production of new varieties of ornamental plants once the breeding programme is complete.

Botanical medicines, personal care and cosmetic products

Benefit-sharing in the botanical medicine and personal care and cosmetic sectors has developed primarily in the context of the supply of raw materials for the manufacture of products. These industries do not depend upon large numbers of samples for screening programmes (with the exception of large cosmetic companies, which have recently incorporated high-throughput screening as a discovery tool). The development of new products tends to be targeted and based on information derived from literature, databases, trade shows and intermediaries. In some cases, companies have established partnerships for the sourcing of raw materials for manufacture that include the transfer of technology and capacity-building.

Access is often severed from benefit-sharing in these industries, both when traditional knowledge of a species is used (customarily acquired from literature and databases), and when use is made of the genetic resource itself (which might be grown outside its native habitat, or treated as a commodity). Demand for access to new species is increasing in these sectors, alongside developments in scientific and technological capacity that allow for more efficient and affordable study and the testing of natural products. It is therefore likely that companies in these industries will require closer relationships with source countries and communities in the future. In these circumstances, benefit-sharing packages can be designed to link not only raw material supply, but also commercial research and product development activities, to local capacity- and institution-building. Source countries benefit to only a limited extent when they act solely as raw-material providers; benefits are best captured when source country institutions and companies partic-

BOX 8.11: INNOVATIVE MECHANISMS FOR SHARING BENEFITS: GEOGRAPHIC INDICATIONS AND TRADEMARKS

David R Downes and Sarah A Laird

Two forms of intellectual property have received relatively little attention to date in discussions of sustainable use or sharing of benefits derived from bioresources and traditional knowledge: geographic indications and trademarks (particularly trademarks relating to labels or symbols placed on products that communicate designated information to consumers on the social, cultural and environmental conditions of product sourcing). These forms of intellectual property could potentially serve as tools to help holders of traditional knowledge to benefit more equitably than they have in the past from the commercial use of their knowledge, and could also help prevent its unauthorized use by outsiders. They are particularly useful in the food, beverage, botanical medicine, cosmetic and personal care industries, and in other sectors in which consumers shop selectively. Where products are relatively easily done without or where there are available substitutes, companies are fairly close to consumers, and so consumer choice can more directly influence corporate practice.

Geographic indications are defined under the Trade Related Aspects of Intellectual Property Rights (TRIPS) agreement as 'indications which identify a good as originating in the territory of a [World Trade Organization] member, or a region or locality in that territory, where a given quality, reputation or other characteristic of the good is essentially attributable to its geographic origin' (Article 22.1). Based on an 'underlying philosophy of the distinctiveness of local and regional products' (Moran, 1993), geographical indications enhance the power of local producers to sell their distinctive products in a global marketplace, often at a premium. They allow small local producers to enhance their reputations, and potentially to sell directly to the final consumer, thus competing more effectively with large multinational companies. As a type of intellectual property that is linked to territory, they enable the relevant social and industrial groups to distinguish their products, not by company or brand, but by linking them to their origin in a particular territory and the natural and cultural characteristic of that territory relevant to the distinct character of the product (Moran, 1993; Downes, 1997).

An important criterion for determining whether a product qualifies for a geographical indication is, of course, whether it was produced in the relevant region. In addition, geographical indications typically have four types of criteria for determining whether a product meets the standards for carrying the indication: variety or species (of plant or animal); yield; production methods; and processing methods. The best-known type of geographical indication is the appellation *d'origine*, a well-developed system employed in France that includes 400 designations for wine, 32 for cheeses and others for spirits, walnuts and poultry (Moran, 1993; Dutfield, 1998). Geographic indications have significant potential as tools for the protection of traditional ecological knowledge and management of species, because they:

*   are based on collective traditions and a collective decision-making process;
*   protect and reward traditions while allowing evolution;
*   emphasize the relationships between culture, land, resources and environment;
*   are not freely transferable from one owner to another and are not subject to unconditional control by a private owner; and
*   can be maintained as long as the collective tradition is maintained.

Geographic indications might prove particularly useful in the case of kava (*Piper methysticum*), the South Pacific anti-anxiety root that has found widespread adoption by European and US consumers. The production techniques for kava are based on the 'long histories of empirical experimentation and experience' characteristic of products that may be protected by geographic indications (Moran, 1993). Although traditional practices continue to evolve over time, a core of propagation, cultivation and processing techniques combine to produce the optimally effective kava product. A local consortium organized under the auspices of the Kava Forum Secretariat is undertaking research into the potential for collective trademarks and geographic indications in order to help claim the 'true' kava for South Pacific islanders.

A trademark is a form of intellectual property right that protects a distinctive symbol, design, word or series of words, typically placed on a product label or advertisement of a firm that owns the right to use the mark. Article 15 of TRIPS provides that 'any sign, or any combination of signs, capable of distinguishing the goods or services of one undertaking from those of other undertakings shall be capable of constituting a trademark'. Trademarks serve as marketing tools that highlight a producer's claim to authentic or distinctive products or services. Specific types of trademarks that are particularly relevant for genetic resource-based products are collective marks and certification marks. Collective marks are trademarks or service marks used by the members of a cooperative, an association or another collective group. Certification marks are 'used in connection with the products or services of one or more persons other than the owner of the mark to certify regional or other origin, material, mode of manufacture, quality, accuracy or other characteristics of such goods or services' (Blacks Law Dictionary, 1979).

Trademarks are used in the UK, for example, by Stilton cheese makers, who limit the use of the 'Stilton' certification trademark to cheese produced in, or near, the village of Stilton in accordance with traditional manufacturing techniques, and making use of traditional ingredients (Dutfield, 1998; 1999). Such marks have also been used by some indigenous and local communities, including agricultural products made by native American Indians, certified as such by the Intertribal Agriculture Council, and Inuit soapstone carvings, certified by the Canadian Department of Indian and Northern Affairs (Dutfield, 1997).

Intellectual property systems have evolved primarily to serve industrial commercial interests and to emphasize private ownership, in contrast to the collective and communal property traditions of many indigenous and local communities. Geographic indications and trademarks, however, have the potential to respond to the concerns of local and indigenous communities more effectively than do other intellectual property rights.

While copyright and patents are intended to reward investments in innovation, geographical indications and trademarks reward producers who invest in building the reputation of a product over time. They are designed to reward good will and reputation created or built up by a producer or group of producers over many years or even centuries. They reward producers who maintain a traditional high standard of quality, while at the same time allowing flexibility for innovation and improvement in the context of that tradition.

A preliminary assessment suggested that geographic indications and trademarks may have potential as incentives for conservation and sustainable use for some, but not all, products from five well-known plant species or varieties traditionally used in certain regions of Africa, Asia, South America and the Pacific (see Downes and Laird, 1999). Products examined include: kava, rooibos (*Aspalathus linearis*), Quinoa (*Chenopodium quinoa*), basmati (*Oryza sativa*) and Neem (*Azadirachtica inidca*).

Source: excerpted from David R Downes and Sarah A Laird, 1999, *Innovative Mechanisms for Sharing Benefits of Biodiversity and Related Knowledge: Case Studies on Geographical Indications and Trademarks*, UNCTAD Biotrade

ipate at a higher level in the value chain. This has the added benefit of providing the basis from which source-country groups can develop domestic markets for processed products, which are generally far less fickle than international (particularly US) botanical medicine markets.

Few botanical medicine products are patented. However, an increasing emphasis within the botanical medicine industry on 'branding' or trademarked lines of products as a tool to distinguish products from competitors, and establish product equity, has concentrated financial returns in some cases. Branded products based on species native to a given region, or traditional knowledge of a defined group – such as those for kava or various ginsengs – should generate financial revenues for countries and communities of origin. The Kava Forum Secretariat is investigating the potential for developing the intellectual property tools of geographic indications and trademarked products to protect and promote 'true' kava products, sourced sustainably and in ways that benefit local communities in the Pacific Islands from which it originates (Downes and Laird, 1999; see Box 8.11).

Corporate steps towards standards of best practice

Company responses to the Convention on Biological Diversity

Awareness and experience of partnerships that reflect the Convention on Biological Diversity vary enormously between and within sectors, and even within single companies. Companies within the pharmaceutical, crop-protection, seed and biotechnology industries appear most aware of the Convention, although its direct impact on corporate business practices is most evident in the pharmaceutical industry. Horticulture, botanical medicine and personal care and cosmetic companies are largely unaware of the content of the Convention on Biological Diversity (ten Kate and Laird, 1999). In general, however, awareness is on the rise, and an increasing number of companies are responding by changing business practices. The most common responses include:

- a decrease in corporate collecting activities; consolidation of collecting programmes into fewer countries, or even solely domestic-collecting activities;
- greater recourse to material from ex-situ collections, such as culture collections and compound libraries, in place of samples acquired through field-collecting activities;
- an increased role for intermediaries as brokers of access and benefit-sharing relationships, as well as suppliers of samples;
- the increasing use of material transfer agreements (MTAs) to clarify the terms of exchange; and
- the development of basic standards of benefit-sharing best practice to guide staff within companies – for example, through policies and internal guidelines.

Material transfer agreements

As mentioned earlier, companies are increasingly using MTAs to clarify their own rights and responsibilities and those of the organizations supplying them with samples or working with them on discovery and development. While MTAs of intermediary institutions, such as gene banks and botanic gardens, are typically freely available, more sophisticated access and benefit-sharing agreements between companies and their suppliers are generally confidential. These contractual agreements, more than any other documents, reflect emerging best practice within the industry. The fact that the parties to such agreements tend to insist on keeping them confidential makes it difficult to compare agreements and gauge best practice. However, it is common for these agreements to contain benefit-sharing commitments comprising a 'package' of monetary and non-monetary benefits. The core elements of commercial agreements are examined in Chapters 9 and 10.

Corporate policies

Development of a corporate or institutional policy on access and benefit-sharing offers several advantages to a company or other organization. Preparation of a policy provides an opportunity and a mechanism for a company to familiarize itself with the letter and spirit of the Convention and access legislation, and will result in a management tool that can protect the company from liability by ensuring compliance with required standards and procedures. A corporate policy can enable more proactive companies to design tools for continuous improvement in their supplier and user chains, and can contribute to the development of a company's R&D strategy. The process of developing such a policy will help the company identify parameters such as the number of countries it is likely to work in, its main suppliers and collaborators and the monetary and 'non-monetary' costs of partnerships. A policy also provides a tool for 'transparency' and good corporate

citizenship, enabling companies to communicate their positions and commitments to suppliers and other outside collaborators. Finally, a good policy is a vehicle for positive public relations. Some elements that could be included in corporate and institutional policies on the CBD are set out in Box 8.12 (see also Chapter 3).

To date, very few companies have developed policies in response to the CBD, let alone clear and detailed public documents designed to ensure and to demonstrate compliance with the CBD and national laws on access. As explored by ten Kate and Laird (1999), pharmaceutical companies that have developed policies on acquiring genetic resources include: Glaxo Wellcome (*Discovering New Medicines from Nature: Policy for the Acquisition of Natural Product Source Materials*, 1992); Novo Nordisk (*Acquisition of Natural Resources for the Development of New Pharmaceuticals*, 1995); Xenova Discovery Ltd (*Policy for the Acquisition of Natural Product Source Materials*, 1998); and Shaman Pharmaceuticals (*Agreement of Principles*, 1995).

In its *Discovering New Medicines from Nature: Policy for the Acquisition of Natural Product Source Materials*, Glaxo Wellcome acknowledges the need 'to conserve rare species and not to imperil biodiversity' and sets out the company's views and mode of conduct. The policy addresses the quantities of material sourced; the kind of institutions with which the company will collaborate; the requirement of supplier organizations to provide written evidence of proof of prior informed consent and government permission to supply samples; and benefit-sharing. Other than reimbursement of costs, reward for expertise and 'financial benefits' whose magnitude 'will recognize the relative contribution of the discovery of the bio-active principle to the subsequent development of the commer-

Box 8.12 Possible elements for inclusion in corporate and institutional policies developed in response to the Convention on Biological Diversity

Scope and standard

Included in this category are:

- the scope of activities and resources covered by the policy;
- reference to the Convention on Biological Diversity, its access and benefit-sharing provisions and to national law; and
- standard of effort.

Prior informed consent (PIC) and legal title

This category covers:

- PIC for collection from all interested parties (eg government, research institutions, local communities);
- requirement of proof that an organization supplying genetic resources has title to the materials and is authorized to supply them to the company for product discovery and development; and
- respect for the traditional resource rights of local communities.

Benefit-sharing

This comprises:

- monetary and non-monetary benefits;
- timing of benefit-sharing;
- sharing of benefits arising from use of pre-CBD materials; and
- sharing benefits with a range of stakeholders (eg government, research institutions, local communities).

Conservation and sustainable use

This category comprises:

- sustainable sourcing for manufacture;
- dedication of benefits to conservation; and
- commitment to not overharvest species during collections.

Process and indicators

This includes:

- objectively verifiable indicators that the policy has been applied;
- options for scrutiny; and
- continual improvement.

Source: ten Kate and Laird, 1999

cial products', the nature of monetary or non-monetary benefits is not discussed. The policy refers to covering costs and sharing benefits in the event of commercialization. It does not stipulate the timing during which benefits will be shared; but, in practice, the company shares benefits in the short, medium and long term (Melanie O'Neill, pers comm, 1998).

In another example, in 1995 Novo Nordisk Health Care Discovery developed a document concerning *Acquisition of Natural Resources for the Development of New Pharmaceuticals*, which stated the company's respect for the sovereign rights of nations to their own natural resources, and acknowledged that 'benefits arising from the utilization of natural resources by any other party should be shared fairly and equitably with the donor country'. The policy affirmed the company's intention to establish research agreements with organizations supplying material in compliance with national legislation and international law; affirmed its requirement for supplying organizations to provide documentary evidence of 'all necessary authorizations and permits' to dispose and make use of the material; and upheld benefit-sharing. The company's approach to access and benefit-sharing evolved in the next two years and, in its 1997 report on environment and bioethics, it set out 'Guiding Principles for Novo Nordisk's Implementation of the Convention', which applied to both its health-care and enzyme business.

By 1998, the company's *Environmental and Bioethics Report* reported on progress in implementing the principles in its partnerships in several countries, and identified the need for countries to establish effective systems for establishing prior informed consent without too much bureaucracy. It also highlighted the need for users to be able to identify whose prior consent for access is required. The documents do not explicitly distinguish between monetary and non-monetary benefit-sharing, or state when benefits will be shared; but the 1998 *Environmental and Bioethics Report* sets out examples of 'collaborations with organizations from different regions of the world involving both monetary and non-monetary benefits to the providing country'. As with other policies adopted by companies, the scope of Novo Nordisk's policy appears to be restricted to post-CBD materials. Beyond endorsing the CBD's objective of conservation, the document makes no mention of conservation or sustainable sourcing.

The company's use of published targets demonstrates its commitment to the continual improvement of its policy on implementing the CBD. The target for 1998 was to develop formal corporate requirements on the use of, and access to, genetic resources in keeping with the Convention on Biological Diversity. This accomplished, the target for 1999 was that all relevant patent applications and publications submitted from 1999 onwards should state the country of origin of genetic material. The company's target for 1999–2000 was to develop procedures for monitoring the implementation of company requirements on the use of, and access to, genetic resources.

Personal care and cosmetic companies that have developed policies include Aveda Corporation, which launched a process to develop a manifesto regarding the use of traditional knowledge following the United Nations Conference on Environment and Development (UNCED; commonly known as the Earth Summit) in Rio de Janeiro in 1992. In 1994, The Body Shop initiated a process to develop an Intellectual Property Rights Agreement to guide their collaboration with the Kayapo Indians in Brazil, including the development of new commercial products.

In addition to specific companies, industry and professional associations have taken steps to address broader social and environmental responsibility in business. These networks and associations – including the Social Venture Network, Businesses for Social Responsibility and the Coalition for Environmentally Responsible Economies – might be encouraged to take up issues growing from the CBD, including access and benefit-sharing (Box 8.13).

BOX 8.13. NETWORKS AND ASSOCIATIONS FOR CORPORATE SOCIAL AND ENVIRONMENTAL RESPONSIBILITY

A number of companies participate in industry-wide efforts to promote environmental and socially responsible business practices. These networks and associations play a range of roles: the supply of services to companies seeking to move forward in this area (eg advice, conferences, publications); establishing social and environmental standards of best practice; ranking companies according to achievement of criteria; and presenting awards to outstanding companies. All argue that reporting and transparency help not only consumers but companies, communities and investors who want value over time. None of these groups has tackled the issues raised in the Convention on Biological Diversity specifically, although some address issues of equity and the sharing of benefits in partnerships with developing-country communities and groups. These might be useful fora in which to promote the concepts of 'access and benefit-sharing' or 'equitable research partnerships' as critical elements of corporate social and environmental responsibility in policy and practice. A brief review of a few of these groups follows.

Businesses for Social Responsibility (BSR)

Founded in 1992, Businesses for Social Responsibility (BSR) is a US-based global membership organization that works to help companies 'be commercially successful in ways that demonstrate respect for ethical values, people, communities and the environment. Through socially responsible business policies and practices, companies create value for investors, customers, employees, local communities and other stakeholders.' BSR offers membership services and holds conferences to help companies become socially responsible. There are currently 1400 companies that are members or affiliated with BSR, which collectively employ more than six million workers and have total annual revenues of more than US$1.5 trillion. Companies reflect an enormous range in sales and represent 'nearly every sector in the global economy'. They include, for example: American Express, AT&T, British Telecom, Bristol-Myers Squibb, Johnson & Johnson, Patagonia, Starbucks, Time Warner, Tom's of Maine and Stonyfield Farm Yogurt.

BSR is also part of a growing global network of business membership organizations that focuses on corporate social responsibility and has formal partnerships with the Ethos Institute (Brazil) and *Empresa Privada para la Responsabilidad Social Empresarial* (Panama); special relationships with Business in the Community (UK) and Peru 20/21; and is a founding member of EMPRESA, the Forum on Business and Social Responsibility in the Americas, a new coalition of business organizations established to strengthen and establish national and regional business organizations committed to social and environmental responsibility in Latin America (www.bsr.org, 1999).

Coalition for Environmentally Responsible Economies (CERES)

Formed in 1989, the Coalition for Environmentally Responsible Economies (CERES) is a coalition of environmental groups, socially responsible investors and companies. Companies endorse the CERES principles and thereby formalize their dedication to environmental awareness and accountability. The principles address the following ten areas: protection of the biosphere; sustainable use of natural resources; reduction and disposal of wastes; energy conservation; risk reduction; safe products and services; environmental restoration; informing the public; management commitment; and audits and reports. In the early years, (1989–1992), CERES principles were mainly adopted by 'green' companies, such as The Body Shop, Ben and Jerry's, Seventh Generation and Aveda Corporation. But in 1993, following lengthy negotiations, Sun Oil became the first Fortune 500 company to endorse the CERES principles. Today, 46 companies have endorsed the CERES principles, including General Motors, Polaroid and Bethlehem Steel (www.ceres.org, 1999).

Council on Economic Priorities (CEP)

Since 1975, the Council on Economic Priorities (CEP) has been rating companies on criteria such as environmental stewardship, treatment of employees (women, minorities, family benefits, workplace issues), charitable giving, community outreach, animal welfare, weapons contracts and social disclosure. CEP is not an industry association or network, but acts as an important and well-respected 'carrot-and-stick' group, working closely with the media. CEP offers companies both the 'stick' – bad ratings – and the 'carrot' – good ratings and corporate awards. Corporate Conscience Award Winners for 1999 included Pfizer Inc, which – in a partnership with the World Health Organization (WHO) and the Edna McConnell Clark Foundation – is collaborating on a US$66 million programme to eliminate trachoma, a treatable disease that has caused blindness in six million people and afflicts 150 million. Pfizer is donating enough azithrmycin to treat three million people over the next two years in Ghana, Mali, Morocco, Tanzania and Vietnam. SmithKline Beecham also won a Corporate Conscience Award for its partnership with WHO in a joint venture to eradicate lymphatic filariasis, which currently affects 120 million people in 73 countries and can be treated with Albendazole and another anti-parasitic drug with 99 per cent success rates (www.cepnyc.org, 1999).

Social Venture Network (SVN)

Social Venture Network (SVN) was established in the United States in 1987, and SVN Europe in 1993. SVN is 'an association of companies and individual business leaders who believe they can – and must – make a significant contribution to solve social and environmental problems locally and globally'. SVN works to advance the movement for responsible business in a variety of ways, including developing Standards for Corporate Social Responsibility; the Social Venture Institute; and the Sustainable Trade Initiative, which promotes international trade that is socially, economically and environmentally sustainable, benefiting the local economies and communities of marginalized producers and workers (SVN, 1999). SVN Europe members include Auchan Group, The Body Shop, the Ecover Group, Joh Grundlach KG, Max Havelaar, Naturwaren, Nature et Decouvertes, Rabobank, and Weleda A G (www.svn.org; www.svneurope.com, 1999).

Conclusion

Companies from a very diverse range of industry sectors are engaged in biodiversity prospecting. Within each sector, the extent and nature of biodiversity prospecting activities is equally diverse. The annual market for products, the sales by individual companies and the costs of product discovery and development vary dramatically between and within sectors, as does the role of genetic resources in those sales, and the relationship between genetic resources and final products.

One consistent conclusion that can be drawn from this chapter is that it is difficult to generalize about biodiversity prospecting. This is a critical point for policy-makers and others who might otherwise seek a 'one-size-fits-all' approach to regulating access to genetic resources by all of these industries. Many policy-makers are now aiming to develop national environment and development strategies (such as national biodiversity strategies and action plans), and legislation regulating access to genetic resources and benefit-sharing. For these measures to succeed in practice, it is essential for those who design and will administer the measures to understand the complex scientific, technological and economic basis for biodiversity prospecting, and constantly to update their knowledge in the light of the rapid developments in this field.

While complex and diverse, the commercial use of genetic resources is not unfathomable. Nor is it impossible to develop innovative ways to balance demand for access with conservation and equitable benefit-sharing. Over the past ten years, there has been a constant refinement of best practice in benefit-sharing, particularly in the pharmaceutical industry, to the point that many of the demands of provider countries, regarded as novel ten years ago, are now common practice (eg advance payments and royalties, technology transfer, collaborative research). Since access legislation is a feature of the last five years, many of the developments in access and benefit-sharing agreements pre-date it and took place outside of a detailed legal framework.

Access legislation has struggled to keep up with developments in science and technology and with practice in benefit-sharing emerging from experiences in partnerships around the world. It has not always succeeded in making workable, general prescriptions for what has emerged through case-by-case negotiation of mutually agreed terms. The shortcomings of access legislation and the uneven results of access and benefit-sharing agreements reflect the trials and errors of, and lessons learned along the way by, research institutions, companies, NGOs and other groups. The more information that is available to all of the actors on the commercial use of genetic resources in a range of sectors, the better informed will be access legislation and the more equitable the access and benefit-sharing agreements struck. We hope this chapter will contribute to the growing volume of such information.

Note

1   The following sections are based in large part on research conducted for the European Commission-sponsored book *The Commercial Use of Biodiversity: Access to Genetic Resources and Benefit-Sharing* by Kerry ten Kate and Sarah A Laird (1999). This book – published by Earthscan (www.earthscan.co.uk) – provides a far more comprehensive analysis of the commercial use of genetic resources, and should be consulted for more detailed coverage of the information and issues briefly presented in this chapter.

Chapter 9

Biodiversity prospecting contracts: the search for equitable agreements

Brendan Tobin

Introduction

Biodiversity prospecting contracts (BPCs) are the most frequently used tool for establishing formal legally binding relationships between providers and users of genetic resources. Agreements come in all shapes and sizes, from those for collection of material for taxonomic research purposes, to multimillion-dollar projects for access to, and screening of, medicinal plant varieties. Conditions may be formally included in written documents or acknowledged with a shake of the hand. Contracts may involve the supply of biological raw material, isolated active compounds or material subject to patents. Samples may be provided by governments, landowners, indigenous and local communities, research institutions or gene banks. Access may be sought by pharmaceutical companies, plant breeders, post-graduate students, research institutes or local communities. Resources may be used for a range of purposes including commercial enrichment, scientific investigation and global health programmes. Benefits may be of monetary or non-monetary nature, and may be shared by a wide variety of public and private sector actors, including local and indigenous communities. The range of conditions, relationships and materials covered in agreements is significant and diverse.

Similarly, the forms contracts may take are varied, including contracts for the sale of raw material, material transfer agreements (MTAs), licensing regimes and memoranda of understanding (MOU) (see Chapter 10). At heart, however, all contracts basically serve the same purpose: they identify the parties, define the subject matter, specify uses which may be made of it, provide for compensation of a monetary, technological or in-kind basis, regulate rights over intellectual property in the event of development and marketing of products, and define the period of the agreement and conditions for termination, as well as for breach of contract and the jurisdiction and law of the contract.

Written contracts have potential benefits for both providers and users of resources. For providers, they offer an opportunity to control the use of their resources, both within and beyond the bounds of national jurisdiction. For users, contracts offer a measure of legal certainty with regard to the right to use resources for research and development purposes.

Furthermore, national authorities may find that contracts provide a measure of security for protection of sovereign rights over genetic resources, even where specific access legislation has not been adopted. Indigenous peoples may use agreements over traditional knowledge as a means to excercise control over biological resources considered to be national patrimony (Tobin, 1999).

This chapter reviews the possibilities and limitations of BPCs for securing realization of the Convention on Biological Diversity's (CBD's) objectives. It pays particular attention to the manner in which BPCs have attempted to resolve some of the thorniest issues surrounding biodiversity prospecting, including questions of prior informed consent (PIC), intellectual property rights (IPRs), benefit-sharing and enforcement of agreements. Also included is a brief review of basic negotiating strategies.

The national policy and legal context

Discussion of the relative merits and limitations of biodiversity prospecting agreements in realizing the objectives of the CBD has been the subject of a polarized and often emotional debate. For some, BPCs are merely the new tools of biopiracy, providing a cloak of respectability to arrangements viewed as inherently inequitable due to the disproportionate negotiating strength of multinational corporations, and the potential for misappropriation and monopolization of common goods through utilization of IPR regimes (Bell, 1997). Those holding such views regard any form of biodiversity prospecting as a step towards enclosure of the commons (Shiva, 1998) and as biopiracy (Mooney, 2000).

Conversely, there is evidence that BPCs have, in some cases, provided a means by which source countries, and indigenous and local communities, have obtained more equitable participation in the benefits derived from utilization of their resources. Progressive and incremental advances in developing innovative contractual arrangements have broken new ground, creating precedents that have secured increasing control by providers over the use of their resources, promoted capacity-building in source countries and promoted awareness regarding the value of genetic resources and traditional knowledge, not only for commercial markets but also for national and local survival, food and health needs (Guerin-McManus, 1998; Iwu et al, 1998; Tobin, 1997; Laird and Lisinge, 1998).

Despite widespread promotion of the benefits of biodiversity prospecting agreements, impediments to independent third-party investigation of the terms and conditions, including the commercial provisions, of relevant contracts make reliance on unsubstantiated claims of the merits of existing agreements inadvisable. In a salutary report, the Expert Panel on Access and Benefit-Sharing, a body of 50 international experts meeting at the invitation of the Secretariat to the CBD in Costa Rica in 1999, came to the conclusion that legislative and administrative frameworks are essential to ensuring that contractual agreements serve local, national and international objectives, and promote equitable partnerships. At the same time, it must be recognized that whether access legislation exists or not, contracts are likely to become the primary means for parties not only to authorize access to genetic resources, but also to agree on a return of benefits from subsequent use (Glowka, 1994). However, it is clear that in an unregulated environment the negotiation of agreements does not favour source countries or indigenous and local communities as much as bioprospectors. While the adoption of voluntary codes of conduct by professional bodies and the private sector are to be welcomed, they are no substitute for legal protection under national laws in both provider and user countries (Tobin, 2001).

Biodiversity prospecting contracts and national legislation

A range of issues will affect the outcome of any negotiation and the merits of any final agreement, including:

- what induces parties to negotiate agreements;
- respective negotiating strengths and weaknesses;
- competition for provision of resources and the level of private-sector interest in accessing resources;
- whether there is clear national legislation regarding ownership of resources.

BPCs can act as a disincentive to legislators to develop national access and benefit-sharing (ABS) measures; however, the negotiation of highly visible BPCs has tended to raise public awareness of the issues surrounding biodiversity prospecting. For example, the participation of indigenous and local communities in such agreements has led to renewed interest in, and increased respect for, traditional knowledge systems. Concerns relating to the impact of agreements have also drawn the attention of indigenous and local communities to international intellectual property rights issues (COICA, 1999). ABS legislation appears to have developed

faster in those countries where highly visible biodiversity prospecting activities have led to increased public interest and national debate. In Costa Rica, interest in and concerns about the activities of the National Institute of Biodiversity (InBio) helped foment a participatory national debate that culminated in the adoption of a comprehensive national biodiversity law in 1999 (see Chapter 12). Likewise, in Cameroon the need to ensure adequate protection of medicinal plants in an agreement with the US National Cancer Institute (NCI) led to the inclusion of access and benefit-sharing provisions for genetic resources in the new 1994 Forestry Law (Laird and Lisinge, 1998).

In Peru, the know-how licensing regime adopted by the International Cooperative Biodiversity Groups (ICBG) project strongly influenced the preparation of a draft law for the protection of indigenous collective property rights (Ruiz, 2000). The draft law was originally published in the official press during October 1999; following public comment a revised version was published in August 2000. While marking a significant step towards the development of sui generis legislation to protect traditional knowledge rights, the Peruvian process has highlighted conflicts of perspective, legal vision and interests that must be overcome in order to prepare measures that respond to indigenous and local community priorities rather than serving the interests of the commercial sector and national elites (Tobin, 2001; Tobin and Swiderska, 2001) Negotiation of a BPC involving the Verata in Fiji is considered to have played an important role in the development of guidelines on biodiversity prospecting by the commercial and academic parties to the agreement (Aalbersberg, 1998). In the state of Sarawak in Malaysia new state ABS legislation came into effect on 1 January 1998, spurred on by an agreement between the

NCI, a US pharmaceutical company and the state government (see Chapter 12).

Setting national objectives for biodiversity prospecting contracts

National governments can send, through their policies, a clear message to public- and private-sector negotiators about what is expected of contractual arrangements for access and benefit-sharing, including the level of control they wish to have over the use of resources and clear guidelines on benefit-sharing (Caillaux et al, 1999).

Among the many objectives that underlie a decision to enter into BPCs, some of the most commonly cited are:

- regulate the relationship between provider and user in accordance with the objectives of the CBD;
- develop potential medicinal or veterinary products or their precursors;
- carry out characterization, synthesis and isolation of natural products;
- provide a taxonomy and inventory of biological diversity;
- improve source-country scientific infrastructure;
- develop national scientific capacity to conserve and sustainably use biological resources;
- strengthen source-country capacity to add value to resources in the country;
- build local capacity for pharmaceutical production;
- build capacity of para-professionals in collection, taxonomy and ethnobotany, and build local community support for, and participation in, conservation activities;
- conserve biological diversity;
- protect indigenous knowledge systems;
- enhance local community development opportunities;
- secure equitable benefit-sharing with source-country organizations and individuals involved in collection;
- define and control intellectual property rights over products;
- revalue and strengthen traditional knowledge systems.

The Andean Pact countries have defined a number of objectives that should guide decisions on access and promote the inclusion of provisions in contracts that are conducive to realizing those objectives (see Box 9.1). In the Philippines, Executive Order 247 establishes access regulations that include terms for research and commercial agreements (see Chapter 12).

National authorities and biodiversity prospecting contracts

In some countries, national authorities may take an active role in the preparation, negotiation and implementation of contracts, while in others there may be a policy of limiting involvement to revising contracts within an approvals process. Although the CBD recognizes the sovereign right of states to determine access to resources, this does not always mean that the state must be a party to access agreements. And the state, in many cases, may not be entitled to provide rights to access without the participation and/or prior approval of other parties. In Fiji, for instance, indigenous peoples have property rights over the resources on their territories, and are entitled to negotiate rights of access on their own. In the Philippines and in the Andean Pact countries, access legislation recognizes the need to seek consent of indigenous and local communities in order to collect on their lands, and to access and use their knowledge, innovations and practices (La Vina et al, 1997; Caillaux and Ruiz, 1998). National law pertaining to ownership of resources will be a determining factor in identifying the level of state participation required in contract preparation.

> ## Box 9.1 Andean Pact Decision 391 and contracts
>
> The Andean Pact Decision 391 specifies that agreements should include provisions that deal with the following issues:
>
> - participation of regional scientists in research project activities;
> - assistance with investigations in the region that support conservation or sustainable use of biological diversity;
> - strengthening of mechanisms for the transfer of technologies and associated know-how, including biotechnology, that are culturally, socially and environmentally sound and safe;
> - provision of information on the background, state of the science etc that contributes the highest level of knowledge of the state of science relating to genetic resources, derived and synthetic products, as well as associated knowledge;
> - strengthening of national and regional capacity relating to genetic resources and associated knowledge;
> - strengthening and development of local, Afro-American and indigenous communities in relation to their knowledge, innovations and practices;
> - obligation to put duplicate copies of all material collected in institutions nominated by the source-country authorities;
> - obligation to inform the national authorities of the source-country of investigation results;
> - terms for transfer of resources to third parties.
>
> *Source:* Caillaux and Ruiz, 1998

Negotiating Contracts

'Negotiation is always just the beginning of a longer process of learning, adjustments and building relationships. No agreement is perfect. Unexpected situations arise, and there are disputes over the original meaning of the words used. Adjustments are always necessary, and the most important product of a successful negotiation is a level of trust and commitment on both sides, which facilitates these later adjustments as well as agreements on other topics.' (Barsh and Bastien, 1997)

Negotiation implies the existence of two or more rights holders who are prepared to enter into discussions in order to determine whether there is an issue of mutual interest over which they can agree. It also implies that they have an interest in entering into a legally binding arrangement under which the parties will each assume obligations in return for some compensation or benefit. Negotiations will normally commence following the demonstration by one party of its interest in accessing or providing resources, and a demonstrated interest in providing resources or in acquiring them by another party. Within the framework of the CBD, this negotiation process may be seen as fundamental

291

to arriving at 'mutually agreed terms' (CBD, Article 15 (4)).

Mutually agreed terms

Attempting to define what constitutes mutually agreed terms (MATs) is a thankless and perhaps fruitless task. For some, mutually agreed terms may be perceived as being the market rate for resources. For others, determination of MAT requires inclusion of the notion of equity, in order to create greater equality between strong commercial parties and weak providing nations or indigenous and local communities. Although the tendency is to consider providers as weaker parties to negotiations, this will not always be the case. The CBD requires that access is obtained with prior informed consent (PIC). This implies that the parties were aware of the potential value of resources, and of the costs or impacts of access, and that where PIC has been obtained a BPC may be deemed to demonstrate mutually agreed terms. However, provision of independent third-party review of contractual relations is necessary to ensure equity of benefit-sharing provisions (Bystrom et al, 1999).

Knowing what the other party wants is key to achieving a good agreement. The value of any specific resource or service to users and providers may be completely different, and will probably be determined based upon differing criteria and information (Tobin, 1997). It is important to consider both perceptions of value when negotiating. Industry, for instance, looks for reliability, quality control and clear access to resources, not clouded by bureaucratic procedures and in line with national and international law (Sittenfeld, 1997). This search for legal certainty will – at the end of the day – guide the negotiations. Knowledge of the existing market for resources and the generally acceptable forms of doing business in the natural-product marketplace are essential. There is an ever-growing body of material available that may help negotiators determine the value of their resources, as well as of the types of agreement that may be used to protect them (ten Kate and Laird, 1999).

Parties wishing to negotiate an agreement that will survive with time and that will continue to be supported by all parties should seek to achieve a win–win situation. Where any one or more parties find the agreement has not adequately respected their rights or interests, their commitment to respecting its terms and conditions is weakened. This leads to an alternative definition of mutually agreed terms as being those terms that provide sufficient benefit and incentive to the parties to ensure their continued compliance with their responsibilities during the lifetime of an agreement. This definition would accord more with the principles of equity than with the strictures of contract legislation. As the intention of the CBD is to promote equity, the possibility to review whether or not agreements include PIC and MAT must involve consideration of the conditions that pertained at the time of making the agreement (ABS Expert Panel, 1999).

Although it may be difficult to secure agreement on the equity of any particular agreement, it may be possible to agree upon:

- *means* that are likely to render the outcome more equitable;
- *indications* of the degree to which a specific outcome is equitable;
- *procedural guidelines* that will increase the fairness of the process (Bystrom et al, 1999).

Identifying the resources and the parties who are the basis for negotiation

Whichever party initiates the negotiation, there are a number of basic steps that must be followed prior to commencing the negotiation proper. Firstly, it is necessary to identify the subject matter of the biodiversity prospecting activity (ie what resources and/or associated knowledge are being sought or are being offered). Secondly, it is crucial to decide with whom to negotiate. This requires identification of a party with the legal right to enter into an agreement regarding the proposed genetic resources (ie who is entitled to provide access to resources or knowledge).

Contracts are only binding upon the parties and can only be enforced by the parties. This is of particular importance in relation to benefit-sharing and protection of interests regarding the subject matter of a contract. As contracts are only binding on the parties, it is important to ensure that any collector is in a position to indemnify the provider for any losses, including lost profits that may arise due to their failure to protect the resources from third-party unapproved use. For these reasons, it is important to be clear about where resources may be deposited and under what conditions, as well as to ensure that any transfer to third parties obliges compliance with the terms under which the resources were originally provided.

Establishing rules for negotiation

Negotiation may not be the first step in the process of developing a BPC. Parties often begin by establishing contact, exchanging information and entering into dialogue and consultation, before commencing negotiation. It is important that the parties are aware when actual negotiations begin, and it may prove useful to establish clear guidelines for the negotiation process. Preparation of a timetable for meetings, including proposed dates for termination of negotiations, can help to focus the process. Arrangements on the confidentiality of meeting reports and information exchanged, and other relevant procedures, may be set down in a letter of intent, with parties committing to carry out good faith negotiations. On occasion, parties may agree not to enter into parallel negotiations with other parties for the same subject matter during a fixed period.

Amongst the issues parties may wish to agree upon are: how and where negotiations are to be carried out, the language of negotiations and procedures for preparing draft contracts, including translation where appropriate. Who will carry out negotiations (ie are they to be carried out directly by the parties or by their lawyers)? How are offers and counter offers to be presented? What time scale is to apply? Where will negotiation take place? It is always preferable to ensure that negotiations are carried out face to face, where possible. Negotiation is a personal as well as a professional skill, and bringing together those responsible for decision-making on both sides of a negotiation can often help to resolve issues which intermediaries, or those without decision-making power, cannot decide.

To avoid frustrations, unnecessary delays and piecemeal negotiations, it is advisable to be clear from the outset about the authority of each party's negotiators and their right to make commitments. Does the university professor represent the commercial partners to a collaborative programme, such as the ICBG? Does the provider of the biological resource have the power to grant rights to use its genetic content? Does the leader of the community have the authority to grant rights to use

---

Box 9.2 Preparing for negotiation

As a first step in negotiations, it is important to identify:

- a negotiating team and strategy (eg promote scientific uses or restrict commercial use);
- individuals or parties with whom to negotiate and their capacity to make decisions;
- all stakeholders, including national authorities, who have rights to be involved in negotiation;
- parties whose opposition or support may affect the possibility of implementing any negotiated agreement;
- subject matter (ie genetic resources and knowledge, etc and intended uses);
- sources of information on the value of resources and potential impacts of access;
- alternatives to proposed agreement.

Establishing a negotiation team and strategy is vital. This may be done at a company or research institute level, by a community or by indigenous peoples, or by the state or any combination of the above. Where various providers are involved, it may prove appropriate to establish a joint negotiating team. In establishing a negotiating team it is necessary to:

- identify the resources needed, in terms of leadership, representation, negotiating skills and social, cultural and environmental impact assessors, as well as contractual law expertise;
- define team leadership and internal decision-making process;
- identify support needed for making decisions, including access to information, etc;
- decide whether decisions are to be made by the team leader or the whole group;
- establish means to avoid conflicts within the team during negotiations;
- have all communications channelled to the team leader and copied to other relevant members of the negotiating team;
- ensure that all relevant decisions, agreements, etc are recorded in writing;
- establish lines of communication with other stakeholders or negotiators to promote coordinated negotiation;
- ensure that adequate legal and technical support is available as necessary.

---

traditional knowledge? Does the head of collection activities for a pharmaceutical company have the right to commit to sharing intellectual property rights with a local community (Aalbersberg et al, 1998)?

Care should be taken to ensure that legal advisers are, in fact, representing the position of their clients in negotiations. Efforts should be made to keep negotiations simple and to avoid the use of a technical vocabulary that may marginalize some stakeholders. When obtaining legal and commercial advice, it is important to consider the following:

- Seek advisers in whom you have confidence.
- Good advisers are those who inform you of what you need to know in order to make a decision – not what they think you need to know or think you want to hear.
- Any legal team for commercial contracts should include advisers with

BOX 9.3 CHECKLIST FOR INDIGENOUS PEOPLES ON NEGOTIATIONS

Before beginning

Before beginning negotions, it is important to perform the following:

- Mobilize the community's own technical capacity (eg traditional ecological knowledge).
- Ascertain where you need outside technical expertise.
- Organize community meetings to build consensus around a negotiating plan.
- Identify all other relevant parties, the needs of their leaders and constituents.
- Identify the real decision-makers and ensure their involvement in negotiations.
- Identify similar negotiations or agreements as precedents.
- Select your own negotiators through a public process.
- Build a negotiating team reflecting the diversity of skills and viewpoints in the community.

Developing strategy

This involves the following:

- Use preliminary meetings with other parties to listen and learn.
- Get to know the people who represent other parties. Assess their personal beliefs and influence within their organization.
- Think about ways in which other parties might satisfy their real needs without sacrificing your needs.

Equalizing power

Equalizing power entails the following:

- Meet on your own ground and follow your own traditional procedures. Create situations in which the other parties' negotiators must adapt to your own way of conducting business and must learn to respect and adjust to your own language and culture.
- Find ways in which to ensure that the other parties appreciate the solidarity of your community and legitimacy of its leaders.
- Expose inconsistencies in what other parties say and do.
- Help the other parties to appreciate the value of building a long-term relationship.
- Show other parties how taking advantage of you could be costly and unprofitable in the future.

Managing pressure tactics

Tactics include the following:

- Don't respond to pressure tactics. Let the other parties know that you understand what they are trying to do and that it will not succeed.
- Don't agree to unrealistic timetables.
- Meet frequently with all members of your team and have them share everything they have been told by the negotiators who represent the other parties.

- Never hesitate to say: 'I don't understand this' and stop the discussion. Insist that everyone uses plain, non-technical language. If someone cannot express an idea in plain language, they either do not understand it or intend to deceive you.
- Stay clear about your goals. Never allow yourself to be persuaded that your community's goals are unjust, unreasonable or excessive.
- If you must bring pressure to bear on other parties, try to get others to do so (NGOs, mass media, etc).

Always keep a clear idea of the next best strategy that will achieve your goals, so you know when to quit and have the confidence to do so.

Source: Barsh and Bastien, 1997

a firm knowledge of commercial and contractual law, and experience in negotiating agreements.

- When selecting advisers, take into consideration your objectives and make your selection based upon the capacity of the adviser to provide the expertise necessary to assist in realizing your objectives (eg if it is hoped to develop a new form of licensing agreement to protect indigenous rights, a patent lawyer may be more help than an environmental lawyer; if the goal is to prevent overexploitation of resources, the reverse may be true).
- Ensure your legal advisers have obtained access to relevant information regarding the laws of the countries in which resources are to be used.
- Some major law firms in developed countries, in particular, have programmes for the provision of free – or pro bono – legal advice. In the event that access to such advice is sought by stakeholders in developing countries, local legal advisers should also be included in the process, where possible. This will help to ensure that national law and practice are duly considered and national capacity is developed.

Role of mediating institutions

In some cases, mediating institutions may play an important role in securing the interests of source countries and indigenous and local communities. Entities assisting negotiations have included non-governmental organizations (NGOs) and national research institutions, as well as individual legal consultants. Intermediaries may provide services to both end-users, ensuring compliance with national access laws, collection and provision of resources, and can contribute to national capacity-building and maximization of the provider country's share of benefits (ABS Expert Panel, 1999). While intermediaries can bring skills to the negotiation that one or all of the parties lack, they are as yet unregulated and their intervention in BPC negotiation can hide the institutional, legislative, administrative and policy weaknesses that inhibit providers from securing their rights and an equitable share in benefits. Furthermore, there exists potential for unscrupulous or technically incompetent entities to move into the field (ABS Expert Panel, 1999).

When designing a national policy for biodiversity prospecting, the state should consider the possible role that intermediaries may play in promoting equity in BPCs. Private-sector institutions may have opportunities to develop expertise in the

---

BOX 9.4 CONTRACTS AND BENEFIT-SHARING: KEY POINTS TO CONSIDER

Key points include the following:

- Negotiations of access agreements are commercial negotiations.
- The potential commercial value of genetic resources, and of traditional knowledge, innovations and practices, may be exhausted in the first contract for its use (eg where a patent over an active compound is obtained under the first agreement).
- Benefits may be both monetary and non-monetary and may include intrinsic benefits derived from the existence of resources and rights of free access and use.
- Negotiating any agreement on benefits requires a vision of the whole agreement and not just its parts, in order that the final sharing of benefits is equitable.
- Royalties are potential payments and are not guaranteed; a balance between guaranteed payments and potential future income should be sought in order to prevent frustration of expectations and to secure benefit-sharing as early as possible in the R&D cycle (Rosenthal, 1998).
- Be aware of possibilities that may exist to promote the development of national capacity, to identify value, negotiate, monitor compliance and add value to resources.
- Identify potential opportunities to get national industry involved in the manufacture or distribution of products, as well as in research and development.
- Possibilities for joint ventures may prove the best form for ensuring equitable benefit-sharing.
- Appreciate the value of training abroad in screening, etc.
- There is a need to protect confidential information where, for instance, there is a desire to protect secrecy regarding the source of an active compound, etc.
- It is important to be able to trace the use of resources. For this end, access to laboratory notes may be useful, so that if necessary you can trace back the origin of genetic resources used in developing a product.
- Ensure that the BPC fully represents the agreement between the parties and avoids ambiguous language and provisions. It is particularly important to ensure that all payments and other benefits are viewed as compensation and not as gifts.
- BPCs should include a clear conflict-resolution procedure.

negotiation, monitoring and implementation of BPCs capable of offering support services to national authorities or other providers of resources or knowledge. A legal framework that provides incentives for developing such skills may be an important part of a national access and benefit-sharing strategy.

Provision of unbiased advisory services, conflict resolution and free legal aid as appropriate may all assist in ensuring greater equity in biodiversity prospecting activities. A fundamental question for those considering the establishment of an honest brokerage is whether its purpose is to facilitate and promote biodiversity prospecting or to assist in ensuring equity in the negotiation of agreements.

BOX 9.5 INTERMEDIARIES AND BIODIVERSITY PROSPECTING CONTRACTS: TWO CASES

Two cases may serve to demonstrate the benefits and difficulties associated with the empowerment of mediating institutions to act on behalf of the national interest, or on behalf of indigenous and local communities, in the absence of relevant national legislation.

In Costa Rica, the National Institute of Biodiversity (InBio) has for over ten years taken responsibility for protecting the national interest in negotiating contracts with foreign companies for the use of genetic resources in research and development activities. This has proved a valuable experience for Costa Rica, bringing international renown and assistance for the development of InBio and the national biotechnological industry. InBio has received media attention and acclaim for its biodiversity prospecting agreement with Merck, which brought it to international attention. However, negotiation of this agreement would not have been possible had it not been for the capacity of the Guanacaste Conservation Area (GCA) to offer a guarantee of continuous access to resources, including repeat collections, during the period of the agreement. However, under Costa Rica's legislation, as a national protected area the GCA was not entitled to enter into commercial agreements for use of natural resources, thus demonstrating the need for collaboration with InBio. At the same time, lack of unambiguous regulations to provide InBio with the legal mandate to enter into such contracts led to a protracted and often acrimonious national debate on access, and much criticism of InBio's operations. Costa Rica has recently adopted biodiversity legislation, which includes provisions relating to access agreements. This will not only provide guidance for InBio in future negotiations, but also will ensure that the interests of those parties negotiating for access are legally secured.

Another interesting case is that of the Suriname–International Cooperative Biodiversity Groups (ICBG) agreement, where the NGO Conservation International (CI) was a party to the agreement, with the aim of protecting the interests of indigenous peoples. CI has worked over many years with the indigenous peoples of Suriname, and the Suriname–ICBG agreement has provided the country's indigenous peoples with numerous benefits, which most probably would not have been realized without CI's intervention. However, there was no legal basis for the recognition by the ICBG programme of CI as a representative of Suriname's indigenous peoples. Under the Suriname–ICBG agreement, the relevant indigenous peoples are not a party to the final agreement and therefore have limited rights to seek its enforcement. While the involvement of highly qualified external lawyers working for Conservation International has resulted in an interesting contractual arrangement, the indigenous peoples do not control the process, which has led some to question the extent to which its objectives and terms reflect their aspirations, rather than those of the negotiators. Capacity-building within indigenous groups, however, will allow them to negotiate more effectively on their own behalf in the future.

Prior informed consent and traditional knowledge rights

Who are the 'providers'?

Determining who is legally entitled to provide consent for the use of genetic resources is at present a difficult task in most countries. Even where access legislation is in force, identification of whose prior informed consent is required is not always clear. Genetic resources may be sourced in provider countries from state bodies, national research institutions, ex-situ collections, farmers and local and indigenous communities, as well as from ex-situ collections held outside of the country of origin. Although the CBD establishes the requirement that access to genetic resources is secured with the prior informed consent of the country of origin, regional and national access legislation has effectively extended this obligation to indigenous and local communities as well. Depending upon regulations in the source country, any one or combination of parties may act solely or jointly as providers of resources.

Issues raised in acquiring PIC for traditional knowledge

The acquisition of prior informed consent (PIC) for use of traditional knowledge relating to biological resources is a complex and unresolved issue. In the Philippines, the issue of prior informed consent of communities has been identified as the most difficult element in implementing national legislation regulating access to genetic resources.

Difficult questions associated with contracts and traditional knowledge include the following (Tobin, 1999):

- Can all communities and custodians of relevant knowledge be identified and, if so, is it feasible that they all be required to give consent for its use?
- What happens when communities live in neighbouring countries?
- Is it possible to prevent the use of material in the public domain?
- How can equitable sharing of benefits within communities be secured without state paternalism?
- Can equitable sharing amongst communities be achieved, in particular between communities who do not have a history of cooperation, again without resorting to paternalism?
- In what form can information be held (eg in a register) and for what purpose?
- If the value of the knowledge is in keeping it confidential, how can it be ensured that potential users are aware of which communities must be consulted for use of the knowledge?
- How can transaction costs be kept down? If the system is overly expensive, benefits will end up being consumed by its maintenance and will not reach communities.

Coupled to these questions we can add those of the private sector:

- With whom should the private sector negotiate: all communities, all custodians of particular knowledge, all community members, or only with shamans, healers, leaders, etc?
- How can legal certainty be secured, in order to ensure that the company is protected against future claims for benefits brought by other custodians of knowledge following the development of an interesting product?
- Should warranties be sought from indigenous peoples regarding their rights to enter into agreements?

- Can indigenous peoples be required to accept confidentiality obligations regarding research and development reports and, if so, will they be in a position to comply?
- To what extent are companies responsible for ensuring equity in distribution of benefits within and amongst communities?
- Are companies obliged to pay royalties after patents expire?
- What happens when competitors do not pay royalties for information in the public domain? Is it fair that companies who entered into agreements should be prejudiced in their competition with companies who do not pay royalties?

Determining which individual, community or organization may grant rights to use traditional knowledge is very complicated, and users are right to be concerned that they obtain a defensible legal right to use resources. Numerous examples exist of the difficulties associated with negotiating biodiversity prospecting agreements where lack of consensus amongst organizations representing sections of the same indigenous peoples prevents the establishment of a collective indigenous position on whether to negotiate or not. This is particularly difficult where various potential providers exist, legislation is non-existent and the rights of representative organizations to negotiate are not well established.

In India, for example, the Kanis are divided over the adequacy and nature of benefits provided in agreements for the use of Aarogyappacha (Anuradha, 1998). While two Kanis who provided information regarding use of medicinal plants to external collectors were retained by them as consultants, a group of nine healers objected to the sale of their knowledge to private companies. This case provides evidence of the way in which the trade in

natural products may serve as a divisive force within indigenous peoples and their communities. In Peru, the 1996 ICBG agreement also led to conflict between organizations representing Aguaruna communities, as well as at a national level (see Box 9.6).

Incorporating traditional knowledge within contracts

Where indigenous peoples are involved in biodiversity prospecting agreements, they may participate as providers of wild and domesticated biological resources, as well as of associated traditional knowledge. Indigenous and local communities may, therefore, participate in agreements on a number of different levels, each of which may carry rights to control access and to share in benefits. Under Decision 391 of the Andean Pact, for example, an agreement with indigenous peoples is required in order to carry out collection of genetic resources on their lands. If they also provide access to traditional knowledge, then a separate agreement for collection and use of that knowledge is required (Caillaux et al, 1999). This knowledge may take different forms, however, requiring different types of PIC and benefit-sharing, and may include knowledge of the use of plants, recipes for preparation and the management of species. Different levels of specialization and complexity in knowledge – different types of what some would call indigenous peoples' trade secrets (Ruiz, 2000) – should be paralleled by an increase in financial benefits, including royalties.

There is an ever-growing awareness of the need for a comprehensive international regime to protect rights over traditional knowledge, innovations and practices. Such a regime will require legislation in both provider and user countries; creation of umbrella international legislation; and

---

BOX 9.6 THE PERUVIAN ICBG AGREEMENT

The Peruvian International Cooperative Biodiversity Groups (ICBG) agreement is, in fact, a tale of two contracts and two separate negotiations. In the first, Washington University (WU), awarded an ICBG grant in January 1993, entered into a letter of intent with the Consejo Aguaruna and Huambisa (CAH), a regional federation representing Aguaruna and Huambisa communities of the north-western Peruvian Amazon territories. WU had, in parallel, signed agreements with Searle & Co, the pharmaceutical arm of the Monsanto corporation, for provision of medicinal plants with known use by their communities. The negotiations between the CAH and WU did not prosper and were terminated by the CAH. Subsequently, WU entered into negotiations with three local Aguaruna federations and their national representative organization for provision of resources; as a result, a biodiversity collection agreement was signed by the parties in September 1996.

Throughout this second round of negotiations, and since the signing of the agreement, there has been criticism of the negotiations by the CAH and by national and international indigenous organizations, to which it is affiliated, as well as by certain well-known international non-governmental organizations (NGOs). The lack of national legislation governing rights over collective property, and the apparent lack of any operative customary law to assist in decision-making regarding entry into BPCs, have resulted in an ongoing conflict, which acts as a divisive force within the Aguarunas.

---

a *sui generis* regime for recognizing and protecting rights over traditional knowledge, innovations and practices, founded upon respect for, and compliance with, customary law and practices. Any such regime must be developed with the full and informed participation of indigenous peoples and must respond to their stated priorities and concerns (Tobin, 2001).

Biodiversity prospecting and intellectual property rights

It is important that parties who consider entering into BPCs understand the different ways in which intellectual property rights (IPRs) may apply to their business, and the ways in which IPR laws can be used to protect the rights and interests of countries of origin, and those of indigenous and local communities (see Box 12.6). Firstly, contracts may treat biodiversity and traditional knowledge as information technology capable of protection in a manner similar to software (Greaves, 1994). Secondly, contracts may be used to control research and development (R&D) activities in order to prevent the acquisition of IPRs over genetic resources and associated knowledge, and to limit the effects of IPRs over the use of genetic resources and traditional knowledge. Thirdly, contracts may define the ownership of IPRs over developed products, the working of patents and the granting of licences for R&D activities.

Genetic resources as information technology

The commercial value of genetic resources lies in the information that they hold, and which may be utilized for product development. Proposals for treating traditional knowledge as trade secrets or as know-how have grown in recent years (eg Vogel, 1997). The Peruvian ICBG agreement includes a licence between Searle & Co and the Aguaruna people of Peru. This licence conditions the use of genetic resources on the continued maintenance in force of the licence for the use of associated knowledge (Tobin, 1997). Licensing offers distinct advantages for maximizing benefit-sharing without the transfer of full property rights over the licensed resources. The biotechnology industry utilizes licensing as one of the main tools of the trade, and its application to protect the rights of providers of genetic resources and associated knowledge is a logical and equitable step.

Limiting IPRs

Providers may be concerned to ensure that IPRs, obtained following research and development work utilizing the provider's resources, are not used to restrict the provider's rights to continue using genetic resources or knowledge, or to restrict the licensing of third parties to use such resources. Similarly, a provider may, for moral, ethical or other grounds, wish to prevent the user from obtaining patents over particular products, such as life forms or products based primarily upon traditional knowledge.

Contracts may be designed to respond to such fears. In many cases, the definition of scope of use in the agreement will be adequate to give providers the confidence and protection they seek. However, on occasion it may be necessary to explicitly prohibit the user from seeking patents over certain products. The Peruvian ICBG agreement specifically prohibits the use of genetic resources for developing genetically modified organisms, and for applying IPRs over any life forms that may result directly or indirectly from R&D activities. It also prohibits the use of patents to impede the use, sharing or sale of traditional medicinal products (Tobin, 1997; WIPO, 2000). Agreements could also incorporate provisions stating that no patent applications are to be made for any product that would not be entitled to protection under the laws of the source country.

Protecting IPRs over new products and processes

When entering into contracts for the use of genetic resources or traditional knowledge it is important to specify who will be entitled, if anyone, to apply for IPRs over products. In many cases, agreements vest IPRs in the industrial partner, with obligations to maintain patents and pay royalties to the providers of resources. Increasingly, there is recognition that securing joint ownership of patents, where appropriate, is desirable.

Some agreements propose the possibility of indigenous peoples jointly holding patents. There may be difficulties in having patents granted in the joint names of an indigenous people and a company. The patent regime normally requires identification of the individual(s) responsible for the invention. The possibility of having patents granted in the name of an individual member of an indigenous people, such as a healer or shaman, is also problematic because it individualizes a collective right. To overcome such difficulties, the parties may consider the advisability of establishing some form of joint venture to hold patent rights, license them and distribute benefits. In such cases, indigenous peoples could be partners in the joint venture and receive benefits in the form of shareholding.

Preparing and defending patents

Whoever owns an invention will usually be responsible for preparing the patent application and for defending it. Contracts may provide that the costs of patent preparation and prosecution are borne by corporate parties. It might also be considered advisable to include obligations, requiring commercial partners to assist providers in the application for IPR protection, where they have developed patentable material.

It is not uncommon for provision to be made for recouping the costs of applying for and maintaining patents from royalties. If this is the case, there should be a limit on the amount to which royalties in any one payment period may be reduced to cover such costs. In some cases, no more than 50 per cent of royalties may be apportioned for the costs of preparing and defending patents.

IPR applications, prior art and the public domain

Including traditional knowledge in the description of prior art, or as part of the description of a product process, places information in the public domain where it may be used by anyone, free of charge. Where access agreements involve research activities or other actions that may lead to preparing publications, provision may be made to ensure that all publications are vetted in advance by providers. Agreements can require that acknowledge-ment is given to local and indigenous communities recognizing their assistance (Barton and Siebeck, 1994; see Chapter 4).

Obligations to produce products and bring to market

Providers must be careful to ensure that users do not obtain patent rights over products with the intention of impeding third parties from making developments while the patent holder is not actually working the patent.

Source countries may seek rights to produce and market products covered by patents developed under a biodiversity prospecting agreement. In the African ICBG agreements, for instance, the governments of the US, Nigeria and Cameroon were all granted paid-up, royalty-free licences to all IPRs – a unique arrangement resulting from the fact that the African ICBG has no industrial partners (Iwu and Laird, 1998).

Grant-back clause

It is standard practice for private-sector actors to include a requirement in a licence for use of their technology, obliging the licensee to give the provider rights to use patented inventions. This is intended to protect the provider's competitive position in the event that the licensee develops a major improvement (Barton and Siebeck, 1994). Extending this principle to protect the competitive position of indigenous peoples, the Peruvian ICBG provides the Aguarunas with grant-back rights that entitle them to use all patents developed under the agreement on a royalty-free basis for research and development.

Enforcing contracts and securing equity

Validity of agreements

The Convention on Biological Diversity establishes two underlying principles regarding contracts that were intended to secure the CBD's objectives. These refer to the need for agreements to be based on 'mutually agreed terms' and 'prior informed consent'. It is arguable that where these conditions are not present, any agreement may be void or voidable. It remains to be seen whether such a premise would be upheld by a court reviewing a contract in accordance with national laws and conflict-of-laws legislation. Where two parties have entered into an agreement without coercion, it would be difficult to claim that the terms of the agreement had not been mutually agreed upon. On the other hand, a decision on what amounts to informed consent may depend upon subjective analysis.

Providers should use all reasonable efforts to obtain necessary information regarding the proposed activities, the user's business, the value of resources, as well as any potential impacts of access. In the event that a party who seeks access knowingly provides false information, or fails to make known information that it has (or should reasonably have obtained) regarding its intended activities, value of resources and impacts that its activities are likely to have, the validity of a contract may be open to challenge. Knowledge of foreign law may be required in order to determine whether contracts will be enforceable in the country where the resources are to be used. Decisions regarding the law governing the contract and the jurisdiction for lodging claims will also depend upon the possibilities of obtaining a favourable and adequate judgement and compensation in the event of a breach of contract.

Although the conditions which must be met in order to establish binding contracts may vary from country to country, a number of basic requirements are likely to be found in most jurisdictions, including offer and acceptance, compensation and confidentiality.

Offer and acceptance

Agreements are generally based upon the making of an offer by one party, and its acceptance by another party. This requires action on both sides. Acceptance may take many forms; some jurisdictions may recognize oral acceptance, while others will require written proof. It is also possible that the recipient of the original offer will respond with a counter offer, in which case the process of acceptance is reversed. Whether a contract has, in fact, been concluded will depend upon the law of the country where the agreement is deemed to have been made. In the event that the contract is silent on this point, it will usually be the place where acceptance has been made – a complex issue in itself. The existence of an agreement may also be inferred from the actions of the parties.

Compensation

A second fundamental element of contracts is the almost universal requirement that there is some form of consideration (ie economic or other benefit) in return for obtaining rights under an agreement. For this reason, a promise to grant access to resources will not usually be enforceable, unless the party seeking access has undertaken to provide compensation. Whether the level of compensation must be fair and equitable, as the CBD promotes, or may be nominal will depend upon national legislation. The principle of equity in benefit sharing is set down in the CBD and in some national access laws. There is, however, no security that a contract would be overturned in the event that it is found that the provider had received less than the market rate for such resources.

Confidentiality

Questions of confidentiality arise with regard to the contract itself and its provisions, as well as to material (including trade secrets provided under the agreement) and research-and-product development reports. Obliging the recipient to protect the confidentiality of information provided under the agreement is standard practice. At their most basic, conditions usually require that recipients protect information received with as much diligence as they would protect their own, and at least with a reasonable level of care. This will normally exclude information which is in the public domain or which has been received without restrictions from a third party who was entitled to provide it, as well as information which recipients already had or which they have developed independently.

Confidential information may include trade secrets, methods for doing business and commercial practices. It may also include indigenous knowledge. Whether traditional knowledge, which has been widely distributed amongst indigenous and local communities, is considered to exist within the public domain may be disputed. Even where information regarding indigenous knowledge has been published, this should not be presumed to remove rights to control its use and to impose limitations on further distribution and diffusion. Applying occidental principles of the public domain, as a means to legitimize the expropriation of traditional knowledge not knowingly shared for commercial purposes or for publication, would amount to a breach of human rights (Dutfield, 2000; Tobin, 2001).

The extension of confidentiality to the results of R&D activities serves a number of purposes; it prevents information from falling into the hands of competitors before developing a final product. It may also be necessary to maintain confidentiality in order to obtain patents, as release of information may lead to a loss of IPRs. Questions may arise regarding the ability of developing country authorities and indigenous peoples to protect confidential information against industrial espionage. Parties will need to ensure that concerns of this nature are not used as an excuse to deprive providers of access to relevant information regarding ongoing development activities and their results.

To date, BPCs have been assigned an inordinate level of commercial confidentiality that has raised concerns about the nature of these agreements and, in particular, their treatment of intellectual property rights and benefit-sharing. Why, for instance, should contracts for exploitation of genetic resources be subjected to greater levels of secrecy than oil concessions, as is the case in some Latin American countries? The right for private-sector actors to claim commercial confidentiality over negotiations pertaining to elements of national patrimony is questionable (Tobin, 1997). The costs of commercial confidentiality to date have entailed a loss of public confidence, both in relation to the adequacy of agreements to protect the national interest and to ensure equitable benefit-sharing.

Dispute resolution

Disputes between the parties should, if possible, be resolved without recourse to judicial proceedings. There is, as yet, limited experience in courts to deal with issues relating to equity and rights of providers. Many agreements now provide for arbitration of disputes, which may prove an interesting alternative. Care should be taken to ensure that any board of arbitrators includes those with experience and understanding of the law and practice in both the source country and in the country of use. Amongst the main things to consider in determining which process is best suited to ensuring that disputes are equitably resolved are accessibility and independence of the process. Providers may be advised to include a requirement in agreements that the costs of arbitration will be borne by the user, and that arbitration proceedings will be held in the source country.

The choice of the applicable rules for arbitration is, like the choice of law, one which should be made taking into consideration the possibilities of ensuring enforcement and obtaining relief for damages. It may, in fact, be better to have arbitration under the laws of a foreign country, which offers the greatest possibility of recovering lost profits and securing enforcement against the party in breach.

Where conflicts arise with regard to agreements involving traditional knowledge, dispute resolution procedures should be designed to take into consideration customary laws and practices of the relevant people or community. Any board of arbitration dealing with a matter involving traditional knowledge should include indigenous peoples or local community representatives as appropriate. Indigenous peoples may wish to subject resolution of conflicts to their own customary decision-making bodies.

Control mechanisms

Various measures may be adopted to monitor compliance relating to the use and maintenance of resources, benefit-sharing and protection of information. These include confidentiality arrangements; audit of royalty reports; control of the application for, and protection of, IPRs; access to internal documents recording R&D activities; and report of advances in scientific research and R&D activities in general.

Most biodiversity prospecting agreements now require the user to report advances in research and development activities. The provider should always retain the right of review in order to require modification or withholding of publications and IPR applications to the extent that their submission or publication would run counter to the terms of the agreement, infringe on the provider's rights, or fail to give appropriate recognition to providers of resources and knowledge. However, when negotiating agreements it is advisable to avoid creating unnecessary obligations that may unduly delay publications or IPR or product applications. This may, in fact, be counterproductive, providing opportunities for competitors to obtain IPR protection at an earlier date.

It is imperative that providers are able to identify the use of their resources and therefore of any rights to royalties, etc. To achieve this end it is common practice in the science industries to require access to the licensee's laboratory notes. In order to make sure that royalties are paid as due and owing, contracts should oblige users to maintain records for at least three years from the date of the payment, in their main place of business, with a right for the provider to audit these documents at least once a year. All overdue payments should be subject to interest payments.

BOX 9.7 WARRANTIES, BREACH OF CONTRACT AND LOSS OF RIGHTS

During the negotiation of the Peruvian–International Cooperative Biodiversity Groups (ICBG) agreement, Searle & Co requested a warranty from the Aguarunas that the knowledge provided was free of any third-party right. They also proposed that in the event of a breach of this warranty, Searle should be free to use the traditional knowledge free of any obligations to pay royalties to the Aguarunas. The contracting Aguaruna federations would, therefore, have lost their rights to all royalties, in the event that other indigenous peoples using the same knowledge took an action against Searle & Co claiming rights to share benefits, etc. Searle & Co did not propose a reduction of royalties by the amount that might have been payable to other indigenous peoples, but sought to revoke all rights to receive benefits, solely on the basis that other indigenous peoples demonstrated a right over the same knowledge. In the present unregulated environment, indigenous peoples would be advised not to provide any warranty beyond their right to provide traditional knowledge free of any known obligation to third parties.

Warranties, indemnities and disclaimers of liability

Warranties

Warranties are a standard element of most contracts and may cover the right to enter into an agreement, the right to provide resources for use, and the right to use the resources provided for a particular purpose. Since breach of warranty may lead to a loss of rights, care should be taken to ensure that any warranties included in the agreement can, in fact, be complied with. This is of particular importance with regard to transgenic material, where the supplier wishes to avoid responsibility in the event that the recipient fails to obtain appropriate biosafety clearance (Barton and Siebeck, 1994). Indigenous and local communities should pay extreme caution to warranties regarding the right to use traditional knowledge, particularly in cases where all custodians of such knowledge are not party to the agreement (see Box 9.7).

Indemnities

Indemnities provide contracting parties with protection against any claim or action for loss or damages, including loss of life, arising from any act or omission on the part of the other party. Considering the nature of the biotechnology and pharmaceutical industries, it is quite possible that at some stage in the future an action may arise for damages due to use or distribution, including release into the environment, of a product developed using the resources provided under a BPC. An action might conceivably be brought against the provider of resources for the damage caused by the release of a genetically modified organism, or for the side effects of a drug, especially in the event where they have received economic benefits from the activities. Seeking an indemnity against such claims is a means of transferring any potential liability from the provider to the user in such cases. The provider may also wish to be indemnified for any injury that may be suffered by the collectors, indigenous and local communities and others during the contract's operations; this includes acts arising from any hidden or other dangers associated with collection on their lands.

Disclaimers of fitness for purpose

Providers of resources may be well advised to include in their agreements a disclaimer regarding the resources provided. The purpose of this clause is to clearly deny the making of any implied warranties regarding the merchantability of the resources provided or their suitability for a particular purpose. This would be very appropriate to incorporate in all agreements for the collection and use of genetic resources, traditional knowledge, innovations and practices.

Insurance policies

It is always advisable to require that evidence of adequate insurance is demonstrated before signing an agreement. However, demonstration of insurance cover is not a sure sign of a responsible company and of solvency. Failure to provide evidence of cover is a clear sign that something is not right.

Equity in biodiversity prospecting contracts?

Originating in England as a quasi extra-judicial remedy for redress of the excesses and injustices arising through the rigid application of the law, equity began as a form of relief dependent upon subjective interpretation of justice. The subsequent case law gradually evolved into that branch of law known in common law systems as 'equity'.

In requiring the application of principles of equity to biodiversity prospecting arrangements, the CBD may be seen as acknowledging the injustices of the existing legal regime relating to access and use of genetic resources and traditional knowledge. This implies the need for the development of a new body of international legal principles in order to determine equity in relationships between providers and users of genetic resources and traditional knowledge. This will need to be based upon concepts of justice developed with full consideration and sensitivity to the philosophy underlying differing legal systems, including the customary law and practice of local and indigenous communities.

The need for the evolution of a new body of case law to assist in formulating the rules to govern biodiversity prospecting arrangements would appear self-evident. Existing experiences in the negotiation and preparation of BPCs provide a rich source of such precedents. Their value lies not only in the success stories, but equally in the failures.

There is little question that many of these agreements and approaches could, with hindsight, have been improved upon, both in their content and in the process for their negotiation. However, this should not blind us to the merits of their achievements, which through pragmatic compromise have secured incremental advances in protecting the rights of providers. Many biodiversity prospecting agreements to date have shown a level of innovation in utilizing novel contractual arrangements that cumulatively help to establish precedents that are now finding resonance in access law and national biodiversity prospecting strategies. These agreements have, in some cases, required major changes in the practices of private-sector actors that could not have been achieved without commitment on both sides to exploring new territory (Aalbersberg et al, 1998; Tobin, 2001). On the other hand, lax negotiation and failure to ensure that agreements protect the national interest of source countries, and are in harmony with the customary law and cosmo-vision of indigenous and local communities, may lead to the loss of rights. Either knowingly or inadvertently, they may also have acted as an aid to biopiracy.

It is doubtful that any one person or ideological position can answer the complex question of how to reorder the international trade in genetic resources and traditional knowledge in accordance with the rights of providers, while considering the interests of users – and in a way that promotes the welfare of humankind as a whole. The search for that answer requires greater commitment by all those wishing to secure the CBD's objectives to increased participation, transparency, tolerance, humility and a willingness to commit to securing legislative, administrative and policy measures in both provider and user countries as a prerequisite for facilitating access to genetic resources and promoting the wider use of the knowledge innovations and the practices of indigenous and local communities. It is necessary to conform with the call for rights first, and access only once those have been addressed.

Chapter 10

Elements of commercial biodiversity prospecting agreements

Michael A Gollin

Commercial biodiversity prospecting contracts – agreements relating to the collection, exchange and commercial development of biological resources – fall into a unique category. Given the recent origins of commercial biodiversity prospecting contracts, in most cases, participants have had to start from scratch in structuring and negotiating these agreements. Each agreement or set of agreements is unique, but fortunately there is a growing base of models from which to draw. Some authors have published proposed contractual forms in books and articles as possible starting points for negotiations (eg Downes et al, 1993; Putterman, 1996). Several dozen biodiversity prospecting agreements have been completed this decade in different countries and representing a range of

partnerships (Rosenthal, 1996; ten Kate and Laird, 1999). Agreements cover pharmaceuticals, agricultural products, botanicals, cosmetics and other industrial products.

This chapter draws from the work done to date, describing the key features of commercial biodiversity prospecting agreements in the hope that familiarity can help source-country researchers and local groups structure and negotiate better agreements. The chapter includes a discussion of the national legal context, models for biodiversity prospecting agreements, structures for the agreements and the elements of such agreements. Annex 10.1 includes detailed outlines of issues and provisions to help negotiators start the process of reaching agreement.

National legal context for biodiversity prospecting agreements

Biodiversity prospecting agreements are subject to a variety of national laws in each country where the activities take place (Gollin and Laird, 1996). For example, contract law governs the formation, scope and enforcement of agreements; intellectual property law defines the rights of the

parties to their creations; environmental, conservation and natural-resources laws regulate the use of land and resources; and trade laws govern the import and export of biological materials.

National laws influencing biodiversity prospecting agreements are in a state of rapid reform as countries take steps to implement international agreements, principally the Convention on Biological Diversity (CBD) and the agreement on Trade Related Aspects of Intellectual Property Rights (TRIPS) (see Chapter 12). Some countries have no applicable legal or regulatory framework; others have a framework to facilitate the formation of agreements; and yet others, such as the Philippines, virtually preclude the establishment of new commercial arrangements (see Chapter 12). Given the rapid rate of change in national laws, and the highly political nature of many of the decisions involved in biodiversity prospecting, generalizations about contractual features and elements must be analysed and verified for compliance with local law. Accordingly, it is critically important for any effective agreement to have input from individuals knowledgeable about the legal and regulatory framework in each country involved. Any other approach invites challenge, delay and unenforceability.

Models for biodiversity prospecting agreements

Although we are beginning to benefit from the existence of a pool of negotiated biodiversity prospecting agreements that can be used as forms on their own, it is helpful to begin by comparing bioprospecting agreements to types of agreements with which practitioners have far greater experience. The analogous types of agreements include **general commercial contracts, biological material transfer agreements, environmental permits, intellectual property licences, software 'shrinkwrap' licences, option agreements, real estate leases** and **letters of intent.** Biodiversity prospecting agreements are an unusual hybrid of these models, integrating aspects of each of them. Understanding these other types of agreements sheds light on how biodiversity prospecting agreements are put together.

When asked to fashion a new type of agreement, practitioners rarely invent an entirely new approach. Instead, they look for guidance to analogous situations with which they are familiar and build on them. Biodiversity prospecting agreements have been developed from several other types of agreements. This section compares and contrasts biodiversity prospecting agreements with the better-known types of agreements. The other agreements provide fertile ground for precedent in situations that are not dealt with in this chapter or other materials focused specifically on biodiversity prospecting.

Commercial contracts in general

As with any agreement, biodiversity prospecting contracts come into being when two or more parties together commit to each other in order to exchange money or materials or to do (or not do) certain actions (Gollin and Laird, 1996). In general, the essential elements of any contract, throughout the world, include:

- competent parties able to be bound by the agreement through their representatives;
- meeting of the minds regarding the subject of the agreement – an understanding of what will be done or not done;
- mutual assent – a voluntary commitment to perform under the agreement;
- consideration – an exchange of valuable tangible things, money, promises or rights;

- enforceability – the promises of the parties must comply with legal requirements; a formality such as a written document or a ritual such as handshake or sharing a kava drink may be required, depending upon the jurisdiction.

The laws governing these requirements vary from country to country. In particular, national legislation implementing the CBD may make agreements unenforceable unless they include provisions governing prior informed consent (PIC) and benefit-sharing. The best practice in negotiating is to elucidate the main special national requirements – such as restrictions on collecting and exporting plants, land-access regulations and the need for a permit from the national environmental agency – early in the process, and then to verify compliance at the end of the process. Any changes that are required at that point are usually dealt with quite simply when the important terms of the arrangement have already been worked out.

Intellectual property licences

There are several definitions of intellectual property that are often used interchangeably in negotiations, causing significant misunderstandings. It is important for the parties to clarify what, specifically, they mean by the term.

Lawyers use the term intellectual property to represent a combination of doctrines from industrial property (patents, trade secrets, trademarks) and literary property (copyright). A discussion of the details of each of these legal fields is far beyond the scope of this chapter. A lay person's dictionary definition is that intellectual property is something intangible, created by the use of mental ability, to which legal rights attach. Typically, the rights relate to new creations by individu-

als. Economists and business people look at intellectual property as a tool for converting human capital into value by defining and capturing new knowledge. In the last decade, intellectual property has taken on an expanded meaning as part of the term 'intellectual property rights', and is used to represent an ethical principal valuing all knowledge, including old and collective knowledge.

In an intellectual property licence, the owner of the right grants a licence to the recipient in exchange for payment of some kind. A licence is essentially an agreement by the licensor–proprietor not to assert his or her rights against the licensee. Typically, an intellectual property licence includes separate granting clauses for patents, trade secrets/know-how, trademarks and copyright, because the legal requirements for each differ and an enforceable grant needs to be tailored to the type of intellectual property being licensed. Furthermore, the scope and term of each type of intellectual property may differ, so that it is good practice to have separate consideration (payment) for each grant. The simplest licences relate to an existing intellectual property asset such as an issued patent, but licences frequently cover prospective rights such as improvements or new inventions that have not yet been made.

A biodiversity prospecting agreement has aspects of the latter type of intellectual property licence (a 'reach-through licence' as discussed below) in that it allocates rights in inventions and trade secrets before they have been made. For example, the parties may agree that all patents will be owned by the developer, but that the collector or provider will have a licence to practise any inventions relating to locally significant diseases.

A biodiversity prospecting agreement is more complex than many intellectual property licences in that there is typically a need under the CBD for governmental consent and benefit-sharing that flows back to the source country. These terms are not typically the subject of intellectual property licences. Also, a significant aspect of a biodiversity prospecting deal typically involves physical transfer of biological materials, which is typically not a part of a simple intellectual property licence and requires special treatment as discussed below.

Material transfer agreements

Material transfer agreements (MTAs) are used widely in academic, governmental and corporate research. The transaction is typically a transfer of biological material from a provider to a recipient with restrictions on what the recipient may do with the material. The property rights involved are tangible (physical) property rights, but are often considered to fall within the meaning of 'intellectual property'. Although the narrow legal definition of intellectual property (intangible property) does not apply to tangible materials, the broader lay definitions discussed above would include biological materials. Thus, biological materials can be viewed as another category of legal rights along with trade secrets, patents, copyrights and trademarks. In practice, MTAs often include licences of related intellectual property rights and vice versa. But because of the important difference between real, tangible biological materials and intangible, purely legal intellectual property rights, different approaches are needed in MTAs (Gollin, 1995).

In an MTA, the provider agrees to give the physical material itself to the recipient, and the recipient agrees to restrict the use of the material – for example, restrict use to screen for an activity but not to transfer the material further to third parties. The biological material may be replicating (seeds, bacteria, cell lines, DNA) or not

(leaves, extracts). The need for control over replicating material may be greater than with non-replicating material, as recipients of a one-time transfer may be able to produce all that they need. In contrast, the recipient of non-replicating material will probably need to come back to the source for more.

There are countless thousands of MTAs in effect throughout the world. Indeed, the diversity of different MTAs and the transaction costs of negotiating each one anew has been a continuing source of concern to technology-transfer professionals. MTAs are common in the biotechnology industry and academic and government research for replicating materials (cell lines, genetic material, microbes, plants). In an effort to simplify, streamline and speed the process of entering into MTAs, in 1995 the US National Institutes of Health (NIH) and the Association of University Technology Managers propounded the Uniform Biological Material Transfer Agreement. This effort is slowly gaining support and has over 150 signatories (http://www.autm.net/ubmta/index.html). However, most organizations continue to use their own forms, and each time there is a transfer of material, the two parties must reconcile their forms and approaches and typically fashion yet a new form (ten Kate and Laird, 1999, p244).

A standardized MTA with limited focus is used by the Consultative Group on International Agricultural Research (CGIAR) centres for material covered under the Food and Agriculture Organization (FAO) Trust agreement. The CGIAR centres acquire (import) germplasm under a Germplasm Acquisition Agreement (www.singer.cgiar.org) providing that the centres may use the material for research and to place the material in trust for the benefit of humanity. The centres transfer (export) germplasm through MTAs that prevent the recipient from obtaining intellectual property on the germplasm (although the recipient may protect improved varieties).

Biodiversity prospecting agreements generally involve the transfer of biological materials so they may be considered to be examples of MTAs. However, biodiversity prospecting agreements are more complicated than most MTAs. One reason for the complexity is that the rights of the provider of the material go beyond simple property rights ('I own it and can do what I want with it') and include issues raised under the CBD, such as sovereign rights, prior informed consent, access to land and resources, 'fair and equitable' benefit-sharing, conservation and environmental permitting. Nonetheless, the basic principles of MTAs are helpful in understanding and finding precedent for biodiversity prospecting agreements. Indeed, as discussed below, in a biodiversity prospecting agreement of the type $A \rightarrow B$ and $B \rightarrow C$, the second agreement may fall within the parameters of normal MTAs.

MTAs for research tools outside the biodiversity prospecting context often include 'reach-through' licensing terms (Goldstein, 1999). Here, the material is useful not as a product on its own, but as a research tool for discovering another compound or method that, in turn, will be a commercial product. Reach-through clauses are common in biodiversity prospecting agreements. For example, a plant may be the source of a chemical that guides research into derivatives or analogues. Because the immediate value of the plant is unknown, the provider requires the recipient to promise a royalty on the proceeds of any commercial product that is discovered using the plant extract. The recipient is willing to provide such a royalty in order to get access to the material at a low initial cost. The benefit-sharing language of the CBD encourages source-country providers to ask for such a 'reach through'. The value of the biological resource is speculative, and recipients tend to be willing to share the potentially large up side of a commercially successful product. It is crucial to remember, though, that a reach-through clause covers a highly unlikely event.

Environmental permits

In many jurisdictions around the world, a permit is required to fish, to hunt game, to cut lumber, to drill for oil or to mine minerals. Some countries require project developers to conduct an environmental impact review and to commit to the least destructive alternative. Likewise, under the CBD, countries are encouraged to require collectors of biological resources to obtain a permit before collecting. Even in countries that have not established a regulatory framework for obtaining a permit for biodiversity prospecting, collectors are well advised to obtain explicit permission for the collection from the responsible government agency. Typically, the responsible agency is that which is charged with environmental protection or natural resource management. Consequently, one of the parties to a biodiversity prospecting agreement is often the responsible government agency.

A biodiversity prospecting agreement may reflect one of two models of environmental permitting – pure permit and negotiated contract models. In a pure permit regime, the government grants to the collector and/or recipient permission to collect according to a particular plan. The government does not act as a party, and due to its sovereign immunity is not subject to many of the affirmative conditions to which a private party would be subject (including providing services and dispute resolution). The terms may be simple and the fee for the permit may be minimal (eg US$50 for a six-month collecting permit).

In contrast, in a negotiated contract model, the government acts like a private party. It may waive sovereign immunity and undertakes promises for certain activities (eg assistance, information-sharing). US agencies sometimes use a Cooperative Research and Development Agreement (CRADA) between federal laboratories; for example, the West Africa ICBG is a CRADA with Walter Reed Army Institute of Research, the Bioresources Development and Conservation Programme (BDCP) and the other ICBG members (Iwu and Laird, 1998).

But the CRADA approach avoids the environmental review that is required for an environmental permit. In 1995, the United States National Park Service entered into a Cooperative Research and Development Agreement with Diversa Corporation, whereby the US committed to cooperate with Diversa in researching and cataloguing biodiversity in Yellowstone National Park (YNP), and Diversa promised to share the benefits resulting from its work. However, several non-governmental organizations (NGOs) filed a lawsuit, which resulted in a 24 March 1999 ruling that the US government must conduct an environmental assessment, and in suspending implementation of the CRADA: Edmonds Institute versus Babbit, No 98-561 (DDC, 24 March 1999), available at http://www.edmonds-institute.org/ yellowstone.html. One practical lesson from this history is that a collector should encourage early environmental assessments to avoid legal challenges at a later date.

Real estate leases/land tenure

Biodiversity prospecting agreements may have attributes of a real estate lease. The owner or tenant of land generally has the right to control access to the land and to receive money or other compensation in exchange for letting the visitor onto the land. With biodiversity prospecting agreements, the landowner is typically the national government, in which case the permit models discussed above apply.

However, the land where the collection occurs may belong to a private community, a not-for-profit organization, a corporation or a private individual. In these cases, the biodiversity prospecting agreement must also account for the interests of the local landowner or resident. A common example is found with private botanical gardens that allow collectors to sample plants growing on their grounds in exchange for a fee or share of benefits. The collector is given access to the land for a period of time in order to carry out certain activities – explore, collect, prepare samples, and so on – and the landlord receives compensation in the form of up-front payment, reach-through payments, and so on. Such agreements have some similarities to timber leases, tenant farmer arrangements and mining leases, where a private landowner may share in the revenues obtained by the tenant. Even with private collections, national legislation under the CBD may require that the interest of the national government needs to be satisfied as well, at least with a simple permit.

Shrinkwrap licence

Software manufacturers pioneered the technology transfer approach known as the shrinkwrap licence during the 1980s. The shrinkwrap licence has several fundamental attributes. It relates to copyright in the software, it is a licence, not a sale, and it is formalized as an offer by the manufacturer which is accepted by the 'buyer' by opening the package of software without signing a written agreement. In the modern era of the Internet, such licences have been adopted as 'webwrap' licences, where the reader clicks on a button manifesting agreement with the licensor's offer before being given access to the software.

Bioprospecting arrangements are not yet common enough for many people to have attempted a shrinkwrap licence approach, at least not with newly collected materials. Such one-sided, non-negotiated arrangements often leave open the issue of whether there was truly a meeting of minds and prior informed consent. Downstream transfers (such as from the collector to an industrial company or a research institution) are more likely to occur under the auspices of an MTA that could be structured as a shrinkwrap licence. For example, the CGIAR centres have adopted a standard MTA form that is intended to be used as a shrinkwrap licence. That is, when someone requests germplasm from one of the centres, the request form refers to the terms of transfer; and when the centre sends the material out, enclosed with it is a form agreement listing the restrictions on further use of the material. Under evolving laws in the US and some other countries, such an approach works best when there is some manifestation of assent by the recipient, and an opportunity to return the material if the recipient does not accept the terms.

Option agreements

In an option agreement, the 'optionor' gives the 'optionee' the right to obtain a licence or other right on mutually agreed terms, but postpones the commitment and makes it at the discretion of the optionee. The optionee typically pays an option fee, sometimes renewable, for this 'right to think about' making a commitment, while the optionor forbears granting a licence to a third party. Likewise, biodiversity prospecting agreements may be structured as include options on the part of the developer to maintain exclusivity with respect to certain samples, to obtain patents, to recollect material and so on.

Letters of intent

A letter of intent may or may not be an enforceable contract depending upon whether the terms are defined and the parties manifest an intent to be bound by the document. A letter of intent may simply reflect a willingness to negotiate towards a binding agreement, thus serving more of a business or political purpose than a legal one (Laird, 1993; Downes, 1993). Or it may go further, spelling out certain obligations and identifying a range for negotiation. For example, the parties may agree that there will be a royalty on commercialization of plant samples, but that they will negotiate a rate in a range of 1 per cent to 4 per cent. The US National Cancer Institute (NCI) has titled its forms as a letter of intent (LOI), letter of collection, and memorandum of understanding (MOU), and each creates binding obligations. They spell out the rights of the NCI to conduct research on plants collected under the agreement, and the obligations of the NCI to restrict access by commercial entities to the plants or derivatives. The most recent form is an MOU that requires the NCI to obligate downstream recipients to gain approval from the source country before commercializing the results of the research (ten Kate and Laird, 1999).

An MOU is more commonly less binding than a letter of intent, although the two terms are often used interchangeably. Even if non-binding, an MOU or a LOI may have the same significance as a step toward formalizing a collaborative undertaking without full legal formalities.

Structures for biodiversity prospecting agreements

Given the range of parties and interests that may be covered in a biodiversity prospecting agreement, it is no surprise that many different structures have evolved in the past decade. For convenience, we group these different approaches into two categories: **hub and spoke**, and **consortium** or 'club' structures. Both approaches allow a group of separate entities to approximate a single vertically integrated company that can handle the entire chain of production, from sourcing material from its own property, to collecting, extracting, screening, developing and marketing products.

Consortium

For present purposes, this chapter defines a consortium as a multilateral venture in which numerous parties join together in one group to develop industrially significant products from wild species or other biological materials. The consortium is similar to a vertically integrated company because it is able to carry out all the activities needed to discover, develop and commercialize a natural product (see Figure 10.1). Figure 10.1 shows four parties linked together, each with obligations to all the other parties.

A leading example of the consortium approach is the International Cooperative Biodiversity Groups (ICBG) grant programme of the US NIH and USDA. The ICBG grants bring together public and private corporations, conservation groups, academic and research institutions and economic development agencies from various countries around the world. In the so-called 'One Contract' model of some of the ICBG projects – for example, the project in Costa Rica involving the National Institute of Biodiversity (InBio), Cornell University and Bristol-Myers Squibb – all of the parties join together in one contract that sets forth all the promises of the parties in one document (Rosenthal, 1996). However, most of the ICBG projects that received funding adopted a hub-and-spoke arrangement for various reasons, discussed in the following section.

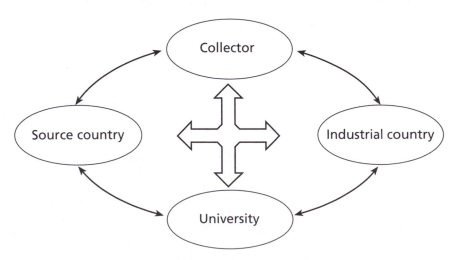

Figure 10.1 *Consortium 1*

The Consultative Group on International Agricultural Research (CGIAR), although not organized explicitly as such, may be considered another example of a biodiversity prospecting consortium. The CGIAR is an association of the 16 international agricultural research centres (IARCs), the World Bank, the United Nations Environment Programme (UNEP), the Food and Agriculture Organization (FAO), donor countries and countries who host the IARCs and collaborate with them. The CGIAR has no constitution, bylaws or officers, and so lacks many attributes of a legal entity (www.cgiar.org). However, the CGIAR holds copyright in its website and publications, and collectively manages some intellectual property for its member centres (such as the germplasm acquisition agreement (GAA) and MTA under the FAO Trust agreement). The CGIAR also sponsors system-wide initiatives such as the System-Wide Genetic Resource Programme (SGRP), which operates a website that indexes information about the collections of all the centres and provides a central place where people can request materials.

A consortium may combine the advantages of public and private entities in satisfying environmental, economic, equitable and ethical goals. However, because they are multilateral, it is difficult and complicated to determine the roles of each party, and negotiations may be more challenging because no deal is done until all parties agree and are ready to sign the same document.

With respect to intellectual property rights, the parties must select between several different approaches. In one, the consortium itself holds the intellectual property in common, and the parties have limited rights to practice the technology, presumably on an as-needed basis. Benefits are pooled at the consortium level and are shared equitably among the members. This is essentially the model of the Africa ICBG.

A second approach to intellectual property is for each party to separately retain the rights to the intellectual property that it creates, with some cross-licensing of rights between the parties. This approach becomes more akin to a hub-and-spoke arrangement, as there are a variety of different licensing arrangements between the different parties.

We can distinguish between a full and partial consortium approach. In a full

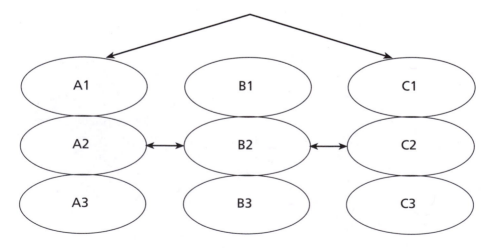

Figure 10.2 *Consortium 2*

consortium, all the parties, *A*, *B* and *C* (source/provider, collector and commercial-product developer) agree in a single document to common terms. Figure 10.2 illustrates the relationships in a full consortium, including groups of organizations involved in providing access (*A* parties), collecting (*B* parties) and developing products (*C* parties). All nine parties agree to obligations to each other, as reflected by the double-sided arrows.

In practice, it is more common to have a partial consortium, where some but not all of the parties agree to obligations to each other. One type of partial consortium includes biodiversity providers *A*, *A'* and *A"* who all enter into an agreement to provide materials to a single collector *B*. Figure 10.2 depicts the partial consortium of the *A* parties, on the left side of the figure. The biodiversity provider parties may be, for example, a local community *A1*, a national regulatory agency *A2* and a conservation trust fund *A3*, chartered to work with the communities to direct benefits into conservation of the targeted biological resources. The source parties may agree to permit a collection project to proceed, and to share commonly in any benefits that result. In this partial consortium, the parties would not have the direct relationship with the developer parties *C*, reflected by the arrow shown at the top of Figure 10.2. This type of providers' consortium model may be referred to as a benefit-sharing club. A benefit-sharing club is employed by Shaman Pharmaceuticals (now Shaman Botanicals). Shaman's approach may be viewed as a consortium with the Healing Forest Conservancy for sharing profits with all indigenous communities and countries who collaborated with Shaman, regardless of the source of the plant or information leading to the profit-generating product. The benefit-sharing club is not necessarily a consortium because there does not need to be any

interaction between the various sources (Moran, 1996).

A second type of partial consortium is a collectors' consortium, involving plant collectors *B1*, *B2* and *B3*, who join together in the collection project. The middle portion of Figure 10.2 shows the relationships between these parties. For example, a national museum *B1*, a national university *B2* and a foreign botanical garden *B3* together sign an agreement with the government in source country *A* (home of the university and museum) to field a team that includes representatives of all three collectors.

Finally, there can be a research and development (R&D) consortium with respect to discovery, development and commercialization of products, with company *C1*, national research institute *C2* and university *C3* together signing an agreement with collector *B2*, as shown on the right side of Figure 10.2. The agreement would set forth divided responsibilities for screening and assaying samples, developing products and marketing them. As with the providers' consortium, the distinction from the full consortium is that there would be no direct relationship with the provider parties. Of course, this type of approach may also be implemented through a hub-and-spoke arrangement, discussed in the following section.

Hub and spoke

For the purposes of this chapter, we consider a hub-and-spoke arrangement to involve more than one contract (the spokes) with one entity common to each of the contracts (the hub). A simple example could be depicted as *A* → *B* and *B* → *C*, where *A* is a public agency of the biodiversity source country, *B* is a not-for-profit research organization and *C* is a for-profit corporation. The arrows represent the transfer of biological resources and related information. Benefits flow in the opposite direction $A \leftarrow B$ and $B \leftarrow C$. There are many other examples of parties A, B and C, as discussed in the context of a consortium model.

Figure 10.3 shows a prototypical hub-and-spoke arrangement that has the same parties as in the consortium model shown in Figure 10.2. In the example shown here, all the parties except $B2$, a source-country university, have a contractual relationship (or 'privity') with a single party, $B2$. $B2$, in turn, has a contractual relationship with all the other parties.

The hub-and-spoke model is exemplified by the ICBG agreements between the University of Arizona and several different countries, research organizations and companies (Rosenthal, 1996). A simpler variant (referred to by Rosenthal as a dual contract model) includes two contracts: a collections/benefit-sharing agreement and a commercial R&D agreement.

An example of the dual contract approach is the Biodiversity Conservation Network (BCN) grant-sponsored project in Fiji where the Verata Tikina community agreed to provide materials to the University of the South Pacific (USP) in one agreement, and USP agreed to provide extracts to the Strathclyde Institute of Drug Research (SIDR) in a second agreement (see Box 10.1). The parties opted for a hub-and-spoke style dual contract arrangement after considering a triangular consortium model in which all three parties A, B and C would have signed a single contract. The flexibility of the dual-contract arrangement made it easier to substitute a new commercial partner when the original company withdrew from the project.

The main advantage of the hub-and-spoke approach is that bilateral agreements are easier to negotiate, and easier to change if the parties or terms change, than a consortium agreement. Furthermore, from

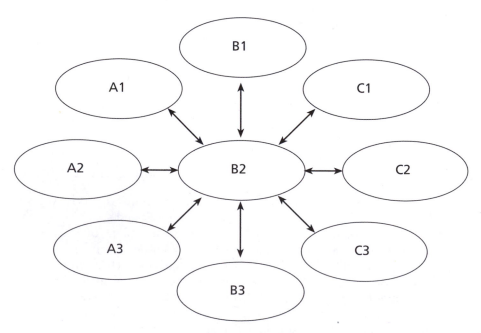

Figure 10.3 *Hub and spoke*

BOX 10.1 DEVELOPING BIOPROSPECTING AGREEMENTS IN FIJI

*William G Aalbersberg (Professor of Natural Products Chemistry,
University of the South Pacific)*

This case study describes the process of designing an equitable bioprospecting agreement and developing community-based activities that included the University of the South Pacific (USP, headquartered in Fiji), pharmaceutical companies, the Fiji government, non-governmental organizations (NGOs) and local communities.

In 1995, USP applied for and received a planning grant from the Biodiversity Conservation Network (BCN).[1] USP approached a coastal community, the Verata, due to its biodiversity and interest in conservation, and Dr Brad Carté of SmithKline Beecham (SKB), an experienced marine sample collector, who responded positively.

After the national government approved the project in principle, USP approached the provincial governments for native affairs with jurisdiction over Verata. The heads of the provincial government were also traditional leaders and had close connections with USP. In Fiji, the indigenous peoples own the land, traditional authority is respected and government is seen as protecting traditional rights. Thus, following traditional protocols facilitated approval by the community, after lively discussions of the proposed project.

To develop the formal bioprospecting agreement, the project team recruited the Natural Rights and Resources Programme at Rainforest Alliance, to advise on equity issues, and Michael Gollin, an attorney experienced with bioprospecting contracts, to facilitate negotiations. In October 1995, USP, SKB and other members of the project team met with a representative of the Fiji government and the Verata community. Discussion was facilitated with an outline prepared from responses to a questionnaire asking stakeholders what they wanted from the agreement, what they were willing to provide and any constraints they felt in joining it.

One of the first points of discussion was whether there should be a three-way agreement between SKB, USP and the Verata, or whether separate SKB–USP and USP–Verata contracts were preferable. On the one hand, contracts that involve the communities as equal partners recognize the crucial role of communities in conserving resources, knowledge and national development. On the other hand, drug companies have legal constraints and favour paying benefits only to legally constituted bodies.

By the end of the week, the parties reached agreement on having two separate contracts and on most other points. SKB was to write a final draft of the agreement to be translated into Fijian for conclusive discussions with the communities.

Surprisingly, in April 1996, SKB closed down their natural products discovery division in the US. USP immediately began a search for another partner. The project team contacted the Strathclyde Institute of Drug Research (SIDR) at Strathclyde University in Glasgow, Scotland, to serve as a broker. SIDR was, at that time, in the process of signing an agreement with a Japanese drug company to provide 5000 samples, and so they were quite keen to become a partner. Strathclyde's agreements provide 60 per cent of all funds obtained from licensing samples to the source country. Although they retain a substantial 40 per cent, there are several advantages to this type of arrangement:

- SIDR has greater credibility and negotiating power compared to a developing country institution and thus can obtain higher fees from drug companies. As an example, SKB had agreed to pay USP US$100 per sample, while the sample fee in

the SIDR agreement comes out toUS$200 for USP (as 60 per cent of SIDR's total fee).
- Because it shares fees with the host-country institution, SIDR is a partner in the bioprospecting. It is thus more likely that SIDR will represent the interests of the source country. This kind of agreement is different from negotiating directly with a drug company, who must place their profits first.
- Bioprospecting partners, such as the government, non-governmental organizations (NGOs) and community groups, perceive that an entity associated with a university will be more likely to honour its contractual commitments than a large multinational drug company.
- The 60:40 split compares favourably with that offered by other collectors/brokers, which may be as low as 10:90.
- It is possible that SIDR can license the samples to other companies once the original licensing period expires, thus increasing the benefit.

The main disadvantage of the SIDR arrangement was that it offered few in-kind benefits. Another limitation is that the bioprospecting contract had to conform to the contract between SIDR and the drug companies, which precluded giving the community the right of prior informed consent on commercial development of a product based on their resource.

SIDR has a simple pro-forma contract that was used as the basis of the USP agreement, which fits into the two-contract model. This approach also allows USP greater flexibility to work with different communities. The SKB draft contract was used as a model to suggest changes and additions to the SIDR contract. Further comments came from stakeholders and the Rainforest Alliance reference group, a group of international experts in bioprospecting.

An associated USP–Verata contract was subjected to the same process, translated into Fijian and reviewed by a community lawyer. The openness of the process was important to concluding a satisfactory set of agreements.

Except for the possibility of joint ownership of any commercial products and a recognition of their stewardship of their resources, intellectual property rights (IPRs) issues are not central to these contracts because the collections are not based on traditional uses. (However, the communities can hold back medicinal plants for which they want their traditional knowledge to be separately rewarded.)

A key feature of these contracts is that a small amount of sample is licensed through SIDR for a limited period (usually one year). This sample remains the property of the community and, if not under a licensing agreement, can be reclaimed by the community. These agreements set out a broad definition of 'sample' to include derived chemicals and products. They also give the Verata first right of recollection and provide for appropriately qualified people from the Verata community to be employed by the project.

Because USP currently covers its collection costs with the BCN grant, all royalty fees are passed on to the Verata. Collection and processing fees and equipment overhead come to about US$30 per sample, for 500 samples. Under the agreement, the division of royalty benefits will be set within two years. This timing allows further discussion in Fiji and the rest of the Pacific on how benefits can be most equitably shared and best used for conservation and development.

the point of view of a commercial researcher, this approach avoids culturally and politically sensitive negotiation with local communities and agencies. Such negotiations require a different set of skills than many business people from industrialized countries are familiar with. In turn, public opposition to biotechnology companies in developing countries may be less if the hub organization is locally known and trusted, and the industrial corporation remains in the background rather than in a direct contractual relationship with the source country.

The main disadvantage of a hub-and-spoke model is that the hub institution must carry the principal burden of negotiation and coordination between the contracts. Each of the contracts must be very carefully reviewed to ensure that it is consistent with the other contracts. There is a risk that a court might impose obligations among the parties on the periphery or rim in a hub-and-spoke arrangement if they are found to be 'third-party beneficiaries' of each other. Third-party beneficiary obligations created inadvertently can make the hub-and-spoke arrangement more similar to a consortium approach. In addition, in some situations source communities and countries may favour a one-contract consortium approach because the process can provide education, empowerment and more direct bargaining power over commercial terms. However, if there is one lead organization who can serve as the hub, the hub-and-spoke arrangement brings flexibility and other benefits, and is feasible in situations where a pure consortium might be impossible.

The ICBG project involving the Smithsonian Tropical Research Institute (STRI), the government and research institutions in Panama, and Monsanto Co followed the hub-and-spoke model (see Box 10.2). The negotiations under the hub-and-spoke structure allowed each national organization to be on an equal footing with STRI and provided opportunities for good public relations and education. Ultimately, as the saying goes, the best contracts – whether established under a consortium or hub-and-spoke model – are rarely referred to after they are signed and the parties begin to work together.

In any hub-and-spoke model, the $A \rightarrow B$ spoke is more like an environmental permit than the $B \rightarrow C$ relationship in that the permissions for sourcing the material must be present (with other complex terms, as discussed above). There may be multiple As (ie multiple agencies, communities or countries providing material to the same collector in sourcing agreements). The $B \rightarrow C$ spoke is more like a conventional MTA. There may be multiple Cs, each requiring separate transfer agreements.

Hub-and-spoke contracts create a problem in that there is no direct contractual relationship (privity) between A and C. Likewise there is no privity between A and D, E or F (downstream recipients), so that A cannot enforce its rights if B transfers to C, consistent with an MTA, but C transfers to D without restrictions. Also, B could not enforce its rights against D, E or F, and so on. One solution to this problem as between A, B and C was presented with the approach of triangular privity as employed by the National Cancer Institute (NCI) of the National Institutes of Health (NIH). As explained above regarding letters of intent, the NCI as collector B requires recipient C to enter into a direct contract with provider A. Furthermore, the Peru ICBG involves a triangular relationship that employs a collecting agreement (Aguaruna people–Washington University), a licence option (Washington University–Monsanto) and a know-how licence (Aguaruna people–Monsanto) (Rosenthal, 1996).

BOX 10.2 BIOPROSPECTING IN PANAMA: STRATEGIES FOR MAXIMIZING THE PARTICIPATION OF HOST-COUNTRY INSTITUTIONS

Todd Capson (Research Associate, Smithsonian Tropical Research Institute, Republic of Panama)

Working through the Smithsonian Tropical Research Institute (STRI) with funding through the International Cooperative Biodiversity Groups (ICBG) programme, we have developed a bioprospecting programme that maximizes the participation of Panamanian institutions from government, academia and the conservation community. The scientific collaborations that have been established call for Panamanian scientists to carry out key components of the research programme, such as the screening and purification of natural products. Only those components of the bioprospecting research that cannot be practically carried out in Panama are accomplished in collaboration with US-based colleagues in academia and industry. To provide the contractual and legal framework for our work in Panama, a series of two-party agreements between STRI and each of the institutions involved have been drafted and signed. The agreements are coordinated, straightforward and mutually consistent. The absence of any applicable model agreements required that all of our agreements were developed from scratch.

There is a single governmental entity in Panama, the Autoridad Nacional del Ambiente (ANAM) that has jurisdiction over the use of biological materials in Panama. Over a period of two years, drafts of legal agreements were presented to ANAM that were subsequently discussed and refined. Throughout the process, we sought the input of attorneys from both the private sector and the US-based non-governmental organization (NGO) Conservation International (CI).

The scientific collaborations in Panama involve six different laboratories from two institutions and focus primarily on the screening of biological materials and the purification of natural products. We are currently collaborating with the University of Panama, where plant extracts are tested for activity against cancer, HIV and agricultural pests, and the Gorgas Memorial Institute for Health Research (GMIHR), a component of Panama's Ministry of Health that specializes in tropical diseases. In the GMIHR, biological materials are tested for activity against malaria, leishmaniasis and *Trypanosoma cruzi*. The use of whole-cell assays in Panama complements the more specific receptor- and enzyme-based assays of our pharmaceutical collaborators.

At both the University of Panama and the GMIHR, the presence of highly qualified personnel and basic infrastructure for scientific research is complemented by money for supplies, salaries and equipment. We consulted extensively with our Panama-based colleagues on the design of the collaboration. The writing of the research proposal for the International Cooperative Biodiversity Groups (ICBG) proved to be helpful for clearly defining the goals of the proposed collaboration and the means by which those goals were to be achieved, all within a specified period of time and with a defined budget.

Once the nature of the collaborations was identified at the GMIHR and the University of Panama, we worked closely with our colleagues in designing legal agreements. The contractual provisions for the ownership of intellectual property developed in Panama stipulate that the ownership will be shared among the institutions of the inventors, in this case, the University of Panama, the GMIHR and STRI. For the sake of simplicity, STRI will manage all of the intellectual property associated with the project, such as the filing of patent applications. The legal agreements stipulate that the largest share of revenues that may result from milestones and royalties will be deposited in an environmental trust fund that will be administered by a local foundation that promotes biodiversity conservation. The second largest share of revenue will go to ANAM, which will use the funds for maintaining and establishing national parks. The remaining share of revenues will be split equally between the GMIHR, the University of Panama and STRI, irrespective of their relative contribution. The latter provision is designed to contribute to a free flow of information and ideas during the bioprospecting research, as well as to eliminate any potential disputes that may result from determining the relative contributions to the development of a successful invention after the fact.

Our ICBG programme has required the export to the US of biological materials for testing in the facilities of both academic and industrial collaborators. Obtaining the necessary permission from ANAM to export materials to our US-based collaborators has been greatly facilitated by our complementary efforts to involve the Panamanian scientific community in our bioprospecting research.

In the absence of a formal triangular relationship, the various spoke parties may nonetheless have rights in the other agreement spokes, even though they are not parties, under the legal principle of third-party beneficiary. This principle provides that if two parties to a contract intend to benefit a third party (who is not a party to the contract), then the third party may have a contractual right to intercede and make a claim against the contracting parties to enforce the third party's rights. However, if the agreements do not specifically provide the third-party beneficiaries with express rights, then the third-party beneficiary rights are only implied and subject to interpretation by a dispute-resolution forum.

Elements of biodiversity prospecting agreements

A biodiversity prospecting agreement should address issues such as the identities of the parties; the resources to be collected and exported; ownership over resources; compensation and benefits provided in exchange for access; technology transfer; restrictions on third-party transfer; measures to promote conservation; data reporting; intellectual property ownership; exclusivity; and confidentiality (ten Kate, 1995; Rosenthal, 1996).

This section provides an outline of issues that are typically addressed in biodiversity prospecting agreements, and examples of clauses that deal with these issues. The outline is a compilation or checklist of issues that may arise in a single contract consortium, a simple hub-and-spoke arrangement or a complex hub-and-spoke/wheel arrangement. The outline will not serve as a template for any one of those approaches.

Readers contemplating entering into a biodiversity prospecting agreement, whether source countries, collectors or the ultimate transferee, are encouraged, firstly, to consider the overall structure that will best suit their needs as described in the previous section. Secondly, they should review the issues in the following outline and consider, for each issue, if it applies to their situation. If so, what is their position on each of the points raised? This should be sufficient to prepare a plain language outline of the structure and salient points of any agreements that need to be prepared. At that point or earlier, input from legal counsel should be sought to structure the arrangement and to formalize the plain language into a more thorough contractual arrangement that deals with issues the parties may not include in the short outline. Thirdly, the reader should review existing contracts and published models for guidance regarding language that might be used to effectuate the points of agreement they wish to formalize. Examples of a range of clauses from such agreements are provided in Annex 10.1. The collection of clauses might appear, at first glance, to represent a model agreement such as those previously published (eg in Downes et al, 1993, and Putterman, 1996). While readers are encouraged to review those models, a major distinction here is that the clauses we include have actually been incorporated within negotiated executed agreements. Practitioners will find the form language interesting for that reason. Also, instead of providing a single model structure, this collection of clauses is intended to cover a wide cross-section of types of agreements and terms, some of which would be inconsistent if they appeared in the same agreement. Thus, readers will need to pick and choose which approach seems to fit the circumstances of their particular situation.

Conclusion

Each biodiversity prospecting relationship is unique, but each shares some features with others and with contracts in general. Those involved in negotiating, commenting on or acting under a biodiversity prospecting contract should be aware of the common features and the principal options they face. The more experience with these contracts that we gain, the easier it should become to structure good, fair, satisfying relationships that support sustainable development and the conservation of biodiversity.

Note

1   Funded by the US Agency for International Development (USAID) under the Biodiversity Support Programme, which is a consortium of WWF, World Resources Institute (WRI) and Nature Conservancy.

Annex 10.1 Outline of issues to address and language to comsider in a biodiversity prospecting agreement

Michael A Gollin[*]

This annex outlines the common issues faced by those structuring a biodiversity prospecting contract. A sample of relevant clauses found in existing agreements is available on the People and Plants website at www.rbgkew.org.uk/peopleplants/manuals/biological/annexes2.htm.

As discussed in Chapter 10, there are three types of actors involved in biodiversity prospecting agreements:

1 the party with jurisdiction over the source of biological material (usually a government agency, but this would also include local communities, private landowners, and others);
2 a collector who obtains the material; and
3 a transferee (commercial developer) who studies and typically plans to commercialize products of the material.

Thus, a typical flow of materials is as follows:

Source ➔ Collector ➔ Transferee.

A typical flow of benefits is the reverse:

Transferee ➔ Collector ➔ Source.

There are numerous variations and combinations of these parties. In a consortium they are all together in one contract. In a hub-and-spoke arrangement, one party (typically a collector) has individual arrangements with each other party.

Each party has certain goals that caused it to enter into a contract, and certain obligations it was willing to undertake in order to encourage other parties to enter into the contract. The goals and obligations may differ from party to party and contract to contract. It is therefore impossible to provide a 'one-size-fits-all' form agreement, and this annex does not provide such a form. Rather, the objective is to provide broad outlines of common issues and provisions that have been used in bioprospecting agreements and that can be used as a checklist for crafting new arrangements.

[*] The assistance of Abe Zachariah and Zayd Alathari in compiling this annex is gratefully acknowledged.

Outline of issues to consider in bioprospecting agreements

Italicized text in parentheses following certain issues or 'heads of agreement' listed here refers to paragraphs in the 'Outline of clauses from biodiversity prospecting agreements' (Gollin, 2001) that contain examples of suitable language.

Some of the categories are redundant. Others are mutually exclusive. Therefore, no agreement will have an outline that is the same as this one.

1 Parties
    1.1 Source and collector *(para 0.A)*
    1.2 Collector and transferee *(para 0.B)*
    1.3 Source, collector and transferee *(para 0.C)*
2 Framework (eg, recitals or whereas clauses)
    2.1 Benefits for collectors and source countries *(paras 0.C, 0.D, 0.F)*
    2.2 Expertise in collecting *(paras 0.A, 0.B, 0.C)*
    2.3 Valuable indigenous knowledge *(paras 0.F, 0.G)*
3 Access to material and indigenous knowledge
    3.1 Identify plant material to be collected or transferred *(para 1-Definition of 'material')*
        3.1.1 Actual plant *(para 1-Definition of 'material')*
        3.1.2 Plant extract *(para 1-Definition of 'extracts')*
        3.1.3 Methods of determining what to collect *(para 2.J)*
    3.2 Responsibility for collecting
        3.2.1 Collector *(paras 0.B, 2.D, 2.E, 2.F, 2.G, 2.I, 2.K)*
        3.2.2 Sub-contracting *(para 2.D)*
        3.2.3 Country/agency
    3.3 Access to indigenous knowledge *(paras 11.A, 15.B)*
        3.3.1 Uses
        3.3.2 Right to license
    3.4 Certifications *(paras 2.F, 2.I)*
        3.4.1 Plant material identity (ie correct plant)
            3.4.1.1 Expert botanist
            3.4.1.2 Chemical/forensic evidence
        3.4.2 Plant material source (ie country/location)
        3.4.3 Collected according to the local, regional and national laws of source country and international law *(paras 15.A, 19.B)*
            3.4.3.1 Proper affiliation
            3.4.3.2 Visas
            3.4.3.3 Customs clearances
            3.4.3.4 Export controls
            3.4.3.5 Environmental issues or standards *(paras 2.C, 2.M, 19.C)*
                3.4.3.5.1 Environmental laws
                3.4.3.5.2 Environmental assessment *(paras 0.J, 1-Definition of 'environmental assessment', 2.C)*
                3.4.3.5.3 Obligation to minimize environmental impact while collecting *(paras 0.H, 2.C)*
        3.4.4 Collected according to specified standards of conservation, resource and ecology management *(para 19.C)*
        3.4.5 Collected according to professional standards of conduct *(para 19.A)*
        3.4.6 Collected in accordance with wishes of indigenous peoples *(paras 11.A, 15.B)*

3.4.7 Collected in accordance with the customs of the source region or country

3.4.8 Collected in accordance with requirements of private landowner *(para 15.B)*

3.5 Notice prior to access

3.6 Documentation of collection *(paras 2.F, 2.I, 20.A)*

    3.6.1 Collector's name, date, location of collection, sample code number, habitat, taxonomic identification

    3.6.2 Procedures

    3.6.3 Preservation

    3.6.4 Photographs

    3.6.5 Matters to be certified (see above)

3.7 Source review of specimens

    3.7.1 Deposit

    3.7.2 Testing

4 Amount to be delivered

4.1 On time

4.2 Upon request

4.3 Recurring or resupply *(paras 2.B, 2.G, 20.A)*

4.4 Minimum amount *(paras 2.A,2.E)*

    4.4.1 Plant material

    4.4.2 Extracts

5 Cost of material/fees/compensation

5.1 Per sample

5.2 Collecting fee

    5.2.1 By collector

    5.2.2 By source *(para 5.E)*

5.3 Handling fee

5.4 Fixed fee

    5.4.1 One time

    5.4.2 Recurring

    5.4.3 Staged (different fees for different periods)

5.5 Revenue sharing/royalty

    5.5.1 Percentage of revenue from testing activities

    5.5.2 Percentage of revenue of middleman from supply activities

    5.5.3 Percentage of net sales (as defined) of covered products (as defined) *(para 5.B)*

5.6 Other compensation

    5.6.1 Fund and facilitate education programmes and other expertise and technology transfer initiatives

        5.6.1.1 Build schools

        5.6.1.2 Exchange programmes for scientists

        5.6.1.3 Educate source-country personnel *(para 5.G)*

            5.6.1.3.1 Provide instructors

            5.6.1.3.2 Collect techniques

            5.6.1.3.3 Bioassays

            5.6.1.3.4 Chemical screening

        5.6.1.4 Land-use programmes

        5.6.1.5 Drug development and research efforts

        5.6.1.6 Joint ventures with third-party institutions to develop and commercialize natural compounds or synthesized chemicals

    5.6.2 Fund conservation programmes

      5.6.2   Fund cultural programmes
      5.6.3   Fund and/or educate source's own drug development and research efforts
      5.6.4   Fund infrastructure projects
      5.6.5   Provide equipment *(para 5.E)*
  5.7 Per use (see below for uses)
  5.8 Provide funds or personnel for services *(para 5.E)*
  5.9 Trust fund
  5.10 Offset or deductions from amounts owed
      5.10.1 Royalties to third parties
      5.10.2 Failure to provide samples in prior periods
      5.10.3 Recouping of out-of-pocket expenses *(para 5.F)*
            5.10.3.1 Costs of licensing
            5.10.3.2 Costs of obtaining industrial (including patent) protection
      5.10.4 Costs of suing or defending against suits for intellectual property infringement
      5.10.5 Costs of collection or sub-contractors

6 Uses of material
  6.1 Non-commercial or non-profit use
      6.1.1   Evaluation or testing *(para 3.E)*
      6.1.2   Research
  6.2 Commercial use
      6.2.1   Use of indigenous knowledge
      6.2.2   Evaluation or testing
            6.2.2.1 For any commercial uses
            6.2.2.2 For uses specific to source country
      6.2.3   Research
      6.2.4   Products
      6.2.5   Sale
  6.3 Documentation of uses
      6.3.1   Periodic reports
            6.3.1.1 Language (native and English)
            6.3.1.2 Accounting *(para 20.C)*
                  6.3.1.2.1   Uses
                  6.3.1.2.2   Quantities
                  6.3.1.2.3   Payments
                  6.3.1.2.4   Maintain records for a period of time *(paras 20.A, 20.B)*
            6.3.1.3 Source agency to receive reports
      6.3.2   Tests taken or to be taken on specimens
            6.3.2.1 Reasons for tests
            6.3.2.2 Summary of tests and test results/data
            6.3.2.3 New chemicals
            6.3.2.4 Problems
            6.3.2.5 Prospects
                  6.3.2.5.1   Collection
                  6.3.2.5.2   Analysis
                  6.3.2.5.3   Uses
  6.4 Documentation by source and source agencies/groups regarding project, compensation, uses of compensation, suggestions to facilitate and improve relationship between collector and source

7 Intellectual property rights allocated between source, collector and transferee
  7.1 Right to distribute to third parties
  7.2 Rights to use (see above)
  7.3 Data *(para 1-Definition of 'data')*
  7.4 Publication
      7.4.1 Each side free to do as it wishes subject to protecting intellectual property rights
      7.4.2 One party given all rights
      7.4.3 Each party makes own publication, but waits to release simultaneously *(para 17.B)*
      7.4.4 Collaboration
      7.4.5 Source has veto right over publications by transferee *(para 17.C)*
  7.5 Patent *(para 7)*
      7.5.1 Collector gets all rights
      7.5.2 Source retains all rights
      7.5.3 Transferee gets all rights *(para 6.G)*
      7.5.4 Joint ownership *(para 6.F)*
      7.5.5 Collector gets all rights except that source retains licence
      7.5.6 Allocate rights according to contribution
          7.5.6.1 Whoever creates invention gets patent *(para 6.D)*
          7.5.6.2 Other
      7.5.7 Right to license to third parties
      7.5.8 Option to purchase exclusive licence
      7.5.9 Obligation to disclose patentable inventions
      7.5.10 Right to file patent application
      7.5.11 Reporting inventions to other parties *(para 6.E)*
  7.6 Trade secrets *(para 10.A)*
  7.7 Copyright *(para 8.A)*
  7.8 Trademark and publicity *(para 9.A)*
      7.8.1 No endorsement/use of name
  7.9 Revenue
  7.10 Exclusivity
      7.10.1 Source outgoing (supply only to transferee) *(paras 7.A, 7.C, 7.D, 7.E)*
      7.10.2 Supply (obtain only from source/collector) *(paras 2.C, 2.L)*
      7.10.3 Use *(paras 4.C, 7.B)*
  7.11 Licence
      7.11.1 Parties retain non-exclusive licence to intellectual property rights
      7.11.2 Reasonable efforts to license
  7.12 Right to negotiate commercial terms with third parties
      7.12.1 If extract is of interest, then additional supply
  7.13 Absence of intellectual property right protection
  7.14 Obligation to sue infringers of intellectual property rights *(para 6.C)*
8 Termination
  8.1 Term or indefinite
  8.2 Termination at will upon notice
  8.3 Unresolved good faith dispute
  8.4 Failure to pay minimum revenue threshold
  8.5 Breach of agreement
  8.6 Bankruptcy of collector
  8.7 Embargo or other action against source country by country of collector's domicile

9   Confidentiality
    9.1   Existence of agreement *(para 17.D)*
    9.2   Terms of agreement *(para 17.D)*
    9.3   Activities
    9.4   Other
10 Warranties
    10.1 None given *(para 14.A)*
    10.2 Authority to enter into agreement *(para 15.A)*
11 Liability/limitation of liability
    11.1 For breach
    11.2 For breach by third parties
    11.3 Illness, injuries, damages from collection, testing, development of samples or
         products *(para 13.B)*
    11.4 No liability *(para 14.B)*
12 Indemnification
    12.1 By source
    12.4 By collector
    12.3 By transferee
13 Assignment
14 Governing law
15 Conflict resolution
    15.1 Jurisdiction
    15.2 Dispute resolution
        15.2.1   Meeting of the parties
        15.2.2   Dispute regarding ownership of invention
        15.2.3   Courts
        15.2.4   Mediation
        15.2.5   Arbitration
    15.3 Costs
    15.4 Right to sue transferees
        15.4.1   Source retains absolute and sole right
        15.4.2   Collector has first right and source can sue only if collector fails to sue
        15.4.3   Collector has sole right to sue
16 Miscellaneous
    16.1 Independent contractors
    16.2 Survival of terms
    16.3 Access to documents filed with the US Food and Drug Administration
    16.4 Severability
    16.5 Notice
    16.6 *Force majeure*
    16.7 Entire agreement (integration)

Outline of clauses from biodiversity prospecting agreements

The outline of clauses relevant to bioprospecting agreements – which can be read in conjunction with the outline of issues in this annex – is available on the People and Plants website at www.rbgkew.org.uk/peopleplants/manuals/biological/annexes2.htm.

Chapter 11

Sharing financial benefits: trust funds for biodiversity prospecting

Marianne Guerin-McManus, Kent C Nnadozie, and Sarah A Laird

Introduction

Sharing the benefits associated with the commercialization of genetic and other biological resources involves not only determination of the nature and size of the benefits, but also the mode of distribution of those benefits to a range of stakeholders, and in a fashion that serves defined objectives over time. Several different models have been advocated or are already in place to share financial benefits. Trust funds – the subject of this chapter – are one model that has been employed to date, building upon experience with delivery mechanisms employed in other areas of conservation and development. There is a short but well-documented history of the use of trust funds in the conservation and development community upon which biodiversity prospecting projects can draw.

The trust fund model is well suited to the bioprospecting field because it can accommodate the long-term time frame of biodiversity prospecting projects, which typically encompass several years of collection, research and drug development and where some of the financial benefits might accrue as long as decades after field activities are completed. Trust funds provide a stable and enduring structure that can last over these long periods of time for the purpose of channelling benefits in a controlled and consistent manner. Trusts can also be structured to operate under specific guiding principles, overseen by a diverse board of trustees, in such a way that the long-term interests of a group or country rather than the short-term gain of individuals, are served.

The process of developing a trust fund may also be an invaluable exercise in itself, in that it requires the definition of goals and objectives and the identification of potential beneficiaries. It also promotes a dialogue on what constitutes equitable benefit-sharing. A trust fund charter might also provide a much needed public record of the principles and objectives that biodiversity prospecting activities are intended to serve, thereby offering a window into the complexity of projects and making the logic of commercial agreements available to a wider public.

This chapter will discuss the origins of the trust fund concept, its development in the context of conservation and its application in biodiversity prospecting. It will highlight the basic principles that should be taken into consideration and the issues to be addressed in designing a trust fund framework. Finally, the chapter will describe concrete steps to develop and implement a biodiversity prospecting trust fund and will relate, through specific case studies, some of the lessons learned from past experiences.

Trust funds: general background

What is a trust fund?

A trust fund is a 'sum of money that is legally set aside and whose use is restricted to specific purposes for designated beneficiaries' (Mikitin, 1995). The concept behind a trust is that assets are managed by a person or a group (the trustees) for the identified goals or benefits of a second group (the beneficiaries). Funds may be organized in several different ways, including non-profit corporations, foundations, government-formed trusts and common law trusts. While this chapter focuses primarily on common law trusts, the concepts involved in their creation apply to the other forms as well.

The law of trusts grows from the Anglo-American legal tradition, including current or former members of the Commonwealth and the US (common law countries). Trusts have been employed for centuries, primarily by families to ensure the financial health of future generations; in England, for example, their first reported use dates back to the 11th century. During the Crusades, Englishmen going to war would 'give' their property to someone to hold in trust until their return from the Holy Land or to pass on to heirs if necessary.

The most analogous counterpart to common-law charitable trusts in civil law systems is the *foundation*, which exists in most modern legal systems in continental Europe and is widely used by environmental institutions in these countries. A well-known example of a foundation is the WWF, which was established in 1961 as a foundation in Switzerland, a civil law country (Mikitin, 1995). While foundations are essentially functional alternatives to common law trusts and adopt most or all of their principles, a major difference is that a foundation legally acquires a separate personality and has the capacity to own property, as opposed to the trust, where legal title is held by the trustees (Mikitin, 1995).

Latin American countries employ the trust concept, using the term *fideicomiso*, in national legislation. In the 1920s, Mexico introduced the trust concept in modified form, by way of national legislation patterned on Anglo-American experience. In other parts of Latin America the trust concept can be traced back to Roman civil law, as transferred by the Spanish. The original intent of *fideicomisos* was to provide for future generations – much as in Europe – so early laws limited beneficiaries to private individuals and did not permit public charities. Today in Latin America, however, trusts can be employed as public charities.

The trusts described above for Latin America grow directly from European legal traditions. There are numerous non-Western trust-like concepts, as well. For example, parallels have been drawn to institutions such as the Islamic *waaf*, which historically served as a legal device for the establishment of perpetual public charities, and to the Asian *yayasan*, which are non-profit organizations treated as legal institutions capable of entering into

BOX 11.1 KEY TERMS

Conservation trust fund: a trust fund whose designated beneficiaries are conservation programmes and activities identified, selected and developed by the fund trustees.

Non-profit corporation: a corporation whose income is not distributed to its members, directors or officers but is used instead to fund ongoing activities of the corporation.

Common law trust: a trust organized so that the trustees have responsibility for the fund's assets and manage its affairs, while benefits accrue to either private parties (individuals who are specifically identified) or the public (not specific individuals, but a community or segment of a community).

Trust established by an act of national government: a trust made possible by a national government for the benefit of the people in that country. Consequently, the aims and objectives of the trust are considered to be in the national interest.

Foundation: a trust-like arrangement used in civil law countries, where the resulting institution is a legal entity able to own assets (as opposed to the trust where assets are held by the trustees).

Debt-for-nature swap: cancellation of foreign debt in exchange for a commitment to mobilize domestic resources for the environment.

Common law: a body of law based primarily on judicial decisions employed, for example, in the US, UK and former Commonwealth countries.

Civil law: a body of law based upon legislative enactments (laws created by statute) employed, for example, in France and Switzerland and most former colonies of France, Spain, Belgium and Portugal.

By-laws: a document that sets out the governing and operating rules to be followed by a board of trustees.

Charter: a document issued by the government to a corporation or non-profit corporation assuring them certain rights, liberties or powers in exchange for fulfilling certain requirements. In the context of trust funds, the charter is analogous to a deed, by-laws or a constitution.

Deed: a document that records the goals of a trust, its structure, the identities of the beneficiaries, the trustees and the obligations of the trustees to the trust and beneficiaries.

Board of trustees: the individual or group of individuals responsible for managing a trust's assets and affairs and distributing revenues to beneficiaries.

legal contracts and civil actions. The scope of these trust-like concepts, however, can be more limited than the common law trust, especially with regard to beneficiaries.

The history of conservation trust funds

Trust funds have only recently been employed to achieve conservation objectives. They arose in response to various issues that surfaced in the late 1980s – in particular, 'debt-for-nature swaps' or transactions in which a developing country's foreign debt is cancelled in return for a commitment to domestic conservation investment (Conservation International, 1991). Debt-for-nature transactions generated large amounts of local currency that local beneficiaries could not adequately absorb. At the same time, there existed an increasing need for long-term financing of conservation projects, such as the recurrent costs of park management; but a visible, transparent and intermediary structure between various sources of financing and numerous biodiversity conservation projects was lacking.

In response to these concerns, the trust fund concept was carried from the estate-planning field to the conservation world. The benefits of the trust fund concept included: promotion of financial security unaffected by fluctuations in international donor or foundation money; building of local institutional capacity on the part of countries, projects and others; increased community confidence in the longevity of conservation projects; and, by including representative stakeholders in the governance and management of funds, the promotion of consensus-building and a sense of ownership over a nation's natural resources (see Box 11.2).

There is clearly a great deal of diversity in the manner and way in which trust funds can operate, and the breadth of the objectives they serve. By building upon expertise acquired through conservation trust funds, 'biodiversity prospecting funds' should be able to bypass some of the mistakes made earlier on, and draw from these models to facilitate quicker implementation and to establish better track records. Furthermore, considering that trust funds can, in practically all jurisdictions, acquire a tax-exempt status and also enjoy certain other immunities and privileges, they present an added advantage because all of the monies contributed to the fund can be applied entirely for the benefit of the intended beneficiaries. In the same vein, profits derived from the investment of part or all of the fund are fully utilized without any tax burden or deductions.

BOX 11.2 CONSERVATION TRUST FUNDS

Conservation trust funds have proven valuable for a range of reasons, including the following:

- The involvement of broad private- and public-sector participation.
- They meet recurrent costs that might otherwise be very difficult to fund, although this requires a system of careful monitoring and evaluation.
- They improve absorptive capacity (ie the ability to hold and use large sums of money over an extended period of time).
- They provide small grant-making capacity by 'retailing' large international grants to a wide range of smaller projects.
- They provide sustained funding, mitigating risks of unexpected stoppage of funds due to political changes, budget cuts, economic austerity programmes, etc.
- They enjoy privileges such as tax exemption that enable full application of available funds to designated beneficiaries.

Size and scope of trust funds

Trust funds can range in size and scope. For example, Suriname's Forest People's Fund, which was established to facilitate benefit-sharing from biodiversity prospecting and foster biodiversity conservation in a small community, began with start-up capital of US$50,000 (see Case Study 11.1). Nigeria's Fund for Integrated Rural Development and Traditional Medicine (FIRD-TM) received original financing of US$40,000 (see Case Study 11.2). Although the start-up funding in these cases is relatively small, both funds are designed to receive additional financial benefits over time. At the other end of the spectrum, Colombia's ECOFONDO, designed to promote the nation's environmental conservation and sustainable development, received US$41.6 million in local currency paid as counterpart to debt cancellation, over four years, by the Colombian government. (ECOFONDO, 1996)

Trust funds are also administered at different levels. The Suriname trust fund operates at the community level; Nigeria's is a national fund. Trust funds can be administered by governments, research institutions, non-profit organizations or community associations. For example, in Fiji, a community-based trust fund – the Verata Tikina Biodiversity Trust Fund – has been developed as part of a three-year project of the University of the South Pacific (USP), the Verata Tikina communities and commercial partners. This project is intended to link pharmaceutical drug development with conservation and community development. Initiated in 1995 with commercial partner SmithKline Beecham (SKB), the fund subsequently changed its partnership to the Strathclyde Institute of Drug Research (SIDR), which works with numerous commercial companies. The Verata community members receive per-sample fees, totalling as much as US$100,000, as a short-term financial benefit, which they are managing through the community-based trust fund (Putzel and Zerner, 1998).

Establishing a biodiversity prospecting trust fund

Biodiversity prospecting projects can generate financial benefits over many years. Usually, an upfront payment, or fees per sample, are made by a company to the collector or local community for the right to prospect. Then, over the course of what may be many years, payments are made in connection with each research milestone – these are known as 'milestone payments'. Eventually, royalties may be paid when products are commercialized. This course of financing sets up several potential problems if a framework for the distribution of the benefits, and an overarching plan for their use, is not in place. The establishment of a biodiversity prospecting trust fund must take these factors into consideration.

Establishment of an environmental trust fund generally moves through three phases of development:

1 Feasibility study.
2 Design.
3 Implementation.

The following sections describe the considerations and actions that should take place during each phase.

CASE STUDY 11.1 THE FOREST PEOPLE FUND OF SURINAME

CASE STUDY 11.1

Marianne Guérin-McManus, Lisa M Famolare, Ian A Bowles, Stanley A J Malone, Russell A Mittermeier and Amy B Rosenfeld (Conservation International, US and Surinam)

The creation of the Forest People Fund (FPF) of Suriname arose out of the International Cooperative Biodiversity Groups (ICBG) project, which started in 1993 in Suriname and is expected to provide a long-term compensation-sharing mechanism for revenues arising out of genetic resources and ethnobotanical knowledge.[1]

The Suriname ICBG involves five different institutions, including Virginia Polytechnic Institute and State University (VPISU), Conservation International (CI), international non-governmental conservation organization Bedrijf Geneesmiddelen Voorziening Suriname (BGVS), a pharmaceutical company owned by the Surinamese government, the Missouri Botanical Garden (MBG), a US botanical research institution, two US pharmaceutical companies, Bristol-Myers Squibb Pharmaceutical Research Institute (B-MS) and, since 1998, Dow. Each institution carries out a specific role, including botanical and ethnobotanical collections and inventory, extraction, screening, chemistry and drug development. The main focus of the Suriname ICBG project is to promote the discovery of biologically active plants for drug development and biodiversity conservation, as well as to ensure that communities and the source country derive maximum benefits for their biological resources and their intellectual contribution.

The Suriname ICBG group works with local tribal people to conduct some of the bioprospecting activities. The majority of the local participants are Bushnegros, or Maroons, who are descendants of runaway African slaves who escaped Dutch plantations on the coast over 300 years ago and settled along the river in central Suriname. Six distinct Maroon tribes live in the interior and depend upon their extensive knowledge of forest resources for their survival. When the Maroons first fled into the forest, they experimented with medicinal uses for the plants, and through a process of trial and error identified plants that were effective for various illnesses. They based their experiments in part on their memories of the healing traditions and plants in their native Africa and on information learned from Amerindians in Suriname's interior. This knowledge has developed into a rich and expansive understanding of the medicinal qualities of Suriname's forest plants.

While the ICBG contract and a statement of understanding govern the means by which future financial gains from bioprospecting are to be distributed, a separate trust fund was established to ensure that the tribal communities would benefit immediately from the access granted to their forest resources. The fund was also to serve as an instrument to capture additional longer-term revenues. The fund compensates these communities for their ethnobotanical contributions to the ICBG project, creates conservation incentives, finances sustainable management projects, provides research and training exchanges, and supports other socially and environmentally sound projects.

The Forest People Fund was established in 1994 with a US$50,000 contribution from B-MS, followed by another US$10,000 donation in 1996. Additional contributions will be made of US$20,000 each year as part of the renewed ICBG project until 2003. The Forest People Fund Foundation is headquartered in Paramaribo, Suriname, and administers the Forest People Fund according to the foundation's by-laws. These by-laws were written by the Surinamese participants and are governed by the laws of Suriname.

The by-laws require the board to meet at least four times a year and whenever deemed necessary to manage the fund's day-to-day operations and finances, and to handle legal arrangements. The board of directors is comprised of five members, including two representatives at large, two representatives from CI, and one who is nominated by BGVS. One Amerindian and one Maroon must fill the position of the members at large. CI's representatives are the president of CI, based in Washington, and the director of CI-Suriname. Richene Libretto, a district representative of the people to Suriname's central government for the interior who is part Maroon, is the current representative of BGVS. Paul Abena is the representative of the Maroon communities and Armand Karwafodi is the representative of the Amerindian communities. Each member is limited to a five-year term and may cast one vote in the board's decisions.

The main activity of the board of directors is to review project proposals. Any tribal person in Suriname, community or foundation that has an idea for a project can submit a proposal. CI-Suriname staff members are available to assist interested parties in their project design and proposal. The board then determines whether to grant funding according to whether the project advances the purpose of the fund, which is to 'stimulate residents of the interior and related living persons who contribute to, and participate in, the preservation and long-term protection of biodiversity and to provide them with social, educational and economic assistance'.

The Forest People Fund supports local communities in the interior of Suriname in projects involving community development, biodiversity conservation and health care. To date, projects funded by the Forest People Fund include:

- a project designed to transport people and goods bound for Paramaribo by boat to Ajonia, the furthest village accessible by road from Paramaribo; this project facilitated travel for people living in the interior while avoiding the creation of new roads, which cause environmental damage in the forest;
- a sewing project, organized by Afinga, which acquired sewing machines and material to make clothes.

Feasibility study

The feasibility phase involves consultations with a representative group of stakeholders, including government representatives, scientists, conservationists, business representatives and community leaders. The group will determine the priority needs of the community/region/country, the objectives of the fund and the types of conservation and development projects it will finance. This exercise might be facilitated by an international expert on trust funds, in conjunction with a local counterpart, in order to help assess the feasibility of the trust fund model in the domestic context. The local counterpart can provide technical assistance regarding the national legal framework and determination of the appropriate form of trust (eg a foundation versus a common law trust according to national law). Experts and stakeholder groups will also need to define the financial and banking structures most appropriate to the situation, and make preliminary determinations about potential board members and the availability of management expertise for fund staff. The

CASE STUDY 11.2

CASE STUDY 11.2 NIGERIA'S FUND FOR INTEGRATED RURAL DEVELOPMENT AND TRADITIONAL MEDICINE (FIRD-TM)

Kent C Nnadozie, Maurice M Iwu, Elijah N Sokomba and Cosmas Obialor

The Fund for Integrated Rural Development and Traditional Medicine (FIRD-TM) was established in Nigeria at the initiative of the Bioresources Development and Conservation Programme (BDCP) as an autonomous body to address the issues relating to the bioprospecting and equitable benefit-sharing aspects of the Convention on Biological Diversity (CBD) within the framework of existing laws. It was a response to the major institutional gap and the lack of an appropriate and effective vehicle to receive and channel benefits in an equitable and consistent manner in order to source communities from which commercially useful genetic resources and specialized knowledge are derived. In establishing the fund as an independent body with constituents from across all sectors, including the government and grassroots, it is anticipated that the principal problem of getting benefits to the localities (and knowledge) that are the sources and custodians of the relevant biotic materials will be overcome.

Background

BDCP is primarily focused on establishing integrated programmes for the discovery of biologically active plants for drug development and on promoting the conservation and sustainable use of biodiversity, while ensuring that local source communities derive maximum benefits for their resources and their intellectual contribution. The basis for the establishment of the fund is also linked to the International Cooperative Biodiversity Groups (ICBG), which are networks of bioprospecting projects that involve several countries and national and international institutions. The African ICBG, one of the networks, is a collaboration of the BDCP, Walter Reed Army Institute of Research, Washington, DC, the Smithsonian Tropical Research Institute, the University of Dschang (Cameroon), the International Centre for Ethnomedicine and Drug Development (Nigeria) and 13 other institutions in Africa and the United States.

Goals and objectives

The fund was registered under the relevant laws in order to give it a legal personality capable of owning property and maintaining and defending actions. This position also bestowed it with a legal tax-exempt status as a non-profit organization. The fund was established as a private non-governmental and non-profit body primarily to facilitate and ensure the equitable distribution of benefits derived from biological diversity and the knowledge of rural communities. It will provide short- and medium-term benefits in the form of immediate cash payments to individuals or groups and the sponsorship of development projects in communities. Long-term benefits in the form of royalties will depend upon the final outcome of the bioprospecting activities. It will also apply revenues available to it to projects or ventures that promote conservation and the sustainable use of biodiversity. It is expected to create the interface that ensures the establishment of mutual respect and to bridge the gap of misunderstanding through the inclusive participation of relevant community and traditional medical practitioners, along with conventional scientists in the benefit-distribution process and the sharing of information.

Structure and governance

FIRD-TM is governed by a constitution that stipulates its aims and objectives, its structure, the nature of its principal organs, its financial matters and conditions for dissolution.

The fund has three principal organs:

1   The *board of trustees*: the property of the fund legally resides within the board of trustees; but it has no executive capacity with respect to the day-to-day running of the body.
2   The *advisory board*: its capacity is purely advisory and it consists of distinguished experts in fields that are related to the objectives of the fund, as well as eminent leaders and individuals who can contribute positively to the fulfillment of those objectives.
3   The *board of management*: this is the executive/administrative organ of the fund. The members serve for a period of five years each and may be reappointed for a further five-year term. There are currently ten members of the board of management, drawn from a wide spectrum of interests and constituencies, including traditional leaders, traditional healers, government representatives and independent experts. All members are currently serving on a voluntary basis and receive no remuneration or allowance for their input except for costs incurred directly in the performance of their duties with respect to the fund.

The constitution provides for a full-time *administrative secretary* who will administer the secretariat and the day-to-day business of the fund, including maintaining a record of the fund's activities and overseeing all other staff of the fund.

Funding

The principal source of funding at the initial stage came from BDCP and its collaborators, especially through the ICBG programme. At the inauguration of the board, an initial donation of US$40,000 was received from the Healing Forest Conservancy as part of the benefit-sharing programme of Shaman Pharmaceuticals Inc. This is yet to be disbursed. Further substantial donations were received from Orange Drugs Limited, an indigenous pharmaceutical company, as well as from the Indigenous Pharmaceutical Manufacturers' Association of Nigeria. There have also been pledges of further support and assistance from various sources, both in the public and private sectors. Although the law requires the auditing of its accounts at regular intervals, the constitution further stipulates for the annual audit of the fund's accounts by external auditors, as well as the preparation of the annual report. Copies of the report will be made available to necessary and interested parties. There is a statutory prohibition against the distribution of profits or dividends to the members or trustees, even upon dissolution. Upon dissolution or 'winding up', assets can only be transferred to another organization having similar objectives or can only be applied to another charity's objectives, as determined by the board of trustees.

Criteria for fund disbursement and compensation

The board of management manages all of the affairs of the fund, decides on issues of policy and budget, reviews and approves proposals and work plans but does not undertake direct participation in the implementation of approved projects. It does, however, exercise a direct supervisory role with regard to approved projects. The board has adopted a fund allocation formula for disbursement to the various targets within the mandate of the fund. Targets include biodiversity conservation activities/national interest activities; educational interests; traditional healers' associations for group projects or micro-credit funds; community development associations/village projects; women's (especially widows) and children's welfare. The board has ongoing consultations with village heads and the professional guild of healers in determining the nature of compensation or forthcoming projects in any given locality. In executing its mandate, priority is to be given to such projects and activities that promote or encourage biodiversity conservation and sustainable development.

Prospects and anticipated problems

One of the initial problems experienced at its inception was the misconception, in some circles, regarding the actual roles of the fund, especially concerning target communities. However, efforts are being made to educate the relevant parties of the true roles and position of the fund, especially its community-development and conservation-oriented focus.

Other key problems that have arisen or are anticipated and which might impede progress include the following:

- Lack of adequate resources: because of the nature of expected benefits to be shared (often uncertain and long term), there is bound to be pressure on the fund, especially in the light of pressing needs and pervasive poverty. Apart from external funding, the fund is ultimately expected to become self-financing, and part of the approach to address this is the development of a reasonably secure and sustainable investment portfolio. The board is also engaged in local fund-raising drives to supplement external funding and to broaden its resource base.
- Competing demands: the board intends to follow clearly outlined modalities and criteria in order to assist it in choosing projects to sponsor and communities that will benefit. It had, however, resolved (especially at this initial stage) to embark on small manageable projects that touch the people closely, rather than to undertake major or large projects that might prove wasteful or be of little benefit. It is currently evaluating several projects that have already commenced or were planned by local community-development associations and herbalist unions for the purpose of advancing additional support or sponsorships, where appropriate.

Key lessons

- A participatory process, exemplified by a cross-cultural membership of the board of trustees/management, is key to the acceptance and cooperation of stakeholders, and is necessary for balanced and informed decision-making.
- Recognition of, and adaptation to, local socio-political realities is essential to achieving stability and sustainability.
- Ongoing communication and consultation with stakeholders enhances profile and the relevance of the trust fund.

feasibility study will seek to answer the following questions.

Will the trust fund concept work in the target community?

Given the legalistic and seemingly bureaucratic nature of trust funds, some have suggested that they run counter to the ways in which local communities traditionally manage and distribute benefits. In fact, in traditional societies who communally own resources, the use of community development associations and cooperatives for rural development and renewal is common. Biodiversity prospecting is likely a culturally foreign activity; however, trust funds are generally not unfamiliar.

Is there a legal framework in the host country to support the trust?

A trust fund must operate within the context of national and international law and policy. As an initial step, local and national laws must be analysed to determine if provisions are made for trusts or trust-like devices. Depending upon national laws, other options might need to be considered, such as government and private partnerships, or a trust established by an act of the legislature. Another option to consider is the integration of a biodiversity prospecting fund within an existing institutional structure (eg creation of a biodiversity prospecting sub-account as part of a national conservation fund; see Case Study 11.3).

The feasibility study should also include an analysis of other relevant law and policy, including intellectual property, trade, environment, natural resources and access and benefit-sharing measures. The activities that generate revenue for the fund, and the objectives served by the fund, should fit within the wider legal and policy context of a country and region. A conservation trust fund should also

endeavour to support a country's national environmental strategy, but should not be a substitute for governmental financial support for environmental management and enforcement of existing laws. Some trusts have explicitly addressed the issue in their by-laws by including a pledge from the government to maintain its current level of support for conservation and development programmes.

A feasibility phase should also pay attention to, and try to maximize, the wider objectives that trust funds can serve – beyond the specific goals of the fund itself. A well-designed trust fund can generate a range of benefits that contribute in non-specific ways to the development of sustainable societies. For example, by making financing available in absorbable amounts, funds build the capacity of local implementing organizations. The transparent participatory processes that characterize trust funds can strengthen civil society (Curtis et al, 1998). Additional benefits of current conservation trust funds include the creation of new parks, as well as strengthened capacity among non-governmental organizations (NGOs) or governments for generating and managing financial resources, a feeling of 'ownership' among stakeholders resulting from direct participation, increased conservation awareness, and increased community involvement (GEF, 1998).

Designing the trust fund: the 'nuts and bolts'

Goals and objectives

Defining a fund's objective(s) is crucial to a trust fund's success, since the structure of a fund depends upon, and responds to, its goals and objectives. This should be the first step in the process of fund establishment. One of the key lessons learned from the establishment of conservation funds is

CASE STUDY 11.3

CASE STUDY 11.3 THE PANAMA ICBG TRUST FUND: THE NATIONAL ENVIRONMENT FUND OF THE FUNDACIÓN NATURA

Todd Capson (Smithsonian Tropical Institute, Panama)

To couple biodiversity conservation with bioprospecting, we chose to establish a fund that works through a Panama-based foundation that promotes the study, conservation and sustainable use of biological diversity. The foundation we work with, Fundación Natura, has supported projects throughout Panama. The fund we established, the National Environment Fund, will provide financing that will be available for conservation and development projects, including biodiversity prospecting, accessible through Fundación Natura's existing competitive grants programme. The National Environment Fund will receive a portion of all access fees, milestones and royalties that are generated by International Cooperative Biodiversity Groups (ICBG) bioprospecting activities in Panama.

Fundación Natura

To appreciate the context in which the National Environment Fund will operate, background information on Fundación Natura is helpful. Fundación Natura was legally incorporated in 1991 with endowments from the US Agency for International Development (USAID) (as principal donor), the government of Panama and The Nature Conservancy as donors to a permanent fund (IUCN 1996). The Nature Conservancy serves as fiduciary. The objective of Fundación Natura is to manage this permanent fund, known as FIDECO. The fund is used to finance projects that promote knowledge, management and conservation of the environment in Panama, with a special emphasis in the Panama Canal watershed.

An additional goal of Fundación Natura is the enhancement of infrastructure within Panama for conservation and sustainable development, primarily through strengthening of the institutions, such as non-governmental organizations (NGOs), that implement those projects. The endowment for Fundación Natura is currently US$33 million, the interest from which provides Fundación Natura's operating budget and revenue for the programmes that it supports. Fundación Natura has ten full-time staff who work on project-funding programmes, accounting and administration.

All proposals submitted to Fundación Natura for funding are reviewed by a technical committee, a group of highly capable volunteer professionals with different areas of expertise. The technical committee reviews applications and makes recommendations with regard to the proposals received by Fundación Natura, in addition to assisting Fundación Natura's technical staff in the supervision of ongoing projects. The technical committee makes recommendations for funding to Fundación Natura's board of directors, the foundation's highest authority.

How the National Environment Fund will work with Fundación Natura

As the majority of the revenue received by Fundación Natura from FIDECO must be spent in the Panama Canal watershed, Fundación Natura is actively seeking new donors – in particular, donors who will allow the foundation to support projects aimed at conservation and sustainable development in areas outside of the Panama Canal watershed. There are ecosystems in Panama of global importance that reside outside of the watershed, such as those found in the provinces of Bocas del Toro, Chiriquí, San Blas and Darién. Donors to the National Environment Fund can specify that projects are supported in regions of Panama that would otherwise receive a small fraction of Fundación Natura's support.

In the contract that has been developed between the Smithsonian Tropical Research Institute (STRI) and the government of Panama, a percentage of 30 per cent of the revenues flowing to Panama, such as access fees, royalties and milestones, has been committed to the National Environment Fund. We envision that when the National Environment Fund has enough capital to generate significant amounts of interest, then the principal be will invested while the interest will he used to support projects. Until that point is reached, meritorious projects can be directly supported by simply providing funds directly to Fundación Natura, to be spent according to well-defined criteria provided by both Fundación Natura and the coordinators of the National Environment Fund. Among Fundación Natura's most successful projects are those that were funded through their Small Grants Programme, in which no award is greater than US$5000. Thus, even if our initial contributions to Fundación Natura are through access fees (US$75,000 per year), we will be in a position to make substantive contributions to biodiversity conservation in Panama.

In summary, Fundación Natura plays an innovative and important role in the ICBG Panama programme. The infrastructure of Fundación Natura – in particular, the rigorous peer-review process by qualified professionals that is the heart of its competitive grants programme – makes it an extremely attractive beneficiary for funds that may result from our biological prospecting work in Panama. The National Environment Fund was established explicitly to receive funds from biological prospecting initiatives in Panama. As donors to Fundación Natura, we can explicitly include sustainable biological-prospecting projects as among those that are supported by our fund. Thus, the National Environment Fund is an important step along the road to a long-term sustainable biological-prospecting programme. As a well-known, highly regarded foundation, both within Panama and internationally, our association with Fundación Natura also provides legitimacy, transparency and credibility to our biological prospecting work in Panama.

that it is critical to have the basic vision of the fund in place before making decisions on design. In deciding on the scope of the fund, it will be necessary, firstly, to define the issues to be addressed; secondly, it is important to identify the types of activities or beneficiaries that a fund could support in order to respond to these issues.

A common objective of most conservation funds is to provide a stable source of financing to meet the recurrent costs of operating and maintaining protected areas and/or to ensure the sustainable use of natural resources through community support (Mikitin, 1995). However, these objectives vary in breadth and depth. They may be narrowly focused, such as the maintenance of a park or park system. For example, the Jamaica National Parks Trust Fund was established to fund two pilot national parks and to establish a National Parks and Protected Areas System in Jamaica (USAID, 1996). One of the principal goals of Suriname's International Cooperative Biodiversity Groups (ICBG) project and conservation trust fund is to record and secure the value of tribal knowledge (see Case Study 11.1).

BOX 11.3 KEY FACTORS FOR SUCCESS

Key factors for success include the following:

- A well-balanced board, reflecting a range of society – government, scientists, local communities, non-governmental organizations (NGOs), etc.
- Dialogue and regular communication between involved parties.
- Transparency that allows independent monitoring, avoidance of mistakes and discourages misuse of funds.
- High visibility of the structure to the public, as well as domestic and foreign donors.
- Government commitment to development and conservation.
- Adequate funding.
- Dynamic and skilled organizers and managers.
- Diverse representation and involvement of stakeholders.
- Well-defined objectives.
- Ongoing monitoring and evaluation.
- Regular reporting and feedback on activities to the public.

Advocates of specific, clear-cut goals such as these point out that when the objectives of a trust fund are narrow, they are easy to understand and communicate, and room for disagreement among governing board members is limited (IPG, 1995).

At the other end of the spectrum are funds that incorporate broad goals. For example, the main objective of Peru's National Fund for State-Protected Natural Areas (PROFONANPE) is to finance protected area projects in Peru (ECOFONDO, 1996). Such all-encompassing goals can tie into national environmental agendas and allow experimentation with new forms of partnerships between the public and private sectors (IPG, 1995).

Generally, funds that focus goals and objectives on a specific range of activities that are selected for strategic impact and feasibility (and which can be carried out quickly to build a track record) do better than those that start out with an 'open-door' policy, which reacts to whatever is proposed. The scope of a fund can always be broadened later, if appropriate.

Alternatively, if a fund starts out with a fairly broad mission and objectives, a 'pilot phase' can be declared in which the fund concentrates on a focused area before accepting proposals from other areas. There are several practical reasons for taking this approach:

- A fund can only process so many proposals and finance even fewer. It is better for a fund to narrow its focus, receive fewer proposals and select as many high-quality proposals as can be funded, in order to establish a track record.
- A narrow focus will allow selection of fund staff and advisory committees with specific technical skills in mind (taxonomy, pharmacology, sustainable development), avoiding the necessity of staffing for multiple disciplines.
- Fund-raising for a fund with a narrow focus will be more directed and will therefore be able to achieve quicker results.
- A narrower focus will enable the fund's management or trustees to acquire

expertise and competencies that, over time, will translate into greater efficiency in the handling of operations. Lessons and skills acquired could subsequently be applied to other areas.

Reaching agreement on the goals and objectives of a trust fund will normally entail stakeholder meetings to discuss the fund's focus. However, if consensus cannot be reached in a collegial setting, an outside facilitator may be hired to help build consensus and arrive at a set of goals and objectives.

Goals and objectives specific to funds financed through bioprospecting activities

Biodiversity prospecting funds are distinct from conservation funds in that financial benefits are directly linked to a set of commercial activities. They seek to facilitate and ensure the equitable distribution of the benefits derived from biodiversity prospecting activities and the sustainable use of biological resources associated with prospecting. Their goals might include:

- Serve as the channel through which the benefits and economic rewards are distributed to the areas from which source species for drug or other product development are found.
- Improve the standard of living in target areas through community development initiatives, information, health care, education and communication. This would include support and assistance to rural families, particularly women and children and to other activities that will help alleviate poverty.
- Apply revenues to projects or ventures that will promote the conservation of biological diversity. For example, in the case of the Nigerian trust fund, biodiversity prospecting activities are intended to promote conservation, but through sustainable management of species in ways that promote biodiversity conservation, rather than support for protected areas (see Case Study 11.2).

- Promote improved ways of seeking the prior informed consent (PIC) of stakeholders. This would include collaboration and consultation with government, research institutions, and town associations, village heads and professional guilds of healers in order to determine the nature of compensation and priority projects in their localities.
- Improve domestic capacity to research local biodiversity, including capacity to conduct research on, and to standardize, traditional medical systems, participate in drug development efforts at a higher level and research tropical diseases. This would include technology transfer and capacity-building in forms such as the provision of equipment, know-how and training.

Origination document (constitution, charter, deed, articles of incorporation)

There are four kinds of origination documents:

1 Constitution.
2 Charter.
3 Deed.
4 Articles of incorporation and/or by-laws.

Despite the differences in name, the substance of the documents is the same. Origination documents are the legal documents that set up the trust, establishing the fund's goals and objectives, and institute the mechanisms by which grants will be awarded and other benefits distributed. Fundamentally, the origination document is the 'law' by which the new fund will be administered and by which the activities of the board and the fund will be directed and ultimately judged. While the document establishes the legal right in the board to initiate suits on behalf of the trust to effect its objectives, it also forms the basis for removing the board, or perhaps dissolving the trust when the goals and objectives are not carried out or there is wrong-doing.

The Constitution of the Verata Tikina Biodiversity Trust Fund and the Trust Fund Committee, created by the Verata Tikina Council in Fiji, specifies that the objective of the fund is to promote the sustainable development of Verata Tikina and its people. Specifically, the trust fund and its committee will invest the funds to ensure long-term sources of funds for sustainable development projects; select projects in priority areas of conservation, education and training, health and micro-enterprise, providing financial and technical resources for their implementation; and provide advice to the Tikina Council on sustainable development issues.

The Healing Forest Conservancy (HFC) (see Case Study 11.4) has developed a model constitution based upon its work with Shaman Pharmaceuticals' biodiversity prospecting activities in several countries. The HFC constitution includes general information about biodiversity-prospecting fund structures, as well as specific guidelines for the distribution of benefits and suggestions for the creation of technical committees that can be helpful in meeting the goals and objectives of the fund. Such committees are particularly important because boards typically only meet two or three times a year and need to rely on other bodies meeting more frequently to perform the groundwork, or to make on-the-spot decisions.

Governing structure

The governing board is made up of stakeholder representatives who make important decisions about the fund, such as defining the guiding principles for proposal selection and grant-making. The governing board's decisions should be open and transparent, and an internal checks-and-balances system should be in place (see Box 11.4).

The composition of the board is of the utmost importance because it can make or break the fund. A primary requirement of governing boards is that they represent the interests of all stakeholders, including government, community, industry and NGO members. As mentioned earlier, the board members must be dynamic, enthusiastic, well connected to the constituency they represent on the board (eg government, communities, scientists, private sector) and committed to conservation and sustainable development. Some consideration should also be given to how well the board members will work together. In some cases, successful boards have one 'super board member' (usually the chairman) who leads and shepherds the board and the fund to success during its infancy.

The board of the Nigerian Fund for Integrated Rural Development and Traditional Medicine (FIRD-TM) includes one traditional healer, four traditional medical practitioners, one representative from the Nigerian Federal Ministry of Health, a representative from the National Agency for Science and Engineering Infrastructure in the Nigerian Ministry of Science and Technology, a professor of medicine with extensive experience in traditional medicine, and a professor of pharmacology associated with the pharmaceutical industry. The professional and sectoral, as well as ethnic, diversity of the membership is part of a deliberate policy to ensure that as many relevant national

CASE STUDY 11.4 THE HEALING FOREST CONSERVANCY: TRUST FUND CONSTITUTION[2]

Katy Moran and Tom Mays

At the time of its incorporation in 1990 as a for-profit corporation, Shaman Pharmaceuticals, Inc founded the Healing Forest Conservancy (HFC), an independent non-profit foundation. HFC was established specifically to develop and implement a process to return long-term benefits to Shaman's collaborating countries and cultures after a product is commercialized.

The company provides immediate and medium-term benefits to collaborating cultures and countries during the drug discovery process. Through HFC, Shaman will donate a percentage of profits from commercial products to all company collaborators (some 30 other countries and culture groups) for as long as Shaman has a profit. HFC will distribute these long-term benefits, equally, to all the countries and cultures that are Shaman collaborators, regardless of where the plant sample or traditional knowledge that was commercialized originated. In such a financially unpredictable industry, spreading the benefits and risks among all Shaman collaborators increases opportunities for benefits.

Trust funds are proposed as financial mechanisms that receive and disburse long-term revenues generated from the commercial use of bioresources to a variety of stakeholders whose representatives serve as board members. Critical to the success of a fund is a constitution that serves as the general operative document, establishing the goals, objectives, rights and duties of the fund. A constitution also supplies a legally enforceable mechanism, under domestic law, for a trust fund. Trustees of the fund, as a collective entity, may institute legal proceedings in their capacity to achieve trust fund objectives.

HFC's constitution is a template to use for the benefit-sharing actions of the conservancy in many different countries. As stated under the mission of the conservancy, the model constitution is a legal document that is flexible enough to respond to unique conditions in the numerous countries where Shaman collaborates. It supplies a legal mechanism to widely disburse financial resources, over a long time frame, and within varied sectors of society. Highlights follow.

Sponsoring entity

The use of a sponsoring entity, such as a non-governmental organization (NGO), in the constitution is intended to facilitate the establishment of the fund. Such an entity may not exist in every country, however, and it may be necessary, in certain cases, to rely on other sponsors, such as governmental entities or universities, to establish the fund. It may also be possible to have the fund established independently by various groups joining together as founding members.

Healers' associations and culture groups

It is also possible to structure the fund without a membership and have the fund managed directly by a board of directors. The template constitution incorporates a membership component in order to promote greater community participation in the activities of the fund. The fund must be an open forum, and it should be easy to become a member. The provision requiring a two-thirds majority vote of all members ensures general agreement for the admission of a new member. It is possible that a sponsoring entity of the fund may insist on having ultimate approval for the admission of new members. While the sponsoring entity should be advised on who is made a new member of the fund, the sponsor should not be able to veto the admission of new members.

Unlike the admission of a member, removal of a member is intentionally made difficult and is subject to a unanimous vote requirement. This is in order to ensure that a single member is not removed by a simple majority of the members, due to some disagreement over one or more policies of the fund. Permitting non-members to serve on the board is designed to have the same effect as an outside director who can provide objective advice to the board. Inclusion of the reference to the selection of board members without regard to their ethnic, political or other background is particularly important for countries where the absence of such a provision may result in disparate treatment among various ethnic or other groups.

Governments

It is important to acknowledge the consent and support of each host-country government for the activities of the fund in order to minimize the risk that the fund is perceived as a threat to the sovereign right of the host-country government to exploit its own natural resources. However, this acknowledgement should not be viewed as undermining the independence of the fund and its autonomous operating authority as an NGO. The precise legal status of the fund will depend upon the laws of the host country wherein the fund is established. It is important that the fund is able to obtain the benefits normally associated with non-profit and charitable entities, such as exemption from taxation. The international character of the fund is intended to permit it to collaborate with similar entities established in other countries. The NGO status of the fund is equally important, as it reinforces its independence from the host government and permits it to participate in other NGO fora.

Distribution of benefits

Article VIII of the model constitution provides for the distribution of benefits to all stakeholders in accordance with the following guidelines:

- At least 50 per cent, but not more than 70 per cent, of available funds will be distributed to traditional healers' organizations and community development funds.
- At least 10 per cent, but not more than 15 per cent, of available funds will be distributed to national universities and other national institutions that share a commitment to the aims and objectives of the fund.
- At least 10 per cent, but not more than 15 per cent, of available funds will be distributed to the sponsoring entity for its furtherance of conservation and development activities.

Committees

The model constitution designates committees that are intended to assist the board of directors in allocating the benefits to be distributed by the fund. It is not intended that the committee membership is limited to members of the fund.

Benefits allocation committee
This committee will ensure that the benefits provided by the fund are allocated consistent with Article VIII of this constitution.

Training committee
This committee will serve as the liaison between the fund and scientists, traditional healers and any other individuals or organizations as the committee sees appropriate. It will actively promote the implementation of programmes or other mechanisms designed to train individuals in the areas of biodiversity conservation and traditional medicinal knowledge.

Educational committee
This committee will serve as the liaison between the fund and universities and other educational institutions and support university departments, and other individuals or groups who are committed to the education of individuals in the areas of biodiversity conservation and traditional medicinal knowledge.

Credit union committee
This committee will supervise the activities of the fund with respect to its lending programmes and make recommendations to the board of directors as to appropriate credit activities of the fund.

Other committees
The board of directors may, by resolution, approve the establishment of such other committees as may be required to achieve the objectives of the fund and as permitted by law.

constituents are represented as possible. The board's composition is intentionally diverse in order to encourage the meaningful exchange of ideas and to capture the range of experiences represented by individual members (see Case Study 11.2).

In comparison, the board of the Forest People's Fund in Suriname is relatively small, with only five members, including two representatives from the Saramaka Maroons, two representatives from Conservation International (CI) and one representative from the Surinamese pharmaceutical partner. The smaller size of this board reflects the regional and community focus of the fund (see Case Study 11.1).

Equally important when deciding upon the composition of the board is the fact that the structure of the board affects outside perceptions of, and attitudes towards, the fund. For example, if a board does not have government representation, the government may distrust the organization and believe that it is trying to usurp its right to determine the disposition of natural resources. On the other hand, if there are too many government representatives, NGOs, communities, researchers and other stakeholders, it may feel that the fund serves only the national government's agenda. The US Agency for International Development (USAID) and the Global Environment Facility (GEF), for example – both donors to conservation funds – will not contribute to the capital of a fund whose board has more than 50 per cent government representatives. These structural dynamics reflect some aid agencies' desire to promote and build civil societies.

Securing the explicit support and goodwill of the national government is very desirable and could be achieved by affording it limited or nominal participation without sacrificing the independence or objectivity of the board. Operating procedures for boards should also be clarified to ensure transparency, checks and balances and the maintenance of standards over time. While an emphasis may naturally be placed on the financial activities of the fund, provisions for the monitoring and evaluation of the grant-making process should also be instituted. Mechanisms such as audits and annual financial reporting must be designed and implemented to measure both financial management and grant-making aspects of the fund's work. In many cases, provisions to that effect are imposed by the donors in the grant agreement.

Financial structure

The financial structure of a trust fund can vary depending upon the time period and goals of the fund. There are four main options for the structure of a trust fund:

1 Endowment.
2 Revolving fund.
3 Sinking fund.
4 A combination of two or more of these structures.

An **endowment** is a fund that maintains a bulk sum of money as principal and only disburses the income earned on that amount (IPG, 1995). Only under specific circumstances can the capital (*corpus*) of an endowment be invaded. The Mexican Fund for Nature Conservation (FMCN) is an endowment whose one main objective is to support and strengthen the capacity of Mexican NGOs through mid- and long-term financing of initiatives for conservation and sustainable natural-resource use. The initial capital of the fund was US$36 million in 1994, including US$16 million granted by the GEF for protected area management and US$20 million from USAID for sustainable development (ECOFONDO, 1996).

A **revolving fund** is a fund to which new assets are added periodically (annually, for example) through fees, taxes or levies collected (IPG, 1995). The Belize Protected Areas Conservation Trust is a revolving fund whose capital comes

---

BOX 11.4 POSSIBLE CHECKS AND BALANCES FOR FUND MANAGEMENT

Checks and balances include the following requirements:

- Advisory committees should include outside participants who will provide a fresh perspective.
- Give certain board members veto power or require super-majorities (75 per cent, 80 per cent or 100 per cent) on certain issues.
- Stagger board membership terms, with members serving terms that expire at different times.
- Institute international arbitration and dispute-resolution provisions.
- Include detailed provisions on auditing, accounting and reporting requirements.

Source: Spergel, 1993

partially from a US$3.75 visitor fee, as well as 20 per cent of all site entry fees, recreation licences and permits and cruise ship fees. Five per cent of the collected revenues are managed as a permanent endowment for emergency purposes (ECOFONDO, 1996).

A **sinking fund** is designed to disburse its entire capital, including its income, over a designated period of time (IPG, 1995). This type of structure can be well adapted to the funding of projects with development or income-generating potential that are expected to become self-sufficient after an initial seed money or startup phase. The Dominican Republic's Pronatura exemplifies a sinking fund: donations are converted to national currency as they are received and are immediately deposited in separate accounts for each project (Mikitin, 1995). Sinking funds are rare, however, partially because of the perception that the time and effort necessary for their creation merit a more permanent structure. Furthermore, most conservation-oriented projects require long-term funding that sinking funds cannot guarantee. Therefore, most sinking components end up being one composite feature of more complex structures.

As expertise builds in the field of conservation funds, the people in charge of their design have come to realize that the most useful structures may involve a combination of two or three funding mechanisms. For example, it is good to bear in mind that, at the onset of most structures, the fund will be under pressure to demonstrate results and success quite rapidly; but it must not lose sight of, or sacrifice, its long-term sustainability. It might therefore be advisable to sink a percentage of the fund and finance some priority exercises or projects so that immediate impact can be felt by the different stakeholders, while the remainder of the funds remains as an endowment. In the case of biodiversity prospecting funds, staggered revenues, such as milestone payments or royalties, can contribute to the fund in a revolving manner; they can also be expended to increase the endowment.

Sources of funding

Conservation trust funds traditionally receive funding from three categories of donors: multilateral donors, bilateral donors and private and NGO donors. In some cases a fourth category is represented by host-government donations. Examples of multilateral donor organizations are the World Bank/Global Environment Facility (GEF) and the United Nations Development Programme (UNDP). The United States and Canada are examples of countries who contribute bilaterally to environmental funds through agencies such as the USAID and the Canadian Agency for International Development (CIDA). The MacArthur Foundation has supported training and design work for the creation of conservation funds, and has contributed to capitalization. Some national governments have also committed specific amounts to funds in their own countries. For example, the Royal Thai government has earmarked specific budgetary items to be disbursed directly to the Thailand Environmental Fund and indirectly through support programmes. Most of these institutions are potential sources of initial startup funding, or seed money, for funds.

Although startup funds are crucial to any fund's development, ongoing capitalization is equally important. Sustained funding ensures that activities and programmes continue and that there are funds available for new projects and increased need for existing ones. Biodiversity prospecting funds derive income across time from sample fees and upfront payments, milestone payments and royalties (see Chapter 8). Milestone payments are attached to various stages of drug discovery (eg screening and identification of active compounds) and development (eg pharmacology, safety studies, phase I, II and III clinical trials, or other steps linked to government regulatory requirements). As a promising sample moves through discovery and development, payments can automatically be made to a fund. Long-term fund revenues might come from licensing fees and royalties on net sales of a commercial product (see Chapter 8).

Funds created in order to be capitalized primarily from biodiversity prospecting projects might also receive additional financing from donors, as long as the fund's goals match the donor's priorities. In some situations, it may be advisable to widen the funds' goals to cover general conservation objectives, or create a biodiversity prospecting 'sub-account' in an existing conservation trust fund. By linking biodiversity-prospecting trust funds to conservation funds, a track record of successful programming and fiscal responsibility might more easily be established that would increase chances of funding from the donor community.

Location of trust and assets

Trusts must be physically located in a selected country. Two main components of trusts that must have a physical base are the trust's board of trustees and the trust's assets. The components may be located in different countries, depending upon various factors and may result in either of the following two possible scenarios (see Box 11.5):

1 A domestic trust with a domestic and/or off-shore asset management account.
2 An off-shore trust with off-shore asset management.

In determining where to locate a trust, the following should be considered:

- Are there good reasons not to locate the trust in the country? For example, is the government stable? Does the local economy offer sufficient investment opportunities?
- Even if the country's government is stable, is there a legal framework to support a trust, foundation, etc?
- What types of investment laws exist in the country? Will the country prohibit off-shore investment? Is the local economy stable? Is there enough technical expertise to manage the assets domestically?
- Are the intended beneficiaries located in only one country?

If the answers to these questions are affirmative, then a local trust would be advisable. If negative, then an off-shore fund would be best. Cases will not always be clear, however, and it may be necessary to come up with a creative solution. Other options may include: establishing a trust by national act; obtaining a government exemption to invest abroad; establishing a trust under the auspices of the United Nations or other international agency; and/or establishing a two-tier trust. This last mechanism may work particularly well because it allows an off-shore trust to be combined with local beneficiaries.

Implementation

There are several important steps which must be completed in order to implement a biodiversity prospecting fund. They include the following:

- *Draft the foundation's deed and its by-laws.* These legal documents establish the legal identity of the fund, state its

---

BOX 11.5 PROS AND CONS OF TRUST LOCATION

Domestic funds are local institutions whose boards hold title to their assets. Their capital, however, can be invested domestically or offshore. Domestic management of funds can increase local management capacity as well as the perception of national ownership, and can even contribute to domestic awareness and community participation in environmental issues (Mikitin, 1995). However, domestically managed funds can suffer from political instability, thin capital markets, currency devaluation or legal status conflicts with other countries. Bolivia's domestically managed National Environmental Fund, for example, lost much of its autonomy when a new government took control in 1993 (ECOFONDO, 1996). Domestic management of the fund, along with the fund's close ties to the national government, led to significant political influence on the fund, which impaired the fund's activities and undermined its principles.

Off-shore funds can be advantageous because they provide a secure hard-currency market and access to professional asset managers, both of which foster donor confidence. Off-shore management, on the other hand, does not foster domestic capacity-building or a sense of national ownership of assets, as can be the case with domestically managed funds. In addition, this type of management may not respond as promptly and effectively to the needs of the designated beneficiaries. It may also result in a lost 'connection' with the intended objectives and targets if the line of communication is not properly established.

Domestic fund with off-shore asset management or a 'two-tier' structure allows a domestic fund to be paired with an off-shore trust. The off-shore trust holds title to the assets invested off shore, ensuring that hard-currency investments are located within an account in a secure market. The local fund is designated as the sole beneficiary of the trust and ensures that local stakeholders are fully represented. The local fund holds title to local assets (eg proceeds from a debt swap) and can choose to invest some of the benefits domestically (eg government bonds or interest-bearing accounts in a local bank).

---

purpose and goals and create its governing structure.

- *Select the members of the board.* The members should represent different backgrounds – culturally, professionally, sectorally (private, government, non-profit) and be willing to use their expertise as advocates for the fund and not to act simply as managers.

- *Develop operation manuals.* Of particular importance is the drafting of guidelines and rules for the grant process, including required materials, criteria for successful applicants and defined areas of funding. The fund may need to engage a consultant in order to help draft these manuals and to implement the guidelines through the training of staff. With more than 40 new or emerging conservation funds throughout the world, there is now a good selection of existing manuals in several languages that can be used as models.

- *Select administrative staff and management.* These professionals will prepare budgets and work plans; develop and administer the grant process; develop and implement financial management systems; arrange for external auditing; and develop fund-raising strategies.

BOX 11.6 SOME LESSONS LEARNED IN THE DESIGN OF TRUST FUNDS

Case-specific lessons learned

Protected Areas Conservation Trust (PACT), Belize

Recurrent costs (salaries for existing and additional park guards, forest rangers and other field staff) were not accounted for in the original list of funded activities (ECOFONDO, 1996). The lesson learned was that planning must include consideration of existing short-term, ongoing and long-term costs, in addition to those of new programmes.

National Fund for State-Protected Natural Areas (PROFONANPE), Peru

Without a tradition of charitable giving to environmental or other non-profit organizations, organizers had to look beyond in-country giving and rely on outside sources of funds, primarily debt-swaps (ECOFONDO, 1996). The lesson learned was that debt swaps are excellent opportunities for countries where there is great economic hardship. Debt-swap proceeds, however, were restricted to certain activities and did not include the fund's own operating costs. It is important to secure ongoing funding for day-to-day operations of the fund until income begins to accrue. Peru's PROFONANPE has also demonstrated that small administrative bodies can run successful funds. In 1996, the permanent staff included only four personnel: a coordinator, accounting coordinator, secretary/assistant and driver/messenger.

Fund for Integrated Rural Development and Traditional Medicine (FIRD-TM), Nigeria

The principal lesson learned in developing the fund – still in its early stages – is that a fully participatory process, involving all stakeholders, is the key to the successful design of a fund. Furthermore, a fund that considers the local/political peculiarities on the ground is essential in order to fund stability and reduce potential areas of conflict or friction (see Case Study 11.2).

Forest People's Fund, Suriname

The biodiversity prospecting project, as a whole, including the agreement process among NGOs and the private sector, must be based upon clear communication, reliability, honesty, and trust. Experience has also shown that some communities may need significant help from fund staff to develop and write proposals, and to participate in the application process itself (see Case Study 11.1).

National Environment Fund, Panama

This project yielded lessons on the value of collaborating with existing funds. The bioprospecting fund is capitalized by a biodiversity prospecting project, currently organized as a sub-account within a larger national fund, Fundación Natura. The fund contributes overhead to the larger institution in exchange for the use of administrative structure. This arrangement allows the bioprospecting fund to focus on fund-raising and implementation of other activities (see Case Study 11.3).

General lesson learned: the importance of champions

During the early stages of organization, there needs to be one person who shoulders the responsibility of driving the process forward. This person may or may not be from the host country, but should be chosen by the organizing group and have the skills that help to catalyse the process. This person will:

- contact local legal counsel and assess the requirements for setting up a trust, and engage his or her services to advise the forming trust;
- scout for additional organizers, qualified personnel and facilities, and begin to pre-select a possible board, keeping in mind the guidelines mentioned below;
- coordinate efforts by the group to enlist donors, including making contacts with international agencies and NGOs;
- hire a consultant skilled in the development of conservation trust funds.

Once the initial stages are complete, this person would likely become the executive director of the fund.

- *Establish technical committees to advise the board.* For example, a finance committee would advise and inform the board about the fund's economic health and potential investments, and can aid the management team. Scientific committees might advise on research priorities.
- *Train the board, managers and administrative staff.* These groups will need training in fund management and identification of priorities for the fund's constituents.
- *Inform potential fund beneficiaries about the fund's activities and grant application process.* Provisions in the operations manual may need to include outreach to local communities to inform them, help them develop proposals and assist with the grant-making process as a whole.
- *Draft a monitoring and evaluation plan.* These plans are essential to ensure that the fund meets its goals and continues to be responsive to changing needs.

Criteria for fund disbursement and compensation

Once the feasibility and design phases are settled, criteria for disbursement of income must be agreed upon. In the case of biodiversity prospecting funds, the relative contribution of different stakeholders must be assessed and difficult issues addressed, such as sharing of benefits with individuals versus communities/institutions; distribution of benefits across communities and society, including to those not directly involved in research; and the most effective ways in which to promote conservation and sustainable development objectives (see Box 11.7).

Criteria such as the following can act as a starting point for the development of more detailed criteria that are used in evaluating grant proposals:

- Does the project conform with the underlying principles of the fund?
- Will it help to promote the conservation of biodiversity and sustainable development?

BOX 11.7 FUND DISTRIBUTION

Suriname fund distribution mechanisms

A multifaceted approach was developed in the Suriname project to distribute benefits, including:

- a long-term research agreement that controls the ownership, licensing and royalty fee structure for any potential drug development;
- a statement of understanding that further defines the parties' intentions regarding the distribution of royalties among Surinamese institutions;
- a trust document establishing the Forest People's Fund (which is capitalized in part with upfront payments);
- provision for the transfer of technology and other forms of non-monetary compensation to the Suriname.

FIRD-TM formula and criteria for fund disbursement

Apart from deciding upon the sectoral allocation of funds to targets and beneficiaries, the board of management has some general guidelines and criteria stipulated to guide it in allocating and disbursing funds.

Guidelines and criteria for project funding include the following:

- The project must have clear, definite and identifiable results.
- The project must be sustainable and should have a reasonably attainable endpoint.
- The board should, as much as possible, maintain a fairly balanced geographical spread in approving projects for funding.

Guidelines and criteria for the funding of individuals include:

- Consideration of the relative contribution to the discovery of useful materials or drug development.

- Will it meet the priority needs of target communities/institutions/stakeholders, as defined by these groups?
- Does it recognize and reward the contributions of stakeholders (eg communities, scientists, government, research institutions, conservation projects) to the biodiversity prospecting project?
- Will it promote the development of domestic and local capacity to study biodiversity; to conduct research on tropical or other locally important diseases; to standardize traditional medical systems; and to improve capacity to participate at a higher level in drug discovery and development?

A clearly defined set of criteria, a reasonably simple application and a transparent evaluation process are all necessary in order to facilitate prompt response to potential grantees and the release of funds to approved beneficiaries or projects.

Flexibility and efficiency

The creation of a trust fund will not be the answer to all organizational needs. Sometimes it may be more efficient to channel money through a local NGO or to integrate a biodiversity prospecting trust fund into an existing conservation fund as a 'sub-account', thereby reducing the costs associated with building a fund from the ground up. An integrated fund might be particularly attractive in the context of biodiversity prospecting because financial benefits often arrive after a number of years (sometimes decades), or in smaller sums spread across many years. Without a steady source of income, a biodiversity prospecting fund risks running out of operating finances and risks jeopardizing its new programmes. By associating with an already established fund, a biodiversity prospecting fund could focus its resources on substantive activities, and is thereby allowed greater flexibility in the formation process.

Conclusion

One of the principal lessons learned from existing funds is that a system predicated on a wide consultative and participatory process will increase the chances of acceptance by the principal stakeholders and, therefore, of the fund's success. Furthermore, since many countries have yet to enact relevant access and benefit-sharing (ABS) measures, parties need not wait for legislation in order to commence a process of compensating relevant stakeholders, especially where the prospects of such enactment are not immediate. Even in cases where national legislation has been passed, the sharing of financial benefits continues to present numerous challenges, and many governments are calling for the establishment of trust funds. Benefit-sharing systems are sought that are based on fairness, are transparent and support the objectives of the Convention on Biological Diversity (CBD). These systems should also be flexible and should allow incorporation of the multisectoral, multistakeholder agendas that characterize biodiversity prospecting relationships. The trust-fund model presents an opportunity to develop this type of system for the sharing of financial benefits resulting from biodiversity prospecting partnerships.

Notes

1   The International Cooperative Biodiversity Groups (ICBG) is a US government-funded programme sponsored by the National Institutes of Health (NIH), the National Science Foundation (NSF) and the US Agency for International Development (USAID).
2   For a copy of the Trust Fund Constitution, visit the HFC website at www.shaman.com/healing-forest.html or the People and Plants website at www.rbgkew.org.uk/peopleplants/.

Section V

NATIONAL POLICY CONTEXT

Photograph by Sarah A Laird

A group of researchers, NGOs, government representatives and others meet in the Limbe Botanic Garden in 1995. In this photograph, they are standing before a specimen of Ancistrocladus korupensis *which yields the promising anti-HIV compound michellamine-B, and raised widespread discussion within Cameroon on access and benefit-sharing issues*

Chapter 12

Developing and implementing national measures for genetic resources access regulation and benefit-sharing

Charles V Barber, Lyle Glowka and Antonio G M La Viña

Introduction

Prior to December 1993, when the Convention on Biological Diversity (CBD) came into force, no international legal regime existed to regulate access to genetic resources and to promote the sharing of benefits arising from their commercial and scientific use. While many countries have long possessed regulations governing access, and use of, *biological* resources – such as timber, fisheries resources and botanical or zoological samples – these measures do not deal with the specifically genetic component of biological resources. In recent decades, however, technological changes have given genetic resources more potential economic value as raw material for the development of pharmaceuticals and other products, and they emerged as a contentious political and legal issue during the negotiation of the CBD.[1]

On the one hand, the industrialized nations generally argued that unfettered exchange of genetic resources among countries was essential for the continued progress of scientific research and the development of new products in agriculture and industry. On the other hand,

developing countries argued that direct benefits from the use of genetic resources removed from their territories accrued largely to developed countries with the capacities to collect, modify and market them (Hendrickx et al, 1994; Mugabe et al, 1997a).

At the same time, developing countries – relatively rich in biological diversity – were increasingly pressured by developed countries to conserve and sustainably use their biological resources for the benefit of the world at large. The developing countries therefore proposed that the CBD include the establishment of international legal obligations that would provide the broad contours of a new international approach to ensuring the sharing of benefits from the use of genetic resources, as between parties to the convention. This view prevailed and is embodied in CBD Article 15 on 'Access to Genetic Resources', complemented (and sometimes complicated) by a number of other CBD provisions (Barber, 1994).

This chapter reviews this new international legal framework and discusses its

> ## BOX 12.1 WHAT ARE 'GENETIC RESOURCES' UNDER THE CONVENTION ON BIOLOGICAL DIVERSITY?
>
> The CBD defines genetic resources as genetic material of actual or potential value, and defines genetic material as 'any material of plant, animal, microbial or other origin containing functional units of heredity'. Functional units of heredity include all genetic elements containing DNA (deoxyribonucleic acid) and, in some cases RNA (ribonucleic acid). Thus, 'genetic material' under the CBD includes, for example, a seed, cuttings, semen or an individual organism, as well as DNA extracted from a plant, animal or microbe, such as a chromosome or gene. On the other hand, a biochemical extract is not genetic material if it does not contain functional units of heredity (although national-level access and benefit-sharing (ABS) measures often cover biochemicals). The CBD does not cover human genetic resources.
>
> Article 15 (3) makes it clear that the CBD's provisions on access and benefit-sharing only apply to genetic resources collected after the CBD's entry into force in a particular state. Therefore, parties with collections of genetic resources that were collected originally from other parties before the entry into force of the convention are not obliged to share the benefits derived from their use with the latter. Nevertheless, many are seeking to do so in an effort to uphold the 'spirit' of the CBD.

implications for countries as they develop their own legal frameworks governing genetic resources access and benefit-sharing (ABS) in accordance with the mandate of the CBD. The chapter's primary focus is on the scope and content of ABS legislation. However, it also discusses the broader policy decisions that must underlie and direct specific legislative choices, the importance of a participatory multistakeholder legislative development process and issues of administration and institutional capacity that must be addressed if legislation is to be effectively implemented. Examples of national and sub-national measures already in place or under development are used throughout. Finally, the experience of the Philippines – where national ABS measures have been in place since 1995 – is presented in some detail to illuminate the practical challenges other countries are likely to face as they develop their own ABS regimes.

Access and benefit-sharing provisions in the Convention on Biological Diversity

The CBD's provisions on access are premised on five fundamental concepts:

1   Sovereignty over genetic resources.
2   Facilitating access to genetic resources between parties.
3   Access subject to mutually agreed terms.
4   Access subject to prior informed consent (PIC).
5   Equitable sharing of benefits arising from the utilization of genetic resources.

Sovereignty over genetic resources

CBD Article 15 (1) states that 'Recognizing the sovereign rights of States over their natural resources, the authority to determine access to genetic resources rests with the national governments and is subject to national legislation'. This provision does not *require* countries to restrict access to genetic resources, it merely recognizes their right to do so. It is also important to note that the CBD's recognition of state 'sovereignty' over genetic resources does not grant states a property right over genetic resources. Indeed, ownership of genetic resources is not addressed at all by the CBD and is a function of national or sub-national law. Most current national law, however, does not address the question of who actually owns genetic resources (as distinct from biological resources), and this is one of the key questions that national policy and legislation must address at the outset.

Facilitating access

State sovereignty over genetic resources gives governments wide leeway in how they may decide to determine and regulate access to such resources, but it is not an absolute right. CBD Article 15 (2) makes it clear that national measures must not unduly restrict access, stating that 'Each Contracting Party shall endeavour to create conditions to facilitate access to genetic resources for environmentally sound uses by other Contracting Parties and not to impose restrictions that run counter to the objectives of this Convention'. Blanket prohibitions on access to genetic resources, if applied to other parties, would therefore contravene the terms of the CBD. If, however, a country decided that it needed to severely restrict access until such time as it could put in place an effective system for deter-mining and regulating access and for ensuring the sharing of benefits, it would not be violating either the spirit or the letter of the CBD.

Mutually agreed terms

Article 15 (4) of the CBD states that access, where granted, will be on 'mutually agreed terms' between the party providing genetic resources and a potential user, implying a negotiation between the two. A successful negotiation will thus result in an 'access agreement' of some kind, which might be in the form of a contract, a material transfer agreement (MTA) or a research agreement (see Chapter 10). Whatever the form, such agreements will be the primary means to:

- authorize access to genetic resources;
- control their subsequent uses; and
- establish the terms and procedures for the sharing of benefits.

Access agreements do not necessarily have to be negotiated with the national government in every situation; it depends upon a country's legal framework. Where national legislation in a particular country places ownership or other rights over genetic resources in the hands of sub-national government units, research institutions, indigenous groups, individuals or local communities, these entities might be the primary party to contract with the entity seeking access. The role of the state might be to set minimum terms and conditions for such contracts and to approve each one. Alternatively, the state might conclude a separate contract with potential users specifying those conditions, or there might be a third party in a tripartite contract. A state might retain ownership rights but delegate the exercise of those rights to another entity – such as a local government or research institution.

Prior informed consent (PIC)

Article 15 (5) of the CBD established that 'access to genetic resources shall be subject to prior informed consent of the Contracting Party providing such resources'. This means that *prior* to a potential user gaining access to genetic resources, it must obtain the consent of the government based on *information* provided by the potential user, such as how the genetic resources will be collected, used and passed to third parties. The specifics of what constitutes PIC, and the procedures for ensuring that it has been obtained, are not dealt with in the CBD and must be spelt out in national legislation.

> *'The CBD has many good ideas. The practical relevance of these good ideas, however, remains to be seen... Such practical relevance can perhaps only evolve as responses to any specific situation. The law and policy can provide the wider framework for action. The rest would to a large extent depend on political will to achieve equity and fairness'* R V Anuradha, lawyer and activist, New Delhi, India (Anuradha, 1998).

Article 15 (5) requires only that national governments give prior informed consent, but other CBD provisions – as well as the national laws of many countries – imply that PIC should also be obtained from the local or indigenous communities from whose territories genetic resources are taken. Article 8 (j), for example, calls on each contracting party to:

'*...subject to its national legislation, respect, preserve and maintain knowledge, innovations and practices of indigenous and local communities embodying traditional lifestyles relevant for the conservation and sustainable use of biological diversity and promote their wider application with the approval and involvement of the holders of such knowledge, innovations and practices and* encourage the equitable sharing of the benefits arising from the utilization of such knowledge, innovations and practices' [emphasis added].

This provision not only calls on the state to ensure that local and indigenous knowledge, practices and rights are protected, but also that the communities approve the use of their knowledge and resources. This is enhanced by Article 10 (c), which calls on the state to 'protect and encourage customary use of biological resources in accordance with traditional cultural practices that are compatible with conservation or sustainable use requirements'. It can thus be inferred that access to genetic resources owned by local or indigenous communities, or located within their customary land and water territories, is subject to customary law (laws of traditional communities) where such law is established. To ensure that customary law and practices are enforced and respected, it is important that the communities' prior informed consent is obtained before accessing and collecting genetic resources within their customary sphere of authority and control.

> *'I wish the politicians and diplomats who write these policies would go out in the field and try and get prior informed consent'* biotechnology firm representative, 1998 (ten Kate and Laird, 1999).

'Our peoples have for generations been involved in the discovery, improvement and conservation of innumerable plant species and animal breeds for the benefit of themselves and mankind as a whole. Nevertheless, under the cover of international treaties and national laws imposed in our countries, we have looked on helplessly as companies and research institutes have made use of our knowledge, appropriated our resources and made money from what they call "their inventions"' Antonio Jacanimijoy, Coordinating Body of Indigenous Organizations of the Amazon Basin (COICA) (Jacanamijoy, 1998).

Benefit-sharing

Article 15 (7) of the CBD requires each contracting party to take:

'...legislative, administrative or policy measures...with the aim of sharing in a fair and equitable way the results of research and development and benefits arising from the commercial and other utilization of genetic resources with the Contracting Party providing such resources. Such sharing shall be upon mutually agreed terms.'

In formulating measures to regulate access to its genetic resources, therefore, a country needs to pay particular attention to terms and methods for the sharing of benefits, since benefit-sharing is the core objective of regulating access.

In addition, a country where genetic resources obtained from another country are being utilized – whether directly by the state or by a person or legal entity resident by law within the state's jurisdiction – has an obligation to institute measures to ensure benefit-sharing with the providing country. Such 'user-country' measures provide 'provider countries' with an incentive to simplify regulations and thereby facilitate access. As the CBD-constituted Expert Panel on Access to Genetic Resources and Benefit-Sharing concluded in October 1999:

'The degree of legislative simplicity in countries providing genetic resources will increase to the extent that countries and organizations receiving genetic resources take the legislative, administrative or policy measures to offer security to providers that these resources are utilized in accordance with the terms of the Convention' (SCBD, 1999).

Examples of potential benefits that a country might obtain from the use of its genetic resources are noted in the CBD and include:

- participation in scientific research (Article 15 (6));
- a share in commercial benefits generated by use of genetic resources (Article 15 (7));
- access to and transfer of technology making use of genetic resources (Article 16 (3));
- participation in biotechnological research based on genetic resources (Article 19 (3)); and
- priority access to results and benefits resulting from biotechnological use of any genetic resources provided (Article 19 (2)).

None of the benefit-sharing provisions in the CBD, however, actual *require* benefit-sharing. This probably reflects the political reality that most such benefits are generated by the private sector, while the CBD benefit-sharing provisions apply only between its parties – national governments (Glowka, 1998). Individual governments, therefore, are left to develop their own approaches to – and conduct their own negotiations with – the private sector with respect to benefit-sharing. Considerable experience already exists, however, with various arrangements for sharing different kinds of benefits that have been worked out under contractual arrangements (see Table 12.1).

Initial choices that will influence development of national access and benefit-sharing measures

Before moving to the stage of actually developing specific legislative or regulatory enactments, countries seeking to develop national ABS measures must establish a broad policy framework within which to do so. Firstly, countries must decide what their basic stance on the utilization of genetic resources is. Should it be state policy to encourage, tolerate or discourage bioprospecting activities? Secondly, countries need to determine the best strategy for developing ABS measures within their own legal and political contexts. Choices include modification of existing laws and regulations, integration of ABS concerns in new framework environmental or biodiversity laws, and the creation of new stand-alone legal instruments focused specifically on ABS issues. In countries with federal systems, the division of authority to regulate ABS between central and sub-national governments will also have to be clarified (see Box 12.2). Thirdly, countries must decide to what extent intellectual property rights (IPRs) issues will be addressed by proposed ABS measures, if at all. Fourthly, countries need to elaborate a strategic approach to benefit-sharing. What are the scientific, technological, commercial, conservation and development needs of the country and how might ABS measures strategically address them?

Establishing national policy on the utilization of genetic resources

Policy-makers and other stakeholders need to reach an initial consensus on general policy towards the use of genetic resources, especially bioprospecting activities. A country may choose to promote, tolerate or discourage bioprospecting, based on assessment of its own interests and objectives. This is largely a political decision rather than a technical matter, but the decision has important legal and technical implications.

> *'Western scientists worry about a gene war here, that China will close its doors. But we get more from an open door'* Zhu Lihuang, Deputy Director, Institute of Genetics, Beijing, China (*Time*, 1998).

If, like Costa Rica, a country decides that it wishes to encourage bioprospecting as part of a national biodiversity policy, there are at least two implications for the development of national ABS measures. Firstly, the system put in place must be relatively simple and attractive to the private sector and international research institutions, without unduly burdensome transaction costs and bureaucratic red tape (see Box 12.3). Practically, this means that state regulation will be fairly minimal, provid-

Table 12.1 *Benefit-sharing arrangements in selected genetic resource access agreements*

Resource type	Parties to agreement	Short-term benefits	Long-term benefits
Trychopus zeylanicus, a wild plant with anti-fatigue properties known to the Kani tribe of Kerala, India, and developed into a drug (Jeevni) by the Tropical Botanic Garden and Research Institute (TBGRI).	• Kani tribal community • TBGRI • pharmaceutical company to which TBGRI licensed the drug	• licence fee from pharmaceutical firm to TBGRI • TBGRI shares 50 per cent of licence fee with Kani tribal community	• 2 per cent royalty at ex-factory prices to be paid to TBGRI • TBGRI pays 50 per cent of royalty payments it receives to Kani tribal community • additional Kani income and employment through cultivation of plant • protection of associated tree species by cultivation of plant
Micro-organisms capable of surviving in extreme conditions found in thermal features of Yellowstone National Park (YNP), US.	• Yellowstone National Park (YNP), US • Diversa Corporation (firm conducting bioprospecting of the micro-organisms)	• US$100,000 payment from Diversa to YNP, over five years, to be offset against future royalties • transfer of DNA extraction kits to YNP • training of YNP staff in sampling and DNA fingerprinting techniques	• undisclosed royalties of up to 10 per cent to be paid by Diversa to YNP upon commercialization of a product derived from genetic resources sourced in YNP; royalty rates based on a sliding scale depending upon end use of research result and magnitude of sales
Calophyllum spp, a group of species found in Sarawak, Malaysia, containing compounds (calanolides) that are promising for the development of anti-HIV compounds.	• University of Illinois, Chicago • National Cancer Institute (NCI), US • Sarawak state government • Medichem Research, Inc	• input of international scientific expertise to Sarawak • training for local scientists in bioprospecting lab techniques • establishment of a joint venture between Sarawak government and Medichem Research encompassing all patents held on Calanolides	• 50 per cent of future royalties on any drug developed with patents held by joint venture to be paid to Sarawak government (the remaining 50 per cent paid to Medichem)

369

Resource type	Parties to agreement	Short-term benefits	Long-term benefits
Wild genetic resources found in the forests of Suriname, which are being collected and analysed for potential pharmaceutical uses. Collection is carried out in part on the basis of traditional knowledge held by local tribes about the medicinal qualities of various forest species.	• Virginia Polytechnic Institute and State University (VPISU), US • Conservation International (CI: a conservation NGO), US • Bedrijf Geneesmiddelen Voorziening Suriname (BGVS: local pharmaceutical firm owned by Suriname government) • Missouri Botanical Garden (MBG), US • Bristol-Myers Squibb (B-MS: multinational pharmaceutical firm) • Walter Reed Army Hospital, US (screening plants for anti-malarial properties) • local tribal groups with traditional knowledge of medicinal plants	• employment/incomes for traditional healers, field collectors and others • training and technology transfer for Surinamese research institutions • building capacity for local pharmaceutical production • strengthening the national botanical inventory • recording and securing of tribal knowledge • establishment of Forest People Fund (FPF) for community development, health care and conservation projects	• joint ownership of patents by tribal groups where their knowledge is a basis for development of a product. • payment of royalties on future products to Suriname on a sliding scale depending upon proportion of local genetic resources/traditional knowledge contribution • potential discovery of more effective treatments for malaria

Source: SCBD, 1998

BOX 12.2 DEVELOPING ACCESS AND BENEFIT-SHARING MEASURES IN COUNTRIES WITH FEDERAL SYSTEMS

In some countries, significant powers over natural resources are vested in states or provinces, and national legislation may be limited to creating or amending one or more framework laws, promoting harmonization and coordination, and providing follow-up assistance to provincial or state governments in developing their own, more detailed, rules. Since regulating access to genetic resources is a new area of law and policy that is generally not envisioned or mentioned in constitutional provisions allocating powers between federal and state or provincial governments, clarifying the constitutional legal status of genetic resources is a crucial first step in countries with federal systems.

A key first step for federal countries is authoritative legal analysis that can form the basis for a consensual political decision on the relative powers of central and state or provincial governments. Legal analysts advising the government of Malaysia, for example, have concluded that the incorporation of relevant access and benefit-sharing (ABS) provisions under an all-encompassing federal act would supersede the constitutional power of the federal government, but that their incorporation in existing sectoral framework laws on forestry, fisheries and wildlife is constitutionally sound (Mullard, 1998; see also Box 12.4).

A similar assessment was undertaken in 1998 by the Australian Commonwealth-State Working Group on Access to Biological Resources, which proposed that the country strive to develop a 'nationally consistent' approach on the part of the states and territories, in light of the legal, administrative and political difficulties that developing a uniform national policy would entail (Blakeney, 1998).

In India, a draft biological diversity act under consideration during 1999 proposes the creation of a national biodiversity authority, as well as state biodiversity boards, the powers and mandates of each reflecting the relative powers of the state and federal governments over various aspects of biological and genetic resources (Kothari, 1999).

By contrast, Brazil has not conducted this type of analysis, with the result that both state governments (Amapa, Acre, Sao Paulo) and the federal government have taken the initiative to draft or enact their own access laws before resolving the constitutional federalism questions. Indeed, the federal government has proposed a constitutional amendment that would firmly establish the federal government's power over ABS issues, a move which has created consternation at the state level (Environmental Policy Studies Workshop, 1999).

ing minimum standards (such as prior informed consent, mutually agreed terms and some form of benefit-sharing), but largely leaving the details of access agreements to private contracts entered into between providers and users (eg a local university and a foreign pharmaceutical firm) for access to, and use of, particular genetic resources.

Secondly, a country who wishes to encourage bioprospecting needs to add value to its stock of genetic resources, which involves investing in building scientific capacity. Costa Rica's National Institute of Biodiversity (InBio), for example, provides bioprospectors much more than access to raw genetic material. By building up its own scientific capacity in taxonomy and creating an efficient information system on its collections, it is able to offer access to genetic resources in a systematic, reliable and efficient manner

BOX 12.3 INDUSTRY REACTIONS TO CBD PROVISIONS AND NATIONAL MEASURES CONCERNING GENETIC RESOURCES ACCESS AND BENEFIT-SHARING

The CBD is a treaty between states, but it is of central importance to business. Provisions of the CBD on access and benefit-sharing (ABS) and the national laws that implement them set the scene for any company or individual seeking access to samples of genetic resources for scientific research, or as the starting point for commercial development.

Just as the CBD is important to business, so the involvement of the private sector is essential for the successful implementation of the CBD and national provisions on ABS; this is for at least two related reasons. Firstly, monitoring and enforcing access legislation and agreements are difficult since this involves tracking and identifying the source and date of collection of specimens and also a product's movement through the discovery and development pipeline – typically, across national boundaries. Secondly, since user countries show little inclination to introduce laws to support the enforcement of access agreements in the countries where companies conduct their research and development, voluntary compliance by industry is essential.

Companies seeking access to genetic resources and countries providing them clearly have strong incentives to find mutually acceptable ABS terms and procedures. Progress in finding practical solutions has been stymied, however, by several factors.

Firstly, the international debate on 'bioprospecting' has become highly polarized and rhetorical. In simplified and somewhat caricatured terms, many source countries and non-governmental organizations (NGOs) view all companies – and even academic collectors – as 'biopirates'. and all source countries and communities as their vulnerable victims. On the other side, a caricature of the 'business perspective' is that the CBD's ABS provisions and related national laws are driven by grasping politicians who overestimate the value of their genetic resources, will hold companies to 'ransom' by withholding their consent to the commercialization of products after companies have invested hundreds of millions of dollars in research and development, and will not spend a penny of any shared 'benefits' on biodiversity conservation or assistance to communities in areas where genetic resources have been collected.

A second impediment to progress is the fact that industry is generally ill informed about the CBD and access legislation, often basing its opinions on second-hand and inaccurate information. A recent survey (ten Kate and Laird, 1999) of 185 industry figures whose businesses involve access to genetic resources (pharmaceutical, agro-industry, botanical medicines, horticulture, cosmetics, etc) found that 74 per cent had heard of the CBD; but this general awareness does not signify understanding. More than six years after the CBD entered into force, a large proportion of companies have only a very rudimentary grasp of its objectives and provisions. Very few, for example, knew that sustainable use and benefit-sharing were CBD objectives along with conservation. This misconception led one natural products researcher at a large pharmaceutical company to say that: 'Pharmaceutical research is not connected to conservation... Natural products research decisions have nothing to do with the CBD – there is no link whatsoever.' Many were unaware that the CBD covers access to traditional knowledge, as well as plants and animals.

Common *misconceptions* about the CBD that are widely held by industry include the following:

- The CBD does not apply to our industry if we do not use endangered species or overexploit raw materials.
- The CBD does not apply to materials with no known value, derivatives such as proteins or compounds, micro-organisms or ex-situ collections.
- The CBD does not apply to common species with a wide distribution.
- The CBD has no implications for organizations that do not collect genetic resources themselves.
- The CBD does not apply to academic research – only commercial benefits need to be shared.

Some 63 per cent of interviewees believed that the CBD was a 'positive' (versus 'negative' or 'neutral') influence because it promotes equitable relationships; promotes the conservation of potentially valuable genetic resources; potentially clarifies issues relating to ownership and access procedures; and supports best practice in industry. This assertion was generally qualified, however, to mean 'positive in principle', and there is great trepidation about the direction that national ABS legislation is taking. In the words of one natural products research director at a pharmaceutical firm:

'The CBD has had an overall counterproductive effect on natural products research. Expectations are unrealistic, administrative hassles and red tape overwhelming, and if you can get to drug leads in other ways, why still bother to do inherently expensive natural products research in such a politicized environment? From the beginning, the big companies were seen as thieves that come in the night and take things away. There exists a totally unrealistic notion that pharmaceutical companies routinely make billions of dollars from natural sources.'

Negative industry views of the CBD and the national ABS legislation it has spawned revolve around three major areas of concern.

Lack of clarity, a policy vacuum, and the resulting impasse

By far the most common industry complaint concerns the lack of clarity in individual countries about access procedures. Companies from all around the world feel that the CBD has created obligations in circumstances where the procedures do not exist to comply with them, and that while the CBD and ABS laws are fine in theory, there is no practical way to implement, monitor and enforce them. Many companies say that they cannot even get reliable information on what a country's rules are. Often they depend upon local collaborators for this information; but, as one source put it: 'Many of the in-country institutions are so poor that they will say anything to get some cash.' Another researcher observed that: 'The access and benefit-sharing discussion at the national level is not really moving, and companies and collectors are operating in a vacuum.'

Bureaucracy and transaction costs

In countries where clear access rules do exist, interviewees often complained that the rules were too cumbersome for them to wish to work there. Many expressed frustration with the growing divergence between ABS measures introduced by policy-makers and what is feasible to implement on the ground. There is a widely shared concern that these new ABS regulations, rather than encouraging equitable partnerships, are, in fact, restricting scientific advancement and running counter to CBD parties' Article 15 (2) obligation to facilitate access to their genetic resources.

Lack of business understanding

The third common concern shared by companies is that regulators and providers of genetic resources do not understand the interests, activities and proper role of business. Interviewees cited three common misperceptions harboured by governments and institutions who provide genetic resources:

1   'Raw' genetic resource are more valuable than companies believe them to be, leading to unrealistic demands for upfront payment.
2   Business should be involved in, or pay for, conservation and strive for social equity, when many companies do not see this as their role.
3   Companies would be prepared to put up with lengthy national and local procedures to obtain access, when, in fact, it is not cost effective for them to do so and their interest in access is fairly limited.

Many interviewees reported that CBD-driven ABS developments at the national level were leading to changes in business practice. These include:

- a decrease in corporate-collecting activities;
- consolidation of collecting programmes into few countries;
- a concentration, in some cases, on domestic collections;
- greater recourse to material from ex-situ collections;
- an increased role for intermediaries as brokers of ABS relationships as well as suppliers of samples; and
- the increased use of material transfer agreements (MTAs) to ensure that samples have been obtained legally.

Countries developing (or amending) national ABS legislation or other measures may, or may not be, interested in attracting industry to seek access to genetic resources. To the extent that they are, however, policy-makers would do well to take these widely held industry views into account, and realistically assess the impacts of existing or proposed ABS measures on the prospects for collaboration with the private sector in developing the country's genetic resources. 'It would be nice,' concluded one pharmaceutical executive, 'to give some thought to how the CBD could help developing countries attract equitable and more forward-looking natural products research rather than discouraging research altogether.'

Source: adapted from ten Kate and Laird, 1999

– raising the value of the resources relative to what other countries can offer. In turn, its bioprospecting partners have contributed to the strengthening of that scientific capacity through benefit-sharing arrangements included in bioprospecting contracts with InBio (Tobin, 1997; Sittenfeld and Gámez, 1993).

A country might, on the other hand, take a neutral stance, instituting provisions that make bioprospecting possible but give great weight to protecting against biopiracy and safeguarding other national interests and values – such as the prior informed consent of local and indigenous communities. This approach allows for a higher level of legal safeguards, but will not put a country in a competitive position against, say, Costa Rica.

Finally, a country may wish to largely discourage commercial access to its genetic resources, at least for a number of years while it develops ABS measures. Outright prohibition of access to genetic resources would clearly violate CBD Article 15 (2)'s requirement that parties facilitate access by other CBD parties; but a time-bounded ban, a proscription on access by non-parties or a prohibition on commercial uses (as opposed to scientific uses) would not run into this problem. In any case, the practical effect of any highly regulatory regime will be to largely discourage bioprospecting activities, even if the regime does not specifically hold this out as an objective.

As a general matter, the more that a country wishes to encourage bioprospecting activities, the more it will rely on private contracting – with minimal state regulation and intervention. States should be aware, therefore, that a decision to adopt a comprehensive and complicated regulatory system is also, de facto, a decision to discourage those who may seek access to the country's genetic resources. This has been the case in the Philippines, where a fairly complex regulation on access to genetic resources, in effect since 1996, has for all intents and purposes discouraged commercial bioprospectors from seeking access to genetic resources in that country.

Choosing a legislative strategy

The approaches that different countries take in order to establish a legal regime on genetic resources access will necessarily vary with their unique legal, institutional,

economic and cultural conditions. Comparative analysis of existing and draft access legislation reveals five basic approaches that countries are taking (see Table 12.2).

The first approach includes general environmental framework laws, such as those in Gambia, Kenya, Malawi, Republic of Korea and Uganda. Since they relate to ABS issues, these enactments are basically enabling laws that merely charge a competent national authority to examine ABS issues in order to provide guidance for more specific legislation or regulation in the future. They do not, in themselves, establish any sort of national legal or administrative framework. One advantage of a 'gradualistic' approach that begins with this kind of general enabling legislation is that it can be set up rather quickly, but allows countries to prepare themselves adequately before formulating more detailed national legislation or regulations. A gradualistic approach could even involve a temporary prohibition on all genetic resources exports until sound national legislation is set up. A limited period of export prohibition might not contradict CBD Article 15 (2) (which requires countries to facilitate access) so long as the prohibition is meant to allow the country sufficient time to develop a sound regime that effectively facilitates access and ensures that there is fair and equitable sharing of benefits.

The second approach involves inclusion of ABS issues in framework sustainable development, nature conservation or biodiversity laws, with examples found in Costa Rica, Eritrea, Fiji, Mexico and Peru. These laws tend to be more detailed than the framework enabling environmental laws noted earlier. All of them, for example, clearly establish the principles of mutually agreed terms and prior informed consent. Nevertheless, they require further implementing regulation in

Table 12.2 *Legislative options for genetic resources access and benefit-sharing, and selected countries considering or pursuing each option*

ABS legislative strategy options	Selected countries pursuing these options
General environmental framework laws (which only enable future legislation on ABS)	Gambia, Kenya, Malawi, Republic of Korea, Uganda
Framework sustainable development, nature conservation or biodiversity laws (which establish some ABS principles but require further legislation)	Costa Rica, Eritrea, Fiji, Mexico, Peru
Specific stand-alone national laws or executive orders that regulate access to genetic resources	the Philippines and, at the state level, Sarawak (Malaysia)
Modification of existing laws and regulations – such as those governing wildlife, national parks, forestry and fisheries – to include ABS provisions	Nigeria, Malaysia and, at the state level, Western Australia
Regional framework legislation (establishing common principles and procedures but requiring follow-up national legislation)	Countries of the Andean Pact (Bolivia, Colombia, Ecuador, Peru and Venezuela); regional framework agreements or legislation also under discussion by countries grouped in the Association of South-East Asian Nations (ASEAN) and the Organization of African Unity (OAU)

Source: Glowka, 1998

order to set a functioning ABS regime in place.

A third approach is the development of specific stand-alone national laws or executive orders on access to genetic resources. The Philippines system is the only operational example of this approach, and was instituted by way of a presidential executive order in 1995, followed by issuance of implementing rules and regulations in 1996. Experience under this regime is discussed in detail later (see 'Lessons from the Philippines').

A fourth approach is to modify existing laws and regulations – such as those governing wildlife, national parks, forestry and fisheries – to include provisions on genetic resources ABS. This is the model that Nigeria has followed so far, working primarily with its law on national parks (Nnadozie, 1999). One advantage of reforming existing natural resources laws to introduce PIC, benefit-sharing and other provisions is that the country can largely use existing administrative measures, policies and institutional structures. Depending upon the functions and capacities of existing structures and institutions, this may be the more efficient and cost-effective way, particularly for developing countries with limited financial resources. However, it requires substantial capacity-building within the existing institutions and their staff. At the sub-national level, both Western Australia and Malaysia's Sarawak state have both followed this approach.

Finally, legislative action can be taken at the regional level. The only existing example of a regional approach is Decision 391 of the Andean Pact (1996), which creates a common regime on access to genetic resources (see Box 12.5). The countries in the Association of South-East Asian Nations (ASEAN) also initiated discussions during 1998 aimed at creating a common ASEAN policy framework on access (DENR, 1999). In Africa, Model Legislation on Community Rights and Access to Biological Resources, prepared

BOX 12.4 ACCESS AND BENEFIT-SHARING MEASURES IN MALAYSIA

Sally Mullard, Ceclia Oh and Wendy Yap

There is no legislation specific to biodiversity commercialization, access to genetic resources or benefit-sharing at the national level in Malaysia. Some national access controls are in place for foreign researchers, and the Customs Act 1967 governs the export of biological resources; but they predate the CBD.

In response to the importance of the issue at both international and national levels, the Task Force on Access to Genetic Resources – one of the main working groups under the National Committee on Biological Diversity, which was created in 1994 – was established. The task force is chaired by an academic and comprises representatives from the government agencies with responsibility for managing biodiversity in the country, the attorney general's (AG's) chambers, which is the federal government's main legal advisory body, and various research institutions.

In 1996, a national framework approach was proposed by the AG's chambers recommending introduction of an access-licensing scheme through the amendment of existing federal legislation on wildlife protection, forestry and fisheries. The scheme is rather fragmented, however, and there is little clarity on how it would be implemented. The proposed sectoral legislative approach would not cover all the country's biodiversity, and it is unclear how the access system would be coordinated among the various sectors and agencies. In addition, there is no provision for monitoring and little clarification on the respective roles of the federal and state governments.

One of the main difficulties encountered in Malaysia, in terms of developing a legal framework, is the shared legal governance over the country's biodiversity mandated by the federal constitution. Each of the 13 states in Malaysia has its own respective legislatures, and their law-making powers are defined by the constitution in the federal, state and concurrent lists (Schedule 9). 'Biological diversity', per se, is not enumerated on any of the three lists. As a general rule, matters that concern land and natural resources, such as forests and water, are on the state list and thus come under the exclusive jurisdiction of the states. However, others do not. Marine fisheries appear on the federal list and wildlife protection on the concurrent list (that is, competency is shared). It is this division of legal status that complicates the process of implementing the provisions of the CBD.

The constitution does, however, grant a coordinating role to the federal government. It may legislate:

- in order to fulfil obligations under international treaties; and
- for the purpose of promoting uniformity of the laws of two or more states (although for such a law to become operational, the states must adopt their own implementing legislation).

Therefore, constitutionally, it would be possible for the federal parliament to pass legislation on access and benefit-sharing (ABS). It has thus been proposed that the federal government introduce framework legislation on ABS, with the support and approval of the states, with both levels of government being fully involved in the implementation process. This approach is currently favoured over the approach proposed earlier by the AG's chambers, and the federal government is in the process of drafting framework legislation on ABS.

The states of Sabah and Sarawak, lying on the north coast of the island of Borneo where some of Malaysia's richest biodiversity is found, have greater legal autonomy than the peninsular states with respect to natural resources. There is also a relatively high level of awareness about ABS issues in Sarawak because the state has been attracting bioprospectors for many years and the state government has some experience of negotiating ABS agreements. A notable example is the agreement with the National Cancer Institute (NCI) and a US pharmaceutical company for the collection of samples from a *Calophyllum* species for the synthesis of Calanolide A, a promising anti-HIV compound. Spurred, in part, by this case, new state legislation came into effect on 1 January 1998 (the Sarawak Biodiversity Ordinance of 1997) creating a new legal and administrative regime for controlling access to Sarawak's biodiversity. A key feature of the scheme is the establishment of the Sarawak Biodiversity Centre, which will act as the focal point for biodiversity and access issues. Operation of the centre is to be overseen by the Sarawak Biodiversity Council, which has powers to regulate the 'access, collection, study and research, experiment, protection and utilization of the biodiversity of Sarawak, including the removal of any of the biodiversity from the State'.

Under the ordinance, any person wanting access will be required to obtain a permit. The legislation also introduces new provisions for monitoring and enforcement. Anyone caught trying to remove genetic resources from the state without a permit will be subject to a fine of 20,000 Malaysian ringgit (about US$6000), imprisonment for three years or both. However, it is still too soon to know how the legislation will be implemented in practice and whether sufficient resources will be forthcoming to ensure effective enforcement.

Source: adapted from Mullard, 1998

by the Scientific, Technical and Research Commission of the Organization of African Unity (OAU), was recommended for adoption by the OAU ministerial council in June 1998 (Ekpere, 1999; Nnadozie, 1999). The OAU effort is not a regional agreement per se, but rather an effort to get OAU member states to adopt a common position as they develop national legislation, and to give them a well-informed starting point in doing so.

Intellectual property rights and national access and benefit-sharing measures

The relationship between intellectual property rights (IPRs) regimes and ABS issues is complex and contentious, as discussed in Box 12.6 (see also Dutfield, 2000; Dutfield and Posey, 1996; SCBD, 1996; WWF, 1995; Crucible Group, 1994;

Greaves, 1994.) IPRs overlap with ABS issues with respect to the patenting of inventions (such as drugs) based on either a country's genetic resources, traditional knowledge held by its citizens or both. There is considerable tension between existing IPR regimes and the ongoing efforts of countries to develop ABS regimes, as discussed in Box 12.6.

Countries who develop ABS measures need to make a basic decision on whether or not – and if so, how – to address IPR issues in the ABS context. The Philippines, for example, decided that effective measures to regulate access could be put in place without addressing IPR issues in the ABS law, and that inclusion of IPR issues in the debate would slow and complicate the process of putting a regime in place. One contentious IPR issue, however – the question of rights over indigenous knowledge associated with

Box 12.5 Decision 391: the Common Regime on Access to Genetic Resources in the Andean Pact

Manuel Ruiz (Peruvian Society for Environmental Law)

Background

Decision 391 of the Andean Pact (now called the Andean Community of Nations) on a Common Regime on Access to Genetic Resources was adopted, and entered into force, in July 1996. The Andean Community is an economic and social integration treaty formed by Venezuela, Colombia, Ecuador, Peru and Bolivia and was established in 1969.

Article 15 of the CBD and Decision 345 of the Andean Pact on a Common Regime for the Protection of New Plant Varieties – the plant breeders' rights system in force since 1993 – were the legal basis for the development of Decision 391's provisions. In particular, Decision 345 included a provision specifically calling for the development of a system to regulate access to genetic resources in the sub-region.

The background rationale for developing a common set of rules for all Andean Pact member states was the fact that most biodiversity in the Andean–Amazonian region is shared by these five countries. This situation thus made it necessary to develop a system which would:

- prevent unnecessary competition among countries; and
- establish benefit-sharing mechanisms that would ensure an equitable participation of countries sharing common genetic resources in the benefits derived from access to, and use of, those resources.

In response to these concerns, the pact initiated a process in 1994 to design a legal framework on access and benefit-sharing (ABS). The Environmental Law Centre of the International Union for Conservation of Nature and Natural Resources (IUCN) and the Peruvian Society for Environmental Law carried out a regional consultative process that included international agricultural research centres, indigenous peoples' representatives, non-governmental organizations (NGOs) and international technical experts, thus providing the pact with legal and technical assistance in preparing an initial set of elements for draft ABS regulation. After considerable negotiation among member states, revisions and additions, Decision 391 was issued two years later.

Decision 391 establishes a common regulatory framework of minimum standards and procedures applicable to all of the pact's member states, who may implement the rules directly (by officially acknowledging Decision 391 as national law) or through complementary national implementing legislation. At present, Colombia is applying Decision 391 directly, while Bolivia has enacted specific secondary legislation (Supreme Decree No 24676). Peru is also in the process of doing so (*Draft Regulation on Access*, pre-published in May 1998). Venezuela and Ecuador are undergoing an internal process to assess the best option for implementing Decision 391.

General provisions

Decision 391 establishes definitions and a general procedure for determining access to genetic resources. Contracts are the main mechanism, particularly a primary access contract between the applicant seeking access to genetic resources and the 'competent authority' designated by the government of the country in question. This contract specifies the basic conditions for ABS.

The state must be a party to this primary ABS contract because Decision 391 affirms that genetic resources and their derived products are patrimony of the nation or goods of the states, pursuant to member states' specific internal natural-resources laws, policies and regulations. Thus, since only states have rights over genetic resources, the state must be party to any agreement granting access to, and use of, these resources (Article 6).

'Access' is defined in Decision 391 as physical access to, and use of, genetic resources (from either in-situ or ex-situ sources), derived products (molecules or extracts from live or dead biological sources) and 'the intangible component' (knowledge, innovations and practices related to these resources) (Article 1). The scope of Decision 391 thus extends beyond raw genetic resources (such as plant material) to cover purified or processed extracts from such resources, as well as knowledge, innovations and practices associated with the resources (Article 3). Human genetic resources and traditional exchange of resources among indigenous communities are, however, excluded from its scope (Article 4).

With respect to indigenous and local knowledge associated with genetic resources, Decision 391 says that 'Member States, in accordance with this Decision and their complementary national legislation, recognize and value the rights and decision-making capacity of indigenous, Afro-American and local communities over their traditional knowledge, innovations and practices associated with genetic resources and their derived products' (Article 7, unofficial translation). Where genetic resources have an associated 'intangible component' (traditional knowledge associated with the specific genetic resources sought), a discrete access contract (included as an annex to the primary ABS contract) must be negotiated and signed by the applicant, the state and the provider of the associated knowledge (Article 35). This presumably demonstrates the consent of the provider to use the knowledge, although the decision has no explicit provision referring to prior informed consent (PIC) of local and indigenous communities for use of their knowledge. The rights of the providers of such knowledge, however, are to be 'safeguarded' by the competent national authorities of each member state (Article 50 (d)).

Procedure

In order for an applicant to gain access to genetic resources, an application must be presented to, and assessed by, the national competent authority (Article 26). An extract of this application will be published in the national official gazette in order for third parties to be notified about access activities and eventually present their observations if they deem it necessary (Articles 26, 27 and 28).

Once the competent national authority approves the application, the applicant may proceed to the negotiation and drafting of the access contract. The specific content of the contract is left open, subject to its adherence to certain minimum conditions set out in Decision 391 (Article 17). These include, inter alia, participation of national researchers in access activities; an element of technology and know-how transfer; support for in-country research; deposit of duplicate samples in national institutions; and specific terms governing transfer of materials to third parties.

Agreements may be of three main types:

1 The primary access agreement between the applicant and the state (Article 32), represented by the national competent authority (Article 50). This contract, related to the genetic resources per se (over which the state holds ownership) should, nevertheless, take into account the interests of the providers of the biological resources, such as local and indigenous communities in the area where collection activities are proposed, in which the potentially valuable genetic resources may be found (Article 34).

2 Accessory agreements related to the *biological resources* over which communities, individuals, ex-situ centres or the state may have proprietary rights (Article 41). These agreements could also include agreements for the use of indigenous peoples' knowledge, innovations and practices (Article 35).

3 Framework agreements with ex-situ conservation centres and research institutions. These are agreements oriented towards facilitating the daily activities of ex-situ centres and research institutions where individual agreements for specific collection activities would be bureaucratically burdensome (Articles 36 and 37).

Finally, Decision 391 establishes certain penalties and sanctions (Article 46), as well as the general structure and role of national competent authorities.

Final comments

Although originally conceived to prevent competition among countries and to promote regional benefit-sharing, Decision 391 does not establish the specific mechanisms through which benefits may be shared among member states. This is causing difficulties as countries begin designing practical measures for implementing the decision at the national level. Decision 391's complex procedures and limited recognition of the different types of research and methodologies used in bioprospecting for different activities (eg agro-industrial, pharmaceutical), as well as the different sources of resources (eg marine, microbial, terrestrial), is proving a challenge for countries committed to ensuring its adequate and timely implementation.

current and potential uses of genetic resources found within ancestral domain lands – was comprehensively addressed in the 1997 Indigenous Peoples Rights Act (see Box 12.7). In Peru, a draft law specifically addressing this question was proposed for public comment in late 1999 (see Box 12.8).

The Andean Pact's regional framework law, Decision 391, extends state sovereignty over derivatives of genetic resources, defined as 'a molecule or combination or mixture of natural molecules, including raw extracts of living or dead organisms of biological origin, derived from the metabolism of living organisms'.

Thus, it appears that a biocompound isolated and patented outside of the Andean Community could be subject to the claims of community member states. Decision 391 also introduces the term 'intangible component' to refer to any knowledge, innovation or practice (individual or collective) of actual or potential value associated with a biogenetic resource or derivative, whether or not it is protected by intellectual property rights. The decision thus includes this 'intangible component' within the definition of genetic resources, and provides indigenous peoples and local communities with legal support in contest-

Box 12.6 Intellectual property rights and national access and benefit-sharing measures

David Downes and Glenn Wiser (Centre for International Environmental Law – CIEL)

Intellectual property rights (IPRs), such as patents and copyrights, have traditionally been offered to inventors and creators as rewards for innovation, and as incentives for them to share information with the public to promote more innovation by others. Patents are the main mechanism most countries use to allocate rights over inventions. They give their owners monopoly control over their inventions for a fixed term of years. During that time, owners may restrict or control the commercial use and sale of the invention. Society as a whole benefits by gaining access (for a price) to new and useful products, and by acquiring new knowledge that can be used as a basis for additional research and the creation of new inventions. Patent protection has historically been strongest in the industrialized countries and much weaker (or non-existent) in developing countries.

In recent years, many patent offices have begun issuing patents not only for inventions, but also for discoveries of information already existing in the natural world, such as the genetic sequences of living organisms. They have further extended patent rights to plants, animals and micro-organisms containing genes that have been modified in the laboratory. The Agreement on Trade Related Aspects of Intellectual Property Rights (TRIPS) – one of the new trade agreements administered by the World Trade Organization (WTO) – incorporates these trends, so that all WTO members may be required to offer patent protection or similar alternatives for a broad range of discoveries and inventions involving genetic resources. This trend towards privatization and commodification of biological and genetic information has led countries in both the North and South to increasingly view such information as a proprietary asset having monetary value, instead of as part of humankind's common heritage. That view has, in turn, led countries to agree that they should be able to regulate the access to, and sharing of benefits from, their genetic resources.

The need for access and benefit-sharing (ABS) agreements can thus be seen in large part as a response to trends in national and international IPR systems. Nevertheless, IPR systems, as they currently exist, will be of little use to – and could even hinder – the development of ABS agreements in at least three ways.

Firstly, IPRs such as patents protect and reward some types of innovation, but not others. Discrete individuals or firms may obtain patents for specific innovations made at a particular moment in time. But traditional innovations are often developed over long periods of time – possibly from generation to generation – and may result from the incremental contributions of many individuals. Much indigenous and local knowledge of medicinal plants and food crops stems from this type of collective innovation, making it difficult to point to a particular person or even community who can be identified as the 'inventor'. Traditional patent law considers such knowledge to be part of the public domain. Consequently, present patent systems cannot protect it. This leads to a natural imbalance of power under IPR systems between those who want access to genetic resources and those who provide it. Biotechnology and pharmaceutical companies who market 'new' medicines or genetically modified animals, crops and micro-organisms based on genetic resources obtained from indigenous and local communities can receive worldwide patent protection for their products. The knowledge, innovations and practices that made the 'discovery' of those resources possible, however, is not patentable.

Secondly, because present IPR systems do not reward indigenous and local communities for their traditional knowledge, they do not provide incentives for them to preserve their biodiversity. Governments and local communities may have invested a great deal of capital and labour in conserving an area where, for instance, a plant is discovered that provides the basis for a promising new drug. They may have forgone other uses of their land, such as logging or mining, that could yield them immediate financial returns. Or, they may have forgone lucrative opportunities by adhering to life styles that preserve their traditional knowledge, innovations and practices. Patents are intended, in part, to provide incentives to people who invest their time, effort and money in the process of innovation. They are effective in rewarding the efforts of companies who develop products from naturally occurring genetic resources. However, because they do not recognize traditional knowledge or practices as innovation, they do nothing to provide incentives to owners and stewards of lands where the greatest wealth of genetic resources resides to conserve their knowledge or biodiversity.

Thirdly, developing countries who do not have well-developed, enforceable IPR systems may have difficulty in satisfactorily negotiating with firms for benefit-sharing of new products and technologies based upon their genetic resources. These firms may have invested a great degree of capital in a particular technology. Consequently, they may be reluctant to share it with developing country partners who do not provide the same level of IPR protection that they receive in their home countries.

This last observation implies that developing countries who wish to obtain new technologies through ABS agreements may first need to adopt and implement enforceable IPR systems. The TRIPS agreement requires its developing country members to phase in such systems; this began in the year 2000. The challenge facing these countries is to create IPR systems that are strong enough to give firms confidence that their technologies will be protected, while adequately tailoring the systems to their national circumstances and the needs of their indigenous and local communities. Yet, many countries are developing apparently effective national measures on genetic resources ABS legislation without reference to IPRs, as the examples in this book attest.

Nevertheless, IPRs will likely remain the most powerful vehicle for allocating wealth created from the exploitation of genetic resources. Developing countries and their indigenous and local communities may best maximize their ability to share in that wealth if their contributions to innovation are recognized under IPR systems. This will require cooperative and imaginative collaboration among many diverse constituencies, including the CBD, the TRIPS council, the Food and Agriculture Organization (FAO) and other international institutions; legislators and IPR offices in developed and developing countries; and indigenous and local communities and their respective national governments. At the international level, countries could collectively define guidelines for ABS agreements to discourage weak rules that might lead to a 'race to the bottom', stressing immediate, short-term financial gains over long-term, equitably shared benefits.

Establishing national and international registries of traditional knowledge could protect the intellectual property interests of indigenous peoples by helping to further the recognition of their knowledge by patent offices. In addition, patent offices could require that applicants disclose the country of origin from which any biological materials or traditional knowledge were obtained; state what part traditional knowledge played in identifying the properties and location of materials used in developing the invention; affirm that, to the best of their knowledge, they complied with all applicable laws of the source country; supply evidence that the knowledge was obtained with the prior informed consent of the providers; and require notification to designated authorities in all countries or communities identified in the application as sources of genetic resources.

Box 12.7 The Philippines Indigenous Peoples Rights Act of 1997

The Philippines 1997 Indigenous Peoples Rights Act (IPRA) is one of the strongest national laws protecting indigenous rights in existence. It recognizes a wide range of rights held by the country's numerous indigenous groups, including clear land rights over ancestral domains; a considerable measure of self-government within these territories; the right to 'freely pursue their economic, social and cultural development'; and rights to 'preserve and protect their culture, traditions and institutions'. The state is charged with guaranteeing and upholding these rights, and furthermore must consider them in the formulation of all national plans and policies. The act also establishes a National Commission on Indigenous Peoples to carry out the act's provisions, with members chosen by the president, based on a list of nominations submitted by indigenous communities from around the country.

IPRA deals specifically with the question of rights over indigenous knowledge:

'Indigenous Cultural Communities/Indigenous Peoples are entitled to the recognition of the full ownership and control and protection of their cultural and intellectual rights. They shall have the right to special measures to control, develop and protect their sciences, technologies and cultural manifestations, including human and other genetic resources, seeds, including derivatives of these resources, traditional medicines and health practices, vital medicinal plants, animals and minerals, indigenous knowledge systems and practices, knowledge of the properties of fauna and flora, oral traditions, literature, designs, and visual and performing arts' (Chapter VI, Section 34).

This provision makes it clear that an application for a patent or other intellectual property right (IPR) based on any of the specified elements – when not made with the full prior informed consent (PIC) of the community in question – is illegal and will not be granted by the Philippines. It can also be inferred that should such a patent be recognized in another country, it would not be honoured in the Philippines.

IPRA also recognizes that control over indigenous knowledge related to genetic resources requires that indigenous communities possess the right to regulate biological and genetic resources located within their territories:

'Access to biological and genetic resources and to indigenous knowledge related to the conservation, utilization and enhancement of these resources shall be allowed within ancestral lands and domains of indigenous peoples only with a free and prior informed consent of such communities, obtained in accordance with customary laws of the concerned community' (Chapter VI, Section 35).

These rights over genetic resources and associated knowledge, it is important to note, are premised on a comprehensive set of rights over land and resources themselves. IPRA states that: 'The rights of ownership and possession of (indigenous peoples) to their ancestral domains shall be recognized and protected.' The act goes on to enumerate a long list of these rights, including basic ownership; the right to develop lands and resources; and the right to regulate the entry of migrant settlers and organizations (Chapter III, Section 7). These rights are not unlimited, however, and indigenous groups holding such rights are obliged by IPRA 'to preserve, restore and maintain a balanced ecology in the ancestral domain by protecting the flora and fauna, watershed areas and other reserves' (Chapter III, Section 9).

Implementation of this law is at an early stage, but it is currently the most comprehensive example of a national legislative attempt to implement the principles found in the CBD Article 8 (j).

ing patent claims that utilize this 'intangible component' (Dutfield, 1999).

Costa Rica's comprehensive 1998 Biodiversity Law (see Case Study 12.1) – which covers national implementation of all aspects of the CBD – deals specifically with IPRs. Among its provisions is a specific exclusion of certain elements of biodiversity from patent protection in the country, including DNA sequences, plants and animals and inventions 'essentially derived from knowledge associated with traditional biological or cultural biological practices in the public domain' (Dutfield, 1999).

'With the growth of biotechnology, industry and scientists are using intellectual property to gain monopoly control over biological resources and the knowledge of farming communities from the South... This is biopiracy. For farmers and farming communities it may mean having to pay for the products of their own genius. It will certainly mean that they go unrewarded for their contribution to corporate profits' Rural Advancement Foundation International (RAFI, 1996).

Guidelines for the process of developing national access legislation

National consultation processes

Regardless of how countries decide the initial framework issues just discussed, the legislative and institutional framework for genetic resources access that any country develops will only be as good as the process through which it is developed. To actually work once established, development of the legislative framework must have broad support of all relevant sectors of government and society.

Formulating effective access legislation requires participation by a wide range of stakeholders and technical experts. Sectoral agencies – including agriculture, forestry, fisheries, and health – need to be involved, as do representatives of the scientific research community, the private business sector (pharmaceutical and agricultural companies, for example), non-governmental organizations (NGOs), indigenous peoples' groups, and many other actors who will vary from country to country. This kind of broad participatory process takes more time and effort than, say, commissioning a few experts to draft a law, but the benefits far outweigh

Box 12.8 Protecting collective intellectual property rights of indigenous peoples related to biodiversity in Peru

Brendan Tobin

In October 1999, the Peruvian government published for comment a draft law on the protection of the collective knowledge of indigenous peoples relating to biological diversity. Peru thus became the first country to propose a law establishing a regime to regulate access to, and use of, the collective intellectual property rights of indigenous peoples relating to biological resources. The law is intended to serve three broad purposes, to:

1   protect the respect, protection, preservation, wider application and development of collective knowledge of indigenous peoples;
2   promote fair and equitable distribution of benefits derived from use of collective knowledge;
3   promote the use of this knowledge to the benefit of mankind.

The proposed law is based on a number of underlying principles:

- Indigenous peoples' rights over their traditional knowledge exist without the need for action on the part of the state.
- Access to the collective knowledge of indigenous peoples for scientific or commercial purposes requires their prior informed consent (PIC), where such knowledge is not in the public domain. Where use is for a commercial purpose, it is necessary for the parties to enter into a licensing agreement for its use.
- Even where knowledge is in the public domain, indigenous peoples are entitled to share in the benefits derived from its use.
- Traditional knowledge is the collective property and cultural patrimony of indigenous peoples, and as such is inalienable and must be administered by present generations to the benefit of future generations.
- Any community is entitled to grant non-exclusive licences for the use of knowledge, without the need for the approval of other custodians. However, a percentage of all transactions must be paid into an indigenous fund for development purposes.
- Indigenous peoples have a right to share in the commercial benefits derived from the use of their traditional knowledge, whether or not such knowledge is in the public domain. A fixed percentage of the profits of all such trade should be paid into an indigenous development fund, which should be managed by indigenous peoples themselves.
- There is a need to create a balance between the rights of indigenous peoples and the interests of potential users, in order to establish a functional regime to regulate the trade in traditional knowledge.

A working group including representatives of relevant state bodies and the Permanent Commission of Indigenous Peoples of Peru (COPPIP) – a forum bringing together indigenous peoples' and campesino communities' representative organizations – has been established to promote wider participation of indigenous peoples in the revision of the proposed law. A document prepared by the working group, for distribution to indigenous peoples, seeks to explain the reasons why a law is necessary to secure protection of indigenous peoples' rights over their collective knowledge, to explain the draft proposal and to facilitate commentary through use of a questionnaire. Seven areas of particular importance have been identified as requiring specific attention. These comprise the following.

Examination of the objectives of the law

This is to determine whether they meet the aspirations of indigenous peoples. Some observers believe, for example, that the principle of 'balancing the interests' in protecting indigenous knowledge against the interests of others in using that knowledge is a misinterpretation of the state's responsibility, which is to protect the rights of indigenous communities over their knowledge, whether those with an interest in accessing and using traditional knowledge are inconvenienced or not. In this view, only indigenous peoples themselves are entitled to define the extent to which any legislative measure to protect their rights may be designed to facilitate more flexible access for potential users.

Clarification of what knowledge should be protected

Concern has been expressed that by limiting the rights of indigenous peoples over material in the public domain, the result may be to legitimize the historic appropriations of traditional knowledge and its subsequent use. It has therefore been proposed that consideration is given to revising the concept of public domain insofar as it relates to traditional knowledge. Knowledge would, in this view, only be considered to exist within the public domain where its use was so widespread that it would be impossible and unrealistic to require prior informed consent for its use. In all other cases, the intention of the provider at the time that access was granted to the knowledge should be a determining factor in deciding whether the use of the knowledge requires prior informed consent (PIC). In cases where the intention of the original provider cannot be identified, the responsibility for demonstrating a right to use the knowledge without PIC would fall upon the user.

Identifying those entitled to give or withhold consent for use of knowledge

The need to ensure that any law does not lead to divisions within indigenous peoples, or promote competition for the provision of rights to use knowledge, has been clearly identified. Potential conflicts between the need to respect the rights of communities to prevent the use of their knowledge without their consent, and the proposal that individual communities may negotiate without the need for consent of other custodians of the same knowledge, must be resolved before promulgation of a law.

Need to establish mechanisms to identify the existence of knowledge

In order to facilitate effective implementation of any law, it is necessary to ensure that the existence of knowledge, and of the custodians of such knowledge, may be identified. The draft law proposes the establishment of a centralized register, where communities may register their knowledge, if they desire. Non-registration does not, however, have any bearing upon the existence of a right over knowledge. Concerns have been raised, however, over use of information in a centralized register and over the proposal that the authorities may provide this to potential users in order to assist them in identifying the existence of knowledge and of its custodians. The possibilities of developing various tiers of registers at the community, representative-organization and national level might provide mechanisms for ensuring that confidentiality of sensitive information is protected.

Benefit-sharing

The draft law proposes a fixed rate of benefits of an economic nature that must be paid on all transactions for the use of traditional knowledge for commercial purposes. The rate is set at 0.5 per cent of net sales of products developed using traditional knowledge, whether or not in the public domain. All payments are to be made to a fund for the development of indigenous peoples, managed by indigenous peoples themselves. Some commentators have argued that this scheme is too arbitrary because it does not provide for differential rates depending upon the relative importance of the knowledge in the development of the end product.

Resolution of conflicts

The proposal provides administrative procedures for resolving conflicts between indigenous peoples and users of their traditional knowledge. Indigenous peoples may seek relief against the disclosure, acquisition or use of their knowledge without their consent, except where that knowledge is in the public domain (and did not get there through a breach of duty on the part of a user). Conflicts are to be resolved by the office of new inventions of the national intellectual property right (IPR) authority at first instance, with appeal to the Tribunal for Unfair Competition of the same authority. The draft law does not, however, contain provisions for resolving disputes between indigenous communities. To remedy this, it has been proposed that a committee of elders, designated by indigenous peoples, is established to resolve disputes involving communities. Attention has also been drawn to the potential role of customary law in determining such disputes.

Strengthening traditional knowledge systems

The proposed law makes no specific provisions for the strengthening of indigenous traditional knowledge systems. The fund for the development of indigenous peoples may be utilized for this purpose, if the indigenous peoples decide.

Due to the complexity of these issues, and the need for a systematic participatory process to obtain adequate and informed indigenous input, the national patent authority (INDECOPI) in late October 1999 agreed to extend the initial period for receipt of comments on the law from two to four months.

the costs. Not only does the legislative process benefit from the collective experience and technical knowledge of all sectors, but potential opposition to the legislation can be sounded out early and conflicts more easily resolved.

In the cases of the Philippines and the Andean Pact, the formulation of access legislation resulted from quite broad consultative processes involving various governmental agencies, non-governmental organizations, lawyers, private-sector representatives and research institutions. For the draft *Andean Pact Common Regime*, technical aspects were handled by the Junta del Acuerdo de Cartagena (JUNAC) – the Andean Pact administrative organ – with technical assistance from the Environmental Law Centre of the International Union for Conservation of Nature and Natural Resources (IUCN-ELC) and the Peruvian Society for Environmental Law (SPDA). After some initial criticisms that the process was not participatory enough, a series of regional and international consultations and workshops involving a wide range of stakeholders within the region was arranged. In the Philippines, the process was exceptionally open and participatory from the outset. Early drafts of the 1995 executive order on bioprospecting and genetic resources access were debated in a series of well-attended and vocal public fora, as well as within interagency governmental meetings. South Africa provides another interesting example of this kind of process (see Box 12.9).

Drawing on these and other experiences, a good participatory process for developing a genetic resources and ABS regime is likely to have the following objectives:

- Identify and build consensus on national objectives and priorities. Should the country, for example, encourage, discourage or take a neutral position on biodiversity prospecting activities? What scientific, commercial, conservation and development priorities should benefit-sharing measures serve?
- Identify and mobilize various stakeholders (eg representatives of local communities, NGOs, government departments, political institutions, intergovernmental institutions, the private sector, the scientific community, etc).

- Identify and mobilize required expertise, as well as form working groups or committees to address various aspects of ABS issues – such as options for prior informed consent processes, intellectual property rights issues, potential impacts on domestic scientific research and capacity-building, etc.
- Conduct an inventory of existing institutional, policy and legal measures relating to access to genetic resource regulation and benefit-sharing requirements (remembering that these may not be explicit, but will instead require extrapolation from general existing provisions on natural resources, scientific research, export of specimens, etc).
- Create a national body or focal point to coordinate development of the legislation.
- Hold a series of public fora and expert consultations to seek input to improve successive drafts of the legislation.

The importance of an integrated approach

In formulating genetic resources access legislation, it is also important that countries adopt an integrated approach that does not treat the issue in isolation, but rather places it within the broader set of policies and activities aimed at implementing the CBD as a whole. The discussion on how to regulate genetic resources should thus ideally be built into a national biodiversity planning process – as required by Article 6 of the convention – or at least closely linked to it. A national biodiversity planning process provides the basis for gathering knowledge on the status and distribution of a nation's biodiversity, establishing broad national goals and policies and assessing existing institutions, policies and laws. Knowledge of the distribution of biological diversity is important in determining which regions

Box 12.9 Developing a policy on access and benefit-sharing in South Africa: policy research and public participation

Rachel Wynberg

South Africa is one of few countries in the world to have engaged in a comprehensive policy-planning process prior to the development of access legislation (Swiderska, 1999). This experience has allowed stakeholders the chance to reflect and debate policy and legislative options, and the opportunities and constraints of different approaches. In addition, it has provided opportunities for democratic policy-making and an invaluable meeting ground for the sharing of values between the diversity of South Africa's people (Fakir, 1997). Critics, however, point to the fact that consultation has slowed down and frustrated bioprospecting initiatives, a reproach bolstered by the absence, to date, of any legislation to regulate access to genetic resources and benefit-sharing.

In 1995 South Africa initiated a consultation process to develop a national biodiversity policy and strategy, largely in response to the country's signing and imminent ratification of the CBD. Guiding the process was a multistakeholder reference group, comprising representatives from a range of central and provincial government departments, statutory boards and non-governmental organizations. Additional structures included a steering committee to manage the policy process and an editorial committee, tasked with drafting various policy documents.

Three policy documents were drafted between 1995 and 1997:

1   a discussion document, which described the issues under consideration and outlined some of the policy options that could be adopted (DEAT, 1996a);
2   a Green Paper, which articulated a draft biodiversity policy and strategy (DEAT, 1996b); and
3   a White Paper, which described government policy for the conservation and sustainable use of biodiversity (DEAT, 1997).

Comments were invited widely on these documents. Popular versions of the documents, as well as educational leaflets about biodiversity, also were distributed and translated into several different languages. Stakeholder briefings were held in several of the provinces to raise awareness about the policy process and to discuss key issues. At an early stage in the process, a national conference was held to help formulate policy responses to emerging issues. This was attended by 160 organizations, representing a wide range of interest groups.

Bioprospecting was a major issue identified early on in the consultation process, particularly the expropriation of traditional knowledge and the failure of South Africa to develop and benefit from its phenomenal stores of biodiversity. Tremendous opportunities are available for the commercial development of the country's biodiversity, given that South Africa is ranked as one of the 'megadiverse' countries of the world, with at least 80 per cent of its 18,000–20,000 plant species known to be endemic. There is also a vast traditional knowledge of plant and animal uses, considerable scientific capacity, well-developed infrastructure and well-managed living collections and protected areas. These factors make the country highly attractive to companies seeking novel compounds with medical, agricultural, horticultural or environmental applications.

How should South Africa manage bioprospecting and what policy measures are appropriate to ensure that benefits derived from the use of indigenous genetic resources serve national interests? This question was raised repeatedly by different stakeholders during the policy process, and was evidently central to the formulation of a comprehensive biodiversity policy for South Africa.

Recognizing the importance of the genetic resources access issue, the Land and Agriculture Policy Centre (LAPC), a non-governmental organization (NGO) specializing in policy research, embarked upon a bioprospecting research project in tandem with the policy process. The purpose of the project was to investigate the status quo of bioprospecting in South Africa, to identify emerging issues and key stakeholders and to suggest ways of taking the issues forward into the policy arena (Laird and Wynberg, 1996). Fortuitously, the LAPC was also centrally involved in managing the policy process to develop a biodiversity policy, thus enabling effective links to be established between the research and policy development processes. Thus, through the involvement of a well-resourced and respected NGO, state-of-the-art research informed and directed the development of government policy on access to genetic resources.

The initiation of an independent study on bioprospecting not only allowed for the development of an informed policy, but also facilitated the involvement of several stakeholders who may not otherwise have contributed to the policy process. As part of the research process, interviews and discussions were held on bioprospecting with national and provincial government departments, para-states, tertiary educational institutions, industry, NGOs and traditional healers. Research findings were presented at a national workshop on genetic resources, which included contributions from several stakeholders and researchers. In capturing the views and perspectives of these organizations, an important 'buy-in' process was initiated. The success of this process was evidenced by the general acceptance by all stakeholders of the bioprospecting policy to emerge in the White Paper.

Given that the White Paper was adopted in 1997, it is useful to reflect on how it has been implemented since that time by government and by those engaged in bioprospecting. An agreed priority area identified by the White Paper is the development of legal and administrative mechanisms to regulate bioprospecting, as well as other aspects of access to genetic resources and the sharing of resulting benefits. However, such mechanisms are not yet in place, nor are they being developed. This is extremely problematic and has resulted in a good deal of frustration on the part of potential investors and collaborators, a free-for-all among bioprospecting opportunists, and weak benefit-sharing arrangements for South Africa. Complicating matters is the fact that there are several government departments affected by the issue, each of which is taking it up in a different manner and with little coordination. These frustrations have largely negated the considerable amount of work conducted to develop a consensual position on bioprospecting, and have fuelled public criticism about the value of endless policy processes and about the commitment of government to implement policy.

Seen in a more positive light, the torpor of government could inadvertently result in a legislative framework well adapted to the country's needs. A number of bioprospecting agreements have been negotiated since adoption of the White Paper (see Chapter 3). These provide working examples of the strengths and pitfalls of different relationships and accords, and inform an analysis of the essential components of legislation to regulate access to genetic resources and benefit-sharing. Important next steps are to assess the practical implementation of a new access and benefit-sharing (ABS) law, and the capacity and ability of institutions to administer its provisions.

For a recent examination of stakeholder participation in ABS policy processes, including that in South Africa, see Swiderska (2001).

are most likely to be targets for genetic-resource exploration and whether the resources are shared with other countries.

Institutional capacity

Whatever legislative path a country chooses, laws are only as effective as the institutions charged with carrying them out. Since regulation of access to genetic resources is a new area of law, few countries possess the requisite institutions and human resources to implement these new laws. Building this capacity is a long-term process; but it should begin systematically during the development of the legislation. To do this, legislative drafters should think carefully at every stage about what is necessary on a day-to-day basis in order to implement each aspect of the new law or laws, what existing institutions might be able to do so, what new capacities they would need to develop, and whether, in some cases, wholly new institutions might need to be established.

Producing this kind of 'institutional development and capacity-building checklist' has the added benefit of providing a list of priorities for funding that a country may wish to seek from the CBD's financial mechanism or other funding sources. However, countries should make sure that any ABS institutions and procedures established with financial support from donor institutions can be sustained and funded domestically after donor funding ends.

In addition, legislative drafters should think about which institutional entity is going to take the lead on technical, institutional and human resources development that will be necessary to give effect to the new access regulation regime. It may be desirable to have this spelled out in the access legislation itself, or in a parallel legal enactment.

Taking all of the considerations above into account, it becomes clear that there is a tension between the urgent need for action and the complexity of the kind of process that will yield technically sound and politically robust access legislation. Countries rich in biological diversity may wish to establish ABS regimes as soon as possible, due to the rapid expansion of bioprospecting in their territory. In Cameroon, for example, due to the discovery of an anti-HIV compound in a forest vine by US National Cancer Institute (NCI) researchers, the government felt obliged to take rapid action to regulate commercial access to, and use of, genetic and biochemical resources. The resulting regulations – included in forestry and environmental framework laws – provide that all genetic resources belong to the state of Cameroon and cannot be exploited scientifically, commercially or culturally without prior authorization from the state, and sharing of benefits with it. However, years later it remains unclear how these provisions will interact with other national laws, which ministry will administer the activities and to what extent these benefits will be distributed to local communities, research institutions and other stakeholders (Laird and Lisinge, 1998).

In countries where the traditional knowledge of indigenous peoples about the uses of genetic resources is a factor, special attention needs to be paid to participatory processes for indigenous peoples. In most cases, this will involve considerable preparatory work to educate indigenous peoples about the issues involved, how their interests may be affected and the choices that they face (see Case Study 12.1 for a discussion of Costa Rica's systematic approach to this issue).

CASE STUDY 12.1 THE PROCESS OF DEVELOPING COSTA RICA'S 1998 BIODIVERSITY LAW AND ITS TREATMENT OF GENETIC RESOURCES ACCESS AND BENEFIT-SHARING

Approved on 23 April 1998, Costa Rica's Biodiversity Law is the result of a long process to elaborate a national legal framework to implement the Convention on Biological Diversity (CBD) principles and provisions related to equitable sharing of benefits arising from the commercial use of components of biological diversity.

When the initial draft of the Biodiversity Law was presented in June 1996, six contracts allowing transnational corporations to conduct biodiversity prospecting had already been signed in Costa Rica. These contracts were drawn up in a regulatory vacuum. Laws regulating the uses of specific natural resources – such as the Wildlife Conservation Law (1992), the Forest Law (1996), the Constitutive Law for the National Parks Service (1972) and the Organic Law on the Environment (1995) – were in effect during that time. But a legal gap existed in regulating genetic and biochemical resources, including the sharing of benefits from their commercial utilization.

To fill this legal gap, the International Union for Conservation of Nature and Natural Resources (IUCN) Regional Office for Mesoamerica (ORMA), which is based in Costa Rica, was officially requested to provide technical support in drawing up a draft biodiversity law. As a starting point, ORMA and the environmental commission of the legislative assembly jointly developed a set of guiding principles to serve as the law's philosophical framework:

- equal access to, and distribution of, the benefits arising from the use of the components of biodiversity;
- respect for human rights with particular attention to groups marginalized due to cultural or economic factors;
- sustainable use of biodiversity with respect to the interests of future generations; and
- the importance of democracy in guaranteeing greater participation of all citizens and civil peace in decision-making processes and development options.

On this conceptual basis, an initial consultation process was initiated that included indigenous peoples; people living close to protected areas; small farmers' representatives; legal experts; scientists; civil servants; and private companies. The objective of the consultation was to seek broad input on what should be the basic content of the draft law.

With this input, the preparation of the draft law started. It was agreed that the law should be comprehensive, covering all aspects of Costa Rica's rights and obligations under the CBD in an integrated manner. This strategy deliberately left open the possibility of developing discrete, more detailed regulations in the future for specific issues such as biosafety, biotechnology, access to genetic resources and intellectual property.

The draft was published in June 1996 and widely circulated for public comment. 3000 copies were distributed throughout the country and it was posted on the Internet. The draft excited a great deal of comment, both positive and negative. Based on this input, a revised draft was completed in December 1996. At this point the process bogged down due to polarization of different positions on various issues. To resolve the impasse, the environment commission appointed a special sub-commission consisting of the whole range of national stakeholders in order to produce a consensus draft, which was completed in November 1997, passed by the legislative assembly in April 1998, and signed into law the following month. The resulting law is probably one of the most comprehensive pieces of national legislation to implement the CBD that exists.

Treatment of access to genetic resources and benefit-sharing

Under the law (Article 62), any research programme or bioprospecting requires an access permit, with the exception of exchanges of genetic resources between indigenous peoples and local communities. Basic requirements for granting an access permit include:

- obtaining the prior informed consent of local representatives in the area intended for collection; representatives may be conservation areas' regional councils, private landowners or local indigenous authorities, depending upon the legal status of the territory in question;
- validation of the grant of prior informed consent by the National Commission for Biodiversity Management (CONAGEBIO), which is the multisectoral body charged with evaluating and granting access permits through its technical office;
- provisions for technology transfer and the equitable distribution of any resulting benefits;
- provisions for protection of, and/or compensation for, the use of any local knowledge associated with the genetic resources in question, mutually agreed with the local representatives;
- elaboration of the ways in which the bioprospecting activity will contribute to the conservation of species and ecosystems; and
- in the case of foreign individuals or corporate entities, designation of a legal representative resident in Costa Rica.

The permit and any associated contracts must also specify the resources that are intended to be collected, ensure the deposit of duplicate samples and periodic reporting on collecting activities, and agree to adhere to various other scientific and technical rules established by CONAGEBIO.

Somewhat different requirements are set out for commercial versus non-commercial research. In the case of non-commercial research, it must be established beyond any shadow of a doubt that no economic interests exist. There is also a special procedure for duly registered ex-situ collections to allow them a bit more latitude; but they must still specify the areas and resources intended for collection, and their permits are non-transferable.

As a corollary to the principle of local prior informed consent, the law recognizes the right to 'cultural objection', meaning that local communities and indigenous peoples may deny access to their resources and associated knowledge for cultural, spiritual, social, economic or other reasons.

Intellectual property rights and genetic resources

With respect to the patenting of the components of biodiversity, the law specifically excludes the following from intellectual property protection in Costa Rica: DNA sequences per se; plants and animals; micro-organisms that have not been genetically modified; essential biological processes for the production of plants and animals;

natural processes and cycles themselves; inventions that are essentially derived from knowledge associated with publicly owned traditional or cultural biological practices; and inventions which, on being commercially exploited in a monopolistic manner, could affect agricultural processes or products considered basic for the food security and health of the country's inhabitants.

Both the National Seed Office and the Intellectual Property Office are obliged to consult with CONAGEBIO on innovations that involve biodiversity components before granting any form of intellectual property right (IPR) protection. Any such protection granted by these offices must always be accompanied by a certificate of origin issued by the commission's technical office and a certificate of prior informed consent. Opposition raised by the technical office will effectively prevent registration of any patent or plant breeder's right certificate.

The law also establishes that holders of IPR rights related to or based on biodiversity must cede a compulsory licence to the state in cases of national emergency, where this is required to protect the common welfare.

Intellectual property rights and knowledge associated with genetic resources

The law provides that the state recognizes the existence and validity of all forms of knowledge and innovation, and the need to protect them through appropriate legal means for each specific case, including patents, trade secrets, plant breeders' rights, *sui generis* community intellectual rights, copyright, farmers' rights, and other forms.

The law recognizes and expressly protects, under the umbrella term '*sui generis* community intellectual rights', the knowledge, practices and innovations of indigenous peoples and local communities related to the use of the components of biodiversity. This right exists and is legally recognized by the simple existence of the cultural practice or knowledge – it requires no previous declaration, formal recognition or official registration, although it may cover practices that acquire formal status in the future.

A consultative process, mandated by the law, was carried out in 1998 and 1999 by the commission's technical office, together with indigenous and small farmers' representative groups, in order to determine the nature, scope and requirements of these rights for their future legal elaboration.

This effort is also initiating a process for the establishment of a register of local and indigenous knowledge, innovations and practices to be managed by the commission's technical office. Ultimately, this registry will allow the technical office to reject any new requests for recognition of IPRs over knowledge, innovations and practices already recorded in the registry.

To ensure effective implementation of the law and to strengthen civil society participation in this process, representatives of small farmers, indigenous peoples, environmental non-governmental organizations (NGOs) and academics have formed a monitoring and advocacy network with the following objectives:

- Ensure the direct participation of farmers, indigenous populations, academia and the environmental movement in the regulation of the law.
- Strengthen civil society participation in the law's implementation through representation in CONAGEBIO.
- Strengthen civil society participation in the regional conservation area councils.
- Support the community consultative process mandated by the law to elaborate the scope, means and requirements for effective development and implementation of *sui generis* community intellectual rights.

- Support education in biodiversity conservation and sustainable use.
- Strengthen international relations with organizations who work in this area in order to share experiences and support proposals which benefit local communities.

Lessons learned

- Regulation of activities that are underway and are unregulated (such as bioprospecting) is a process that generates strong opposition and considerable political and economic pressure.
- There is little in the way of systematized experiences or best practices that developing countries can rely on in the area of genetic resources access and benefit-sharing (ABS). Countries must, therefore, be innovative and learn empirically from their own experiences.
- Information available to the general public on biodiversity and the economic, ethical and social implications of its utilization has been very limited. As a result, only a relatively small academic and scientific elite is well informed about the relevant issues.
- Participation by Central America as a region in meetings that deal with CBD implementation issues of highest priority to developing countries – such as access to genetic resources – has been sporadic and inadequate.
- The Costa Rican government is still reluctant to share significant decision-making power over key biodiversity issues with civil society, especially the small farmers and indigenous peoples.

Perhaps the most important lesson learned is that the exercise of drafting a national biodiversity law can create an important opportunity for learning, for widening civil society participation in decision-making and for strengthening capacities. This allows for a real change in the management of power and resources, even if the law, in the end, is not approved.

Source: adapted from Solis and Madrigal, 1999

Potential elements of national access and benefit-sharing measures

Countries vary widely in their legal systems, policy objectives and administrative and enforcement capacities, and national ABS measures will vary accordingly. When surveying existing and draft legislation, however, a flexible set of principles and criteria can be delineated as a basis for national, sub-national or regional measures.

Principles, objectives and definitions

Almost any legislation will need to recite *key principles* upon which the enactment is founded (see Case Study 12.1 for a good example from Costa Rica). These would almost certainly need to include state sovereignty over natural resources – including genetic resources – within its jurisdiction; the authority of the government to determine access to genetic resources; and requirements of prior informed consent (PIC) and mutually agreed terms. In addition, some countries might also include statements of principle concerning the rights of indigenous and local communities over genetic resources within the areas they inhabit or use. Such statements would also concern associated knowledge, innovations and practices; the necessity that access legislation conform with legislation on conservation and sustainable use of biological resources; the desired linkage between ABS and transfer of technology; and the desire to cooperate with other states and ensure benefit-sharing.

A section on *objectives* is useful to specify the goals sought by the legislation. These might include establishing a permanent planning process to address ABS issues; equitable sharing of benefits from the use of genetic resources and associated knowledge; scientific and technological capacity-building; biodiversity conservation; and socio-economic progress.

Definitions of key terms used in the legislation are necessary in at least three situations. Firstly, a term may need to be defined when its meaning is unclear. Secondly, a term may need to be defined when the drafters decide that the meaning of the term in the legal enactment should differ from normal usage. Thirdly, a term may need to be defined in order to clarify the scope of the legislation. As a general matter, drafters should be encouraged to draw their definitions from existing documents – such as the CBD and the FAO *International Code of Conduct for Plant Germplasm Collecting* – since the terms and definitions used there reflect broad international consensus (Glowka, 1998).

Scope of application and the legal status of genetic resources

Properly defining the scope of what access legislation will apply to is one of the most important factors contributing to its future effectiveness. While ABS legislation must be sufficiently comprehensive, setting its scope too broadly may make it impossible to implement effectively. There are at least four important dimensions to scope: what materials and associated knowledge are covered; what geographic locales are included; what specific activities are covered; and which actors fall within the scope of the legislation. If the law's intent is to exclude specific actors, activities, places or materials (eg human genetic resources), those exclusions should also be clearly articulated.

Establishing the legal status of genetic resources

Setting the scope of ABS legislation requires, firstly, clarifying the legal status of genetic resources. While the constitutions and subsidiary enactments of many countries specify the legal status of *biological* resources, few, if any, specifically reference genetic resources. In that situation, one might assume that genetic resources would retain the legal status of the biological materials in which they are expressed. But, in fact, some states are developing legal regimes that treat genetic resources differently from the biological resources in which they are found, creating considerable potential for confusion (Glowka, 1998).

Ideally, the legal status of genetic resources would distinguish between rights over the physical entity (such as an organism or its parts) and the genetic information embodied in the physical entity, since it is this information component that is most valuable to bioprospectors (Glowka, 1998). However, since this intangible informational component cannot yet be described with sufficient specificity to allow the creation of a separate system of rights and owner-

---

BOX 12.10 SOME KEY TERMS AND SAMPLE DEFINITIONS FOR ACCESS AND BENEFIT-SHARING LEGISLATIVE MEASURES

Access to genetic resources: to obtain samples of biological or other material containing genetic material from areas within national jurisdiction for the purposes of research on, conservation of, or commercial or industrial application of the genetic material (Glowka, 1998).

Biological diversity: the variability among living organisms from all sources including, inter alia, terrestrial, marine and other aquatic ecosystems and the natural complexes of which they are part; this includes diversity within species, between species and of ecosystems.

Biological resources: genetic resources, organisms or part thereof, populations, or any other biotic component of ecosystems with actual or potential use or value for humanity.

Biodiversity prospecting (or 'bioprospecting'): the exploration of biodiversity for commercially valuable genetic and biochemical resources (Reid et al, 1993).

Biotechnology: any technological application that uses biological systems, living organisms or derivatives thereof to make or modify products or processes for specific use.

Country of origin of genetic resources: the country which possesses those genetic resources in in-situ conditions.

Country providing genetic resources: the country supplying genetic resources collected from in-situ sources, including populations of both wild and domesticated species, or taken from ex-situ sources, which may or may not have originated in that country.

Derivative: unimproved or unmodified chemical compounds, other than DNA or RNA, that exist in a sample of biological material obtained from an in-situ or ex-situ source and formed by the metabolic processes of the organism.[2]

Domesticated or cultivated species: species in which the evolutionary process has been influenced by humans to meet their needs.

Genetic material: any material of plant, animal, microbial or other origin containing functional units of heredity.

Genetic resources: genetic material of actual or potential value.

Source: unless otherwise noted, all terms are from the CBD (see SCBD, 2001)

---

ship over genetic information on its own, legal approaches will, of necessity, have to focus on controlling access to the physical entities within which genetic information is contained. This approach does not mean, however, that subsequent access agreements cannot specify how the information content of acquired genetic resources can be subsequently used and

how resulting benefits should be shared (Glowka, 1998).

The Andean Pact's Decision 391 distinguishes between the legal status of biological resources – which are subject to private or collective property rights – and genetic resources, which are deemed 'inalienable and imprescriptible and cannot be seized, without prejudice to property regimes applicable to the biological resources which contain them, the land on which they are found, or the associated intangible component meaning, in this law, associated traditional knowledge' (Article 6). Thus, the decision does not alter existing private or communal rights over biological resources; but property owners are not entitled to determine access to genetic resources. Property owners can, however, control access to genetic resources indirectly by controlling the physical access of bioprospectors to the areas or materials containing the genetic resources. Decision 391 envisions that this control will allow these actors to negotiate a share of benefits via 'accessory contracts' – which are distinct from the overall access agreement; this is between the bioprospector and the state.

Types and sources of genetic resources to be covered

ABS legislation must clearly state if it applies to domesticated or cultivated, as well as wild, species, and should specifically state whether it applies or not to microbial species, which are of great potential interest to bioprospectors. The Philippines and Costa Rican systems apply only to wild flora and fauna. In contrast, the Andean Pact Decision applies to all genetic resources for which a member state is a 'country of origin', leaving open the possibility that both wild and domesticated species can fall within the decision's scope. The draft Eritrean law specifically applies to both wild and domesticated species.

Such distinctions are important to make, as they can form the basis for creating different ABS regimes for different categories of genetic resources – such as those used for food and agriculture versus other purposes.

A related question concerns whether legislation covers ex-situ as well as in-situ resources. The Andean Pact Decision, Costa Rican law and the draft Eritrean law all include ex-situ genetic resources within their scope.

Protected areas are a potentially important source of genetic resources, and a number of countries have, or are developing, specific provisions related to access to genetic resources found in these areas (see Chapter 6). Similar special provisions also exist in some countries for the territories of indigenous peoples. These two cases are both examples of territories with specialized, pre-existing legal regimes governing their resources, and where particular values and interests not found in other areas are important.

ABS legislation must clarify the status of 'derivatives' under the law as well. The term is used rather loosely and can refer to two distinct kinds of genetic resources. Firstly, it could refer to unimproved or unmodified chemical compounds, other than DNA and RNA, that are merely associated with targeted biological material but formed by the metabolic processes of the organism. Thus, like DNA and RNA, these exist in raw samples of biological material. Secondly, 'derivatives' might refer to DNA or RNA, or a chemical compound, that has been modified, created or synthesized from materials originally obtained from an in-situ or ex-situ source. Examples might be a breeder's hybrid seed, a traditional healer's medicine or a pharmaceutical firm's synthetic version of an extracted biochemical. Access to the first type of derivatives can clearly be regulated by ABS legislation. The law has only to specify this. But it will be very difficult – technically and politically – to extend ABS legislation to the second context, since the state would, in effect, be regulating access to technologies, not genetic resources per se (Glowka, 1998).

Coverage of associated knowledge and information

In many cases, information associated with genetic resources can be quite valuable. Two types of situation need to be distinguished. First is the situation where access is sought to particular information about genetic resources – such as the knowledge of traditional healers about the medicinal properties of forest plants. Second is the situation where valuable knowledge is subsequently derived, either directly from genetic resources or from knowledge about genetic resources on the part of local and indigenous communities.

It is unlikely that states will try to assert an ownership interest in local knowledge about genetic resources, and thus knowledge of indigenous and local communities would not fall within the scope of access legislation (Glowka, 1998). On the other hand, states should seek to protect the rights of their citizens. ABS legislation can and should include a role for the state in regulating those seeking access to local and indigenous knowledge. ABS legislation can thus set minimum standards for prior informed consent from indigenous and local communities whose knowledge about genetic resources is sought. This is the case in the Philippines Executive Order, the Andean Pact Decision and the draft Fijian Sustainable Development Bill, for example.

In addition to traditional knowledge, the physical collections and databases of ex-situ facilities, research institutions and museums in many countries are potentially valuable sources of information about the country's genetic resources. ABS legislation could potentially regulate access to these sources of information, but this will depend upon the legal status of the institutions and the materials they hold (Glowka, 1998). Distinctions need to be made between public and private institutions, while private institutions who receive significant government funding constitute somewhat of a 'grey' area. And, as with physical access to genetic resources, a distinction may need to be made between access for non-commercial versus commercial purposes, so as not to impede non-commercial scientific research and information exchange.

The situation is very different for information and knowledge derived from genetic resources subsequent to their collection. As is the case with physical derivatives of genetic resources, 'derived information' probably cannot be practically included within the scope of ABS legislation. A better approach is for the legislation to specify minimum terms and conditions for access agreements with respect to the ownership, use and sharing of benefits from the use of such derived information.

Geographic locale

The CBD makes it clear that national sovereignty to determine access to genetic resources covers all land territory within a country's internationally recognized borders, as well as its territorial waters. With respect to a country's exclusive economic zone (EEZ) and continental shelf not part of territorial seas, CBD Article 22 specifies that a country's rights to determine access to genetic resources must be exercised in accordance with the law of the sea (including both the 1982 United Nations Convention on the Law of the Sea – UNCLOS – and customary international law). UNCLOS does not refer to 'genetic resources'; but extrapolating from its provisions concerning 'natural resources', 'living marine resources' and 'living organisms', it can be inferred that states hold sovereign rights over the exploration and exploitation of genetic resources on the continental shelf and within the EEZ. Thus, with respect to a country's EEZ and continental shelf, it can be inferred that coastal states hold sovereign rights over genetic resources for the purposes of exploring and exploiting genetic resources, qualified by conservation and management obligations. Resources of the high seas, including genetic resources, are beyond the limits of any national jurisdiction and are freely accessible by every state (Glowka, 1998).

On land, legislation must specify what areas are covered as well. Depending upon particular circumstances, ABS legislation might or might not apply to communal land and sea territories, private property or, in federal states, lands under the jurisdiction of sub-national government units such as states or provinces.

Activities and actors

ABS legislation should specify to what activities and actors its provisions apply. Access may be sought for either non-commercial (scientific research) or commercial purposes, and some countries (Costa Rica, the Philippines) treat these activities differently, providing a less burdensome regulatory procedure for scientific or academic research that does not have a commercial objective. This is an important consideration so that ABS regulations do not unintentionally restrict scientific activities and capacity development. It is sometimes difficult, however, to distinguish between the two, since academic and other research institutions frequently enter into agreements with the private sector in order to obtain financial support for their activities. A local scientific institution, for example, might collect samples for taxonomic purposes, but also make those samples available to an international private-sector firm with commercial objectives. One way to deal

with the blurred line between 'academic' and 'commercial' is to shift the point of negotiating direct financial benefits for end uses of genetic resources to the time of commercialization instead of at the point of access (Vogel, 1997).

Countries must also decide to whom ABS legislation applies. Ideally, it should apply to nationals and non-nationals equally, since this line, too, is often blurred when international companies have local subsidiaries or local institutions act as intermediaries for international actors. The Philippines Executive Order, for example, applies to 'foreign and local individuals, entities, organizations, whether government or private'. The order does specify, however, that only 'duly recognized' national institutions can enter into non-commercial research agreements with the government. Foreign entities, whether legal or natural persons, must enter into a more restrictive commercial research agreement, no matter what the avowed purpose of their desire to access genetic resources.

Institutions to oversee access to genetic resources

Since ABS regulation is a new area for state policy, new institutional arrangements must be put in place to administer the system. An important threshold question is: at what level of government will the determination of access be made? In federal states where sub-national governments hold authority over biological resources, access determination may take place at that level, with the national government playing a role in harmonizing practice among sub-national government units. Some countries may decide to delegate access determination authority to an academic institution, non-governmental body or private-sector contractor. These decisions will depend upon the circumstances of each state; but in all cases it is crucially important that the competent authority be clearly and publicly identified, so that those who seek access to genetic resources know to whom they must apply and which institution can give them a definitive answer that cannot be subsequently challenged by another agency.

Since the issue of access to genetic resources crosses many sectors, intersectoral coordination is essential for any effective ABS system. Most countries organize their management of natural resources along sectoral lines, but genetic resources access cannot be regulated by any one sectoral agency alone. Therefore, countries will need to establish some form of interagency coordinating body that includes all major agencies concerned with different aspects of genetic resources. One sectoral agency may be designated as the lead, but others must be included in the setup. The Philippines, discussed later in the section on 'Lessons from the Philippines', provides the most developed example of such a system.

In establishing the competent authority to take charge of determining access, countries must make suitable financial provision for its operation. New and additional financial and personnel resources must be allocated for the staffing and running of the competent authority. Its tasks are not, and should not be considered to be, merely an extension of the existing duties of the various agencies that are members of the interagency body. At a minimum – in countries where there is a significant number of applications for access – the competent authority needs to establish a secretariat to run its day-to-day affairs, with staff who do not hold other duties. The lack of such a dedicated budget line and specially assigned staff is a good indication that a country is not really serious in its commitment to regulating its

genetic resources, beyond the relatively easy step of passing a law – a step that is fairly meaningless without the allocation of financial and staff resources to effectively implement the law.

The access determination process

Whatever the structure of a competent authority to determine access to genetic resources, a clear and systematic process needs to be established to review and act upon applications for access. Four key components are likely to be involved: an application submitted to the designated competent authority; review of the application; denial of, or consent to, access (the access determination); and some form of appeals process.

Application to a competent authority

The competent authority needs, firstly, to set out in an application form the information and other requirements that an applicant must provide. One useful way to do this is to develop an 'application package' for prospective applicants, containing all relevant requirements and application forms and clearly explaining the country's access-determination process. In particular, such a package should provide contact details for a specific office or person who can provide additional information and answer questions.

Reviewing the access application

Submitting a completed application would trigger the access-determination process, beginning with a review of the application. Key concerns for legislation here are public notification and availability of the access application for review, and the process of reaching mutually agreed terms.

In order to make an access determination, the competent authority needs to gather sufficient information upon which to base its decision. The primary source of information will, of course, be the applicant, and ABS legislation should specify what information the applicant is required to provide. In addition, however, ABS legislation might establish an advisory board to provide a technical review of applications. Parties potentially affected by the access determination, or with special expertise – such as indigenous or local community representatives, businesses and the scientific community – may also have useful information regarding the application. ABS legislation could, therefore, require the competent authority to publicize receipt of the application and its contents to potentially affected parties.

The presumption should be that all applications for access are freely available for the public to review. If an applicant, however, seeks to keep some elements of an application confidential – elements, for example, related to traditional knowledge, fee and royalty rates, or intellectual property right (IPR) issues – the burden should be on the applicant to demonstrate why the information should be kept confidential. ABS legislation might specify guidelines for such confidentiality exceptions to a general rule of transparency in access determinations.

Where a country specifies that the prior informed consent of local or indigenous communities is necessary for a positive determination of access, the procedure for obtaining that consent should be specified in ABS legislation or in its implementing regulations, as is the case in the Philippines. In cases such as this, the provision of adequate information to local communities will be a substantial task, and will require that at least some information about the application is provided in local languages and through media and fora appropriate to the communities in question.

Since arriving at 'mutually agreed terms' is an integral element of any positive decision on access by the competent authority, ABS legislation needs to spell out exactly what that means and among which parties terms must be agreed. For example, ABS legislation might allow a prospective applicant to negotiate a draft access agreement with the ultimate provider of genetic resources (such as a local community or university), and then review the draft as part of the access-determination process. Or, legislation might not allow any negotiations to proceed – even on a draft basis – until an access application has been submitted and reviewed by the competent authority. Similarly, ABS legislation should specify whether mutually agreed terms must be reached between:

- the applicant and the state;
- the applicant and an ultimate provider of genetic resources; or
- both (Glowka, 1998).

In addition, legislation needs to specify minimum terms and conditions for access agreements. These may apply to minimum arrangements for benefit-sharing, how materials sought can be used and by whom, and limitations related to potential environmental impacts.

The access determination

The actual access determination will be simply a decision to deny or grant consent to access genetic resources as specified in the applicant's application. However, for purposes of transparency and possible appeal (discussed in the following subsection), a rationale for the decision should be provided and made publicly available. ABS legislation should specify the criteria against which applications are judged, and specific reference to those criteria should be included in the rationale for the decision. Whether granted or denied, the determination should be communicated in writing. If access is granted, the written communication might be in the form of a permit specifying the conditions of access, with the access agreement embodying attached mutually agreed terms. Such a permit could be used as a certificate of origin (for import of genetic material into other countries), providing proof that prior informed consent and other source-country legal requirements have been met with respect to the genetic resources in question.

Appeal

ABS legislation should provide for an appeals process, open to both applicants denied access as well as to potentially affected parties whose views may not have been adequately reflected in the decision process. An appeals process is necessary to ensure that the access-determination process is viewed as fair by both applicants and by those who might be affected by the applicant's proposed activities. At the same time, countries should be mindful of the need for finality. Appeals should be allowed, but the process should not drag on too long. Once an appeal has been heard and decided, the decision should be final and legally binding.

Implementation and enforcement provisions

ABS legislation will always be difficult to enforce, due to the nature of genetic resources, particularly their wide availability and ease of dissemination or replication (Glowka, 1998). The threat of civil and criminal penalties for breaches of access agreements is therefore an important tool that should be explicitly provided for in ABS legislation. States can also utilize export controls to ensure that PIC requirements have been fulfilled, both with the state and with others. ABS legislation could state, for example, that the export of genetic resources is prohibited without a valid access agreement, approved by the competent authority, which applies to the particular genetic resources that are to be exported. It is important, however, to ensure that such provisions are narrowly tailored to apply only to genetic resources, not to biological resources in general (which are typically controlled under separate pre-existing regulations).

Lessons from the Philippines: Development and Implementation of Executive Order 247 on Access to Genetic Resources, 1994–1999

In 1994, the country's scientific community, in cooperation with government and a large and active community of non-governmental organizations (NGOs), pushed for a comprehensive policy and a legal and administrative regulatory framework aimed at regulating bioprospecting in the Philippines. This was in response to the mandate of Article 15 of the CBD, and more significantly to remedy what was perceived to be a heightening biopiracy problem.

After one year of multistakeholder consultations and interagency deliberations, Executive Order No 247 'Prescribing a Regulatory Framework for the Prospecting of Biological and Genetic Resources, Their By-Products and

Derivatives, for Scientific and Commercial Purposes, and for Other Purposes' (EO 247) was signed by President Fidel V Ramos in May 1995. A year later, in June 1996, Department Administrative Order 96-20 'Implementing Rules and Regulations on the Prospecting of Biological and Genetic Resources' (DAO 96-20) was issued by the Philippines Department of Environment and Natural Resources (DENR).

EO 247 has been praised by many as a pioneering and systematic effort to put the CBD's principles on genetic resources ABS into practice. It has also been condemned by others as unrealistic and unworkable, and is viewed by many in the commercial sector as the bête noir of the international ABS debate (ten Kate and Laird, 1999). Experience under EO 247 is thus worthy of a close look.

Salient features of the Philippines ABS regime

Legal status of Philippine genetic resources

EO 247 establishes that ultimate ownership of wild genetic resources expressed in plants and animals is vested in the state, stating in the preamble that, in line with the country's constitution, 'wildlife, including flora and fauna, among others, is owned by the State and the disposition, development and utilization thereof are under its full control and supervision'. The status of genetic resources expressed in domesticated plants and animals and in micro-organisms, however, is not mentioned, although the phrase 'among others' may be construed to include these as well (Glowka, 1998).

Research agreement with the state required for access

EO 247 requires anyone seeking access to genetic resources to conclude a research agreement with the Philippine government. Depending upon the actor and the activities proposed, the agreement may be either an academic research agreement (ARA) or a commercial research agreement (CRA), both of which require the applicant to satisfy certain requirements and to undergo an application process.

The important difference between the two types of agreement is the extent of government control over research activities. The ARA – which is available only to Philippine government agencies, academic and research institutions and intergovernmental research organizations (such as the International Rice Research Institute, which is based in the Philippines) – allows these institutions a greater degree of self-regulation and flexibility than is permitted under a CRA. The CRA's provisions are more stringent and are the mechanism to monitor private commercial entities and their academic partners – foreign or domestic – with avowed commercial purposes. In addition, all foreign entities, with the exception of intergovernmental research institutions, are presumed to have commercial intentions – whatever their avowed purposes – and must conclude a CRA. ARAs run for five years while CRAs run for three years. Both are renewable upon review by the Inter-Agency Committee on Biological and Genetic Resources (IACBGR) charged with administering EO 247 (see 'Administrative mechanism').

Minimum terms and conditions

EO 247 sets out a list of minimum terms and conditions that must be included in all research agreements:

- The agreement must specify a limit on samples that the collector may obtain and export.

- A duplicate set of all specimens must be deposited by the collector with the Philippines National Museum or duly designated governmental entity.
- 'All Filipino citizens and Philippine governmental entities' must be guaranteed access to all collected specimens 'and relevant data' whenever these specimens are deposited in depositories abroad.
- The collector (or, if appropriate, the principal on behalf of which the collector is acting) must inform the government 'as well as the affected local and indigenous cultural communities' about all discoveries based on collection activities conducted in the Philippines, 'if a commercial product is derived from such activity', and must include provision for payment of royalties from commercial uses, or must negotiate terms for 'other forms of compensation'.
- In the case of foreign collectors, the agreement must stipulate that 'scientists who are citizens of the Philippines must be actively involved in the research and collection process and, where applicable and appropriate as determined by the Inter-Agency Committee, in the technological development of a product derived from' the resources collected.
- Transfer of collected materials to any third party by the collector must be accomplished by use of a standard materials transfer agreement (MTA) form, appended to the agreement, which includes provisions on confidentiality, restricted use, responsibility of the original collector to enforce compliance with the terms and conditions of the law, and the research agreement by third-party recipients.
- 'A status report of the research and the ecological state of the area and/or species concerned will be submitted to the Inter-Agency Committee regularly.'
- Fixed administrative fees, set by the IACBGR, must be paid.
- The agreement must state that where a commercial product is developed from genetic material found in species endemic to the Philippines, the resulting technology 'must be made available to a designated Philippine institution' without payment of licensing fees or royalties. This controversial provision, however, is qualified by the statement: 'provided, however, that where appropriate and applicable, other agreements may be negotiated'.

Academic research agreements are basically subject to these minimum terms and conditions (except for the ones that apply specifically to commercial uses of genetic resources), but involve a larger degree of self-regulation. An ARA:

> '...may be comprehensive in scope and cover as many areas as may be projected. It may stipulate that all scientists and researchers affiliated with a duly recognized university, academic institution, governmental and intergovernmental entity need not apply for a different Research Agreement but may conduct research and collection activities in accordance with an existing ARA.'

Essentially, eligible institutions receive a blanket research agreement and are delegated the responsibility to ensure that all researchers operating under the agreement comply with its terms. ARAs must make clear, however, that when collection under the ARA develops 'commercial prospects' the collector must apply for a CRA.

Benefit-sharing and technology transfer

EO 247 enumerates several provisions to promote the development of local capacity in science and technology, and to ensure the fair and equitable sharing of benefits arising from commercial uses of genetic resources with the indigenous community, local community, protected area or private landowner concerned.

All discoveries derived from Philippine genetic material must be made available to the Philippine government, as well as to the local communities in whose areas the material was collected. Where commercially valuable inventions or technologies are derived from the genetic material collected under a research agreement, a separate agreement must be made for the transfer of royalties, benefits and technology, although the specific terms of this agreement are left to the parties to negotiate. In addition, capacity-building and joint research – including the active involvement of Philippine scientists in the research and collection, and in the technological development of a product derived from the resource – are also encouraged. The parties to the agreement may also include a stipulation on profit-sharing.

In short, the EO 247 regime mandates benefit-sharing – not only with the nation, but with the local communities where genetic resources are collected; but it does not attempt to specify exactly what benefits must be shared. Rather, the parties are given latitude to negotiate benefit-sharing agreements, which are then scrutinized by the IACBGR to ensure that the minimum terms of the law have been met.

Prior informed consent (PIC)

While Article 15 of the CBD requires only that states providing genetic resources within their territories give PIC for access, EO 247 goes further, requiring that:

'Prospecting of biological and genetic resources shall be allowed within the ancestral lands and domains of indigenous cultural communities only with the prior informed consent of such communities, obtained in accordance with the customary laws of the concerned community.' It goes on to require that the PIC of non-indigenous local communities (represented by their local government) must also be obtained, as well as the consent of private landowners where resources are sought on privately held lands. Where collectors seek materials within protected areas, they must obtain the PIC of the local protected area management board.

Evidence that PIC has been obtained must be presented before any collection of genetic material is permitted. In an ARA, PIC is secured after approval of the agreement but before actual collection begins; in a CRA, PIC is a requirement before an agreement is approved. This provides holders of ARA the flexibility to conduct preliminary assessments of potential study sites.

PIC can be obtained following a process of public notification or sector consultation, or both – or in the case of ancestral lands and domains, in accordance with the customary traditions, practices and mores of the community. The PIC certificate can only be issued after 60 days from submission of the proposal to the recognized head of the indigenous people or local community concerned, to ensure that the community has evaluated and deliberated among themselves on what action to take.

With respect to indigenous communities, PIC is required not only under EO 247 but also by the Indigenous Peoples Rights Act (IPRA), a law passed by the Philippine congress in 1997 that extends a PIC requirement to virtually all potential uses of natural resources found within recognized indigenous territories (see Box 12.7).

Administrative mechanism

EO 247 is the concern of several government agencies, including the Philippine Department of Environment and Natural Resources (DENR), the Department of Health (DOH), the Department of Science and Technology (DOST), the Department of Agriculture (DA) and the Department of Foreign Affairs (DFA). These agencies meet as a group under the umbrella of the Interagency Committee on Biological and Genetic Resources (IACBGR). The IACBGR is the regulatory body tasked to enforce and implement the provisions of EO 247 and its implementing rules and regulations. It is chaired by the DENR and its membership includes representatives of the member agencies and representatives from NGOs and peoples' organizations. It is supported by an interagency technical secretariat.

One of the functions of the IACBGR is to process applications for research agreements. After its evaluation and approval, the body endorses the proposal to the secretary of the government agency concerned for approval. IACBGR also ensures that the conditions of the research agreements are strictly observed.

Experiences in implementation: lessons learned

As the first comprehensive regime of national ABS measures to be developed and implemented in direct response to the CBD, the Philippines' experience with EO 247 has provided useful lessons that will guide future development of national ABS measures in that country. And while the context in which other countries are developing national ABS measures, of course, differs from that of the Philippines, the lessons of experience under EO 247 provide useful input for other countries as well.

It is important to note, however, that between the time the system came into force in mid 1996 and the end of 1999, only 15 applications were received – most of them from local universities seeking academic research agreements – and only one commercial research agreement was approved. Thus, practical experience in managing commercial research agreements for access to genetic resources remains limited. Indeed, some have argued that the perceived complexity and bureaucracy of the EO 247 system has acted as a strong disincentive for commercial bioprospecting activities in the country.

Stakeholder participation is essential in developing, enacting and implementing ABS policies, laws, rules and regulations

From the very beginning, EO 247 was a product of a collective effort of many stakeholders with diverse interests. It was originally proposed by the Philippine Network for the Chemistry of Natural Products, a group of Filipino scientists concerned over the lack of an appropriate regulatory framework to govern the growing number of biodiversity prospecting activities underway in the country. The main issue for these scientists was how the Philippines – in particular, its scientific community – could benefit from these activities. Capacity-building was therefore a priority from the beginning of the process.

Consultations were subsequently broadened to include non-governmental organizations and peoples' organizations (grassroots community organizations) active in issues involving environment and natural resources, agriculture, health and indigenous peoples. These groups generally articulated positions critical of bioprospecting but acknowledged that there was a need for a regulatory mechanism. The rules requiring prior informed consent were developed largely in response to their concerns.

> 'It must be emphasized to the Convention Parties that Bristol-Myers Squibb will not pursue natural products research in those countries that impose requirements similar to those contained in the Philippine Executive Order [247]... Government initiatives that place onerous restrictions on those seeking access to genetic resources or do not afford appropriate protection to intellectual property rights will result in fewer efforts to survey natural resources for pharmaceuticals and that will ultimately work to the detriment of environmental protection... [Consultations during the development of EO 247], to the best of our knowledge...did not include pharmaceutical firms, such as Bristol-Myers Squibb, whose natural products research efforts will be seriously undermined by the Philippines EO and other similar initiatives', excerpt from letter by Manheim, Fox, Bennett and Turner on behalf of Bristol-Myers Squibb to the Hon Timothy Wirth, Undersecretary for Global Affairs, Department of State, US, 3 November 1995 (from ten Kate and Laird, 1999).

The relevant government agencies were also brought into the process and ultimately took the lead in guiding the proposed regulation through the formal government approval process. These included, among others, the departments of environment and natural resources, agriculture, health, education and foreign affairs.

A major gap in the consultative process was the lack of involvement by representatives of private industries potentially affected by the proposed regulation. This was due, in part, because it appeared that there were no significant domestic private-sector players at the outset of the process with a stake in the outcome. By 1997, however, a few industry representatives had engaged in the debate about implementation, particularly from the pharmaceutical and agricultural sectors.

The multistakeholder character of the policy-making process was replicated in the implementation procedures that were established. The IACBGR has representatives from different agencies, as well as representatives from NGOs, peoples' organizations and research institutions. As a result, solutions to implementation problems were also arrived at in a collective manner.

Defining the scope and coverage of a national ABS regulation is a priority concern

The most difficult issues associated with the implementation of EO 247 have arisen due to the order's broad definition of bioprospecting, which covers all activities related to research, collection and utilization of biological and genetic resources, whether for scientific or commercial purposes. It, thus, not only affects commercial bioprospectors, but also scientific and academic institutions, NGOs and Philippine government entities involved in biodiversity conservation work. Indeed, conservation work such as biodiversity inventory, conservation of traditional crop varieties and efforts to conserve endangered and endemic wild fauna cannot be carried out without collection, research and (in some cases, such as plant varieties) utilization of these resources.

The EO 247 preamble would seem to imply that the order is primarily directed at regulating bioprospecting activities linked to biotechnology research and development. However, the subsequent articles are fairly clear in their coverage of almost everybody who collects, utilizes and does research using biological and genetic resources. A scope this broad has posed a range of problems. As a result, after two years of debate within the IACBGR, EO 247's scope and coverage were narrowed. For example, research and collection activities associated with pure conservation work, biodiversity inventory and taxonomic studies are no longer required to adhere to the full access determination process established by the order. Instead, these activities are regulated under the simpler research permit process in place before EO 247 came into force. It is recognized, however, that the IACBGR's narrowing of the order's scope is basically an ad hoc measure borne of necessity, and that a future revision of the order – or its replacement by congressional legislation – should craft a narrower legal definition.

Learning from the Philippine experience in this regard, drafters of ABS measures in other countries should keep in mind that such measures need to be comprehensive enough to cover the fairly complex range of activities that a state may wish to regulate; but they must also be realistic in terms of implementation and enforcement capacities, and should take care in choosing which actors and activities are covered. It is thus important for regulators to know exactly what it is they want to regulate and to be aware of the unintended negative consequences of overregulating.

The potential impacts on scientific research activities must be carefully considered when designing and implementing national ABS measures

The Philippine scientific community supports the objectives of ABS regulation, especially where those seeking genetic resources are foreign entities or individuals. Indeed, it was the scientific community, particularly the natural products chemists, who initially pushed for the development of ABS measures. As it turned out, however, the Philippine scientific and academic community has found that EO 247 has a considerable negative impact on scientific research activities.

From the perspective of the research community, the regime established under EO 247 represents a radical departure from previous practice, when state regulation of taxonomic collection and other such activities was minimal and community-level regulation was non-existent. In addition, the research community is often confused and frustrated by the novelty and complexity of the ABS regulatory process, in tandem with the initially low level of administrative capability on the part of the government to make the process move smoothly. As a result, the domestic scientific-research community has been among the strongest critics of EO 247, complaining that the whole process is too tedious, too costly, too time consuming and too broad, encompassing activities that do not have commercial prospects and thus frustrating efforts to better understand and conserve the country's biodiversity. This is particularly unfortunate since one of the duties of the IACBGR, as set out in EO 247, is to 'develop a conceptual framework...for significantly increasing knowledge of Philippine biodiversity'.

Scientists are particularly critical of the required procedures for obtaining prior informed consent of communities in whose territories they will conduct research. While by no means opposed to obtaining the consent of local communities, they say that the mandated procedure is unrealistic and costly, since it requires several trips to the often remote research site, meaning added expense and lost time. Added cost is a main concern because most researchers depend upon research grants that do not provide for expenditures necessary to obtain local PIC. Supporters of EO 247, however, argue that the researchers – and their funders – ought to adjust to the new regulations and factor in these costs, not the other way around. Indeed, in the case of indigenous peoples, free and prior informed consent of the local community is now required for outsiders' access to all types of natural resources under the 1997 Indigenous Peoples Rights Act, as noted previously.

Another common criticism of the regulation is that, while it contains many requirements and prohibitions, there are no provisions that encourage or give incentives for legitimate bioprospecting work, especially work performed by local scientists. Although the IACBGR is mandated by the EO to develop a national and integrated framework for bioprospecting, there has been little movement towards putting this into place.

Creative approaches to obtaining consent from, and sharing benefits with, local communities, including indigenous peoples, need to be explored and developed

The EO 247 requirement that those seeking access to genetic resources obtain prior informed consent from local or indigenous communities in the area in question is strongly supported by many stakeholders in the Philippines and is, in practical political terms, non-negotiable. Through the PIC process, the capacities and efforts of indigenous peoples and local communities to protect, conserve and manage the natural resources in their areas are acknowledged and supported. It also provides them with leverage to negotiate the terms and conditions for the use of the resource and to capture a share of any subsequent benefits.

The process of securing prior informed consent could, however, be simplified and support mechanisms put in place to assist both the community and the parties seeking access. For example, the waiting period could be shortened from 60 days to a shorter period. The essential point is that those seeking genetic resources in the Philippines must anticipate the need to obtain local PIC and incorporate this consideration into their project plans, budgets and schedules (see Chapter 7).

An important issue that will be faced in the future is finding practical approaches for benefit-sharing with local communities. The local PIC requirement was instituted in order to ensure that this discussion or negotiation on benefit-sharing would, in fact, happen. Benefits that might be negotiated by local communities under the EO 247 framework include:

- upfront payments to local communities for samples collected in their territories, and/or cash 'milestone' payments pegged to stages in the development of a product where its value increases;
- transfers of locally useable technology and local capacity-building, so that the source community may bring added value to its genetic resources; examples might be 'para-taxomony' training and employment – such as Costa Rica's National Institute of Biodiversity (InBio) provides (Sittenfeld, 1993) – or training in the preparation of simple extracts from collected biological materials;
- earmarking of funds for conservation of biodiversity and genetic resources in a community's territory;
- coownership of patents and other intellectual property rights where indigenous knowledge associated with collected genetic resources contributes

to the discovery of a useful compound and/or development of a commercial product; and

- support for infrastructure develop-ments – such as schools, water supplies or roads – desired by a community in whose territory samples are collected.

All of these, however, presuppose that commercial bioprospectors will be willing to operate under the procedures and restrictions of the EO 247 regime. After more than three years of EO 247's imple-mentation, however, this does not, for the most part, appear to be the case.

Even if the generally negative attitude of industry towards the EO 247 regime softens – or if the Philippine government decides to relax some of the current proce-dures – finding practical ways to manage and distribute benefits so that they actually reach local people in a manner that is perceived as equitable will pose formidable challenges. Benefits may be absorbed by central government depart-ments who purport to manage such benefits 'on behalf of the local commu-nity'. The local elite may monopolize benefits, be they in cash or in kind. And there is always the risk of run-of-the-mill corruption. Nevertheless, these problems are characteristic distribution issues in virtually all sectors of local economic development. They are not unique to genetic resources. And they are certainly not unique to the Philippines.

An efficient and effective institutional system should be put into place

Since the issues related to bioprospecting are multidisciplinary, implementation of an ABS regime requires an interagency approach that benefits from the experi-ences and expertise of each agency and allows financial resources, staff and other

'*A mechanism is needed to ensure that the benefits that have been negotiated [under EO 247] will directly accrue to the communities. For now, everything is left to the wisdom and sense of justice of the national government agencies and the local government units... The framers of EO 247 hope that they will always put the interests of the commu-nity and its people in mind when making these decisions. But, as always, the good intentions and desires of some are easily dashed when confronted with the day-to-day realities of temptations, conflicts of interest and other bureaucratic ratio-nalizations*' Elpidio Peria, Philippine NGO activist (Peria, 1998).

logistical support needs to be pooled. Decisions are also easily reached because the expertise is readily available. A multi-sectoral approach such as this also has disadvantages, however.

An interagency committee, such as that created by EO 247 – where sectoral groups are represented and high-level officials are members – can easily fall prey to problems such as unavailability of members, lack of quorum, lack of conti-nuity and endless briefings and updates for absentee members. Officially, the IACBGR is supposed to meet once per quarter to review and make recommendations on applications for ARAs and CRAs. But during the period between the installation of a new national executive administration in mid 1998 and September 1999, for example, the IACBGR only met once.

One of the hurdles that the IACBGR has to contend with, if it is to effectively implement the executive order (EO), is funding. The IACBGR and its technical secretariat do not have their own budget and must rely on member agencies to contribute operating funds.

Central to the issue associated with administrative procedures are the application and processing requirements, time frame, monitoring and enforceability. The procedure for processing applications for ARA and CRA is fairly straightforward; but concerns have been raised over the amount of paperwork and time required before a CRA or ARA is approved. The ARA for the University of the Philippines system, for example, was under negotiation for several years.

Once a CRA or an ARA is approved, monitoring and enforceability problems arise. There is currently no monitoring system in place to verify compliance with the provisions of the EO or the terms and conditions of the ARA or CRA. The IACBGR is Manila-based and relies on field offices of the member agencies to verify compliance. At this point in time, it is doubtful if the field offices of the member agencies can effectively perform this function; only a few agencies, such as the DENR, have been actively disseminating information about the EO.

Executive orders, rather than legislative acts, can be useful means of exploring and testing approaches to regulating ABS; but they are also inadequate

The decision to regulate bioprospecting through an executive order rather than an act of congress enabled the Philippines to rapidly put into place a regulatory framework on ABS. Because executive orders are easier to amend, there was a willingness among all stakeholders to proceed with this experiment. In this way, executive orders can be a useful means of exploring and testing approaches to this novel issue. However, the Philippine experience also shows the limits of this strategy. In particular, no penal sanctions can be imposed for violations of EO 247's provisions, unless the transgression also violates another law that provides for criminal penalties. Dealing effectively with intellectual property rights issues that are related to genetic resources is also not possible without legislative action.

In regions where countries share genetic resources, national frameworks alone are inadequate and regional mechanisms may be required

By going ahead of its neighbours in regulating bioprospecting, it is possible that an unintended consequence is a disincentive for research in the Philippines. While there is no empirical evidence that this is happening, there is a fear among Philippine researchers that the complexity of the access regime could discourage international collaborators from coming into the country. Since the Philippines shares with its neighbours many of the same genetic resources, this is a well-founded fear. The Philippines, from this perspective, has put itself at a comparative disadvantage. For this reason, the Philippines has made the adoption of a regional framework agreement on access among the member states of the Association of South-East Asian Nations (ASEAN) an urgent priority.

Conclusion

There is no blueprint for developing national policies and legislation governing access to genetic resources and the sharing of benefits from their use. For one thing, there is simply not enough mature experience with this new area of law and policy to be able to say with certainty what is the 'right way'. For another, countries vary greatly in their capacities, cultures, legal systems and preferences. Nevertheless, there is already a considerable amount of experience – much of it recounted in this chapter and in the References listed at the end of this book – and countries need not, and should not, begin the process of developing and implementing ABS legislation without taking advantage of the fund of experience that already exists.

Establishment of a firm and workable legislative and regulatory ABS framework is an important step in developing a country's policies to achieve the objectives of the CBD. At the same time, however, it must always be remembered that legislation is not a panacea, and that there are many complementary approaches – discussed in other chapters of this volume – that countries need to consider in tandem with legislative and regulatory development.

Notes

1   For a description of the background to the CBD and its institutional arrangements, full texts of the Articles of the CBD and the decisions of the Conference of the Parties, see the *Handbook of the Convention on Biological Diversity* (SCBD, 2001).
2   The term 'derivative' is (confusingly) used in two quite different contexts. The first context involves unimproved chemical compounds as defined above. In the second context, 'derivative' is sometimes used to refer to DNA or RNA, or a chemical compound, modified, created or synthesized by human intervention from biological materials originally obtained from an in-situ or ex-situ source. ABS legislation could be extended to derivatives in the first context, since the ultimate source of the derived material is likely to be biological material derived from the jurisdiction of a particular state. Access legislation would, however, be very difficult to extend to derivatives in the second context because the government would, in reality, be regulating access to technologies (Glowka, 1998).

Section VI

CONCLUSIONS AND RECOMMENDATIONS

Photograph by Sarah A Laird

John and Christiana Musuka return from collections of plants to be used in traditional medicines, in Likombe, Cameroon

Chapter 13

Conclusion and recommendations

*Sarah A Laird, Charles V Barber, Kelly P Bannister, Lyle Glowka,
Michael A Gollin, Kerry ten Kate, Flavia Noejovich, Brendan Tobin,
Antonio G M La Viña and Rachel Wynberg*

Conclusion

Biodiversity research and prospecting take place today amid rapid technological change, increasing the globalization of scientific and economic activity, as well as considerable legal uncertainty. Therefore, as we have seen, the establishment and implementation of equitable research relationships are daunting tasks that span a wide range of ethical, legal, economic, technological, scientific and institutional issues. Technological and scientific advances have resulted in expanded commercial applications for genetic resources and traditional knowledge, changed the way materials can be used and, in some cases, increased the difficulty in tracking resources through the commercial cycle (see Chapter 8). As genetic resources have become increasingly commodified, claims of ownership over them have expanded and intensified, largely through wider applications of evolving intellectual property rights.

Concurrently, the Convention on Biological Diversity (CBD) has established for the first time an international legal framework for regulating access to genetic resources and promoting the sharing of benefits arising from their commercial and scientific uses. This new framework has catalysed the development of national laws and other measures regulating access to genetic resources in many countries. At the same time, indigenous peoples' and local communities' rights to land, resources and control over their own traditional knowledge are receiving greater recognition than at any time in recent history. As this book goes to press, for example, a draft law to protect indigenous knowledge is under review in Peru – a development unthinkable ten years ago.

Although concern about the ethical implications of research is growing within the biodiversity research community, academic and professional standards for advancement within universities and research institutions remain largely unchanged. Furthermore, the multidisciplinary applied research and equitable partnership arrangements that most effectively serve biodiversity conservation and sustainable development remain poorly rewarded within the academic system. Pressures remain high on biodiversity researchers to publish the results of their research, even if publishing aspects of such information might run contrary to the objectives and needs of source countries and communities. Concepts such as prior informed consent (PIC) and benefit-sharing are expanding, but still too often constitute merely pious rhetoric and remain unrealized in the field.

Creating conditions for equity

In order to build equity into biodiversity research and prospecting partnerships, it is critical that a range of instruments are put in place to create and support the conditions for equitable partnerships. In addition to the development and implementation of international and national policy and law, these include contractual and research agreements, and codes of ethics and institutional policies.

The CBD provides a basic framework of international norms and obligations for access to genetic resources and benefit-sharing, and has established the achievement of equity in biodiversity research and prospecting partnerships as an obligation that all Parties to the Convention must strive to meet. While its provisions are binding only on Parties, the CBD also provides research institutions and commercial firms with a set of ethical principles to use in developing their own policies on access and benefit-sharing (ABS). Parties may also regulate stakeholders' rights and responsibilities through access legislation at the regional, national or local levels. Some 50 countries have now adopted or are developing such laws that will regulate scientists and companies hoping to access genetic resources and, often, traditional knowledge. Moreover, the institutional processes of the CBD provide a wide variety of stakeholders – including indigenous and local communities, conservation advocates, scientists and commercial interests – with an ongoing forum to put forward their interests and engage in dialogue with other stakeholder groups.

While the CBD provides a useful and necessary framework, it is still only an instrument to guide change, and its provisions leave most of the hard work of establishing operational measures on ABS to national governments. The CBD establishes important principles such as PIC and benefit-sharing, but it is the governments of individual countries – and, in some cases, states or provinces within countries – who must create laws and policies to turn those principles into binding legal rules and practical procedures. As we have seen in Chapter 12, countries face many challenges in developing national regimes, but an ABS law is not an insurmountable task, and many countries have done so, or will do so in the near future. More difficult are the tasks of gaining stakeholder consensus on broad policies that should drive the development of a national strategy and legislation, establishing a participatory and multistakeholder legislative development process, and dealing with institutional capacity and administrative practicalities to make the law work. Without sufficient attention to these difficult tasks, even the best ABS law, on paper, will be doomed to ineffectuality and irrelevance.

A significant gap in the development of national measures arises from the fact that the onus of taking action at the national level has *de facto* fallen on 'providing countries' – typically, high-biodiversity developing countries where research institutions and commercial firms from industrialized countries seek access to abundant and previously uninvestigated biodiversity. The CBD calls on *all* Parties to institute measures to ensure equitable ABS arrangements. But 'user' countries in the industrialized world have been slow to develop legal measures to ensure that acquisition and use of genetic material and associated knowledge by persons, institutions and corporations within user-country jurisdiction are carried out in compliance with the laws of the source country and the provisions of the CBD. None of the intellectual property rights (IPRs) systems of the industrialized countries, for example, requires that patent applications for inventions based on genetic resources or associated knowledge acquired in another country prove that the resources or knowledge were acquired in compliance with the CBD or national law in the source country. This abdication of responsibility by the major industrial nations is having two consequences. Firstly, it makes it extremely difficult for source countries to enforce their own laws on access, given the transnational and North–South nature of the trade in genetic resources. Secondly, as a result, 'source' countries are tending to establish very restrictive access laws, which often unintentionally hinder scientific research as well as both domestic and international development.

As important as the development of national ABS measures is, however, it is equally important to remember that the nitty-gritty of biodiversity prospecting partnerships and arrangements is not governed by national legislation, but by contractual agreements. Governments often set minimum contractual terms and standards for contracts and reserve the right to review and approve them. However, it is the parties to bioprospecting contracts – typically, research and academic institutions, commercial firms and sometimes local or indigenous communities – who are, to date, the most important and prolific law-makers on the topic, both in the sense that they develop practical schemes for biodiversity prospecting and because, in doing so, they often drive the establishment of new laws or regulations (see Chapters 9 and 10).

Biodiversity prospecting agreements between companies and source countries thus provide a flexible and intensive 'proving ground' for practical implementation of concepts such as PIC and benefit-sharing. They also allow the parties to push the limits of best practice higher than the minimums mandated in the CBD or by national legislation. On the other hand, the gross imbalances in legal, commercial and scientific knowledge, and human resources (eg between a global pharmaceutical firm and an indigenous community or local university in a developing country) mean that the two sides in a bioprospecting contract negotiation are generally not fairly matched. A truly equitable partnership is difficult to achieve in this situation. This is why governments should help to establish minimum terms and oversee contract negotiations, with an eye to protecting the interests of weaker parties to a proposed contract. It is also the reason that governments, non-governmental organizations (NGOs) and donor organizations need to prioritize and strengthen awareness of the political economy of genetic resources, and build negotiating capacity among weaker providing country stakeholders. In response to this situation, many experts have raised the need for an international conflict resolution mechanism to assist in resolving issues of equity in contractual arrangements.

The development of standard form contracts remains unlikely given the variety of situations faced by those involved in biodiversity prospecting. However, to improve the quality of agreements, the processes by which they are formed and the ability of parties to practise under agreements, there is a need for further study, practice and sharing of experience of both what works and what does not. That need can only be met by education, support and the supply of legal resources.

Biodiversity researchers, in turn, must articulate their standards for best practice – including PIC, benefit-sharing and responsibilities for the distribution and use of collected materials and knowledge – in codes of ethics, research guidelines and institutional policies. Examples of existing professional researcher codes and guidelines include the *International Society of Ethnobiology Code of Ethics* and *Draft Research Guidelines* (1998), the *American Society of Pharmacognosy Guidelines for Members* (1996), the *Pew Conservation Fellows Biodiversity Research Protocols* (1996) and the *Manila Declaration: the Ethical Utilization of Asian Biological Resources* (1992) (see Chapter 2). Institutional policies include early documents drafted by botanic gardens to guide biodiversity prospecting activities, as well as more comprehensive institutional policies developed to address both biodiversity research and prospecting. The latter include the University of the South

Pacific *Guidelines for Biodiversity Research and Bioprospecting*, and the *Common Policy Guidelines for Botanic Gardens on Access to Genetic Resources and Benefit-Sharing*, developed by a consortium of botanic gardens in 1998–1999 (see Chapter 3). Awareness of and compliance with existing codes and guidelines relating to their field of inquiry should be seen as a minimum expectation of all researchers.

Like contractual agreements, codes of ethics, institutional policies and other documents drafted by researchers reflect the rapidly evolving scope of equitable research relationships in a post-CBD world, and many become outdated in content or terminology within a matter of years. Nevertheless, their value has been significant in allowing indigenous peoples and local communities, provider-country research institutions, governments and protected areas managers a greater understanding of the standards to which researchers should adhere. In addition, these documents have proved valuable as reference points for those who draft national and international policy instruments, and have helped to focus dialogue on ethical issues within the biodiversity research community.

Making prior informed consent work in practice

The CBD only explicitly requires that prior informed consent is obtained from parties – states – within whose territory one seeks access to genetic resources and prior approval for the use of the knowledge, innovations and practices of indigenous and local people. But other CBD provisions are generally interpreted to imply that PIC should also be obtained from local or indigenous communities

from whose territories genetic resources are taken, and some countries, such as those of the Andean Pact and the Philippines, have so legislated. Whatever the legal basis, it is clear that for equity to be manifested in practice, clear means of acquiring PIC from local groups must be put in place. Typically, this will involve a participatory process and, in some cases, written agreement (see Chapter 7).

Initial efforts to include local PIC requirements in national ABS measures have proven very difficult to implement. Even if the law requires that consent is obtained in accordance with traditional customary law and practice, the concept of ownership of resources and knowledge implied by PIC may prove alien to many indigenous peoples. Recognition of the diversity within and among indigenous peoples, unique customary legal and organizational structures, cosmo-visions and life styles is required in order to develop flexible and appropriate procedures for local-level PIC. For example, during the consultation process for development of proposed Peruvian legislation to protect indigenous peoples' collective knowledge, the different emphasis for Andean *campesino* communities (landraces) and Amazonian indigenous peoples (medicinal plants) became evident.

In the Philippines, where the PIC of local communities enjoys strong political support and is embodied in the country's 1995 regulation on ABS (and which, in 1997, was extended, for indigenous peoples, to *all* natural resources within their territories), local PIC has become a major obstacle to scientific research by Philippine academic and research institutions, and has dampened interest in commercial bioprospecting, as well. While no one objects to the principle of PIC, many have argued that the procedures mandated by the 1995 regulation are overly bureaucratic, time consuming, costly and do not take into account the realities of scientific research or field and transportation conditions in the rural Philippines. Others have noted that the general level of awareness of bioprospecting and what Philippine law says about it is so low among local officials and community members that obtaining consent that is truly 'informed' requires a massive and time-consuming educational effort that should not be the responsibility of scientific researchers. While some have expressed hope that NGOs might fill this awareness gap, this has not materialized, and many NGOs in the Philippines working on biodiversity prospecting issues instead view 'all bioprospecting as biopiracy', urging communities in all cases to withhold consent.

Apart from the Philippines and Andean Pact countries, experience with PIC and local communities in the ABS context is very limited. But a great deal can be learned from practices in other fields (eg the mining, logging and oil sectors), indigenous peoples' negotiation of agreements to protect natural resource rights and land tenure, demands expressed in indigenous peoples' declarations, experience from the field of development, and advances in professional researcher codes of ethics and institutional policies. For example, within the American Anthropological Association (AAA), interest has increased over the past few decades in research relationships with local groups, including the ways in which informed consent is granted and benefits are shared from the research process. In recent years, indigenous peoples' organizations have repeatedly called for greater control over the research process. A number of communities, such as the Inuit Tapirisat in Canada and the Kuna in Panama, have articulated culturally appropriate ways in which PIC might be sought and consultations undertaken within their territories (see Chapter 7). Dialogue and exchange between initiatives such as these, and those unfolding in the ABS context, are essential to accelerate our learning and experience of best practice for PIC, benefit-sharing and ethical research approaches.

Making benefit-sharing work in practice

The legal and institutional framework for effective benefit-sharing continues to emerge and evolve. As we have seen through a number of cases over the past ten years, a range of approaches has been employed to implement short-, intermediate- and long-term benefit-sharing. These include innovative partnerships that place a larger portion of discovery in provider countries, allowing the local capture of greater benefits, including intellectual property rights (IPRs). More modest partnerships based on the supply of samples or raw material have also been structured to incorporate a range of benefits, such as the provision of literature, training, laboratory equipment and wider capacity-building, as well as monetary benefits such as fees, royalties and milestone payments.

Innovations are also being developed for the distribution, or sharing, of benefits. They include trust funds and other mechanisms, which have been employed to distribute financial benefits to serve a wide range of national interests and stakeholders over time, according to mutually agreed principles (such as conservation, sustainable development, research and development – R&D – and capacity-building). Trust funds implemented for biodiversity prospecting projects in countries as diverse as Suriname, Nigeria, Fiji and Panama serve equally diverse and locally defined objectives, within the broader goals of conservation and sustainable development (see Chapter 11).

The central role of intermediary institutions

Often overlooked in examinations of equity in biodiversity prospecting is the central role of research institutions and other intermediaries. Almost without exception, every biodiversity-prospecting collection effort undertaken on behalf of companies is done through intermediaries. In most cases, these are research institutions, botanic gardens and universities. This is because biodiversity prospecting is, at heart, a scientific undertaking, requiring expertise in field-collection techniques, taxonomy, database and information management, chemistry, pharmacology, as well as other areas. A number of for-profit firms specializing in providing genetic material to the private sector have also appeared in recent years.

These intermediary institutions are, in some cases, fulfilling valuable functions in facilitating access to genetic resources and fair and equitable benefit-sharing on mutually agreed terms, in compliance with the CBD and relevant national legislation. This is the case when intermediaries add value locally to the resource and diligently ensure that all national ABS laws and procedural requirements have been met, thereby providing end-users with reliable guarantees of legal certainty and compliance. When these entities provide such functions, they are of considerable value to commercial end-users, and also assist governments in ensuring that national ABS measures are complied with. Where such entities are established within a country who provides genetic resources and where they add value to genetic resources in-country – for example, through maintaining genetic resources 'libraries', preparing extracts and preliminary screening of samples (as is the case with Costa Rica's InBio) – they can also contribute to local capacity-building and the maximization of benefits within providing countries.

However, since these intermediaries represent a new and largely unregulated sector of activity – and since they have been relatively overlooked in discussions on ABS to date – the potential exists for this role to be filled by unscrupulous or technically incompetent actors. Where such entities do not add value to the resource, or where intentionally false or mistaken assurances are made that genetic material has been legally obtained, they pose a significant threat to the ABS objectives of both the CBD and national policies and legislation. It is also important that – where possible – distinctions between intermediaries' academic and commercial research are made clear, although this is increasingly blurred.

The importance of such intermediary entities needs to be considered by governments in the development of ABS regimes, and legislation should support legitimate intermediaries while discouraging those who are not performing useful or legitimate functions. This suggests the need for benchmarks, transparent and accountable policies and objectively verifiable standards. Contractual arrangements also need to reflect the increasingly multiparty nature of the commercial use of genetic resources, and the central role of intermediaries within the institutional landscape. The ultimate commercial end-users of genetic resources can also play a crucial role by establishing standards for the intermediaries whom they deal with, and insisting on adherence to best practices. It is important, however, that regulation of biodiversity prospecting – a fairly modest research activity in terms of frequency and scale within source countries – does not make academic research that is vital for wider biodiversity conservation and sustainable development impossible to execute.

Putting the pieces together

A major difficulty in putting together the various pieces – including national ABS measures, contracts, codes of ethics, institutional policies and research agreements – in ways that create and support conditions for equity, is the fact that biodiversity research and prospecting are forms of intercultural communication. They cross not only cultural but disciplinary, institutional, commercial, technical and legal boundaries. This is perhaps most evident at the community level, where generalizations about PIC, appropriate consultations, benefit-sharing and research agreements often appear unworkable

upon closer examination of the enormous diversity between and within communities. But intercultural communication is also evident between industrialized and high-biodiversity countries with developing economies; among government, NGO and commercial cultures; and even among the specialists – including lawyers, biologists, economists, chemists and anthropologists – who bring their expertise to bear on the subject.

At the same time, genetic resources have become political, as well as biological and commercial, resources. While there is growing acceptance of the *quid pro quo* argument for benefits in return for access and to support conservation, the focus on genetic resources has also fuelled fears of expropriation and biopiracy. However, through the development, implementation and continuing refinement of a range of tools that support 'fair and equitable' partnerships – as provided in this book – the various parties involved may reach a more comfortable basis for dialogue and equitable exchange.

Recommendations for governments who regulate access

- Understand the different user industries and the differences among them: their demand for access to genetic resources and traditional knowledge; the use made of the resources in product discovery and development; the costs and risks involved and the magnitude and nature of the benefits generated.
- Be aware of the variety of possible partnerships and mechanisms for sharing benefits; there is not a 'one-size-fits-all' formulation, and diversity in approaches should be encouraged, rather than discouraged.
- Keep benefit-sharing requirements in laws simple. Allow parties to innovate and reach mutually agreed terms within this framework. The most effective benefit-sharing partnerships tend to emerge from collaborations designed by the involved parties.
- Develop a realistic expectation about the returns possible from biodiversity prospecting, and the extent to which governments can regulate to achieve intended objectives.
- Undertake national consultations that incorporate the wide range of stakeholders within the country, including government, research institutions, NGOs, companies and indigenous peoples and local community groups. Circulate background materials and help educate stakeholders about the issues prior to consultations, in order to ensure that consultations help develop constructive and concrete frameworks.
- Design access measures flexible enough to deal with different genetic resources and uses. Different industries make varied use of genetic resources and have dramatically different financial, scientific and marketing profiles.
- Keep access procedures and conditions simple, speedy and efficient, without compromising basic equity and conservation principles.
- Establish a national focal point or designate a competent national authority for access with the competence to process unambiguous collecting permits and ABS agreements. Legal and administrative ambiguity is a major obstacle to establishing biodiversity prospecting partnerships.
- Establish a national clearing house for providing information on biodiversity prospecting, including markets for resources, model contracts, negotiating strategies, and business and research opportunities. This clearing house might also serve as the base for a national advisory body that can advise on a case basis.
- Assume or delegate the administrative burden and provide clear guidelines for local-level prior informed consent and benefit-sharing arrangements. Base these procedures on a solid understanding of diverse customary legal, organizational and decision-making structures.

- Build domestic scientific, technological, manufacturing and marketing capacity to attract beneficial partnerships. The greater a country's capacity, the more significant the benefits likely to result from biodiversity prospecting.
- Develop a strategy, based on an assessment of national capacity and needs, that identifies – through the national consultation process – both national and local objectives that biodiversity prospecting partnerships should serve (ie building scientific and commercial capacity; contributing funds to protected area systems; funding environmental education and extension programmes; etc). Frameworks for equitable benefit-sharing and partnerships should grow from these objectives. Don't legislate without a strategy or the capacity to implement the laws introduced.
- Cooperate with other governments to harmonize access regulations within your region and around the world.
- Distinguish between research intended for academic and commercial purposes, while acknowledging the increasing lack of distinction between them. It is necessary, however, to ensure academic research does not bear excessive administrative burdens of the kind more comfortably shouldered by the private sector, since they may act as a disincentive to valuable research.

Recommendations for companies and other organizations who seek access

- Develop an accurate understanding of the CBD and national access legislation and policy. Be aware of the convergence of broad environmental, human rights and trade policies, and attitudes that have created current pressures to regulate commercial use of genetic resources.
- Understand the different priorities of provider countries with regard to commercial partnerships.
- Stay informed about potential liability for non-compliance with good practices under the CBD, and actively market the advantages of compliance to customers in terms of reliability, avoidance of legal and financial risk and good community relations.
- Engage in policy formulation at the international and national levels, whether at CBD meetings or through involvement in national processes (such as the formulation of access legislation or user measures), and whether as an individual company or through industry associations.
- Develop a company or institutional policy that will give governments, research partners and others a clear understanding of the company's principles and practice on ABS. This could include clarifying company commitment to international law, prior informed consent, sustainable sourcing of genetic resources, as well as the process through which the policy will be reviewed and revised.
- Develop tools – such as material transfer agreements and guidelines for employees – to ensure that all staff understand the basis for this policy and that it is implemented and enforced.
- Engage in discussion with professional societies and industry associations about the CBD and its relevance to the private sector; develop industry-wide standards of 'best

practice'. Encourage your industry association to act as a technical resource on these issues for member companies.

- Ensure that indigenous and local communities have access to independent legal and technical advice before undertaking negotiation of agreements. Respect traditional decision-making processes.

Recommendations for researchers

- Encourage innovation and changes in the academic tenure and promotion system. Promote a broader concept of 'service' that includes social responsibilities and accountability to the public for publicly funded research; acknowledge and reward interdisciplinary and applied contributions; and promote the inclusion of ethical concerns in the peer review process.
- Identify potential ethical conflicts in advance of initiating research. Examine the direct and indirect implications of recording and publishing cultural knowledge and data, and of including this information in databases; consider alternatives that protect the rights and better serve the interests of local groups and provider countries; base determination of what these interests are on consultation rather than assumption.
- Be aware that historical relationships may have a significant influence on establishing present relationships with indigenous peoples and local communities.
- Draft institutional policies to guide the activities of researchers in the field; articulate the underlying principles institutional research is intended to serve; hold internal working groups and ongoing policy review to ensure staff dialogue on these issues; and encourage flexibility and responsiveness to changing ethical, legal and scientific contexts.
- Draft professional research society codes of ethics and research guidelines; build in a process for ongoing discussion of ethical issues raised by biodiversity research and the revision of documents in light of changing ethical, legal and scientific contexts.
- Reward the champions. Each society or institution who has developed an effective policy, code of ethics or guidelines has done so as the result of efforts of a few champions. Some people will support the need to address ethical issues while others will go along with what is produced; but only a very few individuals are willing to devote adequate time to developing standards for best practice. Recognize that the individuals who champion these issues do so largely against the status quo. Experience has shown the critical role of champions in ushering through the process, since ethical issues are subject to neglect by committees that rarely meet.
- Give back your research results in forms that are relevant and of value to local groups. An important but largely overlooked form of benefit-sharing is the translation and transmission of research results into forms that assist in local resource-management decision-making and effective policy formulation. Build such activities into project design and research proposals.
- Raise awareness in the research community: researchers need to be informed of the changing context in which their research takes place. They should be brought into the international and national dialogue that is rapidly redefining the biodiversity researcher's role. Advocate the importance of broadened temporal scales and episte-

426

mological bases for biodiversity research, both of which may be essential to meeting community-level expectations of the research.

- Participate in the international policy process: researchers are regularly absent from national and international biodiversity policy fora, including national consultations to develop measures to regulate biodiversity research. Advocate the importance of attendance and participation in these fora by institutions and professional societies. Institutions most effectively represented at these meetings have hired staff to explicitly follow and contribute to policy development.

Recommendations for funders and granting agencies

- Require that all funded projects abide by current standards of best practice, including the active involvement of local collaborators, PIC, benefit-sharing and 'giving back' or return of research results to local groups. The AAA code of ethics, for example, proposes that 'a section raising and responding to potential ethical issues should be part of every research proposal'. The *Pew Conservation Scholars Guidelines* (1996) propose that funders – along with professional societies and academic institutions – encourage the sharing of publications and citation of local contributors; the establishment of a system of registering innovations; the establishment of rules of good conduct and practice for researchers; the recognition and reward of ethical practices in research; and the establishment of bioethics committees.
- Make information available to researchers and the donor community about changing legal, policy and ethical contexts, following on the Convention on Biological Diversity and other international and national instruments drafted to achieve equitable conservation and sustainable development.
- Require overhead support for local institutions in any research funded overseas, in addition to the traditional overhead allocated to Northern institutions; ensure the proposal reflects adequate local capacity-building and training, and the active involvement of local groups in project design and implementation.
- Provide funds and allow adequate time for appropriate consultation and procurement of PIC from local communities, institutions and government; recognize that community consultations may take a relatively long time and require several trips to the research site. Equitable research relationships will require additional time, resources and costs on the part of researchers. Thus, it is essential that funders extend their support to include these new commitments. Base assessments of research and grant renewals on time frames appropriate to attaining these additional research objectives.
- Promote and provide funds for the 'giving back' of research results in forms that are relevant and of value to local and national groups; encourage research proposals that incorporate this element, including collaboration with education and extension groups.

Recommendations for protected area managers

- Build capacity in staff: train staff members in the emerging legal and ethical obligations under the CBD and other international and national law.
- Develop research policies to guide research approaches and researcher conduct within the protected area. Protected area policies are an important tool when ABS measures are in place, and can provide detail to the broad PIC, benefit-sharing and other provisions of a national law, in light of local conditions. In the absence of adequate ABS regulation, protected area policies can serve as a critical tool to inform equitable research practices.
- Participate in and inform the ABS policy-development process. National-level consultations are most effective when informed by case-specific and practical advice of the kind that protected areas managers can provide. Since protected areas are often the site of biodiversity prospecting activities, staff will have useful experiences to share with drafters of national policy and law. In some countries, financial benefits resulting from biodiversity prospecting are channelled to protected area systems, and the active involvement of protected area staff in developing these distribution mechanisms will obviously be required.

Recommendations for indigenous peoples and local community groups

- Familiarize yourselves with emerging legal and ethical norms, and the opportunities afforded by the CBD and other instruments for recognition of traditional resource rights; review indigenous peoples' group declarations and statements on biodiversity research and prospecting issued over the past decade. Know your rights – examine your constitution and other relevant domestic legislation; contact civil rights lawyers and ask for their assistance if you are unsure.
- Participate in international policy and national consultation processes in order to ensure your perspectives are heard and incorporated into national ABS measures; engage with policy-makers and politicians.
- Make known to researchers any protocols to be followed within your community, as well as general guidelines and boundaries for research. Develop standards for appropriate consultation processes, steps to acquire PIC and parameters for equitable benefit-sharing; establish a general framework for research agreements that can be modified on a case basis, as appropriate.
- Always ask for clarification of terms, time frames, objectives and any other areas that remain unclear.
- Identify representatives or representative organizations to whom all requests for PIC should be directed; ensure that respective roles and responsibilities within the community for the research process are clear.
- Participate in meetings and workshops held by indigenous peoples' groups that train and educate participants in the legal, scientific, commercial and other aspects of

biodiversity research and prospecting activities, and that recommend ways to ensure equity in partnerships.
- For any commercial partnerships, ensure necessary legal and technical support are in place, as appropriate, but keep decision-making power firmly within the hands of the community and representative organizations.

Directory of useful contacts and resources

Biodiversity-related secretariats

Convention on Biological Diversity (CBD)
World Trade Centre
393 St Jacques Street, Suite 300, Montreal,
Quebec HEY 1N9, Canada
Tel: +1 518 288 2220
Fax: +1 514 288 6588
www.biodiv.org

Convention to Combat Desertification (CCD)
Secretariat of the Convention to Combat
Desertification
PO Box 260129, Haus Carstanjen, D 53175
Bonn, Germany
Tel: +49 228 815 2800
Fax: +49 228 815 2899
Email: secretariat@unccd.de
www.unccd.ch

**Convention on International Trade in
Endangered Species of Wild Fauna and Flora
(CITES)**
15 Chemin des Anemones, CH-1219
Chatelaine-Geneve, Switzerland
Tel: 41 22 979 9139/40
Fax: 41 22 797 3417
Email: cites@unep.ch
www.cites.org

Convention on Migratory Species (CMS)
Martin Luther King Street, 8 D-53175, Bonn,
Germany
Tel: 49 228 815 2401/02
Fax: 49 228 815 2449
Email: cms@unep.de
www.wcmc.org.uk:80/cms/

Ramsar Convention on Wetlands
Rue Mauverney 28, CH-1196 Gland,
Switzerland
Tel: 41 22 999 0170
Fax: 41 22 999 0169
Email: ramsar@ramsar.org
www.ramsar.org

**United Nations Framework Convention on
Climate Change (UNFCCC)**
PO Box 260124, D-53153, Bonn, Germany
Tel: 49 228 815 1000
Fax: 49 228 815 1999
Email: secretariat @unfccc.org
www.unfccc.org

World Heritage Convention
The World Heritage Centre UNESCO
7 place de Fontenoy, 75352 Paris, 07 SP
France
Tel: 33 145 68 1889
Fax: 33 145 68 5570
Email: wh-info@unesco.org
www.unesco.org/whc/

Selected national government access and benefit-sharing contacts

Australia
Biodiversity Convention and Strategy Section
Biodiversity Conservation Branch, Biodiversity
Group
Environment Australia
Fax: 61 26 250 0723
Email: veronica.biazely@ea.gov.au
www.ea.gov.au

Bolivia
Ministry of Sustainable Development and the
Environment
National Secretariat of Natural Resources and
the Environment
Av Mariscal Santa Cruz No 1092 Piso 6to, La
Paz, Bolivia
Tel: 591 023 30762
Fax: 555 331 273
Email: vmarnaf@coord.rds.org.bo
www.rds.org.bo

Brazil
Divisao do Meio Ambiente (DEMA)
Ministerio das Relacoes Exteriores
Esplanada dos Ministerios, Anexo
Administrativo I, Sala 635 Brasilia DF
70170.900 Brazil
Fax: 55.61.411.6012/224.1079
www.brazil.gov.br

Colombia
Ministerio de Medio Ambiente Calle 37 No 8-
40
Santa fe de Bogota, Colombia
Tel: 571 233 2340
Fax: 571 288 9892
Email: webmaster@minambiente.gov.co
www.minambiente.gov.co

Costa Rica
Ministerio de Ambiente y Energia
Email: root@ns.minae.go.cr
www.minae.go.cr

Ecuador
Instituto Ecuatoriano Forestal y de Areas
Naturales y Vida Silvestre
Eloy Alfaro y Av Amazonas, Piso 8, Quito
Ecuador
Tel: 5932 506 337
Fax: 5932 564 037

Eritrea
Department of Environment
Ministry of Land Water and Environment
PO Box 976, Asmara, Eritrea
Tel: 2911 120 311/125 887
Fax: 2911 126 095
Email: env@env.col.com.er

Fiji
Ministry of Local Government and
Environment
PO Box 2131, Suva, Fiji
Fax: 679 30 3515
Tel: 679 211310
Email: info@fiji.gov.fj

India
Ministry of Environment and Forests,
Paryavaran Bhawan
CGO Complex, Lodhi Road, New Delhi
110003, India
Telefax: 91 11 436 1896 / 4360721
Email: secy@menf.delhi.nic.in
http://envfor.nic.in/mef/mef.html

Malawi
The Secretary to the Genetic Resources
and Biotechnology Committee
National Research Council of Malawi
PO Box 30745, Lilongwe 3, Capital City,
Malawi
Tel: 265 781 111
Fax: 265 781 487
Email: nrcm@sdnp.org.mw
www.sdnp.org.mw/nrcm

Peru
Consejo Nacional del Ambiente
Av San Borja Norte 226, San Borja, Lima,
Peru
Tel: 511 225 370
Fax: 511 225 5369
Email: ddda@conam.gob.pe
www.conam.gob.pe

Seychelles
Ministry of Foreign Affairs, Planning and
Environment
Botanical Gardens, PO Box 656, Victoria,
Mahé, Seychelles
Tel: 248 22 46 88
Fax: 248 22 45 00
Email: mfapesey@seychelles.net

South Africa
Department of Environmental Affairs and
Tourism,
Subcommittee on Sustainable Development
Private Bag X447, Pretoria 0001, South Africa
Tel: 271 2310 3446
Fax: 271 2322 2682
Email: omd_ah@ozone.pwv.gov.za

Venezuela
Ministerio del Ambiente y de los Recursos
Naturales Renovables
La Dirección de Vegetación
Av. Rómulo Gallegos con 2da avenida de
Santa Eduvigis, Caracas
Tel: 0212 2854859
Email: info@marnr.gov.ve
www.marnr.gov.ve

Intergovernmental organizations

**Food and Agriculture Organization of the
United Nations (FAO)**
www.fao.org

FAO Agriculture Department
www.fao.org/ag/

**FAO Commission on Genetic Resources for
Food and Agriculture**
www.fao.org/ag/cgrfa/default.htm

FAO Non Wood Forest Products Database
www.fao.org/forestry/forestry.asp

**FAO Plant Genetic Resources for Food and
Agriculture (PGRFA)**
www.fao.org/ag/cgrfa/PGR.htm

**Global Environment Facility, World Bank
(GEF)**
www.gefweb.org

Intergovernmental Forum on Forests
www.un.org/esa/sustdev/iff.htm

**International Organization for Standardization
(ISO)**
www.iso.ch

**Organisation for Economic Co-operation and
Development (OECD)**
www.oecd.org/ehs/icgb/biodiv.htm

**Organization of African Unity/Scientific,
Technical and Research Commission
(OAU/STRC)**
Email: oaustrcl@rcl.nig.com
www.oau-oua.org

**United Nations Convention on Trade and
Development (UNCTAD)**
www.unctad.org

UNCTAD Biotrade Initiative
www.biotrade.org

**United Nations Environment Programme
(UNEP)**
Email: ipainfo@unep.org
www.unep.org

**United Nations Educational, Social and
Cultural Organization (UNESCO)**
www.unesco.org

United Nations Industrial Development
Organization (UNIDO)
www.unido.org

United Nations Commission for Sustainable
Development (CSD)
www.un.org/esa/sustdev/csd.htm

United Nations Environment Programme
(UNEP)
www.unep.org

United Nations Development Programme
(UNDP)
www.undp.org

World Bank
www.worldbank.org

World Intellectual Property Organization
(WIPO)
www.wipo.org

World Trade Organization (WTO)
www.wto.org/english/tratop_e/envir_e/issu1_e.
htm

Selected NGOs, research institutes and organizations working on biodiversity research and prospecting issues

African Centre for Technology Studies
www.acts.or.ke

Association of University Technology
Managers (AUTM)
www.autm.net

Asia-Pacific Centre for Environmental Law
http://www.sunsite.nus.edu.sg/apcel

Asia Pacific Centre for Environmental
Accountability
www.accg.mq.edu.au/apcea

Asia Pacific Information Network on
Medicinal and Aromatic Plants
www.pchrd.dost.gov.ph/apinmap/

Bank Information Center
www.bicusa.org

Biodiversity Action Network (ECONET)
www.igc.org/igc/gateway/enindex.html

Biodiversity Strategies International
Email: lglowka@csi.com

Bioresources Development and Conservation
Programme
www.bioresources.org

BIOSIS
www.biosis.org

Biotechnology and Biodiversity Resource
Centre
www.sustain.org/biotech

Biowatch South Africa
www.oneworld.org/saep/fordb/biowatch.html

Birdlife International
www.birdlife.net

Botanic Gardens Conservation International
www.rbgkew.org.uk/BGCI

CABI Bioscience
www.cabi-bioscience.org

Canadian Institute for Environmental Law
and Policy
www.cielap.org

Center for Biodiversity and Conservation,
American Museum of Natural History
http://research.amnh.org/biodiversity/

Center for Conservation Biology Network
http://conbio.edu/

Center for International Environmental Law (CIEL)
www.ciel.org
biodiversity and intellectual property page:
www.ciel.org/biodiversity/biodiversityintellectu
alproperty.html

Center for International Forestry Research (CIFOR)
www.cgiar.org/cifor/

Centre for Development and the Environment, University of Oslo
www.sum.uio.no/bioprospecting

Centre for Science and Environment
www.oneworld.org/cse/

Centro Internacional de Agricultura Tropical (CIAT)
www.ciat.cgiar.org

Centro Internacional de Mejoramiento de Maiz y Trigo (CIMMYT)
www.cimmyt.org/

Centro Internacional de la Papa (CIP)
www.cipotato.org

Ciencia y Tecnologia para el Desarrollo (CYTED)
www.cyted.org

Commonwealth Scientific and Industrial Research Organization (CSIRO)
www.csiro.au

Conservation International (CI)
www.conservation.org

Consultative Group on International Agricultural Research (CGIAR)
www.cgiar.org

Council for Scientific and Industrial Research, South Africa (CSIR)
www.csir.co.za

Cultural Survival
www.cs.org

DIVERSITAS
www.icsu.org/diversitas

Eden Foundation
www.eden-foundation.org

Edinburgh Centre for Tropical Forests
www.nmw.ac.uk/ectf/

Edmonds Institute
www.edmonds-institute.org

Environmental Resources Information Network (ERIN)
www.ea.gov.au/sdd/erin

European Working Group on Research and Biodiversity
http://europa.eu.int/comm/research/envir/ewgr
b.html

Forest Stewardship Council
www.fscoax.org

Forests, Trees and People (FTP) Programme and Network
www-trees.slu.se

Foundation for International Environmental Law and Development (FIELD)
www.field.org.uk

Friends of the Earth (International Secretariat) (FoE)
www.foei.org

Gaia's Forest Conservation Portal
www.forests.org/portal/

Gecko Productions (marine conservation education)
Email: nward@mbl.edu

Gene Ethics Network
www.geneethics.org

Genetic Resources Action International (GRAIN)
www.grain.org

Greenpeace International
www.greenpeace.org

Green Net
www.gn.apc.org

Harvard University Center for International Development
www.cid.harvard.edu/cidbiotech/homepage.htm

Healing Forest Conservancy (HFC)
www.shaman.com/healing-forest.html

Horticulture Research International (HRI)
www.hri.ac.uk

Indian Institute of Management/SRISTI
www.sristi.org

Institute of Terrestrial Ecology (ITE)
www.nmw.ac.uk/ite/edin/

Instituto de Gestion Ambiental, Colombia
Email: igea@impsat.net.co

Instituto Nacional de Biodiversidad de Costa Rica (InBio)
www.iabin.org

Inter-American Biodiversity Information Network (IABIN)
www.nbii.gov/iabin/

International Center for Agricultural Research in the Dry Areas (ICARDA)
www.cgiar.org/icarda/

International Center for Living Aquatic Resources Management (ICLARM – The World Fish Center)
www.iclarm.org

International Centre for Genetic Engineering and Biotechnology (ICGEB)
www.icgeb.trieste.it

International Centre for Research in Agroforestry (ICRAF)
www.icraf.org

International Chamber of Commerce (ICC)
www.iccwbo.org

International Crops Research Institute for the Semi-Arid Tropics (OCRISAT)
www.icrisat.org/

International Development Research Centre (IDRC) (Canada)
www.idrc.ca

International Food Policy Research Institute (IFPRI)
www.ifpri.org

International Institute for Environment and Development (IIED)
www.iied.org

International Institute for Sustainable Development (IISD)
www.iisd.ca

IISD, Environmental Negotiations Bulletin
www.iisd.ca/linkages

International Livestock Research Institute (ILRI)
www.ilri.org

International Plant Genetic Resources Institute (IPGRI)
www.ipgri.org

International Rice Research Institute (IRRI)
www.irri.org

International Service for National Agricultural Research (ISNAR)
www.isnar.org

International Union of Forestry Research Organizations
http://iufro.boku.ac.at

International Water Management Institute (IWMI)
www.iwmi.org

IUCN Environmental Law Centre
www.iucn.org/themes/law/index.html

IUCN – The World Conservation Union
www.iucn.org

IUCN Medicinal Plant Specialist Group
www.iucn.org/themes/ssc/sgs/sgs.htm

Maryland Biotechnology Institute
www.umbi.umd.edu

The Max Lock Centre, University of
Westminster
www.wmin.ac.uk/builtenv/env/maxlock/
default.htm

Mexican Centre for Environmental Law
(CEMDA)
www.cemda.org.mx

National Biological Information Infrastructure
(NBII)
www.nbii.gov

National Center for Complementary and
Alternative Medicine (NCCAM)
www.nccam.nih.gov

Natural Resources Defence Council
www.igc.apc.org/nrdc

The Nature Conservancy
http://nature.org

Organisation for Economic Co-operation and
Development (OECD) Megascience Forum
www.oecd.org/dsti/mega

People and Plants Programme
www.rbgkew.org.uk/peopleplants

Peruvian Society for Environmental Law
(SPDA)
www.spda.org.pe

Plant Conservation Alliance (PCA) Medicinal
Plant Working Group
www.nps.gov/plants/medicinal

Rainforest Alliance
www.rainforest-alliance.org

Royal Botanic Garden Edinburgh
www.rbge.org.uk

Royal Botanic Gardens, Kew (RBG)
www.rbgkew.org.uk

Rural Advancement Foundation International
(RAFI)
www.rafi.org

Third World Network
www.twnside.org.sg

TRAFFIC International
www.traffic.org

Tropenbos Foundation
www.tropenbos.nl

Tufts Centre for the Study of Drug
Development
www.tufts.edu/med/research/csdd/

United Plant Savers
www.plantsavers.org

Via Campesina – UNORCA
www.laneta.apc.org/unorca/

Vitae Civilis
www.vitaecivilis.org.br

Von Humboldt Biological Resources Research
Institute
www.humboldt.org.co

West Africa Rice Development Association
(WARDA)
www.warda.org

World Business Council for Sustainable
Development (WBCSD)
www.wbcsd.ch

World Conservation Monitoring Centre
www.wcmc.org.uk

World Economic Forum (Davos Forum)
www.weforum.org

World Foundation for Environment and
Development (WFED)
www.wfed.org

World Resources Institute (WRI)
www.wri.org

Worldwatch Institute
www.worldwatch.org

WWF
(World Wildlife Fund in Canada and the US)
www.wwf.org

WWF International Secretariat
www.panda.org

Selected professional research organizations with codes and guidelines

American Anthropological Association (AAA)
www.aaanet.org

American Society of Pharmacognosy (ASP)
www.phcog.org

American Sociological Association
www.asanet.org/ecoderev.htm

Association of Systematics Collections (ASC)
www.ascoll.org

Centre for Applied Ethics (professional ethics resources on the www)
www.ethics.ubc.ca

International Society of Ethnobiology (ISE)
Code of Ethics
http://users.ox.ac.uk/~wgtrr/isecode.htm

The Pew Conservation Fellows
http://geography.berkeley.edu/ProjectsResources/BRP/BRP.html

Register of Professional Archaeologists
www.rpanet.org

Society for Economic Botany (SEB)
www.econbot.org

The American Folklore Society
www.afsnet.org/ethics.htm

Indigenous peoples' organizations, traditional knowledge and resource rights groups

Aboriginal Studies
www.ciolek.com/WWWL-Aboriginal.html

Assembly of First Nations
www.afn.ca

Australian Indigenous Cultural and Intellectual Property Rights
www.icip.lawnet.com.au

Center for World Indigenous Studies
www.cwis.org

Centre for Indigenous Knowledge for Agriculture and Rural Development (CIKARD)
www.ciesin.org/IC/cikard/CIKARD.html

Consejo Indio de Sudamerica (CEA CISA)
www.puebloindio.org
Coordinating Body for the Indigenous Organizations of the Amazon Basin (COICA)
www.pangea.org/~coam/coica.htm
The COICA Statement on IPRs and Biodiversity:
http://users.ox.ac.uk/~wgtrr/coica.htm

Dialogue Between Nations
www.dialoguebetweennations.com

First Nations Development Institute
www.firstnations.org

Fourth World Documentation Project (FWDP), The Center for the World Indigenous Studies
www.cwis.org

The Honey Bee Network and SRISTI
www.iimahd.ernet.in/~anilg/

Humanity Libraries Project
www.oneworld.org/globalprojects/humcdrom

The Impact of Ecosystem Degradation on Peoples Lives: Searching for Stories from Around the World
www.wri.org/wri/wr2000/

Indigenous Environmental Network
www.ienearth.org

Indigenous Peoples Biodiversity Information Network (IBIN)
www.ibin.org/

Indigenous Peoples Council on Biocolonialism
www.ipcb.org

Indigenous Peoples and the Law
www.kennett.co.nz/law/indigenous/index.html

Indigenous Knowledge and Development Monitor
www.nuffic.nl/ciran/ikdm/index.html

Indigenous Knowledge Initiative (The World Bank Group – Sub-Saharan Africa Region)
www.worldbank.org/afr/ik/ik-web2.htm

International Working Group for Indigenous Affairs (IWGIA)
www.iwgia.org

International Alliance of the Indigenous-Tribal Peoples of the Tropical Forests
www.gn.apc.org/laip

International Indian Treaty Council (IITC)
www.treatycouncil.org

LANIC: Indigenous Peoples
http://lanic.utexaas.edu/la/region/indigenous

Nuffic Centre for International Research and Advisory Networks, Indigenous Knowledge (Nuffic-CIRAN)
www.nuffic.nl/ciran/ik.html

Principles and Guidelines on Indigenous and Traditional Peoples and Protected Areas (WCPA, IUCN, WWF)
www.panda.org/resources/publications/sustainability/indigenous2/index.html

Protection of Traditional Knowledge/Resources Guide Lines (World Council of Indigenous Peoples and CIDA)
www.kivu.com

South and Meso-American Indian Rights Centre (SAIIC)
www.saiic.nativeweb.org

Survival International
www.survival.org.uk

WATU – Accion Indigena
www.servicom.es/watu

WIPO Roundtable on Intellectual Property and Indigenous Peoples
www.wipo.int/eng/meetings/1998/indip/index.htm

World Rainforest Movement
www.wrm.org.uy

Working Group on Traditional Resource Rights
www.users.ox.ac.uk/~wgtrr/wghist.htm

Selected industry associations[1]

Pharmaceutical

Association of the British Pharmaceutical Industry
www.abpi.org.uk

European Agency for the Evaluation of Medicinal Products (EMEA)
www.eudra.org

International Federation of Pharmaceutical Manufacturers Associations (IFPMA)
www.ifpma.org

International Conference on Harmonization
www.ifpma.org/ich1.html

Japanese Pharmaceutical Manufacturers Association (JPMA)
www.jpma.or.jp

Pharmaceutical Research and Manufacturers of America (PhRMA)
www.phrma.org

United States Food and Drug Administration (FDA)
www.fda.gov

Botanical medicine and personal care

American Botanical Council
www.herbalgram.org

American Herbal Products Association (AHPA)
www.ahpa.org

Bundesvereinigung Deutscher Apothekerverbande (ABDA)
www.abda.de

Cosmetic, Toiletry and Fragrance Association
www.ctfa.org

Herb Research Foundation
www.herbs/org

Seed

American Seed Trade Association
www.amseed.com

Federation Internationale du Commerce Semences (FIS)
www.worldseed.org/fis.htm

Horticulture

American Horticultural Society (AHS)
www.ahs.org

International Federation of Agricultural Producers (AIHP)
www.ifap.org

Crop protection

American Crop Protection Association
www.acpa.org

Crop Protection Institute
www.croppro.org

Global Crop Protection Federation
www.gcpf.org

Biotechnology

BioIndustry Association
www.bioindustry.org

Biotechnology Industry Association
www.bio.org

Japan BioIndustry Association
www.jba.or.jp

Socially responsible business organizations

Businesses for Social Responsibility
www.bsr.org

Coalition for Environmentally Responsible Economies (CERES)
www.ceres.org

Social Venture Network
www.svn.org

Online list servers and information networks

AFRICADIV
List server on biodiversity and indigenous knowledge. To subscribe, send message 'subscribe africadiv yourfirst name yourlastname' to lyris@lyris.nuffic.nl
www.nuffic.nl

ASEAN
Review of biodiversity and environmental conservation (includes event calendar and book references)
www.arbec.com.my

BIODIV-CONV
CBD and related information list server. To subscribe, send message 'subscribe biodiv-conv' to majordomo@igc.erg
www.biosis.org

BINAS
Information network and advisory service; service of the United Nations Industrial Development Organization (UNIDO). Monitors global developments in regulatory issues in biotechnology
www.binas.unido.org/binas/ home.html

BIO-IPR
Intellectual property rights related to biodiversity and associated knowledge
Archives: www.cuenet.com/archive/bio-ipr

BIODIV-L
List server on biological diversity. To subscribe, send message 'subscribe biodiv-l' to majordomo@ns.bdt.erg.hr

Bioengineering Action Network
Host of a new list server for activist networking on genetic engineering
www.artactivist.com

Bioline Journal
Fish, insect and tropical biodiversity
www.bdt.org.br/bioline

BIOPLAN
Electronic mailing list for biodiversity planners. To subscribe, send the following message 'subscribe bioplan address (your email address)' to majordomo@undp.org

BIOSAFETY
CBD working group policy and science updates. To subscribe, send message 'subscribe Biosafety listserver' to acfgenetC@peg.apc.org

BioSafety Journal
Online journal.
www.bdt.org.br/bioline/by

BIOWATCH
To subscribe, send message 'subscribe BIOWATCH listserver' to majordomo@sunsite.wits.ac.za

Canadian Institute for Business and the Environment
Gallon letter list server. To subscribe, send message 'subscribe gallon-1, END' to majordomo@list.web.net

CONSBIO
Conservation biology list server. To subscribe, send message 'subscribe consbio yourfirstname yourlastname' to listproc@u.washington.edu
www.earthsystems.org/list/consbio/info.html

CSDGEN
CSD information list server. To subscribe, send message 'subscribe csdgen <your email address>' to majordomo@undp.org

CHM
The Convention on Biological Diversity's clearing-house mechanism
www.biodiv.org

DEVLINE
Institute of Development Studies and the British Library for Development Studies
www.ids.ac.uk

ENV-BIOTECH
Bi-weekly news bulletin, *Intellectual Property and Biodiversity News*. To subscribe, send message 'subscribe env-biotech' to majordomo@igc.apc.org

Environment News Service (ENS)
www.ens.lycos.com

European Working Group on Research and Biodiversity (EWGRB)
Electronic conference on research and biodiversity
www.gencat.es/mediamb/biodiv

G7ENRM
The G7 Environment and Natural Resources Management Project
www.g7.fed.us/enrm

HERB
Medicinal and aromatic plants; cross-cultural medicine and folk/herbal medicine (Anadolu University Medicinal Plants Research Centre). To subscribe, send message to listserv@vm3090.ege.edu.tr
www.tbam.anadolu.edu.tr

INDKNOW
Indigenous knowledge list server. To subscribe, send message 'subscribe indknow' to listproc@u.washington.edu
http://sdgateway.net/mailinglists/list9.htm

Indigenous Knowledge and Development: List server Archive and Summary
www.globalknowledge.org/worldbank/ikd/current

International Institute for Sustainable Development (IISD)
Has a subscription service for the following online journals: *Earth Negotiations Bulletin*, *Linkages* and *Sustainable Development*
www.iisd.ca

IPR-SCIENCE
Intellectual property in science, academic–industry links, sociological/ethical/legal analyses, inventiveness and exploitability. To subscribe, send an email to mailbase@mailbase.ac.uk
www.jiscmail.ac.uk/lists/ipr-science.html

NTFP-BIOCULTURAL-DIGEST
Non-timber forest products and ethnobotany. To subscribe, send message to majordomo@igc.erg and in the body put 'subscribe ntfp-biocultural-digest' (your email address)

SEARICE
Biopiracy, genetic resources, indigenous peoples rights listserver:
antibiopiracy@yahoogroups.com
searice@philonline.com.ph

Science and Technology Update
Research and information of relevance to science, technology and international development. To subscribe, send message to majordomo@ksglist.harvard.edu – write 'tech' (without quotation marks) under the subject. In the body of the message write: command listname email_of_user(optional). For example: Subscribe tech Calestous_Juma@harvard.edu.

US Environmental Protection Agency
Internet newsbrief. To subscribe, leave subject line blank and send message 'subscribe INTERNETNB-L firstname lastname' to listserver@unixmail.rtpnc.epa.gov.

Note

1   See ten Kate and Laird (1999) *Commercial Use of Biodiversity: Access to Genetic Resources and Benefit-Sharing*, Earthscan, London, for a more complete listing.

Contributors' contact information

Chapter authors

Miguel N Alexiades
Department of Anthropology
University of Kent at Canterbury
Canterbury, Kent CT2 7NP, UK
malexiades@hotmail.com

Kelly P Bannister
POLIS Project on Ecological Governance
Environmental Law and Policy
University of Victoria
Victoria, BC V8W 3R4, Canada
kel@uvic.ca

Charles V Barber
Biological Resources Programme
World Resources Institute
14 Cabbage St, Valle Verde 5
Pasig, Metro Manila, the Philippines
Fax: 63 2 631 0406

Lyle Glowka
Biodiversity Strategies International
Agnesstrasse 41
D-53225 Bonn, Germany
lglowka@csi.com

Michael A Gollin
Venable, Baetjer, Howard, & Civiletti, LLP
1201 New York Avenue, NW Suite 1000
Washington, DC 20005–3917, USA
www.venable.com
magollin@venable.com

Marianne Guerin-McManus
Conservation International
2501 M St, NW, Suite 200
Washington, DC 20037, USA
m.guerin-mcmanus@conservation.org

Kerry ten Kate
Conventions and Policy Section
Royal Botanic Gardens, Kew
Richmond, Surrey TW9 3AE, UK

Sarah A Laird
PO Box 222
Waterbury Center, VT 05677, USA
sarahlaird@aol.com

Estherine E Lisinge
WWF Cameroon Programme Office
Immeuble Panda
BAT Compound
BP 6776, Yaounde, Cameroon
elisinge@wwfnet.org

Kent Nnadozie
Bioresources Development and Conservation
Programme
1, Tinuade St, Allen Avenue
PO Box 13940, Ikeja, Lagos, Nigeria
kent@netlane.com

Flavia Noejevich
48 Park Lane
West Harrison, NY 10604, USA
flavia86@hotmail.com

Patricia Shanley
Center for International Forestry Research
PO Box 6596, JKPWB
Jakarta 10065, Indonesia
p.shanley@cgiar.org

Brendan Tobin
brendantobin@yahoo.co.uk

Antonio G M La Viña
World Resources Institute
10 G Street NW, Suite 800, Washington, DC
20002, USA
tonylav@wri.org

Rachel Wynberg
PO Box 69, St James 7946, South Africa
Fax: 27 21 788 9169

Case study authors and other contributors

William G Aalbersberg
Institute of Applied Science
University of the South Pacific
Suva, Fiji
Fax: 679 300 373
aalbersberg@usp.ac.fj

Agnes Lee Agama
People and Plants Initiative, South-East Asia
WWF Malaysia
PO Box 14393, 88850 Kota Kinabalu, Sabah,
Malaysia
Fax: 6088 242 531
junaidi@pc.jaring.my

Paulo Amaral
IMAZON
Para, Brazil
imazon.bel@zaz.com.br

P Balakrishna
Regional Biodiversity Programme
IUCN
48, Vajira Road, Colombo 5, Sri Lanka
pbala@sltnet.lk

Hans Chr Bugge
Department of Public and International Law
University of Oslo
Postbox 6706, St Olavspl, 0130 Oslo,
Norway
h.c.bugge@jus.uio.no

Todd Capson
Smithsonian Tropical Research Institute
Unit 0948, APO AA 34002–0948, Balboa,
Republic of Panama
capsont@tivoli.si.edu

Tatiana Correa
IMAZON
Para, Brazil
imazon.bel@zaz.com.br

Michel De Pauw
BP 793, Bouake 01, Côte d'Ivoire
depauw@africaonline.co.ci

Shivcharn Dhillion
Department of Biology and Nature
Conservation
Agricultural University of Norway
PO Box 5014, N-1432 Ås, Norway
shivcham.dhillon@ibn.nlh.no

David R Downes
Center for International Environmental Law
1367 Connecticut Avenue, NW #300
Washington, DC 20036, USA
ddownes@ciel.org

Graham Dutfield
Working Group on Traditional Resource
Rights
OCEES, Mansfield College
Oxford OX1 3TF, UK
wgtrr.ocees@mansfield.oxford.ac.uk

Anil Gupta
Indian Institute of Management
Ahmedabad 380015, India
anilg@iimahd.ernet.in

Maurice M Iwu
Bioresources Development and Conservation
Program
bdcp@bioresources.org

Sam Johnston
Secretariat, Convention on Biological
Diversity
World Trade Centre
393 St Jacques St
Montreal, Quebec H2Y 1N9, Canada
www.biodiv.org

Thembela Kepe
Programme for Land and Agrarian Studies
School of Government
University of the Western Cape
Private Bag X17, Bellville, 7535, South Africa
tkepe@uwc.ac.za

Isoa Korovulavula
South Pacific Regional Forestry Program,
Forum Secretariat
Suva, Fiji
Fax: 679 315 446
gtz@is.com.fj

RRB Leakey
Agroforestry and Novel Crops Unit
School of Tropical Biology
James Cook University
PO Box 6811, Cairns, Queensland 4870,
Australia
roger.leakey@jcu.edu.au

Patricia Madrigal-Cordero
Apartado Postal 20–1017
San Jose, Costa Rica
Fax: 506 231 0024
patmadri@sol.racsa.co.cr

Bile Mathieu
Faculty of Law
University of Cocody Abidjan
BP V179, Côte d'Ivoire

Thomas D Mays
Morrison and Foerster, LLP
2000 Pennsylvania Ave, NW
Washington, DC 20006–1888, USA
Fax: 202 887 0763
Tmays@mofo.com

William Milliken
Royal Botanic Garden Edinburgh
Edinburgh, EH3 5LR, Scotland UK
w.milliken@rbge.org.uk

Katy Moran
The Healing Forest Conservancy
3521 S Street, NW
Washington, DC 20007–2243, USA
moranhfc@aol.com

Yakobo Moyini
Environmental Monitoring Associates (EMA)
Ltd
Plit 71 Kanjokya ST
PO Box 21598, Kampala, Uganda
Fax: 256 41 348 897
eeau@swiftuganda.com

Lukman Mulumba
Afritech (U) Ltd
Kampala, Uganda

Jackson Mutebi
Development through Conservation
CARE Uganda
Kabale, Uganda

Nouhou Ndam
Limbe Botanic Garden
PO Box 437
Limbe, South West Province, Cameroon
Fax: 237 43 18 83
mcplbg@iccnet.cm

Gonzalo Oveido
People and Conservation Unit
WWF International
27 av du Mont-Blanc, 1196 Gland,
Switzerland
Fax: 41 22 364 5829
goveido@wwfnet.org

Daniela Peluso
Anthropology Department
Columbia University
New York, NY 10027, USA
dmp1@columbia.edu

Manuel Ruiz
Peruvian Society for Environmental Law
manoloruiz@blockbuster.com.pe

Diane Russell
International Centre for Research in
Agroforestry
PO Box 30677, Nairobi, Kenya
drussell@cgiar.org

Vivienne Solis-Riviera
Regional Office for Mesoamerica
World Conservation Union
PO Box 1161–2150, Moravia, Costa Rica
Fax: 506 240 9934
vsolis@orma.iucn.org

Terry Sunderland
African Rattan Research Programme
Limbe Botanic Garden
BP 437, South West Province, Cameroon
afrirattan@aol.com

Hanne Svarstad
Centre for Development and the Environment
University of Oslo
PO Box 1116, Blinderm 0317, Norway
www.sum.uio.no/index.html
hanne.svarstad@sum.uio.no

Tabe Tanjong
WWF Cameroon Programme Office
Immeuble Panda
BAT Compound
BP 6776, Yaounde, Cameroon
ttanjong@wwfnet.org

Martin Tchamba
WWF Cameroon Programme Office
Immeuble Panda
BAT Compound
BP 6776, Yaounde, Cameroon
wwfnsp@iccnet.cm

Nathalie Ward
Boston University Marine Programme
Marine Biological Laboratory
Woods Hole, MA 02543, USA
nward@mbl.edu

Niall Watson
WWF UK
Panda House, Weyside Park
Cattleshall Lane, Godalming, Surrey GU7
1XR, UK
nwatson@wwfnet.org

Adrian Wells
CBD Unit
Royal Botanic Gardens, Kew
Richmond, Surrey TW9 3AE, UK

China Williams
CBD Unit
Royal Botanic Gardens, Kew
Richmond, Surrey TW9 3AE, UK
c.williams@rbgkew.org.uk

Glenn Wiser
Center for International Environmental Law
1367 Connecticut Avenue, NW #300
Washington, DC 20036, USA
gwiser@ciel.org

Wendy Yap
WWF Malaysia
wyap@wwfnet.org

Jeanne Zoundjihekpon
Bd Latrille – Immeuble SOCOCE
06 BP 6403 Abidjan 06, Côte d'Ivoire
Fax: 225 22 42 62 08
j.zoundjih@aviso.ci
wwfabio@globeaccess.net

Acronyms and abbreviations

AAA	American Anthropological Association
AAAS	American Association for the Advancement of Science
ABDA	Bundesvereinigung Deutscher Apothekerverbande
ABPI	Association of the British Pharmaceutical Industry
ABS	access and benefit-sharing
ACTS	African Centre for Technology Studies
AEPS	Arctic Environmental Protection Strategy
AG	attorney general
AHPA	American Herbal Products Association
AHS	American Horticultural Society
AIA	Archaeological Institute of America
AIDS	acquired immune deficiency syndrome
AIHP	International Federation of Agricultural Producers
ANAM	Autoridad Nacional del Ambiente (Panama)
AND	Asociación para la Defensa de los Derechos Naturales (Peru)
ARA	academic research agreement
ASC	Association of Systematics Collections
ASEAN	Association of South-East Asian Nations
ASOMPS	Asian Symposium on the Medicinal Plants, Spices and Other Natural Products
ASA	American Sociological Association
ASP	American Society of Pharmacognosy
ATCC	American Type Culture Collection
AUTM	Association of University Technology Managers
B-MS	Bristol-Myers Squibb
BCN	Biodiversity Conservation Network
BDCP	Bioresources Development and Conservation Programme
BGVS	Bedrijf Geneesmiddelen Voorziening Suriname
BINP	Bwindi Impenetrable National Park
BIONET	Biodiversity Action Network
BPC	biodiversity prospecting contract
BSR	Businesses for Social Responsibility
Bt	*Bacillus thuringiensis*
CAH	Consejo Aguaruna and Huambisa communities (Peru)
CARE-DTC	CARE Development through Conservation (Uganda)
CBD	Convention on Biological Diversity
CD	compact disk
CEMDA	Mexican Centre for Environmental Law
CEP	Council on Economic Priorities

CERES	Coalition for Environmentally Responsible Economies
CFA	Communauté Financière Africaine
CFR	central forest reserve
CFR	US *Code of Federal Regulations*
CGIAR	Consultative Group on International Agricultural Research
CHF	Swiss franc
CI	Conservation International
CIAT	Centro Internacional de Agricultura Tropical
CIDA	Canadian Agency for International Development
CIEL	Centre for International Environmental Law
CIFOR	Center for International Forestry Research
CIFOR	Centre for International Forestry (Indonesia)
CIKARD	Centre for Indigenous Knowledge for Agriculture and Rural Development
CIMMYT	Centro Internacional de Mejoramiento de Maiz y Trigo
CIP	Centro Internacional de la Papa
CITES	Convention on International Trade in Endangered Species of Wild Fauna and Flora
CMS	Convention on Migratory Species
CNPq	Brazilian National Council for Science and Technology
COE	Committee on Ethics
COICA	Coordinating Body of Indigenous Organizations of the Amazon Basin
CONAGEBIO	National Commission for Biodiversity Management (Costa Rica)
CONSEFORH	Honduran Dry Forest Species Conservation and Silviculture Project
COP	Conference of the Parties
COPPIP	Permanent Commission of Indigenous Peoples of Peru
CPG	Common Policy Guidelines
CPNP	Cuc Phong National Park
CRA	commercial research agreement
CRADA	Cooperative Research and Development Agreement
CRE	Centre for Research in Ecology (Côte d'Ivoire)
CSD	United Nations Commission for Sustainable Development
CSIR	Council for Scientific and Industrial Research (South Africa)
CSIRO	Commonwealth Scientific and Industrial Research Organization
CYTED	Ciencia y Tecnologia para el Desarrollo
DA	Department of Agriculture (the Philippines)
DANIDA	Danish International Development Assistance
dbh	diameter at breast height
DEAT	Department of Environmental Affairs and Tourism (South Africa)
DENR	Department of Environment and Natural Resources (the Philippines)
DFA	Department of Foreign Affairs (the Philippines)
DFID	Department for International Development (UK) (*formerly* ODA)
DNA	deoxyribonucleic acid
DOH	Department of Health (the Philippines)
DOST	Department of Science and Technology (the Philippines)
DPN	Department for the Protection of Nature (Cameroon)
EC	European Commission
EC	European Community

ECOSOC	United Nations International Covenant on Economic, Social and Cultural Rights
EEZ	exclusive economic zone
ELC	Environmental Law Centre of the IUCN
EMEA	European Agency for the Evaluation of Medicinal Products
EMPRESA	Forum on Business and Social Responsibility in the Americas
ENS	Environment News Service
EO	executive order
ERIN	Environmental Resources Information Network
EU	European Union
EWGRB	European Working Group on Research and Biodiversity
FAO	Food and Agriculture Organization of the United Nations
FDA	Food and Drug Administration (US)
FFT	Tropical Forest Foundation (Brazil)
FIELD	Foundation for International Environmental Law and Development
FIRD-TM	Fund for Integrated Rural Development and Traditional Medicine (Nigeria)
FIS	International Seed Trade Federation (Federation Internationale du Commerce Semences)
FMCN	Mexican Fund for Nature Conservation
FoE	Friends of the Earth
FPF	Forest People Fund
GAA	germplasm acquisition agreement (FAO–CGIAR)
gbh	girth at breast height
GCA	Guanacaste Conservation Area
GCBCD	Global Coalition for Bio-Cultural Diversity
GDP	gross domestic product
GEF	Global Environment Facility
GIS	geographic information system
GMIHR	Gorgas Memorial Institute for Health Research
GMO	genetically modified organism
GMP	good manufacturing practices
GoC	Government of Cameroon
GPS	global positioning system
GRAIN	Genetic Resources Action International
GRO	grassroots organization
GTZ	Gesellschaft für Technische Zusammenarbeit (Germany)
ha	hectare
HFC	Healing Forest Conservancy
HRI	Horticulture Research International (UK)
IABIN	Inter-American Biodiversity Information Network
IACBGR	Inter-Agency Committee on Biological and Genetic Resources (Philippines)
IARC	an international agricultural research centre
IBIN	Indigenous Peoples Biodiversity Information Network
ICARDA	International Centre for Agricultural Research in the Dry Areas
ICBG	International Cooperative Biodiversity Groups
ICC	International Chamber of Commerce
ICE	International Congress of Ethnobiology

ICGEB	International Centre for Genetic Engineering and Biotechnology
ICLARM	International Centre for Living Aquatic Resources Management
ICRAF	International Centre for Research in Agroforestry
ICTA	International Centre for Technology Assessment
IFAW	International Fund for Animal Welfare
IFPMA	International Federation of Pharmaceutical Manufacturers Associations
IFPRI	International Food Policy Research Institute
IGCP	International Gorilla Conservation Programme
IIED	International Institute for Environment and Development
IISD	International Institute for Sustainable Development
ILO	International Labor Organization
ILRI	International Livestock Research Institute
IMAZON	Institute of People and the Environment of the Amazon
InBio	National Institute of Biodiversity (Costa Rica)
IPAM	Institute of Environmental Research for Amazônia (Brazil)
IPGRI	International Plant Genetic Resources Institute
IPM	integrated pest management
IPR	intellectual property right
IPRA	the Philippines 1997 Indigenous Peoples Rights Act
IRRI	International Rice Research Institute
ISE	International Society of Ethnobiology
ISNAR	International Service for National Agricultural Research
ITE	Institute of Terrestrial Ecology
ITFC	Institute of Tropical Forest Conservation
IUCN	World Conservation Union (*formerly* International Union for Conservation of Nature and Natural Resources)
IWGIA	International Working Group for Indigenous Affairs
IWMI	International Water Management Institute
JPMA	Japan Pharmaceutical Manufacturers Association
JUNAC	Junta del Acuerdo de Cartagena
KfW	Kredietanstalt fur Wiederaufbau, Germany
kg	kilogramme
km	kilometre
LAPC	Land and Agriculture Policy Centre (South Africa)
LBG	Limbe Botanic Garden (Cameroon)
LOI	letter of intent
m	metres
MAA	material acquisition agreement
MAB	Man and the Biosphere Programme
MAT	mutually agreed term
MBG	Missouri Botanical Garden
MESRS	Ministry of Higher Education and Scientific Research (Côte d'Ivoire)
MINAE	Ministry of Environment and Energy (Costa Rica)
MINAGRA	Ministry of Agriculture and Livestock (Côte d'Ivoire)
MINEF	Ministry of Environment and Forestry (Cameroon)
MINREST	Ministry of Scientific and Technical Research (Cameroon)
MKFP	Mount Kupe Forest Project

MOU	memorandum of understanding
MRC	Medical Research Council of Canada
MSA	material supply agreement
MTA	material transfer agreement (FAO–CGIAR)
MUP	Multiple Use Programme
MUST	Mbarara University of Science and Technology
NAPRALERT	NAtural PRoducts ALERT
NARO	National Agricultural Research Organization
NBI	National Botanical Institute
NBII	National Biological Information Infrastructure
NCI	National Cancer Institute (US)
NCRL	Natural Chemotherapeutics Research Laboratory (Uganda)
NCST	National Centre of Science and Technology
NDA	National Drug Authority
NEMA	National Environment Management Authority (Uganda)
NGO	non-governmental organization
NHM	Natural History Museum, London
NIH	National Institutes of Health (US)
NPS	National Park Service (US)
NSERC	Natural Sciences and Engineering Research Council of Canada
NSF	National Science Foundation (US)
NTFP	non-timber forest product
Nuffic-CIRAN	Nuffic Centre for International Research and Advisory Networks, Indigenous Knowledge
NYBG	New York Botanical Garden
OAU	Organization of African Unity
OCRISAT	International Crops Research Institute for the Semi-Arid Tropics
ODA	Overseas Development Agency (UK)
ODI	Overseas Development Institute (UK)
OECD	Organisation for Economic Co-operation and Development
ORMA	IUCN's Regional Office for Mesoamerica
OTC	over-the-counter
PA	protected area
PACT	Protected Areas Conservation Trust (Belize)
PAMSU	Protected Area Management for Sustainable Use Project
PCA	Plant Conservation Alliance
PCR	polymerase chain reaction
PCRPS	Programme for Collaborative Research in the Pharmaceutical Sciences, University of Illinois, Chicago
PEC	Production and Environment Committee (Uganda)
PEMANSKY	Study for the Management of the Forested Area of the Kuna Territory (Panama)
PG	participating garden
PGRFA	FAO Plant Genetic Resources for Food and Agriculture
PhRMA	Pharmaceutical Research and Manufacturers of America (US)
PIC	prior informed consent
PICNIC	prior informed consent or no informed consent
PLAAS	Programme for Land and Agrarian Studies

PMAC	Park Management Advisory Committee (Uganda)
POEMA	Poverty and Environment in Amazonia Programme (*now* Bolsa Amazonia) (Brazil)
PPC	Park Parish Committee (Uganda)
PRA	participatory rural appraisal
PROFONANPE	National Fund for State-Protected Natural Areas (Peru)
PTO	Patent and Trademark Office (US)
RAFI	Rural Advancement Foundation International
RBG	Royal Botanic Gardens, Kew
R&D	research and development
RNA	ribonucleic acid
RPA	Register of Professional Archaeologists
RSP	Revenue-Sharing Programme
SADC	Southern African Development Community
SAIIC	South and Meso-American Indian Rights
SBSTTA	Subsidiary Body on Scientific, Technical and Technological Advice
SCBD	Secretariat of the Convention on Biological Diversity
SEB	Society for Economic Botany
SGRP	System-Wide Genetic Resource Programme
SIDR	Strathclyde Institute of Drug Research
SKB	SmithKline Beecham
SPACHEE	South Pacific Action Committee on Human Ecology and the Environment
SPDA	Peruvian Society for Environmental Law
SSHRC	Social Sciences and Humanities Research Council of Canada
STRI	Smithsonian Tropical Research Institute
SVN	Social Venture Network
TBGRI	Tropical Botanic Garden and Research Institute
TCM	traditional Chinese medicine
TEK	traditional ecological knowledge
TK	traditional knowledge
TNP	Tai National Park
TRACOR	Transkei Agricultural Corporation (South Africa)
TRIPS	Trade Related Aspects of Intellectual Property Rights
TRR	traditional resource rights
UBC	University of British Columbia
UFPA	Federal University of Pará (Brazil)
UIC	University of Illinois, Chicago
UIE	Uganda Institute of Ecology
UK	United Kingdom
UN	United Nations
UNCED	United Nations Conference on Environment and Development
UNCLOS	United Nations Convention on the Law of the Sea
UNCST	Uganda National Council for Science and Technology
UNCTAD	United Nations Convention on Trade and Development
UNDP	United Nations Development Programme
UNEP	United Nations Environment Programme
UNESCO	United Nations Educational, Social and Cultural Organization

UNFCCC	United Nations Framework Convention on Climate Change
UNIDO	United Nations Industrial Development Organization
UPOV	Union for the Protection of New Varieties of Plants
US	United States
USAID	US Agency for International Development
USDA	US Department of Agriculture
Ush	Uganda shillings
USP	University of the South Pacific
UWA	Uganda Wildlife Authority
UWS	Uganda Wildlife Society
VCC	voluntary code of conduct
VPISU	Virginia Polytechnic Institute and State University
WARDA	West Africa Rice Development Association
WBCSD	World Business Council for Sustainable Development
WCPA	World Commission on Protected Areas
WFED	World Foundation for Environment and Development
WGIP	United Nations Working Group on Indigenous Peoples
WHO	World Health Organization
WIPO	World Intellectual Property Organization
WRI	World Resources Institute
WTO	World Trade Organization
WU	Washington University
WWF	*formerly* World Wide Fund For Nature (World Wildlife Fund *in US and Canada*)
YNP	Yellowstone National Park

Glossary

access to genetic resources: To obtain samples of biological or other material containing genetic material from areas within national jurisdiction for purposes of research on, conservation, commercial or industrial application of the genetic material.

assay: A technique that measures a biological response; the determination of the activity or concentration of a chemical (see bioassay).

bacteria: Members of a group of diverse single-celled organisms; organisms lacking a nucleus.

best practice: Standards of practice that are widely regarded by those in the field as representing the highest levels of conduct, and the practical implementation of core underlying principles such as conservation of biodiversity, sustainable use and equitable benefit-sharing.

bioassay: The determination of the activity or concentration of a chemical by its effect on the growth of an organism under experimental conditions.

biochemical: A product produced by chemical reactions in living organisms.

biodiversity: (See biological diversity).

biodiversity prospecting: The exploration of biodiversity for commercially valuable biological and genetic resources.

bioinformatics: A scientific discipline that comprises all aspects of the gathering, storing, handling, analysing, interpreting and spreading of biological information. Involves powerful computers and innovative programmes that handle vast amounts of coding information on genes and proteins from genomics programmes. Comprises the development and application of computational algorithms for the purpose of analysis, interpretation and prediction of data for the design of experiments in the biosciences.

biologics: Vaccines, therapeutic serums, toxoids, antitoxins and analagous biological products used to induce immunity to infectious diseases or harmful substances of biological origin (see biopharmaceuticals).

biological control agent: The use of living organisms to control pests or disease. May be single organisms or a combination of a number of different organisms.

biological diversity (biodiversity): The variability among living organisms from all sources including, *inter alia*, terrestrial, marine and other aquatic ecosystems and the ecological complexes of which they are part; this includes diversity within species, between species and of ecosystems.

biological resources: These include genetic resources, organisms or parts thereof, populations, or any other biotic component of ecosystems with actual or potential use or value for humanity.

biopharmaceutical: Recombinant protein drugs, recombinant vaccines and monoclonal antibodies (for therapeutic roles). Biopharmaceuticals are still only a small part of the pharmaceutical industry, but of increasing importance (see biologics).

biotechnology: Any technological application that uses biological systems, living organisms or derivatives thereof to make or modify products or processes to provide goods and services.

board of trustees: In the context of trust funds, the individual or group of individuals responsible for managing a trust's assets and affairs and distributing revenues to beneficiaries.

botanical: A substance derived from plants; a vegetable drug, especially in its crude state.

botanical medicine: A medicine of plant origin, in crude or processed form; used to represent herbal, or plant-based, medicines that are not consumed as isolated compounds (as are pharmaceuticals).

by-laws: A document that sets out the governing and operating rules to be followed by a board of trustees.

charter: A document issued by the government to a corporation or non-profit corporation assuring them certain rights, liberties or powers in exchange for fulfilling certain requirements. In the context of trust funds, the charter is analogous to a deed, by-laws or a constitution.

civil law: A body of law based upon legislative enactments (laws created by statute), employed, for example, in France, Switzerland and most of the former colonies of France, Spain, Belgium and Portugal.

code of ethics: A public moral system developed to encourage certain types of behaviour and to establish rules that should be followed. They include general principles that underlie and pre-date all equitable research activities, as well as those that specifically guide the research process.

community controlled research: Research in which communities set research agendas and the terms for research projects, including collaborations with outside researchers.

consultation: A dynamic process of engaging affected people and other interested parties in open dialogue through which a range of views and concerns can be expressed in order to inform decision-making and help build consensus.

contract: An agreement between two or more parties to a set of lawful promises that make up a legal obligation resulting from the parties' agreement or understanding, where there is a duty of performance and a remedy of law in the event of a breach or non-performance.

combinatorial chemistry: Automated parallel synthesis of hundreds or thousands of compounds at a time; can be directed to produce 'drug-like' molecules and molecules compatible with molecular-based screens.

commodification: In this context, the influence or appropriation of biodiversity and cultural knowledge by science and market-related forces; this has resulted in biodiversity and cultural knowledge being viewed and treated increasingly as commodities.

common law: A body of law based primarily on judicial decisions employed, for example, in the US, UK and former Commonwealth countries.

common law trust: A trust organized so that trustees have responsibility for the fund's assets and manage its affairs, while benefits accrue to either private parties (individuals who are specifically identified) or the public (not specific individuals, but a community or segment of a community).

cosmeceuticals: Products that straddle the boundary between cosmetics and drugs, with increasingly sophisticated bioactive properties. Unlike cosmetics or general skin-care products which claim only to mask or retard skin ageing, cosmeceuticals change, or claim to change, the structure of the skin.

country of origin of genetic resources: The country who possesses genetic resources in in-situ conditions.

country providing genetic resources: The country supplying genetic resources collected from in-situ sources, including populations of both wild and domesticated species, or taken from ex-situ sources, which may or may not have originated in that country.

cultivars: Distinct form or variety of domesticated plant derived through breeding and selection and maintained through cultivation.

customary law: Enforceable rules and norms of conduct existing within and applying to a tribal group or other community living within a socio-cultural system distinct from the dominant system of the state within whose territory the community resides.

decision of the Conference of the Parties: A formal agreement of the Conference of the Parties (COP) to the Convention on Biological Diversity that leads to binding actions. It becomes part of the agreed body of decisions by the COP and directs the future work of the COP and guides action at the national level.

deed: A document that records the goals of a trust, its structure, the identities of the beneficiaries, the trustees and the obligations of the trustees to the trust and beneficiaries.

deoxyribonucleic acid (DNA): The molecule that generally encodes all genetic information. It consists of two strands or chains of sub-units (known as nucleotides).

derivative: Unimproved or unmodified chemical compounds, other than DNA or RNA, that exist in a sample of biological material obtained from an in-situ or ex-situ source, and formed by the metabolic processes of the organism.

domesticated or cultivated species: A species in which the evolutionary process has been influenced by humans to meet their needs.

drug development: Includes chemical improvements to a drug molecule; animal pharmacology studies; and pharmacokinetic and safety studies in animals, followed by phases I, II and III clinical studies in humans.

drug discovery: The process by which a lead is found, including the acquisition of materials for screening; identification of a disease and therapeutic target of interest; methodology and assay development; advanced screening; and identification of active agents and chemical structure.

ecosystem: A dynamic complex of plant, animal and micro-organism communities and their non-living environment interacting as a functional unit.

ex-situ conservation: The conservation of components of biological diversity outside of their natural habitats.

foundation: A trust-like arrangement used in civil law countries, where the resulting institution is a legal entity able to own assets (as opposed to a trust where assets are held by trustees).

fair and equitable benefit-sharing: The Convention on Biological Diversity (CBD, Article 15 (7)) requires each contracting party – whether developed or developing – to take 'legislative, administrative or policy measures...with the aim of sharing in a fair and equitable way the results of research and development and the benefits arising from the commercial and other utilization of genetic resources with the Contracting Party providing such resources...upon mutually agreed terms'. The CBD does not define 'fair and equitable', but it can be inferred that where the terms of benefit-sharing are mutually agreed between the parties, they meet the standard of 'fair and equitable' (Glowka et al, 1994).

gene: A small section of DNA that contains information for making one protein molecule; a unit of hereditary information that can be passed from one generation to another.

genetic engineering: The manipulation of information in the DNA of an organism in order to alter the characteristics of the organism. Developed in the 1970s, the technique allows the bypassing of biological constraints to genetic exchange and mixing, and may permit the combination of genes from widely different species.

genetic material: Material of plants, animal, microbial or other origin containing functional units of heredity.

genetic resources: Genetic material of actual or potential value.

genetically modified organism (GMO): The modification of the genetic characteristics of a micro-organism, plant or animal by inserting a modified gene or a gene from another variety or species.

genomics: The study of genomes, including genome mapping, gene sequencing and gene function. The use of this information is in the development of therapeutics.

germplasm: The genetic material that forms the physical basis of heredity and which is transmitted from one generation to the next by means of germ cells.

give back: The translation and transfer of research results in a form useful for local groups with whom researchers work.

Global Environment Facility (GEF): The multibillion dollar GEF was established by the World Bank, UNDP and UNEP in 1990. It operates the Convention on Biological Diversity's 'financial mechanism' on an interim basis and funds developing country projects that have global biodiversity benefits.

habitat: The place or type of site where an organism or population naturally occurs.

horticulture: The cultivation of ornamental and vegetable plants in gardens or smallholdings (market gardens). *Hortus* = garden (Latin).

impact assessment: An evaluation of the likely impact on biological diversity of proposed programmes, policies or projects.

indigenous peoples: People regarded as indigenous on account of their descent from the populations who inhabited a country, or geographic region to which the country belongs, at the time of conquest or colonization or the establishment of present state boundaries, and who – irrespective of their legal status – retain some or all of their own social, economic, cultural and political institutions (ILO Convention 169).

integrated pest management (IPM): the challenging or control of pests through a tailored programme of different strategies, including biological control agents and agrochemicals.

in-situ conditions: The conditions where genetic resources exist within ecosystems and natural habitats, and, in the case of domesticated or cultivated species, in the surroundings where they have developed their distinctive properties.

in-situ conservation: The conservation of ecosystems and natural habitats, and the maintenance and recovery of viable populations of species in their natural surroundings and, in the case of domesticated or cultivated species, in the surroundings where they have developed their distinctive properties.

landrace: Farmer-developed cultivars of crop plants that are adapted to local environmental conditions.

letter of intent (LOI): A document signed prior to drafting a contract, in which the parties involved in negotiations determine and broadly outline the basic terms and conditions for an agreement.

life science companies: Companies who combine businesses in pharmaceutical, agricultural chemicals and products, and food and nutrition.

local communities: A group of people having a long-standing social organization that binds them together, often in a defined area.

material transfer agreement (MTA): A special type of contract defining the rights and obligations of all parties, including third parties, during the transfer of biological material from a provider to a recipient. They are used widely in academic, governmental and corporate research.

mechanism-based screening: A receptor- or enzyme-based screen against which a range of materials can be run, including natural products such as plants, marine organisms, fungi and micro-organisms, but also synthetic compounds.

memorandum of understanding (MOU): A document elaborated in the preliminary phase of a negotiation process, where the parties set down the general framework for a future agreement, and which may include references to the agenda and rules for future negotiations, the scope of the proposed discussions and the parties involved.

microbe: Synonymous with micro-organism.

micro-organisms: Groups of microscopic organisms, some of which cannot be detected without the aid of a light or electron microscope, including the viruses, the prokaryotes (bacteria and archaea), and eukaryotic life forms, such as protozoa, filamentous fungi, yeasts and microalgae.

mutually agreed terms: The Convention on Biological Diversity (CBD, Article 15 (4)) states that 'access, where granted, shall be on mutually agreed terms'. Inherent in the phrase 'mutually agreed terms' is the expectation of a negotiation between the contracting party granting access to genetic resources and another entity – an individual, a company, an institution, a community or a state – desiring access to and use of the genetic resources. A successful negotiation could then result in the creation of an access agreement embodying the terms that have been mutually agreed (Glowka et al, 1994).

natural product drugs: Drugs of natural origin classified as original natural products, products derived semi-synthetically from natural products, or synthetic products based on natural product models.

non-governmental organization (NGO): In the context of the Convention on Biological Diversity, NGOs include environmental groups, indigenous peoples' organizations, research institutions, business groups and representatives of city and local government.

prior informed consent (PIC): consent of a party to an activity that is given after receiving full disclosure regarding the reasons for the activity, the specific procedures the activity would entail, the potential risks involved, and the full implications that can realistically be foreseen. In the context of the Convention on Biological Diversity (CBD, Article 15 (5)), prior informed consent (PIC) for access and use of genetic resources contains the following elements:
- consent of the contracting party who is the genetic resources provider (an affirmative act);
- based on information provided by the potential genetic resource user;
- prior to consent for access being granted.

The CBD only requires the PIC of CBD contracting parties (states who have ratified the CBD); but national legislation may extend PIC requirements to other entities, such as sub-national governments, local and indigenous communities or research institutions holding collections of genetic resources.

protected area: An area of land and/or sea especially dedicated to the protection and maintenance of biological diversity, and of natural and associated cultural resources, and managed through legal and other effective means (IUCN et al, 1994); a geographically defined area that is designated or regulated and managed to achieve specific conservation objectives (CBD, Article 2).

random screening: This form of screening treats all samples equally and works through extract and compound libraries. Compounds may be screened singly or in mixtures.

ratification: After signing the Convention on Biological Diversity, a country must ratify it; for this it often needs the approval of the parliament or other designated body. The instruments of ratification are submitted to the UN Secretary General, who acts as the depositary. 90 days later the country becomes a party.

rational drug design: Lead compounds are identified based on a molecular understanding of the drug and its receptor, often by using computer technology to aid in determination of the 3-D structures of molecular targets. Molecular modelling can be used to design new structures from scratch, or to look at a database of existing compounds for screening, or to manipulate naturally occurring molecules.

recombinant DNA (r-DNA): A strand of DNA synthesized in the laboratory by splicing together selected parts of DNA strands from different organic species, or by adding a selected part to an existing DNA strand.

research agreement: An agreement specifying the scope and terms of research on, and collection of, biological or genetic resources, and generally also specifying subsequent uses of the resources and the sharing of expected or potential benefits from their use.

research guidelines: Documents drafted to provide practical detail and guidance on current standards of best practice in research – in particular, special context research. Often appended to codes of ethics.

scope (of law or agreement): Issues or areas covered and regulated by a specific law or agreement.

Secretariat of the Convention on Biological Diversity: Staffed by international civil servants and responsible for serving the Conference of the Parties and ensuring its smooth operation, the Secretariat of the Convention on Biological Diversity makes arrangements for meetings, compiles and prepares reports and coordinates with other relevant international bodies. The Secretariat is administered by UNEP and located in Montreal, Canada.

sovereignty over genetic resources: The right of states to determine access to genetic resources, subject to national legislation, deriving from a state's general sovereign rights over its natural resources. State sovereignty was first explicitly recognized in the Convention on Biological Diversity (CBD, Article 15). Sovereignty does not, however, imply ownership, which must be determined by national legislation (Glowka et al, 1994).

species: A taxonomic rank below a genus, consisting of closely related, morphologically similar individuals capable of exchanging genes or interbreeding.

subsidiary body of the Convention on Biological Diversity: A committee that assists the Conference of the Parties. The CBD defines one permanent committee: the Subsidiary Body for Scientific, Technical and Technological Advice (SBSTTA). The Conference of the Parties may establish additional subsidiary bodies as needed; for example, in 1996 it set up the Open-Ended Ad Hoc Working Group on Biosafety.

sui generis: Latin for 'unique' or 'of its own kind'.

sustainable use: The use of components of biological diversity in a way and at a rate that do not lead to the long-term decline of biological diversity, thereby maintaining its potential to meet the needs and aspirations of present and future generations.

taxonomy: The study of the theory, procedure and rules of the classification of organisms according to the similarities and differences between them.

technology transfer: The transfer of knowledge or equipment to enable the manufacture of a product, the application of a process or the rendering of a service.

traditional environmental or ecological knowledge: A body of knowledge and beliefs transmitted through oral tradition and first-hand observation. It includes a system of classification, a set of empirical observations about the local environment, and a system of self-management that governs resource use. In the Convention on Biological Diversity context, traditional knowledge refers to knowledge, innovations and practices of indigenous and local communities deriving from customary uses of biological resources and associated cultural practices and traditions (CBD, Article 8 (j)).

traditional resources: Tangible and intangible assets and attributes deemed to be of value to indigenous and local communities, including the spiritual, aesthetic, cultural and economic. Includes plants, animals and other material objects that have sacred, ceremonial, heritage or aesthetic and religious qualities, as well as economic and social values.

tribal peoples: People in independent countries whose social, cultural and economic conditions distinguish them from other sections of the national community, and whose status is regulated wholly or partially by their own customs or traditions or by special laws or regulations (ILO Convention 160).

ultra high-throughput screening: Fully automated, around-the-clock screening of compound libraries in a variety of molecular-based assays. The result is the capability to merge the increasing capacity for the development of new screening targets and the production of chemical diversity to reduce cycle times in drug discovery.

variety: A taxonomic rank below sub-species in botany; varieties are usually the result of selective breeding and diverge from the parent species or sub-species in distinct but relatively minor ways. Usage varies in different countries.

References

Introduction

Acharya, Keya (1999) 'UNESCO's upcoming summit to pursue social equity goal', IPS Service, 5 February, www.ips.org

Amaral, W A N and R H Born (1999) *Biodiversity conservation and biotechnology*, Center for International Development at Harvard University, Harvard, wanamara@carpa.ciagri.usp.br

Balick, M J (1997) 'Are we throwing out the baby with the bathwater?' International Union of Biological Sciences, www4.nas.edu/usnc/ethnobot.nsf

Blackman, K (1995) 'Africa–Environment: curbing exploitation of nature's cures', *Inter Press Service*, 29 November

Bowles, I A, D Clark, D Downes and M Guerin-McManus (1996) 'Encouraging private sector support for biodiversity conservation: the use of economic and legal tools', *Conservation International Policy Paper*, vol 1, Washington, DC

Brockaway, L (1979) 'Science and colonial expansion: the role of the British royal botanic gardens', *American Ethnologist*, vol 6, pp449–65

Brooke, L (1993) 'The participation of indigenous peoples and the application of their environmental and ecological knowledge in the Arctic environment protection strategy', Inuit Circumpolar Conference, Ottawa, in *IUCN Intercommission Task Force on Indigenous Peoples, Indigenous Peoples and Sustainability: Cases and Actions*, International Books, Utrecht

Bystrom, M, P Einarsson and G A Nycander (1999) 'Fair and equitable: sharing the benefits from use of genetic resources and traditional knowledge', Report, September, Swedish Scientific Council on Biological Diversity, Stockholm

Christensen, J (2000) 'A romance with a rainforest and its elusive miracles', *The New York Times*, 30 November 1999

Clark, D and D Downes (1995) *What Price Biodiversity? Economic Incentives and Biodiversity Conservation in the United States*, Center for International Environmental Law, Washington, DC

Downes, D (1999) 'CIEL asks US Patent and Trademark Office to boost recognition of traditional knowledge', 3 August, CIEL, Washington, DC

Downes, D R (1994) 'The Convention on Biological Diversity: seeds of green trade?', *Tulane Environmental Law Journal*, vol 8, issue 1

Dove, M R (1996) 'Centre, periphery, and biodiversity: a paradox of governance and a developmental challenge' in S B Brush and D Stabinsky (eds) *Valuing Local Knowledge: Indigenous People and Intellectual Property Rights*, Island press, Washington, DC

Drahos, P (1999) 'Biotechnology patents, markets and morality', *European Intellectual Property Review*, vol 21, issue 9, September, pp441–49,

Dutfield, G (2000) *Intellectual Property Rights, Trade and Biodiversity: Seeds and Plant Varieties*, Earthscan, London

Dutfield, G (1999) 'Biopiracy: the slavery of the new millennium? Surely not', Working Group on Traditional Resource Rights, Oxford, UK

Ekpere, J A (1999) *Biotechnology Research and Development in Africa*, Center for International Development at Harvard University, Harvard, Jekpere@rcl.nig.com

Euromonitor plc (1998) *The World Economy Factbook 1998/99*, sixth edition, Euromonitor plc, London

Forje, L C and J W Forje (1985) 'Critical perspectives on research, high technology, the multinationals and underdevelopment in Africa', *Impact of Science on Society*, no 141, pp37–49

Four Directions Council (1996) *Forests, Indigenous Peoples and Biodiversity*, Four Directions Council, Canada

Glowka, L (1998) 'A guide to undertaking biodiversity legal and institutional profiles', IUCN Environmental Law Centre, *Environmental Policy and Law* Paper no 35, Bonn

Glowka, L (1998) 'A guide to designing legal frameworks to determine access to genetic resources', IUCN Environmental Law Centre, *Environmental Law and Policy* Paper no 34, Bonn

Gollin, M A (1999) 'Legal and practical consequences of biopiracy', *Diversity*, vol 15, no 2

Gollin, M A (1993) 'An intellectual property rights framework for biodiversity prospecting' in W V Reid et al *Biodiversity Prospecting: Using Genetic Resources for Sustainable Development*, World Resources Institute, Washington, DC

Gollin, M A and S A Laird (1996) 'Global Policies, Local Actions: the Role of National Legislation in Sustainable Biodiversity Prospecting, *Boston University Journal of Science and Technology Law*, vol 2, 16 May, L.16

Harry, D (1998) 'Tribes meet to discuss genetic colonization', Report from the Colonialism through Biopiracy Conference, www.niec.net/ipcb

Hoagland, K E (1994) *Guidelines for Institutional Policies and Planning in Natural History Collections*, Association of Systematics Collections (ASC), Washington, DC

Juma, C (1989) *The Gene Hunters: Biotechnology and the Scramble for Seeds*, Princeton University Press, Princeton

ten Kate, K and S A Laird (eds) (1999) *The Commercial Use of Biodiversity: Access to Genetic Resources and Benefit-Sharing*, Earthscan, London

Kiew, R and N H Lajis (1994) *The Commercial Exploitation of Biodiversity with Special Reference to Malaysia*, ASOMPS VIII, Melaka, Malaysia

Kwayera, J (1999) 'Gene banking: UK scientists accused of biopiracy', *All Africa News Agency Wire*, 13 December, www.africanews.org/east/kenya/stories/1999

Lama, A (2000) 'Law to protect native intellectual property', *IPS News Bulletin*, 12 January, www.ips.org

Macilwain, C (1998) 'When rhetoric hits reality in debate on bioprospecting', *Nature*, vol 392, 9 April, pp535–40

Makhubu, L (1998) 'Bioprospecting in an African context', *Science*, vol 282, October, pp41–2

McAfee, K (1999) 'Selling nature to save it? Biodiversity and green developmentalism', *Environment and Planning D: Society and Space* 1999, vol 17, pp133–54

McNeely, J (1999) 'Ethical systems and the Convention on Biological Diversity: Setting the stage', *Diversity*, vol 15, no 1

McNeely, J (1988) *Economics and Biological Diversity: Developing and Using Economic Incentives To Conserve Biological Resources*, IUCN, Gland

MedAdNews (1998) 'Top 50 companies ranked by healthcare revenue', *MedAd News*, September

Mordeno, M C (1999) 'Lumads oppose biopiracy', *Philippine Daily Inquirer*, Manila, 3 January, www1.inquirer.net

Mytelka, L (1999) 'Evolution of the "biotechnology" industry', Paper Presented at the International Conference on Biotechnology in the Global Economy, Center for International Development at Harvard University, Harvard, 2–3 September

Nayak, A R (1999) 'Biotechnology and the integration of the life science industry', Paper Presented at the International Conference on Biotechnology in the Global Economy, Center for International Development at Harvard University, Harvard, 2–3 September

Neto, R B (1998) 'Brazil's scientists warn against "nationalistic" restrictions', *Nature*, vol 392, 9 April, p538

Orr, D (1999) 'Education, careers, and callings: the practice of conservation biology', *Conservation Biology*, vol 13, no 6, December, pp1242–5

Parry, B (2000) 'The fate of the collections: social justice and the annexation of plant genetic resources' in C Zerner (ed) *People, Plants and Justice: The Politics of Nature Conservation*, Columbia University Press, New York

Portillo, Z (1999) 'Biopirateria nueva amenaza para la Amazonia, IPS sevicio de noticias', *Inter Press Service*, Rome, January

Posey, D A (ed) (1999) *The Cultural and Spiritual Values of Biodiversity*, UNEP, Nairobi

Posey, D A (1996) *Traditional Resource Rights: International instruments for protection and compensation for indigenous peoples and local communities*, IUCN, Gland

Posey, D A and G Dutheld (1996) *Beyond Intellectual Property: Toward traditional resource rights for indigenous peoples and local communities*, IDRC, Ottawa

RAFI (1999) 'Biopiracy project in Chiapas, Mexico denounced by Mayan indigenous groups. University of Georgia refuses to halt project', News Release, 1 December

Redford, K H and B D Richter (1999) 'Conservation of biodiversity in a world of use', *Conservation Biology*, vol 13, no 6, December, pp1246–56

Reid, W V, S A Laird, C A Meyer, R Games, A Sittenfeld, D H Janzen, M A Gollin and C Juma (eds) (1993) *Biodiversity Prospecting: Using Genetic Resources for Sustainable Development*, World Resources Institute, Washington, DC

Richter, B D and K H Redford (1999) 'The art (and science) of brokering deals between conservation and use', *Conservation Biology*, vol 13, no 6, December, pp1235–7

Secretariat of the Convention on Biological Diversity (2001) *Handbook of the Convention on Biological Diversity*, Earthscan, London

Shiva, V (1999) 'Biopiracy, blocking TRIPS reform: Seattle and the politics of the WTO/TRIPS review', 12 November; Launch of Global Campaign on Biopiracy and TRIPS Reform

Shiva, V (1998) *Biopiracy: the plunder of nature and knowledge*, Green Books, Devon

Simpson, A (1999), 'Can democracy cope with biotechnology?' *Splice*, vol 5, issue 2, The Genetics Forum, www.geneticsforum.org.uk

Solis Rivera, V and P Madrigal Cordero (1999) 'Costa Rica's Biodiversity Law: sharing the process', paper prepared for the Workshop on Biodiversity Conservation and Intellectual Property Rights, New Delhi, India, 29–31 January

Tobin B, F Noejovich and C Yanez (1998) *Petroleras, Estado y Pueblos Indigenas: El Juego de las Expectativas, Defensoria del Pueblo, Linamientos Preliminares para la consulta de los pueblos indigenas amazonicos del Peru en las actividades de exploracion y explotacion de Hidrocarburos*, Defensoria del Pueblo, Lima

Villamea, L and M Pinto (2000) 'Biopiracy: Indians want patent chiefs to prepare international law suit against scientists who registered indigenous knowledge', *ISTOE Magazine*, www.zaz.com.br/istoe/brasileiros/2000

Vogel, J H (1996) 'The successful use of economic instruments to foster sustainable use of biodiversity: six case studies from Latin America and the Caribbean', White Paper, Bolivia Summit on Sustainable Development, Santa Cruz, 6–8 December

Wilson, E O (ed) (1988) *Biodiversity*, National Academy Press, Washington, DC

Zerner, C (2000) *People, Plants and Justice: The Politics of Nature Conservation*, Columbia University Press, New York

Section I: Biodiversity research relationships

Akeroyd, A (1984) 'Ethics in relation to informants, the profession and governments' in R Ellen (ed) *Ethnographic Research: a Guide to General Conduct*, Academic Press, London

Alexiades, M N (ed) (1996) *Selected Guidelines for Ethnobotanical Research: a Field Manual*, Advances in Economic Botany 10, New York Botanical Garden, New York

Alexiades, M N (in press) *Ethnobotany and Globalization: Science and Ethics at the Turn of the Century*, Advances in Economic Botany, New York Botanical Garden, New York

American Anthropological Association (AAA) (1998) *Code of Ethics*, approved June 1998, AAA, Washington, DC

AAA (1971) 'Statements on ethics: principles of professional responsibility', adopted by the Council of the AAA, May 1971, AAA, Washington, DC

AAA (1969) 'Statement on problems of anthropological research and ethics', adopted by the Council of the AAA, March 1967, AAA, Washington, DC

AAA (1948) 'Resolution on freedom of publication', adopted by the Council of the AAA, December 1948, AAA, Washington, DC

AAA (no date) *Commission to Review the AAA Statements on Ethics*, Final Report, Washington, DC

American Folklore Society (1988) 'A statement of ethics', *AFSNews*, February, vol 17, no 1, www.afsnet.org/ethics.htm

American Society of Pharmacognosy (ASP) (1996) *Guidelines for Members of the American Society of Pharmacognosy*, available at www.phcog.org

American Sociological Association (1997) *Code of Ethics*, www.asanet.org/ecoderev.htm

Archaeological Institute of America (AIA) (1999) *Code of Ethics and the AIA Code of Professional Standards*, www.archeological.org/ethics.html

Association of Systematics Collections (ASC) (1992) 'Report from the ASC Workshop on data sharing and database ethics', *ASC Newsletter*, vol 20 no 6, December

Baker, J et al (1995) 'Natural product drug discovery and development: new perspectives on international collaboration', *Journal of Natural Products*, vol 58, no 9, September, pp1325–57

Balakrishna, P (1999) 'Why share benefits?' *The Hindu*, 23 May, India

Balick, M And R Arvigo (1998) 'The new ethnobotany: sharing with those who shared', *Herbalgram* No 42

Bannister, K P (2000) 'Chemistry rooted in cultural knowledge: exploring the links between antimicrobial properties and traditional knowledge in food and medicinal plant resources of the Secwepemc First Nation', PhD thesis, University of British Columbia, Vancouver, BC

Bannister, K P (1999) 'When promotion and protection conflict: indigenous knowledge and traditional plant resources of the Secwepemc First Nation (BC, Canada)', Paper presented at the 98th Annual Meeting of the American Anthropological Association, 17–21 November, Chicago, Illinois

Bannister, K and K Barrett (in press) 'Weighing the proverbial "ounce of prevention" versus the "pound of cure" in a biocultural context: a role for the precautionary principle in ethnobiological research' in L Maffi, T Carlson and E López-Zent (eds) *Ethnobotany and Conservation of Biocultural Diversity*, Advances in Economic Botany Series, New York Botanical Garden, New York

Bannister, K P and the Secwepemc Cultural Education Society (1997) 'Letter of consent for the Secwepemc Ethnobotany Project: ethnopharmacology of Secwepemc traditional medicines', Submitted in Partial Fulfillment of Ethical Review by the Behavioural Sciences Screening Committee for Research and Other Studies Involving Human Subjects, University of British Columbia, Vancouver, BC

Barnes, J A (1977) *The Ethics of Inquiry in Social Science*, Oxford University Press, Delhi, India

Beaman, J H and R S Beaman (1998) *The Plants of Mount Kinabalu 3: Gymnosperms and Non-Orchid Monocotyledons*, Natural History Publications (Borneo), Kota Kinabalu in association with the Royal Botanic Gardens, Kew, UK

Bhat, KKS (1997) 'Medicinal plant information databases' in Food and Agriculture Organization *Medicinal Plants for Forest Conservation and Health Care*, Non-Wood Forest Products 11, FAO, Rome

Boas, F (1919) 'Correspondence: social scientists as spies', *The Nation*, vol 109, no 2842, December

Brockaway, L (1979) 'Science and colonial expansion: the role of the British royal botanic gardens', *American Ethnologist*, vol 6, pp449–65

Brush, S and D Stabinsky (1996) *Valuing Local Knowledge: Indigenous People and Intellectual Property Rights*, Island Press, Washington, DC

Cassell, J and S E Jacobs (eds) (1987) *Handbook on Ethical Issues in Anthropology*, Special Publication of the American Anthropological Association, No 23, AAA, Washington, DC

Cassell, J and S E Jacobs (1987) 'Introduction' in J Cassell and S E Jacobs (eds) *Handbook on Ethical Issues in Anthropology*, Special Publication of the American Anthropological Association, No 23, AAA, Washington, DC

Centre for Applied Ethics (1999) 'Professional ethics resources on WWW', Centre for Applied Ethics, University of British Columbia, Vancouver, BC, www.ethics.ubc.ca/resources/professional/codes.html

Chambers, R (1983) *Rural Development: Putting the Last First*, Longman, Harlow

Chau Ming, L, P Gaudêncio and V P dos Santos (1997) *Plantas Medicinais. Uso Popular na Reserva Extrativista 'Chico Mendes', Acre*, CEPLAM, UNESP, Botucatu, Brazil

Chiquen, M, J Cutamurajay, C Prado and S Paz (1994) *Estudio comparativo: Arboles y Alimentos en Dos Comunidades Indígenas del Oriente Boliviano*, FTPP-FAO, Cochabamba, Bolivia

Churcher, T (1997) *Biodiversity Research Protocols: Directory of Guidance Documents Relating to Biodiversity and Cultural Knowledge Research and Prospecting*, Compiled for the Biodiversity and Ethics Working Group of Pew Conservation Fellows, University of California, Berkeley

Clement, C and M N Alexiades (2000) 'Etnobotanica e biopirateria na Amazonia' in T B Cavalcanti (ed) *Topicos Atnais em Botanica. Palestras convidadas do 51 Congresso Nacional de Botanica*, EMBRAPA/SBB, Brasilia

Colvin, J (1992) 'Editorial: a code of ethics for research in the Third World', *Conservation Biology*, vol 6 no 3, September, pp 309–11

Cooper, N S and R C J Carling, (1996) *Ecologists and Ethical Judgements*, Chapman and Hall, London

Cragg, G M et al (1997) 'Interactions with source countries: guidelines for members of the American Society of Pharmacognosy', *Journal of Natural Products*, vol 60 no 6, pp654–55

The Crucible Group (1994) *People Plants and Patents*, International Development Research Centre, Ottawa

The CSIR, South Africa (1999) 'Policy on bioprospecting'; 'CSIR's research approach to bioprospecting'; 'CSIR's policy on partnerships for bioprospecting', South Africa, www.csir.co.za

Cunningham, A B (1996) 'Professional ethics in ethnobotanical research' in Alexiades, M N (ed) *Selected Guidelines for Ethnobotanical Research: a Field Manual*, New York Botanical Garden, New York

Cunningham, A B (1993) *Ethics, Ethnobiological Research and Biodiversity*, Research Report, WWF-International, Gland, Switzerland

Cunningham, A B (1993) 'Guidelines for equitable partnerships in new natural products development: recommendations for a code of practice' in *Ethics, Ethnobiological Research and Biodiversity*, Research Report, WWF-International, Gland, Switzerland

Department of Environmental Affairs and Tourism (DEAT) (1999) 'State of the environment in South Africa: an overview', www.ngo.grida.no/soesa/

DEAT (1997) *White Paper on the Conservation and Sustainable Use of South Africa's Biological Diversity*, Notice 1095 of 1997, *Government Gazette*, vol 385, no 18163, South Africa

Diamond, J M and R M May (1985) 'A discipline with a time limit', *Nature*, vol 317, pp111–12

Diversity (1998) vol 14, p15

Dove, A (1998) 'Botanical gardens cope with bioprospecting loophole', *Science*, vol 281, 28 August

Dove, M R (1996) 'Centre, periphery, and biodiversity: a paradox of governance and a developmental challenge' in S B Brush and D Stabinsky (eds) *Valuing local knowledge. Indigenous people and intellectual property rights*, Island Press, Washington, DC, pp 41–67

Downes, D R and S A Laird (1999) *Community Registries of Biodiversity-Related Knowledge: the Role of Intellectual Property in Managing Access and Benefit-Sharing*, Prepared for UNCTAD Biotrade Initiative, Geneva

Elisabetsky, E and D A Posey (1994) 'Ethnopharmacological search for antiviral compounds: treatment of gastrointestinal disorders by Kayapo medical specialists' in D J Chadwick and J Marsh (eds) *Ethnobotany and the Search for New Drugs*, Ciba Foundation Symposium 185, John Wiley & Sons, Chichester, UK

Ellen, R (ed) (1984) *Ethnographic Research: a Guide to General Conduct*, Academic Press, London

Farnsworth, E J and J Rosovsky (1993) 'The ethics of ecological field experimentation', *Conservation Biology*, vol 7, no 3, September, pp 463–72

Food and Agriculture Organization (FAO) (1991) *Draft International Code of Conduct for Plant Germplasm Collecting and Transfer*, FAO, Rome

Foodtek, South Africa (1998) 'South Africa's initiative will triple number of plants ever investigated by mankind', Press Release, 25 September, www.foodtek-int.co.za/biocontent/pressre.htm

Foodtek, South Africa (1999) 'World-class medicinal plant extraction facility opens at CSIR, 19 May 1999', www.foodtek-int.co.za/biocontent/pressre.htm

Fox, R C (1990) 'The evolution of American bioethics: a sociological perspective' in G Weisz (ed) *Social Science Perspectives on Medical Ethics*. University of Pennsylvania Press, Philadelphia, pp201–21

Fowler, C S (1993) 'Ethical dilemmas: intellectual property rights: some considerations for the AAA', *Anthropology Newsletter*, May

Gadgil, M, P R Seshagiri Rao, G Utkarsh and P Pramod (1998) *New Meanings for Old Knowledge: The People's Biodiversity Registers Programme, Ecological Applications*

Galliher, J F (1980) 'Social scientists' ethical responsibilities: looking upward meekly', *Social Problems* (Special Issue), vol 27, pp298–308

Gericke, N (1996) 'Useful guidelines and tips for fieldworkers', *The Indigenous Plant Use Newsletter*, vol 2, no 4, December

Glowka, L (1998) *A Guide to designing Legal Frameworks to Determine Access to Genetic Resources, Environmental Policy and Law*, Paper No 34, IUCN Environmental Law Centre, Bonn

Goldberg, C (1999) 'Urging a freer flow of scientific ideas', *The New York Times*, Tuesday, 6 April, section F, p3

Gosling, M (1999) 'South Africa to sell off plant rights', *Cape Times*, April

Greaves, T (ed) (1994) *Intellectual Property Rights for Indigenous Peoples: A Source Book*, Society for Applied Anthropology, Oklahoma

Grifo, F T (1996) 'Chemical prospecting: an overview of the International Cooperative Biodiversity Groups Program' in *Biodiversity, Biotechnology, and Sustainable Development in Health and Agriculture: Emerging Connections*, San Jose, Costa Rica, pp12–26

Gupta, A K (1999) *Blending Universal with Local Ethic: Accountability Toward Nature, Perfect Stranger, and Society*, IIMA Working Paper No 99-10-05, October

Gupta, A K (1999) 'Ethical dilemmas in the conservation of biodiversity' in S Shantharam and J F Montgomery (eds) *Biotechnology, Biosafety and Biodiversity: Scientific and Ethical Issues for Sustainable Development*, Science Publishers, Inc, New Hampshire, pp93–128

Gupta, A K (1996) 'Social and ethical dimensions of ecological economics', Keynote Paper Presented at the Down to Earth Conference of the International Society of Ecological Economics, Costa Rica, October, 1994, in R Constanza, O Segura and J Martinez-Alier (eds) *Getting Down to Earth: Practical Applications of Ecologial Economics*, Island Press, Washington, DC, pp91–116

Gupta, A K (1995) 'Ethical dilemmas in conservation of biodiversity: towards developing globally acceptable ethical guidelines', *Eubios Journal of Asian and International Bioethics 5* (Japan), March, pp40–6

Gupta, A K (1995) *Accessing Biological Diversity and Associative Knowledge System: Can Ethics Influence Equity?*, IIMA Working Paper No 1340, November, Presented at the Global Biodiversity Forum, Jakarta, 4–5 November

Gupta, A K (1994) *Ethical Issues in Prospecting Biodiversity*, IIMA Working Paper No 1205, August

Gupta, A K (1992) 'Ethics of foreign aid: why is it always ignored?' in F Dolberg (ed) *Criteria for Foreign Aid*, Development Research Working Group, University of Aarhus, Denmark, pp30–50

Gupta, A K et al (1999) 'Blending universal with local ethic: accountability toward nature, perfect stranger and society' in C Potvin, M Kreanzel and G Seutin (eds) *Protecting Biodiversity: Roles and Responsibilities*, McGill–Queens University Press, Toronto

Herskovits, M J (1973) *Cultural Relativism: Perspectives in Cultural Pluralism*, Vintage, New York

Hill, J N (1987) 'The Committee on Ethics: past, present and future' in J Cassell and S E Jacobs (eds) *Handbook on Ethical Issues in Anthropology*, Special Publication of the American Anthropological Association, no 23, AAA, Washington, DC

Hoagland, K E (ed) (1994) *Guidelines for Institutional Policies and Planning in Natural History Collections*, Association of Systematics Collections (ASC), Washington, DC

Hoagland, K E (1993) 'Scientific code of ethics', *Association of Systematics Collections Newsletter*, vol 21, no 1, p10

Howarth, J M (1996) 'Ecology: modern hero or post-modern villain? From scientific trees to phenomenological wood' in N S Cooper and R C J Carling (eds) *Ecologists and Ethical Judgements*, Chapman and Hall, London

International Cooperative Biodiversity Groups (ICBG) Programme (1997) *Principles for the Treatment of Intellectual Property and the Sharing of Benefits Associated with ICBG Sponsored Research* (modified for second request for applications – 15 August), the National Institutes of Health, National Science Foundation, US Agency for International Development, Washington, DC

International Federation of Accountants (1998) 'Codifying power and control: ethical codes in action', *International Management Accounting Study 8*, May, New York

International Society of Ethnobiology (ISE) (1998) *Code of Ethics and Guidelines for Research, Collections, Databases and Publications*, ISE, Aotearoa/New Zealand, November

InterRidge, www.lgs.jussieu.fr

International Union for Conservation of Nature and Natural Resources (IUCN) (1997) *Indigenous Peoples and Sustainability: Cases and Actions*, IUCN Intercommission Task Force on Indigenous Peoples, International Books, the Netherlands

Janzen, D H, W Hallwachs, R Gamez, A Sittenfeld and J Jimenez (1993) 'Research management policies: permits for collecting and research in the tropics' in W V Reid, S A Laird, C A Meyer, R Gamez, A Sittenfeld, D H Janzen, M A Gollin and C Juma (1993) *Biodiversity*

Prospecting: Using Genetic Resources for Sustainable Development, World Resources Institute, Washington, DC

Johns, J S, P Barreto and C Uhl (1996) 'Logging damage in planned and unplanned logging operations in the eastern Amazon', *Forest Ecology and Management*, vol 89, pp59–77

ten Kate, K and S A Laird (1999) *The Commercial Use of Biodiversity: Access to genetic resources and benefit-sharing*, Earthscan, London

ten Kate, K (1999) 'Botanic garden policy on access and benefit-sharing: introduction to information document' in *Secretariat to the Convention on Biological Diversity, Submissions by the UK Government: common policy guidelines for participating botanic gardens on access to genetic resources and benefit-sharing*, UNEP/CBD/ISOC/Inf 2, Intersessional Meeting on the Operations of the Convention, June, Montreal

ten Kate, K (1997) 'Access to ex situ collections: resolving the dilemma?' in J Mugabe et al (eds) *Access to Genetic Resources*, WRI/IUCN/ACTS, Nairobi

ten Kate, K and L J C Touche (1997) *Botanic Garden Policy on Access and Benefit-Sharing: Pilot Project Briefing Note 1*, Royal Botanic Gardens, Kew, UK

King, J and D Stabinsky (1999) 'Patents on cells, genes and organisms undermine the exchange of scientific ideas', *The Chronicle of Higher Education*, 5 February

Koebner, L, J Sokolow, F T Grifo and S Simpson (eds) (1998) *Scientists on Biodiversity*, American Museum of Natural History, New York

Kowal, M and E Padilla (1998) *Collaborative Links between Research and Extension Organizations: Lessons from the CONSEFORH Project Experience in Farm Forestry with Intermediary Agencies*, Rural Development Forestry Network Paper 24c, winter 1998–1999, Overseas Development Institute, London

Lacaze, D and M N Alexiades (1995) *Salud Para Todos: Plantas Medicinales y Salud Indígena en la Cuenca del Río Madre de Dios, Perú. Un Manual Práctico*, CBC, FENAMAD, Cusco, Peru

Laird, S A and R Wynberg (1997) 'Biodiversity prospecting in South Africa: towards the development of equitable partnerships' in J Mugabe, C Barber, G Henne, L Glowka, and A La Viña (eds) *Managing Access to Genetic Resources: Towards Strategies for Benefit-Sharing*, ACTS, Nairobi, and WRI, Washington, DC

Limbe Botanic Garden (LBG) (1998) *Draft Limbe Botanic Garden Policy on Access to Genetic Resources and Benefit-Sharing, Collaborative Research, Data and Information Exchange*, LBG, Limbe, Cameroon

Maffi, L (2001) 'On the interdependence of biological and cultural diversity' in L Maffi (ed) *On Biocultural Diversity: Linking Language, Knowledge, and the Environment*, Smithsonian Institution Press, Washington, DC, pp1–50

Mann, H (1997) *Intellectual Property Rights, Biodiversity and Indigenous Knowledge: a Critical Analysis in the Canadian Context*, Report submitted to the Canadian Working Group on Article 8(j) of the Convention on Biological Diversity

Marshall, P A (1992) 'Anthropology and bioethics', *Medical Anthropology Quarterly*, vol 6, no 1, pp49–73

Martini, A, N Rosa and C Hill (1994) 'An attempt to predict which Amazonian tree species may be threatened by logging activities', *Environment Conservation*, vol 21, pp152–62

The Max Lock Centre (1999) *Improving the Transfer of Research Knowledge* (Ref R7171), University of Westminster, London

McNeely, J (1999) 'Ethical systems and the Convention on Biological Diversity: setting the stage', *Diversity*, vol 15, no 1, pp29–30

Merton, R K (1973) 'The normative structure of science' in *The Sociological of Science: Theoretical and Empirical Investigations*, University of Chicago Press, Chicago

Milliken, W (1997) 'Traditional anti-malarial medicine in Roraima, Brazil', *Economic Botany*, vol 51, no 3, pp212–37

Milliken, W and B Albert (1996) 'The use of medicinal plants by the Yanomami Indians of Brazil', *Economic Botany*, vol 50(1), pp10–25

Missouri Botanical Garden (MBG) (1994) *Natural Products Research Policy*, MBG, St Louis

National Association for the Practice of Anthropology (1998) *Ethical Guidelines for Practitioners*, November, US

National Biological Information Infrastructure (1999) 'Database protocol to usher in open access to biodiversity data', *Access*, vol 2 no 1, January, www.nbii.gov

National Cancer Institute (NCI) (1998) *Memorandum of Understanding and Letter of Collection*, NCI, Bethesda, MD

National Health and Medical Research Council (NHMRC), Commonwealth of Australia (1991) *Guidelines on Ethical Matters in Aboriginal and Torres Strait Islander Health Research*, Approved by the 11th Session of the NHMRC, Brisbane, June

Natural History Museum, London (NHM) (1996) *Bioprospecting Policy*, NHM, London

National Institute of Biodiversity (InBio) *Costa Rica Rights Agreement*, InBio, Costa Rica

New York Botanical Garden (NYBG) (1996) 'Statement of policy regarding biodiversity prospecting with collaborating organizations', NYBG, New York

NIH, NSF, USDA (1998) 'Request for Applications (RFA) International Cooperative Biodiversity Groups', available at www.nih.gov/fic/opportunities/rfa.html

Novacek, M (1998) 'Introduction' in L Koebner, J Sokolow, F T Grifo and S Simpson (eds) *Scientists on Biodiversity*, American Museum of Natural History, New York

O'Riordan, T (1996) 'Foreword' in N S Cooper and R C J Carling, (1996) *Ecologists and Ethical Judgements*, Chapman and Hall, London

Office of Science and Technology Policy (OSTP) (1999) *OSTP Proposed Federal Policy on Research Misconduct to Protect the Integrity of the Research Record*, Federal Register 64(198), pp55722–5

Orr, D (1999) 'Education, careers, and callings: the practice of conservation biology', *Conservation Biology*, vol 13, no 6, December, pp1242–5

Pew Conservation Fellows (1996) *Biodiversity Research Protocols: 1996 Proposed Guidelines for Researchers and Local Communities Interested in Accessing, Exploring and Studying Biodiversity*, Developed by the Biodiversity and Ethics Working Groups of Pew Conservation Fellows, Berkeley, CA

Posey, D A (ed) (1999) *The Cultural and Spiritual Values of Biodiversity*, UNEP, Nairobi

Posey, D A (1996) *Traditional Resource Rights: International Instruments for Protection and Compensation for Indigenous Peoples and Local Communities*, IUCN, Gland, Switzerland

Posey, D A (1995) *Indigenous Peoples and Traditional Resource Rights: A Basis for Equitable Relationships?* Green College Centre for Environmental Policy and Understanding, Oxford

Posey, D A (1994) 'International agreements and intellectual property right protection for indigenous peoples' in T Greaves (ed) *Intellectual Property Rights: a Sourcebook*, Society for Applied Anthropology, Oklahoma

Posey, D A (1990) 'Intellectual property rights and just compensation for indigenous peoples', *Anthropology Today*, vol 6, no 4, pp13–16

Posey, D A (1979) 'Origin, development and maintenance of a mixed-blood community: the Freejacks of Fifth Ward Settlement', *Journal of Ethnohistory*, vol 26, no 2, pp177–93

Posey, D A and G Dutfield (1996) *Beyond Intellectual Property: Towards Traditional Resource Rights for Indigenous Peoples and Local Communities*, IDRC, Ottawa

Posey, D A, G Dutfield, and K Plenderleith (1996) 'Collaborative research and intellectual property rights' in N S Cooper and R C J Carling, (1996) *Ecologists and Ethical Judgements*, Chapman and Hall, London

Punch, M (1986) *The Politics and Ethics of Fieldwork*, Sage, Beverly Hills

Pyke, C R et al (1999) 'Letter to the Editor: a plan for outreach – defining the scope of conservation education', *Conservation Biology*, vol 13, no 6, December, pp1238–9

Redford, K H and B D Richter (1999) 'Conservation of biodiversity in a world of use', *Conservation Biology*, vol 13, no 6, December, pp1246–56

Register of Professional Archaeologists (RPA) (1999) *Code of Conduct and Standards of Research Performance*, Baltimore, MD, www.rpanet.org

Richter, B D and K H Redford (1999) 'The art (and science) of brokering deals between conservation and use', *Conservation Biology*, vol 13, no 6, December, pp1235–7

Rosenthal, J P (1997) 'Equitable sharing of biodiversity benefits: agreements on genetic resources', *Proceedings of the OECD International Conference on Incentive Measures for the Conservation and Sustainable Use of Biological Diversity*, Cairns, Australia, pp253–73

Royal Botanic Gardens, Kew, and Botanic Gardens Conservation International (1996) *The Role of Botanic Gardens in Implementing the Convention on Biological Diversity – with Particular Reference to Articles 6 and 8*, UNEP/CBD/COP/3/Inf 46

Royal Botanic Gardens, Kew (RBG) (1998) *Policy on Access to Genetic Resources and Benefit-Sharing*, RGB, London

Ruiz, M (1998) 'Protecting indigenous peoples' knowledge: policy and legislative developments in Peru', Paper Presented at the International Conference on Medicinal Plants, February, Bangalore, India

Ruppert, D (1994) 'Buying secrets: federal government procurement of intellectual cultural property' in T Greaves (ed) *Intellectual Property Rights for Indigenous Peoples: a Sourcebook*, Society for Applied Anthropology, Oklahoma City

Russell, D and C Harshbarger (in press) *Social Research for Community-Based Conservation*. AltaMira Press, Lanham, MD

Sagoff, M (1985) 'Fact and value in ecological science', *Environmental Ethics*, vol 7, pp99–116

Sanchez, V and C Juma (1994) *Biodiplomacy: Genetic Resources and International Relations*, African Centre for Technology Studies, Nairobi

Schoenhoff, D M (1993) *The Barefoot Expert: the interface of computerized knowledge systems and indigenous knowledge systems*, Greenwood Press, Westport, Connecticut

Schweitzer, J, F G Handley, J Edwards, W F Harris, M R Grever, S A Schepartz, G Cragg, K Snader and A Bhat (1991) 'Commentary: summary of the Workshop on Drug Development, Biological Diversity and Economic Growth', *Journal of the National Cancer Institute*, vol 83, 18 September, pp1294–8

SEB (1999) 'New, exciting and finally...an ethics column', *Plants & People. Society for Economic Botany Newsletter*, vol 13, Fall, SEB, Lawrence, KS, p13, available at www.econbot.org/newsletter/nl_backissues.html

Secretariat to the Convention on Biological Diversity (1999) 'Submissions received by the Executive Secretary concerning decision IV/8, paragraph 2', UNEP/CBD/ISOC/Inf 1, Intersessional Meeting on the Operations of the Convention, June, Montreal

Secretariat to the Convention on Biological Diversity (1999) 'Submissions by the Government of the UK: common policy guidelines for participating botanic gardens on access to genetic resources and benefit-sharing', UNEP/CBD/ISOC/Inf 2, Intersessional Meeting on the Operations of the Convention, June, Montreal

Shanley, P (1999) 'Equity-based environmental education along an Amazon tributary', Paper Presented at the Global Environmental Education and Communication Conference, North American Association of Environmental Education

Shanley, P (1999) 'To market, to market: Brazilian villagers encounter snags in peddling forest fruit', *Natural History Magazine*, October, New York, pp44–51

Shanley, P, M Cymerys and J Galvao (1998) *Fruitiferas da Mata na Vida Amazonica*, Belem, Brazil

Shanley, P, J Galvao and L Luz (1997) 'Limits and strengths of local participation: a case study in Eastern Amazonia', IIED, *PLA Notes*, vol 28, pp64–70

Shanley, P, I Hohn and A Valente da Silva (1996) *Receitas sem Palavras: Plantas Medicinais da Amazonia*, Belem, Brazil

Shanley, P, L Luz, J Galvao and P Cymerys (1997) 'Translating dry data for rural communities: science offers incentives for conservation', Overseas Development Institute, *Rural Development Network News*, vol 19e

Shepard, G H Jr (1999) 'Pharmacognosy and the sense in two Amazonian societies', PhD thesis, Medical Anthropology Programme, University of California, Berkeley

Simon, M M and L Brooke (1993) 'Inuit science: Nunavik's experience in Canada' in IUCN (1997) *Indigenous Peoples and Sustainability: Cases and Actions*, IUCN Intercommission Task Force on Indigenous Peoples, International Books, the Netherlands

Society for Economic Botany (SEB) (1995) *Guidelines of Professional Ethics of the Society for Economic Botany*, SEB, Lawrence, KS

Tyler, V (1994) 'Letter from Dr Varro Tyler to SEB President on code of ethics', *Plants & People. Society for Economic Botany Newsletter*, Fall, SEB, Lawrence, KS, p11

Uhl, C, P Barreto, A Veríssimo, P Amaral, A C Barros, E Vidal, J Gerwing, J Johns, and Jr C Souza (1997) 'An integrated approach for addressing natural resource management problems in the Brazilian Amazon', *Bioscience*, vol 47, no 3, pp160–8

United Nations (1995) *UN Commission on Human Rights on the Protection of the Heritage of Indigenous Peoples*, United Nations, Geneva

University of the South Pacific (USP) (1997) *Guidelines for Biodiversity Research and Bioprospecting*, USP, the Pacific Islands

Universiti Malaysia Sabah Tropical Biology and Conservation Unit and People and Plants Initiative in South-East Asia (WWF/UNESCO/RBG) (1998) *Biodiversity Prospecting: Access Control and Benefit Sharing Recommendations and Findings*, September, Kota Kinabalu, Sabah, Malaysia

Ventocilla, J, H Herrera and V Nuñez (1995) *Plants and Animals in the Life of the Kuna*, University of Texas Press, Austin, Texas

Veríssimo, A, and P Amaral (1996) *Exploração madeireira na Amazônia: situação atual e perspectivas*, Cadernos de propostas da Fase, Rio de Janeiro, pp9–16

Vitae Civilis – Institute for Development, Environment and Peace (1998) *Perception on the Rights of Use of Natural Resources and Intellectual Property: the Case of Jureia*, Sao Paulo, Brazil

Wax, M L (1987) 'Some issues and sources on ethics in anthropology' in J Cassell and S E Jacobs (eds) *Handbook on Ethical Issues in Anthropology*, Special Publication of the American Anthropological Association, no 23, AAA, Washington, DC

WHO/WWF/IUCN (1988) *Chiang Mai Declaration: Saving Lives by Saving Plants*, Chiang Mai Thailand

Wilson, E O (ed) (1988) *Biodiversity*, National Academy Press, Washington, DC

Working Group on Traditional Resource Rights/Linacre College (1998) *Findings and Recommendations from the International Conference Human Impacts on the Environment of the Brazilian Amazon*, June, Linacre College, Oxford University, Oxford

World Resources Institute (WRI) (1999) *Biodiversity*, WRI, Washington, DC, www.wri.com

Wynberg, R (1997) *Future Options and Roles for the National Botanical Institute in Biodiversity Prospecting*, Report Prepared for the National Botanical Institute, July

Section II: Biodiversity research and prospecting in protected areas

Aké Assi, L, (1984) 'Flore de la Côte d'Ivoire: etude descriptive et biogéographique, avec quelques notes ethnobotaniques', PhD thesis, Faculté des Sciences, Département Biologique Végétale, UdA, RCI

Allport, G, C Boesch, G Couturier, J Esser, G Merz and J Piart (1994) 'La faune' in *Le Parc National de Taï*, Tropenbos Séries, vol 8, pp72–93

Bobo Kadiri, S, S Tiawoun and B Boukar (1998) *Etudes prealables a l'exploitation eventuelle des ressources naturelles dans le Parc National de Waza: propositions de recherche*, November, UICN, Projet Waza-Logone, Maroua, Cameroon

Bokwe, A, M Fosi and S Neckmen (1999) *Case studies and other relevant information on the implementation of Article 8(j) of the Convention on Biological Diversity (Decision IV/9 of the Fouth Conference of the Parties to the CBD)*, Presented by the Government of the Republic of Cameroon. Ministry of the Environment and Forests, Yaounde, Cameroon

Borrini-Feyerabend, G (1996) *Collaborative Management of Protected Areas: Tailoring the Approach to the Context*, IUCN, Gland, Switzerland

Brandon, K, K H Redford and S E Sanderson (1998) *Parks in Peril: People, Politics and Protected Areas*, Island Press, Washington, DC

Bridgewater, P, A Phillips, M Green and B Amos (1996) *Biosphere Reserves and the IUCN System of Protected Area Management Categories*, Australian Nature Conservation Bureau, World Conservation Union and UNESCO, Canberra

Brock, T D and H Freeze (1969) '*Thermus aquaticus* gen. n. and sp. n., a non-sporulating extreme thermophile', *Journal of Bacteriology*, vol 98, pp289–97

Burnham, P (2000) 'Whose forest, whose myth? Conceptualisations of community forests in Cameroon' in A Abramson and D Theodossopoulos (eds) *Land, Law and Envvironment: Mythical Land, Legal Boundaries*, Pluto Press, London, pp31–58

Chester, C C (1996) 'Controversy over Yellowstone's biological resources: people, property and bioprospecting', *Environment*, vol 38, no 8, October, pp11–15, 34–6

Chester, C C (1999) 'Reconciling conservation with bioprospecting', Paper Presented at the Center for International Development at Harvard University Conference, Harvard

Colchester, M (1994) *Salvaging Nature: Indigenous Peoples, Protected Areas and Biodiversity Conservation*, Discussion Paper 55, United Nations Research Institute for Social Development, World Rainforest Movement and WWF

Culverwell, J (1997) *Long-Term Recurrent Costs of Protected Area Management in Cameroon: Monitoring of protected areas, donor assistance and external financing, ecological and management priorities of current and potential protected area system*, WWF, Yaounde, Cameroon

Edmonds Institute (1997) Press Release, 3 December 1997 and 5 March 1998

Environmental Law Institute (1996) *Legal Mechanisms Concerning Access to and Compensation For the Use of Genetic Resources in the United States of America*, ELI, Washington, DC

European Chemical News (1997) March

European Chemical News (1988) February

Frey, H P (1998) Letter to H Svarstad, 26 March

Gjersvik, C (1998) 'Opplysninger om Novartis og Sandimmun Neoral', Letter to H Svarstad. 17 March

Government of Cameroon (1998) *Manual of the Procedures for the Attribution, and Norms for the Management, of Community Forests*, Ministry of Environment and Forests, Yaounde, Cameroon

Government of Cameroon (1996) *Loi No 96/12 du 5 August 1996: Portant loi-cadre a la gestion de l'Environnement*, Ministry of Environment and Forests, Yaounde, Cameroon

Government of Cameroon (1994) *Law No 94/01 of 20 January 1994 to Lay Down Forestry, Wildlife and Fisheries Regulations*, Ministry of Environment and Forests, Yaounde, Cameroon

Government of Cameroon (1995) *Decree No 95/531 du 23 August 1995: Fixant les Modalites d'Application du Regime des Forets*, Ministry of Environment and Forests, Yaounde, Cameroon

Guillaumet, J L (1994) 'La flore' in *Le Parc National de Taï*, Tropenbos, Séries 8, pp66–71

Guillaumet, J L (1967) 'Recherches sur la végétation et la flore de la région du Bas–Cavally, Côte d'Ivoire'. *Mémoire ORSTOM*, no 20, p249

Hooper, D, D Hawksworth, and S Dhillion (1995) 'Microbial diversity and ecosystem processes; Section 6, biodiversity and ecosystem functioning: ecosystem analyses' in V H Heywood (ed) *Global Biodiversity Assessment*, Cambridge University Press, Cambridge

International Union for Conservation of Nature and Natural Resources (IUCN) (1992) *Parks for Life*, Report of the IV World Congress on National Parks and Protected Areas (84), IUCN, Gland, Switzerland

IUCN (1993) *Biological Diversity Conservation and the Law: Legal Mechanisms for Conserving Species and Ecosystems; Environmental Policy and Law*, Paper No 29, IUCN, Gland, Switzerland

IUCN (1994) *1993 United Nations List of National Parks and Protected Areas*, IUCN, Gland, Switzerland

IUCN, CNPPA and WCMC (1994) *Guidelines for Protected Area Management Categories*, IUCN, CNPPA and WCMC, Gland, Switzerland

IUCN (1996) *World Conservation Congress*, October, IUCN, Gland, Switzerland

Kempf, E (1993) 'In search of a home' in *The Law of the Mother, Protecting Indigenous Peoples in Protected Areas*, WWF, Gland, Switzerland

James, A and T Anderson (eds) (2000), *The Politics and Economics of Park Management*, Rowman and Littlefield Press, Lantham, MD

Janzen, D H, W Hallwachs, R Gamez, A Sittenfeld and J Jimenez (1993) 'Research management policies: permits for collecting and research in the tropics' in W V Reid, S A Laird, C A Meyer, R Gamez, A Sittenfeld, D H Janzen, M A Gollin, C Juma (eds) *Biodiversity Prospecting: Using Genetic Resources for Sustainable Development*, World Resources Institute, Washington, DC

Johnston, S (2000) *Protected Areas and the Convention on Biological Diversity*

ten Kate, K and S A Laird (1999) *The Commercial Use of Biodiversity: Access to genetic resources and benefit-sharing*, Earthscan, London

ten Kate, K (1999) 'Biotechnology in fields other than healthcare and agriculture' in ten Kate, K and S A Laird (1999) *The Commercial Use of Biodiversity: Access to genetic resources and benefit-sharing*, Earthscan, London

ten Kate, K, L Touche and A Collis (1998) *Yellowstone National Park and the Diversa Corporation: Case Studies on Benefit Sharing Arrangements*, Secretariat of the Convention on Biological Diversity, Fourth Conference of the Parties (COP 4), Bratislava, Slovakia

Laird, S A, A B Cunningham and E E Lisinge (1999) 'One in ten thousand? The Cameroon case of *Ancistrocladus korupensis*' in C Zerner (ed) *People, Plants and Justice: Case Studies of Resources Extraction in Tropical Countries*, Columbia University Press, New York

Larson, P S, M Freudenberger and B Wyckoff Baird (1998) *WWF Integrated Conservation and Development Projects: 10 Lessons from the Field 1985–1996*, World Wildlife Fund, Washington, DC

Lauginie, F (1992) 'La spécificité biologique du Parc national de Taï', Communication orale à la table ronde sur l'avenir du Parc National de Taï, Abidjan, Côte d'Ivoire

Lewis, C (ed) (1996) *Managing Conflicts in Protected Areas*, IUCN, Gland, Switzerland

Lindstrom, R (1997) 'Case study: *Thermus aquaticus*' in J H Vogel (ed) *From Traditional Knowledge to Bioprospecting*, Inter-American Development Bank, Consejo Nacional de Desarrollo del Ecuador

Lyster, S (1985) *International Wildlife Law*, Grotius Publications Limited, Cambridge

Madigan, M T and B L Marrs (1997) 'Extremophiles', *Scientific American*, April

Martin, C (1993) 'Introduction' in *The Law of the Mother, Protecting Indigenous Peoples in Protected Areas*, WWF, Gland, Switzerland

McNeely, J A (1993) *Parks for Life: Report of the Fourth World Congress on National Parks and Protected Areas*, IUCN, Gland, Switzerland

Miller, K R (1996) *Balancing the Scales: Guidelines for Increasing Biodiversity's Chances Through Bioregional Development*, World Resources Institute, Washington, DC

Milstein, M (1995) 'Yellowstone managers stake a claim on hot-springs microbes', *Science*, vol 270, 13 October

Ministère du Logement, du Cadre de Vie et de l'Environnement; Ministère de l'Enseignement Supérieur, de la Recherche et de l'Innovation Technologique; Le Comité National des Ressources Phytogénétiques et le WWF (1997) *Rapport du Séminaire Ouest-Africain sur les plantes médicinales, l'accès aux ressources génétiques et le partage équitable des bénéfices tirés de l'exploitation de ces ressources*, Adiopodoumé, 19–20 June

Mount Kupe Forest Project (1997) *Draft Guidelines for Visiting Researchers at Mount Kupe*, South-West Province, Cameroon

Mutebi, J, L Mulumba and Y Moyini (1997) *Access to Genetic Resources and Benefit Sharing in Bwindi Impenetrable National Park (BINP)*, Case Study Report Prepared by WWF–Eastern Africa, Nairobi

Novartis (1998) *Operational Review 1997*, Novartis, Basel, Switzerland

Novartis Pharma AG (1998) *Transplant Square*, March, www.transplantsquare.com/index.htm

Oates, F (1986) *Action Plan for African Primate Conservation: 1986–1990*, IUCN/SSG, Primate Specialist Group, Gland, Switzerland

Oviedo, G (1998) *Towards a Policy on Indigenous/Traditional Peoples and Protected Areas*, October, WWF International, Gland, Switzerland

Oviedo, G and J Brown (1999) 'Building alliances with indigenous peoples to establish and manage protected areas' in S Stolton and N Dudley (eds) *Partnerships for Protection*, Earthscan, London

Pimbert, M P and J N Pretty (1995) *Parks, People, and Professionals: Putting 'Participation' into Protected Area Management*, UNRISD Discussion Paper, DP 57, Geneva

Riezebos, E P (1994) 'Espace Taï' in *Le Parc National de Taï*, Tropenbos, Séries 8, pp9–11

Riezebos, E P, A P Vooren and J L Guillaumet (eds) (1994) *Le Parc National de Tai, Côte d'Ivoire*, Tropenbos Series No 8, La Fondation Tropenbos, Wageningen

Sittenfeld, A and R Gamez (1993) 'Biodiversity prospecting by InBio' in W V Reid, S A Laird, C A Meyer, R Gamez, A Sittenfeld, D H Janzen, M A Gollin, C Juma (eds) *Biodiversity Prospecting: Using Genetic Resources for Sustainable Development*, World Resources Institute, Washington, DC

Sloot, P H M (1994) 'Aperçu historique' in *Le Parc National de Taï*, Tropenbos, Séries 8, pp12–27

Smith, C (1999) '0.5% royalty on bio-deal too cheap, say critics. Park gave bio-rights away, critics complain', *The Salt Lake Tribune*, 4 October

Solis Rivera, V and P Madrigal Cordero (1999) 'Costa Rica's Biodiversity Law: sharing the process', Prepared for the Workshop on Biodiversity Conservation and Intellectual Property Regime, New Delhi, India, 29–31 January

Stolton, S and N Dudley (eds) (1999) *Partnerships for Protection*, Earthscan, London

Stolton, S and N Dudley (1999) 'Paper Parks, Arborvitae', *The IUN/WWF Forest Conservation Newsletter*, October

Svarstad, H, H C Bugge and S Dhillion, (2000) 'From Norway to Novartis: Cyclosporin from *Tolypocladium inflatum* in an open-access bioprospecting regime', *Biodiversity and Conservation*, vol 9, pp1521–41

Svarstad, H and S Dhillion (eds) (2000)*Responding to Bioprospecting: From Biodivesity in the South to Medicines in the North*, Spartacus Forlag, As, Oslo

Tribe, H T (1998) 'The discovery and development of Cyclosporin', vol 12, pt 1, February

Tuxhill, J and G P Nabhan (1998) *Plants and Protected Areas: a guide to in situ management*, WWF People and Plants Conservation Manual, Stanley Thornes Ltd, Cheltenham; republished (2001) by Earthscan, London

Wolf, R (1994) 'Yellowstone discovery: should US get profits?', *San Jose Mercury News*, Monday, 25 July

WCPA/WWF/IUCN (1999) *Principles and Guidelines on Indigenous and Traditional Peoples and Protected Areas*, WCPA/WWF/IUCN, Gland, Switzerland, www.panda.org/resources/publications/sustainability/indigenous2/index.html

Webster, J (1997) 'Fungal biodiversity (Foreword)', *Biodiversity and Conservation*, vol 6, no 5

WWF/IUCN (1998) *Protected areas for a New Millennium: the Implications of IUCN's Protected Area Categories for Forest Conservation*, WWF/IUCN, Gland, Switzerland

Yellowstone National Park (1997) Letter from the Superintendent, Yellowstone National Park, to the Director, National Park Service, 22 August, Ref N30 (YELL)

Yellowstone National Park (1997) Text of standard letter from the Yellowstone Park Superintendent to Cooperating Researchers, Ref N2621 (YELL)

Yellowstone National Park (1998) 'Research authorization', 'Request to perform research in Yellowstone National Park', 'Permit application', National Park Service, Yellowstone Center for Resources, PO Box 168, Yellowstone National Park, WY 82190, Provided by Bob Lindstrom, 11 February

Yellowstone National Park (1999) 'Yellowstone Media Kit', www.biocat.com/index.html

Section III: Community relationships with researchers

Alexiades, M N (1999) 'Ethnobotany of the Ese Eja: plants, health and change in an Amazonian society', PhD thesis, City University of New York, New York

American Anthropological Association (AAA) (1998) *Code of Ethics of the American Anthropological Association*, available at www.ameranthassn.org/committees/ethics/ethcode.htm

American Sociological Association (ASA) (1997) *Code of Ethics*, ASA, www.asanet.org/ecoderev.htm

Ardito, W (1996) *Los Indígenas y la tierra en las leyes de América Latina*, Survival International, London

Barsh, L L R and K Bastien (1997) *Effective Negotiation by Indigenous People: An Action Guide with Special Reference to North America*, ILO, Ottawa

Borrini-Feyerabend, G (ed), (1997) *Beyond Fences: Seeking Social Sustainability in Conservation*, vol 2 IUCN, Gland, Switzerland

Brooke, L (1993) 'The participation of indigenous peoples and the application of their environmental and ecological knowledge in the Arctic environment protection strategy', Inuit Circumpolar Conference, Ottawa, in *IUCN Intercommission Task Force on Indigenous Peoples, Indigenous Peoples and Sustainability: Cases and Actions*, International Books, Utrecht

Brush, S and D Stabinsky (1996) *Valuing Local Knowledge; Indigenous People and Intellectual Property Rights*, Island Press, Washington, DC

Canadian Medical Association (CMA) (1996) *Code of Ethics of the Canadian Medical Association*, www.cma.ca/inside/policybase/1996/10-15.htm

Chapin, M (1991) 'How the Kuna keep the scientists in line', *Cultural Survival Quarterly*, vol 15, no 3, p17

Crengle, D (1997) 'Perspectives on Maori participation under the Resource Management Act: a case study' in *Indigenous Peoples and Sustainability: Cases and Actions*, IUCN Intercommission Task Force on Indigenous Peoples, International Books, the Netherlands

Daes, E-I (1996) 'Standard setting activitites: evolution of standards concerning the rights of indigenous peoples', Working Paper by the Chairperson-Rapporteur Mrs Erica-Irene Daes, on the Concept of Indigenous People, E/CN.4/Sub2/AC.4/1996/2, 10 June

Davis, M (1999) *Indigenous Rights in Traditional Knowledge and Biological Diversity: Approaches to Protection*, IP Australia

Díaz-Polanco, D (1995) *Etnia y nación en América* Latina.Consejo Nacional para la Cultura y las Artes, México

Downes, D, S A Laird, C Klein and B K Carney (1993) 'Biodiversity prospecting contract' in W V Reid et al (eds) *Biodiversity Prospecting*, World Resources Institute, Washington, DC

Dutfield, G (2000) *Intellectual Property Rights, Trade and Biodiversity: Seeds and Plant Varieties*, Earthscan, London

Emery, A (1997) *Guidelines for Environmental Assessments and Traditional Knowledge*, Report from the Centre for Traditional Knowledge to the World Council of Indigenous People. WCIP, CIDA, Canada, www.kivu.com/environmental.html

Evans, B (1998) *A Guide to Developing (a memorandum of) Understanding Within and Between Parties Involved in Community-Based Recording and Use of Ethnobotanical Knowledge*, WWF-South Pacific, Fiji

Four Directions Council (1996) *Forests, Indigenous Peoples and Biodiversity*, Four Directions Council, Canada

Gadgil, M et al (1998) 'New meanings for old knowledge: the people's biodiversity registers programme', *Ecological Applications*

García Hierro, P (1997) *Guía para leer el Convenio 169*, Racimos de Ungurahui, Lima, Perú

Glowka, L, F Burhenne-Guilmin and H Synge in collaboration with J A McNeely and L Gündling (1994) 'A guide to the Convention on Biological Diversity', *Environmental Policy and Law* Paper No 30, IUCN, Gland, Switzerland, and Cambridge

Glowka, L (1998) *A Guide to Designing Legal Frameworks to Determine Access to Genetic Resources*, IUCN, Gland, Switzerland

Gollin, M and S A Laird (1996) 'Global policies, local actions: the role of national legislation in sustainable biodiversity prospecting', *Boston University Journal of Science and Technology Law*, vol 2, L, p16

Gómez, M (ed) (1997) *Derecho Indígena*, Instituto Nacional Indigenista, México

Grenier, L (1998) *Working with Indigenous Knowledge: a Guide for Researchers*, IDRC, Ottawa

Greaves, T (ed) (1994) *Intellectual Property Rights for Indigenous Peoples: a Sourcebook*, Society for Applied Anthropology, Oklahoma

Grifo, F and D Downes (1996) 'Agreements to collect biodiversity for pharmaceutical research' in S Brush and D Stabinsky (eds) *Valuing Local Knowledge; Indigenous People and Intellectual Property Rights*, Island Press, Washington, DC

Guerin-McManus, M et al (1998) 'Bioprospecting in practice: a case study of the Surinam ICBG Project and benefit-sharing under the CBD' in *Case Studies on Benefit-Sharing Arrangements*, Secretariat, Convention on Biological Diversity, Fourth Conference of the Parties (COP 4), Bratislava, Slovakia

International Alliance of Indigenous–Tribal Peoples of the Tropical Forests and International Work Group for Indigenous Affairs and IWGIA (1997) *Indigenous Peoples, Forest and Biodiversity*

International Alliance of Indigenous–Tribal Peoples of the Tropical Forests (1996) *Guiding Principles: Conservation in Indigenous and Tribal Territories*

International Cooperative Biodiversity Groups (ICBG) (1997) *Principles for the Treatment of Intellectual Property and the Sharing of Benefits Associated with International Cooperative Biodiversity Groups*, NSF/NIH/AID, US

International Finance Corporation (IFC) (1998) *Doing Better Business Through Effective Public Consultation and Disclosure*, IFC, Washington DC

International Society of Ethnobiology (ISE) (1998) *Code of Ethics*, November, ISE, Aotearoa/New Zealand, www.users.ox.ac.uk/~wgtrr/isecode.htm

International Union for Conservation of Nature and Natural Resources (IUCN) (1997) 'Perspectives on Maori participation under the Resource Management Act' in *Indigenous Peoples and Sustainability: Cases and Actions*, IUCN Intercommission Task Force on Indigenous Peoples, International Books, the Netherlands

Inuit Tapirisat (1993) *Negotiating Research Relationships in the North*, Inuit Tapirisat of Canada, Nunavik, Quebec

IUCN (1997) *Indigenous Peoples and Sustainability: Cases and Actions*, IUCN Intercommission Task Force on Indigenous Peoples, International Books, the Netherlands

IUCN and WWF (1998) 'Implementation of Article 8 (j) and related provisions', Policy Recommendations for the Fourth Meeting of the COP to the Convention on Biological Diversity

Iwu, M M and S A Laird (1998) 'The ICBG: drug development and biodiversity conservation in Africa – a case study of a benefit sharing plan' in *Case Studies on Benefit-Sharing Arrangements*, Secretariat, Convention on Biological Diversity, Fourth Conference of the Parties (COP 4), Bratislava, Slovakia

Janzen, D et al (1993) 'Research management policies: permits for collecting and research in the tropics' in W V Reid et al (eds) *Biodiversity Prospecting*, World Resources Institute, Washington, DC

Johnson, M (ed) (1992) *Lore: Capturing Traditional Environmental Knowledge*, The Dene Cultural Institute and IDRC, Ottawa

ten Kate, K and S A Laird (2000) *The Commercial Use of Biodiversity: Access to Genetic Resources and Benefit-Sharing*, Earthscan, London

Kaufert, J M and J D O'Neil (1990) 'Biomedical rituals and informed consent: Native Canadians and the negotiation of clinical trust' in G Weisz (ed) *Social Science Perspectives on Medical Ethics*, University of Pennsylvania Press, Philadelphia, pp41–64

Kepe, T (1997) 'Environmental entitlements' in *Mkambati: Livelihoods, Social Institutions and Environmental Change on the Wild Coast of the Eastern Cape*, Research Report 1, Programme for Land and Agrarian Studies, University of the Western Cape, Bellville

Kepe, T (1999) 'The Problem of defining "community": challenges for the land reform programme in rural South Africa', *Development Southern Africa*, vol 16, no 3

Laird, S A (1993) 'Contracts for biodiversity prospecting' in W V Reid et al (eds) *Biodiversity Prospecting*, World Resources Institute, Washington, DC

Laird, S A and E E Lisinge (1998) 'Sustainable harvest of *Prunus africana* on Mount Cameroon: benefit-sharing between Plantecam company and the village of Mapanja' in *Case Studies on Benefit Sharing Arrangements*, Secretariat, Convention on Biological Diversity, Fourth Conference of the Parties (COP 4), Bratislava, Slovakia

Laird, S A and Wynberg, R (1996) 'Biodiversity prospecting in South Africa: towards the development of equitable partnerships', Discussion Paper Prepared for the Land and Agriculture Policy Centre, Johannesburg

Leticia Declaration and Proposal for Actions (1996)

Marshall, P A (1992) 'Anthropology and bioethics', *Medical Anthropology Quarterly*, vol 6, no 1, pp49–73

Mataatua Declaration on Cultural and Intellectual Property Rights of Indigenous Peoples (1993)

'Memorandum of Understanding among National Park Service, Redwood National Park, California Department of Parks and Recreation, Prairie Creek Redwoods State Park and the Yurok Tribe for Government to Government Relations' (1998 draft)

'Memorandum of Understanding Regarding the Gathering of Plant Resources for American Indian Traditional Cultural–Religious Purposes from National Park Lands among Zion National Park, Cedar Breaks National Monument, Pipe Spring National Monument and the

Kaibab Band of Paiute Indians, the San Juan Southern Paiute Tribe, the Moapa Paiute Tribe, the Las Vega Paiute Tribe and the Paiute Indian Tribes of Utah' (1998 draft)

Metcalf, P (1998) 'The book in the coffin: on the ambivalence of "informants"', *Cultural Anthropology*, vol 13, no 3, pp326–43

Moran, K (1998) 'Mechanisms for benefit-sharing: Nigerian case study' in *Case Studies on Benefit-Sharing Arrangements*, Secretariat, Convention on Biological Diversity, Fourth Conference of the Parties (COP 4), Bratislava, Slovakia

Narby, J (1997) *La Serpiente Cósmica*, Takiwasi, Racimos de Ungurahui, Lima, Perú

Nijar, G (1996) *In Defense of Local Community Knowledge and Biodiversity: a Conceptual Framework and Essential Elements of a Rights Regime*, Third World Network (TWN), Paper 1, TWN, Penang

Northwest Territories Policy 51.06 – Policy on Traditional Knowledge

PACOS (1998) 'Community Protocol Workshop', August, Tambunan, Sabah, Malaysia

Peluso, D M (forthcoming) 'Ese Eja Epona: women's social power in multiple and hybrid worlds', PhD thesis, Columbia University, New York

PEMANSKY (1988) *Programa de Investigaion Monitoreo y Cooperacion Cientifica*, Kuna Yala, Panama

Pew Scholars Initiative (1996) *Proposed Guidelines for Researchers and Local Communities Interested in Accessing, Exploring and Studying Biodiversity*

Pimbert, M P and J N Pretty (1995) *Parks, People and Professionals: Putting 'Participation' into Protected Area Management*, UN Research Institute for Social Development, Discussion Paper DP57, Geneva

Posey, D A (1996) *Traditional Resource Rights: International Instruments for Protection and Compensation for Indigenous Peoples and Local Communities*, IUCN, Gland, Switzerland

Posey, D A (1995) *Indigenous Peoples and Traditional Resource Rights: a Basis for Equitable Relationships?* Green College Centre for Environmental Policy and Understanding, Oxford

Posey, D A (1994) 'The Covenant on Intellectual, Cultural and Scientific Resources' in T Greaves (ed) *Intellectual Property Rights: a Sourcebook*, Society for Applied Anthropology, Oklahoma

Posey, D A and G Dutfield (1996) *Beyond Intellectual Property: Toward Traditional Resource Rights for Indigenous Peoples and Local Communities*, IDRC, Ottawa

Richardson, B J, D Craig and B Boer (1994) *Aboriginal participation and control in environmental planning and management: review of Canadian regional agreements and their potential application to Australia*, North Australian Research Unit, Australian National University, Darwin

Ruiz, M (1999) *The Legal Framework on Access to Genetic Resources in the Americas*, Fundación Tropical de Pesquisas y Tecnología André Tosello, Brazil, www/bdt.org.br

Ruppert, D (1994) 'Buying secrets: federal government procurement of intellectual cultural property' in T Greaves (ed) *Intellectual Property Rights for Indigenous Peoples: a Sourcebook*, Society for Applied Anthropology, Oklahoma

Rural Advancement Foundation International (RAFI) (1994) *Conserving Indigenous Knowledge: Integrating Two Systems of Innovation*, Independent Study by RAFI, United Nations Development Programme, New York

Schwartz, N and Deruyttere, A (1996) 'Community consultation, sustainable development and the Inter-American Development Bank', a Concept Paper, Washington, DC

Secretariat of the Pacific Community (SPC) and UNESCO (1999) 'Declaration on the protection of traditional knowledge and expressions of indigenous cultures in the Pacific Islands', Adopted at a Symposium Held at SPC Headquarters in New Caledonia, 15–19 February

Shanley, P, M Cymerys and J Galvao (1998) *Fruitiferas da Mata na Vida Amazonica*, Belem, Brazil

Shelton, D (1995) *Fair Play, Fair Pay: Strengthening Local Livelihood Systems Through Compensation for Access to and Use of Traditional Knowledge and Biological Resources*, WWF International, Gland, Switzerland

Simon, M M and L Brooke (1997) 'Inuit science: Nuanvik's experience in Canada' in *Indigenous Peoples and Sustainability: Cases and Actions*, IUCN Intercommission Task Force on Indigenous Peoples, International Books, the Netherlands

Stavenhagen, R (1997) 'El marco internacional del derecho indígena' in M Gómez (ed) *Derecho Indígena*, Instituto Nacional Indigenista, México

Sutherland, J et al (1996) 'Workshop Paper', Prepared for the IUCN Environmental Law Commission Workshop on Indigenous Peoples and Environmental Law

Third World Network (TWN) (1994) *Community Intellectual Rights Act*, TWN, Malaysia

Tobin, B (1995) *Protecting Collective Property Rights in Peru*, Asociación Para La Defensa de los Derechos Naturales, Lima, Peru

Tobin, B (1997) 'Certificates of origin: a role for IPR regimes in securing prior informed consent' in Mugabe et al (eds) *Access to Genetic Resources: Strategies for Sharing Benefits*, ACTS Press, Nairobi

Tobin, B, F Noejovich and C Yañez (1998) *Petroleras, Estado y Pueblos Indígenas: el Juego de las Expectativas*, Defensoría del Pueblo, Lima, Perú

Tores, R (ed) (1997) *Entre lo Propio y lo Ajeno: Derechos de los Pueblos Indigenas y Propriedad Intelectual*, Coordinadora de las Organizaciones Indigenous de la Cuenca Amazonica (COICA), Ecuador

UN Commission on Human Rights (1995) Final Report by Mrs Erica-Irene Daes, 'Discrimination against indigenous peoples', June, E/CN.4/Sub 2/1995/26

UN Draft Declaration on the Rights of Indigenous Peoples (1993)

The World Bank (1996) *The World Bank Participation Sourcebook*, Washington DC

WRI/GEA/AC (1993) *El Proceso de Evaluación Rural Participativa, una propuesta metodológica*, WRI/GEA/AC, Washington, DC

WWF and IUCN (1999) *Principles and Guidelines on Indigenous and Traditional Peoples and Protected Areas*, WWF International, Gland, Switzerland

WWF International (1996) 'Statement of principles on indigenous peoples and conservation', WWF International/IUCN, Gland, Switzerland

Wynberg, R and T Kepe (1999) *Land Reform and Conservation Areas in South Africa: Towards a Mutually Beneficial Approach*, IUCN, Department of Environmental Affairs, Department of Land Affairs, South Africa

Section IV: The commercial use of biodiversity and traditional knowledge

Aalbersberg, W G, I Korovulavula, E Johne and D Russell (1998) 'The role of a Fijian community in a bioprospecting project' in Secretariat of the Convention on Biological Diversity *Case Studies on Benefit-Sharing Arrangements*, Fourth Conference of the Parties (COP 4), 4–15 May, Bratislava, Slovakia

ABS Expert Panel (1999) *Report of the Panel of Experts on Access and Benefit-Sharing*, Report of First Meeting, 4–8 October, San José, Costa Rica. UNEP/CBD/COP/5/8, Secretariat of the Convention on Biological Diversity, Montreal

Anderson, J (1996) 'Utilization of natural products in the cosmetics industry', Paper Presented at The Royal Society of Chemistry's Phytochemical Diversity, a Source of New Industrial Products Conference, The University of Sussex, April

Anuradha, R V (1998) 'Sharing with the Kanis: a case study from Kerala, India', *Benefit-Sharing Case Studies*, Fourth Meeting of the Conference of the Parties to the CBD, Bratislava, May, Secretariat of the Convention on Biological Diversity, Montreal

Association of the British Pharmaceutical Industry (ABPI) (1998) *Pharmaceutical Facts and Statistics*, ABPI, London

Baker, J et al (1995) 'Natural product drug discovery and development: new perspectives on international collaboration', *Journal of Natural Products*, vol 58, no 9, September, pp1325–57

Balick, M B, E Elisabetsky and S Laird, S (eds) (1996) *Medicinal Resources of the Tropical Forest: Biodiversity and Its Importance for Human Health*, Columbia University Press, New York

Barsh, L L R and K Bastien (1997) *Effective Negotiation by Indigenous People: An Action Guide with Special Reference to North America*, ILO, Ottawa

Barton, J and W Siebeck (1994) 'Material transfer agreements in genetic resources exchange: the case of the International Agricultural Research Centres', *Issues in Genetic Resources*, no1, May, IPGRI, Rome

Bell, J (1997) 'Biopiracy's latest disguises, seedling', *The Quarterly Newsletter of Genetic Resources Action International*, vol. 14, no 2, June, Barcelona

Blacks Law Dictionary (1979) fifth edition, West Publishing Co, St Paul, Minnesota, p206

Blumenthal, M (1999) 'Herb market levels after five years of boom: 1999 sales in mainstream market up only 11% in first half of 1999 after 55% increase in 1998', *Herbalgram*, no 47

Brevoort, P (1998) 'The booming US botanical medicine market: an overview', *Herbalgram*, no 44, Fall

Bystrom, M, P Einarsson and G A Nycander (1999) 'Fair and equitable: sharing the benefits from use of genetic resources and traditional knowledge', Report, September, Swedish Scientific Council on Biological Diversity, Stockholm

Caillaux, J and M Ruiz (1998) *Acceso a Recursos Geneticos: Propuestas e Instrumentos Juridicos*, SPDA, Lima, Peru

Caillaux, J, M Ruiz and B Tobin (1999) *The Andean Regime on Access to Genetic Resources, Lessons and Experiences*, SPDA/WRI, Lima, Peru

Carte, B (1997) 'Natural products and the changing paradigm in drug discovery: an industry perspective', Paper presented at UNIDO Seminar, Davao, the Philippines, July (unpublished)

Chemical and Engineering News (C&EN) (1998) February

Christoffersen, R E and J J Marr (1995) 'The management of drug discovery' in M E Wolff (ed) *Burger's Medicinal Chemistry and Drug Discovery: Principles and Practice*, fifth edition, vol 1, Wiley, New York

Cohen, J I (ed) (1999) 'Managing agricultural biotechnology: addressing research program needs and policy implications', *Biotechnology in Agriculture Series*, no 23, CABI, Wallingford, UK

Conservation International (CI) (1991) *The Debt-for-Nature Exchange: a Tool for International Conservation*, CI, Washington, DC

Cragg, G M, D J Newman and K M Snader (1997) 'Natural products in drug discovery and development', *Journal of Natural Products*, vol 60, no 1, pp52–60

Crucible Group (1994) *People, Plants and Justice*, International Development and Research Centre, Ottawa

Cunningham, A B (1993) *Ethics, Ethnobiological Research and Biodiversity*, WWF International, Gland, Switzerland

Curtis, R et al (1998) *Designing a Fond Haitien Pour L'Environnement et Le Developpement: Issues and Options*, The Nature Conservancy, Washington, DC

Downes, D R (1998) 'Integrating implementation of the Convention on Biological Diversity and the rules of the World Trade Organization', Law and Policy Discussion Paper, IUCN–CIEL Discussion Paper, Washington, DC

Downes, D R (1997) 'Using intellectual property as a tool to protect traditional knowledge', CIEL Discussion Paper, November, Center for International Environmental Law, Washington, DC

Downes, D R and S A Laird (1999) *Innovative Mechanisms for Sharing Benefits of Biodiversity and Related Knowledge; Case Studies on Geographical Indications and Trademarks*, Prepared for UNCTAD Biotrade Initiative, Geneva

Downes, D, S A Laird, K Klein and B K Carney (1993) 'Biodiversity prospecting contract' in W V Reid et al (eds) *Biodiversity Prospecting: Using Genetic Resources for Sustainable Development*, World Resources Institute

Dutfield, G (1997) *Can the TRIPS Agreement Protect Biological and Cultural Diversity?* Biopolicy International Series No 19, ACTS Press, Nairobi

Dutfield, G (1998) 'Background paper on intellectual property rights in the context of seeds and plant varieties', Draft Paper Prepared for the IUCN Project on the Convention on Biological Diversity and the International Trade Regime, September

Dutfield, G (2000) *Intellectual Property Rights, Trade and Biodiversity: Seeds and Plant Varieties*, Earthscan, London

ECOFONDO (1996) *Regional Consultation on National Environmental Funds (NEFs) in Latin America and the Caribbean*, Case Studies on In-Country Resource Mobilization, 11–14 June, Cartagena, Colombia

The Economist (1998) 'The pharmaceutical industry survey', 21–27 February

Farnsworth, N R, O Akerele, A S Bingel, D D Soejarto and Z Guo (1985) 'Medicinal plants in therapy', *Bulletin of the World Health Organization*, vol 63, pp965–81

Florez, M (ed) (1998) *Diversidad Biologica y Cultural, retos y Propuestas Desde America Latina*, Grupo Ad-hoc sobre Diversidad Biologica, Santafe de Bogota

Fost, D (1997) 'Expanding Asian markets offer new horizons for manufacturers of performance chemicals', *Drug and Cosmetic Industry* (DCI), September, Advanstar Communications, New York, pp33–8

Genetic Engineering News (GEN) (1999) *Directory of Biotechnology Companies*, Mary Ann Liebert Publishers, New York

Global Environment Facility (GEF) (1998) *GEF Evaluation of Experience with Conservation Funds*, GEF Council, GEF/C.12/Inf 6, 10 September

Glowka, L et al (1998) *A Guide to Undertaking Biodiversity Legal and Institutional Profiles*, IUCN, Gland, Switzerland

Goldstein, J A (1999) 'Research tools and reach throughs', ATCC Biotech Patent and Licensing Forum

Gollin, M A (1995) 'Biological materials transfer agreements', *Bio/Technology*, vol 13, p243

Gollin, M A and S A Laird (1996) 'Global Policies, Local Actions: the Role of National Legislation in Sustainable Biodiversity Prospecting, *Boston University Journal of Science and Technology Law*, vol 2, 16 May, L.16

Greaves, T (ed) (1994) *Intellectual Property for Indigenous Peoples. a Source Book*, Society for Applied Anthropology, Oklahoma

Grifo, F T (1994) 'Chemical prospecting: an overview of the International Cooperative Biodiversity Groups Program', Emerging Connections of Biodiversity, Biotechnology and Sustainable Development in Health and Agriculture, Pan American Health Organization Conference, San Jose, Costa Rica

Grifo, F, D J Newman, A S Fairfield, B Bhattacharya and J T Grupenhoff (1996) 'The origins of prescription drugs' in F Grifo and J Rosenthal (eds) *Biodiversity and Human Health*, Island Press, Washington, DC

Gruenwald, J (1999a) 'The international herbal medicine market', *Nutraceuticals World*, January/February

Gruenwald, J (1999b) *The Market and Legal Status of Echinacea Products in Europe*, American Herbal Products Association (AHPA) Report, May/June

Gruenwald, J (1999c) 'The world market for Hypericum products', *Nutraceuticals World*, May/June

Gruenwald and Buettel (1996) 'The European phytotherapeutics market: figures, trends, analyses', *Drugs Made in Germany*, vol 39, no 1

Guerin-McManus, M, L M Famolare, I A Bowles, S A J Malone, R A Mittermeier and A B Rosenfeld (1998) *Bioprospecting in Practice: a Case Study of the Suriname ICBG Project and*

Benefit-Sharing Under the Convention on Biological Diversity, Secretariat to the Convention
on Biological Diversity, Fourth Conference of the Parties (COP 4), Bratislava, Slovakia, May

Hendrickx, F, V Koester and C Prip (1994) 'Access to genetic resources: a legal analysis' in V
Sánchez and C Juma (eds) *Biodiplomacy, Genetic Resources and International Relations*,
ACTS Press, Nairobi

Interagency Planning Group on Environmental Funds (IPG) (1995) *Environmental Funds: the
First Five Years; Issues to Address in Designing and Supporting Green Funds*, Preliminary
Analysis for the OECF/DAC Working Party on Development Assistance and Environment

International Federation of Accountants (1999) *Codifying Power and Control – Ethical Codes in
Action*, International Management Accounting Study 8

Iwu, M M (1995) *Linking Biodiversity and Socio-Economic Development: Bioresources
Development and Conservation Programme*, BDCP, Washington, DC

Iwu, M M (1996) 'Biodiversity prospecting in Nigeria: seeking equity and reciprocity in
intellectual property rights through partnership arrangements and capacity building', *Journal
of Ethnopharmacology*, vol 51, pp209–19

Iwu, M M and S A Laird (1998) 'Health, conservation and economic development: the
International Cooperative Biodiversity Groups "Drug Development and Biodiversity
Conservation Programme in Africa": a benefit-sharing plan' in *Case Studies on Benefit-
Sharing Arrangements*, Secretariat to the Convention on Biological Diversity, Fourth
Conference of the Parties (COP 4), Bratislava, Slovakia, May

Japanese Pharmaceutical Manufacturers Association (JPMA) (1998) *Approval and Licensing of
Drugs*, JPMA, Tokyo

Juma, C (1989) *The Gene Hunters: Biotechnology and the Scramble for Seeds*, Princeton
University Press, Princeton

ten Kate, K (1999a) 'The development of major crops by the seed industry' in K ten Kate and S A
Laird (eds) *The Commercial Use of Biodiversity: Access to Genetic Resources and Benefit-
Sharing*, Earthscan, London

ten Kate, K (1999b) 'Biotechnology in fields other than healthcare and agriculture' in K ten Kate
and S A Laird (eds) *The Commercial Use of Biodiversity: Access to Genetic Resources and
Benefit-Sharing*, Earthscan, London

ten Kate, K (1995) *Biopiracy or Green Petroleum? Expectations and Best Practices in
Bioprospecting*, ODA, London

ten Kate, K and S A Laird (2000) 'Biodiversity and business: coming to terms with the grand
bargain', *International Affairs*, vol 76, no 1, pp241–64

ten Kate, K and S A Laird (eds) (1999) *The Commercial Use of Biodiversity: Access to Genetic
Resources and Benefit-Sharing*, Earthscan, London

Kübler, E (1998) 'Use of natural fibres as reinforcement in composites for vehicles: research
results and experiences' in D E Leihner and T A Mitschein (eds) *A Third Millennium for
Humanity? The Search for Paths of Sustainable Development*, Peter Lang, Frankfurt,
Germany, pp393–402

Laird, S A (1999) 'The botanical medicine industry' in K ten Kate and S A Laird (eds) *The
Commercial Use of Biodiversity: Access to Genetic Resources and Benefit-Sharing*,
Earthscan, London

Laird, S A (1993) 'Contracts for biodiversity prospecting' in W V Reid et al (eds) *Biodiversity
Prospecting: Using Genetic Resources for Sustainable Development*, World Resources
Institute, Washington, DC

Laird, S A and M Burningham (1999) 'The development of a benefit-sharing partnership in
Vietnam: *Panax vietnamensis* – a 'new' ginseng' in K ten Kate and S A Laird (eds) *The
Commercial Use of Biodiversity: Access to Genetic Resources and Benefit-Sharing*,
Earthscan, London

Laird, S A and E Lisinge (1998) *Sustainable Harvesting of Prunus africana on Mount Cameroon:
Benefit-Sharing Between Plantecam Company and the Village of Mapanja*, Secretariat to the

Convention on Biological Diversity, Fourth Conference of the Parties (COP 4), Bratislava, Slovakia, May

Laird, S A and R Wynberg (1996) 'Biodiversity prospecting in South Africa: towards the development of equitable partnerships', Discussion Paper Prepared for the Land and Agriculture Policy Centre, Johannesburg

Lange, D (1998) *Europe's Medicinal and Aromatic Plants: Their Use, Trade and Conservation*, TRAFFIC International, Cambridge

Lange, D (1999) 'Identification training for medicinal and aromatic plants covered by CITES and EU Regulation 2307/97', Lecture Script version 2, German Federal Agency for Nature Conservation, Bonn

La Viña, T, M Caleda and J Baylon (1997) *Regulating Access to Biological and Genetic Resources in the Philippines: a Manual for the Implementation of Executive Order No 247*, FPE and WRI, Manila

Leakey, R R B (1999) 'Potential for novel food products from agroforestry trees: a review', *Food Chemistry*, vol 66, pp1–14

Lesser, W H (1994) 'Attributes of an intellectual property rights system for landraces', Working Paper No R10W, International Academy for the Environment, Geneva

Macilwain, C (1998) 'When rhetoric hits reality in debate ion bioprospecting', *Nature*, vol 392, 9 April, pp535–41

Masood, E (1998) 'A formula for indigenous involvement', *Nature Magazine*, vol. 392, p539

McGowan, J and I Udeinya (1994) 'Collecting traditional medicines in Nigeria: a proposal for IPR compensation' in T Greaves (ed) *Intellectual Property for Indigenous Peoples. a Source Book*, Society for Applied Anthropology, Oklahoma

McNeely, J (1995) *Biodiversity Conservation in the Asia Pacific Region; Constraints and Opportunities*, Asian Development Bank, IUCN, Manila, the Philippines

MedAd News (1999) 'The top 500 prescription drugs by worldwide sales', Eagle Publishing Partners, New Jersey, May

MedAd News (1999) 'The top 50 companies', Eagle Publishing Partners, New Jersey, September

Mikitin, K (1995) *Issues and Options in the Design of GEF Supported Trust Funds for Biodiversity Conservation*, Environment Department Papers, Biodiversity Series, Paper No 011, Global Environment Division, The World Bank, Washington, DC

Miller, A R and M H Davis (1990) *Intellectual Property: Patents, Trademarks and Copyright*

Mirasol, F (1999) 'Drug makers surpass Wall Street expectations', *Chemical Marketing Reporter*, 3 May

Mitschein, T A and P S Miranda (1998) 'POEMA: a proposal for sustainable development in Amazonia' in D E Leihner and T A Mitschein (eds) *A Third Millennium for Humanity? The Search for Paths of Sustainable Development*, Peter Lang, Frankfurt, Germany, pp329–66

Mooney, P R (1994) *Conserving Local Knowledge: Integrating Two Systems of Innovation*, Independent Report Prepared by the Rural Advancement Foundation International and UNDP

Moran, K (1998) *Mechanisms for Benefit-Sharing: Nigerian Case Study for the Convention on Biological Diversity*, The Healing Forest Conservancy, Washington, DC

Moran, K (1996) 'Returning benefits from drug discovery to native communities', *Renewable Resources Journal*, vol. 14, no 1, pp11–16

Moran, W (1993) 'Rural space as intellectual property', *Political Geography*, vol 12, pp263–77

Morris, J and S A Laird (1999) 'Cohune Oil: Marketing a personal care product for community development and conservation in Guatemala – an overview of the Conservation International and Croda Inc partnership' in K ten Kate and S A Laird (eds) *The Commercial Use of Biodiversity: Access to Genetic Resources and Benefit-Sharing*, Earthscan, London

Mugabe, J, C B Barber, G Henne, L Glowka and A La Viña (1997) *Access to Genetic Resources: Strategies for Sharing Benefits*, ACTS Press, Nairobi

Mytelka, L (1999) 'Evolution of the "biotechnology" industry', Paper Presented at the International Conference on Biotechnology in the Global Economy, Center for International

Development at Harvard University, Harvard, 2–3 September

Nayak, A R (1999) 'Biotechnology and the integration of the life science industry', Paper Presented at the International Conference on Biotechnology in the Global Economy, Center for International Development at Harvard University, Harvard, 2–3 September

Newman, D J and S A Laird, (1999) 'The influence of natural products on 1997 pharmaceutical sales figures' in K ten Kate and S A Laird (eds) *The Commercial Use of Biodiversity: Access to Genetic Resources and Benefit-Sharing*, Earthscan, London

Nutrition Business Journal (NBJ) (1998) 'Natural personal care', *Nutrition Business Journal*, vol 3, no 1, January

Panik (1998) 'The use of biodiversity and implications for industrial production' in D E Leihner and T A Mitschein (eds) *A Third Millennium for Humanity? The Search for Paths of Sustainable Development*, Peter Lang, Frankfurt, pp59–73

Parry, B (1999) 'The fate of the collections: social justice and the annexation of plant genetic resources' in C Zerner (ed) *People, Plants and Justice: the Politics of Nature Conservation*, Columbia University Press, New York

PhRMA (1998/1999) *Facts*, PhRMA, Washington, DC

Pombo, D (1998) 'Biodiversidad: una nueva logica para la naturaleza' in M Florez (ed) *Diversidad Biologica y Cultural, retos y Propuestas Desde America Latina*, Grupo Ad-hoc sobre Diversidad Biologica, Santafe de Bogota, p61

Posey, D A (1994a) 'International agreements for protecting indigenous knowledge' in V Sánchez, Vicente and C Juma (eds) *Biodiplomacy, Genetic Resources and International Relations*, ACTS Press, Nairobi

Posey, D A (1994b) 'International agreements and intellectual property right protection for indigenous peoples' in T Greaves (ed) *Intellectual Property for Indigenous Peoples: a Source Book*, Society for Applied Anthropology, Oklahoma

Prendergast, H D V, N L Etkin, D R Harris and P J Houghton (eds) (1998) *Plants for Food and Medicine*, Royal Botanic Gardens, Kew

Purseglove, J W (1979) *Tropical Crops: Dicotyledons*, Longman Publishers, London

Putterman, D M (1996) 'Model material transfer agreements for equitable biodiversity prospecting', *Colorado Journal of International Law and Policy*, vol. 7, no 1, pp145–73, www.users.ox.ac.uk/~wgtrr/mtav9.htm

Putzel, L R and C Zerner (1998) *Community-Based Conservation and Biodiversity Prospecting in Verata, Fiji: a History and Review*. Rainforest Alliance Natural Resources and Rights Programme, New York

Reid, W V, S A Laird, C A Meyer, R Games, A Sittenfeld, D H Janzen, M A Gollin and C Juma (eds) (1993) *Biodiversity Prospecting: Using Genetic Resources for Sustainable Development*, World Resources Institute, Washington, DC

Richman, A and J P Witkowski (1998) 'Herb sales still strong', *Whole Foods*, South Plainfield, New Jersey, October, pp19–26

Robbins, C S (1998) 'Medicinal plant conservation: a priority at TRAFFIC', *Herbalgram*, vol 44, Fall

Rosenthal, J (ed) (1999) 'Drug discovery, economic development and conservation: the International Cooperative Biodiversity Groups', *Pharmaceutical Biology*, vol 37

Rosenthal, J (1998) 'The International Cooperative Biodiversity Groups (ICBG) programme' in *Case Studies on Benefit-Sharing Arrangements*, Fourth Conference of the Parties (COP 4) to the Convention on Biological Diversity, Bratislava, May

Rosenthal, J P (1996) 'Equitable sharing of biodiversity benefits: agreements on genetic resources', Paper Presented at the International Conference on Incentive Measures for the Conservation and the Sustainable Use of Biological Diversity in Cairns, Australia, 22–28 March

Rosenthal, J P (1996) 'Equitable sharing of biodiversity benefits: agreements on genetic resources', *OECD Proceedings: Investing in Biological Diversity*, Cairns, Australia, March

Ruiz, M (1997) 'Report on the Global Biodiversity Forum Workshop on Policy Research to Implement the CBD', *Sustainable Developments*, vol 8, no 1, International Institute for Sustainable Development, 1 September, www.iisd.ca/linkages/sd

Ruiz Muller, M (2000) 'Regulating bioprospecting and protecting indigenous peoples knowledge in the Andean community: Decision 391 and its overall impacts in the region', Paper presented at the UNCTAD Expert Meeting on Traditional Knowledge, Innovations and Practices, 30 October–1 November, Geneva

Sánchez, V and C Juma (eds) (1994) *Biodiplomacy, Genetic Resources and International Relations*, ACTS Press, Nairobi

Science (1999) 'Drug industry looks to the lab instead of rainforest and reef', *Science*, vol 285, 9 July

Shearson Lehman Brothers (1991) *PharmaPipelines: Pharmaceutical Winners and Losers in the 1990s*, Lehman Brothers Securities, London

Sheldon, J W, M J Balick and S A Laird (1997) 'Medicinal plants: can utilization and conservation co-exist?', *Advances in Economic Botany*, vol 12, New York Botanical Garden Scientific Publications Department, New York

Shiva, V (1998) *Biopiracy: the Plunder of Nature and Knowledge*, Green Books, Devon

Shiva V (1995) *Captive Minds, Captive Lives: Ethics, Ecology and Patents on Life*, Research Foundation for Science, Technology and Natural Resource Policy, Dehra Dun, India

Shiva, V and R Holla-Bhal (1993) *Protection of Plants, People and Intellectual Rights: Proposed Amendments to the Draft Plant Varieties Act*, The Research Foundation for Science, Technology and Natural Resource Policy, New Delhi

Situma, F (1997) 'Legal framework for conservation, ownership, access and utilization of African biodiversity: medicinal plants and food crops' Paper Presented at the Organization of African Unity – Scientific, Technical Research Commission/Kenya Industrial Property Office/Development Partners Workshop held at Nairobi, 13–16 April

Spergel, B (1993) *Trust Funds for Conservation*, World Wildlife Fund, Washington, DC

Swanson, T (1997) *Global Action for Biodiversity, An International Framework for Implementing the Convention on Biological Diversity*, Earthscan, London

Tewari, D N (1992) *Monograph on Eucalyptus*, Surya Publications, Dehra Dun

Tobin, B (2001) 'Redefining perspectives in the search for protection of traditional knowledge: a case study from Peru', *Review of European Community and International Environmental Law*, vol 10, no 1

Tobin, B (1999) 'Protecting collective property rights in Peru: the search for an interim solution', Paper Presented at the Seminar on Intellectual, Biological and Cultural Property Rights, Hosted by Conservation Melanesia, NRI, Institute for Medical Research and the Department of Environment and Conservation, Port Moresby, Papua New Guinea, 13–14 August 1997; Spanish translation published in Pablo Ortiz (eds) *Comunidades y Conflictos Socioambientales: Expereincias y Desafios en America Latina*, Quito

Tobin B (1997a) 'Putting the commercial cart before the cultural horse, part II: the search for equity in the International Cooperative Biodiversity Groups (ICBG) project in Peru', unpublished manuscript, September

Tobin, B (1997b) 'Certificates of origin: a role for IPR regimes in securing prior informed consent' in Mugabe et al (eds) *Access to Genetic Resources: Strategies for Sharing Benefits*, ACTS Press, Nairobi

Tobin, B (1994a) 'El problema del acceso y de los derechos de propiedad intelectual sobre la diversidad biologica' in O Dancourt, E Mayer and C Monge (eds) *Peru el Problema Agrario en Debate*, proceedings of the fifth Seminario Permanente de Investigación Agraria (SEPIA V), Lima, July 1993, Universidad Nacional de San Augustín, Lima, p551

Tobin, B (1994b) 'Putting the commercial cart before the cultural horse: a study of the ICBG Agreements', Paper Presented at the Symposium of Indigenous Peoples of Latin America: Indigenous Peoples, Biodiversity and Intellectual Property, Santa Cruz, Bolivia, 27–30 September (on file with the Peruvian Society for Environmental Law: SPDA)

Tobin B, F Noejovich and C Yanez (1998) *Petroleras, Estado y Pueblos Indigenas: El Juego de las Expectativas, Defensoria del Pueblo, Linamientos Preliminares para la consulta de los pueblos indigenas amazonicos del Peru en las actividades de exploracion y explotacion de Hidrocarburos*, Defensoria del Pueblo, Lima

Tobin, B and K Swiderska (2001) *Speaking in Tongues: A Case Study of Indigenous Participation in the Development of a Sui Generis Regime to Protect Traditional Knowledge in Peru*, April, IIED, London

United Nations Environment Programme (UNEP) (1994) *Convention on Biological Diversity: Text and Annexes*, Gland, Switzerland

United States Agency for International Development (USAID) (1996) *Endowments as a Tool for Sustainable Development*, USAID Working Paper No 221, Center for Development Information and Evaluation, Washington, DC

Vaughan, J G and C A Geissler (1997) *The New Oxford Book of Food Plants*, Oxford University Press, Oxford

Vogel, J H (1997) 'Bioprospecting and the justification for a cartel', *Bulletin of the Working Group on Traditional Resource Rights*, winter

Waddington, M and S A Laird (1999) 'The production and marketing of a species in the "public domain": the Yawanawa and Aveda Corporation *Bixa orellana* Project, Brazil' in K ten Kate and S A Laird (eds) *The Commercial Use of Biodiversity: Access to Genetic Resources and Benefit-Sharing*, Earthscan, London

Womens Wear Daily (WWD) (1999) 'The beauty top 100: the who's who of cosmetics', *Womens Wear Daily*, September

World Intellectual Property Organization (WIPO) (2000) 'Annex B Extracts from the Peruvian ICBG Agreements' in 'Report of Peruvian fact finding mission' in WIPO Global Intellectual Property Division *Intellectual Property Needs and Expectations of Tradtional Knowledge, vol 3*, July, draft report, WIPO, Geneva

WIPO (1999) *Intellectual Property and Human Rights*, Publication No 762(E), WIPO, Geneva

Yuquan, W (1998) 'China Medipharm insights', 8 April

Zerner, C (1999) *People, Plants and Justice: the Politics of Nature Conservation*, Columbia University Press, New York

Section V: National policy context

Anuradha, R V (1998) 'Sharing with the Kanis: a case study from Kerala, India' in *Case Studies on Benefit Sharing Arrangements*, Secretariat of the Convention on Biological Diversity, Montreal

Barber, C V (1994) 'Focus on the Convention on Biological Diversity' in *World Resources 1994–1995*, World Resources Institute, Washington DC, pp154–62

Blakeney, M (1998) 'Access to biological resources: domestic and international developments and issues', *E Law – Murdoch University Electronic Journal of Law*, vol 5 no 3, September, Perth, Australia, www.murdoch,edu.au/elaw/issues/v5n3/blakeney53nf.html

Crucible Group (1994) *People, Plants and Patents: the impact of intellectual property on trade, plant biodiversity, and rural society,* International Development Research Centre (IDRC), Ottawa

Department of Environmental Affairs and Tourism (DEAT) (1996a) *Towards a Policy for the Conservation and Sustainable Use of South Africa's Biological Diversity: A Discussion Document*, DEAT, South Africa

DEAT (1996b) *Green Paper on the Conservation and Sustainable Use of South Africa's Biological Diversity*, DEAT, South Africa

DEAT (1997) *White Paper on the Conservation and Sustainable Use of South Africa's Biological Diversity*, July, Notice 1095 of 1997, DEAT, South Africa

Department of Environment and Natural Resources (DENR) (1999) *Workshop on the ASEAN Framework Agreement on Access to Genetic Resources*, Draft Text, DENR, South-East Asia Regional Institute for Community Education (SEARICE) and the Association of South-East Asian Nations (ASEAN), Manila, the Philippines

Dutfield, G (2000) *Intellectual Property Rights, Trade and Biodiversity: Seeds and Plant Varieties*, Earthscan, London

Dutfield, G and Posey, D (1996) *Beyond Intellectual Property: Toward Traditional Resource Rights for Indigenous Peoples and Local Communities*, International Development Research Centre (IDRC), Ottawa

Ekpere, J A (1999) 'Alternative to UPOV for the protection of new plant varieties', May, Scientific, Technical and Research Commission of the Organization of African Unity (OAU), Lagos

Environmental Policy Studies Workshop (1999) *Access to Genetic Resources: an Evaluation of the Development and Implementation of Recent Regulation and Access Agreements*, School of International and Public Affairs, Columbia University, New York

Fakir, S (1997) 'Biodiversity policy in South Africa: finding new values and shifting paradigms', *Biopolicy*, vol 2, paper 8

Glowka, L (1998) *A Guide to Designing Legal Frameworks to Determine Access to Genetic Resources*, IUCN (World Conservation Union) Environmental Policy and Law Paper No 34, IUCN Environmental Law Centre, Gland, Switzerland

Glowka, L (1995) 'Legal and institutional considerations for states providing genetic resources' in J Mugabe, C V Barber, G Henne, L Glowka and A La Viña (eds) *Access to Genetic Resources: Strategies for Sharing Benefits*, ACTS Press, Nairobi, pp33–51

Greaves, T (ed) (1994) *Intellectual Property Rights for Indigenous Peoples: a Source Book*, Society for Applied Anthropology, Oklahoma

Hendrickx, R, V Koester and C Prip (1994) 'Access to genetic resources, a legal analysis' in V Sánchez and C Juma (eds) *Biodiplomacy: Genetic Resources and International Relations*, ACTS Press, Nairobi, pp139–53

Jacanimijoy, A (1998) 'Initiative for the protection of the rights of the possessors of traditional knowledge, indigenous peoples and local communities', Paper Presented on Behalf of the Coordinating Body for the Indigenous Peoples' Organizations of the Amazon Basin (COICA), WIPO (World Intellectual Property Organization) Roundtable on Intellectual Property and Indigenous Peoples, Geneva, 23–24 July

ten Kate, K and S A Laird (eds) (1999) *The Commercial Use of Biodiversity: Access to Genetic Resources and Benefit-Sharing*, Earthscan, London

Kothari, A (1999) 'Intellectual property rights and biodiversity: are India's proposed Biodiversity Act and Plant Varieties Act compatible?', Kalpavriksh, Pune, India (unpublished manuscript)

La Viña, A G M, M J A Caleda and M L L Baylon (eds) (1997) *Regulating Access to Biological and Genetic Resources in the Philippines: a Manual on the Implementation of Executive Order No 247*, Foundation for the Philippine Environment (FPE) and World Resources Institute (WRI), Manila

Laird, S A and E Lisinge (1998) 'Benefit-sharing case studies: *Ancistrocladus korupensis* and *Prunus africana*' in *Case Studies on Benefit-Sharing Arrangements*, Secretariat of the Convention on Biological Diversity, Montreal

Laird, S A and R P Wynberg (1996) *Biodiversity Prospecting in South Africa: Towards the Development of Equitable Partnerships*, Land and Agriculture Policy Centre, Johannesburg

Mugabe, J, C Barber, G Henne, L Glowka and A La Viña (1997a) *Managing Access to Genetic Resources: Towards Strategies for Benefit-Sharing, Biopolicy International*, Paper No 17, ACTS Press, Nairobi

Mugabe, J, C Barber, G Henne, L Glowka and A La Viña (eds) (1997b) *Access to Genetic Resources: Strategies for Sharing Benefits*, ACTS Press, Nairobi

Mullard, S (1998) *Review of the Status of Access and Benefit-Sharing Measures in Malaysia*, WWF Malaysia, Petaling Jaya, Malaysia

Nnadozie, K C (1999) 'Access to genetic resources and intellectual property rights: regulatory and policy framework in Nigeria', Paper Presented at the International Conference on Trade Related Aspects of Intellectual Property Rights (TRIPS) and the Convention on Biological Diversity, 6–7 February, Organized by the African Centre for Technology Studies (ACTS) and the United Nations Environment Programme (UNEP)

Peria, E V (1998) 'Can't we stop and talk awhile?: a Philippine NGO perspective on Executive Order 247', Paper Presented at the Tenth Global Biodiversity Forum, Bratislava, Slovakia, 1–3 May

Reid, W V, S A Laird, C A Meyer, R Gámez, A Sittenfeld, D H Janzen, M A Gollin and C Juma (eds) (1993) *Biodiversity Prospecting: Using Genetic Resources for Sustainable Development*, World Resources Institute, Washington, DC

Ruiz, M (1997) 'Access regime for Andean Pact countries: issues and experiences', in Mugabe et al (eds) *Access to Genetic Resources: Strategies for Sharing Benefits*, ACTS Press, Nairobi, pp187–200

Rural Advancement Foundation International (RAFI) (1996) *Enclosures of the Mind: Intellectual Monopolies – a Resource Kit on Community Knowledge, Biodiversity and Intellectual Property*, RAFI, Ottawa

Sánchez, V and C Juma (eds) (1994) *Biodiplomacy: Genetic Resources and International Relations*, ACTS Press, Nairobi

Secretariat of the Convention on Biological Diversity (SCBD) (1999) *Report of the Panel of Experts on Access and Benefit-Sharing*, UNEP/CBD/COP/5/8, Montreal

SCBD (1998) 'Case studies on benefit-sharing arrangements', SCBD, Montreal

SCBD (1996) *The Impact of Intellectual Property Rights Systems on the Conservation and Sustainable Use of Biological Diversity and on the Equitable Sharing of Benefits from its Use*, UNEP/CBD/COP/3/22, Montreal

SCBD (2001) *Handbook of the Convention on Biological Diversity*, Earthscan, London

Sittenfeld, A and R Gámez (1993) 'Biodiversity prospecting by InBio' in W V Reid et al (eds) *Biodiversity Prospecting: Using Genetic Resources for Sustainable Development*, World Resources Institute, Washington, DC, pp69–97

Solis, R V and P C Madrigal (1999) 'Costa Rica's Biodiversity Law: sharing the process', Paper Prepared for the Workshop on Biodiversity Conservation and the Intellectual Property Regime Organized by the Research and Information System for the Non-Aligned and Other Developing Countries (RIS) with the World Conservation Union (IUCN), New Delhi, India, 29–31 January; Abridged and Edited Jointly with Genetic Resources Action International (GRAIN) for the BIO–IPR Internet List Server (bio-ipr@cuenet.com)

Swiderska, K (2001) 'Stakeholder participation in policy on access to genetic resources, traditional knowledge and benefit-sharing: case studies and recommendations', *Biodiversity and Livelihoods Issues*, No 4, Earthprint Ltd, London

Swiderska, K (1999) *Developing Regulations for Access to Genetic Resources and Traditional Knowledge: Overview of Experience with Stakeholder Participation*, International Institute for Environment and Development (IIED) Bioprospecting Project, London

Time (1998) 'Gene piracy: scientists are ransacking the jungles and rain forests for tomorrow's miracle drugs, but angry people are starting to ask: who owns nature?', *Time*, 30 November

Tobin, B (1997) *Access Laws and Contracts, IPR and Benefit-Sharing: a Study of Law and Practice in Costa Rica and Proposals for the Future*, Report Prepared for the National Institute of Biological Diversity (InBio) under Global Environment Facility (GEF) Grant No 28453, Lima, Peru

Vogel, J H (1997) 'Bioprospecting and the justification for a cartel', *Bulletin of the Working Group on Traditional Resource Rights*, winter

WWF (1995) *Access Controls for Genetic Resources*, WWF, Gland, Switzerland

WWF (1995) *The Biodiversity Convention and Intellectual Property Rights*, WWF, Gland, Switzerland

Index

Page numbers in *italics* refer to boxes, figures and tables